1996

Citizens of the World examines the business and social strategies of the men who developed the British Atlantic community in the eighteenth century. This book focuses on twenty-three London merchants who traded with America in an age of imperial expansion. These associates started their careers as marginal people, sought and took advantage of opportunities around the world, and approached their business and social lives with the integrating and improving ideals of the practical Enlightenment. They were London's success stories in the period before the American Revolution. Contrary to traditional representations of the canonical merchant, they were not born to City fathers, did not become formal City apprentices, and did not enter traditional, established trades; they came to London in midlife as outsiders who had the intelligence, the nose for opportunity, and the nerve to open new commercial trading routes, develop and people new lands, including the establishment of speculative slaving ventures that brought Africans to America, and provision Britain's growing war machine.

Writing in the comprehensive tradition of Charles Andrews and Richard Pares, Professor Hancock combines narrative and statistical sources to reveal how these associates managed the business of the empire and turned themselves into gentlemen: he tracks their shipping over fifty years, investigates their farms and plantations, cumulates their investment portfolios, follows them into their scientific societies, and watches them build country houses and fill them with art. He places all this activity in the context of the developing institutions of Britain's colonies in America and the social world of polite and industrious men and women at home.

Citizens of the World

Citizens of the World

London merchants and the integration
of the British Atlantic community, 1735–1785

DAVID HANCOCK

Harvard University

CAMBRIDGE
UNIVERSITY PRESS

Published by the Press Syndicate of the University of Cambridge
The Pitt Building, Trumpington Street, Cambridge CB2 1RP
40 West 20th Street, New York, NY 10011–4211, USA
10 Stamford Road, Oakleigh, Melbourne 3166, Australia

First published 1995

Printed in the United States of America

Library of Congress Cataloging-in-Publication Data
Hancock, David.
Citizens of the world : London merchants and the integration of
the British Atlantic community, 1735–1785 / David Hancock.
p. cm.
Includes bibliographical references and index.
ISBN 0-521-47430-2
1. Merchants – England – London – History – 18th century. 2. London
(England) – Commerce – United States – History – 18th century.
3. United States – Commerce – England – London – History – 18th century.
4. London (England) – History – 18th century. I. Title.
HF3520.L65H36 1995
382'.092'241 – dc20   94–41566
                                                          CIP

A catalog record for this book is available from the British Library.

ISBN 0-521-47430-2 Hardback

To
A. S. K.

Contents

Acknowledgments

This book is about the integration of the British-Atlantic community by London's transoceanic merchants in the period 1735–85. My object is to analyze the business and social worlds constructed by these traders, and to explore the connections between what have been traditionally treated as separate spheres. In writing a work that is neither wholly business or economic history nor purely social or art history, I have had to draw heavily and frequently on the expertise and work of others. I now wish to express formally my gratitude to them.

First and foremost, I have been blessed with exceptional academic mentors, masters of the craft, to whom I owe an incalculable debt. Edmund Morgan first introduced me to colonial British and American history and pointed me to a style of narrative that imaginatively evokes the lives of real people, past and present. His subjects feel deep emotion, face believable predicaments. Any of his students who can pull back the bow of history half as far as he has is extremely fortunate. To Bernard Bailyn I express my warmest gratitude. This book has its origins in a paper written for his graduate seminar on British-American history. From that first brief essay, through the last version of the dissertation, to the final draft of this book, Bailyn has encouraged my research into the business and social activities of metropolitan entrepreneurs. He monitored the long gestation of the thesis and assisted the project, not with immoderate and inappropriate oversight, but with a skeptical and critical distance that expressed itself in endless, sometimes vexing questions and unexpected bursts of genuine enthusiasm. More important, he has provided a model of an historian who asks big questions and undertakes the archaeology needed to answer them, unearths new evidence and tells new stories from it, and constructs a narrative in which the expression of the idea is an important part of the idea itself. I hope my own scholarly investigations and professional dealings with my students follow the precept of his example.

One of the pleasures of scholarship is interaction with engaging colleagues, and two deserve special mention. John Brewer rendered practical assistance at every stage, urging me to ask large questions of my material, providing information on many fine points of British history, and offering valuable critical advice. Our conversations have contributed to my understanding of the period in ways that should be clear to any reader and have kept alive my desire to combine British and American history. I have likewise benefited from Simon Schama's unique blend of unstinting generosity and critical imagination. His example and prodding did much to guide my attempts at delineating the social lives of these businessmen.

In addition to my advisors and colleagues, numerous scholars generously read this book in its various drafts and revisions; for fear of implicating them in the outcome, I will let them remain anonymous, but must express my deep appreciation. In addition, the readers who reviewed the manuscript for the Press criticized the argument and details with such care that they saved me from numerous errors of fact and infelicities of expression and encouraged me to devise a more workable structure. Throughout the project, Professors Jacob Price and John McCusker unselfishly shared with me their encyclopedic knowledge of oceanic shipping, currency matters, and early-modern terminology; the field of trans-Atlantic commerce would be greatly impoverished without their help and their example. Lastly, other scholars have graciously contributed evidence and helped refine the narrative: Donna Andrew, Frank Bate, Mary Bilder, David Bush, Cary Carson, Barbara De Wolfe, Richard Dell, Donald Fleming, Christopher Fyfe, S. E. D. Fortescue, Mark Girouard, Daryl Hall, Barry Higman, Dale Hoak, Alan Karras, David Kirp, Mark Kishlansky, Hamish Little, Joseph C. Miller, Tessa Murdoch, Walter Ogg, James C. Oldham, James G. Parker, Alistair Rowan, Lord Conrad Russell, Francis Russell, Maurice Schofield, Arlene Shy, Barbara Solow, Tony Smith, Robert Stein, Alan Tait, Anita Tien, Alberto Vieira, Patrick Villiers, and C. J. Ware.

As research assistants, Jason Factor in the United States and Tim Wales in the United Kingdom followed what were often extremely vague leads. The data they unearthed made my job of constructing a more comprehensive narrative much easier. Unstinting help from Harvard's British and American history bibliographers, Carolyn Fawcett and Nathaniel Bunker, further advanced the progress of this book in ways they would seldom have imagined. Their aggressive and efficient search for research materials has made Harvard an unequaled place to undertake historical research and writing. Mary McConnell in the Harvard History Department office eased with her help and cooperation the day-to-day challenge of writing while teaching.

Numerous friends have provided important assistance and much needed diversion along the way: Jonathan Alsop, Margaret Duchess of Argyll, Anthony Athos, Michael Baenen, Antony Beevor and the Hon. Artemis Cooper, Colette Bowe, Peter Dudney, Guy Erwin, Sir Archibald Grant of Monymusk, James Hamilton, Sir Edward Hulton, Frances Kelly, Prince Adam Kurakin, Major R. N. A. Macleod, Cathy Patterson, John Patterson, Hugh Russell, Hugh Poole-Warren, Gary Stahl, Lord Strathspey, and the Hon. Charles Tyrrell.

The work of the historian is not so very different from that of the detective. But I could not have written this attempt at detection without the patient, if sometimes bemused, support of those who own family papers. I am especially grateful to Admiral Sir Julian and Lady Veronica Oswald for introducing me to their family papers and easing my initial stay in England. Their unfailing kindness, perceptive questions, and wry humor furthered this project immeasurably. I am also indebted to the following individuals for allowing me to examine and quote from manuscript collections in their care: the Duke of Argyll, Mr. Hugh Alexander Boyd, the Brodie of Brodie, Mr. Christopher Campbell-Johnston, the Duke of Buccleuch, Mrs. Daphne Burton, the Marquis of Bute, the Earl of Cathcart, Mr. H. P. English, the Duke of Devonshire, the Earl of Elgin, Sir Patrick and Lady Grant of Dalvey, Sir Michael Herries, Baron Home of the Hirsel, Mr. James Hunter-Blair of Blairquhan, the Marquis of Linlithgow, the Earl of Mansfield, Mr. Paul Mellon, Mr. Oliver Russell, the Earl of Shelburne, the Earl of Strathmore, Mrs. Jane Waley, and the Earl and Countess of Yarborough. Similarly, I would also like to express my appreciation to the archivists and librarians at the many libraries and record offices listed in the List of Unpublished Sources. They and their staffs have all showed me the greatest kindness.

The research for the dissertation was assisted by generous fellowships from the Jacob K. Javits Fellowship Program, the Henry Huntington Library, the Krupp Foundation, the Center for European Studies at Harvard University, and the London School of Economics. Subsequent travel, research, and writing were facilitated by assistance from the American Philosophical Society, Harvard University's Clark Fund, and the Henry Huntington Library. To all these sponsors I am grateful.

My parents, Patricia Leigh Hancock and John Darwin Hancock, by raising me in a climate of intellectual curiosity and industriousness, contributed distinctively to the telling of this story.

And, last, but surely not least, I would like to thank Lex Kelso, whose interest in historical matters, whose insight into economic and human problems, and whose personal kindness and support over the years have helped to keep this project always challenging and exciting.

Truro, Massachusetts
July 1, 1994

Tables

Graphs

Illustrations

Abbreviations Used in the Footnotes

Add.Mss.	Additional Manuscripts Collection, British Library, London
ADM	Admiralty Records, Public Record Office – Kew Gardens, London
AO	Audit Office Records, Public Record Office – Kew Gardens, London
B	Court of Bankruptcy Records, Public Record Office, Chancery Lane, London
BCM	Ballindalloch Castle Muniments (Macpherson-Grant Papers), Ballindalloch Castle, near Aviemore, Scotland
BL	British Library – Department of Manuscripts, London
C	Court of Chancery Records, Public Record Office – Chancery Lane, London
CO	Colonial Office Records, Public Record Office – Kew Gardens, London
COLRO	Corporation of London Record Office, London
CP	Court of Common Pleas Records, Public Record Office – Chancery Lane, London
CS	Court of Sessions Records, Scottish Record Office, Edinburgh
CSP(C)	*Calendar of State Papers, Colonial Series, America and West Indies*
E	Court of Exchequer Records, Public Record Office – Chancery Lane, London
EUL	Edinburgh University Library, Edinburgh
EXT	Extracted Papers, Public Record Office – Kew Gardens, London

FO	Foreign Office Records, Public Record Office – Kew Gardens, London
GD	Gifts and Deposits Collection, Scottish Record Office, Edinburgh
IGI	*International Genealogical Index* (Salt Lake City, Utah)
IOL	India Office Library, London
KB	Court of King's Bench Records, Public Record Office – Chancery Lane, London
NLS	National Library of Scotland, Edinburgh
PROB	Last Wills and Testaments filed with the Archbishop of Canterbury's Court, Public Record Office – Chancery Lane, London
PRO-CL	Public Record Office in Chancery Lane, London
PRO-KG	Public Record Office at Kew Gardens, London
RD	Register of Deeds, Scottish Record Office, Edinburgh
RS	Register of Sasines, Scottish Record Office, Edinburgh
SP	State Papers Records, Public Record Office – Kew Gardens, London
Spottes	Spottes, Home of Sir Michael Herries, near Castle Douglas, Scotland
SRA	Strathclyde Regional Archives, Glasgow, Scotland, and Ayr, Scotland
SRO	Scottish Record Office, Edinburgh
Sudlows	Sudlows, Home of Admiral Sir Julian Oswald, Shedfield, England
T	Treasury Papers, Public Record Office – Kew Gardens, London
Trade and Plantations	*Journal of the Commissioners for Trade and Plantations*
T-SK	Stirling of Keir Papers, Strathclyde Regional Archives, Glasgow
WO	War Office Records, Public Record Office – Kew Gardens, London

The following standard abbreviations are also employed:

arr.	arriving	eds.	editors	pt.	part
b.	born	f.	folio	q.	quire
c.	capita	ff.	folios	r.	recto
c.	circa	Geo.	George	r.	reel
ch.	chapter	misc.	miscellaneous	sched.	schedule
chs.	chapters	ms.	manuscript	ser.	series
cl.	clause	mss.	manuscripts	sub.	see under
cls.	clauses	n.	number	trans.	translator
cf.	compare	nn.	numbers	v.	verso
dep.	departing	p.	page	vol.	volume
ed.	editor	pp.	pages	vols.	volumes

All dates before the Gregorian calendar was introduced in 1752 are given in the old style, yet the year reckoned as beginning on January 1.

Letters, spelling, and punctuation have been preserved in the quotation of original passages.

All prices are given in English pounds sterling, unless otherwise noted.

In the text, numbers are rounded; in the footnotes, they are as exact as possible.

Introduction

IN 1773, A SWEDISH BOTANIST NAMED HENRY SMEATHMAN arrived at Bance Island, fifteen miles upstream from the mouth of the Sierra Leone River. On this rock, the site of a West African slave factory owned and operated by six London merchants, and the safest anchorage of the region, Smeathman found an orderly refuge from the confusion of the jungle. Much given to regular ways himself, the "unfortunate flycatcher" was immediately struck by the harmonious arrangement of the place. The unruly growth of the tropics was carefully and frequently cleared away, and there remained "little else but iron, rock & gravel." Favorably comparing these facilities to others along the coast, he wrote that the headquarters of the factory was "a plain neat building" with "a very cool & convenient gallery in the front" where the traders "walk & see everything . . . that is passing about them." Its main spaces boasted large and lofty rooms. But what most fascinated the Swede was not the order and neatness, for the depot certainly had its share of "little, dark & inconvenient" apartments, not the barbarous trade in slaves, but rather the entertainment available there, the myriad ways the factory made up for tropical discomfort with European amusements and necessities.

On his first full day on the island, the botanist and his companions, traders from all parts of America and Europe, played a game of golf. In Britain, golf courses could be found in only two places and, on the continent, they existed only in Holland. In Africa, therefore, a golf course was something of a rare species and, in his diary, Smeathman described what was surely the first course on the African continent, as if it were a new creature omitted by his friend Linnaeus. Two holes, each the size of a man's head, were made in the ground, he recorded, about a quarter of a mile from each other. The balls were the size of tennis balls, and the clubs were made from rare Central American woods. The players formed two parties; each group took its place at one of the holes and then proceeded to strike its ball toward the opposite hole; and so it went, back and forth. These sportsmen were dressed in white cotton shirts and trousers brought from India in the factory proprietors' ships. They were attended by African caddies, draped in loincloths of a tartan design made from wool that had been woven in one of the partners' industrial ventures, a wool factory near Glasgow. Golf was "a very pretty exercise" for the middle of the jungle, since the exertion was minimal and the American and British company congenial. When the game was over, entertainment shifted indoors. The white inhabitants amused themselves before supper with whist and backgammon. They dined on ape, antelope, boar, and fish. After dinner, they drank Madeira wine and smoked Virginia tobacco.[1]

As I read Smeathman's account for the first time, over 200 years later, I was stunned by the bizarre, un-self-conscious parody of African territorial conquest. But I was more surprised by and intrigued with the implications of the image for the larger colonial and imperial world. Golf courses hedged by mangroves, British and American traders in Indian cotton, slaves in tartan, Irish beef and butter, Caribbean rum, Virginian tobacco, German guns, London ships? How did this odd collection come to be, and what did it represent?

This congeries of goods and peoples was the tangible result of the work of a small group of London partners. The six owners of the factory, drawing on their own peripatetic experiences, were working to extend the frontier of Britain's empire, in Africa and in America. They were doing this by marshaling their employees, agents, and clients on four continents to build the outpost, to staff and provision it, to conduct an extensive trade with the African hinterland from it, and to sell its produce, slaves, from Tobago to Jamaica to Rhode Island. This slave entrepot was one of the principal nodes in their far-flung business operations, which embraced victualing stations in India, Jamaica, Nova Scotia, and Germany, plantations in the Caribbean, the American mainland, and India, and an interconnected chain of shipping and trading routes between London and Calcutta, Madeira, the British West Indies, and the North American mainland colonies in the period 1735–85. Building these networks made them wealthy and provided the commercial infrastructure for the development of the British Atlantic world in the eighteenth century.

This study is part of a larger, ongoing research inquiry into how America grew from a small band of settlers scattered along the eastern coastline of the mainland and the Caribbean early in the seventeenth century to a diverse group whose prosperity and confidence nearly 175 years later allowed thirteen colonies "to dissolve the political bands" that had connected them to Britain. The present historical study aims

1. "Extracts from Mr. Smeathman's Letters to Mr. Drury," May 10, 1773, Smeathman Papers, Ms. D26, envelope 2, no. 4, University of Uppsala, Uppsala, Sweden; GD 248/60/1/31, 34, and 248/511/4; and Chapter 6 in the present book.

to understand one critical aspect of that growth: how the British metropolis influenced the American periphery. It focuses on commerce and particularly on the men in the metropolis who traded with America. It shows how one group of London merchants working between 1735 and 1785 seized imperial, largely American opportunities, helped integrate the empire as they integrated their own business operations and worked to improve their surroundings as, by the standards of their day, they improved their positions in British society. In doing so, these merchants actively abetted what Adam Smith called America's rise to "wealth and greatness," even as they enriched themselves.

Historical Writing on Trans-Atlantic Traders

Historians' general assessments of the role of eighteenth-century trans-Atlantic trade have taken one of two forms – statistical analysis or biographical narrative. Each form has its strengths and its weaknesses. The statistical approach constructs arguments about commercial and economic forces based upon aggregate data; it gathers facts compiled in the colonial period and focuses on large sweeps of time. Like much economics, it deals with markets and movements, not principally with people. Statistics enable the historian to define and measure historical forces and lend precision to historical questions.[2] Yet, at the same time, the statistical approach often renders a remote and deracinated account, stripped of reference to the actions and thoughts of the men and women

2. Studies focusing on the statistical dimensions of colonial trade include Gary M. Walton, "Sources of Productivity Change in American Colonial Shipping, 1675–1775," *Economic History Review*, 2nd ser., v. 20 (1967), pp. 67–78; John J. McCusker, "The Rum Trade and the Balance of Payments of the Thirteen Colonies, 1750–1775" (Ph.D. dissert., University of Pittsburgh, 1970); William L. Davisson and Laurence J. Bradley, "New York Maritime Trade: Ship Voyage Patterns, 1715–1765," *New York Historical Society Quarterly*, v. 55 (1971), pp. 309–17; Geoffrey N. Gilbert, "Baltimore's Flour Trade to the West Indies, 1750–1815" (Ph.D. dissert., Johns Hopkins University, 1975); Gary M. Walton and James F. Shepherd, *The Economic Rise of Early America* (Cambridge, 1979); and James H. Levitt, *For Want of Trade: Shipping and the New Jersey Ports, 1680–1783* (Newark, 1981).

For similar studies concerning the trade of the mother country, see Ralph M. Davis, *The Rise of the English Shipping Industry* (London, 1962); Jacob M. Price, "New Time Series for Scotland's and Britain's Trade with the Thirteen Colonies and States, 1740 to 1791," *William and Mary Quarterly*, 3rd ser., v. 32 (1975), pp. 307–25, and *Capital and Credit in British Overseas Trade: The View from the Chesapeake* (Cambridge, Mass., 1980); Jacob M. Price and Paul G. E. Clemens, "A Revolution in Scale in Overseas Trade: British Firms in the Chesapeake Trade," *Journal of Economic History*, v. 47 (1987), pp. 1–43; Christopher J. French, "The Role of London in the Atlantic Slave Trade, 1680–1776" (M.A. thesis, University of Exeter, 1970), and "The Trade and Shipping of the Port of London, 1700–1776" (Ph.D. dissert., University of Exeter, 1980); and Kenneth Morgan, *Bristol & the Atlantic Trade in the Eighteenth Century* (Cambridge, 1993).

who made up society. For example, in one analysis, Geoffrey Gilbert ably establishes that the top 2.5 percent of investors acquired 21 percent of the tonnage in late eighteenth-century Baltimore, but he does not (and, in his defense, probably cannot) show how the distribution of investment affected individual merchants. Statistical answers are general, frequently so general that they bear little connection to the people affected. At times, one is left wondering whether the historical forces existed at all, because the process of historical "number-crunching" often reveals patterns in their entirety of which the participants could not directly have been aware.

Biography provides a ready alternative to statistics. The biographical approach focuses on individual lives or families, or specific commercial groups working in certain geographical areas. As a result, reading biography is often more satisfying than reading the economists' accounts; in focusing the reader's attention on people, it paints a picture more like life as readers experience it. This method has been adopted by James Hedges, who wrote artfully about the Brown family of Rhode Island, Richard Pares, who studied the Pinney family of Nevis and Bristol, Thomas Doerflinger, who carefully dissected the community of Philadelphia merchants, and Jacob Price, who wrote about Glasgow merchants.[3] Yet, with the notable exceptions of Doerflinger's and Price's

3. Studies of American individuals: James B. Hedges, *The Browns of Providence Plantations: Colonial Years* (Cambridge, 1952); William T. Baxter, *The House of Hancock* (Cambridge, 1945); Philip L. White, *The Beekmans of New York in Politics and Commerce, 1647–1877* (New York, 1956); Carl L. Romanek, "John Reynell: Quaker Merchant of Philadelphia" (Ph.D. dissert., Pennsylvania State University, 1969); James D. Anderson, "Thomas Wharton, 1730/31–1784: Merchant in Philadelphia" (Ph.D. dissert., University of Akron, 1977); and Richard R. Johnson, *William Nelson* (Oxford, 1991).

Studies of American groups: Arthur M. Schlesinger's *The Colonial Merchants and the American Revolution, 1763–1776* (New York, 1918), was the first work to isolate merchants for discussion, but it focused solely on political activity. Later scholars placed merchants more squarely in the counting-house. Virginia D. Harrington, *The New York Merchant on the Eve of the Revolution* (New York, 1935); Bernard Bailyn, *The New England Merchants in the Seventeenth Century* (Cambridge, 1955); Thomas Doerflinger, *A Vigorous Spirit of Enterprise: Merchants and Economic Development in Revolutionary Philadelphia* (Chapel Hill, 1986); Oliver A. Rink, *Holland on the Hudson: An Economic and Social History of Dutch New York* (Ithaca, 1986); and S. Stumpf and J. Marshall, "Leading Merchants of Charleston's First 'Golden Age,'" *Essays in Economic and Business History*, v. 4 (1986), pp. 38–46.

Studies of British individuals: Richard Pares, *A West India Fortune* (London, 1950); William L. Roberts III, "Ralph Carr: A Newcastle Merchant and the American Colonial Trade," *Business History Review*, v. 42 (1968), pp. 271–87; Jacob M. Price, "One Family's Empire: The Russell–Lee–Clerk Connection in Maryland, Britain & India," *Maryland Historical Magazine*, v. 72 (1977), pp. 165–225; and Price, *Perry of London* (Cambridge, Mass., 1992).

analyses, these studies, richly detailed and cogently argued as they are, seem incomplete, shackled largely by the state of surviving evidence. Typical is William Roberts's life of Ralph Carr. Roberts carefully recounts how the merchant Carr fails to market European manufactures in New York and New England in the 1750s, but unrealistically describes the failure as resting solely in Carr's inability to accept risk; in this account, contemporary economic and geopolitical realities do not impinge upon his decision-making. In principle, by stressing intentionality or agency, biography should allow the historian to see how individuals react to invisible forces. But whatever the community or the size of the group being studied, it has usually been written as if mercantile lives or businesses took place in a vacuum: biographers have trouble dealing with those aspects of social life not under the direct control of their subjects or those areas not fully evidenced. One seldom comes away from reading merchants' biographies with a sense of the social aggregate into which the individuals fit, or the extent to which they interacted with larger economic and social forces, processes, and circumstances. In this historical genre, the choices the subject made eclipse attention to the alternatives he weighed; the rationalizations the subject adopted for those choices crowd out attention to different, unknown, or unseen motives.[4]

Studies of British groups: Walter E. Minchinton, "The Merchants in England in the Eighteenth Century," in H. G. J. Aitken, ed., *Explorations in Enterprise* (Cambridge, 1965), pp. 278–95; R. J. Wilson, *Gentlemen Merchants: The Merchant Community in Leeds, 1700–1830* (Manchester, 1971); Thomas M. Devine, "Glasgow Merchants and the Collapse of the Tobacco Trade, c. 1700–1815," *Scottish Historical Review*, v. 52 (1973), pp. 50–74; Thomas M. Devine, "An Eighteenth-Century Business Elite: Glasgow–West India Merchants, c. 1750–1815," *Scottish Historical Review*, v. 57 (1978), pp. 40–67; Elizabeth K. Newman, "Anglo-Hamburg Trade in the Late Seventeenth Century and Early Eighteenth Centuries" (Ph.D. dissert., University of London, 1979); Price, *Capital and Credit*; Kenneth J. Morgan, "Bristol Merchants and the Colonial Trades, 1748–1783" (Ph.D. dissert., Oxford University, 1983); Margaret Hunt, "English Urban Families in Trade, 1660–1800: The Culture of English Merchant Capitalism" (Ph.D. dissert., New York University, 1986); Jacob M. Price, "The Great Quaker Business Families of Eighteenth-Century London," in R. S. Dunn and M. M. Dunn, eds., *The World of William Penn* (Philadelphia, 1986), pp. 363–99; John Sainsbury, *Disaffected Patriots: London Supporters of Revolutionary America, 1769–1782* (Kingston, Ontario, 1987); and Peter Earle, *The Making of the English Middle Class* (Berkeley, 1989).
4. Wilson's Leeds clothiers, for example, behave as if their community or the periphery prospered by itself. Wilson, *Gentlemen Merchants*. Perhaps that is a reflection of the cloth trade, but Wilson's approach is paradigmatic of that of students of other groups of merchants. Only recently have historians of eighteenth-century commerce begun to articulate the merchants' involvement in the larger world of empire, a world which the merchants were aware of, affected by, and involved in. Doerflinger, *A Vigorous Spirit*, pp. 97–122, provides a good example of the newer approach.

The challenge of understanding the influence of the metropolis on the periphery is heightened by the fact that neither the statistical nor the biographical approach has done much with the metropolis. London's merchants remain largely unstudied, and the influence of London on trans-Atlantic commerce has seldom been explored, apart from White-hall's policy of mercantilism or the legislation of Parliament.[5] There are some exceptions: Ralph Davis's masterly synthesis of English shipping, a work of immense scope that comprehends London traders even though it is primarily argued from non-London sources; Peter Earle's recent attempt to dissect London business before 1730; two studies of the port of London by Christopher French, who includes some mention of trading circles but bases his conclusions almost exclusively on the extremely spotty port records; and the dozen or so biographical accounts of Augustan London merchants written by Lewis Namier and his followers.[6] But these contributions are noticeably few, given the overall importance of London to the empire, and they focus exclusively on trade. Ignoring the complex dynamics of eighteenth-century life, none takes into account

5. The view from the periphery has won the day, despite Richard Pares's compelling case for a view from the center. "The Economic Factors in the History of the Empire," *Economic History Review*, v. 7 (1937), pp. 114–44.
6. Davis, *The Rise*; Earle, *English Middle Class*; and French, "The Role of London," and "The Trade and Shipping." For Namier and his students, see Lewis Namier, "Brice Fisher, M.P.: A Mid-Eighteenth-Century Merchant," *Journal of Economic and Business History*, v. 1 (1927), pp. 514–32, and "Anthony Bacon, M.P.: An Eighteenth-Century Merchant," *Journal of Economic and Business History*, v. 2 (1929), pp. 20–70; Lucy Sutherland, *A London Merchant, 1695–1774* (Oxford, 1933); Elizabeth Donnan, "Eight-eenth-Century English Merchants: Micajah Perry," *Journal of Economic and Business History*, v. 4 (1938), pp. 70–98; Richard Pares, "A London West Indies Merchant House, 1740–1769," in Richard Pares and A. J. Taylor, eds., *Essays Presented to Sir Lewis Namier* (London, 1956), pp. 75–107; William L. Roberts III, "Samuel Storke: An Eighteenth-Century London Merchant Trading to the American Colonies,"*Business History Review*, v. 39 (1965), pp. 147–70; A. H. John, "Miles Nightingale – Drysalter," *Economic History Review*, 2nd ser., v. 18 (1965), pp. 152–63; Ralph M. Davis, *Aleppo and Devonshire Square: English Traders in the Levant in the Eighteenth Century* (London, 1967); D. W. Thoms, "The Mills Family: London Sugar Merchants of the Eighteenth Century," *Business History*, v. 11 (1969), pp. 3–10; P. W. Kingsford, "A London Merchant: Sir William Baker," *History Today*, v. 21 (1971), pp. 338–48; Dean Rapp, "Social Mobility in the Eighteenth Century: The Whitbreads of Bedfordshire, 1720–1815," *Economic History Review*, 2nd ser., v. 27 (1974), pp. 380–94; Nicholas Rogers, "Money, Land and Lineage: The Big Bourgeoisie of Hanoverian London," *Social History*, v. 4 (1979), pp. 437–54; Price, *Capital and Credit*, "Buchanan and Simson, 1759–1763: A Different Kind of Glasgow Firm Trading to the Chesapeake," *William and Mary Quarterly*, 3rd ser., v. 40 (1983), pp. 3–41, "The Last Phase of the Virginia/London Consignment Trade: James Buchanan & Co., 1758–1768," *William and Mary Quarterly*, 3rd ser., v. 43 (1986), pp. 64–97, and "Great Quaker Business Families," pp. 363–99; Henry Horwitz, "'The Mess of the Middle Class' Revisited: The Case of the 'Big Bourgeoisie' of Augustan London," *Continuity and Change*, v. 2 (1987), pp. 263–96; and Philip Ziegler, *The Sixth Great Power* (New York, 1988).

the merchants' other economic activities, such as manufacturing, farming, or stock-trading, let alone their social lives, their houses, art collections, and the like.[7] The omission is serious, since London's importance in the empire also includes its importance vis-à-vis other urban communities in Britain, its domination of the Home Counties, and its strong influence on the economy and society of rural areas. Furthermore, none of the London studies assesses the contribution made by Londoners to the labor of merchants and entrepreneurs in America. For decades, historians have taken for granted the fact that the mother country was "the central figure, the authoritative and guiding force, the influence of which did more than anything else to shape the course of colonial achievement."[8] There is little serious analysis of how men at the

7. Contrast the narrow approaches taken by British and American writers with the more synthetical approach of students of European and Canadian commerce. For France, see T. J. A. Le Goff, "An Eighteenth-Century Grain Merchant: Ignace Advisse Desruisseaux," in J. F. Bosher, ed., *French Government and Society, 1500–1850* (London, 1973), pp. 94–122; Robert Niklaus, "The Merchant on the French Stage in the Eighteenth Century, or the Rise and Fall of an Eighteenth-Century Myth," in D. J. Mossop et al., eds., *Studies in the French Economy* (Durham, 1978); Norma Perry, "French and English Merchants in the Eighteenth Century: Voltaire Revisited," in *Studies in Eighteenth Century French Literature* (Exeter, 1975), pp. 193–213; and Robert L. Stein, *The French Slave Trade in the Eighteenth Century: An Old Regime Business* (Madison: 1979). Canadian merchants have been the subject of recent investigation. J. F. Bosher, *The Canada Merchants, 1713–1763* (Oxford, 1987). Especially insightful, systematic studies of group composition and career patterns have been written by historians of colonial Latin America. D. A. Brading, *Miners and Merchants in Bourbon Mexico, 1763–1810* (Cambridge, 1971); John E. Kicza, *Colonial Entrepreneurs: Families and Business in Bourbon Mexico City* (Albuquerque, 1983); Brian R. Hamnett, *Politics and Trade in Southern Mexico, 1750–1821* (Cambridge, 1971); Elizabeth A. Kuznesof, "The Role of the Merchants in the Economic Development of São Paulo, 1765–1850," *Hispanic-American Historical Review*, v. 60 (1980), pp. 571–92; and Louisa S. Hoberman, "Merchants in Seventeenth-Century Mexico City: A Preliminary Portrait," *Hispanic-American Historical Review*, v. 57 (1977), pp. 479–503.

Some scholars have come to appreciate more diverse aspects of the merchants' world, yet these are seldom incorporated into larger economic interpretations. Diana Donald, "'Mr. Deputy Dumpling and Family': Satirical Images of the City Merchant," *The Burlington Magazine*, v. 106 (1989), pp. 755–63; Katharine A. Kellock, "London Merchants and the Pre-1776 American Debts," *Guildhall Studies in London History*, v. 1 (October 1974), pp. 109–49; Neil McKendrick, "'Gentlemen and Players' Revisited: The Gentlemanly Ideal, the Business Ideal, and the Professional Ideal in the English Literary Culture," in *Business Life and Public Policy: Essays in Honour of D. C. Coleman* (Cambridge, 1986), pp. 98–136; John McVeagh, *Tradefull Merchants: The Portrayal of the Capitalist in Literature* (London, 1981); Jacob M. Price, "Directions for the Conduct of a Merchant's Counting House, 1766," *Business History*, v. 28 (1986), pp. 134–50; Sainsbury, *Disaffected Patriots*; and Maurice Woolf, "Eighteenth-Century London Jewish Shipowners," *Transactions of the Jewish Historical Society of England*, v. 24 (1974), pp. 198–204.

8. Charles M. Andrews, *The Colonial Period of American History*, v. 1 (New Haven, 1934), p. xi.

metropolitan center actively and creatively managed the economic systems that Americans used to their advantage and then rebelled against.[9] And there is little critical attention paid to what Jacob Price has recently described as "the backward influence of the colonies" on the world of Londoners – a surprising state of affairs, since, in the words of the French historian and philosopher Abbé Raynal, "the whole world" made London "rich and populous."[10]

Inspired by the goals of the founders of the *Annales* school of history – to analyze as well as to narrate historical phenomena, to comprehend a wide range of human behavior rather than political activity alone, and to draw upon other disciplines – and by recent British and American approaches that view the Atlantic as a bridge rather than a barrier, the present study combines statistical and biographical inquiry to open up the boundaries that have limited historical writing on eighteenth-century trans-Atlantic traders, and fill some of the gaps in our understanding of the mutual influence of the center and the periphery on each other. Hoping to mediate between the mass and the individual, as well as between impersonal forces and human reactions, and statistics and biographies, the present study recreates the complex world of some of

9. This is in marked contrast to the systematic study of London's seventeenth-century merchants: J. R. Woodhead, *The Rulers of London, 1660–1689* (London, 1965); Richard Grassby, "English Merchant Capitalism in the Late Seventeenth Century: The Compilation of Business Fortunes," *Past and Present*, v. 46 (1970), pp. 87–107; Richard Grassby, "The Personal Wealth of the Business Community in Seventeenth-Century England," *Economic History Review*, 2nd ser., v. 23 (1970), pp. 220–34; D. W. Jones, "London Overseas-Merchant Groups at the End of the Seventeenth Century" (Ph.D. dissert., Oxford University, 1970); Robert Brenner, "The Civil War and London's Merchant Community," *Past and Present*, v. 58 (1973), pp. 53–107; Robert Brenner, *Merchants and Revolution: Commercial Change, Political Conflict, and London's Overseas Traders, 1550–1663* (Princeton, 1993); R. G. Lang, "Social Origins and Social Aspirations of Jacobean London Merchants," *Economic History Review*, 2nd ser., v. 27 (February 1974), pp. 288–47; and Peter Earle, "Age and Accumulation in the London Business Community, 1665–1720," in Neil McKendrick and R. B. Outhwaite, eds., *Business Life and Public Policy: Essays in Honour of D. C. Coleman* (Cambridge, 1986), pp. 38–63.
10. Abbé G. T. F. Raynal, *A Philosophical and Political History of the Settlements and Trade of the Europeans in the East and West Indies*, v. 6 (London, 1783), p. 412. J. Botsford, in *English Society in the Eighteenth Century as Influenced from Overseas* (New York, 1924), made an erratic start; more recently, H. Bowen analyzed the effects of India events on London's financial world. H. V. Bowen, "Investment and Empire in the Later Eighteenth Century Empire: East India Stockholding, 1756–91," *Economic History Review*, 2nd ser., v. 42 (1989), pp. 186–206. But the best analysis of this influence is Price, "Who Cared about the Colonies? The Impact of the Thirteen Colonies on British Society and Politics, circa 1714–1775," in Bernard Bailyn and Philip Morgan, eds., *Strangers within the Realm* (Chapel Hill, 1991), pp. 395–436. The point was previously made by B. Lenman and P. Lawson, "Robert Clive, 'the Black Jagir,' and British Politics," *Historical Journal* (1983), p. 827.

London's international merchants at a critical moment in the development of the colonies.[11]

This is easier promised than delivered. London merchants, the subjects of this study, seldom made the news. Their record is thin, so thin that neither biographer nor statistician should be satisfied. Their business dealings were usually conducted in conversation, not on paper; businessmen seldom wrote about their work unless forced by distance or law. Though they wrote business letters detailing the comings and goings of ships, the fulfillment of contracts, the honoring of requests, the execution of trusts, and the like, little was said about the harmony or tension that prevailed among partners, the division of responsibilities among those in the counting-house, the physical setting for their business transactions, or their reasons for going into new areas of business. They penned personal missives, but these are relatively few and often uninformative. Too, they appeared in governmental records as entries in customs books, securities ledgers, and other official reports. By combining these materials for personal biographical narrative and aggregate statistical analysis, and by adding to them a discussion of the material artifacts the merchants left behind (houses, gardens, roads, factories, and plantations), I propose to illuminate their world. That is to say, by combining the private and public lives of real people, keeping them at the center of the story, and merging the account of their experiences with the broader explanatory context of the economic and social forces impinging upon men and women in the Atlantic community, I believe we can gain a more accurate and interesting understanding of the influence of the metropolis on British-American trade in the fifty years before the end of the American Revolutionary War.

The Sample of Merchants and the Nature of the Evidence

In the present study, I focus on one cadre of London merchants who traded with America. "Merchant" originally meant any trader in goods, but by the middle of the eighteenth century, its original meaning had been considerably narrowed. General dictionaries, like those written by Samuel Johnson or Thomas Sheridan, defined a merchant as one "who trafficks to remote countries." Trade experts like Timothy Cunningham, the author of a popular treatise on the law of bills of exchange, described

11. Good examples of a "bridge" perspective emphasizing the integrated nature of the empire are Ian K. Steele, *The English Atlantic, 1675–1740* (New York, 1986), Bernard Bailyn, *Voyagers to the West* (New York, 1986), and David Cressy, *Coming Over* (New York, 1987).

a merchant as not "every one who buys or sells" but rather one who moves in the "Way of Commerce" by "Importation or Exportation," who "makes it his Living to buy and sell, and that by a continued Assiduity, or frequent Negotiation in the Mystery of Merchandizing." Most contemporaries agreed that a merchant was a wholesale trader who had dealings with foreign countries. Many groups of critical importance to the domestic economy, such as "artificers" (manufacturers), skilled tradesmen, retailers, and shopkeepers, were not labeled "merchants."[12]

The cadre of trans-Atlantic wholesale merchants I am writing about lived in London for the half-century between 1735 and 1784 and worked regularly with one another, trading on a large scale with Britain's American colonies and around the world. I discovered this group while in my first graduate seminar at Harvard. I was searching for material on the cadre's most famous member, Richard Oswald of Philpot Lane, who served as Britain's representative at the 1782 Paris negotiations that ended the war between the rebellious colonies and the mother country. As I studied Oswald's life and examined his role in the prerevolutionary development of America, I quickly moved beyond diplomacy to the activities of Oswald and others like him that contributed to the integration of the Atlantic community. In response to letters I wrote to Oswald's descendants, I learned that they still had personal and business papers stuffed in hatboxes and sea chests, and they invited me to examine them. I looked at these collections in the ensuing months and quickly realized that Oswald was only one piece of a large puzzle, one character in a complicated story much like the intricate network of Scheherazade's tales, which never completely come together. As I discovered more about the West African slaving operation Oswald managed, I added his five partners in that venture to my search and, when I learned still more about the six partners, I widened my search to all of their known partners. In the end, I identified a group of twenty-three London merchants, associates clustered in four circles of partnership

12. Samuel Johnson, *A Dictionary* (London, 1755); Thomas Sheridan, *A General Dictionary of the English Language*, v. 2 (London, 1780); and Timothy Cunningham, *The Law of Bills of Exchange, Promissory Notes, Bank-Notes, and Insurances* (London, 1761), p. 4 and n. 1. Other contemporary descriptions appear in R. Campbell, *The London Tradesman* (London, 1747), pp. 284–85; Wyndham Beawes, *Lex Mercatoria Rediviva: Or, The Merchant's Directory* (London, 1761), pp. 29–40; and Thomas Mortimer, *The Universal Director*, Part III (London, 1763), pp. 3–4. See also David H. Sacks, *The Widening Gate* (Berkeley, 1991), pp. 125–26; Earle, *English Middle Class*, p. 34; Jacob M. Price, "What Did Merchants Do?" *Journal of Economic History*, v. 49 (1989), p. 282; and Minchinton, "Merchants in England," pp. 62, 69. Minchinton extends the definition of the term to include loan contractors, exchange brokers, stock jobbers, and bullion dealers.

around four individuals: Augustus Boyd, Alexander Grant, John Sargent II, and Richard Oswald:

Boyd Circle
Augustus Boyd (1679–1765)
Sir John Boyd (1719–1800)
John Trevanion (1741–1810)
William Wood (fl. 1763–81)

Oswald Circle
Alexander Anderson (1756–1832)
John Anderson (1747–1808)
Michael Herries (1715–99)
John Levett (1725–1807)
John Mill (1710–71)
Richard Oswald (1705–84)
Robert Scott (d. 1771)

Sargent Circle
George Aufrere (1715–1801)
Thomas Birch (d. 1774)
Christopher Chambers (fl. 1753–83)
William Cooke (d. 1787)
Samuel Gardiner (1723–94)
Robert Rolleston (1747–1826)
John Sargent II (1714–91)
John Sargent III (1750–1831)
Richard Stratton (1704–58)

Grant Circle
John Gardiner (fl. 1749)
Sir Alexander Grant (1705–72)
Alexander Johnston (1698–1775)

For some readers, the use of terms like "associates" and "circles" may raise interpretive problems: "associates," to the modern reader, may connote regular if intermittent, common endeavor. Yet only some of the time did these merchants act together in joint activities; most of the time, they moved independently, albeit along parallel lines. Such problems are semantic. In the pages that follow, I refer to four "circles," and call their members "associates." No formal, legal tie is implied by using such terms, for certainly no such tie existed, and the associates never once used either term to denote their relationships, although they occasionally employed "association." Still, these terms seem appropriate, since they capture the loose, flexible nature of the business ties better than any others. Indeed, one of the defining characteristics of this cadre, its informality, stems from the fact that partnerships in the eighteenth century could still be open-ended. It was possible to be a partner with one person for a venture or two, and to be partners with different individuals or groups at the same time in different ventures. The trading possibilities were numerous: investment partnerships in one shipping venture or ongoing shipping ventures; commercial associations in pursuit of trade, irrespective of ownership of ships or shares, whether through simple partnerships of two merchants, large multimember firms, regulated companies, or joint-stock companies. The "firm," as it has since come to be known, was still evolving in the eighteenth century. While most merchants operated alone or from two- or three-person partnerships sharing premises, this did not stop them from participating in larger, looser, more informal trading consortia that operated like commercial guilds, on the order of the Bristol Merchant Venturers and the Company of Merchants trading to Africa, or pursuing overseas trade directly, as did the twenty-three merchants studied here. In consistently but loosely maintaining links to others, the associates represent a significant subclass of eighteenth-century merchants engaged in the overseas trade. The merchants studied here had common outlooks and experiences which allowed them to come together for some purposes in joint commercial operations, but did not require them to maintain those bonds in all instances.

Although all twenty-three associates are discussed, this book concentrates on the leaders of the four circles – their origins, their varied business activities, and their social and personal lives. The focus on these four men, as well as the issues addressed, are partly a reflection of the survival and the nature of the extant records: on the biographical level, this book deals only with matters for which there is source material. But these are the men we would most want to understand, anyway. They dominated their circles. And they were leaders in London's mercantile community.[13]

In describing their lives, I seek to paint a picture of the work of London merchants who operated in the Atlantic between 1735 and 1785. To understand their lives beyond their businesses, I have considered a wide range of activities, for the associates played many different roles. They were merchants, traders, planters, contractors, lawyers, financiers, politicians, connoisseurs, farmers, industrialists, and philanthropists. I have investigated how they approached nonbusiness subjects like land holding, house building, art collecting, gardening, farming, charitable giving, and road, bridge, and canal building, as well as more purely commercial pursuits, like shipping, planting, slaving, and contracting.

No existing source collections document all of the activities of the associates. The most obvious sources for information are the manuscripts held by their descendants, but such collections are generally uneven in content and document primarily personal, family, or local concerns. The usual materials available to business historians – letters and accounts – scarcely exist for these Georgian merchants. In order to reconstitute as fully as possible the physical and mental furniture of the associates' world, I have had to move beyond family and counting-house papers. To supplement this body of data, I located the communities

---

13. New manuscript collections discovered too late to be incorporated into the present discussion, such as the Cust Papers at the Lincolnshire Archives Office, confirm their dominance.

in which the twenty-three lived and worked around the world, consulted the archives of those communities in search of relevant material and, from them, culled details about their activities and thoughts.

Since the associates' operations stretched from Mexico to Calcutta, from Nova Scotia to the Falkland Islands, the paper trail is long. Nevertheless, it has proved possible to piece together accounts of their business and social activities from 1735, when Augustus Boyd set up shop in the City, to 1784, when Richard Oswald, the best known of the associates, died. In addition to compiling biographies, I have tracked from customs records the comings and goings of the associates' ships over a forty-year period, and amassed statistics recording their use of banking facilities, investment in stocks, and acquisition of land. From national, local, and colonial court records, I have compiled another database which documents how the associates used law to settle disputes and order their affairs.

In the quest for material, the main surprises came as the search ranged farther afield, beyond much-used repositories in America and London to seldom visited record offices in the West Indies, the meticulously arranged archives of German principalities and other European states, the malodorous West Bengal State Archives, and a dank warehouse in suburban London where lay the records of one colony, unused and uncataloged, amid crates strewn with bits of broken coconut shells and old newsprint. In these unexpected places, I discovered richly detailed records of great value in reconstructing the associates' activities. My story expanded as my material expanded, for it was this process of expanding discovery that opened my eyes to the intertwined complexities of British-American commerce and the managerial role played by successful merchants at the center of the empire.

A Larger Picture

The associates were neither wholly unique nor wholly representative of London's merchants. The question of uniqueness or representation is difficult to answer precisely, because we do not know enough about the London mercantile community in the eighteenth century to permit comparisons across the entire group.[14] It is safe to say that the associates

14. It is, of course, relevant to know what percentage of the population the associates represented, and it is possible to hazard some estimates, even though the evidence is thin. Accepting Wrigley's population estimates for London, greater London may have had 675,000 inhabitants at midcentury. A London trade directory for 1749 lists 2,865 merchants, less than half of 1% of the metropolitan population. A names analysis of the merchants in this trade directory shows that Scots merchants made up 4% of that 0.5%. If these figures are to be believed, the 12 Scots in this sample of 23 merchants

were not representative in the sense of a statistical sample; but there is no reason to believe they were unique, either. They were not creators or inventors, but "state-of-the-art" entrepreneurs, commercial practitioners who adopted new practices and products whenever they seemed profitable. Such men were always looking for new techniques to adopt and implement; they were not mired in tradition. Neither, however, were they driven to discover new trade routes, as to the South Seas, or new forms of merchandising, as did Josiah Wedgwood. They were what marketing experts today call "fast followers" – opportunistic in adopting new and useful practices, and in imitating procedures and operations that seemed appropriate. Their greatest distinction may be that they were successful, indeed, colossally successful by eighteenth-century standards, both commercially and socially.

The story of the associates shows the role of an often ignored yet nonetheless powerful kind of international merchant – marginal, opportunistic, global, improving, and integrative – at work in the British Atlantic trading world during the middle decades of the eighteenth century. The associates came from the periphery, physically, commercially, and socially; they were amalgams of two or three distinct traditions or experiences, usually preceded by rejection and migration. I use "marginal" to distinguish the associates from those who fit the cultural norms, did not migrate, and stood as charter members of the economic and social establishment. The associates were "opportunistic," restless men who actively adapted their decisions and actions to the commercial expediency of the moment. They were relentless, even experimental in seeking opportunities to invest; they maintained more than one product or activity at once; they entered new enterprises, often profitably; and, in general, they were flexible in their responses to change. Their opportunism stood in contrast to peers who thought and acted more traditionally. The associates were "global" overseas merchants, whose operations stretched around the world; their fields of action were

made up 10% of the Scots merchants in London at midcentury. E. A. Wrigley, "A Simple Model of London's Importance in Changing English Society and Economy, 1650–1750," *Past and Present*, v. 37 (1967), p. 44; D. V. Glass, "Gregory King's Estimate of the Population of England and Wales, 1695," in D. V. Glass and D. C. Eversley, eds., *Population in History* (London, 1965), p. 203; R. Floud and D. McCloskey, *The Economic History of Britain since 1700*, v. 1 (Cambridge, 1981), pp. 17, 21; P. Deane and W. Cole, *British Economic Growth, 1688–1959* (Cambridge, 1967), p. 6; and K. H. Connell, "Land and Population in Ireland, 1780–1845," *Economic History Review*, 2nd ser., v. 2 (1950), p. 278. For merchants, see Anon., *A Complete Guide* (London, 1749). In a thoughtful new study, Robert Brenner strives to overcome the problem of representation by stressing "internal cohesiveness" – common origins, family and business ties, and entrepreneurial interests – without making them representative of something larger (*Merchants*, p. 182).

primarily neither local nor national. Their reach started early in life with their migrations, and they drew on their far-flung experiences and contacts throughout their careers. In this study, "global" and "globalization" denote the range and breadth of the associates' contacts with commercial points around the globe, especially with lands and peoples not traditionally tied to Britain; it does not mean that any single merchant maintained contact with all points. In this sense, I am not distinguishing "global" from "international."

Using the word "global" also does not imply acceptance of the reasoning of Immanuel Wallerstein and his followers, whose adoption of a global perspective to analyze long-term economic growth and the underdevelopment of the Third World is flawed by an overly selective reliance on old data and an extremely rigid view of the world as a single economic structure made up of core, subperiphery, and periphery components.[15] Each of these components is made up of separate but ultimately fungible states or communities. Wallerstein's neo-Marxian analytical approach considers the rule of law and the exercise of power as epiphenomena, secondary to the possession of wealth and the ownership of property. Such a view, unfortunately, ignores subtle, significant details, from person to person and place to place, which gave each community its character and each empire its history. Rather than imposing a determinative relationship between property and power, as does Wallerstein's approach, a more particularistic approach uncovers mediated, reciprocal relationships. It focuses on political structures like colonies and legal institutions like assemblies, and on cultural ties between the state and the colony, that is, on the day-to-day exercise and acceptance (or rejection) of authority, as well as on the relations between imperial powers – all of which are contingent on time, space, and human agency. Accordingly, I have adopted a particularistic framework for understanding the ways in which merchants like the associates worked and prospered.

The last two characteristics of the associates – improvement and integration – arose within the context of their responses to their marginality and to the expanding international environment they found

15. It is suggestive that, while "global" denoted something globular or spherical in the seventeenth century, the word came to comprehend anything all-inclusive, unified, total, or which pertained to or involved the whole world by the nineteenth century. "International" was widely used in the associates' lifetimes. See, for instance, Jeremy Bentham, *Principles of Legislation* (London, 1780), pp. xvii, 25. For uses of world systems analysis in recent historical writing, see Immanuel Wallerstein, *The Modern World System*, 3 vols. (New York, 1974–88); Samir Amin, *Accumulation on a World Scale* (Sussex, 1974), and *Unequal Development* (Sussex, 1976); Andre Frank, *World Accumulation, 1492–1789* (New York, 1978), and *Dependent Accumulation and Underdevelopment* (New York, 1978).

themselves in. They were the principal impulses driving these men's lives. The associates were "improvers": they were not content with maintaining the status quo. This is clear toward the end of their lives, as they built estates, houses, art collections, gardens, farms, factories, and charities. Improvement, as they defined it, meant more than an increase in crop yields; it touched most aspects of everyday life, and it manifested itself in programs that were at once polite, industrious, and moral. Running through most of their noncommercial activities and even some of their business ventures is an intense drive for a broadly based civility, a persistent attention to the possibility of bettering man's condition: their own, as they became gentlemen, and others', since they believed society as a whole was advancing from barbarism toward civility.

Improvement was a preoccupation that came relatively late in the day. In contrast, integration was an approach they adopted throughout their careers. They helped build the infrastructure of Great Britain's Atlantic empire, by managing their own commercial operations, linking the empire with new American immigrants, both voluntary and involuntary, new American markets, and new scientific and technological innovations. That is, they coordinated people, materials, and capital across market sectors and among geographically dispersed areas. The work of integration is the principal story of the associates' lives, and it ties what they did in the counting-house to what they did in the slave depot visited by Smeathman or the plantation house in America. Whether sending supplies, slaves, or arms to America, planting indigo, rice, or sugar there, shipping American crops to London, distributing bread to the army in Europe, or amassing extensive collections of paintings and statues, the key to their success was in bringing people and products together in flexible and novel ways.

The associates integrated their businesses geographically, combining goods or people from India, Africa, the West Indies, South Carolina, and Germany, and operationally, managing multiple activities, like shipping, planting, and contracting. The geographical range is most apparent. When Smeathman toured Bance Island, he found traders trained in every corner of the British world, and goods that had been grown or manufactured in numerous places between the Yucatan and Bengal. The proprietors drew upon resources from all parts of the world and deployed them with skills sharpened in all parts of the world. A second, related dimension of the associates' business integration was operational: the associates did not build their ventures into unified organizations, but instead managed them as loosely bound sets of plans, projects, and ventures that combined their linked networks of partners, relations, dependents, agents, and contacts. This approach made the system flexible, and enabled this group of imperial enterprisers to control risks and earn profits. Instead of supervising and managing all parts of their operations themselves, they delegated tasks to a variety of equals, dependents, suppliers, agents, and correspondents, and held in reserve others who could serve as alternates in case their original plans broke down.

To separate integration and improvement for the purpose of historical analysis is not to suggest that the two were separate. In fact, the two were deeply intertwined: the patterns and processes the associates used to integrate their businesses – geographical and operational linkages, personal networks, and the like – were the same as those they employed to better their own and their contemporaries' social condition. They improved themselves in British society by introducing foreign styles into British backwaters, instituting new and different programs, techniques, crops, and machines into the countryside, and physically and financially connecting the empire and the city to the country. They improved themselves in business by expanding their entrepreneurial commitments and erecting linked systems of enterprise around the world. Although they did not use the word "integrating," they believed that by linking the world through trade and the discourse of experimentally minded men, they were improving it, raising it from economic barbarism to economic civilization. They applied what they learned in the economic sphere to the conduct of life in the social sphere, and vice versa; patterns and processes learned in one reinforced and altered those in the other.

It is easy to value the legacies that these merchants left from their success in trade, the development of the New World, and their social and charitable projects. For some of these things, we may even admire them as people. One has the sense that many of them would have been good dinner-table companions – Benjamin Franklin and Henry Laurens thought so. To late twentieth-century observers, then, it is incongruous that these same men were active, even eager participants in the slave trade, and made some of their most representative business initiatives in that realm. We cannot justify their participation in the slave trade; and it would be repulsive to admire someone who acted as they did in our century – an age that is more self-conscious about race and social and economic freedom. We can, however, recognize that these merchants' failure to comprehend the immorality of slavery stems from the same habits of mind that led to their achievements elsewhere. Much will be made in this book of their practical, opportunistic, improving approach to the world. With regard to slavery, they are also prime exemplars of the limits of that approach, and of the coldness, indifference, and inhumanity that its unthinking application can lead to. Because of their practical, commonsense focus, they did not reconsider the acceptable, the accepted means of their day. Their few extant comments on the subject do not even recognize the need to justify slavery, the slave trade, or their role in it. At the ends of their lives the associates were self-consciously patrons, concerned to look beyond their personal lives and fortunes to the greater weal of their communities. This is heavy with irony, since the communities were peopled from Africa as well as from Europe, and built with Africans' sweat and blood as well as Europeans'. Their vision was limited by the ideas available in their times, and the common humanity of Africans and Europeans was not part of the ideas available to mundane men of affairs in mid-eighteenth-century London. The irony was lost on them.

Western man's understanding of what he was permitted to do and where he was permitted to go was expanding over the course of what has come to be known as the Age of Reason. Wars were fought on a grander scale, and empires, the outcome of wars, stretched farther around the globe. Science and technology grew; communication became faster; even the very conception of business became broader. Growth was very much a part of the workaday world. Such growth, of course, was not peculiar to the eighteenth century or to Britain. Yet it takes on a new dimension when placed in the eighteenth-century British context of population explosion, the adoption of general principles of mechanization and their application to all parts of the economy, and the unprecedented growth in international commerce. These were exciting, challenging, even disorienting times in which to work. The changes in the business and social environment that accompanied the Age of Reason in Britain and her empire were the results of few dramatic breakthroughs in thinking or technology. Rather, most changes took place steadily, the results of many small, nearly invisible innovations by relatively unknown men like the associates who nibbled away at the boundaries of the familiar and permissible, in such entrepreneurial areas as oceanic shipping and trading, long-distance management of plantations, slaving, military contracting, and rural improvements. In the words of the associates' friend Benjamin Franklin, they seized any opportunity that tended to increase their power "over matter and multiply the conveniences and pleasures of life."[16]

16. Benjamin Franklin, "Proposals for Promoting Useful Knowledge among the British Plantations in America," 1743, in L. W. Labaree, ed., *The Papers of Benjamin Franklin*, v. 2 (New Haven, 1960), pp. 378–83.

Plan of the Study

This study unfolds in three sections. Part I stresses the importance of both the empire and the individual to the conduct of trade. Chapter 1 reviews old and new historical scholarship on the course of the empire in the eighteenth century to show how the world was expanding, how the challenges and opportunities that arose from that expansion presented themselves, and how new ways of handling these challenges and opportunities were being devised and utilized. In essence, it argues that the empire set the framework for their lives by establishing opportunities and channeling energies. Chapter 2 introduces the associates, analyzing the similarities among them and contrasting them to the canonical "merchant" profile devised by historians. It discusses the differences among them in experience and personality by focusing on the four most prominent: Augustus Boyd, Alexander Grant, John Sargent II, and Richard Oswald. The chapter argues that these were diverse, marginal men, who were driven to erase that status through commercial and social opportunism.

Part II (Chapters 3 through 8) takes a closer look at the associates' businesses. Chapter 3 shows the London international merchant at work in his counting-house at the seat of the empire, where he handled correspondents' affairs, directed his own business, and indulged his omnivorous appetite for information. The chapter reconstitutes a merchant's physical surroundings, and articulates one of the central themes of the book – that a key to commercial success was "integration," marked by a wide range of activities that had to be managed simultaneously, and a diversity of skills among partners and employees that had to be knit together. With the aid of a computerized database of contemporary British, colonial, and foreign port records documenting associate shipping, Chapter 4 sketches their shipping and trading businesses: the wide dispersal of the associates' ships, the linkages with which they connected the skills of the men who worked for them, their combining commission merchandising and "principal enterprising," the use of diverse contacts to fill ships, and the insistence on close supervision to prevent tardy vessels.

Chapters 5, 6, and 7 argue that one of the reasons for the associates' commercial success in shipping and trading lies in the "backward integration" of their business interests into three distinct areas of "principal enterprising": planting, slaving, and contracting. In these activities, we see the associates managing the imperatives of each field of business, investing and reinvesting, finding suitable, effective on-site managers, and linking their various business activities. Chapter 8 explores some aspects of the financing of the associates' business ventures. Over their lives, they moved from being users of funds to providers of funds. This chapter discusses how they built their initial stakes from family, previous business, and marriage sources; how they borrowed and lent; how they dealt with banks; and, finally, how they invested in other business and land when they were not plowing cash back into their own businesses.

Part III (Chapters 9 and 10) deals with the associates' preoccupation with increasing their social status and creating a new and better world. It focuses on domestic, noncommercial activities as necessary steps along the road to becoming a gentleman: estate building, house building, art collecting, gardening, farming, and charitable endeavors – road, bridge, and canal building, manufacturing, and philanthropy. These personal and community activities reflected the status the associates had achieved in the mercantile and political worlds, and enhanced and reinforced that status further. Through activities that were polite, industrious, and moral, with programs that combined a practical, commonplace approach with a visionary intent, the associates reshaped people's lives. Closing the book is an epilogue with a comment on the legacies left by the twenty-three international merchants.

As "citizens of the world," London businessmen like the associates were critical to the economic development of the British Atlantic community during the eighteenth century's middle decades. The rubric, a modification of a phrase coined by Joseph Addison and later made famous as the title to Oliver Goldsmith's 1762 commentary on the variety of eighteenth-century life, characterizes these London enterprisers as transnational agents in an international business environment.[17] The deceptively simple conception provides, nonetheless, an important framework within which to understand a wide range of British and colonial endeavors, and in particular a lens through which to see the development of early America, a region strong enough by 1776 to steer its own course. Great Britain's transoceanic empire created and empowered men like the associates: men hailing from Britain's periphery, drawn to its core, and taking part in the commercial organization and management of the lands and peoples they left behind; entrepreneurs working in an empire structured around political, economic, and colonial correspondence between mother country and dependent colonies and attuned to a

17. *The Spectator*, No. 69 (May 19, 1711), in Joseph Addison, *The Works*, ed. Thomas Tickell, v. 1 (London, 1804), pp. 178–79. For subsequent quotation or similar commentary, see Postlethwayt, *Universal Dictionary*, v. 2 (London, 1755), p. 624; and Frederick A. Pottle, ed., *Boswell's London Journal, 1762–1763* (New Haven, 1950), passim.

rational, enlightened Euro-Atlantic culture of refinement. As a contemporary of the associates observed, "none but people of narrow and contracted minds" should "entertain separate ideas of the Island of Great Britain" and her empire. "Without thoroughly understanding and keeping constantly in our minds this natural, this inseparable connection of interests, we shall be liable to continual mistakes."[18] Neither the periphery nor the center prospered by itself; the periphery, in particular, prospered through trade with and help from the center.

Augustus Boyd, Alexander Grant, Richard Oswald, John Sargent, and their associates provided some of the metropolitan trade and help by integrating and improving the British Atlantic community. They served as the colonists' counterparts on the eastern edge of the Atlantic, and they built or organized the economic and, on occasion, social and political structures within which colonial merchants and entrepreneurs conducted their business. The African slave factory that Henry Smeathman visited in 1773 looked as it did because its proprietors were in the business of moving plantation supplies, trade goods, and white and black laborers around the Atlantic, developing hinterlands, economically and socially, at home and abroad, and experimenting with and spreading new ideas and technologies. The same could be said of any of the associates' plantations in America. With a flexible, integrative approach to international operations and a wide-ranging, technique-driven, ideal-laden spirit of improvement, metropolitan entrepreneurs made investments and commitments that promoted economic growth and helped create the commercial success of Britain and America.

18. [John Campbell,] *Candid and Impartial Considerations on the Nature of the Sugar Trade* (London, 1763), pp. 73, 19–20. Some 175 years later, Charles Andrews described the empire in similar terms. *Colonial Period*, v. 4, p. 344.

PART I

The Crucible of Trade

1

A Larger World

THESE RESTLESS FORWARD- AND OUTWARD-LOOKING associates would have understood their characterization as citizens of the world. They were aware of their new-found allegiance to a larger community, talked about it constantly, and attempted to meet its challenges. Out of necessity, they were international thinkers and actors who viewed the world as a connected series of markets that they could integrate and improve. To them, Britain's America was an important link in this international chain. Commercial and social systems that they installed at various points around the Atlantic and in India brought the associates financial success, served as a buffer against the unpredictable swings in the economic cycle, allowed them to be more commercially flexible than most private-sector oceanic traders, and gave them the means to leave a legacy. The associates realized these gains within the context of Britain's expanding global empire, with a growth in territory, governance, trade, consumption, and knowledge occurring all around them. As we shall see in the chapters that follow, they seized and made the most of opportunities this growth created.

The Dimensions of Expansion

Over the course of the eighteenth century, Britain's reach was widening. At home, the eighteenth century opened with the Act of Union (1707) that abolished Scotland's Parliament and combined its national government with that of England and Wales. It closed with another Act of Union (1801) that brought Ireland into the national fold.[1] Abroad, the British were building "a new kind of empire," larger and arguably more unified than the conglomerate that was known as Great Britain. The years from 1655 and the capture of Jamaica to 1763 and the end of the Seven Years' War witnessed a fivefold increase in the extent of the empire and, with it, a dramatic redrawing of colonial boundaries.

---

1. Ian Christie, *Wars and Revolutions: Britain, 1760–1815* (Cambridge, Mass., 1982), passim; and Judith Blow Williams, *British Commercial Policy and Trade Expansion, 1750–1850* (Oxford, 1972), passim.

Whereas, in 1655, the North American mainland colonies had been grouped in four small areas along the Atlantic coast, 108 years later, they ran in an almost unbroken line from the Labrador beaches in the north to the Florida swamps in the south; inland, they penetrated more than 200 miles as far as Montreal and Quebec, Fort Stanwix (New York), Fort Bedford (Pennsylvania), Charlottesville (Virginia), and Wachovia (North Carolina).[2]

The expansion occurred in war-induced spurts.[3] In the War of Spanish Succession (1702–13) and its Peace of Utrecht (1713), Britain wrested from Spain two strategically important naval bases, Gibraltar and Minorca. At the same time, Britain's South Sea Company, which enjoyed a monopoly of all English trade with Central and South America, gained a contract for transporting and selling slaves to Spain's colonies there. From the French, the British acquired Acadia (Nova Scotia), Newfoundland, and the Hudson's Bay territory. In terms of the total amount of land appropriated, the next international war, the War of Austrian Succession (1740–48), had less of an immediate effect on territorial rule, the British returning Cape Breton Isle to France in exchange for the French restoring Madras to Britain. Still, the long-term expansion on the Indian subcontinent and the opportunities to trade in the South Seas that followed therefrom were hardly negligible, for there were important economic interests protected and promoted in this midcentury redrawing of boundaries, and it was precisely these interests that were nurtured in the years that followed. The Seven Years' War (1756–63) in Europe, known as the French and Indian War in America, capped the century-long wave of dynamic growth. Under the terms of its Peace of Paris (1763), Britain gained valuable territory in North America (Spain ceding Florida, and France ceding Canada and Cape Breton Isle), the Caribbean (France ceding the important agricultural islands of Tobago,

2. P. J. Marshall, "Empire and Authority in the Later Eighteenth Century," *Journal of Imperial and Commonwealth History*, v. 15 (1987), pp. 106, 115–16. The redrawing of colonial boundaries was most apparent on the North American mainland. During the 1660s, at least two New England colonies annexed neighboring lands, but the real expansion occurred to the south. The surrender of the Dutch in New Jersey, Delaware, and New York culminated in a grant to Charles II's brother of all land between the western boundary of Connecticut and the eastern shore of the Delaware River. Several years later, Charles II granted William Penn a charter to all land west of the Delaware. The Crown was no less interested in lands farther south: supporting a settlement in the Cape Fear River area of North Carolina; granting to eight proprietors all the land between the 31st and 36th parallels (South and North Carolina); and encouraging speculators to occupy and settle land south of the Savannah River.

3. On the subject of territorial expansion, see *The New Cambridge Modern History*, v. 6: *The Rise of Great Britain and Russia, 1688–1725*, ed. J. S. Bromley (London, 1970), pp. 442–43; and v. 7: *The Old Regime, 1713, 1763*, ed. J. O. Lindsay (Cambridge, 1957), pp. 191–213.

Grenada, St. Vincent, and Dominica), West Africa (France ceding Senegal in exchange for Gorée), and India (Britain allowing France to keep Pondichery and Chandernagor, in return for France acknowledging Britain's de facto supremacy on the subcontinent). As peace was proclaimed in 1763, Britain approached the apogee of her power. Her empire was now a composite structure of an accidental and various design.

At the same time as Britain's imperial territory was growing, her population was rising, and some of the rise was causally related since more lands meant more, often healthier places for Britons to settle and propagate. Britain's total population increased from 6.9 million in 1700 to 10.7 million in 1800; overall, a 55% rise. In England itself, while the seventeenth-century population had grown only 25%, it rose 72% in the eighteenth century, from 5.0 million in 1700 to 8.6 million in 1800. London became Europe's largest city, with nearly 1 million people in 1801.[4] But the periphery witnessed the greatest growth in population. In colonial Jamaica, the population rose from 47,000 in 1698 to 340,000 in 1800, roughly 2% each year. And in Britain's North American colonies, growth was even more pronounced: from roughly 250,000 people in 1700, the European population of North America grew by more than 3% per year to approximately 2,150,000 in 1770.[5]

While her territories and peoples were increasing, Britain's state government was expanding and her administrative grip was tightening. As John Brewer has emphasized, Britain's military successes, which made possible the territorial acquisitions, "would not have been possible without adequate resources in manpower and money." Over the course of the century, British citizens witnessed a remarkable increase in the number of workers who earned a living in the service of the state, and in the amount of money that oiled the bureaucracy and allowed it to keep pace with the increasing lands and peoples it controlled and governed. Between 1692 and 1755, personnel in the offices of the Secretary of State, the Lord High Admiral, the Navy Board, and the Board of Trade all increased fourfold. Some departments grew at a greater rate,

4. P. Mathias, *The Transformation of England* (London, 1979), p. 118; E. Wrigley and R. Schofield, *The Population History of England* (London, 1981), pp. 533–34; and E. Wrigley, "Urban Growth and Agricultural Change: England & the Continent in the Early Modern Period," *Journal of Interdisciplinary History*, v. 15 (1985), pp. 683–728, esp. 693.

5. U.S. Department of Commerce – Bureau of the Census, *Historical Statistics of the United States: Colonial Times to 1970*, Part 2 (Washington, D.C., 1975), p. 1168; and David Watts, *The West Indies* (Cambridge, 1987), Table 7.5, p. 311. McCusker and Menard, *Economy of British America*, Table 3.1, give slightly higher figures and a rise of 762% in the North American colonies; in the British Caribbean colonies, a 226% rise; in all British American colonies, a 570% rise.

others at a lesser, but the overall shift was undeniably upward. Revenue departments, the agencies that were most closely tied to the expansion of a global economy, experienced similar growth: manned with 2,524 in 1690, they had grown to 8,292 by the end of the War for America in 1783.[6]

As expenditures for defending the empire and manning its bureaucracy rose, so public indebtedness mounted to astonishing heights: between 1697 and 1783, the unredeemed public debt increased nearly fifteenfold, lurching upward with each successive war. Empire was expensive: in 1737, nearly 82% of total government expenditure defrayed the charges incurred in defending Britain's territories and maintaining her debt; by 1764, this figure had risen even further to 89%. The debt was "discharged" in two ways: more debt, and more taxation. An increase in debt was the politicians' preferred alternative, but over the course of the century per capita tax revenue (adjusted for inflation) grew two-and-one-half times, from 12 shillings 3 pence in 1700 to 1 pound 11 shillings in 1800 – a rise of 155% in 100 years.[7] Furthermore, as the costs of the wars grew, so did the opportunities for profit-making by government contractors, who were more often than not large-scale London wholesale merchants who traded overseas. These same entrepreneurs were also called on to finance the increasingly militaristic state, by investing heavily in the popular government annuities that were offered to induce the subscription of loans for defraying war costs.

From numerous studies published in the last three decades, we also know that Britain's economy grew relatively slowly during the eighteenth century: per capita national income, for example, increased 0.3% per year in the first eight decades of the century. Only in the area of foreign trade do we find any significant contrast to this slow growth: whereas the output of English industry consumed at home rose by 14% beween 1700 and 1770 and the output of English agriculture rose by 17% in the same period, the output of English industry exported to foreign and colonial markets rose by 156%.[8] During roughly this same

---

6. The discussion in this and the following paragraph owes much to John Brewer's study of the emergence of Britain as an international fiscal and military power in the 1700s. *The Sinews of Power: War, Money and the English State, 1688–1783* (New York, 1989), pp. 64–69, 114–26.

7. Brewer, *Sinews*, pp. 66–67, 114–21; and Mathias, *Transformation*, pp. 118–21.

8. P. Deane and W. Cole, *British Economic Growth, 1688–1959* (Cambridge, 1962), p. 78; and N. F. R. Crafts, *British Economic Growth during the Industrial Revolution* (Oxford, 1985), p. 45. The slow growth of the agricultural sector can be deceiving, for many aspects of change in this prestatistical period are difficult to quantify. There was, we know, an increase in the extent of both estates and farms. There were, too, a proliferation and diffusion of new crops like turnips and breeding techniques, and an increase in seed yields. Peter Mathias, *The First Industrial Nation* (Cambridge, 1983), pp. 66–70.

period (1700–60), exports grew from 24% to 35% of gross industrial output.[9]

The export and re-export sector was the most expansive area of Britain's economy and opened up opportunities that were obvious to merchants in the empire. As foreign trade grew over the eighteenth century, the non-European market rose in importance compared to the European market. Around 1700, more than 80% of England's exports and re-exports went to the "unprotected" markets of Europe, and less than 20% to the "protected" markets of America, Africa, and India, where mercantilistic imperial laws ensured British merchants of customers; just over seventy years later, Europe took only 40%, and overseas dependencies took the remainder. The American market led the rise and, to many, it was apparent that of "all the branches of our commerce" it was "the most valuable." The American colonies alone received 33% of English exports and re-exports in 1774, in contrast to the 13% they had received in 1701. Indeed, North America and the West Indies absorbed slightly more exports from England in the 1770s than England had exported to all parts of the world at the beginning of the century, a fact that partially explains Britain's determination to hold onto her colonies.[10]

Tied to the growth and shift in the export sector was a "consumer boom" that reached "revolutionary proportions" by the time the associates were at the height of their careers. During the eighteenth century, British factories began producing pottery, ceramics, glassware, cutlery,

9. Crafts, *British Economic Growth*, p. 132. Crafts adjusts data for 1700 and 1760 given by Ralph Davis in "English Foreign Trade, 1700–1774," *Economic History Review*, 2nd ser., v. 15 (1962), pp. 285–303.
10. B. R. Mitchell and P. Deane, *Abstract of British Historical Statistics* (Cambridge, 1962), p. 312; Deane and Cole, *British Economic Growth*, p. 87; and Davis, "English Foreign Trade," pp. 285–303. See also [George Lyttelton,] *Considerations upon the Present State of Affairs, at Home and Abroad* (London, 1739). For a recent breakdown of the percentages that accounts for Scottish data, see Price, "Who Cared about the Colonies?" in Bailyn and Morgan, eds., *Strangers within the Realm*, pp. 416–21.

 In correctly focusing on growth in the American sector, one should not ignore other important global shifts that led to dynamic growth in the export area overall. One of the more significant was the slow erosion of the prominence of the Dutch in the trade between Europe and Asia. In this area, the British were big winners. Much had to do with the way competing European companies dealt with China in the tea trade. In 1718, the Dutch Company centered in Batavia offered the Chinese fixed prices for green tea that were much lower than previous prices and then charged the Chinese higher prices for Batavian pepper. Chinese disgust at this treatment led to China allowing Holland's competitors to buy black tea directly from the Chinese. Holden Furber, *Rival Empires of Trade in the Orient, 1600–1800* (Minneapolis, 1976), pp. 129–44; R. Glamann, *Dutch-Asiatic Trade, 1620–1740* (Copenhagen, 1958), pp. 216–43; K. Chaudhuri, *The Trading World of Asia and the English East India Company, 1660–1760* (Cambridge, 1978), p. 388; and Larry Neal, *The Rise of Financial Capitalism* (Cambridge, 1990), p. 131.

leather, and paper goods at unprecedented rates and in unprecedented volumes.[11] Rising disposable incomes which, among the mercantile groups, were frequently tied to the growth in exports, and growing supplies of cheap goods combined to build what has been described as "a major watershed" in British economic life – the emergence of rampant consumption. Newspaper publishing and advertising and a network of permanent retail shops linked the outer reaches of the kingdom to the "goods-rich" metropolis; and the easing of credit removed additional barriers to buying.[12]

Imports soared, too. It is well known that, in this period, tea, tobacco, and sugar grown overseas emerged as staples in the domestic economy, but the influence of overseas trade was not restricted to major commodities. As John Brewer reminds us, small shops like those of Abraham Dent in Westmoreland or the grocer Henry Hancock in Sheffield regularly stocked rice, raisins, currants, prunes, vinegar, oil, hops, pepper, other spices, and brandy obtained from the Mediterranean, the Baltic, India, North America, and the Caribbean.[13] Nor was the rise in consumption confined to England and Wales; the people of Scotland, Ireland, and America all experienced similar shifts in behavior. As one historian has noted, the eighteenth-century American market experienced "an exceptionally rapid expansion of consumer choice." Small peddlers in backcountry America widely distributed finished goods manufactured in Britain, as when, by the outbreak of the Revolution, housewives in plantation-country Carolina eagerly bought, albeit "at a monstrous price," soap that was made in Ireland. Transoceanic merchants served as the conduit for satisfying American consumers.[14] We get an especially vivid illustration of this from New York advertising: whereas, in some months in the 1720s, New York City merchants

11. Maxine Berg, *The Age of Manufactures: Industry, Innovation, and Work in Britain, 1700–1820* (Oxford, 1985), pp. 28–29, 38–40, 274–78.

12. Neil McKendrick, "The Consumer Revolution of Eighteenth-Century England," in Neil McKendrick, John Brewer, and John Plumb, *The Birth of a Consumer Society* (Bloomington, Ind., 1982), pp. 9–34. McKendrick also points to the contributing force of social emulation, but its role has been downplayed in more recent systematic studies. Christine Macleod, *Inventing the Industrial Revolution: The English Patent System, 1660–1800* (Cambridge, 1988); and Hoh-Cheung and Lorna Mui, *Shops and Shopkeeping in Eighteenth-Century England* (Toronto, 1989). The body of scholarship on the subject grows each year. In addition to the foregoing studies, see Roy Porter, *English Society in the Eighteenth Century* (Harmondsworth, 1982); and Lorna Weatherill, *Consumer Behavior and Material Culture in Britain, 1660–1760* (London, 1988).

13. Brewer, *Sinews*, pp. 184–85. See any issue of *The Edinburgh Advertiser* for the increasingly regular advertisement of the sale of exotic foodstuffs in the provinces.

14. Timothy Breen, "'Baubles of Britain': The American and Consumer Revolutions of the Eighteenth Century," *Past and Present*, v. 119 (1988), p. 79. On the colonies, see E. W. and C. M. Andrews, eds., *Journal of a Lady of Quality, . . . 1774 to 1776* (New Haven, 1921), p. 204.

described only fifteen different manufactured goods in newspaper advertisements, and those descriptions were of generic categories, by the 1770s, they were hawking over 9,000 different imported items with specific, elaborate descriptions. No rugs were described in advertisements before 1750, but seven different kinds of rugs were hawked by some merchants during the 1760s. "A vast Demand," Benjamin Franklin observed, was "growing for British Manufactures," abroad and at home, and this demand London's wholesale merchants were all too eager to satisfy.[15]

Alongside the growth in the territory and the economy of the empire, there occurred an expansion in the intellectual sphere: eighteenth-century merchants and their contemporaries witnessed significant advances in geographical investigation, scientific knowledge, and technological technique.[16] This was a time of continuing discovery and exploration, only some of which had to do with a growth in territory: the Bering Straits in 1728; Alaska and the Aleutian Islands in 1741; Tahiti, the Solomon Islands, and New Guinea in the late 1760s; Botany Bay in 1770; and Hawaii in 1778. While James Bruce traced the Blue Nile to its confluence with the White Nile, Horace de Saussure climbed to the summit of Mont Blanc and took weather measurements, and Mungo Park explored the deepest recesses of the Niger River. Others unearthed the Rosetta Stone; and still others mapped the moon. Whole new interior regions – northern Asia and northern North America – were opened to the use of the European. Exploration increasingly took on a more scientific character.[17]

As Captain Cook's voyages demonstrated, this phase of geographical discovery coincided with (indeed, it was facilitated by) profound advance

15. Breen, "Baubles," p. 80; and Benjamin Franklin, "Observations Concerning the Increase of Mankind,..." (1751), in A. H. Smyth, ed., *The Writings of Benjamin Franklin*, v. 3 (1907), p. 66. The studies of "consumer society" in America are less satisfying than those for England. Breen has reviewed this literature in "'Baubles of Britain'," pp. 73–104; and "An Empire of Goods: The Anglicization of Colonial America, 1690–1776," *Journal of British Studies*, v. 25 (1986), pp. 467–99. A good synthesis appears in Carole Shammas, *The Pre-Industrial Consumer in England and America* (Oxford, 1990).
16. Marshall and Williams, *The Great Map of Mankind*, pp. 45–63; and Mathias, *Transformation*, p. 46.
17. An increasing number of writings publicizing these discoveries appeared over the course of the century. On Georgia, see Trevor R. Reese, ed., *The Most Delightful Country of the Universe: Promotional Literature of the Colony of Georgia, 1717–1734* (Savannah, 1972), and *Our First Visit in America: Early Reports from the Colony of Georgia, 1732–1740* (Savannah, 1974). On Hawaii and the Pacific Northwest, see Bernard Smith, *Imagining the Pacific: In the Wake of the Cook Voyages* (New Haven, 1992), pp. 23–31; and John L. Allan, *Lewis and Clark and the Image of the American Northwest* (New York, 1975). For a more general introduction, see Edward Heawood, *A History of Geographical Discovery in the Seventeenth and Eighteenth Centuries* (Cambridge, 1912), pp. 322–49, 408–09.

in experimental science. Newton's *Optics*, Linnaeus's *Systema Naturae*, and Lavoisier's Table of 31 Elements were all published within the associates' lifetimes. Such works, of course, were the delayed harvest of the seventeenth century's "Scientific Revolution," and their insights into the nature of matter and the laws that regulated it found an avid audience with practical and scientific men who were more concerned than their forebears with the development, organization, and functioning of man in society and especially how these relate to the solution of everyday problems. Fittingly linking science and social engineering, the eighteenth century bridged the introduction of an inoculation against the societywide scourge smallpox (1717) and a vaccine against it (1796). The offensive of systematic knowledge against traditional ignorance, a movement which made no distinction between science and engineering, also made inroads in the economic sector. The flying-shuttle loom (1733), steam condenser (1764), spinning mill (1771), steam engine (1775), double-acting rotary steam engine (1782), and cotton gin (1793) changed manufacturing techniques, which in turn led to changes in the organization of industry. Practical and enlightened international merchants were enamored of these new discoveries, inventions, and systems, attempted to acquaint themselves with their benefits wherever feasible, and even introduced them into their daily lives.[18]

In this superheated atmosphere of geographical, scientific, and technological discovery, information and technique were advancing the agenda of commercial and practical men of affairs. One of the advantages of doing business in London was its location at the hub of the empire's governmental and commercial networks, and chief among the advantages was access to the press.[19] During the 1720s, at least 40 London newspapers paid advertising taxes; by the late 1760s, the number had risen to 85. During the 1720s, there were 3 daily papers; by the early 1770s, there were 8. In the counties, the number of papers rose from 22 in 1725 to 50 in 1783.[20] Helped by a growth in safe, dependable

18. Scientific and technological advances are outlined in Abraham Wolf, *A History of Science, Technology, and Philosophy in the Eighteenth Century*, 2nd ed. (London, 1952), pp. 498–667; and Charles Singer et al., eds., *A History of Technology*, v. 4 (Oxford, 1958). The influence of scientific discoveries on Cook's handling of navigation and cartography is discussed in Smith, *Imagining*, pp. 41–49.
19. John Brewer, *Party Ideology and Popular Politics at the Accession of George III* (Cambridge, 1976), p. 142.
20. A. Aspinall, "Statistical Accounts of the London Newspapers during the Eighteenth Century," *English Historical Review*, v. 63 (1948), pp. 210–11, 224–27; and Brewer, *Party Ideology*, p. 142. There is some disagreement on the number of papers. According to G. A. Cranfield, 130 newspapers were established before 1760, 33 of which survived. *The Press and Society from Caxton to Northcliffe* (London, 1978), pp. 179–86. The spread of news was a function of better roads and faster ships, both of which improved dramatically in the seventeenth and eighteenth centuries. Steele, *English Atlantic*, pp. 114–22, 303; Wesley E. Rich, *The History of the United States Post*

road mileage and an increase in sailing speeds, an international merchant could each day devour news from around the world that was printed in the *Gazetteer, Public Advertiser, General Evening Post, London Evening Post, London Chronicle,* and *Lloyd's List,* the indispensable handbook of London's international shippers and traders. News about ships, stocks, commercial matters before the House of Commons or the City's Common Council, and estates for sale was all displayed on their pages. Merchants not only received information; they actively used the dailies to advertise the arrival of their ships, the sale of goods consigned to them, the disposal of their ships, the rental of their estates, and the creation and dissolution of their partnerships.[21]

Books and information societies also became more widespread during the eighteenth century. Published writings on commercial subjects were available as never before, and allowed the merchant "to make the tour of the world in books." A crude count of entries relating to writings on "commerce," "trade and manufactures," "finance," and "the colonies" in the most comprehensive catalog of eighteenth-century economic literature suggests a constant growth and an increasing profusion of commercial information between 1688 and 1768.[22] Guides, handbooks, narratives, and tracts for British merchants appeared in most European languages – English, Swedish, Dutch, German, French, Italian, Spanish, and Portuguese; and these books, having found their way into the libraries of international merchants, allowed them to "make the tour of the world," to receive "the idea of the whole at one view."[23]

Office to the Year 1829 (Cambridge, 1924), pp. 3–48; William Smith, *The History of the Post Office in British North America, 1639–1870* (New York, 1921), pp. 1–73; and Eric Pawson, *Transport and Economy: The Turnpike Roads of Eighteenth-Century Britain* (London, 1977), pp. 113–15.

21. John J. McCusker and Cora Gravesteijn, *The Beginnings of Commercial and Financial Journalism: The Commodity Price Currents, Exchange Rate Currents, and Money Currents of Early Modern Europe* (Amsterdam, 1991), pp. 291–300.

22. Daniel Defoe, *The Compleat English Gentleman,* ed. Karl D. Bulbring (unpublished at Defoe's death in 1731; London, 1890), p. 225; and *The Goldsmiths'-Kress Library of Economic Literature: A Consolidated Guide to . . . the Microfilm Collection,* 4 vols. (Woodbridge, Conn., 1976). On the growth of the book market, see Marjorie Plant, *The English Book Trade: An Economic History of the Making and Sale of Books,* 3rd ed. (London, 1974), pp. 53–58; and Paul Langford, *A Polite and Commercial People: England, 1727–1783* (Oxford, 1989), pp. 90–94.

23. Price, "Who Cared," p. 408. George Aufrere, Thomas Birch, Alexander Johnston, and John Mill, for example, subscribed to John Wright's handbook *The American Negotiator: Or, The Various Currencies.* Price has found that 31 percent of the subscribers of the three editions of Wright's *Negotiator* were merchants. Ibid., pp. 408, 410. John Sargent II's tastes may have been more philosophical, for his only known subscription was to Francis Hutcheson's treatise *A System of Moral Philosophy.* The library at John Boyd's villa was filled with prints of harbors and ports, county maps, geological specimens from around the world, and scientific instruments. On the role of books in self-education, see the unpublished treatise of Daniel Defoe, who died in 1731. Defoe, *Compleat English Gentleman,* p. 225.

The associate Richard Oswald was a particularly apt example of this: he was an especially eager reader of books and pamphlets on international and commercial subjects (it was his habit of reading long into the night that, he believed, impaired his eyesight), and he was quick to recommend commercial, economic, and political works relating to the colonies to his friends.[24] An inventory of his library, drawn up after his death in 1784, suggests the range of his interests, yet, more to the point, it highlights his need for commercial information.[25] The library contained 2,329 books; and these were divided into four categories: theology, philosophy, literature, and history. Under a heading of "Arts" (a subset of "Philosophy"), there were grouped 75 books on agriculture covering such topics as farming, gardening, and rural economy, and another 27 books on trade. Most of the trade books were published after 1745 and, like Wyndham Beawes's *Correct Tables for Calculating the Exchange between London and Some Foreign Places* or John Thomson's *Tables of Interest*, were concerned with everyday matters of practical import. The remaining books on trade addressed the commercial implications of political policy, as in the numerous writings of Malachy Postlethwayt, or the historical and philosophical origins of trade, as in *The Political and Commercial Works of Charles D'Avenant* and Alexander Anderson's *An Historical and Chronological Deduction of the Origins of Commerce.*

Of particular importance to international merchants were maps, globes, marine atlases, printed guides, and other forms of navigational intelligence that assisted them in planning the long-term movements of vessels. In a very graphic way, maps evidenced the expanded horizons of metropolitan merchants. From the reign of William and Mary onward, British cartographers moved away from mapping the estates of the noble and wealthy and the routes of the monopoly and regulated trade companies, to charting the changing balance of international power and producing "large-scale charts of remote, relatively little-visited regions" discovered and protected with the help of merchant capital. By the end of the eighteenth century, nearly all of the major continental coastlines had been more or less reliably mapped and significant areas of the

24. Oswald was keenly interested in the history of colonization and, to correspondents, he frequently suggested the reading of William Barron's *The History of the Colonization of the Free States of Antiquity* and *The Political Connection between Britain and Ireland*, as well as George Chalmers's *History of America.* February 22, April 7, and May 22, 1780, Oswald Papers, Sudlows.

25. "A Catalogue of the Books in the Library of R. A. Oswald, Esq., at Auchincruive," Oswald Papers, Sudlows. The inventory was drawn up at the death of Oswald's nephew George Oswald. George Oswald added to his uncle's library but confined his purchases to literature and history.

interior had been introduced to the European mind. By making himself "master of the geography of the Universe in the maps, attlasses, and measurements of our mathematicians," the merchant could "kno' a thousand times more in doing it than all those illiterate sailors."[26]

Parallel with their exposure to an increasing number of commercial publications was merchants' attendance at the public lectures and discussion groups of commercial societies.[27] By far the most important of these organizations, the Society for the Encouragement of Arts, Manufactures, and Commerce, arose in London in the mid-1750s.[28] The Society met at Rawthmell's Coffee House, near Covent Garden, and in other watering holes near the Strand for five years until, in 1759, it finally settled in the Adelphi. There, aristocrats mixed with commoners in what Tobias Smollet considered alarming "democratical form" and the Society allowed the public free access to its "Repository of Inventions or Industrial Museum."

The Society organized its gatherings into six formal standing committees, whose weekly meetings provided fora for detailed investigations into matters of common interest. From the start, colonial settlement and commercial enterprise headed the agenda. Of the six standing committees on prizes, one concerned itself with the "British Colonies and Trade" and another with "Manufactures"; the former, the Colonies Committee, performed "useful service" by supplying and spreading information on America, publicizing models and machines that could be used there, and distributing sample seeds and crops that might flourish in the New

26. Defoe, *Compleat English Gentleman*, p. 225. On the increase in navigational literature, see Robin Craig, "Printed Guides for Master Mariners as a Source of Productivity Change in Shipping, 1750–1917," *Journal of Transport History*, v. 3 (1982), pp. 23–35. On British and Dutch cartography during the 1690s and early 1700s, see essays by Peter Barber and Dirk De Vries in R. Maccubbin and M. Hamilton-Phillips, eds., *The Age of William III and Mary II* (Williamsburg, 1989), pp. 95–111.
27. On information societies in Glasgow, see David Murray, *Early Burgh Organization in Scotland*, v. 1 (Glasgow, 1924), pp. 446–50; W. R. Scott, "Adam Smith and the Glasgow Merchants," *Economic Journal*, v. 44 (1934), pp. 506–08; W. R. Scott, *Adam Smith as Student and Professor* (Glasgow, 1937), pp. 81–82; and Anon., *View of the Merchants House of Glasgow* (Glasgow, 1866). In London, one set of talks was given by Thomas Mortimer, who outlined his *Elements of Commerce* (London, 1772) in a well-attended series held during the late 1760s. *Dictionary of National Biography*, sub "Thomas Mortimer," p. 1044. At the same time, there existed a "British West India Society" ("Planters Club") and the West India Merchants Committee which, among other things, disseminated useful information and sponsored pamphlets. West India Committee Minutes, sub August 1, 1769, January 2, February 5, 1771, Institute of Commonwealth Studies Archives, London. The associates regularly attended the latter group's meetings at the London Tavern in Bishopsgate.
28. For the history of the Society, which clearly needs rewriting, see Sir Henry T. Wood, *A History of the Royal Society of Arts* (London, 1913); and more recently Derek Hudson and Kenneth Luckhurst, *The Royal Society of Arts, 1754–1954* (London, 1954).

World and bring benefit to the Old. To the weekly committee meetings, where "the greatest freedom of debate" prevailed, came London's overseas merchants. Indeed, most of the members were London merchants, and they joined and attended in large measure to learn about, discuss, and criticize a variety of urban and commercial concerns: ground transportation, food supply to urban areas, colonial developments, and oceanic shipping.[29] In 1757, for example, they investigated a solution to prevent the destruction of ships' bottoms by worms. The following year, they considered the improvement of navigation instruments and life-saving devices, such as cork life-preservers and lighted buoys.[30] On still other occasions, they debated the award of prizes for the growth and shipment of South Carolina silk and East Florida sarsaparilla, or for the import of Philadelphia sturgeon. The explosion and dissemination of information and the development of the empire were here closely linked.[31]

The Consequences of Expansion

The associates and merchants like them viewed commercial enterprise in the middle of the eighteenth century within the context of British expansion. The growing global environment profoundly shaped the ways they did business, at once granting them new opportunities, such as those from the incorporation of peripheral peoples (like the African, Ottoman, Mughal, and Russian empires) into the Europe-dominated trading system or the creation of favor-seeking ("rent-seeking") routines, and, yet, at the same time, subjecting them to the challenges and demands of heightened British oversight and rule.

In the most obvious way, Britain's multifaceted expansion created opportunities for the associates to increase trade and integrate new regions and products into their trading portfolios. It reduced business for some London merchants by increasing their competition from around the world. But for many more merchants, it expanded business, by opening up the opportunities of new customers and commodities. Business could become more sizable, efficient, and profitable, given the new and increased chances to shop around, minimize risks, and expand portfolios. The more enterprising businessmen went about this work of integration by treating clients as suppliers, by buying and selling as part

---

29. Manuscript Subscription Books, Royal Society of Arts, London: George Aufrere, Christopher Chambers, William Cooke, Samuel Gardiner, Sir Alexander Grant, John Mill, Richard Oswald, John Sargent II, John Sargent III, and John Trevanion.
30. Hudson and Luckhurst, *The Royal Society*, pp. 142–47.
31. Committee Minutes, Royal Society of Arts, London – 1764–65: Colonies and Trade (November 2, 27, December 15, 1765), 1765–66: Colonies and Trade (January 21, June 10, 1766).

of a whole, and by rigorously coordinating all parts of that whole. They treated clients as suppliers in both colonial and noncolonial markets: English and French colonists purchased slaves from these merchants and, in turn, provided dyestuffs to them. Furthermore, with more work to supervise, there was more need for planning and less time for inaction. Since more transactions were conducted across greater distances as the decades passed, successful trans-Atlantic merchants had to consider the buying and selling activities of their firms as parts of a whole. It took three months for codfish from Gloucester, Massachusetts to reach Funchal, Madeira, and eighteen months to arrange and execute the distribution of West African slaves to a French slave-trading consortium. A single act, such as the exchange of East Indian cloth for West African slaves, required years of preparation and coordination in the markets of India, England, Holland, France, Africa, and the Americas.[32] Clients' complicated needs could not be satisfied instantaneously or even speedily. Nor could they be handled in isolation. A successful merchant had to manage not just individual transactions but also a portfolio of simultaneous operations, which included the affairs of others, and he increasingly did so under the guise of institutionalized multimember firms and informal consortia of several such firms. A merchant's expanded commitments required him, at the center, to combine with other merchants in other ports around the globe. And they forced him to improve and raise the level of commercial communication – not only to keep in touch with the collection and distribution networks of existing peripheral areas but also to penetrate those of new ones as he had never done before.

The expanding imperial environment did more than influence the conduct of merchants; in creating the need for an infrastructure – shipping and trading services, physical plant, and voluntary and involuntary settlement opportunities – it increasingly provided the precondition for much wealth creation in the new colonies and settlements in North America, the Caribbean, West Africa, and British India. More precisely, it provided opportunities for individuals to profit by building that infrastructure and offering those services which, in turn, set the stage for further wealth creation. Wealth flowed to the metropolitan center, as Adam Smith well knew, but it also flowed to the edge of empire. This outward flow occurred through the cultivation and development of the economies of new regions, the creation of jobs for immigrant whites (most of whom became permanent residents), and the agricultural

---

32. Henry Lloyd Letter Book, 1765–66, Harvard University Business School, Special Collections, cited in Arthur H. Cole, "The Tempo of Mercantile Life in Colonial America," *Business History Review*, v. 33 (1959), pp. 286–87.

improvement of plantations and lands. The conduct of experiments with new hybrids, machines, and cultivation techniques on overseas plantations owned by London merchants was increasingly favored, as was the construction of harbors, roads, bridges, ferries, and the like in the undeveloped hinterland that surrounded these estates. Merchants like the associates helped channel the flow of wealth – their money poured in to Britain, but it also poured out to America and the margins of the empire – and, in doing so, they assured themselves a permanent place in the commercial and social firmament.

The expanding international environment influenced the conduct of merchants in an additional way, by necessitating a change in imperial commercial policy. London's transoceanic shippers and traders working in a global setting became relatively indifferent to national borders. Slowly but surely, merchants pushed ministers and legislators to reconsider and relax many old trade regulations; in the process, they broadened the state's view of the market and competition. If we look closely at their stands on commercial policy, we detect a mild opposition to the state intervention in the management of commerce that was such an integral aspect of the traditional mercantile system. At home, large-scale London wholesale merchants believed that no trade should continue "unless it stand upon its own legs" and that no government should serve as a prop to failing industry. They regarded it as dangerous for Parliament or the assembly to meddle with the correction of commerce, for commerce "must regulate itself by the mutual consent & good will of every individual."[33] Abroad, they generally took exception to the restraints imposed by paternalistic agreements and governmental regulations that granted exclusive trading rights to large state- or Crown-sanctioned monopoly companies or national jurisdictions. The African Trade Act of 1750 and the Free Port Act of 1766 were largely the work of merchants like the associates who, in building a slaving entrepôt in Sierra Leone in the 1750s and 1760s, built their own personal free port. Again and again, they argued for untrammeled access to new regions opening up to private "free" traders around the world. Although London's overseas merchants were not themselves economic thinkers, and they accepted much of the mercantilistic framework of trade regulations, especially the state's protection of the City's interests vis-à-vis the interests of other traders from competing cities or countries, they

33. GD 248/173/4: Ralph Carr to Sir Ludovick Grant, April 1, 1749; GD 345/1168/1762: Ralph Carr to Sir Archibald Grant, February 8, 1762; GD 345/1169/1763: Ralph Carr to Sir Archibald Grant, February 26, 1763; CO 323/17/1; GD 248/221/2: Sir Alexander Grant to Sir Ludovick Grant, April 28, 30, May 7, 1767; and GD 248/99/6/42: Sir Alexander Grant to James Grant, January 12, 1768.

generally pushed for an easing of trade barriers inside and outside the empire, as well as for a flexibility in currency forms and stability in foreign exchange.[34] Individual and official attitudes about policy changed alongside the rise of opportunities to integrate and improve.

~ The institutional structures of the empire channeled individuals' responses. In growing in territory and expanding governance, trade, and knowledge, Britain's empire in the 1700s created opportunities for men like the associates. New regions and new products were waiting to be exploited. New levels of state governance had to be managed. And new consumers in increasingly consumer-oriented markets were waiting to be supplied. Those who were willing to act could take advantage of greater knowledge about the science of their craft and the state of these markets; new pamphlets and treatises even spelled out the commercial possibilities for them. Out of the expansion in empire, state, economy, and knowledge sprang men with an interest (in both senses of that word) in new places, people, products, and techniques. Out of their variegated, marginal beginnings, they found the resources and the turns of mind to capitalize on their interest, integrating their far-flung businesses, and so commercially integrating the empire.

34. Frances Armytage, *The Free Port System in the British West Indies: A Study in Commercial Policy, 1766–1822* (London, 1953), pp. 28–29, 37–42. Edmund Burke claimed that, for the first time in history, a ministry organized public meetings of merchants and acted on their advice in 1766. Men who traded with America, like Trecothick, Fuller, Dalrymple, and Moore, "directed the course of affairs" in the passage of the 1766 Free Port Act. Ibid., p. 39. As we shall see in Chapter 6, there was some precedent for this step in the African legislation pushed forward by the associates in the early 1750s. On rearrangements to be made in the Senegal trade after the Seven Years' War, see CO 388/50: December 16, 1762.

2

Mercantile Origins:
"Passengers Only"

THE ASSOCIATES WERE A LOOSE GROUP of restless outsiders. Overseas merchants based in London, the twenty-three entrepreneurs
conducted business on a large scale, operated as wholesale traders, dealt
primarily though not exclusively with the American colonies, lived in
the metropolis between 1735 and 1785, and worked in "circles" that
formed around four men – Augustus Boyd, Alexander Grant, Richard
Oswald, and John Sargent II – the joint owners of the African slave-
trading factory that Henry Smeathman visited in 1773. The business
connections among the associates were flexible and opportunistic. The
slave factory was, in fact, the only task that all the associates contributed to. Some of the associates were partners in the Bance Island venture, and some were members of the individual commercial partnerships
to which the Bance Island proprietors belonged. Thus representing a
type – a combination of marginal men, metropolitan entrepreneurs, and
imperial and colonial merchants – the associates made the most of the
imperial developments and structures we surveyed in the previous chapter, creating and using new supplies of capital and labor, and funda-
mentally, if not always wittingly, shaping the world in which Britons
and Americans prospered, and in which some of the latter rebelled.

The associates came from middling, Protestant families – Anglican,
Presbyterian, and Huguenot.[1] They were born and raised overseas, in
Scotland, in Ireland, or in England beyond the Home Counties.[2] They

1. Of the 14 associates about whom we know something of their fathers' occupations, 7
fathers were merchants, 4 were ministers, 1 was a farmer, 1 was a mariner, and 1 was
a government clerk. The religious affiliation of the associates' parents is more difficult
to ascertain, since the merchants made almost no mention of the subject in their
correspondence. Birch, the Boyds, Chambers, Samuel Gardiner, Levett, Rolleston, the
Sargents, Stratton, Trevanion, and Wood were listed in Anglican church birth-registers
or were buried in Anglican churchyards; the Andersons, Cooke, John Gardiner, Herries,
Johnston, Mill, Oswald, and Scott had similar links to Presbyterian churches. Some five
were sons of Protestant ministers: Aufrere, Johnston, Oswald, Rolleston, and Trevanion.
2. Some 10 of the 23 were born in Scotland or to Scots parents; 2 in Devon; 1 in
Gloucester; 2 in Derby; and 1 in Turkey. About the remaining four, nothing is known.
Only three were born in London.

lacked material possessions when they were young, although they were never impoverished, and they felt the need for money throughout their lives. Most attended primary and grammar schools through the age of fourteen or fifteen, learning the fundamentals of reading, writing, arithmetic, and accounting, as well as basic Latin. Few, however, received any form of postsecondary education at the universities. Nor was formal apprenticeship and clerkship generally part of their preparation. They did not take the trouble to become members of the livery companies and receive the Freedom of the City, since the right to wholesale trade was no longer contingent upon such marks. They left their birthplaces in their midteens and worked their way up the mercantile ladder in Glasgow or London or overseas.[3] Most became shippers and traders; half did so abroad before settling down in the metropolis. When they established themselves in London, they dealt with those parts of the world they had left behind: the associates who had lived in Jamaica or Virginia, for instance, first turned there for clients and correspondents. At some point in their careers, they all traded with America, having come to believe that it was the future of the empire. Nearly all the associates remained engaged in American commerce until their deaths. Some like Alexander Johnston, Sir John Boyd, and John Sargent II suffered temporary financial embarrassment, but few experienced long-term hardship; none ever went bankrupt.

The associates were success stories. They took advantage of the new imperial commercial opportunities arising around the world in the middle decades of their century. Over half of the group, for instance, entered into a private trade in African slaves, just as the public monopoly of the slave trade was collapsing. Nearly a third purchased American lands which were opening up after Britain's entry into Georgia, Florida, the Ceded Islands, and Nova Scotia, and they built a plantation trade with these new colonies.[4] An equal number served as government contractors in Britain's global wars, and they speculated in the new stocks and securities that funded these wars. The associates succeeded in London by opportunistically moving into areas of enterprise where commercial

3. Only the Andersons, John Boyd, Herries, and Sargent III attended university, although Grant received rudimentary instruction in medicine at the University of Aberdeen. Only Aufrere, Cooke, Gardiner, and Sargent II signed formal articles of apprenticeship. Some eleven of the nineteen associates whose pre-London travels are known traveled to and settled temporarily in India (Levett), Turkey (Stratton), Portugal (Sargent II and Scott), the West Indies (the Boyds, Grant, Johnston, and Oswald) or North America (John Anderson, Chambers, and Oswald).
4. Some nine of the sixteen associates about whom overseas estate ownership is known owned plantations abroad, and eight of these nine owners owned land in the West Indies.

networks, built up over centuries and reluctant to absorb outsiders, were least strong.[5]

More than any other opportunity that the metropolis furnished the associates was the chance to work with men like themselves. According to Sir Alexander Grant, an "Association in Trade" was "the very next thing to Matrimony." It required "similar or well adapted tempers & dispositions & even personal friendship & affection."[6] It was important to the "Association," Grant realized, that it be made up of personalities and skills that complemented one another. Grant, with his flinty personality, was a hands-on manager. He had to know what was going on at all times in his counting-house. He flourished in moments of crisis when a burst of energy and close supervision were needed most. Richard Oswald's behavior was not dissimilar, although he paced himself better than Grant. One senses that Oswald was a distrusting employer: he was always "in his clerks' pockets," constantly checking their work. Neither merchant could easily delegate responsibility. In many things, John Sargent II and Augustus Boyd provided counterpoints to them, being willing to relinquish control, while sharing a love of factual detail. What is most striking about Boyd's role in this group – a role his son John filled after him – was his gift for conceiving ideas. He was an enthusiast, with a flair for articulating a modus operandi for the group and for getting everyone in the group to do their part. He did not enjoy supervising the operations themselves; these he left to his partners. Whereas Boyd and Grant were better in the planning stage, Sargent and Oswald were better in the managing phase. Over the years, the four associates drew upon their differing personal and managerial styles to promote their joint ventures.

Only a third of the associates were active in national politics. As Sir Lewis Namier suggested, "merchant" did not imply "strong political convictions." Those who assumed a place on the national stage tended to shun factional infighting or, at least, their allegiance fluctuated so frequently that partisan politicians could not rely on them. Infrequently voiced, their specific political beliefs appear to have resembled the loose bits of paper and glass in a kaleidoscope. Yet, on closer inspection, a

5. The Boyds, Grant, Mill, Oswald, Sargent II, Scott, and Trevanion served as government contractors during the War of Austrian Succession or the Seven Years' War. Some nineteen associates speculated in the Funds; sixteen voted as stockholders in the various trading and insurance companies; eight served as Directors of monied or insurance companies.

6. Sir Alexander Grant Letter Book, Sir Alexander Grant to John Gordon, October 14, 1769, Grant Papers, Tomintoul House.

pattern of self-interest ran throughout: the associates used politics primarily to safeguard their commercial, social, and personal interests.[7]

In the private realm, the associates had other similarities. Although some belonged to clerical families, few expressed religious sentiments.[8] Most associates married and, although they did not wed members of the aristocracy or greater gentry, they did marry well, for money or land.[9] While most associates were not dynastic in a business sense, they were nevertheless tireless in their efforts to make sure that their heirs lived in comfort and joined the elite of the counties.[10] By acquiring the attributes of gentlemen, they and their families rose in the British social world.[11]

This group portrait is different from the one painted heretofore by the historians of business who discuss the professional paths trod by seventeenth- and eighteenth-century merchants. The associates were neither London-born nor gentle-born. Their careers did not reflect the pattern canonized by students of early-modern business: primary and secondary schooling, formal apprenticeship in the City, receipt of a financial gift from one's father, membership in a livery company, grant

---

7. Namier and Brooke, *House of Commons*, v. 1, p. 131. Despite the fact that each associate was wealthy enough to buy himself a seat in Parliament, only six of the twenty-three sat as M.P.s. Only three held administrative posts: Aufrere was a Prize Commissioner during the Seven Years' War; Oswald served as Britain's negotiator at the peace conference with the Americans in 1782; and Sargent III was a Clerk of Ordnance (1793–1802), Joint Secretary to the Treasury (1802–04), and a Commissioner of Audit (1806–21). Only eight associates ever indicated an opinion on political matters or were noticed for taking a stand: Aufrere, Grant, Herries, Oswald, the Sargents, Stratton, and Trevanion.

8. Apart from the fact that the fathers of some were ministers and that the associates for which there is a record received Christian baptism and burial, little information is known about their religious beliefs and practices. Grant expressed Methodist sentiments and favored Methodist charities, and he once entertained John Wesley; in general, he was noted for his piety. Oswald attended church on at least one recorded occasion. Oswald, Mill, and Herries all assisted the building of Presbyterian Kirks. Aufrere kept a large collection of devotional literature in the library at 38 Mincing Lane. Cooke, at his death, gave to the Presbyterian Fund in London and "the Office for the Relief of the Widows and Children of Poor Protestant Dissenting Ministers." And the Boyds and the members of the Sargent circle married and befriended Huguenots.

9. Some seventeen associates married; four remained single. Only Sargent III married a member of the greater gentry. Less well-endowed yet still wealthy heiresses included the wives of Alexander Anderson, Aufrere, the Boyds, Grant, Oswald, and Trevanion.

10. In only five cases were a father and a son both involved in trade; in another case, a nephew and uncle were involved. The lack of any pattern here does not seem to warrant use of the label "dynastic." Contrast the case of London aldermen in the period 1738–63. Rogers, "Money," p. 450.

11. Two-thirds of the associates bought large estates. These findings confirm Rogers's results for London aldermen between 1738 and 1763. "Money," p. 453. Lang, "Social Origins," p. 47, found the same behavior in the mid-1760s.

of the Freedom of the City, marriage, partnership, retirement, and death at the age of sixty.[12] They began their careers on the margins of London life, with few connections to the City's more powerful families or firms. They did not exit trade as wealth and age advanced. They were interested in land and purchased it in large amounts from middle-age to their death at, on average, seventy. They did not view land as an alternative to commerce, and they did not regard city life as an alternative to country life; they blended the two with ease. This group portrait raises questions about the associates' relation to the larger merchant community in London. The extent to which the careers of the associates matched those of London's Caribbean sugar traders, Chesapeake tobacco traders, Levant silk traders, or Hamburg linen traders, for instance, is unclear, since full-scale profiles of each group's origins, families, education, religion, and politics have yet to be studied and drawn in detail; business histories that discuss the work of these groups tend to concentrate on adult business activities almost exclusively, ignoring antecedents. Given the range of the associates' entrepreneurial undertakings, it is likely they shared many traits with these groups. One probable difference is the associates' extreme opportunism. The Glasgow merchants studied by Price and Devine, for instance, did not push into contracting, slaving, and planting to the degree that the associates did, and it would not be surprising if the fraternity of London tobacco, sugar, or cloth traders similarly restricted their adventures. But further research is sorely needed.

The associates represent an element of London commercial life that is all too often lost in academic accounts of Georgian commerce. They were "marginal" men.[13] That is, they were social amalgams, their lives

12. The canon is most recently articulated by Earle in *English Middle Class*, although see Minchinton, "English Merchants," for an acknowledgment of the diversity in origin, education, and career path. Only four associates became apprentices (Aufrere, Cooke, Samuel Gardiner, and Sargent II). Only five became members of City livery companies (Aufrere, Cooke, Samuel Gardiner, Levett, and Sargent II).

13. The word "marginal" is used here in the sense originally defined by the sociologist R. E. Park in the late 1920s. "Human Migration and the Marginal Man," *American Journal of Sociology*, v. 33 (1927–28), p. 892. See also E. V. Stonequist, *The Marginal Man* (New York, 1937), pp. xv, 3–6. According to Park, a "marginal man" was a social amalgam of two distinct peoples' experiences and traditions that resulted from migration. At least one of the different spheres was antagonistic to the other. The immediate effects of migration, in Park's view, were disorganizing. In this dimension, the case of the Hanoverian Scot in London, especially the rural Scot who moved to the metropolis, seems analogous to the case of the migrant to foreign countries. A provocative study of marginality in trading groups appears in Edna Bonacich, "A Theory of Middlemen Minorities," *American Sociological Review*, v. 38 (1973), pp. 583–94. Ultimately, marginal status might result in creative response. Although (as Georg Simmel has shown) it could as easily result in socially dysfunctional behavior, anomie, and alienation, this over the whole of their lives does not appear to have been

and careers combining two or three distinct experiences and traditions – in most instances, provincial, Scottish, Irish, American, or Caribbean. In midlife, they set themselves up in London on the fringes of mercantile power, with few or no ties to elite institutions or groups such as those enjoyed by the sons of Blackwell Hall drapers or factors who had run London's woolen cloth trade for centuries. They possessed nearly no long-standing geographic connections to the City or the Home Counties – indeed, apart from the Sargent circle, almost no ties to England.[14]

The associates were strangers to the metropolis, and they built their London businesses in an environment that was markedly hostile to foreigners and strangers. Twelve of them were Scots or Scots-Irish, one was French Huguenot, and ten were English. By comparison, over four-fifths of London's merchants at midcentury were of English, miscellaneous, or unknown extraction; only 5% were Scots, another 5% were Jewish, 4% were Huguenot, and less than 1% were Irish. First- and second-generation alike, members of ethnic minorities encountered significant obstacles in eighteenth-century London. The Scots, in particular, were reviled by the English for their food, clothes, accent, financial and political connections, indeed their very success, and they clustered in Aldgate, Broad Street, Cheap, Langbourn, and Wallbrook wards. Scots formed a numerically insignificant group in the City, despite the prominence of intellectuals like David Hume, Tobias Smollett, and William Strahan. No mayors and aldermen hailed from Scotland in the middle decades of the century. Nor were any Scots elected to the Bank of England Directorate between 1740 and 1790.[15]

Like many Scots who had migrated to London out of necessity and

the case with the associates. No connection is seen to more recent applications of the term that extend the meaning of "marginal" to almost every conceivable group. An example of later inapposite extensions appears in Mary E. Wilkie, "Colonials, Marginals and Immigrants," *Comparative Studies in Society and History*, v. 19 (1977), pp. 83–7.

14. On the importance and function of elites in traditional trades, such as the woolen cloth trade, see Westerfield, *Middlemen*, pp. 279–81; and Barry Supple, *Commercial Crisis and Change in England, 1600–1642* (1959), pp. 39–51.

15. *A Complete Guide*, 4th ed. (London, 1749). Study of satirical prints and newspaper articles suggests that hostility to ethnic minorities was voiced in various ways. John Brewer, *The Common People and Politics, 1750–1790s* (Cambridge, 1986), pp. 26–30, 52; Michael Duffy, *The Englishman and the Foreigner* (Cambridge, 1986), pp. 15–22; and George, ed., *British Museum Catalogue of Satirical Prints*, "The Caledonian Voyage to Money-Land" and "The Caledonian Arrival in Money-Land" (May 1762). See also W. M. Acres, *The Bank of England from Within*, v. 2 (London, 1931), pp. 616–23. Only in the East India Company and the Company of Merchants trading to Africa did they find room for maneuver: 11 of 138 India Directors were Scots in 1754–93; 15 percent of the 234 managing committee members of the Africa Company in 1750–75 were Scots. Scots formed a greater percentage of the General Court of Proprietors, and they received a large percentage of the Company's junior appointments to India. Courtesy of J. G. Parker; and T 70/143/146.

in pursuit of opportunity, the associates were propelled forward by their lack of resources and social standing in the localities where they were raised, and their lack of an assured place in the London community into which they had moved. As the biographies of the four men who dominated the four circles of associates suggest, the associates moved between several worlds – their birthplaces, their temporary homes abroad, the metropolis, and the counties – but, in the early years of their London careers, were full citizens of none. Commercial power and social acceptance were hard-won commodities for them.

Augustus Boyd

Augustus Boyd arrived in London in 1735 from St. Christopher in the eastern Caribbean. The status of the outsider was nothing new to him, for his move was just the last in a series of migrations made by a family that had fallen on hard times. The period 1640–1745 was a time of wrenching dislocation for the Boyd clan. Born in Portnacross, County Donegal, Ireland, in 1679 or 1680, Augustus Boyd was distantly related to the Lairds of Kilmarnock. The 9th Lord Boyd had supported the king during the English Civil War and, in recognition, Charles II raised the 10th Lord Boyd to the earldom of Kilmarnock. It was through the illegitimate brother of the 2nd Earl that the associate traced his descent. Such a descent might have granted the Boyds special privileges, of course, but, by the time Augustus Boyd came of age at the turn of the century, his family had turned against the Crown, reconverted to Catholicism, experienced financial hardship, and dispersed in order to make ends meet. The 3rd Earl supported James II and his son in the late seventeenth and early eighteenth centuries, and the 4th Earl fought alongside the Young Pretender in the '45 Rebellion, for which he lost his head.[16]

16. A genealogy of the Boyd family appears in Appendix I.1. On the Scottish and Irish Boyds, see *Appendix to the 26th Report of the Deputy Keeper of the Public Records . . . in Ireland* (Dublin, 1895), pp. 80–1, 958; John Burke, *Genealogical and Heraldic History of the Peerage, Baronetage and Knightage*, pp. 1486–87; James B. Paul, *The Scots Peerage*, v. 1 (Edinburgh, 1904), pp. 172–82; James Paterson, *History of the Counties of Ayr and Wigtoun*, v. 3 (Edinburgh, 1866), pp. 415–22; Rev. George Hill, *An Historical Account of the Macdonnels of Antrim* (Belfast, 1873), pp. 201, 366, 389–93, 440; Belfast, P.R.O. of Northern Ireland, T 828/4: Will of Robert Boyd, 1662; M. Perceval-Maxwell, *The Scottish Migration to Ulster in the Reign of James* (London, 1973), pp. 58, 131, 141, 231, 288, 344–45; George Hill, ed., *The Montgomery Manuscripts, 1603–1706*, v. 1 (Belfast, 1869), pp. 41, 53, 134, 139, 239, 409; *Acts of the Privy Council of England, 1626, June – December*, p. 65; HMC, *Report on the Manuscripts of the Late Reginald R. Hastings*, v. 4 (London, 1947), p. 1818; Raymond Gillespie, *Colonial Ulster: The Settlement of East Ulster, 1600–1641* (Cork, 1985), pp. 29–30, 50, 162, 179, 192; and *The Journals of the House of Commons of the Kingdom of Ireland*, v. 1 (Dublin, 1763), p. 590, v. 2 (Dublin, 1763), p. 354. For Augustus Boyd's descendants, see William Playfair, *British Family Antiquity*, v. 7 (London, 1811), pp. 200–01; G. E. Cokayne, ed., *Complete Baronetage,*

Economically, the Boyds were unable to recoup their losses in Scotland or Ireland, where many moved. Late seventeenth- and early eighteenth-century Ireland, where Augustus was born, was no place for an ambitious young man. A small number of men owned most of the good freehold land; agricultural prices fell and stayed low; agricultural productivity declined; nonagricultural enterprises were incapable of sustaining the economy; and Ireland's share of imperial trade remained minimal. Young Boyd found his opportunities limited.

Boyd turned to the New World, in his case to the eastern Caribbean island of St. Christopher, the home of his mother's brother, Andrew Thauvet, a French Huguenot who had recently been naturalized and become a captain in the militia. There, Boyd found what many immigrants to America found, a mix of Europeans who had claimed the land and ousted native Indians, but only partially exploited its possibilities. St. Christopher – nineteen miles long by six miles wide and cut in two by a volcanic ridge – was rich with potential, highly valued for its healthy climate, fresh water, and high-quality sugar. It was also rife with discord and uncertainty. Since its founding in the late 1620s, when it was divided between the French and English, it had been taken and returned in a dizzying series of reconquests and restorations.[17] It was to this potentially wealthy but constantly disturbed community that Augustus Boyd moved in 1700, when he was twenty years old. Before ten years had passed, he had rented forty-nine slaves and a medium-sized plantation in the English Quarter of the island and begun cultivating sugar; within twenty years, by 1718, he had acquired another 150–acre plantation in what had once been the French Quarter, struck up a trade supplying planters in neighboring islands, and married the only daughter of a prominent planter and the Speaker of the Assembly. Steadily, he worked his way through the ranks of the tiny island community.[18]

Yet, despite these achievements, Augustus Boyd's rise was blocked by powerful English individuals who monopolized all lucrative and powerful governmental offices. Between 1730 and 1732, he struggled unsuccessfully to regain possession of a 110-acre estate in the English Quarter of the island that had been left him by his maternal uncle.[19] Disappointed, he next set his sights on obtaining a seat on the island's Council, but

v. 5 (Exeter, 1909), pp. 184–85; and Joseph Foster, *The Baronetage and Knightage . . . for 1882* (London, 1882), pp. 64–65.
17. HMC, *Report on Various Collections,* v. 8 (London, 1913), pp. 410–11; and Anon., *The Modern Part of the Universal History,* v. 15 (London, 1764), pp. 238–47.
18. On Boyd's plantations, see CO 152/7/L58/1; CO 152/7/L59; CO 152/11/0131/7; CO 152/12/P18/H88; and CO 152/12/P38/H108. Boyd's earliest trading voyage was in 1718. William Smith, *The Natural History of Nevis* (London, 1745), #39. Boyd's wife Lucy Peters was the daughter of John Peters and Elizabeth Henderson. C 54/5818/13–19; and Vere L. Oliver, *Caribbeana,* v. 6 (London, 1919), pp. 28–29.
19. T 98/3/517: Petition of Augustus Boyd, before August 24, 1731; and CO 152/19–20.

the English Governor moved to prevent that. Twice rebuffed, Augustus Boyd turned his back on St. Christopher and looked to Britain where, he surmised, opportunities for greater riches lay.[20] He crossed the Atlantic one last time at the age of fifty-eight to settle in London. There, he lodged with his brother-in-law, the Huguenot James Pechell, and began work as Pechell's partner in a commission merchandising firm, that is, a partnership which supplied goods and services to colonies and sold or re-exported colonial produce consigned to them in turn, for which services commissions from .5 percent to 5 percent were earned.[21] His was one of the loudest voices denouncing the stop, search, and seizure practices of the Spanish *guarda costas* in the late 1730s, one of the more persistent figures appearing before the Ministry and Parliament to defend planter interests, and one of the calmest minds arbitrating West Indian trade disputes.[22] Boyd's ties to the margin of the empire proved to be his strengths – his connections to Irish and Huguenot traders (his brother Paul and the Pechells) gave him reliable sources of goods and merchandise needed in the colonies, his acquaintances in the eastern Caribbean basin brought him cargo and clients (the Duports, Bourryaus, and Jesups), and his plantations produced additional freight. Even after he moved one block west and established his own counting-house in the Huguenot neighborhood of Austin Friars in 1745, he continued to base his business almost exclusively on these foundations, and to move and work in an ethnically enclosed circle of friends and clients.[23] (See Illustration 2.1.)

Sir Alexander Grant

One might suppose that the families of aspiring merchants would have supported them in entering the metropolitan business community, but

20. CO 152/20/3A: December 20, 1733 – January 17, 1734.
21. C 24/1548/17. Pechell's father Samuel (1645–1732) left Montaubun, France, in 1687, on account of the Revocation of the Edict of Nantes two years before. He visited St. Christopher and Jamaica in 1688, served in Ireland with Protestant forces attacking James II's supporters, and eventually settled in Dublin, where his son James (1679–1750) met Jane Boyd. *Sussex Archaeological Collections*, v. 26 (1875), p. 114.
22. As the spokesman of Caribbean planters and merchants, Boyd drafted and signed a 1736 Memorial approving a joint British and French warranty of safe but separate fishing in the Leeward Islands; he notified the British Ministry of a French law prohibiting non-French traders from sailing within one league of French islands; and he opposed unwarranted harassment of French traders by the English Governor William Mathew. Boyd took a dislike to Mathew, who had previously opposed his taking a seat on the St. Christopher Council, but he mended the breach by 1738. CO 152/22/245: December 1736; *CSP(C)*, v. 43 (London, 1963), pp. 27–28, 259; and *Trade and Plantations*, v. 7, p. 256.
23. C 11/1869/15; C 24/1548/17; and C 54/5726/16.

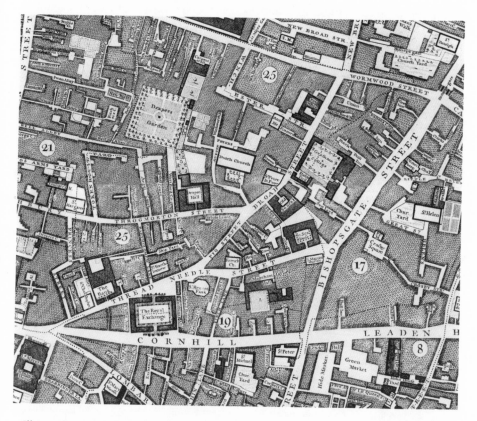

Illustration 2.1 Detail of Map of the City of London, focusing on Austin Friars and Broad Street. *From*: John Rocque and John Pine, *A Plan of the Cities of London and Westminster, and Borough of Southwark* (London, 1746). *Courtesy*: The Harvard Map Collection, Harvard University.

this was seldom the case with the associates. The Boyd clan was incapable of helping Augustus Boyd. The Grant clan was ambivalent and, on occasion, openly hostile to the rise of Sir Alexander Grant who, for much of his career, tried to balance the desires of his Scottish kin with the demands of his London enterprise.

Like Augustus Boyd, Sir Alexander Grant belonged to a once power-ful family whose position had been undermined by its support for the Stuarts. The Grants had deep roots in the Central Highlands of Scot-land, where the associate was born on the farm of Dalvey, Inverness-shire, on July 1, 1705.[24] Like Augustus Boyd, Grant found his prospects at home bleak. At the turn of the century, "North Britain" was an economically depressed region. War with France closed off its export markets; famine ravaged its people; and rising rents, overcrowded tenantries, and England's animosity toward a country where many sup-ported the Pretender stood in the way of assistance from Whitehall. "Necessity" was "a cup" that Grant was forced to "drink deep of" in his youth. With little to hold him to the Spey valley, he completed a rudimentary correspondence course in pharmacy from the University of Aberdeen before he was seventeen, and "went to his travells," moving to Jamaica in search of "prodigious Riches." He first appeared there as a "Practitioner in Physick and Chiurgery" in 1721.[25]

24. Lachlan Shaw, *The History of the Province of Moray*, ed. J. F. S. Gordon, v. 1 (London, 1882), p. 91. The Grant family enters the historical record in the first half of the thirteenth century, when Gregory Le Grant, the Sheriff of Inverness, witnessed several deeds. Gregory was succeeded by his son Sir Laurence, another Sheriff of Inverness, and his grandson Sir John, a renowned warrior who helped William Wallace defend Scotland against the English. Around 1350, Sir John's son, Sir John Grant II, acquired lands southwest of Inverness near Aviemore. The associate Alexander Grant traced his lineage to Sir John Grant II's daughter or niece, Matilda Grant, who, in 1385, married a grandson of Robert II of Scotland, and whose son Patrick adopted her surname. William Fraser, *The Chiefs of Grant*, v. 1 (Edinburgh, 1883), pp. 499–533; Cokayne, ed., *Baronetage*, v. 4 (Exeter, 1904), pp. 358–60; Burke, *Peerage*, 105th ed., v. 1 (London, 1970), pp. 1155–58; v. 3, pp. 2562–64; Burke, *Landed Gentry*, 18th ed., v. 1 (London, 1965), pp. 332–33; and Lord Strathspey, *A History of Clan Grant* (Chichester, 1983), pp. 68–69. A genealogy of the Grant family ap-pears in Appendix I.2. Alexander Grant's father Patrick was born in 1651 or 1654. In 1676, Patrick Grant inherited the lands of Inverlaidnan; twenty-five years later, he acquired the lands of Kinveachy-robie and Lethindie-veole; and, in 1701, he bought the lands of Dalvey. He farmed the Dalvey lands until 1722, when he sold them to the chief of the clan. Alexander Grant's mother, Lydia, was the daughter of William Mackintosh the Improver and the sister of the 1715 rebel William Mackintosh, Jr.

25. IGI; C 24/1700/15A: Interrogatories, October 31, 1759; GD 345/1157/9/56: Patrick Grant to Sir Archibald Grant, December 12, 1740; Charles Leslie, *A New and Exact Account of Jamaica*, 3rd ed. (Edinburgh, 1740), p. 355; and Alexander Grant to Alexander Davidson, January 12, 1770, Grant Papers, Tomintoul House. On the Scottish economy c. 1700, see T. C. Smout, *A History of the Scottish People, 1560–1830* (London, 1969), pp. 196, 224–25, 317–19.

Grant arrived in this "od but yet very pleasant" paradise with high hopes of earning great wealth in Jamaica and returning to Britain in comfort. Initially, he practiced as an itinerant "Country Doctor" in the western parishes where two cousins had settled plantations, curing the ills of transplanted Scots like Robert Rutherford, Rutherford's partner Alexander Ramsay, and Ramsay's only child Mary, who would one day marry Grant's partner Richard Oswald. After nine years, in 1730, he acquired 300 acres in the parish of St. Elizabeth.[26] In the same year, he also moved into trading, leasing an acre in Westmoreland and erecting a brick storehouse from which he and his partner Peter Beckford, Jr., of St. Catharine sold supplies to neighboring planters. Three years later, Grant transferred the business to Kingston and set up a shop along the wharf. There, Beckford introduced him to the only daughter of another St. Catharine planter, Elizabeth Cooke, whom he married in 1737.[27] In Kingston, Grant gathered together a group of friends – Governor Trelawney, James Knight, the planter James Lawes (the son of former Governor Nicholas Lawes) and his wife Elizabeth Gibbons, the Deist Samuel Dicker and his wife Elizabeth Elbridge (Elizabeth Cooke's first cousin), and the merchants Mark Davis and James Watson – who remained close to him for the rest of his life. These men and women, all British emigrants, looked "upon themselves as passengers only," as "fluctuating" adventurers. As his cousin John Grant wrote John Winthrop IV many years later, "the aim of all of us who venture" to Jamaica "is Riches, which however very few of us acquire." Realizing his financial prospects were greater in the metropolis, Grant and his wife set sail in January 1739.[28]

26. The phrase appears in Journal of Thomas Thistlewood, sub February 25–26, 1764, Monson Papers, v. 38, Lincolnshire Record Office, Lincoln; and Lord Adam Gordon, "Journal of an Officer," in Mereness, ed., *Travels in the American Colonies*, p. 380. For Grant's own purchases, see Jamaica Archives, Land Patents, 1/B/11/1/19/160 (May 2, 1730); Island Record Office, Deeds, v. 81, f. 123 (June 1730), v. 83, f. 160 (September 1, 1730), v. 90, f. 16 (January 1, 1732); and Jamaica Archives, Land Patents, 1/B/11/1/21/68 (March 1740). In 1730, Grant also entered into partnership with Peter Beckford Jr. of Spanishtown. *Weekly Jamaica Courant*, June 24, 1730. On Beckford, see PROB 11/686/212–13.
27. Island Record Office, Deeds, v. 102, f. 49 (May 13, 1734). Grant bought the lot from the Scot William Maxwell and sold it to a Scots doctor eight years later. Ibid. (January 1, 1738). Elizabeth Cooke was the daughter of Robert Cooke Sr., a Bristol trader who, in the late 1600s, had emigrated to Jamaica and acquired 1,000 acres in Clarendon and St. Catharine. She was the sister of Robert Jr., a "Practitioner in Physick and Chiurgery." On the Cookes, see Jamaica Archives, Land Patents, 1B/11/1/12; Island Record Office, Deeds, v. 66, f. 80, v. 100, f. 123, v. 160, ff. 239–41, v. 163, f. 44, and Wills, v. 25, ff. 3–4.
28. Island Record Office, Deeds, v. 106, f. 90; Alexander Grant to Earl of Home, January 16, 1750, Douglas-Home Muniments, Box 25 Bundle 4, The Hirsel, Coldstream; and C 24/1700/15A: Interrogatories, October 31, 1759. On Jamaican inhabitants, see

The world into which Grant insinuated himself in London was filled with merchants, erstwhile planters, Scots, Grants, and physicians who had left their homeland, struggled along the imperial periphery, and made enough money to return to Britain. The man with whom Grant set up shop, for instance, Alexander Johnston, had also come from Scotland, practiced medicine and planted sugar in Barbados and, in 1731, settled in London as a wholesale druggist.[29] (See Illustrations 2.2 and 2.3.) The match was a good one, perhaps more so for Johnston, who highly prized "the interest & particular acquaintance" Grant had in Jamaica. From Johnston's shop in Magpie Alley, Fenchurch Street, at the sign of the Golden Steed, the two Scots built a commission merchandising business, Johnston distributing drugs and Grant marketing sugar and plantation supplies.[30] They worked together until 1753, when they divided their cash and stock. Thereafter, on their own, Johnston worked as a drug merchant and a commission agent for wine and sugar houses overseas, and Grant worked alone as a sugar merchant, slave trader, and navy supplier.[31]

Grant strove to reunite his severed family ties on returning to Britain. He acted as the clan's London agent.[32] He was its banker, providing a

Gordon, "Travels," p. 380; Patrick Adam to Earl of Strathmore, September 12, 1741, Strathmore Papers, 104/5/1, Glamis Castle, Dundee; John Grant to John Winthrop, October 9, 1769, Winthrop Family Papers, Ms. G.41.10, v. 1, p. 19, Boston Public Library, Boston; and Long, History of Jamaica, v. 2, pp. 286–87.

29. Alexander Johnston's grandfather was a merchant in Edinburgh; his father was the minister of Girthon, Kirkcudbright. His parents married in 1697 or 1698 and had four children – Alexander who was born in 1704, Samuel who settled in Jamaica, Margaret, and Patrick who settled in Barbados. IGI; Burke, Landed Gentry, pp. 348–49; Burke, Peerage (London, 1906), p. 925; Barbados Supreme Court, Wills, v. 35, p. 260; and James C. Rutnam, The Early Life of Sir Alexander Johnston (Sri Lanka, 1988), p. 2. Johnston first appeared in the 5th Precinct of Aldgate Ward on August 30, 1731. Ms. 11,316/96, Land Tax, COLRO. He married Janet Gordon of Campbelltown, Kirkcudbright, on December 9, 1748; he died in London on November 22, 1775, one of the City's oldest merchants. IGI; and Scots Magazine, v. 37 (1775), p. 638. He was survived by his wife and five children: Peter (1749–1837), Alexander (b. 1750), Samuel (1752–98), Janet (b. 1759), and Jane Margaret (1761–1836).

30. GD 345/1157/9/56x: Patrick Grant to Sir Archibald Grant, December 12, 1740. The Grants lived with the Johnstons in 1740–41. The first official notice of Grant's appearance in London occurred when he moved from Magpie Alley to Hatton Garden on the northwest side of the city before Lady Day 1741. Ms. 10,835, f. 119v, Guildhall Library, London. Five years later, he moved to Billiter Lane. During his first decade in the City, Grant owned a share in at least two vessels that shuttled goods between Kingston and London. Shipping Database: Westmoreland, and Neptune.

31. Stock Ledger, 6/32/1/21 (May 3, 1753; £750 each), British Linen Bank Papers, Bank of Scotland, Edinburgh. Grant's work as shipper and trader, slaver, and victualer are detailed in Chapters 4–7. Riskier adventures in timber, whales, and fish appear in Hancock, "Citizen of the World," pp. 82–86.

32. Grant mainly served two branches of the family: the Grants of Grant, those directly related to the chief of the clan, who resided at Castle Grant, southeast of Inverness; and the Grants of Monymusk, who lived at Monymusk House, northwest of Aberdeen.

full range of cash-management services: accepting, holding, and forwarding cash; paying bills; making loans; and buying lottery tickets.[33] He was its hotelier, and his home often functioned as a boardinghouse for relatives. Grant's spare bedrooms were seldom empty. His pocketbook was usually open to kin.[34] He was also the clan's chief employment officer. His own counting-house employed dozens of nephews and cousins, but it could absorb only so many and Grant cast his net more widely. As early as January 1744, Sir Archibald Grant of Monymusk asked the associate to obtain "anything in the Jamaica Way" for him should Alexander's client the Earl of Home become the Governor of Jamaica. As it turned out, Home's governorship was pure speculation, but the quest was begun and, from 1744 to 1772, Alexander served as his cousin's eyes and ears, even after it became clear how difficult it was to peddle someone who was clearly "no favorite."[35] With other job seekers, he enjoyed greater success. He prevailed upon an old friend, Commander Keppel, to take Sir Archibald's youngest son William to Virginia in 1754 and introduce him to another friend, Lieutenant-Governor Robert Dinwiddie, Jr.[36] As a sizable shareholder of the East India Company and a close friend and sometime partner of Director John Boyd, the only child of Augustus Boyd, Grant was able to find India posts for a number of other relatives. His nephew Alexander Davidson, his cousins Captain Alexander Grant, Walton Steevens, and Ludovick Grant, his great-nephew James Falconar, and distant kinsmen

33. GD 248/168/1/18, 22, 28: Alexander Grant to Ludovick Grant, March 31, April 12, May 7, 1743; and GD 345/1184/6: Alexander Grant to Francis Grant, September 11, 1744. Alexander Grant received the salary that Ludovick Grant received for serving as a Police Commissioner of the Highlands. GD 248/168/7/11, 13, 23, 22: Alexander Grant to Ludovick Grant, October 5, December 21, 28, 1745, March 4, 1746; and GD 248/172/3/12: Alexander Grant to Ludovick Grant, October 11, 1746. Throughout the 1750s, Grant also collected Captain Archibald Grant's army pay. GD 345/1164/1/5: Sir Alexander Grant to Captain Archibald Grant, December 21, 1756.

34. GD 248/175/2: Alexander Grant to Sir Ludovick Grant, December 7, 1752; and GD 345/117/1768: Sir Alexander Grant to Sir Archibald Grant, August 1, 1767.

35. GD 345/1158/4/7: Alexander Grant to Sir Archibald Grant, January 12, 1744; GD 248/168/4/13: Alexander Grant to Sir Ludovick Grant, July 31, 1744; and GD 345/1159/2/16, 17x: Alexander Grant to Sir Archibald Grant, September 8, 10, 1747. On the reasons for the dislike of the scheming Sir Archibald, see A. J. G. Cummings, "The York Buildings Company: A Case Study in Eighteenth-Century Corporation Mismanagement" (University of Strathclyde, Ph.D. dissert., 1980).

36. GD 345/1163/2/31: Alexander Grant to Sir Archibald Grant, November 9, 1754; GD 345/1163/3/39: Alexander Grant to Sir Archibald Grant, December 28, 1754; GD 345/1189/5x: Sir Archibald Grant to William Grant, July 11, 1755; and GD 345/1164/2/53: Sir Alexander Grant to Sir Archibald Grant, January 24, 1756. Sir Alexander had tried to help William Grant by obtaining a recommendation from Richard Oswald. GD 345/1160/4/149: Alexander Grant to Sir Archibald Grant, December 22, 1750.

Illustration 2.2 Alexander Johnston Portrait, attributed to Robert Edge Pine.
Courtesy: Christopher Campbell-Johnston, Esq., Salwarpe, Worcestershire.

Illustration 2.3 Janet Gordon Johnston Portrait, attributed to Robert Edge Pine. *Courtesy*: Christopher Campbell-Johnston, Esq., Salwarpe, Worcestershire.

Abraham Leslie and Robert Innes, all won appointments as Company Writers, Factors, or Free Merchants after Grant intervened.[37]

The tensions that arose between Grant and his family were apparent almost from the beginning of his London career. The associate thought he received little credit for serving his family and, as the years passed, he came to reconsider the necessity of doing so. It was in "the family's interest" to procure jobs for relatives, he realized, but he received little thanks for the work, and it cut his earning potential, consuming much time and earning no commission. In addition, serving "the family interest" threatened the "routine and custom" of his shipping and trading business. As the years passed, he pulled back, focusing less on the needs of his extended family and more on the needs of his own business and that of his "Association" in London. To the end of his days, Sir Alexander was hated and ridiculed by his Highland kin.

Grant insulated himself from his family, not by enmeshing himself in English society, as did Augustus Boyd's son John, but by befriending a cadre of expatriated Scots. The Duke of Argyll and Lords Erskine, Findlater, and Hopeton, the most politically and socially prominent Scots peers of the day, were regular guests at his table. Grant saw much of southern England as the guest of fellow Scots, and frequently visited fashionable spas like Bath and the Bristol Hot Wells in their company. In June 1747, after spending "some time" with the 2nd Earl of Orford at Houghton Hall, Grant and his wife moved on to a party of absentee Scots at the Dickers country house near Bristol. The following year, they gained entry to the royal circle at Hampton Court, Windsor, and Cliveden with the help of high-ranking Scots in the Ministry. Several years later, they spent an entire month with the 3rd Duke of Argyll at his home outside London. No summer or fall was complete without several such excursions.[38]

37. Likewise, as a West Indian trader and planter, he was in a good position to find jobs in British America. Nephews Patrick and Peter Davidson and great-nephew Gilbert Falconar found work on his Caribbean ships as commanders and on his Jamaican estates as overseers. IOL, B 75/247, 469–70, 483, 487, 487–88, 532; and Sir Alexander Grant to Col. Robert Gordon, April 1, 1770, Sir Alexander Grant to James Grant, December 20, 1770, Sir Alexander Grant Letter Book, Grant Papers, Tomintoul House.

38. The Grants' out-of-London jaunts are well documented. Bath and the Bristol Hot Wells were favorite haunts. In September 1744, the Grants went to Bath for several weeks with close friends who had just arrived from the West Indies. Alexander Grant to Earl of Home, September 18, 1744, Douglas-Home Muniments, Box 25, Bundle 4. On the Grants' visits to country houses, see GD 345/1159/2/18: Alexander Grant to Sir Archibald Grant, June 16, 1747; GD 248/173/1: Alexander Grant to Sir Ludovick Grant, August 8, 1748; and GD 345/1161/4/56: Alexander Grant to Sir Archibald Grant, February 1, 1752. Travel decreased after they purchased a villa in Kent, yet they never dispensed with it entirely. In June and July 1764, they visited old Jamaican

One of the few places Grant avoided was his homeland: he traveled north only seven times in fifty years and, on four of these occasions, he was campaigning for a seat in Parliament. Grant came to loathe the idea of living there. Family betrayals and quarrels with the chief weakened his ties to the clan and its territory at a time when the associate was making more congenial and reliable friends in the South.[39] Significantly, it was to Bookham Grove, his villa in Surrey, that Grant planned to retire, and it was in Hampstead that he hoped to be buried; his estates in Scotland may have contributed to his family's political power and clan's strength, but not to his own happiness.

The problems with his family first erupted in the 1740s during a discussion of Grant's acquisition of an estate and the elevation in rank that should accompany the purchase. The matter was complicated, for the two were hopelessly intertwined. Grant claimed a baronetcy that had been granted to an ancestor four generations before, but had fallen dormant. Whether nonuse barred inheritance was the central legal issue; the critical personal matter was that Grant was perceived as "pushing to be at the head of the clan."[40] Seeing in Grant a threat to his own

friends in Surrey and then moved on to Bristol and Bath to take the cure. They returned to Bath in October, Alexander for a bruised foot and Elizabeth for a stomach disorder. GD 345/1180/1764: Sir Alexander Grant to Sir Archibald Grant, June 12, July 17, 1764; and GD 345/1169/1764: Sir Alexander Grant to Sir Archibald Grant, October 10, 1764. In August 1765, they went "sea-bathing" at Margate. GD 248/672/5/55: Sir Alexander Grant to James Grant, July 27, 1765; GD 345/1170/1765: Sir Alexander Grant to Sir Archibald Grant, September 4, 1765. 1767 found them back at the Hot Wells in late Spring, and at Chichester in August. GD 345/1171/1/108: Sir Alexander Grant to Sir Archibald Grant, August 17, 1767. At the end of his life, he and his wife visited Bath for two months in late 1770, and spent the summer of 1771 in "a Northern Tour for Health & Pleasure." Sir Alexander Grant to Patrick Grant, December 6, 1770, Sir Alexander Grant to John Grant, October 14, 1771, Sir Alexander Grant Letter Book, Grant Papers, Tomintoul House.

39. Grant visited Scotland in 1745, 1752, 1754, 1761, 1766, 1768, and 1771. As early as 1756, he owned a villa in Eltham, Kent, to which his wife retired for the entire summer and to which he retreated every weekend from June through August. GD 345/1179/329: Sir Alexander Grant to Captain Archibald Grant, July 10, 1756. He leased the villa until 1769, when he bought the estate of Bookham Grove, near Leatherhead, Surrey. F. B. Benger, "Pen Sketches of Old Houses in this District: 15. Bookham Grove, Great Bookham," *Proceedings of the Leatherhead and District Local History Society*, v. 1 (1955), pp. 21–25; and S. E. D. Fortescue, *People and Places: Great and Little Bookham* (Great Bookham, 1978), pp. 50–53, and *The Story of Two Villages: Great and Little Bookham* (Great Bookham, 1975), p. 29.

40. Alexander Grant's ancestor Sir James Grant of Dalvey had been granted a Nova Scotia baronetcy in 1688, but Sir James died without children and his brother Ludovick did not assume the dignity. Ludovick's second cousin and heir, Sueton Grant, also failed to take up the title and sold the Dalvey estate in Inverness-shire to Patrick Grant, the son of Donald Grant, Sueton's second cousin, in 1701. The baronetcy thus fell into disuse. It was Alexander's contention that his father was the rightful heir as the eldest great-grandson of the heir of the brother of the grandfather of Sir James Grant of Dalvey.

dominance, the chief of the clan tried to settle the matter himself, granting the merchant the extensive barony of Grangehill, between Nairn
and Forres, in Morayshire, but, in order to keep Grant in his place,
denying him full rights to the baronetcy, something which the chief
had no legal power to do. Understandably, Grant was dissatisfied. He
grudgingly accepted the barony, and then applied for and accepted a
Crown charter for it in July 1749, after which he moved his father into
its crumbling mansion house as quickly as possible. Pulling strings in
London and Edinburgh, avoiding his family altogether, he next got his
father officially "returned" as heir to the title of the baronetcy in August 1752. When his father died three years later, the title fell to him.[41]
(See Illustration 2.4.)

Problems with his family did not subside with the grant of the
baronetcy; they permeated his foray into national politics as well. Grant
spent 1750 "making interest" – that is, strengthening his political position by visiting Scotland, loaning money, and making friends – and,
three years later, he called upon these friends to back his election as the
parliamentary representative of the Inverness Burghs. But he campaigned
in vain and was defeated at the General Election in April 1754. In the
Burghs, he had fallen victim of the clan chief's disdain. A deterioration
in family relations quickly ensued. When, in 1761, he was elected Member
of Parliament (M.P.) for the Inverness Burghs, he noted that his success
was ensured, not by the support of his family, but by the support of
political power brokers in the metropolis.[42]

Overall, Grant's experience was one of disappointment, dislocation,
and "outsiderness." He was, in effect, nobody's child. Northern Scotland was unable to support his youthful ambition. In the predominantly
English colony of Jamaica, he was neither native Creole nor transplanted Englishman. Despite the existence of a large Scots community
there, Scots almost always longed to return home and, more often than
their English and Irish counterparts in the colony, they appear to have

41. GD 248/173/1: Alexander Grant to Sir Ludovick Grant, August 8, 1748. Grangehill
    had been previously owned by the impoverished Dunbar family. Register of Sasines,
    July 15, 1749, SRO; and GD 248/175/3: Alexander Grant to Sir Ludovick Grant, July
    2, 1752. A man of small aspirations, Patrick Grant accepted the title to satisfy his
    heirs. Despite all his negotiations, Sir Alexander did not inherit a quiet title. Contro-
    versy over its legitimacy later erupted in a 1760 lawsuit brought by James Grant.
    James Grant v. Sir Alexander Grant, Memorial, August 6, 1760, Grant Muniments,
    London.
42. Grant's political activities are summarized in Namier and Brooke, eds., *House of
    Commons*, v. 2, p. 528. See also GD 248/175/3, 2: Alexander Grant to Sir Ludovick
    Grant, July 17, August 4, September 28, October 26, December 2, 1752; GD 125/27/
    3/27: Alexander Grant to Hugh Rose, September 20, 1752; and GD 125/26/6/55, 54x,
    52: Alexander Grant to Hugh Rose, October 9, 12, 22, 1752.

Illustration 2.4 Crown Charter of Grant of Dalvey family. *Courtesy:* Sir Patrick Grant of Dalvey, Bt., Tomintoul House, Inverness-shire, Scotland.

in fact gone back, not because they had earned "prodigious riches," but because they had become comfortable enough to make another attempt back home. London posed its own problems of adaptation. Even the most casual reading of midcentury letters and journals reveals the pronounced degree of anti-Scots sentiment in the metropolis. On top of this, Grant could not find a home among his extended Scottish family. Although it was not his only perspective, Sir Alexander could look back at the end of his days on a life simultaneously troubled by continual rejection and challenged by the need for creating a society for himself.

Richard Oswald

The associate best known to posterity sat across the table from Benjamin Franklin during the peace negotiations of 1782. Richard Oswald, Britain's representative, was another international merchant of Scottish origin who had experienced disappointment and dislocation, moved beyond his homeland, amalgamated several different cultural traditions, and made the most of Britain's expanding empire. His family had come from the cold and desolate frontierland far to the north of Inverness: farmers in Orkney, they moved south to Caithness in the 1640s and quickly became one of the county's prominent families, supplying magistrates, ministers, and teachers on both sides of the Episcopalian/ Presbyterian divide for four generations.[43] Like the Boyds and the Grants, the Oswalds could not provide for their young in Caithness and they frequently turned to Glasgow, where two brothers, Richard "the Elder" and Alexander, moved south to Glasgow in the early years of the eighteenth century.[44] The brothers were living and trading there as early as

43. A genealogy of the Oswald family appears in Appendix I.3. The family was "founded" by James Oswald I (1590–1633) of Kirkwall, Orkney. His only child, James Oswald II (b. 1620), moved south to Caithness, became the Bailie of Wick, and married Barbara Coghill. Their sons James III (1654–98) and George (1664?–1725) became ministers. James III enrolled as "a Student in Humanitie" at the Thurso school, twenty miles northwest of Wick, in August 1670, and received an M.A. degree from King's College, Aberdeen, in 1674. Returning to Thurso, he served as its schoolmaster from 1679 to 1681, when he became the Episcopal minister of Watten, halfway between Thurso and Wick. James III married Mary Murray, and they raised four children. Their two sons – Richard (1687–1763) and Alexander (1694–1766) – moved to Glasgow when they came of age. James III died in 1698, and the care of his young family fell to his younger brother, George. George's career closely mirrored that of his brother: while he attended an M.A. course at the University of Edinburgh in 1692 and returned to Watten as its schoolmaster, he came to acknowledge "the evil of Prelacy" in 1695 and became an ordained minister in the Presbyterian Church. Caithness, at the time, was ravaged by religious battles between Presbyterians and Episcopalians, and George Oswald became heavily involved in the inquisition of churchgoers who opposed the new Presbyterian ministers. Following conversion, George Oswald married his sister-in-law's sister Margaret Murray and raised five children: James (1703–93), the Presbyterian minister of Dunnet and, after 1750, Methven, Perthshire; Richard (1705–84), the subject of this sketch; and three daughters. On the Oswalds, see IGI; J. B. Craven, *A History of the Episcopal Church in the Diocese of Caithness* (Kirkwall, 1908), pp. 141, 148–49, 162–69, 173, 186, 192–98, 275; Donald Beaton, *Ecclesiastical History of Caithness and Annals of Caithness Parishes* (Wick, 1909), pp. 202–03; Colin Macnaughton, *Church Life in Ross and Sutherland* (Inverness, 1915), pp. 6–11; James Paterson, *History of the Counties of Ayr and Wigtoun* (Edinburgh, 1863–66), pp. 416–18; Burke, *Landed Gentry* (London, 1847; 18th ed., London, 1972); James T. Calder, "The Oswalds of Auchincruive," *John O'Groats Journal* (August 12, 1853); A Native, "Watten in Olden Days," *Northern Ensign* (July 14, 28, 1908); Anon., "The Oswalds of Caithness," *Northern Ensign* (April 19, 26, 1910); John Henderson, *Caithness Family History* (Edinburgh, 1884), pp. 189–93, 232–37, 253–54, 313–16; and Hew Scott, ed., *Fasti Ecclesiae Scoticanae*, v. 4 (Edinburgh, 1923), p. 223, v. 7 (Edinburgh, 1928), pp. 43, 120, 139, 442, v. 8 (Edinburgh, 1950), pp. 368, 676–77.

44. "The Elder" refers to the son of James III, to distinguish him from the son of Rev. George. According to some accounts, Richard the "Elder" applied to be master of the Thurso parish school in 1706, but his candidacy was rejected. James Calder, "The Oswalds of Glasgow," *John O'Groats Journal* (July 15, 1853); George Eyre-Todd, *History of Glasgow*, v. 3 (Glasgow, 1934), pp. 257–64; and George Crawfurd and William Semple, *The History of the Shire of Renfrew* (Paisley, 1782), pp. 22–23.

1713, when the elder became chief clerk in the Port Glasgow Customs House.[45]

Their younger cousin, the associate Richard Oswald, was born in Dunnet, Caithness, probably in 1705, and grew up in the strict, inquisitorial atmosphere of his father's Presbyterian parish. Soon after his father died in 1725, recognizing the constraints upon his advance in Caithness, he joined his cousins in Glasgow, at a time when they were considered "the most Eminent Merchants" there.[46] The brothers were frugal, hardworking, and prosperous merchandisers who found opportunities abroad and turned them to good account. In the early decades of the century, they built a small import/export business that brought tobacco from the Chesapeake, sugar from the Caribbean, and wine from Madeira and the Canary Islands. By 1731, they were the city's fifth largest tobacco firm, importing on average 300,000 pounds of the weed each year. The Oswalds prospered, amassing wealth that was unattainable in Caithness.[47]

In Glasgow, Richard Oswald "the Younger" immersed himself in his

45. Richard the Elder was given lodgings at the Port Glasgow Town House. He held the customs post through the early 1720s. Bogle Papers, April 27, 1713, Mitchell Library, Glasgow. In 1716, he was made a Burgess and Guild Brethren of Glasgow and, in 1719, his brother received the same honor. James R. Anderson, ed., *The Burgesses and Guild Brethren of Glasgow, 1573–1750: Part IV* (Edinburgh, 1924), pp. 318, 347, 371; and Senex [J. M. Reid], *Glasgow Past and Present*, v. 1 (Glasgow, 1884), pp. 29–41.

46. According to the gravestone in the family vault at St. Quivox Parish Church, Ayrshire, Richard Oswald was born in 1700; but most other contemporary accounts state he was born in 1705. Detailed studies of Oswald the Younger's life do not exist. William P. Courtney's entry in *The Dictionary of National Biography*, v. 14, pp. 1,223–1,224, has formed the basis of all subsequent historical mention, but it is filled with errors. For example, Courtney suggests that Oswald was the unsuccessful candidate for the Thurso schoolmastership, but this possibility can be readily discounted on the grounds that he would have been at most six years old when applying for the position. The Thurso Kirk session records, now housed at the Scottish Record Office, contain no mention of any Oswald applying for the post. CH 2/414/2, SRO. For contemporary opinion of the Oswald brothers, see Rev. Alexander Carlyle, *Anecdotes and Characters of the Times*, ed. James Kinsley (London, 1973), p. 45. The Oswalds were active members of the Merchant House, a trade association and discussion group that included Adam Smith and David Hume in its group. Anon., *View of the Merchants House of Glasgow* (Glasgow, 1866); and W. R. Scott, "Adam Smith and the Glasgow Merchants," *The Economic Journal*, v. 44 (1934), pp. 506–08.

47. Jacob Price, "Buchanan & Simson, 1759–1763: A Different Kind of Glasgow Firm Trading to the Chesapeake," *William and Mary Quarterly*, 3rd ser., v. 40 (1983), p. 9, Table 1. A contemporary "Account of Tobacco Imported into Scotland, 1728–1732" presents a slightly different picture: the Oswald brothers imported an annual average of 303,243 pounds, and re-exported the bulk (80%). During this period, they owned shares in nine ships that made fifteen voyages and returned to Port Glasgow and Greenock with tobacco; the total value of ten of these voyages amounted to £182,203. SRO, CD 1/6 (September 19, 1734). From 1733 to 1735, the Oswalds were partners in three new ships that made four separate voyages. Scottish Port Books, E 504 (Port Glasgow and Greenock), SRO.

cousins' tobacco trade. As their clerk, he performed a variety of tasks – filing and storing records, examining and copying accounts, writing letters, drawing bills of exchange, addressing bills for acceptance, and handling customs and insurance matters. For a decade he toiled thus, gaining the respect of his cousins who, as a promotion, sent him to Virginia, Carolina, and Jamaica as their supercargo. Living primarily in the Chesapeake during the late 1730s and early 1740s, young Oswald distributed supplies to planters, negotiated purchases of tobacco, oversaw its packaging and loading, collected payments for debts, dunned tardy debtors, and did whatever else was needed to promote the interests of the firm.[48]

Pleased with his work, the brothers made young Oswald their partner and brought him back to Glasgow in 1741. There, from an office overlooking the Old Green, he managed the daily details of their joint concerns.[49] Until the 1740s, the Oswald brothers had restricted themselves to dealing with two or three countries and to peddling two or three commodities. In that decade, however, with young Richard prodding them onward, they increased their shipping volume and added new trading correspondents. Between July 1742 and March 1747, they held shares in at least 133 different voyages, a ninefold increase over the early 1730s. Previously, their ships had plied Chesapeake waters primarily but, over the course of the 1740s, their operations gradually drifted southward, toward the Caribbean. They moved beyond shipping into related industries, like rope manufacturing, sugar refining, and bottle manufacturing.[50] On his own account, young Richard began to buy

48. At the end of his life, Richard the Younger told Lord Dartmouth that he had traded six years in the vicinity of Norfolk, Virginia. Memorandum, August 15–17, 1781, McGregor Library Acc. 703, McGr-23, University of Virginia, Charlottesville; and W. S. Robinson, Jr., ed., "Bibliographical Note," in *Oswald's Memorandum*, p. 136. For further mention of his early years, see Simmons and Thomas, eds., *Proceedings and Debates*, v. 2, p. 212; BCM 295: Richard Oswald to Governor Grant, July 25, 1764, June 8, 24, 1770; and Smyth, ed., *Writings*, v. 8, p. 528.

49. According to Customs accounts for July 1744, young Oswald supervised the arrival and unloading of *L'Heureuse Marie*, a Martinique vessel that had been taken by *The Hound* (a ship of which he was part owner and which had been commandeered by the navy) and condemned by Port Glasgow's High Court of Admiralty; young Oswald placed the muscovado sugar, coffee, and cocoa nut in the Oswalds' warehouse and later sold it to merchants in Hamburg. By managing several such prize ships, Oswald reputedly earned £15,000. Carlyle, *Anecdotes*, p. 45; and E 504/28/1 (July 11–12, 1744), SRO.

50. During the 1740s, the Oswald brothers forged strong commercial bonds with the West Indies; they manned their West Indian operations with Glaswegians like Robert Hamilton, Lawrence Coloquhoun, or their cousin Richard Oswald. Hamilton of Rozelle Papers, 1735–46, Glasgow University Archives, Glasgow; and Jamaica Archives, Powers, v. 28, pp. 220–21 (March 1, 1738). Sugar and wine became central to their business. They founded a sugar refinery in Glasgow – the United Sugar House – where

shares in trans-Atlantic voyages that imported prunes, cork, and vinegar from Spain and Portugal, sugar, spices, and cotton from the Caribbean, and tobacco from Virginia, and then exported or re-exported bottles, linens, woolens, leather goods, candles, iron and lead products, and hardware.[51]

The experience of Richard Oswald "the Younger" as a principal in a wide range of trans-Atlantic trading ventures was enhanced by his restless, inquisitive, experimental approach to problem-solving. No fact was useless, as far as he was concerned. According to the wit Alexander Carlyle, he was intellectually voracious, spending "his [spare] time almost entirely in Reading." All projects merited at least passing consideration. On one occasion, he became involved in the sale of wigs to Virginia; on another, in the construction of a wool factory in Glasgow; on yet another, in a plan to establish a London-based privateering operation and a Newcastle-based import venture to ship tobacco directly from Tidewater Virginia to northeastern England.[52]

Little came of Oswald's "experiments," but he was not deterred. In early 1746, he was thinking of "fixing at London"; he was resident there by mid-year and scheming in a big way. On one level, the move was a continuation of the trade he had begun elsewhere: Oswald modeled his London operation after the work he had undertaken in Glasgow and America. From a three-story counting-house that he leased at 17 Philpot Lane, he focused primarily on shipping and trading tobacco and became, within a year, the ninth largest metropolitan tobacco trader. A

they could process their own imports. Robert Renwick, ed., *Extracts from the Records of the Burgh of Glasgow*, v. 5 (Glasgow, 1909), pp. 115, 308, 364–65, 440–41, 451, 491–92, v. 6 (Glasgow: 1911), p. 3; and B 10/15/5962 (May 19, 1748). SRA-Glasgow, Glasgow. At the same time, they became the town's supplier of wine. In 1738, they took a three-year lease on the Port Glasgow Ropework buildings. Renwick, ed., *Extracts*, v. 5, p. 493. The site was so small and unsuitable, however, that, in 1742, they built a larger four-story building at the east end of Glasgow's Old Green. *Glasgow Past and Present*, pp. 29–41. In May 1742, three Glasgow merchants also applied to the Town Council to enlarge an old glass factory that had been erected in 1730, and this factory also came to be managed by the Oswalds. Renwick, ed., *Extracts*, v. 6, pp. 114–17, 164, 581; and B 10/15/5699, 5697, 5696, and 6077, SRA-Glasgow, Glasgow.

51. Between January 1743 and January 1746, young Oswald is listed in the Scottish Port Books as a co-partner in fourteen different ships using Port Glasgow and Greenock harbors. E 504 (Port Glasgow and Greenock), SRO; and Shipping Database.

52. Carlyle, *Anecdotes*, p. 45. On hats and wool, see *Virginia Gazette*, June 6, 1745; Renwick, ed., *Extracts*, v. 6, pp. 199–200 (March 26, 1745); T-MJ/584 (May 23, 1743), 551 (September 22, 1761), 584 (September 29, 1766), and 546 (May 7, 1769), SRA-Glasgow, Glasgow. On the London and Newcastle projects, see Add.Mss. 33,052/278–94, BL: Memorial, April 12, 1744; Ralph Carr to Richard Oswald, February 1, 1746, ZCE 10/16/285, Ralph Carr to Richard Oswald, September 19, 1746, March 13, June 13, 1747, ZCE 10/17/96, 312, 408, Carr-Ellison Mss., Northumberland Record Office, Newcastle.

steady stream of vessels brought tobacco from the Chesapeake and returned with plantation supplies; during Oswald's first fourteen months, he shipped tobacco valued at £16,510. At the same time, the move represented a significant increase in the scale of Oswald's trade, and it ushered in a remarkable entrepreneurial efflorescence. He became involved in buying and selling Newcastle horses in 1747. The following year, with the Boyds, Grant, and two others, he acquired Bance Island in West Africa and entered the slave trade.[53] And, during the 1750s, he began to focus more closely on trading West Indian produce.

Like most associates at the beginning of their London careers, Oswald was a man of relatively few financial assets. A strategic marriage eased these constraints. On November 12, 1750, Oswald married Mary Ramsay, a young Scots heiress whom he had met in Jamaica at the home of Alexander Grant, at that time both Oswald's and Ramsay's physician.[54] Mary Ramsay had much to recommend her when the two renewed their acquaintance in London in the late 1740s. She belonged to a large family from northeastern Scotland that had reached prominence in the wilds of western Jamaica.[55] She possessed a substantial

53. T 1/326/121/41: August 1, 1746; and T 1/326/110–14/40: October 24, 1747.
54. Ramsay was not Oswald's first female companion. He had already had a liaison with Agnes Barr of Glasgow. The arrangement ended in 1746 when Oswald moved to London; yet, well into the 1760s, Oswald sent Barr maintenance payments and took care of their two sons – George Oswald (d. 1763) and Richard Jr. (d. 1768). GD 1/618/32–4: Cash Book of George Oswald; and Agnes Barr to Richard Oswald, November 8, 1773, Oswald Papers, EUL. The older son George died in France in August 1763 in the arms of the writer Laurence Sterne; Richard Oswald paid off all creditors. Archibald B. Shepperson, "Yorick as a Ministering Angel," Virginia Quarterly Review, v. 30 (1954), pp. 54–66; Oswald Letter Book, v. 2, ff. 186–89, SRO; and Tobias Smollett, Travels through France and Italy (Oxford, 1981), pp. 101–02 (Letter XI). Oswald's younger son Richard caused even greater heartache. In 1750, Richard Sr. secured for him a clerkship at Cape Coast Castle; and he employed him as his own clerk in Germany during the late 1750s, until the son began to embezzle magazine funds. T 70/143: February 20, 1751; T 70/357/4: May 1, 1751; and Richard Oswald, Jr., to Richard Oswald, Sr., March 31, 1759, Richard Oswald, Jr., to Col. David Graeme, December 11, 1759, Oswald Papers, Sudlows. After Richard Jr. foolishly enlisted in a regiment stationed in Jamaica, Richard Sr. secured his release and ordered his island correspondent to care for him. Back in London by 1765, Richard Jr. lived in a house in Camberwell that was paid for by his father, and took a tour of the Continent the following year. The young prodigal died between 1768 and 1773. Oswald Letter Book, v. 2, ff. 195–201, 348, SRO.
55. Oswald and Ramsay were married at St. Martin in the Fields, London. Bishop of London's Marriage Registry, p. 438, Guildhall Library, London; and John Cathcart to Robert Hamilton, December 1, 1750, Hamilton of Rozelle Papers, Bundle 113, Glasgow University Archives. Ramsay's father Alexander was a member of the Ramsay family of Laithers in Aberdeenshire and Melrose in Banffshire, two Catholic strongholds. In the 1690s, the family was headed by James Ramsay (d. 1693), whose nephew Alexander married Jean Ferguson and, after the birth of Mary in 1719, sailed for Jamaica. Oswald Vault, St. Quivox Kirk, Ayrshire; and Janet Sutherland to Richard Oswald, October 21, 1765, Oswald Papers, Sudlows. For further details on Alexander Ramsay, see Hancock, "Citizen of the World," pp. 121–22.

inheritance (roughly £20,000 sterling) as the only child of a Kingston import/export merchant.[56] And her beauty and dignity, captured by Johann Zoffany (Illustration 2.5) and satirized by Robert Burns, was legendary.[57] Mary Ramsay thus brought Oswald an estate and close ties to Jamaica's merchants and planters. She also brought Oswald the trustees of her dowry, two more Scots who had recently settled in London – John Mill, a coastwise trader from Montrose, and Robert Scott, the head of a large Madeira wine-trading firm.[58] For the next three decades, these three provided Oswald with financial resources and personal camaraderie. Their values – honesty, industry, frugality, and sobriety – reinforced his own; their interests matched his own; and their Scottish and Atlantic contacts helped him open up new areas of enterprise.

What was Richard Oswald like as a person? On the surface, he looked plain and serious. The head-and-shoulders portrait painted by William Denune at the time of his marriage to Ramsay and reproduced here as Illustration 2.6 shows an elongated face, an aquiline nose, and piercing eyes. His full head of dark brown hair was parted in the center and pulled back, and his sober taste in clothes was expressed in a silk waistcoat and white shirt.[59] Yet even this paragon of simplicity was not above a touch of vanity: noticeably absent were the spectacles that enabled him to see and the ear horn that helped him to hear. His clothes, while comfortable, were never those of a dandy. His possessions – his taxable property in 1766 amounted to a light four-wheel carriage, 500 ounces of silver plate, and printed books – were those of a relatively modest merchant.[60] Oswald abhorred the dissipation of contemporary life; he was constantly enjoining his friends to abstain

56. Mary Ramsay's personal estate was valued at £8,285 sterling, her interest in real estate at £11,372, and her contacts inestimable. Island Record Office, Powers of Attorney, v. 29, ff. 7–8 (May 1738), 204 (March 25, 1740). When her father died in 1738, Mary Ramsay was a minor. She and her mother set sail for England, leaving her guardian to manage her affairs. Mary Ramsay received the bulk of her father's estate and later inherited the estate of her uncle James Ferguson, when he died c. 1739.

57. James Kinsley, ed., *The Poems and Songs of Robert Burns*, v. 1 (Oxford, 1968), v. 1, pp. 446–47.

58. Marriage Articles, November 16, 1750, Oswald Papers, Sudlows; and Island Record Office, Deeds, v. 146, ff. 64–67 (Indenture, September 30, 1751). For detailed biographies of Mill and Scott, see Hancock, "Citizen of the World," pp. 146–62.

59. Looks may not have been Oswald's best feature. In the 1780s, it was rumored that Benjamin West's painting of "The Peacemakers" was never finished because Oswald refused to sit for the artist on account of his ugliness. Helmut von Erffa and Allen Staley, *The Paintings of Benjamin West* (New Haven, 1986), pp. 218–19; Sellers, *Benjamin Franklin*, pp. 398–400; and the entry in John Quincy Adams's Diary for July 21, 1817, quoted in *Portraits of John and Abigail Adams* (Cambridge, 1967), p. 43. On his bad eyesight and poor hearing, see John Stevenson to Richard Oswald, September 15, 1767, Oswald Papers, Sudlows.

60. T 47/4: Duty Paid on Coaches, Carriages and Plate, 1764–66, sub Richard Oswald.

Illustration 2.5 Mary Ramsay Oswald Portrait, by Johann Zoffany. *Courtesy:* The Trustees, The National Gallery, London.

Illustration 2.6 Richard Oswald Portrait, by William Denune. *Courtesy:* Private Collection, United Kingdom.

from wine and to drink more seltzer, and lecturing the young to avoid display of any kind. He was a quiet, unobtrusive man, who spoke only when he had something to say.[61] In politics, he played such an invisible role that it is sometimes difficult to reconstruct his beliefs or positions.

61. Henry Laurens to John Laurens, February 28, 1772, and Henry Laurens to John Lewis Gervais, February 28, 1772, *Papers of Henry Laurens*, v. 8, pp. 198–200.

Temperamentally, he was averse "to asking favours from people in power," but, when necessary, he lobbied strenuously for his shipping and trading, slaving, and planting interests. He never held a parliamentary seat, yet was careful to vote in every election between 1764 and 1784. Like most of his associates, he preferred the "invisible" service of informing and persuading policymakers. Political representation in a public forum did not interest him and, when he served as a diplomat in 1782, he did so behind closed doors, much as he would have done as an arbitrator handling a commercial dispute in the City.[62]

Despite this aversion to notoriety and publicity, Oswald was a sociable member of Scots and American society in London. He cast a wide net and, on his guest list, he included such luminaries as the artist Robert Strange, the authors Laurence Sterne and James Boswell, the wit Caleb Whitefoord, the American merchant and statesman Henry Laurens, and the "electric philosopher" Benjamin Franklin. He felt comfortable with both the high and the low. His greater circle of friends included Scots merchants who traded with the colonies, Scots officers and employees he had known in Germany when he served as army contractor during the Seven Years' War, and members of his clubs and charities. He supported his associates, friends, and relatives to an extraordinary degree, providing jobs for some and procuring work for others.[63] With money he was less free, yet he assisted poor Scots in London and Ayrshire and frequently bailed out friends and neighbors who had fallen on hard times.[64] His inner circle of friends contained business partners Mill, Scott, and Herries, a few other associates, his neighbor and attorney the Huguenot Charlton Palmer, and a handful of others, like Sir Alexander's cousin Dr. William Grant.[65]

62. His lobbying efforts for Glasgow in the 1750s, his request for protection of the Tortola traders in 1756, his opposition to the use of paper currency in North Carolina in 1759, and his support for the reduction of import duties on brandy in 1763, appear in CO 152/28/Bb71: March 11, 1756; W. Saunders, ed., *The Colonial Records of North Carolina*, v. 6 (Raleigh, 1888); and T 1/424/115: February 18, 1763.
63. The son of a Thurso alderman became Oswald's clerk in the 1760s; his nephews the Andersons became clerks in 1780; and two other nephews, Harry Robertson and James Anderson, became overseers in Florida in the 1770s and 1780s. Moreover, Oswald procured appointments for a London business acquaintance Robert Forbes, an Ayrshire neighbor Alexander Oliphant, a distant relative of Sir Stuart Threipland, and many of his former contracting employees who needed work. Robert Forbes to Richard Oswald, September 26, 1778, and Alexander Oliphant to Richard Oswald, December 19, 1778, Oswald Papers, Sudlows.
64. Anon., *A Short Account of the Institution, Progress, and Present State of the Scottish Corporation* (London, 1777); and Robert Sandilands to Richard Oswald, February 24, 1780, and Charles Dalrymple to Richard Oswald, June 30, 1780, Oswald Papers, Sudlows.
65. Palmer lived across the street from Oswald at 18 Philpot Lane. The first evidence of his legal practice is the 1750 Oswald/Ramsay Marriage Articles. He specialized in

Plain, unobtrusive, and reserved, Oswald was "a man of parts," highly prized for his knowledge. He was an avid reader. This is hardly surprising, since he, like the other associates, believed that working and learning should proceed hand-in-hand. Before he embarked on any new adventure, he immersed himself in the pertinent literature and emerged "a Man of Great Knowledge and Ready Conversation" who was widely sought as an expert on the subject by family, friends, fellow Scots, business acquaintances, and government servants.[66] Acting on knowledge was central to his character. In business or in society, he knew how to prepare himself for making decisions. He acquired "correct" information before he acted – indeed, he was constitutionally unable to act without such data – and, thus armed, he proceeded carefully, step by step, acting in a manner that appears to have been above reproach.[67]

John Sargent II

In building their businesses at the center of the empire, Boyd, Grant, and Oswald united the distinct experiences they had along the periphery of the empire. Both Boyd and Grant were handicapped by the relative poverty of their families, and all three by the opprobrium in which Scots were held. They were inhibited by the dire economic state of their homeland. They were strangers to London who arrived in the metropolis with comparatively few assets or connections, except ethnic ties and their links to the periphery, which they then used to create business. Their lives provide textbook examples of the destructive and constructive force of marginal status. In many respects, the nine partners in the Sargent circle stood apart from their counterparts in the other three circles: they formed the only group that was born in England (although they were born in the West Country or East Midlands, and not the Home Counties) and trained in London; they were the only participants in commercial guilds; and they were more bound by marriage and cousinage than any other circle. They were, therefore, the least marginal

contracts, deeds, and wills. On his work, see Marriage Articles, November 16, 1750, Oswald Papers, Sudlows; C 12/808/2: Johnson v. Bell; Grenada, St. George's, Supreme Court, Deeds, F 1/1–14 (April 24–25, 1766), S 2/1–33 (April 25–26, 1774), and N 3/236–54 (March 16–17, 1787); Oliver, *Caribbeana*, v. 3 (July 29, 30, August 1, 1777); Plymouth, Montserrat Deed Books, November 4, 1774; and Stowe 366/3–4 (August 27, 1765), Stowe 182 (May 8, 1766), Stowe 7/1 (April 27, 1769) and Stowe 187 (December 7, 1769), Stowe Mss., Huntington Library, San Marino.

66. Carlyle, *Anecdotes*, p. 180.
67. BCM 491: Richard Oswald to James Penman, April 18, 1769, and James Penman to Governor Grant, October 9, 1769.

group, with some ties to the City predating the arrival of each merchant in the circle in London.

The Sargent circle's origins lay in two older London firms whose principals had come from the West Country. The first company was founded by George Arnold, a Devonshire storekeeper's son who, in 1710, at the age of eighteen, left Exeter and established a dry-goods trade in London. He became one of London's prominent merchants and, when he died in 1751, bequeathed his business to a young cousin John Sargent II (Illustration 2.7).[68] A competing company was founded by William Smith, a Dorsetshire farmer's son who, in 1704, at the age of fourteen, left Lyme and served as an apprentice to a London linen-draper. Like Arnold, Smith also came to be regarded as one of London's principal citizens – he was knighted for his loyalty to the Crown in 1745 – and, at his death, his business was divided among his partners, the major share going to the Huguenot George René Aufrere, John Sargent II's third cousin by marriage (Illustration 2.8).[69]

John Sargent II's early years were as itinerant as most of the associates'

68. A genealogy of the Arnold family appears in Appendix I.4. See also IGI, Devon; Beatrix F. Cresswell, *Exeter Churches* (Exeter, 1908), p. 154; and M. M. Rowe and A. M. Jackson, eds., *Exeter Freemen, 1266–1967* (Exeter, 1973), pp. 140, 144, 166, 174–76, 180. George Arnold's father, William Arnell (1656–1720), left the family homestead in north-central Devon and set himself up as a grocer in Exeter. After changing his surname to Arnold, he and his wife Ann raised eleven children. Their ninth child George was born on May 4, 1692 and raised in Exeter. At the age of eighteen, George moved to London, turned from foodstuffs to dry-goods, and rose to prominence in the African trading community. Arnold was slowly drawn into City politics: he joined the Haberdashers' Company before 1722; sat as an Alderman for the Ward of Cheap from 1722 to 1740; acted as Deputy Alderman in 1733; and served as the Master of the Haberdashers in 1735–1736, the Sheriff of London from 1740 to 1751, and President of St. Thomas's Hospital in 1750–51. Alfred B. Beavan, *The Aldermen of the City of London*, v. 1 (London, 1908), pp. 105, 347, and v. 2 (London, 1913), pp. lvii, 30, 128; Anon., *The Poll of the Livery-Men of the City of London at the Election for Members of Parliament* (London, 1722), p. 92; PROB 11/1751 Surrey July 197 (PCC 197 Busby); and Devon Record Office, 216/1/2/64 (January 15, 1752).

69. Smith's family came from Ilminster in Devon and Chard in Somerset. Smith was born in Chard in 1686 and, at the age of five, he inherited his father's substantial estates in Somerset and Dorset. He was apprenticed to Daniel Mason of London, and admitted to the Mercers' Company in 1704. John Hutchins, *The History and Antiquities of the County of Dorset*, 3rd ed., v. 4 (London, 1870), pp. 498–99, 504; Author's Correspondence, Mercers' Company Archivist to David Hancock, November 7, 1988; and Freedom Records, COLRO. In 1718, Smith purchased the estate of Sydling in Dorset. He served as Collector of the Orphan's Coal Duties between 1717 and 1752; he unsuccessfully contested the parliamentary seat for Lyme Regis in 1722; he sat on the London Common Council as a representative for Aldgate from 1722 to 1728; and he served as the City's Sheriff in 1741–42, commanded Colonel Green's militia regiment from 1749 to 1751, and served as Alderman from 1749 to 1752. In February 1745, he was knighted for his support of the Crown. Beavan, *Aldermen*, v. 1, p. 14, and v. 2, pp. 130, 198. His estate stretched from London to York to Devon. PROB 11/793 (1752 London March 77).

Illustration 2.7 John Sargent II Portrait, by Allan Ramsay. *Courtesy:* The Holburne Museum and Craft Studies Centre, Bath.

and laid the foundation for his amalgamation of differing traditions. His father was a grocer in Plymouth who had moved to London to work for the Navy in 1714.[70] For the fifteen years following the birth of John II in 1715, the Sargents were constantly on the move: first

70. A genealogy of the Sargent family appears in Appendix I.4. R. H. D'Elboux and Winifride Ward, trans., *The Registers of St. Dunstan in the East*, Part III (London, 1958), p. 34; and Henry Wagner, "Pedigree of Sargent, Afterwards Arnold, and Sargent," *The Genealogist*, n.s., v. 33 (1917), pp. 189–97.

Illustration 2.8 George Aufrere Portrait, by William Hoare. *Courtesy:* Private Collection, United Kingdom.

Deptford, then Lisbon, later Sheerness and Chatham, and finally back to Deptford where, in 1729, the elder Sargent became the Navy's Clerk of the Survey.[71] On returning to the London area, the Sargents placed

71. Deptford: Accountant for Stores, 1716–18; Lisbon: Agent for Victualing, 1718; Sheerness: Clerk of the Cheque, 1719–28; Chatham: Clerk of the Ropeyard, 1728–29; and Deptford: Clerk of the Survey, 1729–46. John Sargent I held the last position until 1746 when he became the Deptford Yard Transport Agent responsible for loading

their fifteen-year-old son John in the care of their cousin George Arnold. As Arnold's assistant and, on turning eighteen in 1733, as his apprentice, young Sargent learned the ways of the linen trade. After three years of apprenticeship, he joined the Haberdashers Company, received the Freedom of the City, and became Arnold's partner.[72] To the work of the linen-trading firm, Sargent brought his family's familiarity with the vagaries of naval supply and an awareness of the commercial opportunities opening up to British merchants around the world. For a company looking for new sources of supply, India, with its expanding commerce, was a logical choice and, prodded by Sargent, the firm became one of London's largest purchasers of East Indian goods. West Africa provided similar opportunities and, in the years following his purchase of the Bance Island slave factory with the Boyds, Grant, Oswald, and Mill, he steered his firm toward an active role as a supplier of cloth goods to slave traders.[73]

John Sargent II's experience and training enabled him to take charge of Arnold & Co.'s trade with little difficulty following Arnold's death and Sargent's inheritance of the controlling share; Thomas Birch, another London-trained linen-draper who had come from Devon in the early years of the century and joined the Arnold firm in the 1740s, took the minority share. Their experience dealing with Germany and Portugal gave them a familiarity with distant lands, fluency in the language of commerce, an understanding of the web of governmental bureaucracy, a knowledge of contracting, and flexibility in trade – all skills an international trading firm would need if it was to meet the challenges raised by Britain's territorial expansion. Before Arnold was even buried,

---

vessels with naval supplies. Subsequent application for a seat on the Navy Board fell on deaf ears, and he remained Storekeeper until August 1755, when his name disappears from the Deptford Yard Letter Books. ADM 106/3378/381, 384, 389, 106/3379/251, and 106/3380/190. He was, it appears, made a Clerk of the Privy Seal and held that sinecure until his death on September 21, 1762. John Sargent II to Duke of Newcastle, June 27, 1755, Add.Mss. 32,856/321–22, BL; *London Magazine*, v. 24 (1755), p. 397; and *Gentleman's Magazine*, v. 32 (1762), p. 448.

72. Freedom Records, COLRO; and Haberdashers' Freedom Register, January 9, 1736, Ms. 15,857/2/397, Guildhall Library. John Sargent II gained the Freedom of Exeter on June 11, 1733. Rowe and Jackson, eds., *Exeter Freemen*, p. 244.

73. With Sargent as partner, the Arnold firm began to sell North Carolina pitch, tar, and turpentine to the Navy Board. ADM 106/2535: April–June 1741, 106/2556: June 23, 1742, 106/2557: August 4, 1742, and 106/2558: January 5, April 4, 1743. In the late 1740s, Sargent worked to reorganize the African trade. He later recommended Ebenezer Young to the new Company of Merchants as one of its Deputy Agents. T 70/1516: December 19, 1750. His firm supplied the new Company, particularly Young's Cape Coast Castle, with large quantities of East Indian spices, printed linens, carnelian beads, salad oil, and linseed oil. In 1750, for instance, the firm sent 20,000 ounces of silver to India where it purchased diamonds and cloth for the slave trade. CO 388/44–45; T 70/143; and B 71 (1758–64), IOL.

they reconfigured the partnership as "Sargent, Birch & Co." and began operating out of Sargent's house in New Broad Street.[74]

Unlike the associates in the other circles, who seldom, if ever, changed partners, Sargent continually allied himself with new men from his family's Devon or his wife's Derby and Lincoln: first Birch; then Birch and Aufrere; then Aufrere, William Cooke, and Christopher Chambers (a first cousin of Sargent's wife); and, finally, in the 1770s, Chambers, Samuel Gardiner, Robert Rolleston (Sargent's brother-in-law's brother-in-law), and Sargent's younger son John III (Illustrations 2.9 and 2.10).[75] Making sense of Sargent's activities is no easy task, for one must separate individual from joint ventures and, among the latter, keep track of ever-shifting alliances. One way Sargent managed his numerous partners was by not dealing with all of them equally. He limited his close contact to a small core of one or two partners at a time and, in fact, gave the impression that he trusted very few. If the firm required more members, he let the other principals maintain the operation and deal with the other partners and employees.

The Sargent circle was the most English and the most endogamous circle, and it was the circle best connected to London's and England's elite. These ties come from association with George Aufrere, the Huguenot cloth merchant who had taken charge of Sir William Smith's firm and become Sargent's partner in May 1754. Aufrere was the partner to whom Sargent was closest. Through their multidecade partnership, Sargent dealt most with Aufrere, and Aufrere with the others.[76] The two

74. For Thomas Birch, see Hancock, "Citizen of the World," pp. 194–95. Birch and Sargent parted at some point in the early 1750s. As he severed his connection with Sargent, Birch began to operate under his own name in 1755. The break was complete by 1760. Maitland, *The History and Survey of London*, v. 2, p. 902; and T 1/393/19: Memorial, 1759. Birch died at his house in Hatton Street on July 29, 1774, and was "buried in the most private manner in some country church yard by daylight." *London Chronicle*, July 30, 1774, p. 10; *Gentleman's Magazine*, v. 44 (1774), p. 390; and PROB 11/1774 Middlesex August 293 (proved August 27, 1774).

75. On Gardiner, Rolleston, and Sargent III, see Hancock, "Citizen of the World," pp. 229–34.

76. A genealogy of the Aufrere family appears in Appendix I.4. The Aufreres were descended from a French noble family that had held high legal and ecclesiastical office during the fifteenth century, but had been chased out of France after the Revocation of the Edict of Nantes (1685) for adhering to the precepts of Calvin. Aufrere's paternal grandfather settled in Holland. At the turn of the century, he moved to England, where one of his sons, Israel Antoine Aufrere, assumed the ministry of the French Church of the Savoy. From 1701 to 1727, Rev. Aufrere preached at the Savoy Chapel, and it was there that his youngest child George was christened on November 7, 1715. While living in Amsterdam, Rev. Aufrere married Sarah Amsincq, the daughter of a wealthy merchant connected to the Boreel and Fagel families. They raised five children in London: Jeanne (b. 1701); Magdalene (b. 1703); Anthony (1704–81); Marianne (b. 1707); and George René (1715–1801). David Agnew, *Protestant Exiles from France* (Edinburgh, 1886), pp. 334–37, 391–92; Charles P. Stewart, "History of the Aufreres,"

conducted their business out of Aufrere's house at 38 Mincing Lane.[77] Aufrere, a Londoner by birth and upbringing, had what Sargent needed most – valuable commercial and social connections in the metropolis. Aufrere's father had been granted the ministry of the Chapel Royal at St. James Palace. His mother was related to some of Amsterdam's richest trading families. His sister married the King's principal physician. The merchant to whom he was apprenticed was an important City politician. His wife Arabella Bate (Illustration 2.11) was also well-connected. Her brother was the King's principal chaplain. Her aunt and uncle were the 8th Earl and Countess of Exeter. Her nephew Sir Joseph Banks was a President of the Royal Society.[78] And her relatives among the greater Bate family provided Aufrere and Sargent with young partners in Christopher Chambers (Bate's third cousin) and Robert Rolleston (Bate's third cousin by marriage); a small client base in continual need of cloth (the extended Cecil family); and a wife for Sargent (another third cousin of Mrs. Aufrere, Rosamunde Chambers) (Illustration 2.12).[79]

Proceedings of the Huguenot Society of London, v. 9 (1909–11), pp. 145–57; and Winifred Turner, "The Aufrere Papers," *Publications of the Huguenot Society of London*, v. 40 (1940), pp. 63, 112, 162, 184–89, 195, 202.

77. From March 1752 to March 1754, Aufrere, Peregrine Cust, and William Frye, the partners in the old Smith firm, continued along the lines laid down by Smith and Aufrere. Their last recorded transaction was the sale of Indian cowries to the Company of Merchants on March 13, 1754. T 70/143/273. After 1754, Sargent continued to reside in New Broad Street, although he did business in Mincing Lane; all joint affairs were handled in Mincing Lane. *Kent's Directory for the Year 1754* (London, 1754), p. 88; *A Complete Guide* (London, 1755), p. 152, and (London, 1757), p. 146; T 1/367/11: George Aufrere to James West, February 12, 1756; and T 1/368/39: George Aufrere to James West, June 19, 1756.

78. Arabella Bate (1720–1804) married George Aufrere in 1746. Their marriage portraits, painted by William Hoare, now hang at Brocklesby Park. Her paternal great-grandfather Colonel William Bate was a Royalist who had fled to Barbados during the English Civil War and had taken up planting by 1661; his son Richard returned to England and regained the family's Derbyshire lands. Joanne M. Sanders, ed., *Barbados Records: Wills and Administrations*, v. 1 (Marceline, Mo., 1979), p. 20, and v. 3 (Houston, Tex., 1981), pp. 21–22; and PRO-CL, Close Rolls, 10 Wil.III 2–21. Arabella Bate's maternal grandfather was Thomas Chambers, a Governor of the Company of Copper Mines. "Articles between the Copper Mines in England and Thomas Chambers" (London, 1725), p. 4; *The Herald and Genealogist*, v. 7 (1873), pp. 488–89; and Scott, *Constitution*, pp. 430–35. Arabella Bate was the daughter of William Bate of Foston-cum-Scropton, "a gentleman of fashion and estate" (d. 1735), and Arabella Chambers (1701–27). She was orphaned at age fifteen and raised by her aunt Hannah Sophia Chambers, the 8th Countess of Exeter. The Cecil genealogy is found in BL, Egmont Mss. 1075. It was rumored that Bate brought £90,000 to her marriage with Aufrere in 1746, but contemporary legal records suggest that £9,000 is more likely. Cf. Joseph Farington, *The Farington Diary*, ed. James Greig, v. 3 (London, 1924), p. 78; C 12/2288/38: 1734; Will of 8th Countess (1765), Burghley House, Stamford, Lincolnshire; Rev. Robinson to Henry Wagner, February 13, 1897 (extract), Papers of Vere L. Oliver, Society of Genealogists, London; and PROB 11/898/163.

79. Exeter Ms. 45/28, Burghley House, Lincolnshire; and IGI, Derby, August 11, 1747.

Illustration 2.9 Robert Rolleston Engraved Portrait, by James Alderson. *Courtesy:* National Portrait Gallery, London.

Illustration 2.10 John Sargent III Portrait, by George Romney. *Courtesy:* The Holburne Museum and Craft Studies Centre, Bath.

From analyzing the associates' characteristics and retelling the biographies of the four principals, we gain a perspective on their personal mercantile orientation that complemented the rise of imperial opportunities and entrepreneurial challenges. The associates were cultural hybrids. For the most part, they came from the ethnic, religious, and commercial margins of late-seventeenth- and eighteenth-century Britain. They were, to a man, restless, adaptive, protean characters who struggled to overcome the marginal and dependent station they inherited and

Illustration 2.11 Arabella Bate Aufrere Portrait, by William Hoare. *Courtesy:*
Private Collection, United Kingdom.

encountered. Their varied backgrounds were their strength, for they
forced them to combine different traditions and experiences in order to
succeed in taking advantage of imperial opportunities. Their outsiderness
provided the spur to doing so. Their individual personalities, desires,
and experiences combined with the changes in the empire and market
to shape the management of trade.

Illustration 2.12 Rosamunde Chambers Sargent Portrait, by Allan Ramsay. *Courtesy:* The Holburne Museum and Craft Studies Centre, Bath.

PART II

The Management
of Trade

The associates began their London business careers as shippers and traders. Marginal men at the outset, they became mercantile middlemen who, to ply their craft, relied on their personal and commercial links that derived from their positions in the City, at the heart of the empire, and spanned the globe. They concentrated on the colonial trades, in which pre-existing social and financial connections mattered least, and where their connections were the strongest, anyway. They developed specific markets or sectors by using their commodity sources and contacts overseas, combining goods and people from many points around the world, and then managing multiple activities simultaneously. The choice of commission merchandising in the colonial trades was a fortunate one, because Great Britain's colonial territories expanded greatly in their lifetimes. This was not enough, however, to make them truly successful; commission merchandising by itself was a middling business. The associates needed more lucrative ventures that would flourish as the empire expanded. Largely, they found these ventures by doing what is known to modern business as backward integration, first by adding trading on their own accounts to commission merchandising, and later by producing or managing the goods that they had hitherto only brokered or transported.[1] Even before the Seven Years' War, the associates were pushing closer to the source of supply, extending their enterprises into plantation farming and slaving.

The commercially integrative behavior of the associates needs to be viewed from the perspective of imperial growth. Therein, the Seven Years' War can be seen to have promoted the expansion of British trans-Atlantic trade, with the British navy's gaining control of the world's principal shipping lanes and the protection to the colonies that followed

---

1. For an introduction to the use of "backward integration," see Michael Porter, *Competitive Advantage: Creating and Sustaining Superior Performance* (New York, 1985), pp. 276, 308–09; and Alfred D. Chandler Jr., *Scale and Scope: The Dynamics of Industrial Capitalism* (Cambridge, Mass., 1990), pp. 28, 31, 61–62.

therefrom. In this, the war was unique among eighteenth-century military conflicts. It provided knowledgeable merchants with opportunities to expand their colonial business, and to use their merchant skills to integrate backwards into military contracting. Indeed, government contracting during the Seven Years' War was the most lucrative in history, and it provided the associates with the quantum increase in capital that enabled them to increase the scale of other forms of backward integration after the war. The war, for instance, decimated the French as an Atlantic power and especially as a competitive imperial player in the struggle for control of North America. The associates speculated in and developed lands taken from the French which, after 1763, lay open and safe for settlement. The associates speculated in those lands, established plantations there, and transported white people to settle them and black slaves to work them. Moreover, new markets lay ready to exploit. The war, for instance, expanded the sugar industry of America and Britain, multiplied the need for general and related services, and increased the mother country's imports and its share of sugar re-exports to continental Europe. New ventures on a much larger scale involved new risks, but they turned out to be risks worth taking.

Probably the single most profitable venture they undertook with contracting profits was to expand their Sierra Leone slave factory – the one visited by Henry Smeathman. They acquired the entrepôt in 1748, cheaply; and, as we will see, their early endeavors suffered losses. Even though their contacts in the American plantation community kept them well-informed about the need for laborers, the success of the factory was not assured. Indeed, it might never have paid off had not the Seven Years' War turned events to their favor. That war opened the Ceded Islands, Florida, and Nova Scotia to British agricultural development and so to plantation agriculture's insatiable need for unfree laborers. It also destroyed the French slave trade from Senegal and Gorée, and seriously impeded France's supply of slaves to plantations in the French Caribbean. France retained Guadeloupe, Martinique, and St. Domingue, but these islands sorely needed to rebuild their slave forces as much as (perhaps more than) the British did theirs. Despite long-standing national animosities, French slave-trading middlemen turned to Bance Island, just as the British did.

The simultaneous management of factory slaves, Caribbean plantations, and oceangoing vessels positioned the associates to take full advantage of production and marketing opportunities. These areas of activity complemented and reinforced the associates' commission merchandising, as well as each other, by providing opportunities to control more sides of the Atlantic trade polygon. They increased the associates' profit opportunities and their risks. Backward integration was the principal source of the growth and the profitability of their businesses.

Part II examines the associates' entrepreneurial activities, looking at the world of their counting-houses, and the specific businesses they conducted from there. Before we turn to an in-depth look at these enterprises, we should consider what the associates had to manage to make them succeed. Each type of enterprise was guided by its own specific, fundamental business imperatives for making money and achieving success. Keeping their ships full and under sail, for instance, was the key to making money in shipping and trading. Matching crops to the soil and climate of their plantations was a guiding principle of planting. In running a slave entrepôt like the one at Bance Island, the fundamental business imperative was maintaining a steady flow of slaves from suppliers and simultaneously managing multiple channels for bringing slaves to customers. In military contracting, it was necessary to overcome the massive and continuous logistical nightmare of getting food to troops that were on the move, in the face of enemy fire and nonexistent transport, foodstuffs, and workers. The associates' business correspondence is an extended commentary on these imperatives.

In addition to satisfying the fundamental business imperatives in each activity, the associates had to invest and reinvest in their operations. In the case of shipping and trading, they overhauled and improved their vessels to maintain a fleet that had sufficient capacity, was speedy, and required little time or money to be spent on repairs. Plantations required purchasing new lands, clearing forests and swamps, building facilities, supplying equipment, and providing laborers, black and white. To make Bance Island an efficient slave entrepôt, its proprietors had to build fortifications and lodgings, as well as to maintain its military and commercial supplies; later, they found it necessary to erect outfactories for funneling slaves to the main depot. Military contracting likewise required investing – in wagons, mills, bakeries, and storehouses west of the Elbe to provide bread to the army in Germany, and in overseas transport vessels and warehouses to victual the Navy in Kingston and Nova Scotia.

In all of their endeavors, the associates had to find, place, and keep competent, honest, and loyal managers at the places where the goods were produced and the trades were negotiated. Since the associates managed their businesses over long distances and with rudimentary, though gradually improving, transoceanic communications, they had to rely on individuals who could act in their stead. They turned repeatedly to their kinsmen and acquaintances in America, Scotland, Ireland, or the counties, and to those who had worked for them elsewhere in previous endeavors. Some of these people worked directly for the associates, while others assisted their ventures in a worldwide network of correspondents, agents, clients, and suppliers – selling them their slaves, their cargoes of European manufactures, and their shipping and factorage services; buying their American crops and goods for eventual resale in London and Europe; and calling on them to assist them in emergencies and to supply them with information about the day-to-day needs and opportunities of their far-flung business empires. When the stakes were exceptionally high and delays exceedingly costly, as they were for some military contracts, they managed the operations in person.

All these components – managing the imperatives of each business, investing and reinvesting, and finding suitable, effective on-site managers – were ingredients of success for anyone who undertook to be a shipper and trader, an overseas planter, the manager of a slaving depot, or a military contractor. What the associates did that most others did not was to integrate these various business activities. By shipping and trading on their own accounts, and integrating backward into planting and slaving, they provided themselves with additional means to keep their ships full, their plantations staffed with slaves, and their crops moving toward European markets. The coordination that their endeavors required was their greatest challenge. It was also the secret to their success.

3

Managing from a "Merchant's Public Counting-House"

THE ASSOCIATES COULD HAVE FULLY INTEGRATED their diverse collection of businesses only from London – the center of world commerce in the eighteenth century.[1] Inhabitants at the center of the empire, whether in London's walled enclosure or the metropolis that had spilled well beyond the walls, daily encountered a rich assembly of "countrymen and foreigners consulting together upon the private business of mankind, and making this metropolis a kind of emporium for the whole earth." The bustle of the Royal Exchange, for instance, was emblematic of what was going on in the City and empire. Therein was held "a great Council, in which all considerable Nations have their Representatives." The man of letters Joseph Addison, for one, was pleased

> to hear disputes adjusted between an inhabitant of Japan and an alderman of London, or to see a subject of the Great Mogul entering into a league with one of the Czar of Muscovy. Sometimes I am jostled among a body of Armenians; sometimes I am lost in a crowd of Jews; and sometimes make one in a group of Dutchmen.

Looking on such a farrago, the Englishman (for Addison was not alone; many commentators writing later in the century shared his sentiment) fancied himself "a Dane, Swede or Frenchman, at different times" or, better, "like the old philosopher, who, upon being asked what countryman he was, replied . . . 'a citizen of the world.'"[2] The associates, more prosaic than Addison's denizens yet still fitting the description, located themselves as closely as possible to the center of this world, so as to cope best with the international bustle of the "emporium." There, in

---

1. Sir Alexander Grant to Peter Davidson, November 27, 1765, and May 24, 1766, Court of Error Records, 1B/11/1, v. 4, ff. 188–87, Jamaica Archives. The chapter title quotes the title of a handbook by Postlethwayt, *The Merchants Counting House; Or New Mercantile Institution* (London, 1750).
2. *The Spectator*, No. 69 (May 19, 1711), in Addison, *The Works*, ed. Tickell, v. 1, p. 178. See also Ned Ward, *The London Spy* (1703) (London, 1955), pp. 55–57.

their counting-houses, the associates received the day's news and supervised and coordinated the wide range of their own and their partners'
and employees' diverse skills and activities.

The City

By the mid-1730s, London was the largest city in the world. Its chief
claim to primacy lay in "its Number of Houses and Inhabitants," for
it was supposed to exceed "any other capital City in the known World,
either antient or modern." (Contemporary chroniclers seem to have
forgotten about Tokyo or Peking, Constantinople or Tenochtitlan.) More
than one-tenth of the total population of Britain lived in London, two-
thirds of whom had come "from distant Parts." With nearly three-
quarters of a million people in 1700, London was larger than Paris,
Amsterdam, or modern Rome, and it remained so throughout the century. Its citizens enjoyed "an amazing Plenty and Cheapness" of foods
and manufactures, to a degree not matched by any other great city. Its
only serious competition as a market came from Amsterdam but, by
1735, that city was a shell of its former trading self, London having
eclipsed it in all areas but finance.[3] London was the seat of Britain's
government – the King, his court, the Ministry, and the central courts
of justice – and the government was increasingly interested in commerce. But it was not "the influence of government" alone that drew
men like the associates. It was also "the ordinary impulse of men and
things" whose predilections were decidedly commercial and independent
that exerted "a kind of attraction of commerce" on shippers and traders.[4]

Preeminent among European ports, Hanoverian London was, first of
all, a shipping center. Most of Britain's overseas fleet dropped anchor
there, where twenty-nine official "sufferance" wharves for processing
dutiable goods and public "legal" quays for handling all other goods
facilitated the landing of commodities for the market. Most of Britain's
oceangoing vessels were built there, although increasingly the ports of

---

3. William Maitland, *The History and Survey of London*, 3rd ed., v. 2 (London, 1760),
   pp. 750–56; Wrigley, "A Simple Model of London's Importance," p. 44; Jan De Vries,
   The Dutch Rural Economy in the Golden Age, 1500–1700 (New Haven, 1974), p.
   100; Jan De Vries, "The Decline and Rise of the Dutch Economy, 1675–1900," in G.
   Saxonhouse and G. Wright, eds., *Technique, Spirit and Form in Making of Modern
   Economies* (Greenwich, 1984), pp. 149–89; and Jonathan Israel, *Dutch Primacy in
   World Trade, 1585–1740* (Oxford, 1989), pp. 377–98.
4. On the heterogeneity of London, discussed in this and the following paragraphs, see
   Maitland, *History*, v. 2; Abbé Raynal, *A Philosophical and Political History*, v. 6
   (London, 1783), pp. 412–13; Joseph G. Broodbank, *History of the Port of London*
   (London, 1921); George, *London Life*; Penelope Corfield, *The Impact of English Towns,
   1700–1800* (Oxford, 1982); and Keith Wrightson, *English Society, 1580–1680* (Lon-
   don, 1982), p. 128.

northeastern England were cutting into this dominance. And most of Britain's "seamen for navigation, and hands for commerce" were found there, on the quays or in the taverns, inasmuch as, over the century, Britain's largely rural population was slowly breaking up and moving to the capital. Oceanic navigators in search of marine equipment could find no better warehouse of globes, maps, charts, telescopes, or compasses in all Europe. London was, also, a lively trading center. Suppliers abounded. Here were based the Crown-chartered or Parliament-sanctioned monopoly companies, like the East India Company, the South Sea Company, the Royal African Company, and the Levant Company – the sources of valuable re-exports. Here were the markets. Here were found, in the City's wholesale produce stalls and warehouses, commodities of almost every description used in overseas merchandising or victualing: fish (Billingsgate), livestock (Smithfield), vegetables and fruits (Covent Garden), and grain (Bear Key and the Corn Exchange). Farther out, in the suburban communities that ringed the City, could be obtained manufactures of increasing variety or refinement – sugar, rum, beer, or silk. London with its large population of consumers was, of course, a hungry market for overseas commodities, but it was also the dominant transshipment point for inland trade.

London was also a financing center. Finance follows commerce and, in the City, all forms of financing flourished: the Bank of England, smaller private banks, brokers specializing in marine insurance, and a growing market for stocks and shares. Nowhere in Britain's empire was the raising or providing of funds as developed or available. And, finally, London surpassed all other British cities as an education center for the youth of the mercantile classes. When asked about the "mercantile education" of one young man, Sir Alexander Grant noted that "Bristol, Liverpool & all outports pursue only few branches & even that in a limited way" and that young men there "acquire narrow peculiaritys that are unsuitable to commerce in the great universal marts of London, Amsterdam, Hamburgh, & c." "It is true," he admitted, there was less opportunity "for, or temptation to, vice in narrow places, but at the same time there is far less opportunity for instruction." In the outports, there were no chances for an apprentice to learn the "management" of a "business" and to become "known to correspondents" with whom he might later "fix" an intercourse. Outport apprentices "are often as much at a loss what to pursue after their apprenticeships as before." London, Grant believed, provided the best commercial education money could buy.[5]

5. GD 345/1180/1765: Sir Alexander Grant to Captain Archibald Grant, December 27, 1764.

London was a powerful magnet for ambitious outsiders; it had long been so. Augustus Boyd could have returned to Ireland; Grant might have resettled in the Spey Valley; Oswald could have remained in Glasgow. They did not. These opportunists were attracted by the institutions London was famous for – its central governmental offices, its shipping and trading facilities, its highly developed financial sector, and its rich but informal education.

The Neighborhood

Not all parts of the City drew the associates equally. Choosing where to locate a counting-house was one of the most important early decisions aspiring overseas merchants had to make, for only by placing themselves as closely as possible to the center of commercial activity could they hope to move from the margins. In an age when most trading was direct and oral, the closer the neighborhood lay to institutions or people that mattered, the better it enabled a resident to compete in international commerce.

When the Boyds moved into Broad Street Ward in the mid-1730s, they moved to stay, hoping to benefit from the close, interconnected enclave of Scottish, Irish, and Huguenot merchants who lived there. Philpot Lane, the home of Oswald & Co. from 1746 onward, was situated halfway between New Key's five wharves and the banks in Lombard Street, and was lined with the houses of overseas merchants to whom Oswald would turn again and again during his career. Each morning, Oswald's junior partner Herries could easily run to the West End on small errands and be back in time to supervise the work of the junior clerks; less pressed for time in the late afternoon and early evening, he could comfortably walk to the Jamaica Coffeehouse in St. Michael's Alley, just off Cornhill, or similar taverns near the Exchange and there acquaint himself with the trans-Atlantic mercantile news of the day, just as the newspapers were being distributed to subscribers.[6]

Indeed, the usefulness of being close to the center of the "Hotch-Potch" cannot be overstressed, since staying abreast of the news was one of the merchants' chief concerns. Consider the location of Sargent's offices. Mincing Lane in Tower-Street Ward was a "broad and strait" thoroughfare, "filled with very good Houses" leased by "Merchants and persons of Repute." From his counting-house along the southeastern side of the street, Sargent enjoyed an easy walk of five blocks or less to Cloth-Workers Hall at the northern end of the street, the East India

6. Michael Herries to Richard Oswald, August 17, 1765, Oswald Papers, Sudlows.

Company and the Royal African Company in Leadenhall Street, the Hudson's Bay Company in Fenchurch Street, the Bank of England where he was a director in Threadneedle Street, the London Assurance where his partner Aufrere was a director above the Lord Mayor's office in the Royal Exchange, and the two livery companies to which he and his partners belonged – the Haberdashers in Maiden Lane and the Mercers in Cheapside. Within easy reach were nearly a dozen quays, the Customs House, the old Navy Office, and the Trinity House, which was responsible for superintending Thames pilotage, arbitrating maritime disputes, and disseminating advice on merchant shipping.[7]

A well-situated London counting-house offered its partners easy access and direct communication with men "in the know," whether sea captains, brokers, buyers, or competitors. It facilitated shopping around, bargaining, and acquiring information. Where there was "always a choice," a merchant could "go to a second shop" and secure better bargaining terms: the "sure way of making a good market" was to be ever "on the spot" in the right City neighborhood, where similar business or relevant institutions were densely packed. Seeking a second bid was almost second nature to the associates, and they frequently went to several different counting-houses in the two or three streets that abutted their own, before they found a reference for acceptable consignees abroad. News in the City, fresh off incoming ships and buzzing about the counting-houses, filled in the gaps correspondents left in their letters. If they were desirous of making a sale, they made haste to the various coffeehouses known for information about a particular colony or commodity, such as the Colonial in Threadneedle Street or the Pennsylvania in Birchin Lane. If they were willing to gossip in trade "rookeries," like Jonathan's, Lloyd's, or Garraway's, they might gain valuable tips on the impending rise or fall of commodity or share prices.[8] And if they were looking for a new partner, they need look no farther than four or five blocks. When Sargent chose Aufrere as his partner in 1754, for instance, he turned to a merchant who had first apprenticed on Cheapside

---

7. Sewer rate books, window rate books, and general assessment books, esp. Ms. 11,316/182/1755/iii, Guildhall Library, London. *A Complete Guide* (London, 1749) lists Sargent's neighbors. For a discussion of the assets of each neighborhood, see Maitland, *History*, v. 2, pp. 838–53 (Broad Street), 790–93 (Billingsgate), 1031–40 (Tower-Street).
8. Firm principals, like Oswald or Grant, visited certain coffeehouses at specific times each day to conduct business. Price, ed., "Directions," pp. 136–41. When in the counties, they kept themselves abreast of commercial or financial developments by reading newspapers sent via the post. Michael Herries to Richard Oswald, August 17, 1765, Oswald Papers, Sudlows. On finding consignees, see GD 345/1168/1762: Duncan Grant to Sir Archibald Grant, December 10, 1762; and Ms. 12,048, Edward Grace Letter Book, May 23, 1767, and September 28, 1769, Guildhall Library, London.

as Sargent had, and later worked four blocks from Mincing Lane in Leadenhall Street.

London's commercial neighborhoods were not much to look at: Sargent's Mincing Lane, like any minor street, was a close, dank thoroughfare, paved with cobblestone and strewn with straw, food, and feces; the smell of burning coal and the deafening noise of coaches, carts, horses, and dogs pushing their way through the slop was often overwhelming, even to the hardiest citizen. Yet, despite the "confused Babel" and "the Hotch-Potch of half-moon and serpentine Streets, close, dismal, long Lanes, stinking Allies, dark, gloomy Courts, and suffocating Yards," City neighborhoods, if centrally located, allowed one to build on the foundation of being in London at the heart of the empire and make the most of the resources of the City.

The House

The counting-house was the real center of London commerce; it was "the custom" to spend "many hours" there in conversation and negotiation. Unfortunately, eighteenth-century merchants trading overseas seldom described their offices or abodes in their correspondence and, by and large, historians have accepted the silence. Nevertheless, from anecdotal bits strewn about in personal letters, insurance accounts, and testamentary records, one can piece together the appearance and management of the typical London counting-house in the Georgian era, and discern its role in managing a global commerce. Merchants' counting-houses exhibited a wide range in comfort, from lavish palaces to spartan quarters. They unified what seemed at times a welter of different, seemingly incompatible projects and peoples. And they mixed public and private affairs. In the small world of the counting-house, one finds mirrored the larger, more multifarious world of the mercantile classes and, indeed, of the empire.[9]

Architectural designs for City houses in the 1700s did not vary much. In the century that followed the Great Fire of 1666, newly built houses adhered to one of two plans: the rectangular single house, with a regularly spaced three-bay sash-window front; and the square double house, with a five- (or seven-) bay front. Both usually possessed three principal stories, with a cellar below and an attic above. Their roofs were

9. George Maxwell to Benjamin Charnock, November 16, 1743, Lascelles & Maxwell Letter Book, p. 59.

generally tiled, rising at an angle from behind a parapet. Their fronts were usually faced in brick.[10]

The single house was by far the more common of the two forms. In fact, most of London's streets and courtyards in the early 1700s were lined with such narrow-fronted houses whose sites "stretch back to twice their width or more, and . . . have a tiny patch of courtyard or garden – rarely more than the size of a large carpet – at the back." The single house at 17 Philpot Lane into which Oswald moved in mid-1746 was one such house.[11] Located in a small courtyard off the southeastern side of the street, the lot contained three distinct areas: a front house containing both office and dwelling, a yard, and a back warehouse.[12] The front house rose flush with the south side of the court. As depicted in Illustration 3.1, it possessed three stories, plus a cellar and attic. Like so many houses in its day, its exterior was plain: its walls were bricked, its windows set with flush frames and flat arches, and its roof covered with tile.

Little on the outside connoted the bustle within. Entering through the front door on the right side of the entrance facade, visitors confronted a Hall and a staircase connecting cellar to attic. The house followed a two-room, front-and-back pattern, after the plan in Illustration 3.2. Business was conducted on the ground floor: in the front room, to the left of the foyer, clients and visitors were received; behind this office, in

10. John Summerson, *Georgian London*, 3rd ed. (Cambridge, Mass., 1988), pp. 55–56. The subject of merchant housing is a rich field for research. Several contemporary sources are useful in reconstructing facades, floor plans, and decoration. *The Statutes of the Realm*, v. 5 (London, 1819), pp. 601–12 (18 and 19 Car. II, c. 8: An Act for Rebuilding the City of London); and Joseph Moxon, *Mechanick Exercises: Or the Doctrine of Handy-Works*, 3rd ed. (London, 1703), pp. 128–30, 265–68. For more recent scholarship, see Andrew Byre, *London's Georgian Houses* (London, 1986); Dan Cruickshank and Peter Wyld, *London: The Art of Georgian Building* (London, 1975), pp. 24–29; Gunther Hofle, *Das Londoner Stadthaus* (Heidelberg, 1977); and Summerson, *Georgian London*, pp. 39–64. Two authors have provided in-depth analysis of turn-of-the-century forms. A. F. Kelsall, "The London House Plan in the Later 17th Century," *Post-Medieval Archaeology*, v. 8 (1974), pp. 80–91; and M. J. Power, "East London Housing in the Seventeenth Century," in Peter Clark and Paul Slack, eds., *Crisis and Order in English Towns, 1500–1700* (London, 1972), pp. 237–62. The few remaining eighteenth-century City houses are listed in Summerson, *Georgian London*, pp. 297–98. The plans reconstituted here are based upon associates' writings, governmental records, sales catalogues, contemporary building manuals, as well as secondary literature.

11. Details of the interiors of single houses are reported in Kelsall, "London House," pp. 80–91. Details on Oswald's house are found in Sun Office Policy Register, Ms. 11936/289/438, 164, Guildhall Library, London; and Michael Herries to Richard Oswald, July 5, 1766, Oswald Papers, Sudlows.

12. On Oswald's warehouse, see *The Papers of Henry Laurens*, v. 9, pp. 628–30; and Sudlows, Michael Herries to Richard Oswald, July 5, 1766, Oswald Papers, Sudlows.

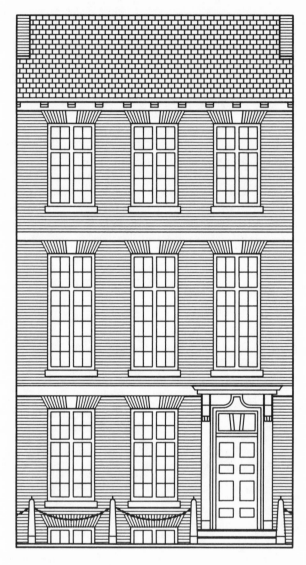

Illustration 3.1 The Single Counting-House: Facade, Drawn by Hugh Adams Russell.

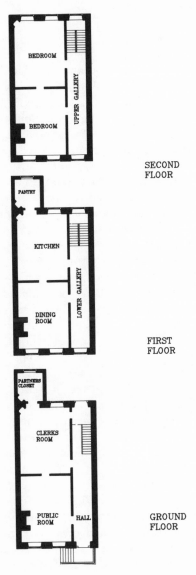

Illustration 3.2 Richard Oswald's Single Counting-House, 17 Philpot Lane: Floor Plans, Drawn by Hugh Adams Russell.

the back room, clerks and employees toiled; and, off the Clerks' Room, Oswald and Mill met in the Partners Closet, where, by the fireside, they wheedled their clients into repaying overdue loans or argued with one another about the price they would charge the Government for supplying the army with bread. Eighteenth-century probate inventories suggest that Oswald's Clerks' Room, if typical, would have contained two writing tables, side tables, chairs, stools, scales and weights, a seven- or eight-day clock and, on the walls, world maps and money charts. Such small ground-floor rooms (at most, 16' × 22') were typically lined with painted pine paneling, heated by marble fireplaces flanked by wooden pilasters, and crowned with molded cornices. The floors above were laid out and appointed in a similarly simple yet comfortable fashion: walls paneled; fireplaces marbled; and cornices molded. The kitchen with its lead sink and the all-white dining room were situated on the first floor; two sleeping chambers – the heated one at the front of the house reserved for the Oswalds or the most senior resident partner, and the other for the managing clerk – were placed on the second floor; at the very top of the house, in the attic, there were two bedrooms for clerks.[13]

If a single house like the Oswald house on Philpot Lane was the more common of City housing forms in the early 1700s and remained so through the end of the century, a double house was an increasingly favorite form selected by large-scale London wholesale merchants who favored large partnerships. At first glance, the house over which John Sargent II presided at 38 Mincing Lane is a good example. It looked much like the merchant's house depicted in Illustration 3.3, which, in turn, was much like Oswald's house, only bigger (47' × 50' rather than 27' × 50'). Its western facade contained the principal entrance. Callers approached the central door from a short flight of stairs, running parallel to the house and guarded by wrought-iron railing, and proceeded into a stone-paved Hall that swept from front to back and was lit by a single square lantern. On this entry-level ground floor, two rooms flanked each side of the Hall (Illustration 3.4). Immediately to the left of the entrance was the Partners' Room, a comfortable space heated by a large fireplace adorned with a fluted frieze and paneled pilasters and furnished with a mahogany Merchant's Bureau, an eight-day clock in a wainscot case made by Whitehurst of Derby, and a painted six-foot cupboard with shelves and doors. Adjoining the Partners' Room was an equally large Kitchen, stocked from floor to ceiling with an array of

13. Although it was usual for the associates' clerks to live in the counting-house, they did not always do so. Trevanion's clerks – Thomas Frith and Jonathan Lindsey – lived in lodgings across town. Cf. Price, ed., "Directions," pp. 136, 141, where clerks lived in rooming houses and dined in taverns.

Illustration 3.3 Capel & Osgood Hanbury's Double Counting-House, 34 Great Tower Street: Facade. *Courtesy*: Royal Commission on Historical Monuments (England).

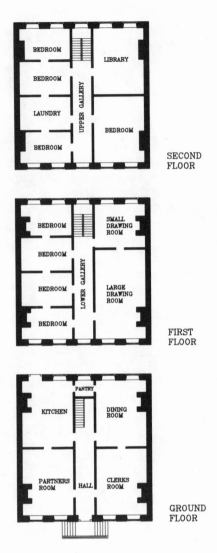

Illustration 3.4 John Sargent II's Double Counting-House, 38 Mincing Lane: Floor Plans, Drawn by Hugh Adams Russell.

cooking implements: a 9′ × 2′ working table, 5 chairs, a wooden meat screen, numerous copper pans and kettles, 13 tin pots, 4 coffee pots, "a quantity of Queen's ware," brown pans, and jars. This was the stuff of any large middle-class London household of the period.[14]

What distinguished Mincing Lane from such homes were the rooms that followed. The Pantry running under the stairs connected the Kitchen and Dining Room, and was home to the better table utensils: mahogany trays, lacquer ware, porcelain service (baking dishes, soup tureens, sauce dishes, butter boats, salad bowls, tart pans, fruit baskets, forty pieces of "blue & white" china, a Derbyshire Spar cream pail, a crystal salver, and fifty-seven British Nankin plates, to name but a few pieces). The Dining Room, where such valuables were used, was one of the grander spaces of the house. Two sets of green woolen curtains were festooned along the edge of the windows; and a Turkey carpet (14′ × 12′) was laid upon the floor. Filling in the dining area were a set of oval mahogany dining tables (each 4′ × 8′), ten mahogany chairs, an octagonal mahogany sideboard, three mahogany knife cases, a large black-and-gold marble side table, two mahogany Pembroke tables, and two small circular mahogany card tables, to which were probably added, when needed, the mahogany oval dining table and eight mahogany horsehair chairs that stood in the Hall. By the material standards of the day, this was an elegant space, graced with polite furniture and trimmed with the trappings of prosperity: mahogany furniture, porcelain dishes, and Turkey carpets. Yet, in an important commentary on its partners, it was not as grand as it could have been; one finds, for instance, no mention of silk, silver, or gold, elements generally mentioned as present in the houses of the aristocracy.[15]

14. As discussed in this and the following paragraphs, Sargent's house is described in Christie's, *A Catalogue of the Household Furniture* (London, December 15–16, 1806). Compare its interior with that of the counting-house at 34 Great Tower Street. Walter Bell, "An Old City Merchant's House," *The Pall Mall Magazine* (1910), pp. 437–44; Royal Commission on Historical Monuments (England), *An Inventory of the Historical Monuments in London*, v. 4: *The City* (London, 1929), p. 185(6); and *Survey of London*, v. 15 (London, 1934), pp. 23–30, pls. 37–61. The Great Tower Street building was one of the last surviving seventeenth-century counting-houses in the City. From the 1740s to the 1760s, it was occupied by John Hanbury, tobacconist, and Capel & Osgood Hanbury, Virginia merchants; it was destroyed in the Blitz. A watercolor of another double house on Threadneedle Street, built and occupied between 1677 and 1734 by Sir John Houblon, a Huguenot merchant, appears as Catalogue No. 418, in Tessa Murdoch, comp., *The Quiet Conquest: The Huguenots, 1685–1985* (London, 1985). General changes in middle-class interior decoration and furnishings between 1727 and 1749 are described in John Wood, *An Essay toward a Description of Bath* (London, 1749).

15. On the lack of silver, see T 47/5 (1757–62) and 47/4 (1764–66). Lorna Weatherill, *Consumer Behaviour and Material Culture in Britain, 1660–1760* (London, 1988), pp. 166–89, provides a fascinating glimpse of material culture in the middle years of

Adjoining the Dining Room at the front of the house was the large
Clerks' Room, the raison d'être of the house. Here sat another mahogany Merchant's Bureau and, nearby, a painted bookcase, a six-foot
wainscot two-flap single desk, two chairs, and an "excellent" mahogany
library desk covered with green leather and resting on casters. On the
walls were tacked maps of the world and charts guiding the wary clerk
through the bog of foreign currency exchange. Five leather stools rose
above the top of the fixed elevated wooden counter. On a normal
working day, every available surface would have been littered with
large pewter inkstands, sandboxes, rulers, and candlesticks.

Two flights of stairs covered by Wilton and cheaper woolen Scotch
carpets brought one to private quarters on the first floor, where again
one is struck by the fact that the house, while the abode of a prosperous
and successful merchant, was relatively free from grand decoration and
ornament. Along the north side of the first floor were arranged four
bedrooms, two heated with stoves, two unheated, and all hung with the
same green woolen cloth that was used below. Across the Lower Gallery on the south side were the Large Drawing Room, the main reception room, and the more intimate Small Drawing Room. There seem to
have been few differences in appointment in these social rooms. The
Large Drawing Room at the front of the house was hung with dyed,
festooned, and tasseled calico cotton curtains; pin-striped woolens for
wintertime hanging remained folded in a chest. Four Sargent family
portraits by Alan Ramsay and George Romney hung between large,
full-length pier glass mirrors. New colors were introduced: a blue-striped
cotton cover on one mahogany sofa, and another green linen damask
on another. A large woven Brussels carpet (20′ × 14′) lay upon the
floor. This was clearly the principal room for entertainment: card tables, games, and music tables were all present. The Small Drawing
Room at the back of the house was a place for civil conversation:
"elegant cotton French curtains," lined and tasseled; two bell ropes;
two pier glasses in gilt frames; a tufted Wilton carpet (12′ × 10′); a
square mahogany card table with fluted legs; a round claw-foot table;
and six "neat" mahogany chairs were all recorded in the inventory as
present. Nevertheless, even in these relatively grand rooms, only a few

the associates' careers. Among other things, she traces an increase in the choice of
"more decorative and expressive household goods, many of them imported from the
Far East." She examines "the gentry" and "the middling rank" down to farmers and
laborers, but she excludes the upper echelons of these groups, especially the elite
"dealers" and tradesmen of London. A trans-Atlantic comparison appears in Carole
Shammas, *The Pre-Industrial Consumer in England and America* (Oxford, 1990), pp.
157–93. There is room for a more thorough investigation of the goods acquired by
the upper and upper-middle classes.

items – a strip of silk or a few gilt frames – bespeak anything more than the common comfort and civility sought by prosperous merchants intent on raising their profile in society without exposing themselves or appearing to succumb to the corruptions of luxury.

The second floor provided bedroom space for apprentice clerks and wage employees. Bedsteads, beds, bolsters, mattresses, pillows, quilts, blankets, and linens filled every room but two. In most rooms, there were two beds but, in two rooms, there were as many as four beds. All in all, the house (including the attic with its three beds) contained twenty-two beds. There were clearly more beds than the partners, wives, and children required. Upstairs, private life and business life merged, as clerks and workers were more or less forced into the family mold. The second-floor rooms, like much of what fell below, were devoid of ornament, perhaps more so: less mahogany was used, and more wool. And their space was shared with the Laundry, crammed full with an oak mangle, a deal ironing board, trestles, tables, chairs, stools, steps, chests, carpets, portraits, a crayon sketch of "Moses Striking the Rock," and a bird cage. The floor served utilitarian purposes, and fittingly it was here that the Library was tucked away in the southeastern corner. As we have already seen, London merchants trading overseas had the wherewithal and inclination to appreciate ideas, and they treated libraries and books as nurseries of the imagination. The Library at Mincing Lane contained 374 books at the time of Aufrere's death: bound newspapers and magazines, records of local information and improvement societies, dictionaries, plays, poems, novels, and treatises; works of philosophy, history, literature, and geography written in English, French, Portuguese, German, Greek, and Latin. Nothing, it seems, was outside the interest of this circle. This room was no retreat from the noisy world of business and family: it served as a schoolhouse for clerks in training (in similar houses, when the clerks had finished their tasks, they were to round out the day "in improving themselves" by reading "the printed Books on Trade bought for the use of the Counting house"); and it doubled as a storehouse for such masculine objects as guns, a shaving stand, and several sets of backgammon and chess.[16]

The partners and their families shared quarters with an army of unmarried clerks, employees, and servants. Through the end of the eighteenth century, if Sargent's and Oswald's houses are any indication, no dramatic separation between public and private zones, no significant

16. See also Price, ed., "Directions," p. 140. A similar "Catalogue of [307] Books belonging to Newton & Gordon," a firm located in Madeira and established in 1758 by the associate Alexander Johnston, appears in Cossart & Gordon Papers, Box 6, Liverpool University Archives, Liverpool.

division of working spaces and living quarters, had occurred. Masters and their families lived with clerks who lived with servants; "academical education" went hand-in-hand with everyday enterprise; service, business, and entertainment rooms were jumbled together in apparent disregard of the neat divisions later historians would impose on them. Lack of privacy, however, was not the same as doing without private comforts. These were the homes of successful merchants and, inside their houses, the owners created or at least adapted a style that was comfortable, neither demotic nor aristocratic. On the one hand, there was no wooden tableware; and there were few pieces made from baser metals like pewter. On the other hand, one looks in vain for the work of London's nameworthy cabinetmakers, pictures of Britain's monarchs, a profusion of silver, ranks of vases for fresh flowers, or the numerous looking glasses that Lorna Weatherill has found are suggestive of "a certain self-awareness and a desire to set the atmosphere of rooms" – all hallmarks of a high, formal style of living.[17] One encounters simply turned furniture made of mahogany (less exotic than it was in the early 1700s), only a few leather chairs, a handful of floor coverings, accessible domestic and foreign china, decent yet still relatively coarse linens and drapes, and only one brand-name clock. Bedsteads were there but without ornate carvings. Mincing Lane sported paneled and painted walls, plastered ceilings, molded chair rails, and dentilled box cornices, but these were probably the limit: there is no mention of expensive polite French wallpapers or gilt parlors. There was nothing that a man of comfortable means could not easily have obtained in the metropolis. In going over the inventory of Mincing Lane and the inventories of the houses occupied by similarly situated merchants, one is, in the end, struck by the practicality of comforts, rather than their display.

A "Merchant's Public Counting-House" was also a home, where entertainment and chaos daily disrupted comfortable order and regularity. Mincing Lane knew its share of fun. The library, as one would guess with this group, provided its own form of entertainment, a pastime that satisfied Sargent's passion for philosophy and Aufrere's interest in religion. In the waning light of the day, illuminated only by candlelight, they would gather on the second floor, Sargent poring over his treatises (he was fond of Hume) and Aufrere his devotional meditations (he frequently read Wesley); often they were joined by their juniors or clerks, sometimes by those more renowned, like Benjamin Franklin. For those more socially inclined, the counting-house contained several sets of backgammon and chess, card games like India quadrille,

17. Weatherill, *Consumer Behavior*, p. 189.

musical instruments, and all the necessary furniture to allow for the musical soirees beloved by Rosamunde Sargent. The atmosphere in Philpot Lane was perhaps more boisterous, enlivened as it was by the continual cluck, chatter, and howl of a menagerie. In the summer of 1764, a parrot named Gallant Piquero whose running nose was being treated with "some Sulphir mixt with Butter" and a monkey who frequently "broke loose out of his chain" and tyrannized the neighbors by smashing their furniture to smithereens were joined by six dogs, another parrot with "a fine Pipe" and a command of Portuguese, and a gazelle.[18] Whatever the entertainment, what one does not find is a clearly defined, self-sealing commercial environment; familial, personal, irrational situations generally intruded into and influenced the conduct of business.

Room use, layout, and decoration suggest the necessity of close supervision of business operations. This is reflected in the lack of privacy. It is also reflected in the insistence on order, whether in the arrangement of furniture or in the cleanliness of a room. On this point, the most imposing and revealing piece of furniture in Sargent's house was an object possessed by nearly every trans-Atlantic merchant in London – the Merchant's Bureau – a piece usually placed in the Clerks' Room. The Bureau figured as a concrete representation of the mastery of detail so integral to commercial success. The typically 7' to 9' tall, 5' wide mahogany "double desk" rose in three stages above the chaos of the surrounding desks and tables: the lower stage, the bottom half, contained sixteen drawers; two doors opening outward revealed the top half, which contained the middle and upper stages, each fitted with shelves, pigeonholes, and small drawers for ledgers and papers. Prominent among the compartments were six divisions used for filing –

London Dock Accounts
Customs House Duties
Contracts
Remittances
Average Documents
Bills of Lading

A double row of horizontal boxes, lettered "A" to "Z," was reserved for correspondence with clients. Order was demanded throughout. A clerk in a typical large counting-house was to take care that he put a letter "up again in the same place or order where he found it" and that "no loose papers remain on the Desks lest they be mislaid or fall into

18. Michael Herries to Richard Oswald, August 2, 6, September 27, 1764, Oswald Letter Book, v. 2, ff. 336, 338, 342, SRO; and Michael Herries to Richard Oswald, July 10, 1764, Oswald Papers, Sudlows.

Books"; on leaving the house, he was "to clear his own Desk." The compartmentalized Merchant's Bureau thus gave substantive meaning to the maxim "a place for everything and everything in its place." Whether in the Clerks' Room or Partners' Closet (Sargent placed one in each), the bureau, a symbol of order, drew the eye of the employer, employee, or visitor. The associates, the message is clear, valued, indeed depended upon, order in their environment.[19]

The ordering influence of certain pieces of furniture was reinforced by the appearance of the house itself. Renovations were generally made about every ten years, usually in the summers when the partners were away in the country.[20] Oswald's first renovation occurred in 1765. It had been clear for some time that changes were needed, but it was not until Herries's neurotic fear of moisture, mold, smoke, and fire, and his obsessive passion for order got the better of him that renovations and refurbishment commenced. Peeling walls were painted, old chimneys refaced with marble, new chimneys installed in the bedrooms to make them "more secure against Fire," and sashes rebuilt to make the house warmer in winter. But annoyed at the fact that the building, with "the papers & everything in it," was "most intolerably dirty & nasty, not having had any sort of cleaning for many years," Herries was not content with minor changes; he undertook a complete top-to-bottom scouring of the premises. Acutely sensitive to unsavory sights and smells, he personally scrubbed the floors and wainscotting, opting for plain soap and water rather than a fresh coat of paint, because the former left "no smell & [was] but a trifling expence." Finally, Herries saw to it that the house would remain attractive and usable. Having once seen advertised a "Machine . . . for warming churches, halls, counting-houses, & other such places" that left no "offensive smell, dirt, ashes, or smoak," he approached the patentee and arranged for the installation of the new contraption.[21]

London merchants like Herries and Oswald thought that the internal management of their houses was directly linked to the external conduct of their business. In orderly surroundings, partners could best synthesize

19. For this desk in Sargent's house, see *A Catalogue*, p. 8. See also Price, "Directions," pp. 149–50; and M. J., "Mahogany Bureaux from Kent and Ireland," *Country Life*, v. 80 (July 18, 1936), pp. 72–73. On the order and filing and storing procedures in a typical London firm, see Price, "Directions," pp. 141, 149–50. A list of stationery supplies used in a counting-house appears in Invoice, May 7, 1774, Cossart & Gordon Papers, Liverpool University Archives, Liverpool.

20. Later work was done in 1778 and 1784. GD 171/54/3: Richard Oswald to William Forbes, August 6, 1778; and C 12/1081/6: Oswald v. Anderson, Complaint, and Answer, sched. 2.

21. Michael Herries to Richard Oswald, August 13, September 13, 17, and October 18, 1765, Oswald Papers, Sudlows; and *Public Advertiser*, July 1765.

and analyze the ins and outs of their international shipping and trading operations and indulge their omnivorous appetite for information, even as they closely oversaw the work of the clerks. Not surprisingly, the simultaneous management of so many activities and people contributed to a schedule that was highly regimented. There is no record of the division of responsibilities among the inhabitants of any associate's counting-house, but the procedures adopted by other firms specify the work of the clerks in nearly every hour of every day. Tight adherence to a schedule was critical to the work of a global firm.

Central to the work of each clerk and, through it, the flow of oceanic business was orderly communication. Since writing was "the usual way of intercourse of merchants with one another" and with overseas clients, "the spinning out a very long letter" was "the common knack" of the successful "London Factor," and was certainly the daily lot of his clerk. "Letters of trade, wrote with judgement, and language suitable to the subject, beget respect and confidence." In fact, "epistolary correspondence" and accounting were the principal subjects of education for apprentices in eighteenth-century business. Since contemporaries realized that "the nature of foreign commerce" was "variable and fluctuating," "the life of a trader" was driven by a need to express oneself in "method and regularity."[22] The associates, in particular, were keenly aware of the importance of the appearance of their letters. Grant was forever lecturing others in the art of writing letters, settling accounts, and balancing books. Business letters, he demanded, should have no political or personal news in them; such material should be reserved for personal letters that did not go into the counting-house for examination and copying. Furthermore, he felt that frequent and

22. Price, ed., "Directions," pp. 138–39. On letter writing, see George Maxwell to Benjamin Charnock, November 16, 1743, Lascelles & Maxwell Letter Book, p. 59; C 12/2349/15: Home v. Home, 1762; C 24/1699/I/30: Home v. Home, July 5, 1759; Postlethwayt, *Universal Dictionary*, sub "British Mercantile College," v. 1, p. 221 and Sir Alexander Grant to Peter Davidson, November 27, 1765, Court of Error Records, 1B/11/1/4/187–88, Jamaica Archives. A good discussion of the uncertainty appears in Douglas Hall, "Incalculability as a Feature of Sugar Production during the Eighteenth Century," *Social and Economic Studies* (1961), pp. 340–52; and Brewer, *Sinews*, pp. 221–30. On the keeping of regular accounts, see Postlethwayt, *Universal Dictionary*, pp. 210–17, 222–23, and *Merchant's Public Counting-House*; Thomas Lazonby, *Merchants Accounts; Or, The Italian Method of Book-Keeping* . . . (London, 1757); John Howard, *An Introduction to the Counting-House, or, a Collection of the Various Forms of Business* . . . (London, 1761); and John Mair, *Book-Keeping Methodiz'd, Or a Methodical Treatise of Merchant Accompts, According to the Italian Form* (Dublin, 1763). One must be careful when interpreting these texts, since many merchants conducted only one audit per year. Earle, *English Middle Class*, pp. 137–38, citing B. S. Yamey, "Book-Keeping and the Rise of Capitalism," *Economic History Review*, 2nd ser., v. 1 (1949), pp. 109–10.

consistent reconciliation would redound to the merchant's profit: all money matters should be resolved at Christmastide, and all books balanced every March 31; Grant's were. Whatever the form, communication should be made neatly on full sheets of paper, not written on small loose scraps in an illegible scrawl.[23]

The Partnership

At midcentury, London merchants trading overseas worked in partnerships, and the associates were no exception.[24] "Even where two or three merchants" were capable of doing business on their own, it was conceded by the author of the century's only compendium of partnership law that it was in the interest of merchants "to join their stock; as this arrangement lets in the advantages of the division of labour" and allows credit to rise "in much more than an equal ratio with the capital on which it rests." A partnership was "a voluntary contract, between two or more persons, for joining together their money, goods, labour, and skill," upon an agreement that "the gain or loss shall be divided proportionably between them" and an understanding that a "fair and open trade" would be advanced and protected. Such a union took many forms. The principal division was between public "partnerships" and private ones. The former, large societies and companies, like the Royal Exchange Assurance Company, had many members and were established "to carry out some important undertaking"; these unincorporated joint-stock syndicates were one of the predecessors of the modern limited liability corporation. Private partnerships, on the other hand, consisted of a handful of merchants. These were, it was thought, the most common in Britain and the most "beneficial to commerce." Compared to public partnerships, private partnerships were managed with "more facility, and frequently with a greater degree of skill, prudence, and economy." In large measure, this was because they could be "general" (contracted "for a long course of dealing and extending to a large stock or capital in trade") or "special" (formed for "a particular concern" or

23. Letters are discussed in GD 345/1168/1762: Sir Alexander Grant to Sir Archibald Grant, May 16, 1764; and GD 345/1167/4/110: Sir Alexander Grant to Sir Archibald Grant, December 7, 1761. Accounts are discussed in GD 345/1180/1764: Sir Alexander Grant to Captain Archibald Grant, May 16, 1764; GD 248/99/6/51: Sir Alexander Grant to Lachlan Grant, December 30, 1769; and John Boyd, Jr., to Sir Robert Murray Keith, December 10, 1784, Add.Mss. 35525/77, BL.

24. Analysis of the 1749 London trade directory, *A Complete Guide* (London, 1749) suggests that, of the 2,857 merchants listed, 1,808 were lone entrepreneurs and 1,049 were members of partnerships. When the sample is reduced to merchants trading overseas, however, the number of lone entrepreneurs becomes statistically insignificant.

"a single dealing or adventure," whether the operation of a specific branch of trade, the ownership of a ship, the management of a cargo, or the control of a chattel).[25]

Because the phenomenon of partnerships is so little understood and because they were the principal organizational structure of eighteenth-century business and the chief means by which the associates knit together the skills at their disposal, a closer look at the associates' private partnerships is warranted. What did they look like? How were they formed? How did they capitalize on the partners' several skills?

To the modern eye, the most striking characteristic of eighteenth-century general private partnerships in London was their size: they were small. With the exception of Sargent's firms, not one of the associates' counting-house partnerships had more than three partners and, in this, they were typical merchant firms. Consider London sugar partnerships as a comparison: Between 1740 and 1775, 21 percent had a single proprietor, and the remainder two to four partners. Small firm size was the norm in other trades as well. The feature was so pronounced, in fact, that it shaped the definition: Thomas Mortimer, an expert on London commerce, described the general private partnership as a "conjunction of 3 or 4 persons, who jointly contribute different or equal sums towards forming a general trade." Later in the century, William Watson in his treatise on partnership law suggested two or three partners.[26]

"No charter or license" was necessary for forming a general private partnership, merely "the bare consent" of the several men involved. Many agreements were reduced to written "articles," yet, if the number of surviving deeds are reliable testimony, more agreements remained implicit. Not one of the collections of associates' papers contains formal articles of partnership. More important than formal deeds was the recognition of the reciprocal choice of those involved, attesting to the mutual advantages gained and liabilities shared. Every individual who joined in "the communion of profit and loss" was considered a partner.[27]

---

25. William Watson, *A Treatise of the Law of Partnership*, 2nd ed. (London, 1807; 1st ed., London, 1794), pp. xxiii, 1, 3–5, 54–55. There is, unfortunately, no modern study of early-modern partnership law.

26. Sheridan, *Sugar and Slavery*, p. 299; Mortimer, *Every Man His Own Broker*, 7th ed., pp. 5–6; and Watson, *Treatise*, pp. 5–6. In contrast, Thomas Devine has argued that Glasgow firms averaged six to nine partners. Devine, "Glasgow Merchants," p. 69. It is not clear, however, whether Devine can be trusted, for he makes no distinction between general and special partnerships. For a good general discussion of the problems connected with determining size from the Naval Office Shipping Lists, see Jacob Price and Paul Clemens, "A Revolution of Scale in Overseas Trade: British Firms in the Chesapeake Trade, 1675–1775," *Journal of Economic History*, v. 47 (1987), pp. 8–9.

27. Watson, *Treatise*, pp. 5–6, 11, 17, 63.

Small general private partnerships could possess any of a number of management structures. Some firms were companies of equals. Tasks and returns were evenly divided. Johnston & Co. and Oswald & Co. operated on this basis. Other firms had unequal divisions of shares or responsibilities. Some were dominated by one individual and filled out with passive or junior partners. This was always the case at Boyd & Co., ruled first by Augustus Boyd, after his death by his son John in name only and, from the early 1770s, by John Trevanion. Grant & Co., after Grant's split with Johnston, was run only by Grant and his clerks, Grant being reluctant to share a scintilla of power. Partnerships could also include "dormant partners," where "all partners in trade do not appear ostensibly to the world, although they share in the profits and loss." This arrangement was suited to "gentlemen of large and independent fortunes" who, "ignorant of the *science* of commerce," were willing to embark considerable sums of money and depend "entirely upon the skill of merchants" but were unwilling to suffer "their names to appear in the copartnership firm." Notwithstanding the usefulness of silent investors, in their general and special partnerships, excepting their ship partnerships, the associates tolerated no dormant partners. Their partners were to be actively useful.[28]

The associates chose new partners from a pool of men with proven talents or obvious assets: blood relation was one possible bond, but not the most important, when building a firm. There were many other reasons why unrelated, skilled general partners came together. Perhaps the most obvious, though often the most difficult to prove, was personal compatibility: they simply liked working with one another. The one associate who was notoriously difficult to deal with, Grant, not surprisingly avoided taking partners after 1750. Apart from friendship, there were other, equally compelling reasons to band together. Especially at the beginning of a career, a merchant could reduce overhead expenses by entering into a partnership. Renting a house or some space on a wharf (all of the associates' houses and wharves were leased), furnishing and staffing the house, and compiling an initial inventory were expensive and, to the lone entrepreneur, could pose a daunting obstacle to entry into business; they could be overcome by joining with other merchants.

Perhaps an even more compelling reason for combining with others was to spread risk. Prudent merchants did not put "all their eggs in one basket": if a ship went down, they did not want their business to go down with it. Most merchants were not rich enough to afford a sufficiently

28. Watson, *Treatise*, p. 46.

wide range of ventures on their own. Thus, partners were extremely valuable. The risk-spreading motivations of partners have captured the interest of many historians, but overemphasis of such concerns does not do justice to the complexity of eighteenth-century enterprise.[29] By itself spreading risk was no reason to prefer a general partnership over a succession of special partnerships. Having a regular partner was easier and quicker, certainly, than having to negotiate new partnership arrangements for each voyage or asset. But Grant's example shows that it was possible to go it alone.

Complementarity of business strengths was a much stronger reason for general partnerships. In nearly every market, there were fluctuations in demand and supply; in such a variable world, both merchants and their customers wanted regular outlets and regular sources. Therefore, they went after complementary partners who could ensure them regularity.[30] On this point, the behavior of the associates is instructive. When they joined with others as partners, they aligned themselves with merchants who specialized in regions, commodities, and services that provided complementary sides of the market. It was clear to Grant that, when Johnston engaged him in 1740, it was because of Grant's "interest & particular acquaintance . . . in the West Indies." Grant would not even have had to reside in London, so long as Johnston, an expert in Britain's inland trade who was keenly interested in exporting quack medicines to America, could use his name and tap his reservoir of western Caribbean connections.[31] Likewise, when Oswald, an expert in North American and West Indian trade, put together his first partnership later in the decade, he looked to John Mill, a general merchant familiar with the coastwise trade between Aberdeen and Newcastle. The complementarity the associates achieved could be geographical or operational. Partnership with Thomas Birch, a director of one of the two companies legally entitled to sell marine insurance, gave Sargent a source of information and influence in the global insurance market. The stockbroker Samuel Gardiner brought Sargent expert representation in the world of London's high finance. Aufrere brought Sargent a tie to the financially and commercially powerful Huguenot community in London and, through it, valuable connections on the Continent; later, in the 1760s and 1770s, Cooke, Chambers, and Rolleston strengthened Sargent's hand with the inland traders of East Anglia, the West Country,

---

29. Davis, *Rise*, p. 89; Minchinton, *"Africa,"* p. 188; Wilson, *Gentlemen Merchants*, p. 65; and Devine, "Glasgow Merchants," p. 69.
30. Pares, "London Sugar Market," pp. 254–70; Sheridan, *Sugar and Slavery*, pp. 389–486; and McCusker and Menard, *Economy of British America*, pp. 118–24, 159–61.
31. GD 345/1157/9/56: Patrick Grant to Sir Archibald Grant, December 12, 1740.

and the Midlands. Whatever their circle, the associates enhanced and developed their internal capabilities so as to adapt to and innovate in an expansive marketplace. With the right partner, a merchant could share overhead expenses and spread risks but, more importantly, he could reduce transaction costs in and structural impediments to global shipping and trading by capturing synergies of separate but interrelated activities.

If the associates' businesses are an accurate representation, general private partnerships were usually long-lived, lasting to the death of one of the senior partners. Throughout their careers, the associates also participated in more short-lived special partnerships.[32] These arrangements served a variety of purposes. Some were put together to pursue slave trading, wool manufacturing, or land speculation; others were established to manage the ownership of a chattel such as a slave or to husband a cargo of goods through to sale. Special partnerships "to build ships, to equip them and [to] keep them in repair" were the most common. In principle, a ship could be owned either by one merchant (a sole owner) in its entirety, or by a group of enterprisers (partial owners) each of whom owned a fractional share and earned a fractional portion of the profits. Some historians have noted that ship partnerships differed from trade partnerships and argued that the chief characteristic of a ship partnership was its large size.[33] But the evidence from the associates' shipping activities suggests contrary conclusions. Generally, the proprietors of a ship formed a small group: on average, the associates' vessels had 2.4 owners, usually the members of one general private partnership.[34] Looking at ownership data recorded in the Naval Office Shipping Lists and other marine lists, we find that the associates controlled nearly 70 percent of the ships they employed as sole owners or partial owners with other associates. Occasionally – in 20 percent of all recorded ship movements – the associates shared control over ships

32. Less than 10 percent of the late seventeenth-century merchants Peter Earle has studied entered into formal bonds of partnership; many more "entered into partnerships for a few years or for a particular trading venture." *English Middle Class*, p. 111.

33. Davis, *The Rise*, pp. 83–91. But Davis's presentation is confusing: he argues for a large number of owners (p. 83), yet notes a decline to a low number in the average number of owners during the first third of the century (pp. 88–91) for all but slaving and coastwise ventures. For an example of partial ownership, see Deed Books, # 1,196, f. 232, Plymouth Court House, Montserrat.

34. Hancock, "Citizen of the World," Table 11. Devine has argued that both partnership law and the desire to avoid risk kept the numbers high. "Glasgow Merchants," p. 69. But Devine does not distinguish among kinds of partnership. And the low number of ship partnerships involving the associates calls in question Devine's risk-spreading argument. More persuasive is Jacob Price, who argues that scarcity of specie in Scotland kept the numbers high, between four and ten. *Capital and Credit*, p. 24.

or cargoes with nonassociates or other firms. In this, they were like the shippers in America, but unlike merchants in Glasgow.[35] Apparently, they relied on other men's ships in only two situations: when accepting the sugar consignments of Caribbean clients and correspondents and, then, only when the consignments exceeded the capacities of their own vessels, or when shipping arms to West Africa or North America during the French and Indian War.[36]

A London counting-house was a commercial beehive, active, ordered, and integrated, a place where the interests of the partners often converged. Mirroring the complementarity of their skills were the skills among the much larger group of men and women who worked for them: from apprentices and wage clerks to runners and scullery maids. Since the need for skilled reliable participants in global operations was great, clerks and employees were often viewed and treated as potential partners or representatives. Almost all but the lowest were introduced to the firm by relatives, friends, or clients of the partners. In larger firms, like the tobacco house run by Michael Herries's cousin Robert Herries, there were two groups of clerks, each with senior and junior positions: one group managed European business, and the other handled British, Irish, and American business. Circumstantial evidence suggests that this was also the practice in Sargent's house. Each clerk worked nine hours per day, Monday through Saturday, from 9 to 2, and, in the afternoon, from 4 to 8, receiving two afternoons off each week. In many of the associates' smaller houses, there were only two clerks.[37]

If and when the associates' commercial networks failed them, they nearly always regarded the failure as the result of a breakdown of communication and the betrayal of a representative. Oswald saw his failures in East Florida planting operations during the 1760s and 1770s

---

35. Hancock, "Citizen of the World," Table 12. Sole ownership was favored in the Middle Colonies. Doerflinger, *A Vigorous Spirit*, pp. 99–102; and Geoffrey Gilbert, "Maritime Enterprise in the New Republic," *Business History Review*, v. 58 (1984), pp. 14–29. In contrast, partial ownership was favored in Glasgow, although high inbound freights and the uncertainties of space caused many tobacco merchants to own their own vessels or charter vessels. Price, *Capital and Credit*, p. 40.

36. Davis, *The Rise*, p. 98. The associates frequently hired out their own vessels to North Americans interested in the West African trade. Henry Laurens to John Nutt, March 26, 1757, in *The Papers of Henry Laurens*, v. 2, pp. 507–09.

37. For a remarkably detailed account of the work performed by clerks in one large London house, see Price, ed., "Directions," pp. 136, 138. The associates' clerks were generally young kinsmen or the children of friends. Oswald's clerks: John Donaldson (May 1751), Mr. Aislabie (July 1766), and Mr. Charles (October 1784). Grant's clerks: Robertson (April 1752), Alexander Davidson and Alexander Harper (March 1756), Alexander Harper and Lewis Gordon (November 1756), Alexander Harper and Hugh Falconer (July 1761), and Hugh Falconer (1764).

as the work of a malingering overseer; conversely, Grant attributed his success in Jamaica to the appointment of his cousin and namesake Achoynanie as his island "doer." To encourage successes like Grant's, counting-house partners preferred to hire and promote experienced men who had traveled overseas, worked abroad, or at least dealt with overseas trade. But such men were not always in abundant supply, and for recruits they turned to their own counting-house staffs. Complementarity and coordination in the wider business world had to be carefully constructed from the outset within the firm.

In educating the uninitiated, the associates were not at a loss for advice; contemporary pundits waxed lyrical on the subject. In *The London Tradesman*, Campbell prescribed a program for the training of employees that required the apprentice to understand

> his Mother Tongue perfectly, write it grammatically, and with Judgement; he must learn all the Trading Languages, French, Dutch, and Portuguese, and be able to write them accurately; he has no great Necessity of Greek and Latin, but a superficial Knowledge of them is soon acquired, and may be useful to him in obtaining the other Languages. He must understand Geography and some navigation, must write a fair legible Hand, and ought to be a compleat Master of figures and merchants Accompts.

Any youth with such accomplishments would be fit for the counting-house; he could "turn out Supercargo to any Port, and may settle as Factor in any of our Plantations, or other Trading Cities in Europe."[38] Equally revealing were Malachy Postlethwayt's 1757 proposals for the foundation of a "British Mercantile College," whose curriculum was to include mercantile computations; exchange arbitrations; foreign currency; customs, usages, and laws; weights and measures; calculation of duties, subsidies, drawbacks, bounties, tariffs, and imposts; writing; and accounts. The minds of the young were not "to be touched by abstracted ideas," a point with which both Grant and Oswald agreed.[39]

Few clerks, representatives, or potential partners scaled such heights of accomplishment, but occasional references to counting-house training

---

38. Campbell, *London Tradesman*, pp. 293–94. Cf. Sir John Barnard, *A Present for an Apprentice* (London, 1740); Martin Clare, *Youth's Introduction to Trade and Business* (London, 1748); William Weston, *The Complete Merchant's Clerk* (London, 1754). Compare Campbell's suggestions to earlier advice, noted in John Browne's *The Marchants Avizo* (1589), ed. Patrick McGrath (Boston, 1957), p. xxii. Much of what Browne says is similar, but not all. He does not require young men training in the Portuguese or Spanish trade, for instance, to learn either the Portuguese or Spanish language. Nor does he concern himself with trades whose connections extend beyond continental Europe.

39. Postlethwayt, *Universal Dictionary*, v. 1, pp. 218–36.

in the letters of the associates and other London merchants suggest that the career manuals were not far off the mark. From their employees, the associates demanded prior mastery and ongoing competence in purposive subjects, such as writing, languages, and arithmetic. "Let him confine his attention to what will be useful" was a constant reply of an associate when asked for suggestions on what to study.[40] In 1774, on Oswald's advice, his nephew Alexander Anderson took up writing, arithmetic, algebra, geometry, and bookkeeping. Grant's list of prerequisites for an overseas clerkship was somewhat shorter than Oswald's, but it made the same point: "To write a fine hand & be a ready accountant is all. To speak French is useful. But losing time in the common academical education in Scotland is really ridiculous." But for letters and numbers, most subjects could be learned in the counting-house itself. Grant, writing here, was discussing how well a clerk could satisfy the needs of his firm, not how best he could rise to partnership. In such a step, knowledge of currency exchanges and of foreign languages, two accomplishments most easily obtained from "academical education," were necessary for advancement to the level of partner in many a counting-house, although this was more true in a cloth-trading house than a West India firm. Certainly, an inability to speak and write German, Dutch, and Spanish checked the rise of Timothy Cockshutt in Smith & Aufrere, and a facility in French worked to Herries's advantage in Philpot Lane.

The associates' own "practical education" had taken place at least partially abroad and, so, to round out their employees' training and to further the work of commercial integration, the partners sent their clerks out as overseas representatives. Arranged beforehand by the associates, work in West Africa and the Caribbean often prepared a young man for later work in the metropolitan counting-house or at least use by the partners. The experiences of the Anderson brothers were typical of those young men who, having been schooled in the counting-house or given hands-on training overseas, later joined the partnership or served its purposes. Oswald had high hopes for all five sons of his younger sister Elizabeth and her husband William Anderson, a merchant who traded salted beef and processed hides in the northernmost mainland county of Caithness. Although Oswald undertook the supervision of his

40. Elizabeth Cust, ed., *Records of the Cust Family, Series II: 1550–1779* (London, 1909), pp. 257–58; James Anderson to Richard Oswald, October 19, 1774, January 11, 1775, v. 2, f. 116, 120, Alexander Anderson to Richard Oswald, October 31, 1774, v. 2, f. 168, Oswald Letter Book, SRO; GD 345/1180/1763: Sir Alexander Grant to Captain Archibald Grant, February 8, 1763; and George Maxwell to James Bruce, January 17, 1744, Lascelles & Maxwell Letter Book, p. 101.

nephews' education directly, not all of his efforts were rewarded. With Oswald's help, George Anderson, the eldest, was apprenticed to a captain shuttling between Glasgow and Jamaica and was asked to gather commercial news for the Londoner along the way. But George's ship was taken by the Spanish and George himself left for dead; on escaping from a Cuban prison, he fled to Philadelphia and inexplicably cut all ties to his family. Equally ill-fated was Oswald's attempt to settle George's brother James, whom he educated at Leyden and sent out to America, but who died within months of taking up a new post as a plantation doctor in Jamaica, a job found by Oswald.[41]

Oswald had better luck with two other nephews. Their early years provide a rare, detailed glimpse of the training of potential partners without ties to the formal apprenticeship system and the City livery companies. John Anderson was born in December 1747, in Wick, Caithness, the younger brother of George and James. Like most inhabitants of northern Scotland, John's prospects for advance were limited; so, at the age of fourteen and with the help of Oswald and Grant, he signed articles of apprenticeship with Baillie James Grant, an Edinburgh merchant closely related to the London baronet. After serving three years in Edinburgh, John returned to the north and founded a herring fishery at Staxigoe, again with money provided by his uncle in London. But this challenge did little to fix John Anderson's goals: when the opportunity arose to captain one of his uncle's African ships, he jumped at the chance and went to Sierra Leone; in 1770, when he got the chance to work for his cousin George Oswald in Glasgow, he leapt again and took over a coalwork; and, then, when the opportunity to relocate to America arose, he moved once more.[42]

As it did many Glaswegians, the Chesapeake irresistibly charmed young John Anderson. With his uncle financing the move, he left Glasgow in early 1775 and worked at a tobacco trading "store" near Baltimore, all the while keeping his uncle abreast of commercial developments in the tumultuous tobacco trade and the even more volatile American political world. When the eruption of hostilities in America

41. William Anderson to Richard Oswald, May 15, 1764, John Anderson to Richard Oswald, January 10, 1775, Richard Anderson to Michael Herries, June 30, August 8, 1775, Richard Anderson to Richard Oswald, September 28, 1775, and December 2, 1776, Oswald Letter Book, v. 2, ff. 241, 67–68, 143, 145, 147, 166, SRO.

42. IGI; William Anderson to Richard Oswald, May 15, 1764, Oswald Letter Book, v. 2, f. 242, SRO; John E. Donaldson, *Caithness in the 18th Century* (Edinburgh, 1938), p. 193; Smith & Baillies to Oswald & Co., February 21, 1768, Oswald Papers, Sudlows; CO 388/57; and GD 58/6/1/4: July 14, 1770. In Glasgow, John Anderson erected a steam engine and served as an overseer at a coalwork outside Glasgow. On George Oswald, see Price, "Buchanan & Simson," pp. 15–17.

called a halt to trading, he returned to Scotland and found himself beset with the same professional restlessness that he had fled years before. With little to do on account of the "damp" wrought by the war, he submitted three plans to his uncle – settling in Caithness; studying literature in Edinburgh or Glasgow; or working in Glasgow. Oswald sneered at them all, particularly those involving Glasgow, contemptuous as he was of backwater Glaswegians' claims to be able to educate a global commercial elite. After visiting his parents in Wick, Anderson eschewed his uncle's advice, settled in Glasgow, and found work in the firm of a relative who had once been a merchant of some repute but whose operations had contracted severely with the onset of war. When Oswald floated an offer of partnership in the summer of 1780, he took no time to decide.[43]

John moved south to London with his brother Alexander, Elizabeth and William Anderson's youngest child. Also born in Wick, in August 1756, Alexander remained in the north until 1772, when his London uncle took him under his wing. The merchant himself devised the boy's educational curriculum: at first, he was to study subjects suitable for a merchant; later, armed with this "useful knowledge" and again with the assistance of his London uncle, he was to hire a private tutor in Glasgow and study Latin two hours a day and mathematics one hour a day. In the back of Oswald's mind was a place in America, a post that would benefit both nephew and uncle. But such a plan required an end to the Revolution, and this was slow in coming. So it was that, after several years lapsed with little progress toward peace, Oswald summoned him, along with his older brother John, to the metropolis. Their education, training, and travels, the London merchant calculated, could be put to better use closer to home. In the end, his hopes were realized. The Andersons took over the shipping and trading work of Philpot Lane; in particular, they revitalized Bance Island's slave trade, pushing Herries from his place in the firm in the process. When Oswald died in November 1784, the two brothers inherited the counting-house business in its entirety.[44]

43. John Anderson to Richard Oswald, October 9, 1771, January 10, 1775, August 26, September 28, October 4, December 5, 1776, February 24, 1777, and September 14, 1780, Oswald Letter Book, v. 2, ff. 66, 67–68, 69, 72–74, 76, 80, 245, SRO. Devine sketches the effect of the American Revolution on the Scottish tobacco "lairds." "Glasgow Merchants and the Collapse of the Tobacco Trade, 1775–1783," *Scottish Historical Review*, v. 52 (1973), pp. 50–74.
44. IGI; George Oswald to Richard Oswald, September 18, 1772, Oswald Papers, EUL; and Alexander Anderson to Richard Oswald, October 31, 1774, May 11, 1776, and August 13, 1778, Oswald Letter Book, v. 2, ff. 168, 170–71, 172–73.

The main challenge facing Alexander and John Anderson's uncle and the other associates was knitting together a diversity of skills and a wide range of activities in order to cope best with the tumultuous competitive business environment that prevailed in the years between the outbreak of the War of Austrian Succession and the close of the American Revolutionary War. Perhaps unique in the extent of their response, Oswald and his cohort were at the same time typical of the many metropolitan overseas merchants in the nature of their strategy. They located themselves as close as possible to the center of commercial power in the empire, and they struggled to coordinate a welter of different projects and people. Ordinary people, like Alexander and John Anderson, were first given their education, training, and travel with the help of a London merchant, and then subsequently enrolled in the work of his firm overseas or placed in positions of responsibility at home in the close, often chaotic confines of the firm's counting-house. There, orderly "conversation" was strictly maintained with "all parts of the known world" and all parts of one's own business empire. Although concern for minute matters of business practice – choosing a neighborhood, filing, cleaning, training, and the like – often seems to hold limited significance for later generations looking back on the eighteenth century, it signaled the beginnings of a revolution in business management only realized in succeeding centuries: attention to such small affairs created "a true bred merchant" who would be "the most intelligent man in the world" and consequently "the most capable" of devising "new ways to live" in a wider commercial world.[45]

45. Postlethwayt, *Universal Dictionary*, v. 1 (1751), p. 553.

4

Shipping and Trading
in an "Empire of the Seas"

SHIPPING AND TRADING were the core of the associates' international businesses. Their ships called at Madeira, Grenada, Jamaica, South Carolina, Nova Scotia, and Calcutta. Their cargoes included wine, gold, ivory, slaves, sugar, tobacco, medicine, and arrack, a spirit distilled from grain or sugarcane. By drawing on their own experiences overseas, taking advantage of openings in the market, and deploying contacts they had cultivated at home and abroad, they made a place for themselves in London's mercantile community. Shipping and trading as factors and agents for others gave them a start, and paved the way for far more lucrative businesses as principals acting on their own account – shipping and trading, planting, slaving, and government contracting. Both demanded a high degree of coordination.

Augustus Boyd took up the task of supplying Caribbean planters and marketing their produce soon after his arrival from St. Christopher in 1735 and, throughout his career, eastern Caribbean connections remained a sturdy foundation to his other enterprises. Grant built upon the base he prepared in the western Caribbean and each year, for thirty years, he sent out to Jamaica at least two ships, laden with metropolitan goods for his own and his clients' plantations and destined to return with cargoes of sugar and rum for the British market. Oswald pursued a similar course, although his interests lay more in North America with tobacco than in the Caribbean with sugar. In North America, he had represented the commercial interests of his two older cousins and, on his return to Glasgow, he pursued joint ventures with them and pushed his own independent operations. When he set up shop in London, he combined the two activities, working as a tobacco trader on his own account and as his cousins' metropolitan agent. John Sargent's business circle looked eastward for linen goods from the Baltic and German principalities, slave-trade goods from the Netherlands, and silk from the Levant.

For centuries, of course, London merchants had traded with British and non-British markets alike but, during the middle decades of the eighteenth century, the number of non-British regions where British entrepreneurs conducted overseas operations from their counting-houses grew significantly. London merchants of the associates' generation also linked operations with other similarly situated merchants to an extent not known before. Most often, as we saw in the previous chapter, they did this by attaching themselves to specialists in complementary regions: West India merchants like Grant and Oswald formed connections with others like Sargent and Stratton whose colonial and foreign regional specializations differed from their own. These counting-house partnerships made money by managing many different people and things at one time. In addition to the range of regional specialties, they managed their ships' cargoes and itineraries, keeping them full and under sail, and built an often unwieldy network of clients, correspondents, agents, and employees around the world. Throughout the associates' careers, we find them constantly juggling different people and roles, different cargoes and ships, and different businesses.

This chapter focuses on the range of the associates' shipping and trading businesses and the way they managed them. Their global reach is seen most emphatically in the wide dispersal of their ships. One very revealing set of evidence of their engagement with the world is a Shipping Database I have constructed that chronicles the nearly 1,000 movements of all ships that the associates are known to have owned or used between 1740 and 1790 – that is, of all ships which an associate wholly or partially owned, as well as all ships in which an associate freighted space for his cargo. The chapter then turns to the associates' work as factors working for others, and as principals shipping and trading on their own accounts. Lastly, it examines how the associates managed this business: how they kept their ships fully utilized, and how they recruited employees and contacts. On the manpower side, they specifically had to meet two separate but related challenges: establishing a network of correspondents and clients overseas, and finding reliable agents and employees to work for them abroad.

Global Destinations

Writing in the late 1740s, the author of *The London Tradesman* was overwhelmed by the wide sweep of the general merchant, whose commercial sphere extended "to all the known World, and gives Life and Vigour to the whole Machine."[1] The associates' shipping patterns provide

1. Campbell, *London Tradesman*, p. 284. An important point to remember is that there were fewer destinations engaged with in the late seventeenth century. Many London merchants were specialized within colonial commerce yet engaged in foreign trade as re-exporters. Few, however, had a large part in the major European trades. Robert C.

the detail that underlay the pamphleteer's words. They reflect both the patterns of British trade over the eighteenth century and the associates' own commerce, which varied over their lives as their business vigor waxed and waned and as the opportunities they found shifted in volume and location. Between 1745 and 1785, the 23 associates backed 456 trading voyages, roughly 11 voyages each year. The total number of vessels the associates used increased by 3.5 times between 1745 and 1765, although, by 1770, it had returned to its 1745 level. During the American War (1775–83), associate shipping more or less stopped.[2] At the height of their shipping in 1765, the associates had 29 ships in the water, 14 of which dropped anchor in the Thames in that year. This fleet comprised 1.6% of the British fleet registered with Lloyds. The associates' ships that went to America constituted a similar fraction of all ships so bound: in 1766, for example, the five associate ships known to have visited South Carolina comprised 1.4% of all ships arriving there.[3] Some 127 of their voyages (28%) were plantation-supply voyages, with the British West Indies as their primary destination; 120 (26%) were slave-trading voyages, involving the west coast of Africa; another 42 (9%) were packet-boat runs, carrying plantation supplies, expectant settlers, and the mail to the Caribbean. By shipping and trading plantation supplies, human cargo, and plantation commodities, the associates contributed to the buildup of Britain's "empire of the seas" (*imperium pelagi*).

The Shipping Database compressed in Table 4.1 records the ports to which the associates dispatched their vessels. The data were collated from newspapers, customs accounts, and port records as arrivals in or departures from particular harbors at particular times. Not surprisingly, the home port of London was the most favored harbor: between 1745 and 1785, 43% of associates' ships' arrivals and departures took place

Nash, "English Trans-Atlantic Trade, 1660–1730: A Quantitative Study" (Ph.D. dissert., University of Cambridge, 1982), p. 135.

2. See Appendix II, Sources for the Shipping Database. The data for "other countries" is almost certainly underrepresented. Take Madeira as an example. The Madeira trade was extremely valuable since Britain procured most of her gold from Portugal, and shipped many of her dry goods there as well. Madeira was the Portuguese port most frequently visited by the British and Americans. The Shipping Database listing of "Port" arrivals and departures does not account for this sector of trade, especially the ships of Robert Scott, whose firm was based in Madeira until he transferred its seat to London in the late 1740s.

3. Data for this comparison is found in Shipping Database; *Lloyd's Register*, 1764[–66]; and Converse D. Clowse, *Measuring Charleston's Overseas Commerce, 1717–1767* (Washington, D.C., 1981), p. 103. The fleet recorded in *Lloyd's Register* for 1765 numbered 1,864 London ships. According to Clowse, there are no reliable South Carolina statistics for 1765; by averaging figures for the years 1762, 1763 and 1766, it is estimated that there were 367 British ships in South Carolina in 1765, 20 of which came from London.

Table 4.1   Regional Distribution of Arrivals and Departures: "Ports," 1745-85

Year	London	England outside London	Scotland	Ireland	Europe	Africa	West Indies	North America	Other	Total
1745	3		8					6		17
	2	1	2	1				1		7
	2	5	8				5	1		21
	4	3	3			1				11
	8	5	4				1	11		29
1750	13	5	2					4		24
	11	1				3		10	1	26
	12					1	4	1		18
	10						4	3		17
	7					1	8	2		18
1755	20	1					9	8		38
	14	9	1			1	2	5		32
	23	16	1				5	2		47
	11	13				8		3		35
	11	11				3	4	6	1	26
1760	9	17						4		30
	21	15					1	2	1	40
	16	13			1	3	8	2		43
	21	5				12	11	1		50
	25	1	2	1		5	12	6		52
1765	21	1	1			17	14	2		56
	25	2				7	11	4		49
	20		1	1		5	9	2	1	39
	19		1	2		2	6	2		32
	11	1	2	1		8	1	2	1	27
1770	11	1				1	2	6		21
	2	3				3	2	3		13
	2	1		1			2	4		10
	6					2		4		12
	12		1	2			1		2	18
1775	7	1		1		2	4			15
	4									4
										0
	1			1						2
	2									2
1780	2									2
										0
										0
										0
	1	1				1	3			6
1785	1									1
Number	390	132	37	11	1	86	129	107	7	900
Percent	43.3%	14.7%	4.1%	1.2%	0.1%	9.6%	14.3%	11.9%	0.8%	100.0%

Sources: Appendix II.

in the waters of the Thames. More interesting is the choice and distribution of the remaining 57%, the 511 arrivals and departures in ports other than London, as depicted in Graph 4.1. Outside the home-port region, the associates' ships visited the British outports most frequently (35% of all non-London arrivals and departures were in other British ports). The vessels also plied the waters of the Caribbean (25%), North America (21%), Africa (17%), and other countries and regions (including Europe, the Mediterranean, and India) (2%).[4]

The peak of the associates' shipping occurred in the mid-1760s and coincided with the height of their Caribbean and African entrepreneurial ventures. Although from 1745 to 1750 Caribbean arrivals and departures constituted only 8% of their non-London arrivals and departures, by the period 1763–67 West Indian ports attracted 43% of their non-London arrivals and departures. These were the years, heady with opportunity, when their slave factory was operating at full capacity to supply slaves to Caribbean planters; these were the years when their own American plantations and those of their friends needed more workers. These were also years which saw shifts within their own Caribbean trade: before and during the Seven Years' War (1756–1763), the associates' Caribbean fleet more often than not went to Jamaica, where sugar planters were experiencing a boom; during the heyday of Bance Island (1763–73), however, their ships began to bypass Jamaica and serve the eastern Caribbean. There, hundreds of new planters (among them, eight associates) in the recently acquired Ceded Islands were building a slave population from scratch, and the older plantations in the Leeward Islands were increasing the size of their labor force.

There was a similar rise in African destinations over the first twenty years of these data. None of their ships are known to have gone to West Africa before 1748. Following their acquisition of the Sierra Leone factory in that year and their development of its capabilities in the years that followed, the number of associate ships visiting African forts rose steadily to seventeen in 1765. The Seven Years' War may have checked the increase slightly but, if so, the setback was temporary and, in the twelve years between 1762 and 1773, the Sierra Leone depot serviced 29% of all non-London arrivals and departures. Only the War for America stopped the associates from linking the coasts of Africa to the shores of America.

Mainland North America harbored more than 20% of the non-London arrivals and departures between 1745 and 1785. A breakdown of

4. The results accord with similar data that recount the port most recently visited ("previous port") and the port about to be visited ("next port") by the associates' ships. Hancock, "Citizen of the World," pp. 349–64.

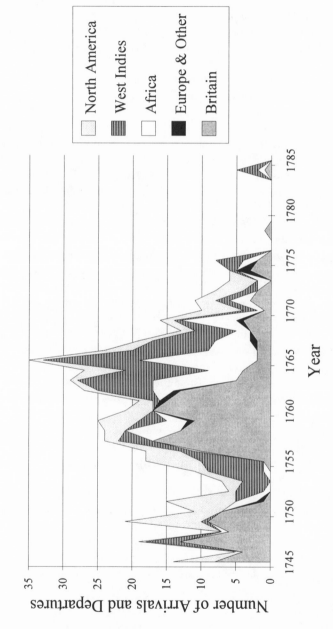

Graph 4.1 Regional Distribution of Ports Other Than London, 1745–85

the ships traveling to and from America suggests a shift within main-land America during that time. Before the outbreak of war in 1755, the associates traded primarily with Maryland, Virginia, and, to a lesser extent, North Carolina: 55% of their ships' non-British arrivals and departures were in these three colonies. By the close of the war in 1763 and for the next twenty-three years, they had little to do with northern North American and Chesapeake shipping. In just nine years, they had turned their backs on the tobacco colonies and fixed their gaze on the rice and sugar economies of South Carolina, Georgia, East Florida, and the Caribbean.[5] Many similarly situated merchants moved out of the northern and Chesapeake colonies at the same time. As trade routes matured, "elites" of the trade established themselves and came to dominate the routes, as the Glaswegians did in the Chesapeake tobacco trade, almost completely eclipsing entry by any but their ilk.

The East Indies also emerged as an increasingly attractive market for the associates after Britain's assumption of military control of the Indian subcontinent, especially in the region around Bengal, between 1757 and 1761 and after the havoc wrought by the commercial and political disturbances in North America in the 1760s and 1770s. The associates sought to bypass the onerous restrictions of what was still a closed market, and invest more heavily in the trade to India: they purchased more shares in East India Company ships; lent more money to the Company on *respondentia* bonds; sent more goods to India as freight on Company ships; and, like John Levett, served there as a "free merchant" or supported others acting in the same capacity. They were extremely quick to invest in Indian ships, Grant owning shares in two Indiamen during the early 1770s and Oswald owning shares in four during the late 1770s. Similarly, they were keenly interested in freight opportunities. Grant and Oswald were especially close to India "husbands" like Andrew Moffatt and Laurence Dundas, having known them since childhood, and with their help Oswald, for instance, consistently bought space in nine Indiamen throughout the decade, purchasing the privilege to do so from the officers known to the husband.[6] Such ventures

5. On the post-1740 withdrawal of slave traders from Virginia, see Herbert S. Klein, "Slaves and Shipping in Eighteenth-Century Virginia," *Journal of Interdisciplinary History*, v. 5 (1975), p. 409. The terrible depression in the northern and Chesapeake provinces following the French and Indian War further encouraged the withdrawal.

6. Until the 1770s, the prospects for private traders like the associate John Levett were bleak but, when reforms in the 1770s made it increasingly difficult for India Company officials to engage in private trade, the number of private "free merchants" and "agency houses" rose. For regulations proving the relatively unfree nature of the India trade and the easing of restrictions on private trade during the 1770s, see Charles Hardy, *A Register of Ships* (London, 1813), pp. 58–61, 92–93, 96–99; Peter J. Marshall, "British Merchants in Eighteenth-Century Bengal," *Bengal Past and Present*, v. 95 (1976),

were few and, although post-1785 movements are not formally tracked by the Shipping Database, the increase in India as a destination in the period after the American Revolutionary War suggests that the early Indian ventures prefigured what was to come later for those associates who continued to ship and trade after 1785.

Notable for their absence in Table 4.1's "Other" category are destinations in Northern Europe and the Mediterranean, especially Italy and the Levant. Before 1745, several of the merchants possessed strong ties to northern Germany (Sargent and Aufrere had traded there) and the Levant (Stratton, Cooke, and Levett had worked there), but the associates' ships generally skirted these regions thereafter. As they became aware that growth in trade with these regions was improbable and that the continual presence of war in the Baltic and Levant frustrated commerce, the associates looked less to these regions as outlets for exports and sources of imports.[7] In the Levant, for instance, internal disturbances, wars between the Ottomans and Persians, subsistence crises, and plaguelike epidemics sweeping through Iran and Syria combined after 1722 to cripple production of exquisite silk fabrics until 1747. Adversely affected by such obstacles, British traders' share of the Levant silk trade with Europe declined. British consumers preferred Persian silk; they never took to its replacement, Syrian silk, viewing it as less desirable than the cheaper Indian or Chinese silks or the more luxurious Italian silk. As a result, British traders began to look elsewhere for substitutes for Levant silk, as they did for Levant cotton and coffee. By the late 1700s, only 1% of total English trade occurred with the eastern Mediterranean, down from 10% in the 1600s.[8]

    pp. 152–54; and James G. Parker, "Scottish Enterprise in India, 1750–1914," in *The Scots Abroad* (London, 1985), pp. 190–98. A *respondentia* bond was an advance on the security of merchandise in a ship. A "husband" managed the dispatch of an India ship.

7. On the perception of a declining trade, see *London Magazine*, v. 18 (1748), pp. 405–06; Sir Matthew Decker, *An Essay on the Causes of the Decline of the Foreign Trade* (London, 1744); Davis, *The Rise*, p. 29; Elizabeth K. Newman, "Anglo-Hamburg Trade in the Late Seventeenth and Early Eighteenth Centuries" (Ph.D. dissert., University of London, 1979), pp. 229, 193.

8. The standard narrative of the British trade with the Levant remains Ralph Davis, *Aleppo and Devonshire Square*. On the production of luxurious silk fabrics and the complicated factors affecting the decline of the caravan trade and Britain's share of the Levant trade, see Abraham Marcus, *The Middle East on the Eve of Modernity* (New York, 1989), pp. 146–153; Bruce Masters, *The Origins of Western Economic Dominance in the Middle East: Mercantilism and the Islamic Economy in Aleppo, 1600–1750* (New York, 1988), pp. 30–33; and Kristoff Glamann, *Dutch-Asiatic Trade, 1620–1740* (Copenhagen, 1958). In any region, the short-term effects of war on shipping were anything but positive. At the outset of the Seven Years' War, Grant noted that "our being now engaged in a declared war will greatly affect our concerns. . . . It will oppress the Planter which will in a great measure put it out of his power to pay his debts and all of us will suffer thereby, as there can be less dependence than even heretofore on remittances." GD 345/1164/3/26, 96: Sir Alexander Grant to Sir Archibald Grant, May 29, June 15, 1756.

Although they represent the largest single block of the associates' non-London arrivals and departures (35%), the large number of ports in Ireland, Scotland, and England other than London is somewhat deceiving. The associates were not significant players in the British coastwise trade; indeed, their coastwise ventures played almost no role in their use of outports after Grant's short-lived attempt during the 1740s to link Garmouth in Morayshire, Newcastle, and London in a timber trade.[9] During the Seven Years' War, over one-third of the associates' ships (37%) made use of outports, but this fact stemmed from the loading of arms manufactured in western England and directed to employees in Africa or correspondents in America. Their ships stopped outside London for three reasons that were seldom tied to coastwise trading: they were in transit, having just arrived in Britain and preparing to moor in the Thames, or having just left the metropolis and en route to Africa or America; they were supplying a correspondent, usually in the West Country or Glasgow; or they were carrying the personal effects of an associate. Shipments to Scotland, for instance, were not considered "business" ventures per se since they were mainly parcels of private goods, such as china for Lady Grant, turtles for John Mill, or wainscot for Richard Oswald. None of these reasons suggests an increased and sustained reliance upon peripheral domestic trading centers.

The London associates, as outsiders to the established trading elites, stayed alert to the possibilities of new business ventures: they worked new commodities such as sugar, rice, naval stores, and India goods into their trading portfolios, moved into different regions opened up to British settlement for the first time, and adopted more varied trading patterns. In these new areas, ties to old trading elites were not important, since elites were seldom well-formed or deeply entrenched; experience or speed of response could count in their stead. Likewise, these new trades involved new growth commodities in increasing demand in Britain and Europe.[10]

Factors and Principals

The need for shipping and trading services for colonists arose with the advent of economically successful colonies. Colonists produced a surplus of commodities that could be sold in the mother country, allowing

---

9. On the whole, this was also the common pattern in the seventeenth century. Overseas merchants rarely engaged in coastwise traffic, which was almost entirely in the hands of specialists.
10. For quantitative description of London's shipping patterns, and for proof that London merchants compensated for "problems in traditional markets by expanding their extra-European trade," see French, "Trade and Shipping," pp. 172–85, esp. 174.

them, in turn, to become consumers of the capital's finished goods. Doing so required merchants who could ship and sell for them. Some of these merchants became "factors," that is, men who traded in their own names, possessed the goods, and usually did not reveal the names of the people for whom they were acting. A factor's misfeasance could not lead to a suit against the principal; he was not an "agent," who was considered to be acting for a principal or employer and whose misfeasance allowed a third party to sue the principal. Although the practice of working as commercial representatives had prevailed for at least a century before the founding of Jamestown, the specific act of Londoners' serving as the factor of American correspondents and clients appears to have sprung up first in the 1660s. By the time the associates arrived in London in the second quarter of the eighteenth century, most international merchants, whether or not they were involved in the American trade, were "in some respects Factors"; indeed, as the author of a popular trade directory noted, it was "very hard to distinguish the Merchants that are not Factors."[11]

Although the "commission merchandising" system employed by factors has been sketched by Richard Sheridan, it is worth reviewing here with special reference to the associates, who all began their London careers acting as factors for others. In principle, a factor's work was simple. He performed a variety of shipping and trading services for provincial, colonial, and foreign merchants, planters, and professionals. A London factor for African traders – in Oswald's case, a factor for agents in the employ of the Company of Merchants trading to Africa who were technically prohibited from trading in African goods, but who were doing so all the same – conducted his business

> by buying goods and merchandizes such as Iron guns, British Spirits, cotton goods, . . . and sending the same in his own ships and vessels to Africa where the same have been bartered for slaves which have been carried to the West Indies and the produce [of slave sales] remitted to him in bills of exchange. And also by importing Sugar

11. For descriptions of the work of factors, see *An Essay on the Increase and Decline of Trade, in London and the Out-Ports* (London, 1749), pp. 32–35; Postlethwayt, *Universal Dictionary*, v. 1, sub "agent" and "factor"; Mortimer, *Universal Director*, pt. 3, p. 4; and Wyndham Beawes, *Lex Mercatoria Rediviva* (London, 1761), pp. 41–44. On traditional practice and the rise of commission merchandising in Britain's foreign trades, see K. G. Davies, "The Origins of the Commission System in the West India Trade," *Transactions of the Royal Historical Society*, 5th ser., v. 2 (1952), pp. 89–107; Davis, *The Rise*, p. 81; Pares, "A London West-India Merchant House," and "The London Sugar Market"; and Sheridan, *Sugar and Slavery*, p. 282, who uses the terms "commission agents," "sugar factors," and "West India merchants" as synonyms. Only in Scotland were "agent" and "factor" synonyms. Reappraisal of the emergence of the system appears in Nash, "English Trans-Atlantic Trade," pp. 129–91.

and Rum from the West Indies and selling the same upon commission and by purchasing and sending to the West Indies divers Goods and Merchandizes also on commission.[12]

The task that defined the factor's relations with his clients was a two-way trade in supplies and produce. For example, Oswald's long-time business acquaintance with James Murray of North Carolina, a childhood friend of his partner Robert Scott, began by honoring Murray's request for plantation supplies. In return, acting on the business principle that "obligations ought to be mutual," Murray consigned his tobacco and indigo to Oswald. On the arrival of Murray's ships in the Thames, Oswald reserved a portion of the produce as payment of his commission, sold the remainder of the cargo, paid the expenses incurred in handling and selling it, and credited the remainder to Murray's account. Oswald earned a commission fee which was negotiable, customarily between $1/2\%$ and $2^{1}/_{2}\%$ of the value of the transaction.[13] This system facilitated a continuous flow of goods and services around the empire. If the associates were typical factors (and there is every reason to believe they were), London factorage was not restricted to one or two commodities or trades; they sold logwood, tortoise shell, palm oil, guinea grain, gold, silver, silk, wine, and arrack, as well as sugar and tobacco.[14]

A factor new to the job, as each associate was in the 1730s and 1740s, spent much of his time deciding "how to sell . . . & to buy Goods in the best manner." Such decision-making was eased most by a deep and complex "Knowledge of the Times & Seasons when to sell

12. C 12/808/2.
13. In providing factor services to Laurens, Murray, Mackaill, Melville, Stevens, or Young, the associate earned at most a fee of 2 1/2%. Some 1/8% was charged for the transfer of stock, 1% for receiving money at the Treasury, 2 1/2% for handling and selling American crops or negotiating bills of exchange, and 5% for loaning money. C 12/808/2: Johnson v. Oswald, Answer, scheds. 1–4 sub October 20, 1753, and August 31, 1755; Peter Davidson's Account Current, sub August 1, 1770, Court of Error Records, v. 4, ff. 197–98, Jamaica Archives; and Pares, "London Sugar Market, 1740–1769," p. 255. Rates varied according to geography: 1.5 to 2% prevailed in the Holland and Hamburg trade; 3% in the Levant trade; and 5% in the Caribbean trade. Earle, *English Middle Class*, p. 347, n. 62.
14. GD 248/174/1: Walter Grant to Sir Ludovick Grant, September 6, 1750; C 54/6864/13/7–9: August 8, 1788. Shipping and trading, not financing (as Richard Sheridan avers), was the primary function of the factor. *Sugar and Slavery*, p. 282. Examples here and in the following paragraphs are drawn from Stevens Family Papers, MG 409 (April 20, November 3, 1742, May 11–July 6, 1746), New Jersey Historical Society, Newark; James Murray Papers, Letter Books, passim, Massachusetts Historical Society, Boston; C 12/808/2: Johnson v. Oswald, scheds. 1–5; Henry Lloyd Letter Book (1765–67), ff. 219, 224, 226, 234–35, 248–50, 321, Harvard Business School Special Collections, Boston; and Letters of Johnston & Jolly to Newton & Gordon, 1758–70, Cossart & Gordon Papers, Liverpool University Archives, Liverpool.

and when to keep," since "those who can sell the best commodity cheapest" and quickest "will always command the market." The factor who possessed such expertise exercised a great deal of control over his clients' shipping and trading matters: he suggested what commodities should be shipped and when, and he managed their sale. Robert Scott's Madeira and London firm of Scott, Pringle & Scott, for example, was the factor for John Stevens of Perth Amboy in New Jersey. Throughout the 1740s, Scott marketed Stevens's wheat and flour in Funchal, as well as the odd lot of gammon, iron, and staves for making wine casks of various sizes; in return, at Stevens's request, Scott bought and shipped wine to Stevens's New York market. Scott's "Knowledge of the Times & Seasons" was usually good, but nothing was certain. In the spring of 1746, for instance, Scott received Stevens's wheat, but he decided that the price was too low for an immediate sale. Scott held out for higher prices but, in the end, was "deceived": the price remained low throughout the summer, until the week after Scott sold, when it began to rise. Yet, despite occasional miscalculations, Scott's depth of experience in handling sales in Madeira, especially his watch upon the market, made him a formidable factor.[15]

A knowledgeable and successful factor was above all patient. Having lived in Jamaica for several decades, Alexander Grant was especially appreciative of the difficulty in dealing in a volatile commodity like sugar, and he resigned himself to accepting unpredictable or slow remittances. Sugar could be a formidable business to manage: Jamaican affairs were "slow & dillatory," and Grant knew of "no remedy but perseverance & patience." So many things occurred "to postpone & often to defeat" his business that he never flattered himself "with a certainty long beforehand." The sugar might not arrive; there might be less than expected; or the quality might vary with the season.[16] After the crop arrived in London, "dull markets" might slow its sale for months and, even if the price was high, difficult brokers, grocers, and bakers might confound matters. Grant's response to such complications was to overlook "neglects & omissions" and move quickly, to "push on": his approach was to ship as soon as possible, unload quickly, and sell early. Holding on to sugar "in order to get the height of the Market" sounded good in principle, but more often than not the cost of handling and

15. [Campbell,] *Candid and Impartial Considerations*, p. 19.
16. Sir Alexander Grant to John Gordon, October 15, 1769, Crant Papers, Tomintoul House; GD 345/1163/3/143: Alexander Grant to Sir Archibald Grant, June 7, 1755; GD 345/1180/1765: Sir Alexander Grant to Captain Archibald Grant, March 23, 1765; GD 345/1171/1768: Sir Alexander Grant to Sir Archibald Grant, September 2, 1768; GD 345/1162/5/25: Alexander Grant to Sir Archibald Grant, November 17, 1753; GD 345/1171/2/29: Sir Alexander Grant to Sir Archibald Grant, February 21, 1767.

storage outweighed the increase in price. Casks were frequently ill-made, and leaks were a common occurrence. Sugars were often improperly weighed in America or plundered shipboard. The "waste of weight, high warehouse rent on so bulky a commodity, & interest on the duty & freight paid on its landing" generally exceeded "any advance that may arise on keeping it."[17] Most of the associates shared Grant's approach.[18]

Other tasks were involved in the satisfaction of trans-oceanic shipping and trading needs. Factors commonly procured insurance and paid premiums, outset costs, and customs duties. In pounds and pence, handling insurance was probably the most important of these ancillary services, for few colonial shipping centers offered reliable marine insurance at competitive prices; James Murray, for instance, always asked Oswald to obtain insurance for the cargoes he shipped to the Caribbean or Britain. Managing money was another service factors provided their clients. Often factors kept clients' accounts and collected monies owed them, as Oswald did in the 1750s for Matthew Mackaill, Thomas Melville, Jr., and Ebenezer Young, three young Scots who had contracted with the Company of Merchants to provide services to slave traders at Cape Coast Castle. From accounting and debt collecting, it

17. GD 345/1163/2/35: Alexander Grant to Sir Archibald Grant, September 6, 1754; and Sir Alexander Grant to John Grant, October 14, December 24, 1771, Sir Alexander Grant to John Gordon, January 25, 1772, Sir Alexander Grant Letter Book, Grant Papers, Tomintoul House. The organization of the London sugar market bore striking similarity to that of the Bristol sugar market. Pares, *A West India Fortune,* "London Sugar Market," and "London West India Merchant House." Information on handling sugar is drawn from these sources, as well as the Lascelles & Maxwell Letter Book, 1743–46, esp. ff. 16, 21, 24, 33, 151, 220, 234.

18. GD 345/1163/2/38: Alexander Grant to Sir Archibald Grant, January 29, 1754; GD 345/1169/1763: Sir Alexander Grant to Sir Archibald Grant, November 26, 1763; and Walter Tullideph to Patrick Grant, March 5, 1754, and Walter Tullideph to Grant, Tew & Russell, December 31, 1757, Tullideph Letter Book, SRO; GD 345/1163/2/35: Alexander Grant to Sir Archibald Grant, September 6, 1754; GD 345/1171/1768: Sir Alexander Grant to Sir Archibald Grant, September 2, 1768; and Pares, "London Sugar Market," p. 257. Selling early may have involved employing a sugar broker. Although metropolitan enterprisers commonly employed intermediaries, middlemen have seldom been the subject of study. Brief mention of brokers appears in Westerfield, *Middlemen*; Davis, *The Rise*, pp. 162, 165; Sheridan, *Sugar and Slavery*, p. 330; and Earle, *English Middle Class*, p. 41. Price provides an illuminating sketch of London's cloth brokers in *Capital and Credit*, but the work of sugar, stock, and insurance brokers still awaits investigation. Some information on insurance brokers is in E 112/1614/1279: Bewicke v. Fraser; Henry Laurens to John Lewis Gervais, September 14, 1774, in *The Papers of Henry Laurens*, v. 9, pp. 557–58; Michael Herries to Richard Oswald, July 12, August 6, 1765, Oswald Papers, Sudlows; C 11/1117/2: Drake v. Todenhorst a.k.a. Drake v. Long. On wine brokers, see Johnston & Jolly to Newton & Gordon, March 5, 1765, May 18, 1766, Cossart & Gordon Papers, Box 3, Liverpool University Archives. Brokers could also serve as independent assessors of the condition or value of goods. C 12/1081/6: Oswald v. Anderson, Answer, July 28, 1787.

was only a small step to managing funds. Oswald and Mill supervised the three young Scots' stock and security portfolios: they sold Bank stock for Mackaill, cashed Navy Bills for Melville, and bought lottery tickets for Young. Like Oswald's, each factor's counting-house was a bank for his clients; the client might send cash but, more frequently, he drew on the factor as one would draw a check on a modern-day bank. Others, too, knowing the client's relation to the factor, drew on the factor for money due from the client.[19]

Factors also moved into managing property. The London associates negotiated the purchase or sale of British estates or American plantations for their clients. As factors, they supervised the clients' legal affairs, hiring lawyers to draft conveyances, contracts, agreements, and wills, since American planters commonly distrusted the ability of colonial attorneys and rested easy in the often unwarranted assumption that deeds drafted in Britain could be fully litigated in the colonies. Factors supervised clients' court cases in the central courts of London. Property matters were also not beyond their ken. After purchasing a plantation for a client, the associates selected overseers and hired laborers. It was not unusual for them to make regular visits to London's charity schools, orphanages, and hospitals, first making the acquaintance of the boys and then returning in search of young workers. If the plantations would not produce, the factors finally might take the extreme step of taking over the management of the estates themselves, as Grant did when tending to the troubled finances of the Earl of Home.[20]

London agents attended to more human concerns, as well, and this rise in an "intimate social relationship" seems to have been new to the eighteenth century.[21] Grant cared for his clients' relatives in London; often he lodged them in his house or found them a job with his firm. Other associates stood similar watch over their clients' relatives when they attended Oxford, Cambridge, or the Inns of Court. Oswald and his wife Mary, for instance, cared for Henry Laurens's children when they were living in London in the early 1770s, and he introduced John Laurens to London's leading legal lights several years later. Oswald also

19. James Murray to Elizabeth Murray, September 4, 1749, James Murray Letter Books, Massachusetts Historical Society, Boston. See also five instances of Robert Scott's paying insurance fees for Boston merchants in 1752. D. S. Greenough Papers, Box 1751–58, Folders 1752, Massachusetts Historical Society. As Pares and Sheridan have shown, factors extended financial assistance to their clients, giving cash or credit and, in return, taking notes, bonds, court judgments, or secured mortgages. Pares, "London Sugar Market," pp. 98–107; and Sheridan, *Sugar and Slavery.*
20. George Maxwell to Michael Longbotham, February 24, 1745, Lascelles & Maxwell Letter Book, ff. 236–37.
21. Davies, "Origins," p. 99.

paid clients' relatives their legacies, as when each year he paid James Murray's sister Barbara Clark of Kelso £60 from an account he kept in Murray's name, and he acted as executor, trustee, or guardian for clients who had lived or owned plantations abroad. He carried out more mundane tasks, too. Oswald sent fashionable wigs ("full grizel bobs") each year to Murray in Carolina, Mackaill, Melville, and Young in Africa, and Levett in Calcutta. White hats, children's shoes, cloth, books, stockings, gold watches, French magazines, a spirit-proof thermometer, beer, wine, coffee, tea: clients demanded and factors provided "goods of the newest fashion as well as of the best kind." This line of service was far from the world of traditional shipping and trading but, as factors, the associates were also governesses, haberdashers, booksellers, and interlocutors.[22]

"Intimate social relationships" could lead factors into less seemly matters, and Henry Laurens's attack on Sir Egerton Leigh is revealing on this point. Leigh, married to Henry Laurens's niece, had been derelict in caring for his wife's younger sister. The girl had been raped in St. James Park in March 1772 when visiting Leigh; she had informed him of it, but he had done nothing to pursue and prosecute the offender. Nine months later back in Charleston, without benefit of a midwife, she gave birth to a boy and intentionally allowed him to die of starvation, again while Leigh stood by. Leigh then bundled her aboard a vessel and shipped her back to London. Laurens was outraged and turned to Oswald for help in orchestrating a lawsuit. Oswald hired his own lawyer and neighbor Charlton Palmer to examine the young woman and the ship's captain, and filed their declarations with the Lord Mayor's Court in London. Eventually, in September 1774, Oswald wrung from Leigh a confession of neglect and monetary reparations.[23]

Less sensational subjects – advising and lobbying on political concerns – were more common, and capped the work of the factor. As a group, London factors worked together to defeat passage of a 1744 parliamentary bill that would have imposed an additional duty on sugar grown by their clients. They waited on Henry Pelham, chief minister. They printed an abstract of their "Case," publishing it in the *Evening Post* and sending a copy to the townhouse of every MP and to every seaport. "[F]requent meetings of the Agents, Planters & Factors interested in Sugar Colonies" were held at the King's Arms and small groups

22. James Murray Letter Books, December 12, 1749, March 20, 1753, Massachusetts Historical Society, Boston; Lascelles & Maxwell Letter Book, f. 28; and Pares, "London Sugar Market," pp. 95–98.

23. *The Papers of Henry Laurens*, v. 8, pp. 269, 339–41, 579–82. 630–39, 645; v. 9, pp. 7, 53–54, 571–74, 628; and v. 10, p. 15.

"personally waited on every MP." In short, nothing was wanting "to make the Clamour popular, and . . . get this damned Bill" blocked. Five years later, acting as Murray's factor, Oswald approached Earl Granville with Murray's request to be made the "Receiver" of the rents on Granville's extensive properties in North and South Carolina. Before Oswald could push Murray's petition further, Murray lost interest in the job; but Oswald's willingness to approach the "people above" on Murray's behalf persisted. Six years later, in 1755, again at Murray's request, Oswald lobbied the Board of Trade and the Admiralty to grant a bounty on the export of North Carolina cypress, Murray being a substantial cypress planter.[24]

The wide range of services that a factor performed in the 1750s was the subject of heated discussion. In 1759, in a grim report on the *State of the British Sugar-Colony Trade*, the writer Joseph Massie took up the subject. Chief among the causes of the mother country's declining commerce and profit, he argued, was the "dwindling" of British merchants "into the diminutive Characters of Agents, Factors, & c. instead of appearing as PRINCIPALS in the TRADE of their OWN COUNTRY." Compared to London enterprisers in the preceding century, Massie claimed, London merchants no longer shipped "on their own account"; instead, they acted on behalf of other merchants and planters, earning commission fees for their work and appearing as little more than servants of colonists.[25] Although in hindsight any "dwindling" occurred well before Massie said it did, at the time he wrote much evidence seemed to support his claims of professional realignment.[26]

24. Lascelles & Maxwell Letter Book, ff. 82–83 (January 17, 1744); James Murray to Earl Granville, July 24, 1749, and James Murray to Richard Oswald, February 28, 1755, James Murray Letter Books, Massachusetts Historical Society, Boston; *London Evening Post*, January 3, 1744; and Pares, "London Sugar Market," pp. 93–95. See also Alison G. Olson, *Making the Empire Work: London and American Interest Groups, 1690–1790* (Cambridge, Mass., 1992), pp. 94–125. On advice on who and how to lobby, see Oswald and Mill telling a Presbyterian minister in London to raise funds for the College of New Jersey to apply to the Board of Trade, in George W. Pilcher, ed., *The Reverend Samuel Davies Abroad: The Diary of a Journey to England and Scotland, 1753–55* (Urbana, 1967), p. 71.
25. Joseph Massie, *A State of the British Sugar-Colony Trade* (London, 1759), pp. 48–49.
26. Grant managed the import and sale of sugar for many absentee planters. Accounts, 1749–55, Douglas-Home Muniments, 26/3; "An Account," 1759, and Thomas Stratton to Robert Hamilton, April 20, June 12, 1760, Hamilton of Rozelle Papers, Glasgow University Archives, Glasgow; C 107/68/one of two tied bundles: "An Account of Zachary Bayly . . ." 1763; CO 142/18: August 10, 1763; and C 12/1014/13: Barclay v. Grant, Bill of Complaint, 1763. Grant's services mirrored those of other associates. Richard Oswald to James Murray, September 4, 1749, James Murray Letter Books, Massachusetts Historical Society, Boston; and C 12/808/2: Johnson v. Oswald, scheds. 1–4 sub August 13, 1754, August 23, 1755. Kenneth Morgan recounts the work of Grant's Kingston comrade and Bristol correspondent Mark Davis in "Bristol Merchants and the Colonial Trades, 1743–83" (Ph.D. dissert., University of Oxford, 1983), Appendix C, pp. 338–59.

But Massie set up a false dichotomy, and unfortunately historians have accepted his analysis.[27] Massie's explanation was as much prescriptive as descriptive, and does not do justice to the complexity of actual trading portfolios. As a reconstitution of the associates' daily business activities suggests, large-scale London merchants trading overseas marketed their own goods as well as their clients' produce – a point that is frequently overlooked. On the outbound voyages, to Virginia in the 1750s and to Florida in the 1760s, Oswald and Mill frequently seized the initiative, bore the risk of sea and market, and speculatively sent to colonial planters and merchants goods that they thought would satisfy colonial demand. As we will see in Chapter 6, they did much the same in their forays into the slave markets of the eastern Caribbean, despite the frequent dire predictions of American correspondents like Henry Laurens. On the more profitable inbound voyages, whether it was Augustus and John Boyd carrying back the produce of their St. Kitts plantations on their ship the *Domville* in 1749, Oswald carrying the proceeds of his wife's estate in Jamaica during the 1750s, or Grant shipping the nearly 2.5 million pounds of sugar produced each year by his own Jamaican plantations during the 1760s aboard his *Albion*, *Elizabeth*, *Dawkins*, and *St. Mary*, the story was the same: the associates divided their holds between their own "& other Gentlemens crops."[28] Factorage was not an alternative but a basis for and complement to principal enterprising – to shipping and trading on their own accounts, as well as to planting, slaving, and victualing.[29] For the associates, outsiders at the start of their careers, commission merchandising served as an easy point of entry into colonial trades in which City financial and social connections mattered least; subsequently, it provided a continual stream of business throughout their careers, and introduced them to a wide range of activities and people that were necessary for the pursuit of other ventures, but the bulk of their fortunes was made in principal enterprising.

Making Money in Shipping and Trading

The activities involved in shipping and trading for oneself were nearly identical to those in working for others as a factor. In either case, the

27. Sheridan's *Sugar and Slavery* and Price's *Capital and Credit* are only the two most prominent books whose themes are shaped by Massie's argument. See also Morgan, "Bristol Merchants," pp. 257–58.
28. T 1/340/86–92; CO 142/16/182–84, 152–53, 145–47; Thomas Newton Letter Book, passim, Madeira Wine Co. Archives; and Sir Alexander Grant to John Gordon, October 17, 1769, September 20, 1770, March 12, October 14, 1771, Grant Letter Book, Tomintoul House.
29. For contemporary recognition of dependance on noncommission earnings, see GD 248/50/3/5x: Sir Alexander Grant to James Grant, January 1772.

associates bought or hired ships, recruited captains, outfitted voyages, bought merchandise for their overseers or clients, and guessed where goods sent out on speculation might sell, what might be brought back, and who might buy it. In the Caribbean or North America, they faced two particular challenges to making money in this business: utilizing ships to their full potential, so that these expensive resources did not lie idle, and building an international network of suppliers, clients, correspondents, agents, factors, and employers.

The associates had to keep their ships full and moving. A full hold was perhaps the best indicator of the success of a transoceanic voyage, and few of their ships departed the metropolis in ballast. Careful attention was paid to the outbound voyage, stocking it with supplies that would satisfy the needs of clients or overseers or that could be sold on speculation, and using the opportunity to carry passengers for a fee.[30] Being located in the metropolis helped the associates fill their holds. London was the emporium of the world; everything was sold there. To the task of procuring plantation supplies, the associates brought their contracting and victualing expertise in obtaining bread, beef, butter, and assorted foods from inland English and Irish suppliers. To the job of acquiring goods used in the slave trade, they brought their experience buying cotton goods from the East India Company.

In addition, not one of the associates' ships leaving a record of its contents departed America with an empty hold. Only seven instances of "ballast only" were recorded by American port authorities, and these situations arose on shuttles between West Indian islands and North American ports.[31] Unless war intervened, full inbound ships became almost a certainly by the 1760s, when the associates were best equipped to provision and stock their slave factory in Sierra Leone and sugar plantations in the Caribbean with goods from India, Europe, Madeira, and America, to supply their clients with wine from Europe, and slaves from Africa, and to carry American commodities back to London.[32] In America, the associates did not have to confront the all-too-common problem of procuring return cargoes at ordinary prices, because they owned highly productive plantations in the Lower South and in the British West Indies and maintained friendly relations with regular clients

---

30. Grant's *Neptune*, for example, brought eight settlers and sixty soldiers to Jamaica in 1747; twenty years later, Oswald's *Charlotte* carried indentured servants to Florida. CO 5/573/129: May 31, 1769.

31. *St. Paul* (July 17, 1745; arr Hampton); *Rose* (April 28, 1747; arr Kingston); *Pelham* (August 19, 1752; arr Hampton); *St. Andrew* (November 24, 1752; arr Williamsburg); *Dawkins* (March 22, 1757; arr Kingston); *Alexander* (February 25, 1763; arr Kingston); and *Industrious Friends* (March 31, 1767; arr Charleston).

32. According to French, ships trading between Jamaica and London carried more sugar per ton in the 1760s than they had in previous decades. "Trade and Shipping," p. 303.

whose products they shipped regularly. They seldom experienced the difficulties in obtaining goods, financing ventures, or procuring return cargoes that outport or colonial merchants encountered.[33]

In addition to keeping their ships full of cargo, the savvy shipper kept them under sail. This meant tackling the problem of "tardy vessels" by paying close attention to the calendar. London shipping "moved in step with the seasons in other parts of the globe"; the arrival and departure of the associates' ships "varied with the winds that blew in distant lands." Overall, they clustered their departures between October and February (54%), and their arrivals between June and November (80%). Grant, Oswald & Co.'s African fleet generally left the metropolis between November and February and returned between June and September, thereby avoiding the Caribbean's hurricane season of August and September. The Jamaican vessels of the Boyds, Grant, and Mill departed London from November to March and arrived back between July and September, again avoiding hurricane season. Oswald's London departures for Virginia and Carolina were fairly evenly distributed throughout the year, with a slightly higher concentration between February and June, so as to coincide with the time at which packed tobacco was most available in the Chesapeake (the packing season ended in June) and in which the weather was least hospitable to the ship-timber-eating *teredo* worm which flourished in the heat.[34]

Brief port times and fast turnaround times were additional keys to keeping ships moving.[35] The associates' ships usually lay 112 days in the Thames, 95 days in Jamaican ports, and 44 days in Falmouth harbor between voyages, and these port times seem to adhere to levels maintained by a significant number of other English merchants' ships.[36] The

33. Inikori, "Market Structure," pp. 753–58, convincingly depicts the difficulty merchants in the outports experienced obtaining guns, textiles, and credit. Almost the reverse situation prevailed in London. For an instance when the associates did not have their way, see IOL, Mss.Eur./D.624/2/299–304.

34. Anon., *An Essay on the Increase and Decline of Trade*, p. 33; Ashton, *Economic Fluctuations*, p. 10; Alan Burns, *The History of the West Indies*, 2nd ed. (London, 1965), p. 757; and Davis, *Rise*, p. 285.

35. Davis discusses these problems briefly in *Rise*, pp. 190–94, 281.

36. Hancock, "Citizen of the World," Table 14, Graph 19, and Appendix 23. Few ports have been studied; London's average, for instance, has yet to be computed, so adequate comparison is impossible. The time spent in port was a function of the facilities of the port and the capabilities of the master and ship. London being the warehouse and treasury of the empire, vessels necessarily stayed a longer time in the Thames than elsewhere. Slaving vessels lying in Jamaican ports during 1744–67 took ninety-six days. Roger M. Dancey, "Shipping in the Jamaica Slave Trade, 1686–1807" (M.A. thesis, University of Exeter, 1971), p. 55. For briefer stays in the colonies and the outports, see Gary M. Walton, "Sources of productivity in American colonial shipping, 1675–1775," *Economic History Review*, 2nd ser. (1967), p. 76; and Richard F. Dell, "The Operational Record of the Clyde Tobacco Fleet, 1747–1775," *Scottish Economic and Social History*, v. 2 (1982), pp. 7–8, 12.

associates' ships averaged one voyage per ship per year – 304 days, or
11 months on each Atlantic voyage between 1748 and 1770. This rate
prevailed whether the ships went to the Chesapeake or the Caribbean,
and stood in contrast to their Glasgow competitors' Chesapeake ships,
which managed to make at least two voyages per year because of the
shorter route and the fewer destinations. Individual ships owned by the
associates and commanded by certain masters developed a reputation
for cutting time and increasing frequency, and Sargent and Stratton
consistently managed to make two voyages per year with the packet
fleet to the West Indies. But generally the associates' times were "state-
of-the-art": one voyage per year prevailed with each of their ships, as
it did with ships of most of their English private-sector competitors.[37]

Another way a merchant could keep his ships' port times brief and
turnaround times fast was through the replacement of his ships with
newer, larger, and heavier vessels. An old or small vessel was more
likely to need repairs in port or to take a longer time crossing the seas.
In keeping his fleet young and well-equipped, the merchant was trading
high purchase price and more expensive insurance for the freedom from
problems and the shortness of times; in addition, John Anderson was
quick to note, a new vessel "would sell for £500 to £800, when the old
ship will bring nothing." On more than one occasion, the associates
came round to reasoning that the high outlay for new ships would be
recovered in a few years time.[38] Again and again in their correspondence, tying the performance of their fleet to its age, they adhered to
norms of their day: from 1745 to 1779, the average age of their large
and heavy ships for which ages were ascertainable was 7.7 years,[39] an

37. Turnaround times involving specific regions are best studied by examining the voyages
of the following vessels in the Shipping Database: for North America, the *Lark* (1748–
50) and the *St. Andrew* (1752–57); for the West Indies, *St. Kitts Planter* (1753–70),
Grace (1752–59), and *Dunnikier* (1764–69). Mill's *Industrious Friends* (Robert Clark
and Walter Tod, masters) and Grant's *Dawkins* (Robert Ballantyne, master) were two
ships that consistently traveled faster than the average turnaround time. There has
been little agreement on and little study of turnaround time. Contrast a contemporary
insurance expert's report that an average round-trip touching at England, Africa, and
America took four to five months, with modern studies' suggestion of eight to twelve
months. Cunningham, *Bills of Exchange*, pp. 338–39; Davis, *Rise*, pp. 190–94, 281;
and Dell, "Operational Record," pp. 7–8, 12.
38. John Anderson to Richard Oswald, September 28, October 5, 7, 1780, Oswald Letter
Book, v. 2, SRO; and Alexander Manson to Richard Oswald, September 28, 1780,
Oswald Papers, Sudlows.
39. Hancock, "Citizen of the World," Table 16, Graph 20, and Appendix 20. Other
features affecting the speed of the vessel were its size, rigging, and shape. The associates preferred large full-rigged ships (45%) or snows (14%), square sterns (89%),
and large registered tonnages (180 tons on average) typical of London's fleet, larger,
that is, relative to outport- or colony-owned ships after 1752. Ibid., Tables 16–18;
and French, "Trade and Shipping," pp. 204–12, 281; Dell, "Operational Record,"

age that was wholly typical of the ships of most Jamaica or Virginia traders visiting the port of London.[40]

The challenges of keeping ships fully loaded and under sail show up in a financial report which constituted part of the evidence that was presented in a dispute over a 1747–48 voyage backed by three associates in Britain's Court of Chancery.[41] The dispute arose over the contract between three associates – Alexander Grant, Alexander Johnston, and John Gardiner – and the captain they appointed to manage their vessel, the *Neptune*, on its voyage between London and Jamaica – Alexander Ogilvie.[42] The three associates had begun by purchasing the vessel and selecting a captain. The ship was bought easily enough, for it belonged to an associate. A three-masted, square-rigged ship of 110 registered tons, it had been built in Boston twelve years before and had been acquired by Gardiner for his individual mercantile fleet. Nor was Ogilvie's selection as captain difficult, since Ogilvie, a native of Scotland temporarily residing in Shadwell on London's suburban fringe, was distantly related to Grant. In the venture, each of the partners (but, surprisingly, not Ogilvie) owned an equal share, a common configuration for bilateral trans-Atlantic voyages. In moving the project along, there were many things to do to ready the ship for sail: it was necessary

> to go over the ship carefully to determine her repair needs, major and minor; to make arrangements, if necessary, for graving and resheathing, and for replacements of timbers, spars and sails. A new voyage had to be determined on, some thought perhaps given to alternatives among fellow-merchants, the ship stored and provisioned

p. 14; and Walton, "Productivity change," p. 70. The effect of the shape of the stern was and remains a hotly debated issue. The square sterns favored by the associates were easier to build, more economical in timber, and had greater stowage space allowing easier access; "round" sterns, probably meaning full round sterns, not just round tuck sterns characteristic of Dutch and Dutch-influenced shipbuilding, were probably stronger and more seaworthy. William Hutchinson, *A Treatise on Naval Architecture* (Liverpool, 1794), p. 28.

40. The average age of London/Jamaica traders was 7.6 years in 1744–48, 6 years in 1752–55, and 8.1 years in 1762–65; the average of London/Virginia traders was 8.6 years (1739–48), 7.1 years (1749–55), 6.9 years (1756–63), and 6.4 years (1764–69). British-built vessels lasted longer than colonial-built ships. "Trade and Shipping," pp. 285–86. Among English slavers entering Jamaica in 1744–67, England-built vessels averaged 9.2 years, and colony-built ships 8.1. Dancey, "Shipping," p. 31.

41. Davis, *Rise*, pp. 159–74.

42. C 11/631/32: Ogilvie v. Grant; and NOSL, Jamaica, for July 3, 1747. In almost every detail, the voyage was typical. Cf. Sir Alexander Grant to Capt. John McNeill, March 12, 1771, Sir Alexander Grant Letter Book, Tomintoul House; Davis, *Rise*, pp. 105. 174; Sheridan, *Sugar and Slavery*, p. 335; Richardson, "Costs of Survival," p. 191; and W. E. Minchinton, "The Voyage of the Snow *Africa*," *Mariner's Mirror*, v. 37 (July 1951), pp. 191–92.

for her next outset. In time of war or stress, passes and protections for the crew must be negotiated with the Admiralty; there was a crew to be hired and customs formalities to be completed.[43]

No exact rule determined who performed these tasks, although, in the case of the *Neptune*, the partners handled financial and commercial matters, whereas Ogilvie performed the maritime and personnel tasks.

On this occasion, the partners took full advantage of the fact that London was where the wholesalers and "monied men chiefly reside."[44] Ballast goods (5,000 bricks, 3 tons of chalk, and 11 hogsheads of coal), for example, posed no difficulty. These weighed down the light outbound vessel (Britain-to-Jamaica vessels generally left with little cargo) and were later sold on the other side of the ocean to planters in need of durable building materials, fertilizer, and fuel.[45] Drawing on their suppliers, they procured most major provisions needed for the voyage: barley, pepper and other spices, 60 pounds of tea, 60 gallons of rum, and gin. In addition, the partners provided voyage and plantation goods from their commercial networks: Gardiner with his West Country and Midlands ties secured guns and ammunition for Grant's correspondents and Kingston's fort, which the Boyds were supplying with sea provisions; and Grant drew on the Boyds' victualing network to feed the ship's crew and provision his clients' plantations (3 hundredweight of bread and 38 puncheons of wine). Finally, the *Neptune* was filled with human cargo: some 60 soldiers bound for Kingston, who paid £1 per person (£10 for their captain); and 8 civilians, mostly relatives of the owners. Financial matters also came under the purview of the partners. Although it was common practice for partners to procure insurance, there is no evidence that the associates did so in this case. But they did register ownership of the ship with the customs commissioners. At the London Customs House, they gave bond warranting that, should they load any enumerated American commodities like sugar or tobacco, they would carry them to a legal destination and there pay legal duty. Captain Ogilvie handled most matters concerning the ship. He interviewed and hired two mates, a surgeon, boatswain, carpenter, gunner, four sailors, a cook, and a boy, and paid them their preliminary wages. He oversaw repairs like glazing the windows, outfitted the ship with marine supplies like thread and sail, and paid most minor fees relating

---

43. Davis, *The Rise*, p. 159.
44. Anon., *An Essay on the Increase and Decline of Trade* (London, 1749), p. 6.
45. On obtaining coal in London, see Westerfield, *Middlemen*, pp. 218–39; M. W. Flinn, *The History of the British Coal Industry*, v. 2 (Oxford, 1984); and R. Smith, *Sea Coal for London: History of the Coal Factors in the London Market* (London, 1961), pp. 34–46.

to the ship's stay in the river – moorage, anchorage, and pilotage out to sea.[46]

The *Neptune* was ready to sail by April 6, 1747. After the partners' customary farewell dinner on board the ship and a minor delay brought on by inclement weather, the crew hoisted anchor two weeks later and slowly and carefully sailed down the Thames with the assistance of an official pilot boat to steer the vessel clear of other ships and dangerous shoals. Once free of the Thames, the Atlantic crossing took only eight weeks, everything running according to plan. Following his orders to the letter, Ogilvie arrived in Barbados in mid-June, progressed to St. Christopher, and reached Jamaica in early July.

Captain Ogilvie had left Gravesend with specific instructions to call on the partners' correspondents in the West Indies and to procure new cargo as quickly as possible for the return voyage.[47] But, in Jamaica, the plans broke down, and he remained in its waters for six months. At the start, he was bogged down in bureaucratic minutiae, spending his first full week on the island traveling the thirty miles to Spanishtown to pay port, carriage, and other fees at the offices of the Island Secretary, Comptroller of Customs, Collector of Customs, Naval Officer, and Receiver General.[48] When he was not filing papers with the government,

46. On average, the associates paid £2.12.0 per person, excluding the master, on a monthly basis. Partial advances were given to all but the master, mates, surgeon, and boy. On the development of marine insurance, see Sutherland, *A London Merchant*, pp. 42–80. Bond and registration were mandated by parliamentary statute – Danby Pickering, ed., *The Statutes at Large*, v. 7, pp. 459–60 (bond: 12 Car.II, c. 18, cl. 19), and v. 9, pp. 428–37 (registration: 7 & 8 Wil.III, c. 22, cls. 17–18); they are discussed in Lawrence A. Harper, *The English Navigation Laws* (New York, 1973), pp. 161–62; Charles M. Andrews, *The Colonial Period of American History*, v. 4 (New Haven, 1938), pp. 118–21, 172–74; and Elizabeth Hoon, *The Organization of the English Customs System, 1696–1786* (New York, 1938) pp. 125–45. Once purchased, the cargo was brought to one of the 19 "free" wharves lining the river between Tower Bridge and London Bridge. Each wharf was specialized by region and commodity and run as a partnership: a partner paid £50 "to enjoy loading and landing"; a nonpartner paid much more. C 11/1651/16: Lateward v. St. Quintin, June 9, 1749, continued as C 12/826/30: Gascoigne v. Lateward, February 24, 1762; and John Chartres, "Trade and Shipping in the Port of London: Wiggans Key in the Later Seventeenth Century," *Journal of Transport History*, v. 1 (1980), pp. 29–47.
47. Davis, *Rise*, p. 168. While some instructions like the *Neptune*'s strictly mapped the captain's route, others merely suggested that he seek the best market.
48. A list of goods subject of duty twenty years later appears in Samuel E. Morison, ed., *Sources and Documents Illustrating the American Revolution, 1764–1788*, 2nd ed. (New York, 1965), pp. 78–82. On colonial customs practice and organization, see Thomas C. Barrow, *Trade and Empire: The British Customs Service in Colonial America, 1660–1775* (Cambridge, Mass., 1967), pp. 73–78. The work of collector, comptroller, surveyor, searcher, landwaiter, tidewaiter, and lesser employees is discussed in detail by Barrow, but no one has yet undertaken a detailed analysis of the related work of more senior colony officials involved in commercial affairs. Edward Brathwaite, *The Development of Creole Society in Jamaica, 1770–1820* (Oxford, 1971), pp. 9–20, provides the only rough outline of their activities.

he turned to repairing the vessel, unloading her cargo, for which task he had to rent local slaves, and reprovisioning the ship. Sea provisions of beef, pork, butter, fish, sugar, and water had to be replenished. Broken ropes in the ship's rigging had to be replaced. Thread for sewing sails, axes for chopping wood, coarse cotton osnaburg for making new sails, white lead for the ship's bottom, firewood for cooking food, slaves for transporting goods, even burial cloths for two sailors who died ashore – all had to be procured at great cost. And, when the outfitting was complete, the entire bureaucratic wheel of filing and payment was set in motion again. There was, in short, comparatively little time to procure an inbound cargo, at least in Kingston.

Only in September, two months after arrival, could Ogilvie turn in earnest to the commercial concerns of the voyage, distributing supplies, selling goods and, most importantly, accepting consignments of sugar and rum. He refused to call upon the associates' friends and contacts in Kingston, especially Grant's cousin who headed one of Kingston's largest mercantile houses and against whom he seems to have had some personal vendetta. Instead, Ogilvie went to the associates' friends outside Kingston directly. In a slow circuit, he rounded the eastern tip of the island and proceeded westward along its north coast. Each time he dropped anchor – at Martha Brae near Montego Bay, Lucea farther west, and Savanna-la-Mar on the southwestern end of the island – he delivered or sold provisions to Grant's relatives or friends like the Beckfords in exchange for their sugar and rum. In Westmoreland Parish, where Grant had practiced as a "Country Doctor" for over twelve years, Ogilvie hired a long boat, three canoes, and four slaves and spent fifty days filling the hold with Grant's former patients' crops. When he finally set sail for London in late November, Ogilvie carried with him more than 200 hogsheads of sugar, 76 puncheons of rum, and 6 bags of cotton.

With the arrival of the *Neptune* in the Thames, the partners could not help but confront the challenges to making money in shipping and trading, for Ogilvie had failed to fill the cargo as fully as the partners had hoped, in large part because he had avoided dealing with their principal supplier, and he had kept the ship in Jamaica waters for an inordinate length of time. Closing the account with Ogilvie proved troublesome; he claimed more than the partners were willing to pay him, and he formally demanded they render an accounting to a Chancery Master. With custom and reason on their side, they never answered Ogilvie's Complaint, and paid him according to their reckoning of the time the voyage should have taken.

The problems with Ogilvie reveal the challenge of utilizing a ship to its full potential. They also highlight a second great challenge facing transoceanic shippers and traders: establishing a network of correspondents and clients around the world. International contacts were critical to the associates' commercial success, and were as much an indication of an involvement in the larger world as the number of the places to which they sent their ships. It is, therefore, worth examining in detail the wide range of their contacts and the way they linked them together in order to develop a strong worldwide information and distribution system.

Consider the case of Oswald. Having left Glasgow for London, he drew upon his cousins, as later he relied upon his nephew, to handle his affairs in the west of Scotland; to a lesser extent, he called upon his cousins' Glasgow friends, such as John Jamieson, James Buchanan, and Alexander Spiers, to serve as his correspondents in regions where his cousins' expertise and contacts were less strong. When he needed an agent in northern England, he commenced a correspondence with his cousins' agent Ralph Carr; likewise, when he needed an agent across the ocean in America, he appointed their clients Alexander Mackie, James Clarke, and Walter Buchanan of Virginia, and in Jamaica he turned to Alexander Spiers's correspondents, Messrs. Moffat, Davis & Bell.

Oswald did not rely exclusively on Glasgow connections. Over time, he built up from London his own commercial network that extended across national boundaries and spanned the oceans to an extent not enjoyed by his cousins or their friends. As we have already seen, the preparation for this London network occurred through the acquaintances he made in the late 1740s. His wife, the heiress Mary Ramsay, brought him ties to powerful mercantile and planting families in Jamaica and London. Her trustees Robert Scott and John Mill brought him contacts in the Wine Islands and along the east coast of Britain. Erstwhile Glasgow friends who had also moved to London, like William Dunbar or Robert Dinwiddie, Jr. (once a Glasgow merchant, then a Bermuda customs collector, and eventually lieutenant-governor of Virginia), secured him the correspondence of American planters and merchants like James Murray of North Carolina. The recommendation of Augustus Boyd brought Oswald the commission work of Henry Laurens of South Carolina. Replicating these arrangements, Oswald later established correspondent ties with local merchants in other colonies as his own commercial interests shifted southward: Georgia (John Graham, a relative of Oswald's army contracting partner David Graeme); East Florida (James Penman, an employee in Oswald's German bread magazines); St. Christopher (Smith & Baillies, the Boyds' island attorneys); Antigua (John Wilkins, a distant relative of Aufrere); and Grenada (David

Mill, a cousin of Oswald's partner John Mill). And, at the same time, he established correspondent relations across Europe: with general merchants in Germany (Hamburg, Cassel, and Stralsund) and the Netherlands (the Hopes of Amsterdam, and childhood friends the Mansons, who had settled in Rotterdam); with slave merchants in the Netherlands (Baalde of Rotterdam) and France (Foache of LeHavre, Premord of Honfleur, Hornetener of Rouen, and Lambert of Paris); with agents of the French tobacco "farm" (Nantes enterprisers who had traded extensively with Michael Herries's cousin Robert Herries); and with Mediterranean traders (Francis Levett of Leghorn, Italy). In Calcutta, Oswald dealt with Francis Levett's brother, John, who had previously managed Oswald's German bread magazines. And, on the African coast, a distant relative of his wife, Thomas Melville, Jr., served as Oswald's principal link with the Company of Merchants' African operations during Melville's tenure as Governor of Cape Coast Castle. The names on this list are not, in themselves, significant. What are important are the relations they bear to the associate in London.

Commercial linkages to men with established, tested skills were culled and cultivated from a collection of blood, ethnic, and neighborhood connections. Dogged persistence in finding contacts in the colonies was critical. Two days after the death of London merchant Vincent Biscoe of Austin Friars, who had enjoyed "many of the most valuable correspondents all over the island," Grant commanded his Jamaica superintendent to seek out Biscoe's contacts, and would not rest until he had secured the custom of three of them. Relentless perseverance in establishing correspondents in the colonies was equally important. Grant, for instance, set up Walter Murray and Thomas Robertson in a Kingston partnership and "advanced a large sum for that purpose." Later, he approached his friend John Pownall, the Secretary of the Board of Trade, and obtained for Murray the post of Naval Officer in Jamaica, with the understanding that Murray would be "pleased to use me as his Correspondent in Business."[49] Relatives, friends, friends of friends, and fellow countrymen with an understanding of the larger commercial world assumed prominent positions in the associates' business empires.

Many of the associates' contacts, correspondents, and clients had lived long overseas. Fewer of their employees had done so. As a result, the burden was on the associate to provide the employee with an international perspective, and much of the training of the clerks in the counting-houses served this purpose. In almost all of the cases of

49. Sir Alexander Grant to John Gordon, May 3, 1770, October 15, 17, 1769, Sir Alexander Grant Letter Book, Grant Papers, Tomintoul House.

in-house employees (whose early training we know about) becoming overseas representatives, the associates first assigned them to colonial and foreign accounts in their firms, watched their progress for several years, and then sent them overseas, to America, Africa, or India. There, as attorney, superintendent, overseer, or captain, they carried out the associates' business and reported on peripheral distribution systems, commercial regulations, and client and consumer preferences.

The placement of Grant's nephews the Davidsons illustrates this marshaling of in-house representatives. Alexander Davidson first worked as a clerk in Grant's Billiter Lane counting-house, where he managed the firm's African accounts, before he went out to Bance Island in the late 1750s to serve as one of the slave factory's two agents. In the following decade, Grant found him a post in India, where, in turn, Davidson filled Grant's requests for India goods and assisted the promotion of other Grant protégés on the subcontinent. During the same twenty-year period, his brother Patrick Davidson received an apprenticeship in Grant's Thames-side warehouse operations before moving on to serve Grant "in the Jamaica way" as the lead captain in the baronet's Kingston-to-London fleet. Another brother, Peter Davidson, underwent similar training in London and, in time, became the most important person in Grant's Caribbean operations: at first, a sea captain; later, the overseer on Grant's largest Jamaica plantation; and, finally, the "General Superintendent" of all Grant's plantations.[50]

Much of the success of Grant's day-to-day operations in West Africa, the Caribbean, or East India can be traced to his insistence on full utilization of his fleet and his employment of representatives, mainly relatives, whom he had educated globally and from whom he could usually expect continued respect and obedience. These two stratagems were linked; as the case of the Davidsons demonstrates, they reinforced each other to cope with the worldwide dispersal of their ships and the broad range of their services and activities.

This approach to international coordination of merchant shipping and trading was widely shared by the associates.[51] When Alexander Johnston was still working as Grant's partner, for instance, he sent one of their clerks, Francis Newton, to Madeira in 1748 and helped him enter the wine business there. Johnston and Grant both sensed the

50. On Bance Island, Alexander Davidson joined his cousin John Davidson, who had gone out to serve as an accountant after years of toiling over Billiter Lane's books. Shipping Database; State and Condition of Bance Island, May 1763, May 1765, July 1766, Main Papers, House of Lords, London.

51. Cossart & Gordon Papers, Boxes 1–6, Liverpool University Archives, Liverpool.

importance of having a reliable personal contact in this critical shipping rendezvous, probably the most important shipping services node in the entire Atlantic commercial system. Its source of fresh water and sea provisions, its supply of trade goods in heavy demand by Americans, and its access to non-British markets further solidified their fledgling trading practice in medicine and sugar, and allowed them to develop a side trade in dry goods. In 1758, five years after he separated from Grant, Johnston sent out another clerk, Thomas Gordon, his young brother-in-law, and provided the capital for Gordon's establishing a partnership with Francis Newton. In founding the partnership of Newton & Gordon and then serving as a principal "sharer" in its "interests," Johnston added another node to his web of international business relations, and this helped him further coordinate the whole of his enterprise. John Scott in Denmark, Messrs. Crop in France, Bewicke & Timerman in Spain, Parminter & Montgomery in Lisbon, the Pasley Brothers in Teneriffe, Francis Newton, Thomas Gordon, nephew William Johnston, and former apprentice David Young in Madeira, John Rowe in Boston, Thomas Newton in New York, Francis & Tilghman of Philadelphia, Alexander Newton and the Riddel Brothers of Virginia, brother Samuel Johnston, Charles Irvine, and Samuel Bean of Jamaica, John Welch and William Kirkpatrick of St. Kitts, Ross & Nesbitt of Nevis, Cholet & Bize of St. Eustatia, Alexander Gordon of Montserrat, William Snaip of Antigua, brother Patrick Johnston of Barbados, and James Baillie of Grenada: All drew on Johnston for shipping and trading services, requesting European merchandise or, on inbound voyages to London, cargo space for their goods. In turn, each saw that Johnston's ships and requests for goods were not delayed in his own port, by helping him fill the hold, assisting the repairs, or buying new ships. The demands and the consignments that came Johnston's way as a result of forming Newton & Gordon kept his ships in the water; the firm's contacts and skills kept them moving forward. Johnston's ships, laden with cloth and other commodities, destined for Madeira and beyond, and consigned to his relatives and their contacts, represent the associates' and the empire's commercial organization at large: satisfying the demands of one correspondent or customer meant marshaling the forces of many.

5

Planting: "A Great Fund of Riches and of Strength to Great Britain"

THE ASSOCIATES' SHIPPING AND TRADING on their own account complemented their work as factors. But they did not stop acting as principals here: over their London careers, they integrated backward into planting and, later, into slaving and military contracting. Purposely entering new fields of enterprise, they undertook work their correspondents and suppliers had previously performed and thereby substantially reduced transaction costs.[1] The associates' move to planting arose perhaps most easily, given their prior experiences in the colonies, as both managers and owners of plantations there. Moreover, as shippers and traders, they were in constant contact with plantation markets, keeping close watch on what was possible and profitable. The work of planting, even for these men, however, was hardly effortless. In order for their American plantations to flourish, they had to match crops to soil, invest heavily in facilities and labor, and impose a close, reliable watch upon their operations.

Forces Driving American Planting: Necessity and Opportunity

In the early and middle parts of their careers, well before the outbreak of the Seven Years' War, the associates occasionally invested in American plantations and farms. Augustus Boyd purchased several sugar estates in St. Christopher between 1700 and 1730, having previously managed them for other planters. To the west, in Jamaica, between 1720 and 1740, Alexander Grant received 1,000 acres of sugar land from the colonial government and then leased the land to other aspiring Scots planters. In the 1750s, he increased his holdings substantially

---

1. The drive to be more productive as planters and slavers did not exclude (indeed, it assisted) the desire to appear landed. The latter will be discussed at length in Part III.

when he began accepting the management of plantations belonging to former friends. John Boyd inherited several working estates on St. Christopher from his maternal grandmother in 1745. And Richard Oswald obtained a financial interest in a large sugar-producing plantation in western Jamaica through his marriage to the heiress Mary Ramsay in 1749. During this time, the associates' planting interests were restricted to the Caribbean; only Oswald and Herries expressed an interest in settling the mainland, and their scheme for settling Georgia in the early 1750s never went beyond applying for, and then withdrawing from, a grant. Their initial investments in settled colonies were of moderate size, remained relatively stable, and seem to have given them little difficulty.

The associates started making substantial investments abroad only after the Peace of 1763. By then, they were well established in the commercial world of the City and, increasingly, the social world of the county. Their successes in shipping and trading and government contracting businesses were paying off, and they saw the settlement of America as an opportunity to invest in a rich gold mine. Despite their comfort and age in 1763 (Oswald and Grant were fifty-eight, Sargent II forty-eight, and John Boyd forty-four), perhaps because of them, the associates jumped at the chance to make another commercial "strike." Whereas they collectively owned 9,000 acres at the end of 1750 and 21,000 acres at the end of 1763, they owned 130,000 acres by the end of 1775.[2]

Most of these lands were in America, where the attractions of rich agricultural soil and low population density were not lost on the associates. They favored plantation lands in the British West Indies (Jamaica, the Leeward Islands, and the Ceded Islands), with the undeveloped lands of the mainland's Lower South (South Carolina, Georgia, and East Florida) not far behind. Oswald established plantations in South Carolina[3]; Oswald, Mill, Herries, and Grant pursued planting in East Florida; and the Boyds, Grant, Mill, Oswald, Scott, Trevanion, and Wood settled plantations in the Windward Islands.[4] These estates were all part of the vast territory stretching from Nova Scotia to Florida and

2. Appendix VI.
3. *The Papers of Henry Laurens*, v. 4, pp. 331–33, 395–96, 426–28.
4. Many associates favored the Caribbean. Richard Oswald to Governor Grant, May 23, 1765, February 12, 1766, BCM 295. Mill acquired plantations in Carriacou and Tobago, and Scott bought a plantation in northern Grenada. In 1764, Oswald was asked to join Mill and two other Scots in purchasing a Carriacou plantation, but he declined. Richard Oswald to Governor Grant, July 25, 1764, BCM 295. Later, through mortgage foreclosures, he acquired property in the eastern Caribbean, as did Boyd, Trevanion, and Wood. On the value of the Ceded Islands, see CO 323/15/101–07: May 5, 1765.

then south along the eastern edge of the Caribbean to Tobago that had been opened up by the Peace to hundreds of British and American grantees and planters and, with their assistance, thousands of settlers; the planting of "uninhabited countries" and "the appropriation of the waste and luxuriant bounties of nature" gave rise, in the minds of planters like the associates, to "a great number of pleasing ideas" and profitable dreams.[5] In addition to these interests in the West Indies and the Lower South, the associates entertained a wider range of plantation schemes. Levett planted cornfields in Bengal.[6] John Sargent II played a dominant role in the management of the Ohio Company.[7] And Grant, Mill, and Oswald all toyed with the settlement of Nova Scotia.[8]

The associates used a variety of means to acquire their properties. John Boyd inherited four estates from his grandmother and father and Grant inherited two plantations from his friends the Dickers,[9] while Grant, Mill, Trevanion, and John Boyd bought directly from Caribbean planters, and Oswald bought indirectly at private auction in London.[10]

5. Bailyn, *Voyagers*, pp. 10–16; Samuel Johnson, *Lives of the English Poets*, ed. G. B. Hill, v. 2 (New York, 1905), p. 393; John Campbell, *Candid and Impartial Considerations in the Nature of the Sugar Trade* (London, 1763), pp. 203–04, 225; and GD 248/49/2/57: Sir Archibald Grant to Sir Alexander Grant, March 7, 1764.

6. John Levett to Richard Oswald, December 10, 1772, December 3, 1774, Herries Papers, Spottes; and Richard Oswald to John Levett, December 18, 1772, December 1, 1774, Oswald Papers, Sudlows.

7. John Sargent II was one of the principals in the single most ambitious scheme of the 1760s – the Grand Ohio Company or, as it was variously known, the Vandalia or Walpole Company (after Thomas Walpole, its chief organizer); it is not to be confused with the Ohio Company of Virginia or the Mississippi Company. The first action of the Grand Ohio Company took place in 1769, but Sargent had been working for several years to put together an investor group. A draft of a royal grant was prepared in early 1775, but the execution of the grant was suspended until the end of the American Revolution. The post-1769 work of the Grand Ohio Company has been given short shrift. Kenneth P. Bailey, *The Ohio Company Papers, 1753–1817* (Arcata, Calif., 1947); Lois Mulkearn, ed., *Papers Relating to the Ohio Company of Virginia* (Pittsburgh, 1954); Washington, D.C., Paul Mellon, Featherstonehaugh/Wharton Papers; *The Papers of Benjamin Franklin*, v. 13, p. 415, v. 16, p. 165, v. 17, p. 8, and v. 22, pp. 19–27; and T 29/40/164, 174–75, 218. Sargent's attorney, Charlton Palmer, was involved in most of these companies. He had served as the solicitor for the Ohio Company of Virginia between October 1760 and April 1764, and assisted its merger with Sargent's Grand Ohio Company in 1770. Mulkearn, ed., *Papers*, pp. 46, 182, 185. He was also the attorney of the Boyds, Grant, Oswald, and Mill.

8. CO 217/20/II/238; *Acts of the Privy Council, Colonial*, v. 4, p. 816, v. 6, p. 368; CO 217/20/II/217, 220, 232, 275, 291; and Map of Egmont's Grant in Nova Scotia, Add.Mss. 47054B, BL.

9. PROB 11/1336/q. 82/ff. 255–58 (proved February 5, 1800); and Powers of Attorney, v. 54, f. 56, v. 66, ff. 1–4, Jamaica Archives.

10. Oswald's attempt to acquire the 1,100-acre Rhine plantation in Jamaica, where he thought his Florida slaves would be more productive, is set out in C 12/1060/10, 12/1054/16, 12/1078/8, 12/1081/6. (1) The auction was to take place at Garraway's coffeehouse at noon on March 3, 1778; (2) a description of the property was available

More important to the postwar acquisitions were two other means. A dozen or so plantations came their way by foreclosing on mortgages they had received as securities for loans they had granted to cash-starved planters when the planters finally found themselves unable to repay: Boyd and Scott, for instance, acquired several plantations in Grenada and St. Vincent this way, and Oswald and Grant did the same in Jamaica.[11] The associates also participated in the large-scale Crown-backed settlement programs set up in the Ceded Islands and North America in the wake of the war to allow many others, both large-scale developers and small-scale yeomen, to invest in plantations.[12]

The time was right for planting America: the period 1745–1785 was a "golden age" for American produce. Consider the case of Caribbean sugar. (One could equally well make the case with North American rice or indigo.) This period was marked by sustained growth in the cultivation, processing, shipment, and sale of sugar and rum.[13] The weight of

beforehand there or at the chambers of the seller's attorney; (3) the highest bidder was to be the purchaser; (4) if there was any dispute, the plantation was to be put up for roup again; (5) £20 was to be paid at the auction, 10 percent two months later, 40 percent on December 1, 1779, and the remainder by December 1, 1780; (6) title and possession were to pass at the second payment; (7) the buyer was to pay one-half of the Crown sales tax; and (8) if the buyer failed to comply with the terms, the seller was free to resell the property. As it turned out, the March auction was the second auction of the plantation; the previous buyer, Alderman Woolridge, failed to pay the deposit. For this second sale, notices appeared several times in late February and early March 1778. The auction started on time in the rooms above Garraway's; Oswald, arriving late, noticed his friend Mr. Cracraft. Oswald asked Cracraft to bid £26,000 on his behalf; after some discussion, Oswald was declared "best Purchaser" and he "took receipt on side of the Printed Particulars" for his down-payment. On Grant's purchases, see Deeds, v. 229, f. 203, v. 213, f. 39, v. 215, f. 135, v. 218, f. 160, 197–98, v. 226, f. 236, Island Record Office. On Boyd's purchases, see Grenada Supreme Court Registry, Deeds, v. 1772/D/2/268–90, v. 1788/R/3/113–34; on Trevanion's purchases, see ibid., 1785/K/3/1–24; on Mill's purchases, see ibid., v. 1766/D/1/330–46.

11. Grenada Supreme Court Registry, Deeds, vv. 1772/D/2/1–16; 1774/R/2/349–58; 1769/ N/1/412–33; 1766/F/1/1–14; 1774/R/2/528–29; Deeds, v. 226, ff. 276–88, v. 227, f. 113, v. 241, f. 11, Island Record Office, Jamaica; and General/Grant Court Records, v. 170, f. 87, v. 168, f. 43, Jamaica Archives; and Sederunt Book, Grant Papers, Tomintoul House. See also n. 17 below.

12. Grants could be obtained either by application to the Privy Council in London or by application to the governor and council in the colony. Bailyn, *Voyagers*, p. 432.

13. The times were good for sugar planters and traders. In the twenty-five years between 1747 and 1772, Britain was at war only nine years. In peace, seas were relatively safe for shipping produce. Freight and insurance rates fell after 1763 and rose again in 1776. Gary Walton, "Sources of Productivity Change in American Colonial Shipping, 1675–1775," *Economic History Review*, 2nd ser., v. 20 (1967), pp. 67–78, and "A Measure of Productivity Change in American Colonial Shipping," *Economic History Review*, 2nd ser., v. 21 (1968), pp. 268–82. Furthermore, during the second half of the century, both the average price of Jamaican sugar and the exchange rate between Jamaican and British currencies remained stable. McCusker, *Money and Exchange*, p. 253. The situation for sugar refiners was more complicated. London's refining world

sugar shipments to Britain increased more than fourfold, from 430 million pounds in 1700 to 1,900 million pounds in 1775; and their value rose nearly as much, from £630,000 at the beginning of the eighteenth century (1699–1701) to £2,364,000 just before the outbreak of the American war (1772–74). By the third quarter of the century, Jamaica had taken the lead and was the largest producer of sugar in the empire; in 1770, it was raising and shipping three times as much sugar as Barbados, the next largest grower and exporter. In 1670, Jamaica had large tracts of uncultivated land and 57 sugar plantations; by 1701–05, there were 124 sugar plantations and, by 1786, there were 1,601 sugar plantations. The slave population rose along with the number of plantations, from 9,500 in 1675, to 45,000 in 1703, to 226,000 in 1788. In the same period, across the waters, London was the most important sugar port in the country: it received more of the sweet substance than did any other British port; and sugar and rum were the City's most sizable and valuable import.[14]

Grant's extensive records reveal how he got involved in planting, and then invested heavily after the war when he was in a position to take advantage of the American boom. During his stay in Jamaica during the 1730s, when he worked primarily as a doctor and merchant, he acquired 1,000 acres of plantation land, but grew nothing for export. Only after he left the island did he turn to planting in a serious way and

suffered a setback in the 1770s and 1780s: in 1766, there were 159 sugar houses; in 1772, 117; in 1781, 125; and in 1792, only 97. Some 62 firms closed during this period, and no firms opened. *British Parliamentary Papers, Accounts & Papers, 1792*, v. 93, pp. 1, 2, 5; and Sheila Lambert, ed., *House of Commons Sessional Papers*, v. 37: *Reports and Papers, 1781–83* (Wilmington, Del., 1975), pp. 57–58, 70. While the amount of sugar being refined increased, the number of refiners decreased after 1770. This is consistent with an interpretation where some refiners are getting better off, while there is a "shake-out" among weaker refiners. Other crops largely ignored by Caribbean historians show similar growth in production in the period. On the rise of rice and indigo, see Peter A. Coclanis, *The Shadow of a Dream: Economic Life and Death in the South Carolina Low Country, 1670–1920* (New York, 1989), pp. 82–84.

14. John J. McCusker, "The Rum Trade and the Balance of Payments of the Thirteen Continental Colonies, 1650–1775" (Ph.D. dissert., University of Pittsburgh, 1970), pp. 232, 891–93; and French, "Trade and Shipping," p. 146. Michael Craton and James Walvin, *A Jamaican Plantation: The History of Worthy Park, 1670–1970* (Toronto, 1970), pp. 73, 75, graph the 1730–75 rise in Jamaican sugar production. In contrast, Lowell J. Ragatz provides a grim picture of unremitting decline in plantation output between 1750 and 1834, in *The Downfall of the Planter Class* (New York, 1928). On the rise in the number of sugar plantations in Jamaica, see Sheridan, *Sugar and Slavery*, pp. 215–17; and Barry W. Higman, *Jamaica Surveyed: Plantation Maps and Plans of the Eighteenth and Nineteenth Centuries* (Kingston, 1988), p. 10. Statistics for the slave population are presented in David Watts, *The West Indies: Patterns of Development, Culture and Environmental Change since 1492* (Cambridge, 1987), Table 7.5, p. 311.

then "it was necessity (not choice)" that drove him "into large possessions in Jamaica."[15] The pretext was the supervision of the estates of his
friend Patrick Adam, who had recently died. Along with his cousin
Achoynanie, Grant assumed the management of Adam's two St. Mary
plantations, Albion and Eden, in the early 1750s. Grant administered
Adam's estates much as he did the property of any other client. In 1752,
his overseer filed a report with the Island Secretary in Spanishtown,
declaring that the two estates produced 115 hogsheads of sugar and 19
puncheons of rum; five years later, the estate was producing 172 hogsheads of sugar and 90 puncheons of rum.[16]

Grant began to augment his own real estate portfolio about the same
time, leasing 903 acres in St. Thomas in the Vale in 1752, buying 111
acres in St. John the following year, and beginning the long process of
buying up the shares of the Adam property in the late 1750s. By the
time of his death in 1772, his seven Jamaican plantations totaled nearly
11,000 acres and were valued at £96,700 sterling. Production rose
rapidly, especially after the war: between 1766 and 1771, Grant's sugar
production doubled from 486,000 pounds (valued at £9,300) to 964,000
pounds (£18,000) and rum distillation more than doubled from 17,000
gallons (£9,300) to 36,000 gallons (£17,000).[17]

Grant's planting complemented his shipping and trading, for the output
from his Jamaican estates allowed him to meet the challenge of keeping
his ships filled. By the 1760s, Grant's ships carried his own sugar as
often as they carried his clients' produce. In 1762, four ships – *Albion*,
Dawkins, *Elizabeth*, and *St. Mary* – left Kingston with 606,000 pounds
on average of his own sugar and 5,500 gallons of his own rum, that is,
one-third of their overall carrying capacity, in addition to cargo for

---

15. Sir Alexander Grant to John Grant, December 24, 1771, Sir Alexander Grant Letter
    Book, Grant Papers, Tomintoul House.
16. Appendix III.
17. £96,700 in 1772 amounts to £5,633,034 or $8,378,462 in 1994. Grant's purchases
    of sugar plantations surged at two different times: the mid-1750s, when he foreclosed
    on the Charlemont leasehold in St. Thomas in the Vale Parish and the Albion and
    Eden freehold in St. Mary Parish; and the mid-1760s, when he foreclosed on four
    mortgages he had previously taken from planters. At the end of the century, the
    Charlemont, Berwick, and Rio Magno plantations were still in the possession of the
    Grant family. *British Parliamentary Papers: The Slave Trade*, v. 61 (Shannon, Ireland,
    1971), pp. 245–48. His continual shuffling of estates is reported in Sir Alexander
    Grant to John Gordon, September 20, 1770, Sir Alexander Grant to John Grant,
    December 20, 1770, Sir Alexander Grant Letter Book, Grant Papers, Tomintoul House.
    Oswald's plantation interests followed a similar trajectory. At Spring Garden estate in
    western Jamaica during the 1740s, factors reported average annual production of 90
    hogsheads of sugar; from 1763 to 1767, 127 hogsheads; from 1767 to 1772, 159
    hogsheads. Crop Accounts, v. 4, ff. 38–39, 90, 127, 163, v. 5, ff. 137, 140, 200, v.
    6, ff. 36, 159, 218, Jamaica Archives.

others. At the time of his death ten years later, his plantations were producing almost 1 million pounds of sugar per year, a crop that alone would have filled the holds of several average-sized sugar ships and earned him £18,000 in the London market.[18] Profits could be considerable. Grant's factor filed crop accounts between 1766 and 1771, and it appears his plantations produced £20,000 worth of produce, or £3,450 per year on average. These earnings represent a return of at least 29 percent per year on the money Grant invested in plantations.[19]

"Constant Circumspection and Economy"

How did the associates make this kind of money from planting? There were four key factors.[20] First, a planter had to tend to the agronomic fundamentals and match the crop to the site, soil, and climate. This may seem an obvious consideration, but finding the right crop in a new land could be difficult. Grant's experience in Jamaica during the 1720s and 1730s gave him a good knowledge of terrain and weather, as well as of the ways of nonresidents' employees. Having lived in Jamaica as a "Country Doctor" and visited "the plantations of a whole parish," Grant learned something of Jamaica's terrain and weather patterns, as well as of the "stale excuses" of overseers. Since "it was thought unnecessary to conceal fraudulent practices" or the facts from him, since his position was (he thought) "undervalued," Grant acquired a cache of information about sugar cultivation that few Londoners possessed. His rule of judging plantation success was "by the produce": "Till I see fruits, I am diffident," he was fond of announcing, and success in production he usually attributed to the site, soil, and climate. He was constantly on the lookout for estates with better soil and greater access to fresh, running water. When he found them, he was quick to move his slaves and works to take advantage of the more felicitous

18. £18,000 in 1772 amounts to £1,048,548 or $1,559,490. Voyages in Shipping Database, sub June 14, 17, 1762; and Author's Correspondence, John J. McCusker to David J. Hancock, May 7, 1992. An average-sized ship of 150 registered tons could carry 6,600 hundredweight of sugar. Accounts of the Boyds carrying their own produce on their own ships are recorded in T 1/340/86–92: 1749–50.

19. £20,000 in 1766–71 amounts to £1,341,527 or $1,995,360 in 1994. Grant's rate of return is calculated in Appendix IV. Cf. Stein, *French Sugar Business*, pp. 84–85 (5–6%). On the dependence on estate revenue, see GD 248/50/3/5/x: Sir Alexander Grant to James Grant, January 1772; and John Boyd, Jr., to Sir Robert Murray Keith, 1778–80, Add. Mss. 35516–18, BL.

20. James Stirling to Patrick Stirling, September 29, 1767, T-St.K 11/2/64, SRA-Glasgow, Glasgow; Alexander Douglass, March 21, 1766, Stapleton-Cotton Mss. 20 (iii), Department of Manuscripts, University College of North Wales, Bangor; and Anon., "Review" of *American Husbandry*, in *The Monthly Review or Literary Journal*, v. 54 (1776).

situation. Managers he could handle, largely by dismissing them, but nature could only be patiently withstood; it was all the more imperative, then, to understand fully the natural resources one was dealing with.[21]

Secondly, plantations needed investments in facilities, slaves, and technologies. Keenly aware that there was never "so great a pickpocket" as an underequipped Caribbean estate, Grant strove to increase the productivity of his plantations by expanding and enhancing their facilities, showering upon them "constant circumspection and economy." He ordered his superintendent to erect "plain convenient buildings of every kind," although he was quick to admonish him that these be "nothing ornamental."[22] With a buildup in facilities went an increase in laborers and, throughout the 1760s and early 1770s, he approved the addition of approximately twenty to thirty new slaves on each plantation each year to replace those who had died or become infirm.[23] Likewise, until his death, he adapted old and sought out new technologies, such as the two steam engines he installed on Albion and Eden in 1767. Grant was especially keen on introducing new ways of harnessing water and steam to the task of planting, at various times in the last years of his life instructing his overseers to adopt (a) the Hispaniola technique of overflowing level land, (b) the Bristol and Edinburgh technique of using a fire engine to raise water for turning a waterwheel mill, (c) the Antigua technique, advocated by Samuel Martin, the writer on plantership, of using seawater in the fermentation cisterns for making rum, (d) the Windward Islands technique of managing the blast with a lime concoction, and (e) a new technique for claying sugar.[24]

The third key element in making money in American planting was finding competent and trustworthy people to man and supervise the operations. This factor was one of the most important. It was difficult to find competent, honest, energetic employees who would not leave to

21. Sir Alexander Grant to Peter Davidson, September 20, 1770, Sir Alexander Grant Letter Book, Grant Papers, Tomintoul House.
22. Sir Alexander Grant to John Gordon, October 18, 1769, and Sir Alexander Grant to John Grant, December 22, 1770, Sir Alexander Grant Letter Book, Grant Papers, Tomintoul House. On refurbishment, see J. Johnston, "The Stapleton Sugar Plantations in the Leeward Islands," *Bulletin of the John Rylands Library*, v. 48 (1965), pp. 192–96.
23. Sir Alexander Grant to John Gordon, March 12, 1771, Sir Alexander Grant Letter Book, Grant Papers, Tomintoul House.
24. Sir Alexander Grant to John Grant, October 14, 1771, Sir Alexander Grant Letter Book, Tomintoul House. The introduction of the steam engine is mentioned in Books of the Committee of Colonies and Trade, v. B, nos. 29, 31, Royal Society of Arts, London; and John Stewart, *A Description of a Machine or Invention to Work Mills, by the Power of a Fire Engine, But Particularly Useful and Profitable in Grinding Sugar Canes* (London, 1767). On productivity increases through technical changes, generally, see Paul David, *Technical Choice, Innovation, and Economic Growth* (New York, 1975), pp. 174–91.

take advantage of the opportunities that the New World offered them. Absentee planters like the associates sought such people among their extended families and their employees from previous operations. For example, throughout the 1760s, when Grant was transforming the production capacity of his plantations, he relied primarily on one particularly dynamic manager – his cousin Alexander Grant of Achoynanie – whose "local & circumstantial experience" made him a "far better judge . . . on the spot" of the merchant's technology-driven schemes for economies.[25] To induce fidelity and service, he fed and housed his laborers and managers well, but the primary bond was his prior relationships with them. Grant's partner Oswald similarly drew upon his network of skilled workers around the world. Typically, after he sold an African trading vessel in 1770, he placed its captain as an overseer on one of his plantations.[26] He also drew upon the networks of other men whose interests he had nurtured. When Oswald desired German or Dutch workers for his Florida plantations, he called upon correspondents in Cassel and Amsterdam. When he wanted Italian settlers, he wrote to Francis Levett, a merchant in Leghorn, Italy, who was the brother of the associate John Levett. When he wanted Chinese laborers for his estates, he approached John Levett in India, who had already imported some Chinese into Bengal to man his arrack distillery.[27] Less satisfactorily, on the rare occasion when his own or his friends' networks failed him, Oswald tapped into the remarkable flow of potential emigrants in London and the provinces. When he wanted to hire skilled workmen for Florida in the autumn of 1768, he contacted a former employee in Aberdeen, had one of his partners in a Scottish woolen factory place announcements at the market crosses at Kilmarnock and Beith, and had a nephew run advertisements in the Glasgow and Edinburgh papers.[28]

25. Sir Alexander Grant to Peter Davidson, November 27, 1765, May 24, 1766, November 27, 1765, Court of Error Records, 1B/11/1/4/188–87, 198–97, Jamaica Archives; and Sir Alexander Grant to Peter Davidson, May 3, 1770, Sir Alexander Grant to John Grant, October 13, 1771, Grant Papers, Tomintoul House. In Achoynanie's absence from Jamaica in 1766–71, he forged similar bonds with Peter Davidson, John Gordon, and John Grant. Compare the pay of one "doer" (£300 per year) with that of a deputy-assistant commissary in the army (£365). Hamish Little, "The Emergence of a Commissariat during the Seven Years' War in Germany," *Journal of the Society for Army Historical Research*, v. 61 (1983/84), p. 209.
26. Richard Oswald to Governor Grant, July 27, 1770, BCM 295.
27. John Wilson to Richard Oswald, December 9, 1768, Oswald Papers, Sudlows; *Glasgow Journal*, December 15, 29, 1768; GD 345/1170/1766: Sir Alexander Grant to Sir Archibald Grant, October 27, 1766; BCM 470: Richard Oswald to Governor Grant, May 3, 1764; and John Levett to Richard Oswald, December 10, 1772, Herries Papers, Spottes.
28. The recruitment of whites appears in Robert Selby to Richard Oswald, October 2, 1768, John Wilson Jr. to Richard Oswald, December 9, 1768, Oswald Papers, Sudlows; *Glasgow Journal*, December 15, 29, 1768; *Caledonian Mercury*, January 11, 1769; and Richard Oswald to Governor Grant, September 18, 1768 (postscript), BCM 295.

Maintaining the quality of the supervision of American plantations extended beyond finding managers and laborers to comprehend their relationship with fellow planters, partners, correspondents, and contacts. Here, too, the associates employed their tried and true methods of putting together groups of prior acquaintance, relying on the network of friends and correspondents they had already developed in other areas of business. Many erstwhile West Indians banded together to pursue plantation schemes in the Ceded Islands. Oswald brought many more "old acquaintances" together to settle East Florida, where society, according to one grantee, was "as agreeable as could be wish'd."[29] Some grantees had shared experiences in the West Indies; others had served in or worked for the British army in Germany during the Seven Years' War, and at least a dozen had worked in Oswald's bread magazines there.[30] Still others were bound by business, and the importance of this bond grew as planting progressed. On the American side of the Atlantic, former commercial ties also facilitated the progress of settlement. Oswald's established correspondent relations in Charleston (Henry Laurens) and Savannah (John Graham) helped him supervise and supply his plantations, and appoint new workers.

Lastly, the associates exploited their capabilities in international shipping and trading to further their planting schemes. Grant added new stops along his ships' Caribbean circuit to incorporate his new Jamaican plantations. When he bought estates in the easternmost Jamaican parish of St. Thomas in the East, he commanded the captain of the *Elizabeth* to stop there regularly and to load the produce of his estates. Likewise, when Oswald needed a ship to carry settlers to Florida in 1769 and to shuttle between St. Augustine and Sierra Leone with supplies of slaves, he commandeered the *Charlotte*, a vessel he had previously used to carry coal and lime between Ayr and northern Ireland. It was Oswald's desire that "she shall be at their [the planters'] service in any shape they please," in "a constant employ in their Trade to Africa & Britain."[31] The associates deployed the same array of goods and workers in

---

29. William Makdougall to George Makdougall, September 1, 1771, Scott of Gala Muniments, Box 3, Bundle 1, Gala House, Galashiels.
30. To this personal dimension, the experience of wartime contracting added an equally important psychological dimension. The management of assets and the handling of amounts on a scale previously unknown, the experimentation of new ways of arranging and moving goods and services, the movement into new lands and markets, and the unavoidable frustration – all worked to break down existing mental barriers to large-scale global enterprise.
31. Richard Oswald to Governor Grant, September 18, 1768, BCM 295. For a similar scheme devised two years before, see Richard Oswald to Governor Grant, February 12, 1766, BCM 295.

developing plantations as they did in their other commercial ventures. If they desired supplies, they could direct a ship from London or any of her outports. Timely delivery was more likely because they were already in the position to know about such needs, as they were in the business of providing plantation goods as general commission merchants. If they wanted slaves, they could send a ship to the factory in Sierra Leone where, as we will see in the following chapter, they possessed a fully developed slaving entrepôt.

"A Mosquito's Bite"

The associates' Florida estates provide an intriguing case study in American planting. Their projects there, particularly Oswald's, produced a greater amount of correspondence and accounts than have survived from their Caribbean ventures. As a result, despite the fact that the Florida project was ultimately a failure, as were most plantation projects in that colony, it is revealing about the way the associates integrated backward into agricultural production, by matching crops to soil and climate, investing in plant, slaves, and equipment, finding competent, trustworthy managers, and linking their several businesses.

The idea of settling Britain's newly conquered lands in North America and the Caribbean after the war was first broached in Oswald's bread magazine at Cassel, Germany, during an inebriated late-night conversation between Oswald and Colonel Thomas Pownall, the former Governor of Massachusetts and the brother of the Secretary of the Board of Trade. Returning to London with his purse bulging from contract payments, and his appetite for building "a town in his closet" whetted by Pownall's descriptions, Oswald plunged. The range of possible investments in America was quite wide. With Pownall, Oswald had specifically discussed the settlement of the Ceded Islands – Dominica, St. Vincent, the Grenadines, Grenada, and Tobago. But after the war, he set his sights northward, having come to the conclusion that a man who was able to buy land should not "risk his life and fortune to purchase in a sickly island when there is a great choice of valuable land at North America to be had for small consideration."[32] Nova Scotia seemed a safer place to reap rewards. With Pownall, Oswald joined an impressive cadre of planters who shared his hopes of settling the colony; but, eventually, he found their attempts "a little confused" and began to

---

32. GD 345/1169/1764: Duncan Grant to Sir Archibald Grant, September 20, 1764; and Robert Grant to Governor Grant, April 20, 1767, BCM 413.

look elsewhere for a place to plant.[33] It took little time. In the spring of 1764, Oswald was working to establish "a Farm plantation & Vineyard" in the backcountry of South Carolina; by the fall of 1765, he was holding a grant to 8,000 acres on Hard Labor Creek, in Granville County, roughly 150 miles inland from Charleston. But this project, too, soon died, and he relinquished his claim in early 1768, having done nothing by way of agricultural improvement. He was looking for a "blank page," and Carolina (even the backcountry) was not that.[34]

The project he finally selected was what he playfully described as his "Mosquito's Bite" – a 20,000-acre "scratch" of land that he had been granted in July 1764 along the east coast of Florida, 250 miles south of Charleston and 45 miles south of St. Augustine.[35] Florida captured Oswald's imagination in a way that the Ceded Islands, Nova Scotia, and South Carolina had not. Idealizing metaphors tumbled forth from his pen whenever he sat down to write about the possibilities for Florida planting. It was a "Paradise," a "New Canaan," a "desert in bloom" in the New World. How and why Oswald was first drawn to planting a country that was "by no means known" is not exactly clear, since Oswald was no pioneer: generally, he and the other associates moved into a region after it was clear that planting would succeed. But the

---

33. Contemporary descriptions of Nova Scotia appear in: Narrative (1755), Inglis Papers, Flourish Walls, near Greenlaw; CO 217/18/245: 1762; and CO 217/21/II/388–91: 1765. The Nova Scotia group included a former Governor (Pownall), the royal cartographer (Mitchell), an M.P. (Jackson), an M.P. and Paymaster of the Marines (Tucker), and a Judge of the Marshalsea who was a cousin of Michael Herries (Blackburne). On the proposal and grant, see CO 217/20/II/238, and CO 217/20/ MPG 290: December 23, 1763; Ontario, Ottawa, Public Archives of Canada, H3/220/ Charlotte, 1763; and *Acts of the Privy Council, Colonial*, v. 4, p. 816, v. 6, p. 368. Tucker and Blackburne were also excluded from the warrant's list of grantees, replaced by Thomas Thoroton, the brother-in-law and secretary of the Marquis of Granby and a cousin of Michael Herries. The stated aim of the settlement was to promote "the protection of Hemp, Naval Stores, and other Important Articles of Commerce" and, since it was to be near the border, "to prevent the outlaws of neighboring colonies sheltering themselves from the Hands of Justice." Oswald's change of heart is chronicled in Richard Oswald to Governor Grant, July 27, 1764, BCM 295.
34. Henry Laurens to Richard Oswald, July 7, 1764, in *The Papers of Henry Laurens*, v. 4, pp. 331–33. An account of the Hard Labor Creek grant is found in Henry Laurens to Rossel and Gervais, September 4, 1764, Henry Laurens to Richard Oswald, October 10, 1764, in *The Papers of Henry Laurens*, v. 4, pp. 395–96, 426–68, and v. 5, p. 34, n. 6. The grants occurred not in 1764, as the editors of *The Papers of Henry Laurens* state, but in 1765. By providing security for Oswald, Laurens became Oswald's partner. Laurens successfully petitioned the Governor and Council for a regrant of the 8,000 acres. Henry Laurens to Richard Oswald, August 12, 1766, Grant, April 29, 1768, Petition, February 3, 1768, *The Papers of Henry Laurens*, v. 5, pp. 155–60, 670, 581–83.
35. *Acts*, v. 4, p. 814.

"good reports" he heard about this territory in early 1764 meshed with his planting aspirations: he believed he could make money by establishing a plantation and reselling it in five or seven years; and it gave him an opportunity to conduct experiments and promote improvements that would satisfy his love of new techniques.

Oswald had to move quickly, for the settlement of Florida proceeded at a brisk pace. George III opened up the land to settlers on October 7, 1763, and appointed Colonel James Grant its Governor the following day. Public advertisements requesting private applications to the Board of Trade soon appeared in metropolitan, regional, and colonial newspapers and magazines. Eventually, the settlement of Florida came to dwarf all other contemporaneous plantation schemes in the number of acres granted.[36] In addition to establishing his own plantations, Oswald was the single most important force in putting and keeping together a Florida planter group.[37] He "plumped" for the colony by getting friends and acquaintances to become grantees, by supplying them with material assistance, and by providing them with moral support once they were bitten by the Florida bug.

As an impresario, Oswald made his greatest contribution in attracting planters. Of the 286 Privy Council orders authorizing survey of plantation lands, 62 (22%) went to men whom Oswald had known before 1763 in his capacity as commission merchant, army contractor, or Scots expatriate. To friends and strangers alike, he boasted that "no people in the world" live "more comfortably than the people in America." Oswald described the country in compelling terms to all who would listen. With a pitch combining uncharacteristic hyperbole with commonsense argument, he gathered together a group of grantees remarkable

36. *Gentleman's Magazine*, v. 33 (1763), p. 518; *Scot's Magazine*, v. 25 (1763), p. 627; *The Edinburgh Advertiser*, January 6, 1764; T 1/436/6/39–48; and Charles L. Mowat, "The First Campaign of Publicity for Florida," *The Mississippi Valley Historical Review*, v. 30 (1943), pp. 359–76. Much of the information about Florida prospects was spread by word of mouth. Oswald's factor John Maxwell, for instance, was approached by a farmer who had "some thoughts of going to settle with his family in America or the West Indies" and asked for information concerning "what Encouragement is proposed to such." Since Maxwell had only the vaguest idea, he wrote to his landlord in London for details as to "How can one be informed of these findings, for I can't find it in our magazines." John Maxwell to William Johnstone, February 13, 1764, Pulteney Papers, PU 1,535, Huntington Library, San Marino. For the Governor's plan, see Governor Grant to Lord Hillsborough, before June 1, 1764, in Grant, *James Grant*, pp. 72–74; and George Douglass to John Hussey Delaval, June 6, 1771, Delaval Papers, 2DE/ 4/7/42, Northumberland Record Office, Newcastle. Nearly 2.9 million acres in East Florida were granted, in contrast to 2.1 million acres in Quebec, Nova Scotia, West Florida, and New York.

37. See Governor Grant's high estimation of Oswald in CO 5/549/77–78: Governor Grant to Earl of Hillsborough, March 12, 1768.

for its "note and ability."[38] Military and contracting contacts formed the core. Such men, he believed, were well equipped to cope with the social dislocation of new communities; they were used to dealing with unknown peoples and regions; and their skills could be put to good use in taming a wilderness. With military men among the planters, there "would be still a greater degree of Security in a New Settlement." Merchants, too, shared many of the same qualities, and Oswald called on others like himself, especially those who possessed an army experience and an international clientele, to settle estates in Florida's hinterland.[39]

Oswald also used his position as a commission merchant to assist operations in the new colony. To other planters, he recommended surveyors, overseers, and skilled laborers. Because he was in the business of supplying American planters with provisions, Oswald was able to send what the Florida estates needed, often before the planters knew that they needed it. Their greatest need was manpower, especially slaves, and among the grantees Oswald was the only slave trader. By 1770, he had sent three ships laden with slave cargo from his slave factory in Sierra Leone to East Florida. In the metropolis, he received planters' crops, chiefly indigo, and handled their sale.[40]

Oswald also provided moral support to the planters. Known as "the Oracle" of "the East Florida Society," an informal drinking, discussion, and information group of Florida investors who met at the Shakespeare's Head in the West End of the City to discuss mutual planting concerns, Oswald gave freely to its members, in order to keep them "in good humour" and "to inspire better hopes." In an informal setting, whether coffeehouse, counting-house, or townhouse, Oswald did what he could "to spirit on those who had taken up the Idea" of planting,

38. Simmons and Thomas, eds., *Proceedings and Debates of the British Parliaments*, v. 2, p. 275 (February 17, 1766); and Doctor William Stork to Governor Grant, July 8, 1766, BCM 243.
39. Richard Oswald to Governor Grant, February 19, 1768, BCM 295. In addition to officers and contractors, Scots with some prior connection to Oswald figured prominently. To some, it appeared that the project would "be in a great measure a Scottish colony." GD 345/1170/1766: Sir Alexander Grant to Sir Archibald Grant, October 27, 1766; John Bowman Jr. to Richard Oswald, November 5, 13, 1768, Oswald Papers, EUL; and Richard Oswald to Governor Grant, January 28, 29, 1769, BCM 295.
40. Governor Grant to Earl of Hillsborough, January 6, 1771, BCM Bound Letter Book 1766–1771. For discussion of Oswald's previous work as a colony slaver, see Shipping Database; Richard Oswald to Governor Grant, March 15, April 8, May 20, 1767, April 4, 1770, Richard Oswald to Captain Richard Savery, May 25, 1767, BCM 295; List of Negroes, May 13, 1770, BCM 305; Earl of Egmont to Richard Oswald, July 21, 1770, Richard Oswald to Governor Grant, June 8, 1770, BCM 295; and Robert Grant to Governor Grant, August 6, 1772, BCM 661.

encouraging the disheartened and reviving flagging energies with practical observations about the possibilities for agricultural improvement.[41]

As a grantee, Oswald wasted no time in pursuing his own project. In early May 1764, he devised an extensive plan of settlement, proposing a joint plantation venture with Governor Grant and outlining the expected stages of development in a lengthy memorandum; several months later, in early July, he was the third to file a request for land with the Privy Council; and, within ten days, he received an authorization to proceed with a survey of 20,000 acres. The Governor arrived in the colony in late August 1764 and, after two unsuccessful attempts, succeeded in fixing the boundaries of his and Oswald's settlement.[42]

The 20,000 acres were located in the wedge formed by the confluence of the Halifax River and the Timoka Creek, approximately forty-five miles south of St. Augustine, a land generally referred to as "the Mosquitoes" after the nearby Mosquito Inlet (now, the Ponce de Leon Inlet) which opened onto the Atlantic (Illustration 5.1). Oswald divided the grant into five settlements and focused his attention on the Mount Oswald Settlement, at the northernmost tip of the grant. His slaves cleared 400 acres, a quarter of which were river swamp dammed "with large and sufficient banks, drains, floodgates, &c.," and then readied them for indigo. Above the marsh, they raised a superintendent's dwelling

41. Governor Grant to James Grant, July 20, 1767, June 17, 1768, BCM Bound Letter Book 1766–177. The makeup of the East Florida Society appears in Rogers, "East Florida Society," pp. 479–96. Rogers unfortunately does not discuss the work of the society. For its activities, see BCM 474: Lord Adam Gordon to Governor Grant, February 14, 1767; BCM 295: Richard Oswald to Governor Grant, March 15, 1767, April 3, 1769; GD 345/1171/1/125: Sir Alexander Grant to Sir Archibald Grant, December 5, 1767. On Oswald's role as moral supporter, see Richard Oswald to Governor Grant, June 9, 1766, September 18, 1768, BCM 295; Peter Taylor to Governor Grant, July 23, 1766, BCM 491; GD 345/1171/1768: Sir Alexander Grant to Sir Archibald Grant, January 16, 1767; and Governor Grant to Richard Oswald, ca. June 17, 1768, BCM Bound Letter Book 1766–71. For an instance of Oswald giving advice to an Ayr neighbor, see Earl of Cassilis to Governor Grant, April 8, 1769, BCM 412. Cf. GD 345/5/15x: Richard Oswald to Robert Innes, November 1, 1767. Sir Alexander Grant served much the same function, moving grants for kin through the bureaucratic machine and assisting the lobbying work of the Florida Society during his tenure as M.P. GD 345/1171/2/88, 86: Sir Alexander Grant to Sir Archibald Grant, April 14, May 14, 1767. See also Richard Oswald to Governor Grant, June 24, 1770, BCM 295.

42. Richard Oswald, "Sketch of a Plan," May 3, 1764, BCM 517; Richard Oswald to Governor Grant, May 3, 1764, Richard Oswald, "Sketch of a Plan," May 5, 1764, BCM 470; and Sir Alexander Grant to Governor Grant, February 1, 1769, BCM 502. For Oswald's problems with the survey, see Governor Grant to Henry Laurens, November 18, 1764, BCM Bound Letter Book 1764–66. The completion of the survey is mentioned in a letter from Grant to Oswald, dated February 12, 1765, in BCM Bound Letter Book 1764–1766. The land was set by Grant and surveyed by Rossel.

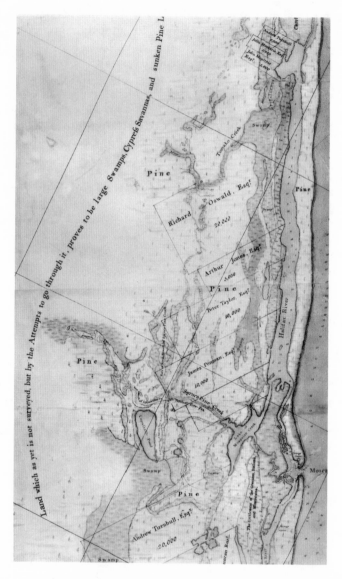

Illustration 5.1 A Map of Florida grants, from Timoka Basin to the Mosquito Inlet. *From*: William G. DeBrahm's "Plan of Part of the Coast of East Florida" (1769). *Courtesy*: Map Library, British Library, London.

house (40′ × 20′) that was "framed, & weather-boarded, shingled & glazed," an overseer's house (20′ × 16′), a kitchen, a large barn (60′ × 30′), a corn warehouse, a stable, and other outbuildings.[43] Toward the end of the decade, they built a string of lesser settlements. The Ferry Settlement, four miles south of Mount Oswald along Timoka Creek, complete with a ferry house, blacksmith's shop, overseer's house, slave huts, and barn, supplied provision corn for the plantation, and grew indigo for export. The Adia Settlement's 100 acres of cleared land farther south was a smaller version of the Ferry Settlement. Cowpens Settlement served as "a small clearing for cattle" and a breeding ground for livestock. But it was on the fifth settlement, ominously called "Swamp," that Oswald expended his greatest energies, for it was at Swamp that he processed sugar. Here, in 1770, he erected a single-story overseer's house "built of very good materials and good workmanship," grain and sugar warehouses, a distillery, and a mill; he cleared 300 acres on the high, relatively dry ground between the Halifax and the Timoka; and he planted them with cane.

Despite the excitement, the Florida planting experiment failed. Oswald's grant was a bog, useless for anything but "indifferent" indigo or rice; and East Florida was, for Oswald and most planters, a swamp of an investment. By the time of the peace negotiations of 1782, while conferring with Laurens and Franklin, Oswald's characteristic understatement took on a tone of bitterness: East Florida was "a more tempting Country than it really is."[44] Oswald and others witnessed (indeed, tolerated) one loss after another. Only 6 percent of the original Privy Council orders authorizing survey were processed and planted, comprising 1 percent of Florida territory. Apart from Governor Grant and perhaps one or two other planters, no large-scale grantee made a profit. Until 1770, the colony sent next to nothing to market. While the customs records for the port of St. Augustine stop in 1769, the papers of Florida landowners suggest that, after that date, little was exported but the produce of one or two plantations. Individual undertakings were a profound disappointment. The Earl of Egmont's estate on Amelia Island cost him £12,000 but brought him nothing. While perhaps the most dramatic, Egmont's loss was mirrored by that of many other Florida grantees. Laurens had been saying it for a long time: East Florida was

---

43. The various settlements erected on Oswald's 20,000 acres are sketched in detail in the depositions exhibited by the East Florida Loyalist Claims Commission in 1784–86. They are reproduced in Wilbur H. Siebert, ed., *Loyalists in East Florida, 1774 to 1785*, v. 2 (Deland, FL, 1929), pp. 54–61.
44. Richard Oswald to James Brown, February 14, 1774, Oswald Papers, Sudlows; and Shelburne Papers, September 11, 1782 (boundaries enclosure), Clements Library, Ann Arbor.

"a Paradise from whose Bourn no Money e'er returns." During the American Revolution, the grantees' properties fell to enemy hands, employees deserted, and slaves rebelled. Independence and the return of Florida to Spain settled the matter.[45]

Historians have identified three systemic causes for the failure of the foray of Britons and Americans into Florida: the poor soil and climate, the lack of infrastructure, and the pervasive use of slaves. Florida's soil was not suited for the grandiose schemes sketched by the planters. A giant spit of oolitic limestone, sand, clay, and muck, the Florida peninsula paled in comparison to the rich agricultural soil to the north. The average elevation of Florida was only 100 feet above sea level, so planters continually faced problems of poor drainage and chronic inundation from springs, swamps, and the high tides that accompanied the hurricanes that swept over the coastal lowlands in late summer and early fall. Its bogs defied even the efforts of confirmed ditchers, drainers, and dikers like Oswald. Florida's soil, ever wet, could not produce sugar the likes of which had made Jamaica "a mine"; nor could it produce indigo of sufficient quality to compete with the product of the French colonies or even South Carolina. If the soil had been better, most of the young colony's other problems would have been "obstacles to overcome," rather than "reasons for failure." But Florida was a swamp.[46]

Compounding "the nature of the climate & the soil" was a second problem – a want of infrastructure. The absence of basic facilities necessary for the growth and functioning of a productive plantation economy frustrated the progress of settlement. Two years into the project, it was clear to Laurens that little progress would ever be made "for want of Neighbours, Navigation & Markets convenient either for disposing . . . of your produce, as well as the distance from the eye & attention of faithful friends." A population of 100 white families, scattered over

---

45. Bailyn, *Voyagers*, p. 469 and n. 50, relies too heavily on the Governor's assertion that Mount Oswald was showing a profit. In fact, before the war, Oswald in London received only twenty-five pounds of indigo from his agent Fairlamb. Richard Oswald to Governor Grant, November 7, 1770, BCM 295. Cf. James Laurens to Richard Oswald, January 24, 1772, Laurens Papers, South Carolina Historical Society, Charleston. On Egmont's case, see Trustees of the Earl of Egmont to Governor Grant, February 27, 1771, BCM 522; William Makdougall to George Makdougall, September 1, 1771, Scott of Gala Muniments, Box 3, Bundle 1, Gala House, Galashiels; State of the Adventure, March 8, 1774, Callendar Papers, Argyll Muniments, Inveraray Castle, Inveraray; Richard Oswald to Governor Grant, June 24, 1770, BCM 295; and Henry Laurens to Richard Oswald, May 28, 1771, *The Papers of Henry Laurens*, v. 7, p. 501.

46. Charles Bernard to Earl of Moira, June 18, 1768, HM 9565, ff. 13–42, Huntington Library, San Marino; Richard Oswald to Governor Grant, February 19, September 18, 1768, April 4, 1770, BCM 295; GD 1/32/38/2: John Farquharson to Sir Archibald Grant, May 1, 1771; James Anderson to Richard Oswald, March 8, 1776, Oswald Letter Book, v. 2, ff. 133–34, SRO; and Bailyn, *Voyagers*, p. 471.

3,750 square miles, and served by one town (St. Augustine), a shallow and treacherous harbor, and Indian trails (after ten years, only two "King's" roads) was insufficient.[47]

The third factor historians have identified as inhibiting the Florida experiment emanated from "the necessary character of the labor force." The imperial government in 1763 had mandated the settlement of free white Protestants in Florida, but this approach turned out to be unrealistic. "The situation, environmental and legal," was "not conducive to the recruitment of a population of free householders," because free white Protestants could not be forced to perform needed work in the same way that chattel slaves could. Denys Rolle's Rollestown and Andrew Turnbull's New Smyrna are dramatic evidence of this fact. Rollestown and New Smyrna are extreme examples, where the planters shared the Government's vision of virtuous, free, white husbandmen and actively strove to implement it, giving up only late in the day. Oswald believed that it was wise to give "these People a part of the Land," sending them out "successively, upon Wages, for the term of 3 years" and, "after their time is out" finding them money to buy several slaves and settling them "on their own acct, either upon my own land or in the neighborhood of it where they can have it."[48] But even with such lucrative terms, he was forced to explain to the Governor, "the People" in Scotland "have all employmt, & are not so fond of going abroad as formerly."[49]

More commonly, planters like Oswald almost immediately introduced black slavery, and paid only "lip service" to the Government's mandates

47. Henry Laurens to Richard Oswald, August 12, 1766, *The Papers of Henry Laurens*, v. 5, p. 156.
48. Richard Oswald to Governor Grant, March 15, 1767, BCM 295. Such sentiments were apparently shared by the Governor, for the previous year James Grant had written that "Africans are the only people to go to work with in a warm climate." Governor Grant to Richard Oswald, August 31, 1766, BCM Bound Letter Book 1764–66. For different incentives offered to whites, see GD 25/9/27/1/1: Dr. William Stork to Earl of Cassilis, June 13, 1767; and John Callendar to Alexander Bald, October 11, 21, 28, 1766, Callendar Papers, Argyll Muniments, Inveraray Castle, Inveraray. Callendar offered a four-year wage contract and fifty acres at the end of the term to "a young, Clever Plowman"; to "husbandmen," he agreed to pay wages for seven years and provide fifty acres free of charge for seven years, at the end of which they would have to pay him the value of one-third of the seven years' produce.
49. On Oswald's white laborers, see Governor Grant to Richard Oswald, November 7, 1767, BCM Bound Letter Book; Richard Oswald to Governor Grant, February 19, 1768, BCM 295; and Governor Grant to Richard Oswald, March 20, 1770, BCM Bound Letter Book 1766–771. Although Scots, especially Glaswegians, were highly prized as adventurers, they were a burden as laborers. Richard Oswald to Governor Grant, January 29, 1769, BCM 295; and GD 1/32/38/12: John Farquharson to Sir Archibald Grant, May 1, 1771. On the particular "laziness of an American born," see Richard Oswald to Governor Grant, August 5, 1768, BCM 295. For similar estimations of Scots, see James Montgomery to John Mackenzie, April 14, 1770, Delvine Collection, Montgomery Papers, Ms. 1,399/20–21, NLS.

on race. The first people Oswald actually placed on the land were forty black slaves whom he bought in the Charleston market. He experienced no serious difficulties in procuring black slaves, since he could draw on Henry Laurens, one of Charleston's largest slave middlemen, and commandeer slaves from his own slave factory in West Africa. By 1780, he was told by an overseer, there were as many as 230 slaves at work at Mount Oswald, most of whom had come from the factory.[50] Most planters recognized the need for slaves, since "the obligation of introducing such a number of White People" was "a great discouragement, & to most People an absolute Bar." Even Oswald, who, with his German and Dutch commercial and military connections, was better placed than most grantees to tap the outward flow of European emigrants, peopled his estates with unskilled labor of African origin. Since there was no practical barrier to using black labor, economic reality prevailed over legal nicety.[51]

Oswald's experiences as an East Florida planter shed light on these three explanations for failure, confirming the poverty of the soil and climate and the lack of infrastructure, while casting the manpower problem in a somewhat different light, and adding a fourth reason to the list – conflicting impulses. One first glimpses the problems that afflicted the scheme in Oswald's inability to select a suitable crop for cultivation in Florida's soil and conditions. Here the blame rests squarely on the shoulders of the planter. Like nearly all the Florida planters, Oswald could not decide what to plant, nor would he stick with a crop long enough to make it pay. Under his original joint venture scheme, he vehemently rejected Laurens's idea of planting rice, thinking it was the wrong crop for a virtuous farmer to cultivate and preferring cotton and

50. Bailyn, *Voyagers*, p. 451; Richard Oswald to Governor Grant, May 5, 1764, BCM 470; *South Carolina Gazette*, February 25, 1765; Account, April 20, 1765, BCM 359. For later talk of Oswald "bringing Slaves from the Coast of Guinea" and "sending out some Palatines," see Governor Grant to Henry Laurens, August 31, 1766, BCM Bound Letter Book 1764–66. By 1771, there were 120 slaves at Mount Oswald. Felix Worley to Richard Oswald, September 21, 1771, Laurens Papers, South Carolina Historical Society, Charleston; Richard Oswald to Governor Grant, May 20, 1767, February 1, 1769, BCM 295. The first load of 103 slaves from Bance Island arrived in St. Augustine in September 1767 on the *St. Augustine Packet*. The only difficulty Oswald encountered was that the slave factory's contract with the French slaving society prevented him from taking slaves directly, since the factory's prime slaves were promised to the Society. The 1780 levels are recorded in Siebert, ed., *Loyalists*, v. 2, p. 58.
51. Sir Alexander Grant to Governor Grant, June 19, 1767, BCM 344. The best discussion of Florida labor appears in Bailyn, *Voyagers*, pp. 471–72. Bailyn thinks that bad soil is "not sufficient to explain" the disaster and that labor is "the decisive factor." But Bailyn explains only that it was not attractive to thousands of settlers seeking employment or land and that Florida could only be tilled by slave labor. From a different angle, I explain why it was not attractive to planters and why it was a failure from a business standpoint.

sugar, before acquiescing in Governor Grant's desire to cultivate indigo. After his partnership with Grant was dissolved, any semblance of a focused, coordinated crop program vanished. Oswald had never been interested in indigo and, perhaps on the suggestion of Laurens, he shifted his attentions among grapes, figs, cotton, and sugar. No one crop ever gave structure to Oswald's operations in Florida.[52]

When he returned to his original idea of growing sugar, the merchant took sides in a rivalry that was dividing the absentee planters in London – a contest between "Grant College," the indigo producers, and "Muskettoe University," the sugar producers. Spurred on by the Governor's own candid admissions that sugar was turning out well and other accounts reporting indigo "indifferent," Oswald resolved "to go vigorously" into sugar so as to one day "vye with the West Indies in that Article."[53] Oswald's selection of sugar was an academic, metropolitan exercise, and his sugar-works were little more than a laboratory for European improvement, well-equipped with the latest technical apparatus and informed by the latest technical knowledge, much like his hothouse in Scotland. Indeed, the two structures were physically linked, since Oswald grew sugar in his hothouse and sent its seedlings to Florida, where he devoted the Swamp settlement to their cultivation. From Jamaica, he brought an expert in sugar cultivation to supervise the planting. In 1775, he adopted a new French method for cutting sugar that had been successfully tried in New Orleans, and he erected a grinding mill according to the latest design.[54]

The mill was as much a miscalculation as the sugar it ground, since

52. Richard Oswald Governor Grant, July 25, 1764, BCM 295; Governor Grant to Richard Oswald, February 12, 1765, BCM Bound Letter Book 1764–66; Richard Oswald to Governor Grant, February 24, 1766, BCM 295; Henry Laurens to Richard Oswald, October 10, 1764, *The Papers of Henry Laurens*, v. 4, pp. 462–67; and Richard Oswald to Governor Grant, June 14, 1766, BCM 295. Many planters' inability to stick with a crop for a viable period was noted by William Makdougall in 1771. William Makdougall to George Makdougall, September 1, 1771, Scott of Gala Muniments, Box 3, Bundle 1, Gala House, Galashiels. On the variety of crops purportedly grown in Florida, see Mowat, "The First Campaign," pp. 360–63; and [Alexander Cluny,] *The American Traveller* (London, 1764), pp. 105–08. Similar to the inability to choose a crop was the misapprehension of models for labor. Confusion arose from the fact that most grantees assumed West Indian practice, which required younger, more fit, and more numerous slaves, yet staffed their plantations with Virginia-sized labor forces of ten to thirty slaves. Richard Oswald to Governor Grant, February 29, 1768, BCM 295.
53. Governor Grant to Earl of Hillsborough, December 14, 1770, BCM Bound Letter Book 1764–71; John Tucker to Governor Grant, June 7, 1771, BCM 253; and James Penman to Governor Grant, August 11, 1771, BCM 491.
54. John Ohlson to Richard Oswald, August 24, 1774, Oswald Papers, Sudlows; and Frederick Mulcaster to Governor Grant, July 19, 1775, BCM 521. Even with the much maligned indigo, Oswald introduced the latest methods, steeping the weed at a higher temperature and liming it to a greater extent, as numerous contemporary articles and treatises advised him to do.

it produced only a small amount of sugar each day and, when used, broke the slaves' legs. Both mistakes are revealing of the error underlying the entire plantation scheme: improvement programs devised and approved in Britain were not a sure guide to success in plantation America. The Swamp Settlement, it turned out, was "too far to the Northward for a Sugar Plantation"; its poor, sandy soil prevented the cultivation of any crop there but the one that Oswald absolutely refused to plant – rice. Studying and performing experiments in an Ayrshire library and greenhouse were no ways to produce a successful Florida export crop. Despite all the sobering information he received about Florida's soil and climate, Oswald pushed ahead with his "experiments."

Oswald's planting schemes were also frustrated by a lack of infrastructure, both informational and material, and he worked to eradicate the problem. With respect to news about his plantation, this merchant who feasted on facts received a meager, unsatisfactory diet. Early reports on Florida planting by Adam Gordon, William Stork, Andrew Turnbull, and writers for the *Gentleman's Magazine* were positive, but vague. Subsequent overseers' accounts were no better. As late as May 1769, Oswald was still "pretty much in the dark"; suspense vexed him and, he believed, killed the interest of others. The planters, he explained to Governor Grant, were "fond of the notion of their foreign possessions"; they liked to talk about them and, "sometimes like us Farmers, to illustrate [them] to the utmost." Yet the planters never received accurate, detailed accounts of the lands they had been granted: reports were never sent, and remittances were "in suspense."[55]

Oswald's grant had been surveyed in late 1764, and a patent issued on the strength of the survey, yet Oswald never received a copy of either the survey or a map of the plantation.[56] In mid-1766, Henry Laurens traveled to St. Augustine to resurvey the land, but he was unable to make it to the Mosquitoes, since the only conveyance was a small pilot

55. Richard Oswald to Governor Grant, May 15, 1769, and June 24, 1770, BCM 295.
56. For a good example of the usual survey experience, consider the case of Sir Alexander, Sir Archibald, and Duncan Grant. They authorized William Stork to conduct the survey, but Stork took their money and fabricated a report. In desperation, they threw themselves on the mercy of the Governor, but he had never liked the three and only grudgingly supervised a survey of their lands on Lake Grant (now Lake George). Governor Grant to James Grant, July 20, 1767, BCM Bound Letter Book 1766–71; Sir Alexander Grant to Governor Grant, February 1, 1769, BCM 402; Governor Grant to Sir Archibald Grant, April 10, June 28, 1769, BCM Bound Letter Book 1766–71; Sir Alexander Grant to Governor Grant, July 20, August 25, 1769, and February 8, 1770, BCM 402; Sir Archibald Grant to Governor Grant, 1770, BCM 470; Map, July 1, 1770, BCM 471; and Sir Alexander Grant to Governor Grant, July 10, 1770, BCM 470. Sir Archibald's grant, which was warranted on March 22, 1768 and surveyed by DeBrahm the following May, was not signed by the Governor until April 1771. GD 345/1235.

boat packed with Oswald's slaves and overseer. A Scots engineer named James Moncrieff did manage to squeeze into the boat, visit the plantation, and make a favorable report, yet even this account did not contain the level of specificity desired by Oswald or Laurens. Oswald continually pleaded with his overseers to send frequent and full reports of every aspect of plantation life. In response to one overseer's account, which he found "very general or rather imperfect," he outlined the contents of a model report:

> Where there's a surface of 30 sqr miles, I should think a good many particulars might be furnished that would be entertaining to a party concerned, such as – the Trees & Vegetables – in the different soils, the sort of soils – proportion of each – their fitness for differt products – pasture – levels – game – fish & ca. – Oeconomie & expence of Slaves – Regulations on the managing & working them & ca.[57]

So it was that he grilled his employees with plantation questions and plagued them with requests for botanical specimens. It was Oswald's firm belief that his overseers should spend several hours each week writing him memoranda on the state of the estate. By autumn 1769, one overseer had had enough, and went so far as to beg the Governor to "stop his [Oswald's] mouth," but Grant knew it was useless. The only things that would satisfy the omnivore would be "twelve sheets of answers," plus vials of soil.[58]

A lack of reliable information about his plantations went hand-in-hand with a lack of material infrastructure. Oswald reveled in the chance "of making some new Experiments Sutable to the nature of the Climate & Soil" which the "generality of New Settlers could not venture to attempt," for he believed that the experiments would not only build a richer, more workable soil and vegetation base but also, with the additional people involved in the administration of the experiments, facilitate the flow of information. When he introduced sugar, he brought in Jamaica experts who had mastered the art of cultivating cane; when he planted corn, he sought advice from Bengal. To his Florida plantations, he brought not only new machines like a contraption for pounding rice and new animals bred for strength in swamp cultivation and resistant to swamp disease, but also experts from other colonies and countries

57. Henry Laurens to Richard Oswald, August 12, 1766, *The Papers of Henry Laurens*, v. 5, pp. 155–56; Richard Oswald to James Penman, April 18, 1769, BCM 491; and Richard Oswald to Governor Grant, May 15, 1769, BCM 295.
58. Richard Oswald to James Brown, February 14, 1774, Oswald Papers, Sudlows; James Penman to Governor Grant, October 9, 1769, BCM 491; and Richard Oswald to Governor Grant, June 24, 1770, BCM 295.

whom he could trust to report back to him. Yet, at the same time, he knew that the soil and mechanical experiments conducted by these experts would come to nought if no attention was paid to "other Circumstances of the Country," even if he was fully apprised of the outcome.[59] Since improved plantations were useless if isolated, Oswald, as well as Mill, Herries, and Grant, backed numerous public works projects in Florida: lighthouses, harbors, canals, bridges, and roads. Their most successful project – a 150-mile carriage road from Fort Barrington to St. Augustine that was funded primarily by private subscription – strove to create "an universal Communication easy in time" where before had stood only a trail that was easily flooded and completely lacking in bridges or ferries.[60]

In addition to the difficulty of isolating appropriate crops, and wanting usable infrastructure, finding reliable managers also bedeviled Oswald's planting in Florida. The traditional interpretation of the manpower issue offered by historians has focused on the choice between slaves and free yeomen, but in Oswald's case the problem of finding honest, competent managers ruined him, not the problem of securing and managing laborers. Trustworthy supervisors were difficult to find, yet the success of the operation depended on them. Oswald had hoped to rely on direct acquaintance, as usual. Contacts he made in Germany were an important source. He invited a Mr. Gessner who had worked for him for four years in Germany and now wanted a job in

59. John Tucker to Governor Grant, March 31, 1769, BCM 412; Richard Oswald to Governor Grant, May 15, 1769, BCM 295; Richard Oswald to James Brown, February 14, 1774, Oswald Papers, Sudlows; Richard Oswald to Governor Grant, February 12, June 14, 1766, BCM 295; Governor Grant to Lord Bute, Governor Grant to Lord Shelburne, January 20, 1767, BCM Bound Letter Book; Henry Laurens to Richard Oswald, October 10, 1767, Henry Laurens to Governor Grant, January 28, 1768, *The Papers of Henry Laurens*, v. 5, pp. 349, 576–77; Richard Oswald to Governor Grant, March 15, 1767, BCM 295; and Richard Oswald to Governor Grant, May 3, 1764, BCM 470.

60. On lighthouses, see Taylor, "Settling a Colony," p. 49. On harbors, see Richard Oswald to Governor Grant, May 25, 1767, BCM 295; and CO 5/544/37–42: Governor Grant to Earl of Hillsborough, August 29, 1768; T 1/476/181–82: January 30, 1770; Petition to the Earl of Hillsborough, February 9, 1770, BCM 320; Sir Archibald Grant to Governor Grant, February 9, 1770, BCM 470; Governor Grant to Richard Oswald, October 18, 1770, BCM Bound Letter Book 1770–72, 73/659; and Richard Oswald to Governor Grant, late December 1770, BCM 295. On canals and roads, see Taylor, "Settling a Colony," pp. 51–52, 93; and Richard Oswald to Governor Grant, May 15, 1769, BCM 295. The first and biggest was the road from St. Augustine to Fort Barrington (Georgia). Governor Grant to Henry Laurens, March 12, 1765, BCM Bound Letter Book 1764–66; *Glasgow Journal*, April 11, 1765; Account, BCM 471; Charles Bockelman, *The King's Road to Florida: The Stagecoach Route* (St. Augustine, 1975), pp. 12–18. Other subscription roads followed: from St. Augustine south to the Mosquito Inlet and New Smyrna, cutting through Oswald's land; and from St. Augustine to Rollestown on the St. John's River.

America. Gessner was "clever enough, active, & faithful," he spoke and wrote German, French, and English well and, best, as a European, he could be used to attract Germans "from the Northwd & back Settlements." When Gessner declined the invitation, Oswald turned to his men already in America. He delegated the responsibility for making an application of survey to his friend and correspondent John Graham of Savannah. Soon after a patent was granted, he named Governor Grant to manage lower-level appointments and on-site operations, and he asked Henry Laurens to supply provisions and laborers.[61]

At this point, Oswald's planning broke down, and he ceased to rely on known men for his planting. A string of inept overseers, whose appointments he had allowed others to make and whose backgrounds he knew but sketchily, obstructed progress. A chronology of Oswald's mishaps is instructive. His first overseer – Samuel Huey – was found by Laurens, and accompanied the Charlestonian to Florida in May 1766. But Huey was "a drunken, good for nothing fellow," unfit "for the sole management of a Plantation." The Deputy Clerk of the Florida Council visited the estate several times that fall and "put Hewie upon his guard," but all for nought. The overseer was idle and negligent, incurred extraordinary expenses, and embezzled the plantation of its provisions. While fishing one day late in the year, he drowned while plantation slaves looked on. His death was barely lamented; the loss of the two slaves who went down in the same boat was greater.[62]

Oswald hoped that Huey's successor, an American Indian named Johnson whom Laurens also hired, would "behave above the rank of common Carolinian Fugitives, to save his Scalp a whole Year." It was believed that he "must be discreet & carry a steady command," if he was to avoid a similar fate, since the blacks, who had allowed Huey to drown, "love those of their own colour least." (The Europeans believed that black slaves considered the Indians as blacks.) The Governor directed Johnson to raise provisions and plant indigo. At the same time, he placed him under the surveillance of two of Oswald's friends who had moved to Florida to supervise their own plantations. Johnson executed his job well for the first year and became "a favorite" of the

61. Richard Oswald to Governor Grant, May 3, 24, 1764, BCM 470. For the involvement of Georgia's John Graham, see Richard Oswald to John Graham, July 27, 1764, BCM 295. Oswald's problems with his survey seem mild when compared to those that plagued most other landowners.
62. "For Mr. Oswald's Plantation" and Accounts, June 22–26, 1765, BCM 359; Henry Laurens to Richard Oswald, August 12, 1766, *The Papers of Henry Laurens*, v. 5, pp. 155–56; Governor Grant to Richard Oswald, August 31, 1766, BCM Bound Letter Book 1764–66; and Governor Grant to Richard Oswald, January 20, 1767, BCM Bound Letter Book 1766–71.

neighbors. Finding "everything neglected & in confusion," he raised enough provisions to supply the slaves already in place and feed the thirty who were sent there during the course of the year. But Johnson had "a wandering disposition," and the Governor could not prevail upon him to stay at his post. One day in 1767 he walked off into the swamp and was not heard from again.[63]

Oswald generally experienced problems with his white managers.[64] He was unable to procure and keep seasoned, reliable overseers; those he employed provided him with useless information, if that. For most of the time, he was "pretty much in the dark as to data."[65] So, in the early 1770s, he returned to the pool of army and commercial talent with which he was personally acquainted. When one of his mariners talked of retiring after fourteen years of service in the shipping lanes, and when another of his captains was to be deprived of his livelihood by the sale of a ship, Oswald moved them to "the Mosquitoes" where they served as overseers.[66] Only in the years just preceding the outbreak of the Revolution did Oswald begin to send overseers who possessed some commitment to service, and some experience growing plantation crops and living in the American hinterland. But by then it was too late.

Despite his hopes, Oswald's superintendents and overseers were "unseasoned" men unused to the climate and uneducated in the ways of plantation cultivation. As Sir Alexander pointed out, "estates never thrive under new [or young] Overseers." By the time the overseers gained experience, they figured out that they could make more money managing their own estates elsewhere, and fled. The economic incentives to break one's contract and leave before the indenture had expired

63. Governor Grant to Richard Oswald, January 20, 1767, BCM Bound Letter Book 1766–71; Henry Laurens to Governor Grant, January 30, June 27, 1767, *The Papers of Henry Laurens*, v. 5, pp. 227–69; and Governor Grant to Richard Oswald, July 20, November 7, 1767, BCM Bound Letter Book 1766–71. By November 1767, another overseer named Parry was working on the estate.

64. On Oswald's overseers, see Richard Oswald to James Brown, February 14, 1774, John Ohlson to Richard Oswald, April 20, 1770, James Brown to Richard Oswald, June 22, 1774, Richard Oswald to James Brown, July 11, 1774, and John Ohlson to Richard Oswald, August 24, 1774, Oswald Papers, Sudlows.

65. John Tucker to Governor Grant, June 12, 1767, BCM 253; Richard Oswald to Governor Grant, June 19, 1767, BCM 295; GD 345/1171/1/60x: Duncan Grant to Sir Archibald Grant, June 21, 1767; Shipping Database; Richard Oswald to Governor Grant, February 24, 1766, February 19, 1768, February 1, 1769, BCM 295; and Governor Grant to Richard Oswald, March 20, 1770, BCM Bound Letter Book 1766–71. On problems with managers, see Taylor, "Settling a Colony," pp. 34–36; and Richard Oswald to Governor Grant, February 24, 1766, May 15, 1769, BCM 295.

66. Richard Oswald to Governor Grant, July 27, 1770, BCM 295. Oswald also worked to find a place for former Bance Island employees. Richard Oswald to Governor Grant, June 24, 1770, BCM 295.

were great. And even when an overseer stayed long enough to write an account of his activities, it was difficult to obtain information from a man coping with a wilderness. The situation faced by a Florida planter vis-à-vis a Florida overseer was dramatically different from that faced by a Grenada planter vis-à-vis his employee. A Caribbean planter had other ways to learn about the state of affairs of his island and the operation on his plantation; a Florida landowner did not. Thus, only three years into his planting, Oswald realized that the grant was a morass into which sank all employees with whom he had no "personal knowledge." These Florida investments never saw a return, in large measure because on-site supervision by reliable relatives or friends was not sustained, as it was on the associates' more successful Caribbean estates to the south. Business success in East Florida, Oswald came to realize, was prevented by "taking up wrong notions." These he likened to an arch: "if one brick fails, the whole fabrick falls." In his own estimation, "wrong notions" were the work of unreliable managers whose imprecise, vague reporting and lack of commitment had led him astray.[67]

In addition to these three reasons for the failure of the Florida project – difficulties in isolating crops, obtaining information and infrastructure, and finding reliable managers – Oswald's own plantations suffered from the additional handicap of an ambivalence about his goals. To Oswald, America represented not only a business venture but also an unlimited opportunity to conduct experiments and promote "improvements." As Jack Greene reminds us, "The people who created and perpetuated the new societies of colonial British America sought not merely wealth and personal independence as individuals and the welfare of their families, but also the social goal of improved societies that would guarantee the independence they hoped to achieve and enable them to enjoy its fruits."[68] This was true for both settlers and planters.

67. Sir Alexander Grant to John Gordon, October 15, 1769, October 14, 1771, Grant Papers, Tomintoul House; and Sir Alexander Grant to Governor Grant, February 8, 1770, BCM 402.
68. Jack Greene, *Imperatives, Behaviors, and Identities: Essays in Early American Cultural History* (Charlottesville, 1992), p. 103. Numerous pamphleteers and writers observed the overlap of American settlement and agricultural improvement. [Campbell], *Candid and Impartial Considerations*, pp. 13–14, 69, 222; James Grainger, *The Sugar-Cane: A Poem* (London, 1764), bk. I, ll. 278–85; John Dovaston, "Agricultura Americana, or Improvements in West-India Husbandry, Considered wherein the Present System of Husbandry used in England is applyed to the Cultivation of growing Sugar Canes to Advantage" (1774) [Ms. in 2 vols.], John Carter Brown Library, Providence; and Franklin Papers, v. 49, f. 14: "Thoughts on the West Indian Trade," American Philosophical Society, Philadelphia. On the meaning of "improvement" in British America, see Greene, *Imperatives*, pp. 103–4, 190–92.

But the combination of motivations could have dire consequences. Florida was a business venture that Oswald kept treating as an experiment, with neither a clear model to copy nor a clear road to follow. Oswald's uncertainty about crops never allowed any one crop to reach wide-scale cultivation, and his penchant for throwing good money after bad severely retarded his plantations.[69] Experiment marked the entire Florida scheme to an extent not known in Oswald's other commercial ventures.

The associate's Florida planting had an eleemosynary, sometimes utopian aspect to it.[70] "The desire of promoting an enterprize productive of both national advantage and private interest" propelled him to lay down "the strictest conditions of Improvement," not only for his investments but also for new settlers he had never met and with whom he had little in common. So Oswald strove to relieve the destitute but deserving poor of Britain by providing them a home in Florida, in much the same way that Grant worked to establish "a good retreat" for penitent prostitutes of London there, and for "indigent familys who struggle under many difficulties in a less favourable soil & climate."[71] Although this strain of philanthropy, expressing little concern for profit, was entirely foreign to the associates' more purely commercial undertakings, it surfaced late in life in their American planting. In planting America, Oswald thought of himself as a virtuous leader in a community where agriculture and commerce were linked.

Long after Oswald's Florida plantation collapsed, one still finds a county crisscrossed with the canals and dams raised with his slaves and scented by the indigo that he never fully supported, as well as an Oswald Field, an Oswald Bluff, a Mount Oswald, a Ramsay Bay, and an Oswald Key. Oswald moved into planting in order to exert better control over the goods he shipped and traded, but his success was mixed. In the eastern Caribbean, like Grant in Jamaica, he matched his crops to the site, soil,

69. Only after the Revolutionary War threw Oswald's overseers onto their own devices was sugar abandoned. Other miscalculations are cited in Franklin Papers, v. 49, f. 14, American Philosophical Society, Philadelphia.
70. GD 1/32/38/24: Sir Alexander Grant to Sir Archibald Grant, June 8, 1767.
71. Richard Oswald to Governor Grant, May 3, 1764, BCM 470; GD 248/49/2/57: Sir Archibald Grant to Sir Alexander Grant, March 7, 1764; James Montgomery to John Mackenzie, April 14, 1770, Delvine Collection, Ms. 1,399, ff. 70–71; GD 1/32/38/22: Sir Alexander Grant to Sir Archibald Grant, May 23, 1767; Sir Alexander Grant to Governor Grant, June 19, 1767, BCM 344; Henry Laurens to Richard Oswald, April 27, 1768, *The Papers of Henry Laurens*, v. 5, p. 666; Anon., *Considerations Which May Tend to Promote The Settlement of Our New West India Colonies, By Encouraging Individuals to Embark in the Undertaking* (London, 1764), p. 1; and Richard Oswald to James Oswald, August 4, 1763, James Oswald Papers, Hockworthy House, Wellington, Somerset.

and climate, and found competent, trustworthy managers to oversee the operation, in much the same way that he had kept his ships full and moving, and staffed his shipping and trading business. This is the story one expects to hear of successful merchants like the associates. But there is another side to it. In Florida, Oswald's twin desires of improving new lands and producing what he shipped and marketed contributed to, but also frustrated, building plantations. The link between improvement and integration was widely heralded. In the words of the Registrar of the Society for the Encouragement of Arts, Manufactures, and Commerce, whose appointment Oswald and Grant had backed,

> ARTS, and COMMERCE, in Britannia's Isle;
> To distant Isles, with Hearts benevolent,
> And North America's wide Continent,
> Shou'd stretch their Hands, replete with friendly Aid,
> To planting Schemes, and beneficial Trade.[72]

Yet, as Oswald and Grant discovered, the linkage of agriculture and commerce was not easy, and commercial imperatives often clashed with the ostensibly compatible spirit of improvement. When inappropriate crops, unreliable managers, and experimental designs were allowed to persist, the attempt at backward integration failed to generate any commercial return.

72. George Cockings, *Arts, Manufactures, and Commerce: A Poem* (London, 1765), p. 3.

6

Slaving: Bance Island's "General Rendezvous"

FROM THE FOREGOING PAGES, a picture of large-scale London wholesale enterprisers in the eighteenth century has gradually emerged. These marginal, opportunistic, global, and integrative merchants combined commission merchandising as London factors with shipping and trading on their own account. But one of the reasons for their commercial success in shipping and trading is that they did not stop there; rather, they integrated their business interests backward so that they could exert better control over the production of goods that they shipped and traded. They moved into planting almost from the day they stepped ashore in British America, and pushed it with vigor in the last decades of their lives.

In 1748, six of them seized the single most lucrative shipping and trading opportunity of their careers when they acquired the slave "trade castle" in the Sierra Leone River on the Windward Coast of Africa that Henry Smeathman visited in 1773, and integrated into the full-scale slave trade. The history of their operations on Bance Island highlights many of the entrepreneurial themes that run throughout all their business ventures: opportunism in entry and trading styles; global scale; linkage of commercial networks, combining distinct products, peoples, and systems for the purpose of furthering trade; and dogged supervision of the internal economies of the operation. As an alembic in which to distill these themes and, at the same time, as another expression of backward integration, its management merits careful attention.

A Castle in Paradise

The "trade castle" was situated on Bance Island near the mouth of the Sierra Leone River – an unusual setting for a London enterprise (Illustration 6.1).[1] Here fantasy and reality existed side by side. Those who

---

1. The name of the island has varied over the years. In the present study, it is referred to as "Bance" Island, as it is known today, although it has also been called "Bence," "Bunce," and "George." It lies eighteen miles up the Sierra Leone River, now on the outskirts of Freetown, Sierra Leone.

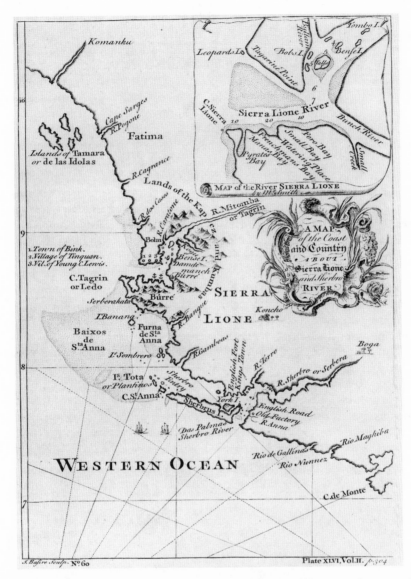

Illustration 6.1 A Map of the Coast and Country about Sierra Leone and Sherbro River (Inset: Map of the River Sierra Leone, by William Smith). *From:* John Green, comp., *A New General Collection of Voyages and Travels,* v. 2 (London, 1745), before p. 305, pl. 46. *Courtesy:* The Houghton Library, Harvard University.

arrived at the river initially thrilled to its more sublime aspects. Their hearts were "gladdened" at the sight of the mountains that ringed the estuary and rose "gradually from the sea to a stupendous height." The area was "richly wooded, beautifully ornamented by the hand of nature, with a variety of delightful prospects." Perfumed plants, singing birds, capricious monkeys, and the "smokes" (thick fog) provided an exhilarating contrast to London life.[2] Over time, visitors' attention turned to the region's commercial advantages. The river, broad and deep, disgorged into many small protected bays that were "safe and convenient for Cleaning and Watering" ships. Trees and brush grew down to its edge and provided timber that could be used for the repair of ships. Sandy soils nourished a wide variety of vegetables and fruits (yams, plantains, pineapples, limes, oranges, papayas, and palmnuts) and the waters fed a "variety of good Fish" (mullet, skate, cavalloes, barracudas, sucking fish, catfish, numbfish, bream, turtle, and oysters). Beyond sprang freshwater streams that provided an abundant supply of drinking water.[3] It was easy to see why a trading concern would establish operations in this region, even with the obvious limitations fixed by the jungle. Lions, leopards, and jackals might roam the woods, boiled ape might be the local delicacy, but the neighborhood possessed "as healthy and pleasant a situation as is to be met with in Africa," "lasting and useful timber," and "various kinds of delicious fish" and comestibles. Slaves and ivory were not far away.[4]

Any explanation of the success of the Bance Island experiment, however, lies less in its geographical setting and natural resources than in the precise historical moment in which it was conducted. The associates purchased the factory at a time when they could capitalize on the growth

2. Anna Maria Falconbridge, *Narrative of Two Voyages to the River Sierra Leone* (first published, 1791–93) (London, 1967), pp. 18–19, 48–49; and "Diary of Lieutenant [John] Clarkson, R.N.," *Sierra Leone Studies*, v. 8 (1927), p. 103; Zachary Macaulay's Journal sub December 27, 1796, MY 418/Box 20/Folder 17, Huntington Library, San Marino; and F. B. Spilsbury, *An Account of a Voyage to the Western Coast of Africa . . . 1805* (London, 1807), p. 19.

3. John Barbot, "A Description of the Coasts of North and South-Guinea," in John Churchill, *A Collection of Voyages and Travels*, v. 5 (London, 1732), pp. 98–106; Christopher Fyfe, *Sierra Leone Inheritance* (London, 1964), pp. 3, 69–70 (John Johnson, 1735); and John Atkins, *A Voyage to Guinea, Brazil, and the West Indies* (London, 1735), pp. 38–57. Later accounts contained similar reports. *Journals of the House of Commons*, v. 26, p. 248 (May 21, 1751); Silvanus M. X. Golberry, *Travels in Africa*, v. 2 (first published, 1787) (London, 1802), pp. 246–47; CO 267/9: Robert Norris to Secretary of State, May 29, 1790; and *Journals of the House of Commons*, v. 46, pp. 414–55.

4. [James Tweed,] *Considerations and Remarks on the Present State of the Trade to Africa* (London, 1771), pp. 81–83. The Tweed attribution is made by the anonymous author of *A Treatise upon the Trade from Great Britain to Africa* (London, 1772), Appendix H, p. 53, who paraphrases Tweed's pamphlet.

in consumer demand for sugar, the rise of plantation economies in Europe's colonies across the Americas, and the fall of the slave-trade monopoly. The demand for sugar in Britain and Europe was fast outstripping the supply in the Americas, encouraging the building of new plantations in the colonies and increasing their demand for labor. Between 1701 and 1770, the British shipped nearly 1.4 million slaves from Africa across the Atlantic. The number of human exports more than doubled, from 12,000 per year in the 1700s to 27,200 per year in the 1760s; over the same period, exports from the Windward Coast, including Bance Island, rose from 1,740 to 4,970.[5] At the same time, the Royal African Company (RAC), the Crown-sanctioned slave-trade monopoly, was finally collapsing, its decline having begun as far back as the 1690s, accelerated in the 1720s when it abandoned the fort at Bance, and culminated in the late 1740s when its funds were exhausted and its charter revoked. The removal of its monopoly opened the way for private British slave traders to litter the coast with their vessels and compete with the French slave traders rushing to satisfy the labor needs of French West Indian planters.[6]

On Bance Island, the associates found a base for slave-trading operations that lay ready to use. The fort and factory had been built in the 1670s by the RAC with an eye to its strategic location (Illustration 6.2). Their base lay near the mouth of the river, surrounded by several islands (Robanna, Tumbo, Tasso, Marabump, and Bob) which were favored by Portuguese, French, and Dutch slave traders alike, as well as pirates of all nations. Fearing attack from competitors, the RAC chose the most defensible island and erected a fortified depot on its northern tip.[7] For

---

5. Curtin, *Atlantic Slave Trade*, p. 150; and David Richardson, "The Eighteenth-Century British Slave Trade," *Research in Economic History*, v. 12 (1989), p. 170. Cf. a similar rise in French trading. Stein, *French Sugar Business*, p. 21.

6. K. G. Davies, *The Royal African Company* (London, 1957), p. 345; David Galenson, *Traders, Planters, and Slaves* (Cambridge, 1986); and Jacob M. Price, "Credit in the Slave Trade and Plantation Economies," in Barbara L. Solow, ed., *Slavery and the Rise of the Atlantic System* (Cambridge, 1991), pp. 299–300, 305. For a discussion of the rivalry between RAC officials and private traders, see *Considerations on the Trade to Guinea* (London, 1708), pp. 13, 25–30; *The Falsities of Private Traders Discover'd, and the Mischiefs They Occasion Demonstrated* (London, 1708); and Board of Trade Report on the Trade to Africa, 1709, in Elizabeth Donnan, *Documents Illustrative of the Slave Trade*, v. 2 (Washington, D.C., 1931), p. 49.

7. Winterbottom, *Account*, p. 19; Lawrence, *Castles*, p. 77; and Barbot, "Description," p. 99. The fort was well situated for protection. "Being established on an elevated soil, thirty feet above the level of the river and having a platform of twenty-five feet, its batteries have an immense advantage and great superiority over ships, which cannot arrive at the isle without their pendants being perceived for an hour before." Golberry, *Travels*, v. 2, p. 246. Only small craft could navigate the narrow, shallow waters beyond the island. Joseph Corry, *Observations upon the Windward Coast* (London, 1807), p. 3. For descriptions of surrounding islands, see Falconbridge, *Narrative*, p. 19; and Spilsbury, *Account*, p. 35.

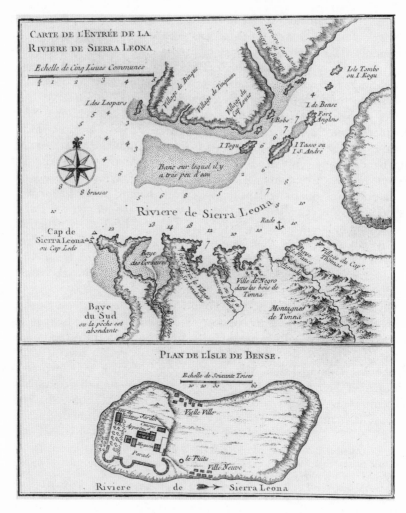

Illustration 6.2 A Map of the Entrance of the Sierra Leone River (Inset: Plan of Bance Island). *From:* Jacques Bellin's *Le petit atlas maritime* (Paris, 1764), v. 3, n. 103. *Courtesy:* The Houghton Library, Harvard University.

nearly fifty years, the RAC operated the fort and factory more or less successfully. Only in 1728, when Africans under the leadership of an Afro-Portuguese trader drove out the agent, blew up the magazine, and burned down the fort, did the RAC abandon it.[8] The island lay unused

8. Fyfe, *Sierra Leone Inheritance*, p. 3; and T 70/1465: Diary of Walter Charles, 1728, cited in Walter Rodney, *A History of the Upper Guinea Coast* (Oxford, 1970), p. 19 n. 2.

for roughly ten years, until a London slave trader named George Fryer found it a safe place "for the . . . Keeping of his Goods, and for a Defence against the French in War Time." From the king of the country, Fryer obtained permission to trade, leased the fort, and struggled for four years to turn a profit.[9] But what at first seemed a gold mine turned out to be quicksand: despite annual shipments of 4,000 slaves, 200 tons of camwood (roughly £6,400 worth), and 15 tons of elephant ivory (£3,600), Fryer never made enough to cover his costs.[10]

In early 1748, a financially straitened Fryer found a buyer in Richard Oswald, with whom he signed Articles of Bargain and Sale on July 8, transferring the island and its dependencies. Simultaneously, Oswald signed a Deed of Copartnership with Augustus and John Boyd (who had introduced him to Fryer), Alexander Grant, John Mill, and John Sargent II. The capitalization of the partnership was divided into nine shares: the Boyds took a joint ninth; Mill and Sargent each a ninth; Grant three ninths; and Oswald three ninths. The six did business as "Grant, Oswald & Co."; and Oswald and Mill served as the company's managing partners.[11] Fryer transferred the land to them free of charge, on the condition that they purchase his inventory, valued at £4,303.[12]

Two contemporary surveys drawn up at the new owners' request record its appearance (Illustrations 6.3 and 6.4).[13] The fort was situated on a steep hill at the northeastern end of the island. On the south bastion were mounted several nine- and three-pound cannon; on the north bastion, or saluting battery, several small cannon; and, on the western demibastion, several nine-pound guns. On these facades, those

9. "Documentos acerca a Serra Leona," *Arquivo Colonial*, cited in Rodney, *Upper Guinea Coast*, p. 248. George Fryer's Bance Island activities are documented in *Journal of the House of Commons*, v. 26, pp. 247–48, 258–59 (May 21, 1751). In 1744, Fryer paid £100 in trade goods to the African king as entry money and £480 in gold bars as five years' land rent. During the late 1740s, Fryer oversaw the execution of the Boyds' victualing contracts in Jamaica.

10. CO 388/43/Bb105: John Boyce to Captain Boyce, February 2, 1744.

11. Among branches of British commerce, the African trade required the largest amount of trading capital. J. E. Inikori, "Market Structure and the Profits of the British African Trade," *Journal of Economic History*, v. 41 (1981), p. 756. In 1749, the Bance Island partners took a loan of £4,500 to sustain trading operations during the first six years. *Journals of the House of Commons*, v. 26, p. 247. If this amount constituted the entire initial capitalization, then Inikori's claims need to be reconsidered.

12. £4,303 in 1748 amounts to £358,951 or $533,897 in 1994. The inventory is listed in *Journals of the House of Commons*, v. 26, pp. 247–48, 258–59: refuse and unsorted goods, £2,777; 28 Africans, £843; slaving ships and their stores, £442; wood and ivory, £303; guns and military stores, £227; and sundries.

13. CO 700/Sierra Leone/1B: "A Prospect of the West Side of George Island"; and CO 700/Sierra Leone/1A: "A Plan of the Fort and Factory." These drawings are confirmed by U.S. Peace Corps, "Recommendations for the Protection and Management of Bunce Island National Historic Site, Sierra Leone" (September 1989), pp. 7–10.

Illustration 6.3 A Prospect of the West Side of George [Bance] Island (1749), by John Wade. *Courtesy:* Public Record Office, CO 700/SL/1A, London.

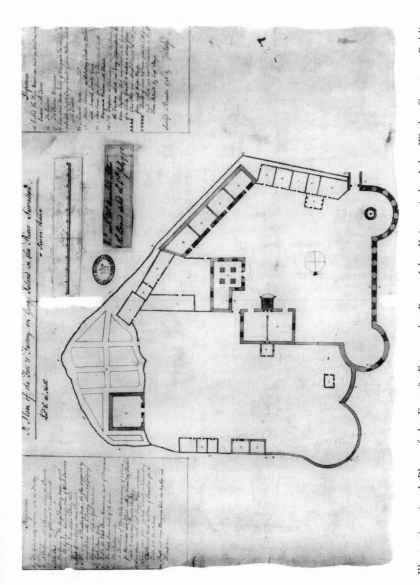

Illustration 6.4 A Plan of the Fort & Factory [at Bance Island] (1749), by John Wade. *Courtesy:* Public Record Office, CO 700/SL/1B, London.

most vulnerable to enemy bombardment, the walls were thick by African standards (30 inches thick), tall (16 feet), and durable, made from lime mortar, broken brick, and laterite stone and plastered with stucco in a European style. Some 16 feet above the level of the yard at the back of the factory was raised a strong, tall fence, a local "Trapado or Pallisadoes" made in the African manner.[14] High above these medieval-looking rubble and wooden walls, towers, and gates, and visible for miles around flapped the Union Jack, the symbolic focal point for the settlement: Britannia looking down upon the comings and goings of her merchants.

The fortified factory occupied the upper quarter of the 15-acre island, where the narrow pebble beaches became wider and sandier. About 150 feet west of the fort, the surveyor's "Prospect" details a jetty made from quarry stone and, further downshore, houses for black workers, lime kilns for making bricks, a "Captain of the Ports" flag, and a graveyard. Within the central yard itself stood the Old Dwelling House that had once served as the residential and administrative headquarters of the RAC, but by 1748 had been reduced to a ruined heap of ramparts, stairs, and walls; a small room at the back of the house had been added but did little to dispel the impression of neglect. Rather than rework the main structure, Fryer had built a new L-shaped Dwelling House that skirted the eastern boundary of the yard. It was in every way an improvement: more spacious – three lodging rooms and a dining room on the first floor and a warehouse below – and extremely secure, with walls 5 feet thick.[15] On the southern and eastern ends of the yard also stood two blocks of houses. One "very desirable" block with plastered walls and a terraced roof contained four large rooms (each 48' × 20') providing lodgings, offices, and storerooms for the whites. The rooms were "arched & paved with Purbeck stone" imported from Britain and considered by all who saw them to be "the finest in Africa." Nearby stood five small slave "houses" (each 15' × 17') that were made from mangrove and mud and designed to hold captives awaiting shipment overseas (Illustration 6.5).[16] Finally, toward the end of the row stood the

14. The 16-foot-high fence was made by planting tall "Potoon sticks" close together and letting them take root and grow together. European bricks were used to frame the arches, corners, and trim of windows and doors; likewise, European stairs were worked into the design.
15. Northeast of the New Dwelling House there was a service yard for the whites. Here was a Cook's Room and Warehouse; a Poultry House; a Rum House; a Garden; a Powder Magazine; a Livestock House; a Smith Shop and Forge; a Lumber House; and a Store House for tar and pitch.
16. The Bance slave houses in Illustration 6.5 bear a marked similarity to the houses of John Thomas, a captain living on one of the islands in the Sierra Leone River in the second half of the seventeenth century, that are depicted in Barbot, "Description," p. 99,

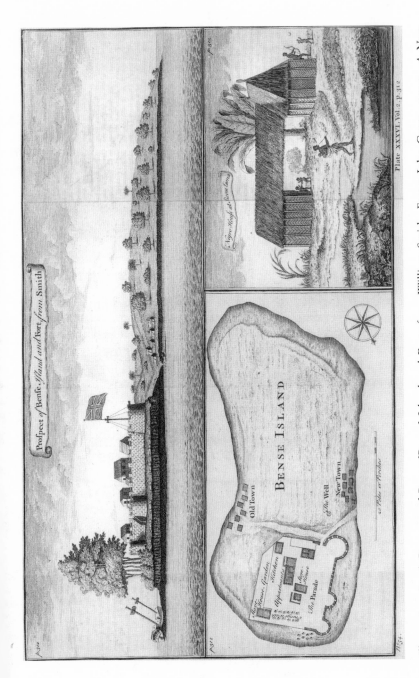

Illustration 6.5 A Prospect of Bense [Bance] Island and Fort, from William Smith. *From:* John Green, comp., *A New General Collection of Voyages and Travels,* v. 2 (London, 1745), after p. 312, pl. 36. *Courtesy:* The Houghton Library, Harvard University.

Palaver House, a small "Place of Reception" (10′ × 15′) where factory agents met African chiefs and arranged the barter of slaves, ivory, and dyestuffs.[17]

The Fight for "Quiet Possession"

The associates acquired this collection of buildings to traffic in slaves: in short order, they sent a surveyor to sketch the factory, compile an inventory, and make an initial foray into trade; employed a factor to supervise subsequent trading; and dispatched three ships from London with English and Irish provisions. But the activity is deceiving: the firm did little else in its first three years; and only two loads of slaves left its wharf. Instead, the associates turned their attention to reorganizing the African trade as a whole and seeking legal confirmation of their title in London. Only after they had safeguarded their opportunity did the proprietors pursue the trade with vigor.

The need for reorganizing the African trade was great. The monopoly company system that had governed it for at least seventy-five years was unable to keep up with the pace of expansion. Similar change and clamor for reorganization had occurred in other trades. During the 1730s, the East India Company's right to its monopoly over the trade between Britain and India came under heavy fire, as private entrepreneurs sought to gain entry to a lucrative rising market. In the following decade, a similar debate ensued over the trade to the Baltic and the Levant.[18] The attack on the RAC's control of the African trade should be viewed in this context. Problems had arisen with the deterioration of the RAC's monopoly, its unprofitability, and its chronic indebtedness.[19]

pl. E. For African houses in seventeenth-century Gambia, see Richard Jobson, *The Golden Trade, or a Discovery of the River Gambia* (London, 1623), pp. 47–48, 53–54. The size and construction of the Bance slave houses also bear some similarity to that of the recreated Carter's Grove slave quarters near Williamsburg, Virginia, where as many as ten slaves lived in a single room (12′ × 16′) with rough walls ("unhewn logs or riven siding nailed to unfinished framing"), dirt floors, and unfinished ceilings. Edward A. Chappell, "Social Responsibility and the American History Museum," *Winterthur Portfolio* (1989), pp. 261–62. If these rooms are representative of slave housing in mainland America, Bance Island's houses were better appointed and more commodious.

17. John Aird to Richard Oswald, October 2, 1764, Oswald Papers, Sudlows.
18. *The Craftsman*, v. 3 (London, 1731), p. 113; *A Proof of the Decay of the Turkey Trade* (London, 1744); Sir Matthew Decker, *An Essay on the Causes of the Decline of the Foreign Trade*, 4th ed. (Dublin, 1751), p. 10; *The London Magazine*, v. 17 (1748), pp. 405–06; and Newman, "Anglo-Hamburg Trade," pp. 228–29, 293.
19. *The Case of the Royal African Company* (London, 1744); *The Importance of Effectually Supporting the Royal African Company* (London, 1744); *The Present State of the British and French Trade to Africa and America* (London, 1745); Malachy Postlethwayt, *The African Trade* (London, 1745), *The National and Private Advantages of the African Trade* (London, 1746); and CO 388/44: Pocock to Admiralty, February 9, 1746.

The increasing inability of the RAC to control private trade and pay its creditors, the sale of the South Sea Company's stores, the termination of the Asiento Contract, and the reentry of the French into the African trade after the Peace of 1748 provided a confusing mélange of decline and opportunity. But unlike the clamor concerning other trades, the agitation over African trade resulted in market reorganization.

The associates eagerly entered the negotiations over the future of the trade in order to work the parliamentary machine to their advantage.[20] Late in 1747, the RAC asked the Government for additional funds to support its forts, but was turned away; even the clamor of prominent merchants, the RAC's creditors, failed to rouse the Commons,[21] and the 1747–48 parliamentary session ended with no changes.[22] Alarmism remained the order of the day in the pamphlet press. In the midst of this confusion, the six partners purchased Bance Island. The debate amid which the purchase occurred took place largely beyond the walls of Parliament and Whitehall, within the smoky and noisy confines of the City's coffeehouses and taverns. In early 1749, merchants of Bristol and Liverpool proposed a bill that contained four fundamental principles – freedom of trade; the separation of trade and defense; the importance of defensible forts; and the necessity of "an open Company, without any Joint Stock or Power to trade as a Corporation under proper Regulation" – and these principles formed the backbone of the African Trade

20. The history of the reorganization of the African trade and of the new Company of Merchants that succeeded the RAC remains largely unwritten. Few historians mention these subjects, or when they do they provide incorrect support. An exception is Eveline Martin, *The British West Africa Settlements, 1750–1821* (London, 1927), pp. 29–56; Eveline Martin, ed., *Journal of a Slave-Dealer* (London, 1930), Intro.; and, although it contains numerous errors, Rawley, *Slave Trade*, pp. 163–64, 175–76, 236–37.

21. *Seasonable Observations on the Trade to Africa in a Letter to a Member of Parliament* (London, 1748), p. 10; and *Journals of the House of Commons*, v. 26, p. 526 (February 16, 1748). The RAC suggested an imaginative way of defraying expenses – the licensing of pawnbrokers in Britain. The idea caught the fancy of "the most Eminent Merchants of the City" but stirred grave doubts among M.P.s; it was judged unconstitutional. M. O'Connor, *Considerations on the Trade to Africa* (London, 1749), p. 52.

22. The response of the commercial classes is detailed in *Journals of the House of Commons*, v. 26, p. 565. London was the first to air its grievances, and even at this early stage the associates were involved. Sargent's uncle and employer George Arnold, one of the largest of the London suppliers of the RAC, faced considerable loss. He decried the "very declining Way" of London's trade with Africa and predicted that only "effectual Provision for the Preservation and Encouragement of this most valuable and necessary Trade" could halt the slide. According to Richardson, Arnold was correct: the share of the trade captured by London reached a century low in the 1740s – 12–15 percent. "Eighteenth-Century British Slave Trade," p. 170. To date, no one has offered a satisfactory explanation why London buckled under the weight of outport competition.

Act of 1750. This Act set the terms of the slave trade that prevailed until the abolition of the slave trade fifty-seven years later.[23]

The African Trade Act of 1750 represented a triumph for Grant, Oswald, and other private traders of London, Liverpool, and Bristol who had lobbied for market principles. It opened the trade to all British subjects between Sallee, in the north near Marrakech, and the Cape of Good Hope, at the southern tip of the continent.[24] Those who traded between Cape Blanco, 1,000 miles south of Sallee, and the Cape of Good Hope were incorporated under the name of "The Company of Merchants Trading to Africa." The RAC's old forts would be vested in this new company and used only "for the protection, encouragement, and defence" of the trade. To ensure "free and open" use, the Act prohibited the new African Company from trading in its corporate capacity and encouraged private traders by giving them greater access to Company facilities and protection.[25]

23. A brief sketch of the 1748–49 parliamentary activity relating to Africa appears in *The London Magazine*, v. 18 (1749), pp. 406–09; and *Journals of the House of Commons*, v. 25, pp. 697–98, 732–33, 777–78, 829–30. The committee was headed by the African trader and London Alderman Slingsby Bethell. London, Bristol, and Liverpool slaving interests were well represented on the committee, but not all members were slave traders. For a breakdown of the interests of the members of this and all subsequent committees, see Hancock, "Citizen of the World," ch. 9. For the new proposal, see *Journals of the House of Commons*, v. 25, p. 856. It sparked a series of new petitions and inquiries. *Journals of the House of Commons*, v. 25, pp. 861–62, 868. In the end, the Commons decided that "a reasonable compensation should be given" to defray the payment of bona fide debtors. It instructed the bill committee to conduct an examination of facilities and debts. The draft was read for a third time on June 6, passed in its entirety, and sent to the Lords who quashed it. *Journals of the House of Commons*, v. 25, pp. 868, 880, 885–86; and *Journals of the House of Lords*, v. 27, p. 364.
24. The Committee of the Whole House debated the petitions, and, the Commons adopted four resolutions and ordered the preparation of a new bill. *Journals of the House of Commons*, v. 25, pp. 977–82; and *London Magazine*, v. 19 (September 1750), pp. 405–06. Passage encountered few obstacles, and the bill received the royal imprimatur on April 12. *Journals of the House of Commons*, v. 25, pp. 1028, 1031, 1042–48, 1050, 1057–59, 1102, 1105–06, 1114.
25. The complete text of the law, 23 Geo. II, c. 31, can be found in Danby Pickering, ed., *The Statutes at Large*, v. 20 (London, 1765), pp. 112–25. Most provisions attempted to ensure that the trade was conducted according to mercantile principles. This is quite apparent in the structure of the new company. Management of African affairs was assigned to a nine-man committee. Meeting in London as often as necessary, its members were to give orders "for the governing, maintaining, preserving, and improving the forts and factories already built," to appoint or remove civil and military officers who would supervise the daily operations, and to devise rules by which the officers would manage the forts. Committeemen, like Scott, Aufrere, Chambers, or Dicker, were elected by merchants who paid 40 shillings each year in dues. The conduct of the committee meetings was prescribed by law. Except for the first year, elections were held on July 3 or 4. The first meeting of the year was held on the first Monday of August, thereafter as often as necessary. The place of business was set in London; as a result, members were always Londoners. No one could serve more than

With the passage of control of African affairs from government monopolists to private traders, the Bance Island partners moved to confirm the title to their lands in the Sierra Leone river basin. As the old monopoly company began settling its affairs, it notified Grant, Oswald & Co. that it included Bance Island among its holdings, a pronouncement the proprietors greeted with alarm. To counteract this, Grant, Oswald & Co. asked the Commons in April 1751 to postpone a decision on who had control of the island until the House had inquired into the rights of the partners or, if those rights were found insupportable, their compensation for interim expenses.[26] Parliament delayed for a year before responding; but when it did, the associates were pleased. The 1752 Act for "Making Compensation" stripped the RAC of its African possessions and gave them to the new Company, and it did the same to contracts previously made with "any of the kings, princes or natives of any of the countries or places on the said coast" – Bance Island specifically excepted. Under the Act, the new Company had no jurisdiction over this "general rendezvous." Given the RAC's abandonment of the fort in 1728, Parliament decided that the RAC's claim had lapsed, and the associates' more recent contract with the local African king stood in its stead. Because of their previous expenditures, Parliament decided that just and reasonable compensation for their interim expenses should take the form of a "liberty . . . to continue in the quiet possession of the said island, fort and buildings," and that the associates' possession should continue as long as the grant was secured "to and for their own use and benefit."[27]

three years in a row; and partners could not serve together. Each meeting, a chairman was chosen by lot. A plurality of votes determined policy decisions. Sessions were designed to avoid the dominance of any one member and to minimize the extent of policy review. The actions were subject to review by the Board of Trade and by the freemen.

26. *Journals of the House of Commons*, v. 26, pp. 193–94. On May 21, the House interviewed Oswald, his bookkeeper, Fryer's agent, RAC officials, members of the nine-man committee, and naval captains. On the subsequent work of the Commons, see *Journals of the House of Commons*, v. 26, pp. 269–70.

27. The preparation of the bill is recounted in *The London Magazine*, v. 21 (1752), pp. 267–68. On the progress of the bill, see *Journals of the House of Commons*, v. 26, pp. 342–43, 360, 494, 499, 515. While they waited for a decision from Parliament, the proprietors called on Robert Scott and through him procured the new Company's support for the repayment of their prior expenditures should the House bar the firm from ownership. T 70/143/129: February 12, 1752. The Act appears in Pickering, ed., *Statutes at Large*, v. 20 (London, 1765), pp. 384–401. The Act also benefited the associates, insofar as it recognized certain old claims against the RAC as valid, and all others as groundless; prominent among the valid claims were sums owed John Sargent's firm, George Arnold & Co., which was to gain £1,822. The only restriction was that they could not grant "their right and interest" to any foreigners.

Managing "a Territory Where My Dominion Is Most Absolute"

Now secure in their possession, the proprietors felt free to promote the Bance Island enterprise without hindrance from the state.[28] Over the next eleven years, they overhauled and supervised the factory's defenses, facilities, supplies, and manpower. Military and commercial defense (in this setting, contemporaries would not have distinguished the two) were not foremost among the proprietors' thoughts during the early years of their ownership. Like most African traders, they did not try to maintain a defensible establishment at the outset of their venture; on the contrary, with the history of the RAC etched in their memories, they viewed protective measures as a drain on capital.

In the conduct of trade, they depended not on security but on "a good understanding with the Natives."[29] But agreement was not always easy to obtain. The Sierra Leone River had long been a haunt of the enemy. Throughout the period of associate control, Sierra Leone's Windward Coast was one of three regions favored by interloping French slave traders: when the British regained control over the coast in the 1740s, the French were driven back into isolated creeks, but they maintained a presence through the 1780s. Time and again, through an assiduous use of "chicane and low cunning," the French sought to "worm" the British "out of the trade," boldly insinuating to the African coastal kings that, if the Africans "could by any means get quit of the English," the French would put the trade "on a very advantageous footing" for the Africans.[30]

These overtures were frequent and sometimes successful. On one occasion in the 1760s, a French ship arrived at the island's jetty and its captain offered trade goods at specified prices to the island's agent James Tweed, promising that if the British should purchase the cargo, the French would leave the coast. Tweed felt that a strong stand was important: since the Frenchman was "the first of that nation who had come into that territory since the Peace" of 1763, Tweed should either

---

28. Cunningham, *The Law of Bills of Exchange*, p. 2. Some steps were taken before 1752. Oswald, for example, had arranged financing months before confirmation was certain. Island Record Office, Deeds, v. 146, pp. 64–67 (September 30, 1751). Oswald raised £5,000 by assigning part of his new wife's dowry to his partner Robert Scott.

29. *Journals of the Commissioners for Trade and Plantations*, v. 1749/50–1753, p. 335 (June 24, 1752), 335–36 (June 25, 1752); and CO 388/45/II/68: July 6, 1752. CO 388/45/II/86: August 29, 1751, contains a list of items deemed necessary; and CO 388/45/II/84: April 24, 1752, itemizes goods actually sent for a trade "with the Natives."

30. GD 345/1180/1762: James Low to Captain Archibald Grant, March 19, April 8, 1762; and Tweed, *Considerations*, p. 26.

purchase his entire cargo or command his departure "without trading" anywhere else along the coast. The proprietors, however, made "light of the matter," and suggested that the Frenchman could "do his worst." Tweed refused his cargo and sent him packing. Later he learned that the French sailed up an adjacent creek and sold the entire cargo to the Africans for a third more than the French had asked from the British. Only after Tweed subsequently "brought the leading men of the country into an agreement to receive no more French" was the factory's commercial dominance resecured.[31]

As attempts at foreign encroachment rose, so too did the maintenance of defense. The island was anything but secure in 1748. The initial survey noted the "very bad repair" of the platforms and carriages of thirteen cannon and the bastions on which they were mounted, and the many subsequent surveys all bore the same message. By 1750, the fort was "in very indifferent repair," with much of the surrounding wooden palisade having fallen down.[32] The phrase "out of repair" came to haunt the proprietors. The walls were a continual source of grievance to the firm's employees, who stood in fear of French pirates; too, they were the chief cause of concern to a Ministry obsessed by the possibility of French encroachment.[33] In the minds of the British in Africa, walls were a tangible symbol of power, and their deterioration had a profound impact on those on both sides. As the agents on the island rightly surmised, the French, desirous of a good anchorage, were emboldened by a crumbling state of defense to "tamper" with "the King of the Place" and to oust the British.[34] At the same time, the Africans were

31. Tweed, *Considerations*, pp. 28–30.
32. CO 388/44: December 19, 1748; and T 70/176/3: November 18, 1750, by Captain Baird. See T 70/176/3–4: 1750, for a similar report by Captain Jasper.
33. Among imperial administrators, however, concern with foreign competition in British West Africa was feverish. During the period 1740–80, slave exports from the northern coast of western Central Africa more than tripled, but increasingly the French controlled this trade and thus forced the British to look northward (along the Gold Coast and in Senegambia). Joseph Miller, *Way of Death: Merchant Capitalism and the Angolan Slave Trade, 1730–1830* (Madison, 1988), pp. 227, 233. The fear of French encroachment led to continual investigation. Typical of the warnings issued was that of July 1752, in which the Board of Trade urged the partners to "preserve the fort and settlement" in such "a condition and to endeavour to keep up such a good correspondence and understanding with the natives as may prevent this important place falling into the hands of any other power." *Journals of the Commissioners for Trade and Plantations*, v. 1749/50–1753, p. 344 (July 9, 1752).
34. CO 388/44/CC69: Agent Samuel Staple, August 9, 1751; CC71-70: Captain Richard Howe, *Glory*, August 19, 1751; CC75-74: Captain Daniel, *Assurance*, January 2, 1752; and CC76: Captain Daniel, *Assurance*, March 1, 1752. In the early 1750s, the French threat was mainly commercial. T 70/143/63: March 22, 1752. During the Seven Years' War, it became military. GD 345/1180/1762: James Low to Captain Archibald Grant, April 8, 1762.

often encouraged to behave in an "Insolent" manner by the fact that the British, without any "house or place of security," could not defend themselves for any length of time.[35]

By August 1756, dramatic changes had taken place and everything was "in good repair."[36] Walls, guns, and men were now plentiful, in place, and usable. The change in preparedness can be best tracked in the "States and Conditions of Bance Island" that were intermittently filed with the Admiralty.[37] Manpower was clearly critical. The number of white employees on the island, which had averaged 10 between 1748 and 1751, increased more than threefold to an average of 35 between 1756 and 1773.[38] Munitions mounted apace. The number of cannon nearly tripled from 12 during 1748–52 to 34 in 1756–76. The kind of cannon changed, too, with more large 12-pounders and small saluting one- and two-pounders appearing in the later period. Likewise, the number of rounds of shot grew, from 387 in the earlier period to 920 in the later period.[39] In its buildup of manpower and artillery, Bance Island became one of the more heavily manned and fortified settlements along the west coast of Africa.[40] Present by the outbreak of Britain's Seven Years' War against France and persisting for twenty years, secure defenses made the island nearly unique among the commercial forts in West Africa. It was better equipped to defend itself than all but one of the other British forts, despite the fact that the others could draw upon public funds.[41]

35. CO 388/44/CC 69, 74–75. Without a "place of defence," the agents were forced either to give the local king "everything he sends for" or to endure the constant threat of war.
36. T 70/176/31.
37. See the fifteen quantitative reports on "The State and Condition of Bance Island" that were written between 1748 and 1776 and filed with the Admiralty; they are scattered throughout the House of Lords Main Papers, the Colonial Office files, and the Treasury Papers, but are tabled in Appendix V.
38. At the same time, the average number of blacks employed by the factory each year rose from 48 in 1750–51 to 128 in 1756–73 (a 267% increase). If the amount for slaves in 1769 is excluded on the grounds that it is only a partial listing of slaves, the 1756–76 black manpower level rose to 142 (a 296% increase). The rise contributed directly to the increasing sense of jeopardy felt by the island's agents.
39. All along the coast, large numbers of guns and quantities of gunpowder were annually imported into West Africa for slaving, crop protection, and decoration. Inikori, "Import," pp. 339–68. For numerous requests made by the associates' various firms for permission to send large shipments of guns and powder to West Africa in 1756 and 1757, see T 1 (requests for export licenses) and T 52 (issues of warrants for licenses), for instance T 1/365/88: Richard Oswald to Ordnance Board, November 1, 1756.
40. Cf. the 1749 levels reported for nine other forts in *Statutes at Large*, 25 Geo. II, c. 40, pp. 397–400. Cape Coast Castle topped the list of forts with 266 black employees, 84 guns, 4,616 rounds of shot, 27 muskets, and 7 vessels. The average numbers of the other eight forts were much lower: 41 black employees, 30 guns, 454 rounds, 26 muskets, and 4 vessels.
41. Egerton Manuscripts, 1162B, ff. 78–80, BL. A copy of this account appears in T 70/1532: November 30, 1773. Only one surveyor felt that the condition was unacceptable. CO 267/15/16, 18: Captain Alexander Scott to Philip Stephens, February 16, 1770.

At the same time they were restoring its defenses, Grant, Oswald & Co. were expanding its operations. Between July 1748 and April 1751, the proprietors appointed two agents and several employees; purchased an Irish ship, the *Swallow*, for permanent use on the Windward Coast, and another larger vessel, the *Mercury*, for shuttle voyaging between England and Africa; and stocked the fort with beef, butter, and pork from Cork and medicines from London. But they did little in the way of trade and, as a result, the factory experienced initial losses: through mid-1751, costs (£2,932) for provisions and wages outstripped returns (£2,351) from the two shipments of slaves, ivory tusks, and camwood.[42]

An extensive list of stores that agent Samuel Staple requested in 1751 gives us a glimpse of the variety of the needs of the entrepot as its proprietors contemplated expanding its operations.[43] Household supplies appeared on the list as a matter of course: flour "and provision of all kinds"; spices; "good beans" for the captives; medicines; tallow and pewter candle molds; coffee cups and teacups, kettles, pots, and spoons; stationery; and hawks' bells. Construction materials – planks and deals, nails, paint, linseed oil, turpentine, and paint brushes – were required to undertake repairs. Shipping supplies were also needed. Small boats and related supplies were wanted to negotiate the treacherous shoals of the Bance and Sierra Leone Rivers and, upstream, the creeks and inlets: a 10- to 12-ton shallop (a small boat); mooring chains to hold vessels; pumps and gears to load them; canvas, thread, twine and cordage to repair them; brimstone; and "Red Bottom, such as they put on the vessels out of Liverpool" to "keep the worm from eating" and destabilizing hulls.[44] To make use of such goods, Staple needed men, especially a carpenter, cooper, smith, and mason to outfit or repair ships.

Since the fort was to serve primarily as a slaving entrepôt, Staple requested 100 shackles, 100 handcuffs, 1,000 forelocks (fastening devices), and 6 strong chains. And, finally, there was the merchandise to be exchanged for slaves. The trade goods filling half of his lengthy indent fell into five groups: clothing and cloth (the largest commodity in

---

42. *Journals of the House of Commons*, v. 26, p. 258 (Appendix 5).
43. CO 388/45/II/86: Indent, August 29, 1751, and CO 388/45/II/84: Bill, April 24, 1752.
44. "Brimstone," the common name for sulfur, was used in solutions for painting and protecting the underside of ships. "Red Bottom" may have been an early form of copper sheathing, used to protect wooden vessels from a mollusk that attacks the wood of ships under water. Grant Uden and Richard Cooper, *A Dictionary of British Ships and Seamen* (New York, 1980), p. 101. More likely, it is a variation on Brown Stuff and White Stuff. Brown Stuff was a mixture of tar and pitch; White Stuff was a mixture of whale train oil, rosin, and brimstone or sulfur. Such fluids were used in combination with sheathing, that is extra planking fixed below the waterline, to stop the entrance of worm. I am indebted to C. J. Ware, of the National Maritime Museum, for this information.

demand) from East India, the Levant, Germany, and Britain; armaments (such as elephant guns, muskets, small guns, pistols, flints, gunpowder, lead shot, and cutlasses); metalware (brass kettles and pans, pewter basins, pint and quart tankards, fire tongs, hangers, iron and lead bars, cutlery, nails, and locks); agricultural commodities (muscovado and refined sugar, and tobacco); and miscellaneous goods (beads, coral, crystal, and 50 pairs of "good shoes").[45]

Lading a ship with 2 bales, 7 barrels, 9 bundles, 33 casks, and 49 chests of goods and supplies, the proprietors satisfied Staple's request in April 1752. Yet such attentiveness to trade per se was not maintained in subsequent years. Having mended the walls and stockpiled the munitions and provisions, the proprietors next turned their attention to revivifying facilities and manpower. When Grant, Oswald & Co. acquired Bance Island in 1748, many of the facilities for conducting an entrepôt trade were already in place: administrative headquarters, lodgings and offices for whites, a conference hall in which to dicker with Africans, holding rooms for captives, warehouses, and outbuildings. Unlike the defensive structure, the commercial complex had remained sound, and construction and upkeep costs remained relatively low during the first decade of associate ownership.

But by the late 1750s, the facilities began to show wear and tear, and the owners began considering various building schemes in earnest. With their promotion of the accountant John Aird to the command of the factory in 1758, they inaugurated their first building program. Before the year was up, Aird had started to repair the lodgings for whites, and to attach a "Tradesmen's Gallery," a two-story block of offices where 90 visiting traders could display their wares in 9 different stores at the same time. On top of the Palaver House, Aird raised a Rice House and covered it with a pavilion roof made of fireproof slate. He subsequently erected a new Cook House, Meat House, Bake House, and Dwelling Houses for the slaves employed on the island (not for the slaves who were shipped overseas).[46] Aird was also extremely sensitive to the danger

---

45. CO 388/45/II/78–79: Richard Oswald to Board of Trade, July 6, 1752. Given the lack of concern for defense in the early years of the venture, the proprietors did not send the model of a strong house that Staple had requested. There "was no occasion for it," they wrote, since the level of trade was low and there were "dwelling houses, warehouses, slave houses, shops, magazines & other conveniencies sufficient for all the Trade that can be carried on at that Settlement."

46. GD 345/1180/118: James Low to Captain Archibald Grant, October 3, 1761. John Aird's father had been Provost of Glasgow in the first decade of the century, and been a close friend of Richard and Alexander Oswald. Aird had arrived at Bance Island in 1754. For an account of his first building program, see John Aird to Richard Oswald, October 2, 1764, Oswald Papers, Sudlows.

posed by the large number and heavy density of captive slaves within the walls of his fort; so he expended great efforts to reduce the chances of successful revolt. He walled in the slave yard, so that "in the event of an insurrection 10 Men are better able to quell it now than 30 could formerly." For the same reason, in a less accessible corner of the fort, he built an "arched & bomb-proof" magazine that could hold more gunpowder (at least 5,000 kegs) and could withstand attack better than its predecessor.

Aird's first renovations improved the capacity, efficiency, and security of the factory. Even so, the facilities could not withstand the strains to which they were subsequently subjected, as the worldwide demand for slaves exploded in the aftermath of the Seven Years' War. As the proprietors forged new contracts with foreigners, developed overseas plantations, and made new contacts with colonial planters, the flow of slaves through the factory turned into a flood. In particular, since the factory was too small to hold all the slaves and too removed from the inland sources of supply to obtain enough slaves, the proprietors established "outfactories" on nearby islands and creeks. Several trading posts had already been set up by August 1761, and the end of the Seven Years' War quickened the expansion. Depots were set up to the north of Bance Island at Sousoos, the Iles de Los, Turraduggy, Woncopong, Barrica, and Malagea, and to the south at Kissy, the Turtle Islands, and Sherbro Island. Later in the decade, three more posts were established after the agents gained the approval of local chiefs – one thirty miles northeast of Bance at Port Lago, one east at Rokel, and another southwest along the coast at Galinhas.[47]

To cope with the 1760s drive to expand, Aird laid out a second plan of renovations: cover the trade galleries; raise the walls of the New Dwelling House; convert the slave houses to whites use by raising their walls and then covering them; build a new slave quarter by raising two blocks of houses in the center of the walled square and placing these houses on "short arches" so as to keep the slaves from the damp ground[48]; build a hospital with "different divisions in it for different ranks of

---

47. Adjacent Bob Island and Tumbo Island, which had been acquired in 1748, came to be used as holding stations for captives; nearby Tasso Island had been annexed as a place for housing free blacks and growing African provisions. The outfactories are listed in the Admiralty reports.

48. The blocks were to extend the whole length of the square, the doors of the houses of the first block facing north and those of the second facing south. The arrangement separated the slaves so that, in case of revolt, there was "only one half to deal with at a Time, and . . . they never have an opportunity of knowing their whole Strength, nor of forming Plots." The division would also minimize intertribal conflict by separating Africans at war with one another.

people, all equally commodious tho' perhaps not equally nice"[49]; build a new wharf with cranes that would "twist" the goods out of a ship, lift them over the walls of the fort, and deposit them in a warehouse, thereby obviating use of "the ugly rugged hill to roll & carry every bit of goods"; and finally rebuild the gun house.[50]

Whenever possible, Aird opted for renovation in this second phase of building. But the proprietors were inclined toward even more drastic change: razing the settlement and rebuilding it on the south side of the island where they believed the situation to be healthier. Here they would deal with the mounting number of slaves by erecting a combined yard for blacks and whites and housing the slaves on an upper – hence, airier, healthier, and safer – story. But a "Train of Inconveniences" rendered the proprietors' replacement plan impracticable. Informed by those familiar with "the nature of slaves," they decided that a combined yard would not only interrupt the work of white tradesmen but also provide opportunities for the slaves to steal tools. Even more unworkable were the upper-story slave-rooms. How, Aird wondered, could slaves "that never saw stairs in their lives be trained to go up & down them in irons without the daylie Risque of breaking their Limbs, perhaps their Necks?" The most dire consequences would result during a slave insurrection: if the slaves were able to free themselves from their chains, then they could "tumble the people appointed to open the doors down before them & force their own way down in spite of opposition."

Aird prevailed, and the second phase of building proceeded according to his plan. Under his watchful eye, the Bance Island entrepôt underwent a thoroughgoing transformation. In the process, it became known as one of the finest forts along the coast, in terms of living accommodations, commercial facilities, and defensible fortifications. Merchants, traders, captains, and occasional observers all praised its capacity and comfort.

As the factory's facilities grew and diversified, so too did its population. Between 1751 and 1756, on average, 10 whites and 48 black slaves ("Grametas," that is, island blacks permanently attached to the

49. The "house for the sick" was to be made of "this Country's wood and worked round basket-fashion with small twiggs, . . . plaster'd with a thin covering of mud, whitewashed on both sides & thatched on top." Aird was a firm believer in thatched construction and a strong opponent of stone housing; the "damp arising from stone walls in the rains & their not admitting a proper quantity of air in the days" contributed to a high level of sickness and death.

50. The state of the gun house raised concern: its foundation weakened with each rainfall, and its situation allowed for no defense. Aird suggested that he raze the "long room" and gun house underneath it, and erect a new semicircular house in their place. The lower floor would serve as a gun room, and the upper story would provide an airy outlook for six large cannon that could defend the island at night.

factory and not for sale) lived within the fortifications of Bance Island.[51] From the outbreak of the Seven Years' War to the start of the American Revolution, the numbers rose to 35 whites and 142 Grametas.[52] However, these averages mask a considerable fluctuation of personnel. They also fail to show Bance Island's reliance on new recruits and the increasing variety of skills the factory employed. The island to which new recruits were drawn developed an occupational hierarchy not unlike the villages and towns of early-modern Britain they were leaving behind.[53] In command on the island were two agents appointed by the proprietors. One managed the ships, the other supervised the fort and outfactories. Directly under their control worked the factors, whose primary responsibility was to procure slaves. Each of the three to five factors supervised the work of a handful of outfactors and, in particular, acted as "a poise upon" the outfactors' conduct. An outfactor, sometimes "one of the most reputable of the natives," ran the outfactories situated alongside the creeks and inlets.[54] Side-by-side with these men who conducted the slave trade worked an army of others who made that trade possible. The "State and Condition" for 1763 notes 21 whites in 12 occupations at work on the island – surgeon, storekeeper, warehousemen, clerks, stewards, sailmakers, tailor, ship carpenters, cooper, joiners, masons, and laborer. In addition, the roster notes 38 Grametas in 12 occupations – factors, underfactors, ship masters, ship carpenters, joiners, coopers, blacksmiths, armorer, masons, gardener, surgeon's assistant, slavekeepers, and porter – which, while lower in status, ranked equal to or (in some cases) greater than the whites in skill. No longer were the Grametas classified according to where they worked, as they had been ten years before; what they did had become more important. With greater frequency, blacks were asked to conduct trade, captain ships, and manage outfactories. As for goods, the whites depended on the blacks for a wide range of services.

The extent to which the island agents employed and maintained friendly

51. Barbot, "Description," p. 99; Atkins, *Voyage*, p. 40; Lambert, ed., *Sessional Papers*, v. 68, pp. 262, 282 (June 22, 1789); and Corry, *Observations*, p. 4. Free blacks were divided into two groups – "factory" slaves who worked within the walls, and "company" or "shipping" slaves who worked with the ships and lived on the south side of the island.

52. According to the Admiralty reports, population peaked in 1763 at 233, but official accounts probably registered only the quickly detectable minimum; visitors, new recruits, men working in the outfactories, and captives were more often than not omitted from official reports. A more reliable estimate was provided by Aird who placed the population at "sometimes upward of 700." John Aird to Richard Oswald, October 2, 1764, Oswald Papers, Sudlows. For post-1755 population figures, see note 38 above.

53. GD 345/1180/1762: Sir Alexander Grant to Captain Archibald Grant, May 25, 1762.

54. GD 345/1180/1762: James Low to Captain Archibald Grant, May 10, 1762.

relations with a large number of skilled black laborers, always at least four times greater than the white population, is remarkable and perhaps exceptional. No such harmony prevailed among the whites. They were an extremely varied lot, whose service was as erratic as their sources were mixed. Much detail suggests that the factory was a funnel for young, ambitious, and often scurrilous provincials of the middling rank who possessed little prospects of advancement at home. Occasionally the factory workers were strangers directly recruited by the agents. John Aird, for example, hired men who answered the advertisement he had placed in London newspapers.[55] Usually, however, the employees were relatives, friends, or friends of relatives or friends. A significant number of white workers were close relatives of partners: the Grants, Mackintoshes, Callendars, Davidsons, and Falconars were cousins and nephews of Grant; the Murrays, Andersons, Cogills, and Robertsons kinsmen of Oswald; and the Arnolds relatives of Sargent. More often, they were the children of mere acquaintances who called upon the associates and, invoking the elusive concept of "family interest" or prior friendship, gained a place for their sons. To many, Bance Island seemed little more than an outpost for the Spey Valley (Grant's birthplace), Caithness (Oswald's), or Glasgow and southwestern Scotland (areas in which Oswald lived).[56]

The kin and countrymen who came to work on the island were often "the dregs of society." Many arrived under a cloud of guilt or suspicion and, at times, even the owners were forced to admit that the settlement resembled more a reformatory than a warehouse. Sir Alexander Grant, for example, took pity on his "poor unfortunate Friend" John Gray, who was using an assumed name in London to hide from the law. To escape, Gray could have gone to the East or West Indies, but Grant believed he would be most secure in Sierra Leone, where "he can be safe & unquestioned for his late offence" and, "if he cann reform & become sober and industrious, he may be in a better scituation than ever before." Grant gave him command of an outfactory and dangled the prospect of preferment: should Gray become "accustomed to the trade of the place & manners of the people," he would be allowed to trade

55. GD 345/1180/91: James Low to Captain Archibald Grant, August 22, 1761.
56. The Scots connection was the strongest of all bonds. Between 1751 and 1773, when we know enough about the employees to analyze their names for ethnic origin, it appears that a quarter were born in Scotland or to Scots parents. Scots ties certainly influenced the selection of agents and clerks. From 1748 to 1776, there were thirteen agents: Melwin, Staple, McLeod, McLeish, Stephens, Aird, James, Tweed, Stirling, Teise, Knight, Davidson, and McIntosh; nine were Scots. The agent John Aird and the clerk John Bowman were sons of prominent Glasgow merchants whom Oswald had known in the 1730s and 1740s.

on his own behalf under the protection of the factory. Bance Island, Grant believed, was "the happiest establishment a man in his unfortunate scituation could have."[57]

For men like Gray, the factory was both an escape from an old life and an entry into a new one. Many used service there as a steppingstone to a career as captain, correspondent, overseer, or trader in America.[58] But not all of the island employees used the opportunity to their advantage, and the quality of individual service varied greatly. One disgruntled clerk reported in 1762 that only men "of the meanest capacity" filled the office of outfactor: many "idlers" could neither spell their names nor keep proper accounts; others toiled more for their own profit than that of the company. Others, with perhaps an excess of scruple, were beaten down by the strangeness of the place and the barbarity of unsavory companions.[59]

The strange, sad story of James Low depicts the plight of the factory worker. Young Low came from Aberdeenshire, where he had worked for the celebrated agricultural improver and notorious financial wastrel Sir Archibald Grant of Monymusk, Sir Alexander's cousin. During his stay at Monymusk, Low decided he wanted to pursue a more virtuous life: he had been exposed "to so many bad Company, and witness to so many not only mean & despicable but destructive ways which many of my society run on into" that he now wanted to avoid plunging himself "headlong into an endless abyss of destruction." In search of "a rational plan," Low sought counsel from Sir Archibald, who sent him to Sir Alexander.[60]

Low arrived in London on August 2, 1761, and presented himself in Billiter Lane. Despite the fact that the baronet was in desperate need of

---

57. GD 248/350/2/25: Sir Alexander Grant to Sir Ludovick Grant of Grant, April 27, 1765; and GD 248/49/3/20: Sir Alexander Grant to Sir Ludovick Grant, January 1, 1765. Gray succeeded. For his later career, as the accountant of the Sierra Leone Company, see Robin Hallett, *The Penetration of Africa* (New York, 1965), p. 273. Cf. Miller's recent description of European immigrants who settled in western Central Africa. *Way of Death*, pp. 246–51.
58. See text at note 115 below.
59. GD 345/1180/1762: James Low to Captain Archibald Grant, May 10, 1762. Miscreants filled many posts. Clerks often behaved badly: the company books were generally in a disorderly state, on account of the carelessness of writers who, "when they get opportunity (which is frequent there upon account of their trade with the West Indies), drink away their senses," and thereby ruined themselves and harmed the company. GD 345/1180/118: James Low to Captain Archibald Grant, October 3, 1761.
60. GD 345/1166/3/36: James Low to Sir Archibald Grant, August 27, 1760. Low's thoughts first turned to small-scale farming or, given his "genius" for geography and astronomy and "a boundless ambition to see and know the world," the service of the East India Company.

"a sober, industrious young man that writes a good hand & is master of figures," Sir Alexander did little at first, and young Low spent four lonely days wandering about the metropolis.[61] He finally met the proprietors on the August 5, but, even then, the reception was anything but warm. Grant asked Low what money and equipment he possessed and, when Low candidly itemized his meager resources, Grant flew into a rage. "In his usual way," Grant fumed that it "was often the case" that his friends sent him recruits completely "naked" and expected him to clothe them. Why, he pilloried the hapless Low, would anyone advance money to a poor young Scot before he reaped "any benefit by him?" Low kept his tongue, and Grant penitently ordered Oswald's clerk "to lay in comfortable provision" for a young man unused to the sea.[62]

Low spent most of the month settling the terms of his apprenticeship. Under a standard factory contract, he agreed to serve for three years as a clerk in exchange for free passage outward, free bed, board, and washing "as other writers or clerks in his station are allowed," and £75 in wages (£20 for the first year, £25 for the second, and £30 for the third), with free passage home at the end.[63] With little money for necessities, no relatives or friends in London, and certainly no money with which to socialize with new acquaintances, Low found the city a cold and lonely place. Still, the young, wistful Scot who had left home in search of virtue patiently bided his time, acting as John Aird's personal secretary until he set sail from Portsmouth in December.[64]

From the moment Low set foot on Bance Island's sandy soil, reality

61. GD 345/1180/140: Sir Alexander Grant to Captain Archibald Grant, July 14, 1761. Sir Alexander was out of town and, later, busy servicing the West India fleet, and thus unable to discuss the position. On the way to find lodgings, which were procured with difficulty, he was stopped by a press gang and liberated only when he showed the leader Monymusk's letter of recommendation.
62. GD 345/1180/146: James Low to Captain Archibald Grant, August 5, 1761.
63. GD 345/1180/91: Agreement, August 20, 1761; GD 345/1180/144: James Low to Captain Archibald Grant, August 13, 1761. On signing the agreement, Low was given £10 to buy clothing and bedding. The company agreed to provide bedding, but suggested that Low procure his own, since the island's supply was "generally very unwholesome, as probably some one or other has died upon it." GD 345/1180/115: James Low to Captain Archibald Grant, October 27, 1761.
64. "I live in the frugallest manner possible," Low lamented in mid-September. He estimated his weekly expenses at seven shillings: "I pay 14 d. per week for my bed & lodging, & finds myself otherways in victualls, as in my idle situation I have opportunity to stroll about and takes a meal where I can get it cheapest, and frequently converts two into one, all to save expences." GD 345/1180/1120: James Low to Captain Archibald Grant, September 17, 1761; and GD 345/1180/91, 93: James Low to Captain Archibald Grant, August 22, 25, 1761. His contract did not cover costs incurred before departure. Returning to London to meet with the proprietors and recruit new workers, Aird hired Low to transcribe factory accounts and papers. GD 345/1180/118: James Low to Captain Archibald Grant, October 3, 1761.

dampened his expectations: the African experience, much like London life, proved to be a test of endurance and probity.[65] On Bance, Low and three others were employed to examine and update the 1761 accounts. To his surprise, he found few errors in recordkeeping, yet he found much else to complain about, both real and imaginary. His apprenticeship agreement, he suspected, had not been sent, nor had any letter of recommendation. Moreover, neither bedding nor washing was provided and he was forced to pay six pence for his weekly ration of soap. The most galling aspect of servitude was his pay, and he constantly complained about receiving "the least wages upon the island."[66] Despite such disappointments, Low experienced few real hardships. He always sat with the agents at their table in the dining hall, he was exempted from watch duty at night, and he gained respect for his work as an accountant. By mid-February 1762, he had closed the 1761 books to everyone's satisfaction and been promoted chief clerk. "Diligent, honest and sober" ways paid off.[67]

Yet, as his stock rose, his spirits sank. The fact that "the way of life here and my disposition will not coincide" profoundly disturbed him. He ignored all signs of favor and focused exclusively on his inferior economic station, his superior moral position, and his precarious state of health. What Low had hoped to escape in Aberdeenshire he found rampant in Africa. He saw vice, alcoholic and sexual, all around him, increasingly threatening not only his peace of mind but also, he feared, his fitness of body.[68] Shunning the appearance of depravity, hoping to

---

65. GD 345/1180/1762: James Low to Captain Archibald Grant, January 30, 1762.

66. GD 345/1180/1762: James Low to Captain Archibald Grant, May 10, 1762, accounts for the clamor over wages. The early 1760s were a time of rapid upheaval in personnel. Many of the outfactors were offering their resignations, with the intention of returning home or settling and trading inland. Employees were in short supply, and new arrivals from England could not fill old vacancies or new positions fast enough. The agents often offered £30 to £40 per year "to people from the ships that are presently here that can barely write their names." "People when here by accident," Low grumbled, "get better encouragement than they would do in Europe." One such person, an old school friend from Aberdeen, had arrived in a slave ship that the factory had hired; knowing him to be honest and diligent, Low recommended him to the agents, but, to Low's mortification, the agents offered his friend £36 per year for the first two years and £48 for the third year to work with another white at an outfactory. GD 345/1180/1762: James Low to Captain Archibald Grant, February 10, 22, 1762.

67. GD 345/1180/1762: James Low to Captain Archibald Grant, February 10, 1762.

68. Low took "daily warning by other people's folly." The workers were dissolute and the traders unprincipled, he thought, and the ways of both groups led to sickness and death. GD 345/1180/1762: James Low to Captain Archibald Grant, March 29, 1762. The factory, he observed, was bad for the blacks but worse for the whites: on average, whereas probably one-sixth (80–90 blacks) of the black population died each year on the island, nearly one-half of the white population died. GD 345/1180/1762: James Low to Captain Archibald Grant, March 29, 1762; and Hancock, "Citizen of the

avoid indisposition, he immersed himself in accounting and sought curiosities for Sir Archibald's museum at Monymusk House. Low's last letter from Bance bears the date August 9, 1762. Despite all his precautions, he fell a victim of the summer rains. His own regularity and virtue were not enough to avoid illness, and he ended his days in much the same way as his more dissolute comrades.[69]

The slave factory – white man's grave, social penitentiary, or commercial college – grew in size and increased in complexity during the period 1748–63. Through dogged overhaul and supervision of its defenses, facilities, supplies, and labor, the proprietors transformed the operation. Despite the mortality and the inhumanity of the operation against the blacks, the proprietors succeeded in creating a showpiece for eighteenth-century British imperial enterprisers. It was a workable, if deadly paradise, and a place that Sir Alexander Grant could brag was "a Territory where my Dominion is most absolute." It was, also, by 1763, ready to do business on a larger scale.[70]

"Negroes Really Support My Affluence"

From the outset of the experiment, the six partners' Bance Island slave trade deviated from the reorganized system under the Company of Merchants Trading to Africa that they themselves had helped to introduce. Under this system, which organized Britain's slave trade from 1750 to 1807, slaving was usually conducted from the decks of

---

World," p. 681. For greater estimates of the numbers who died, see Philip D. Curtin, *The Image of Africa* (Madison, 1964), pp. 71, 483–84 (46% of the white European settlers of Freedom (Sierra Leone) died within the first year during the late 1780s and early 1790s; 39% of the blacks died); and H. M. Feinberg, "New Data on European Mortality in West Africa: The Dutch on the Gold Coast, 1719–1760," *Journal of African History*, v. 15 (1974), pp. 363–66 (18% of the whites on the Dutch Gold Coast died per year between 1719 and 1760). Despite these high numbers, workers continued to view the island as a gold mine, in large measure because few reports of the deaths trickled back to Britain. Record of white deaths was kept in the island's "Black Roll." GD 345/1170/1765: Sir Alexander Grant to Sir Archibald Grant, March 9, 1765. The agents generally attributed the high incidence of death to social origin: those that died were "mostly trade people and others of hard labour, . . . the dregs of society." The way of life that the employees had followed in Britain, the proprietors believed, "will naturally follow" on Bance Island, and that style of living soon put "a period to their days." Low agreed that the "frequent mortality in this part of the world is as much owing to people's irregular way of life as to any bad effects of the climate." GD 345/1180/117: James Low to Captain Archibald Grant, October 1761; and GD 345/1180/1762: James Low to Captain Archibald Grant, May 25, 1762.
69. On Low's death, see GD 345/1180/1763: Sir Archibald Grant to Captain Archibald Grant, March 24, 1763; GD 345/1169/1763: David Low to Sir Archibald Grant, November 22, 1763; and GD 345/1170/1765: Sir Alexander Grant to Sir Archibald Grant, July 11, 1764.
70. GD 248/350/2/25: Sir Alexander Grant to Sir Ludovick Grant, April 27, 1765.

ships.[71] Rather than adhere to the customary "ship trade," however, the Bance Island owners focused on a stationary settlement under the control of a single company.[72] In this "fort trade," which had previously been employed by the RAC, captives were brought by Africans to fort employees, who paid for the slaves and sold them to European or Afro-European shippers. At work was a trade-off between slave prices and slaving times. For collecting and "inventorying" slaves, Bance Island could charge a premium because its operations shortened the time "ship trade" slavers spent on the coast. The savings in time was particularly critical in an undeveloped area like the Windward Coast where the business of gathering slaves was usually slow. A full load with a quick turnaround suited slavers who sought the competitive advantage of being the first each year to arrive in American markets.

For the most part, the Bance Island partners' "fort trade" combined barter exchanges with middleman services. With the passage of time, however, as the island's commercial facilities expanded and demands upon them increased, the London owners modified their way of doing business and incorporated elements of a ship trade that pushed inland, closer to the source of supply. Underlying both approaches was the bedrock of barter. The first command the proprietors issued was "to employ" European goods "in a Barter Trade."[73] Their agents were neither to kidnap the slaves nor to wage war on the tribes, although they could feed "the wars inland" when the country was heavily populated with Africans or could take advantage of drought and famine conditions which induced Africans to sell themselves into slavery. As the agents reckoned, factory interests were best served if the agents removed "every obstruction" to the Africans' "coming down" and used "all their influence" to give "free access to the coast & a safe conduct." Acquiring

71. "A Description of Africa," c. September 1782, Bedfordshire Record Office, L 29/339, Bedford; and Robert P. Thomas and Richard N. Bean, "The Fishers of Men: The Profits of the Slave Trade," *Journal of Economic History*, 2nd ser., v. 34 (1974), p. 899.

72. The exceptional nature of Bance Island may be overstated. Certainly, no other company received royal warranty of its property, and no other firm had such an elaborate settlement; still, a few competing firms maintained fixed facilities along the coast. Smeathman mentions the buildings belonging to Barber & Co. of Liverpool in the Sherbro River. Smeathman Diary, envelope 2, Ms. D26 sub May 23, 1773, University of Uppsala Library, Uppsala. Inikori, "Market Structure," p. 764, refers to at least two large factories built in the 1790s in the vicinity of the Sierra Leone River. Bance Island may better exemplify not a deviation from a rule but an altogether new rule that was followed by others. Cf. Richard Brew's Brew castle, on the Gold Coast, which was begun later (1763) and more focused on the supply of Anomabu Fort. Margaret Priestley, *West African Trade and Coast Society* (London, 1969).

73. CO 388/45/II/78–79: Richard Oswald to Board of Trade, July 6, 1752. An exchange for slaves was the factory's raison d'être, but a barter for camwood and ivory also took place. CO 388/43/Bb105: John Boyce to Captain Boyce, February 2, 1744; CO 388/44/CC73: Captain Pye to Admiralty Secretary, March 18, 1750; CO 388/44/CC75-4: State, January 2, 1752; and Lambert, ed., *Sessional Papers*, v. 68, p. 259.

Africans through barter was easier, more efficient, and more effective than direct capture.[74]

The manufactured goods that merchants like Grant and Oswald brought to the barter varied in character and origin, and show how they marshaled their extensive international networks to support their slaving.[75] The bills of lading and account books itemizing goods the associates sent out to the new Company of Merchants list large quantities of East India goods (Smith, Aufrere & Co.; Arnold & Co.; Sargent, Birch & Co.; and Sargent, Aufrere & Co.), tobacco (Oswald & Co.), and medicines (Johnston & Co.).[76] They sent similar assortments to their own Bance Island. One 1751 list indicates that they thought it prudent to lay up seventeen different kinds of cloth, as well as a wide assortment of beads, coral, crystal, and guns.[77] Over twenty years later,

74. On no recorded occasion did the agents engineer or sanction the capture of Africans by factory employees. Better serving the interests of harmony and economy, their way was to leave enslavement to the Africans. *A Short View*, p. 14; and Thomas and Bean, "Fishers," pp. 905–06. Still, enslavement seems to have been largely a function of white demand. According to Chief Namina Modoro of Port Lago, people inland "go to war on purpose to make slaves. If there is no demand they won't go to war." Zachary Macaulay's Journal, November 28, 1793, MY 418/Folder 2, Huntington Library, San Marino; and Edward Grace to Amable Doct, June 6, July 25, 1768, Edward Grace Letter Book, Guildhall Library Ms. 12048. According to the agent Tweed, "a great many very populous empires and kingdoms, extended along the coast, and reaching above six weeks' journey inland," and these regions were "governed by princes of a warlike and achieving turn," whose disputes brought Africans and commodities to market. Tweed, *Considerations*, pp. 61–63. Occasionally, enslavement was openly encouraged by whites. According to Namina Modoro's summary of practice prevailing since the 1760s, whites "were in the practice also of exciting the natives to make war on each other, giving arms & ammunition to both parties." Macaulay's Journal, November 28, 1793, MY 418/Folder 2, Huntington Library, San Marino. On famines, see George E. Brooks, *Landlords and Strangers*, p. 319.

75. French, in "Trade and Shipping," pp. 58–68, outlines the goods merchants like the associates would have obtained from the various regions: the northern Baltic states (naval stores, iron, potash, and furs); Denmark (guns); Germany (yarn, linen, and tin); Holland (thread, linen, tape, whale, and madder); India (silk, calicoes, cottons, muslin, tea, and drugs); and Turkey (oil, dyestuffs, drugs, soap, and silks). See also Inikori, "Import," pp. 360–61. The point that most goods were British manufactures was incorrectly made by [Campbell,] *Candid and Impartial Considerations*, p. 21.

76. PRO-CL, Ext 1/299/ 86E-H, 61A-C; CO 388/49/118–23; and T 70/357–58. During the 1760s, Sargent's firm provided the new African Company with almost £10,000 in India goods. Chief among these were saltpetre, cottons, and pepper. See also IOL, B 72/92, 236, 315, 483, 546; B 73/7, 43, 118, 363, 373; B 84/485–86; and B 86/12. "Brawles, Bandannahs, Basts, Byrampants, Chints, Corridarries, Coopees, ... Guinea stuffs, Chucklaes, Photaes, Old Sheets, Taffetas," topsails, beads, and cowries were obtained by the associates at the India Company's auctions in Leadenhall Street and sold to the new Company. For a description of sale by auction, see Marshall, *Problems of Empire*, pp. 79, 82.

77. CO 388/45/II/86, 84: Indent, August 29, 1751. Admiralty reports confirm the continued importance of cloth and armament to the island's trade. State and Condition, June 28, 1758, House of Lords Main Papers; CO 388/54: State and Condition, May

at the outbreak of the American Revolution, they were still shipping similar cargoes; one typical large ship bound for the factory bore toys, glassware, hardware (particularly Dutch knives), spirits (sometimes as much as 14,000 gallons), British cloth, French guns, and gunpowder.[78]

Notwithstanding the international source of most barter goods, the exchange was a relatively simple affair. An African king brought to the agent the Africans that his men had captured or the crops his people had grown. After negotiating a sale, the agent gave the king the agreed-upon manufactures for the captives, foodstuffs, or luxury goods.[79] The accountant James Low left us a eyewitness report of the mechanics of ordinary barter in early 1762. On that occasion, the Africans came to the factory in search of European commodities, bringing with them slaves, rice, and ivory. Since there was "no specie current in the Country, at least in this part of it," small shells brought from India, each worth one bar (roughly five shillings), served as counters, as well as a form of real money. In terms of shells, "each piece of European goods" as well as each African commodity had a fixed price, "be it good or bad"; a "prime slave" in 1762–63 averaged sixty-five bars. Calculations and transfers were made by the buyer and seller under the roof of the Palaver House. The kings would leave with trinkets, rum, tobacco, or gunpowder, and the agents would remain with slaves, ivory, or food.[80]

In British West Africa during this period, the native African commercial infrastructure was highly developed, characterized by "a high level of [African] administrative control" not matched in other regions of the continent. Since they could rely on African suppliers, the British had

9, 1765; and CO 388/50/Ji65: State and Condition, May 26, 1765. The Government prohibited the export of guns in wartime but excepted their export to Africa. T 1 (requests) and T 52 (warrants) for the stockpiling of guns, esp. T 1/370/33: George Aufrere to Ordnance Board, May 17, 1756, and T 1/365/88: Richard Oswald to Treasury Board, November 1, 1756.

78. Mss.Eur./D.624/2/299–304, IOL. Not just any goods would do. The Africans of Sierra Leone preferred India goods above all others. When Sargent petitioned the India Company to increase the amounts it imported from India, he cautioned its Directors not to think that all goods and manufactures were the same. "Indian Goods" commanded "a Preference over every other" among the inhabitants of the Windward Coast. See also Donnan, ed., *Documents*, v. 2, pp. 468–69.

79. It was always possible for a slave trader to bring to the negotiation only a promise to deliver goods or slaves. Such promises encouraged the growth of a credit economy in the hinterland.

80. GD 345/1180/1762: James Low to Captain Archibald Grant, January 30, 1762; and Tweed, *Considerations*, pp. 65–67. The most common shell in use was the India cowrie. See B/1/53/88 (April 18, 1770), IOL, for an instance of Sargent purchasing 3.5 tons of cowries from the India Company. The standard iron bar served as the unit of account, in lieu of precious metals on the African coast. On cowry shells, see Jan Hogendorn and Marion Johnson, *The Shell Money of the Slave Trade* (Cambridge, 1986).

little need to involve themselves in the interior to the degree that, say, the Portuguese did in Angola or the French did in Galam.[81] In Sierra Leone, there seem to have been no African or mixed-race caravan or village communities specializing in slaving; nor on the European side was there anything like the bureaucracy or the regulation of tight-packing of slaves in ships and smuggling. Along the Windward Coast, the kings were the primary agents. The kings and their chiefs set rents which the Bance Islanders paid for permission to trade and, later, the Africans often fixed the sale prices of their slaves. From what little evidence survives, it appears that the kings also commonly fixed the value of a healthy man slave and the number of goods per slave. Once the rates were set, the kings and chiefs were the first to trade at the factory or its outpost. In Sierra Leone, it is not clear exactly how the kings obtained their slaves, or from where. Intertribal warfare, the product of hinterland political, social, economic, and demographic change heightened by European demand, created slaving opportunities for Africans. But whatever their means of procurement, the kings carried their own tribe's conquests or passed along the victims of the intertribal violence of other tribes to the company's factories. The Bance Islanders operated in a system that was tightly structured by the Africans.[82]

Over the years, the associates' bartering moved upstream and inland. From the arrival of the first slavers in the vicinity of Sierra Leone, the jungle, a dense and usually impenetrable barrier to trade, made the interior less accessible than, say, the savannah land of the Slave Coast or Portuguese Loango-Angola was. There was also the distinctly British aversion to going inland, if the examples of India and the Hudson's Bay Territory are any indication. Only slowly were these obstacles broken down by the associates. The change was beginning when the accountant James Low stepped ashore in 1762 and, as the decade unfolded, there came to be "very little trade made upon the island itself," the bulk of the trade having passed to "the craft who ply into the rivers and creeks, and the outfactorys." Rather than wait for the chiefs to come to them,

---

81. Robin Law, *The Slave Coast of West Africa, 1550–1750* (Oxford, 1991), pp. 206–19; Miller, *Way of Death*; and Abdoulaye Bathily, "La Traité Atlantique et ses Effets Economiques et Sociaux en Afrique," *Journal of African History*, v. 27 (1986), pp. 269–93.
82. Observations about the Sierra Leone region are taken from Tweed, *Considerations*, pp. 60–69; and Zachary Macaulay's Diary, 1780s–90s, MY 2, and Zachary Macaulay's Journal, 1793–99, MY 418, Huntington Library, San Marino. On the relation between war and the supply of slaves, see Edward Grace to Amable Doct, September 4, 1768, Edward Grace Letter Book, Guildhall Library. Robert Stein, in *French Sugar Business*, pp. 27–32, notes that the average French slaver spent five months in Africa.

the agents went to the chiefs. They set up twelve new outfactories over the course of the decade, and placed great pressure on the factors and outfactors to perform. It became customary to give the factors, who either

> travel into the country themselves, or deal with other factors still further up the river, a quantity of European goods on credit (a great part of them gunpowder and spirits) and if the man in possession of the goods wastes or consumes them, so as not to fulfill his obligation of bringing the stipulated slave or slaves in return, he is taken for a slave himself; or if he does not return in a certain time, any one of his family is taken.[83]

The recorded history of the Bance Island venture lacks any specific account of the Africans and the slaves themselves: where they came from, how they were captured, their life on the island, how they were shipped out, and the kind of life they had when they got to America. We glean precious few details from hints scattered in spotty and disparate sources. Low noted that as many as eighty or ninety blacks died each year. Oswald once ordered his captains to ignore international custom, forgo branding slaves with hot irons, and instead place "checkered beads round the arms" of Bance Island slaves. Later he ordered his Florida overseers to keep slave families from Bance Island together on the same plantation.[84] But these are the only hints we have. The records documenting the work of the factory are sadly cool and businesslike. The modern reader, who wants to know about the inhumanity of its owners and agents, is frustrated at every step by silence. With little moral censure from their contemporaries during the 1750, 1760s, and early 1770s, British slave traders, having existed well over a century, had accommodated themselves to ambiguity: in many respects, Oswald viewed himself as a benevolent head of a family, fussing over the health of his captives, worrying about branding, and trying to keep their families intact; yet, at the same time, he was a calculating merchant who never once forgot that these slaves were inferior members of the extended family he headed. A proprietor of the day valued slaves' productivity over their happiness or liberty. Sitting in his faraway

83. GD 345/1180/1762: James Low to Captain Archibald Grant, May 10, 1762.
84. GD 345/1180/1762: James Low to Captain Archibald Grant, March 29, 1762; C 12/1036/12; Richard Oswald to Governor Grant, May 25, 1767, BCM 295; Henry Laurens to Richard Oswald, August 16, 1783, Henry Laurens Papers, South Carolina Historical Society; Richard Oswald to Captain Smith, July 10, 1774, Sir Alexander Grant to John Gordon, May 3, 1770, and Sir Alexander Grant to John Grant, September 20, 1770, Grant Papers, Tomintoul House.

London counting-house, Oswald did not think a great deal about the inhumanity. He expressed concern from time to time, but nonetheless he allowed himself to be distanced and dissociated from the non-commercial aspects of slaving.

The partners' chief concern was providing slaves to Europeans, Afro-Europeans, and Americans by combining four different systems: partners' proprietary sales to satisfy their own and their clients' needs for slaves; selling slaves by private trades with coast traders; undertaking speculative company ventures that transported slaves to the New World; and providing foreign companies with slaves under long-term contracts.

As Table 6.1 and Graph 6.1 suggest, during the thirty-six years of associate control, partners' proprietary sales accounted for only 18 percent of the captives brought to the island. The partners used the first years of their ownership to satisfy their own plantations' needs or those of their planter-correspondents. During the period of "languid" control through 1752, 16 slaves were shipped in one vessel to the Boyds' sugar plantations in St. Christopher, and 314 slaves were put aboard other ships and sent to Oswald's business clients in tidewater Virginia. After 1752, the partners supplied their own American plantations on only three known occasions. In 1767, Oswald shipped 106 slaves to his plantations in Florida; and he sent similar contingents in 1771 and 1772. Instead, in the years following parliamentary title confirmation, most slaves were directed to Oswald's plantation customers in America. Only a few were sent to the clients of other associates.[85]

Nearly the same number of slaves was involved in private trades with coast traders not directly linked to the partners as correspondents. Records show that traders other than the associates purchased slaves on eleven recorded occasions in forty-five years, and took away 17 percent of the total number of slaves exported by the factory. These figures surely underestimate the frequency of this type of transaction, however, since many of these exchanges were "private" between slave ships and island agents, and may not have been reported to London. Throughout the second half of the century, the island was regarded as a desirable "general rendezvous." Numerous nonquantifiable references suggest that

---

85. For rare use by other associates, see ships sent by Mill in 1763 and 1765 and by Grant in 1765. The numbers might have been greater, but circumstances often intervened. Sir Alexander Grant, for example, generally bought his laborers in Jamaica, but, on at least one occasion, he tried to buy several factory slaves for some new estates he had recently acquired in northern Jamaica, and he was frustrated by the fact that his captain could not procure a full cargo of slaves on the Windward Coast. Sir Alexander Grant to John Gordon, October 15, 1769, Sir Alexander Grant Letter Book, Grant Papers, Tomintoul House.

Table 6.1   Slave Exports from Bance Island and West Africa by Grant, Oswald & Co., 1748-84

Year	Total	Large Contract	Company Venture	Private Trade	Proprietary Sale
1748	0				
	53				53
1750	152				152
	4				4
	121				121
	0				
	0				
1755	0				
	423			276	147
	0				
	230		230		
	440		240		200
1760	337		337		
	300		300		
	240		240		
	1,213	905			308
	700	700			
1765	1,956	800	732		424
	1,718	1,461		257	
	1,199	581	515		103
	477	400	77		
	145		145		
1770	348			348	
	1,444		480	726	238
	884		218	571	95
	358				358
	0				
1775	0				
	37			37	
	0				
	0				
	0				
1780	0				
	0				
	0				
	0				
1784	150				150
Total	12,929	4,847	3,514	2,215	2,353
Percent	100%	0%	27%	17%	18%

Sources: See source notes for Table 4.1.

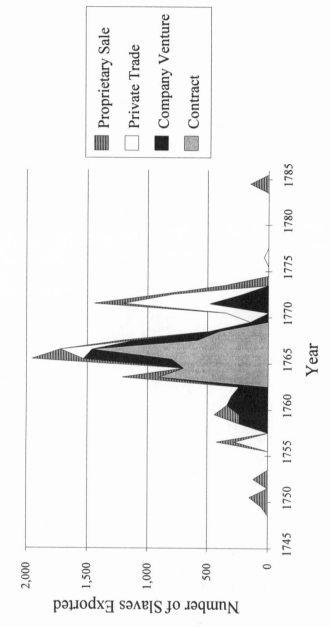

Graph 6.1 Slave Exports from West Africa by Grant, Oswald & Co., 1748–84

more British, French, Danish, Dutch, and Portuguese ships came there than we can attach figures to.[86]

As the slave factory became established, satisfying the needs of partners' plantations or overseas clients declined in importance, and the company's own ventures came to assume a more substantial part of the trade, in terms of the number of slaves shipped and voyages made. Beginning in 1758, Grant, Oswald & Co. backed voyages in the *Betsey*, *Bance Island*, *Nancy*, *Africa*, *Rockhall*, and *King George*. The proprietors sent one or two of these vessels to the island each year with orders to procure a full load of 400 slaves and then carry them to South Carolina, Georgia, St. Christopher, or Grenada. There the captives were sold by the captains or delivered to the associates' correspondents.[87]

The last outlet to be adopted, the large contract, became the most important. The contract was a form of company venture that sold slaves to foreigners, but neither transported them to nor sold them in the American market. During the thirty-six-year period of associate direction, 37 percent of the slaves exported from the island were shipped on one factory contract alone (Table 6.2). Such large-scale trading with foreigners was an uncommon arrangement, and Bance Island's contracts with the Dutch and the French were almost certainly the first of their kind along the coast.[88] The largest of these contracts was drawn

86. The absence of such transactions may also reflect the paucity of sources: whereas the letters of the partners evidence the satisfaction of their own personal needs as commission merchants and plantation owners, few other parallel bodies of records document the dealings of other traders with Bance Island. It may reflect, too, the imprecision of reporting. While there is record of only one Liverpool ship (December 1758) and one Bristol ship (1769) departing Bance Island, many more ships departed surrounding areas, like Sherbro, the Bananas, and the Isles de Los, where the outfactories stood. BT 6/3; and David Richardson, ed., *Bristol, Africa and the Eighteenth-Century Slave Trade to America* (Bristol, 1991), p. 232. For the presence of European ships at Bance Island's wharf, see *Lloyd's List*, March 26, 1751, and April 21, 1752; and France, Orleans, Foache Collection, Letters, 1759 and 1761, cited in Patrick Villiers, "Les Bases Internationales de L'Armement Maritime: Les Foache et la Guerre de Sept-Ans," in Francois M. Crouzet, ed., *Le Négoce Internationale XIIIe–XXe siècle* (Paris, 1989), pp. 171–75.

87. Finding a correspondent for joint ventures could be difficult. In 1767, Grant walked to Messrs. Truman & Neave in search of a possible consignee in St. Christopher; finding Truman out of town and Neave "haughty and supercilious," he went to Ross & Mill, who were also away; he finally secured a contact through Maitland & Boddington. Sir Alexander Grant to Richard Oswald, August 29, 1767, Oswald Papers, Sudlows. Henry Laurens got his Charleston relatives to serve as Richard Oswald's consignees in that port. Higgins, "Charleston," pp. 123–24.

88. Such a contract was sanctioned by the experts. Postlethwayt, for instance, thought that "the peaceable arm of commerce" was one way "to put it out of the power of France to hurt" England. *Universal Dictionary*, v. 1, p. 355, sub "Britain." The earliest of the contracts was with the sugar broker Michiel Baalde of Rotterdam in 1759–63, and with Stanislas Foache of LeHavre in 1761–63. Villiers, "Les Bases," p. 176. Before August 1760, Oswald had agreed to supply Baalde's clients with 250

Table 6.2   Deliveries to Honfleur Contract Ships, 1763-68

Year	Number of Slaves	Ship
1763	350	*La Marie Gabrielle*
	157	*La Jeanne Gentille*
	398	*La Marquise de Brancas*
1764	400	*La Marie Rose*
	300	*La Marie Gabrielle*
1765	400	*La Marquise de Brancas*
	300	*Le Prince de Lamballe*
1766	300	*La Marie Gabrielle*
	391	*La Marquise de Brancas*
	390	*Le Roland*
	380	*Le Côte d'Or*
1767	385	*Le Prince de Lamballe*
	196	*La Madeleine*
1768	400	*La Marquise de Brancas*
Total	4,847	
Average		
year	969	
ship	346	

Source: Mettas, *Repertoire*, v. 2.

up in 1762. Two groups were involved. On the English side was Grant, Oswald & Co.; and on the French side was the "Société pour la Rivière de Sierralionne," a company based in Honfleur. The Society was capitalized at 500,000 livre tournois (roughly £22,000 pounds sterling) which was divided in eighths among four Honfleur merchants. One of the merchants, Jean Baptiste Premord, acted as general manager and chief spokesman.[89] Ordinarily, Premord would have assumed responsibility for financial matters himself, but in this instance he delegated it to the Paris banker Sir John Lambert, an English baronet whose connections to the associates won them the Premord contract.[90]

The chief objective of the Society was to procure slaves for French

slaves. In that month, Baalde advised Foache to procure the same from Oswald in London. Baalde was married to Maria Geertruyda van Coopstad, the daughter of a partner in Rotterdam's principal slave-trading firm, Coopstad & Rochussen; he died in 1770. Register of Marine Permissions for Ships (Old Archives # 2,518), 1759–62, Gemeente Archief, Rotterdam; and Patrick Villiers, "Armateurs et Navires Negriers en Temps de Guerre: La Correspondence Foache, Négociants au Havre, 1759–1762," in *De La Traité a L'Esclavage*, v. 1 (Nantes, 1985), pp. 469–73. For further information on Foache, see M. B. Demeaux, *Mémorial d'Une Famille du Havre*, v. 1 (Paris, 1971), Tables I–IV. Foache's ships had visited Bance Island in 1754 and 1755. Mettas, *Répertoire*, v. 2, pp. 418–19. The contract Foache discussed with Oswald in Fall 1760 involved 500 slaves, at £18 per head; this was to be a concealed expedition, sailing under a Spanish flag, since Britain and France were at war with each other. In 1763, in response to a query made by the Board of Trade Secretary (who was also Oswald's neighbor and friend), the new Company of Merchants replied that it thought contracts with foreigners were "at present Confin'd within a Small Compass"; in fact, the only contracts the committee could think of were those between Bance Island and the French, yet it suspected that the number of slaves exported on contracts would rise with similar contracts. T 70/29/308r: Company of Merchants to John Pownall, December 21, 1763.

89. £22,000 in 1762 amounts £172,193 or $256,116 in 1994. Situated between Caen and LeHavre on the Normandy coast, Honfleur was the fifth largest slave-trading port of France. Jean Mettas, "Honfleur et la traité des Noirs au XVIIIe siècle," *Revue Française d'Histoire d'Outre-Mer*, v. 60 (1973), p. 5. The four merchants were Jean Baptiste Premord, who held a 3/8 interest; Louis Julien, 2/8; Hornetener, 2/8; and DePaterne, 1/8. On the life of Premord, see Mettas, "Honfleur," pp. 14–18; Robert Stein, *The French Slave Trade in the Eighteenth Century: An Old Regime Business* (Madison, 1979), p. 153; and A. Vintras, *Archives du Calvados: Repertoire Numérique des Archives Municipales de Honfleur* (Caen, 1923). Premord came from an old Honfleur family: his grandfather served as an alderman and sheriff; his father supervised armaments for the slaving Compagnie de Senegal. Premord had already launched the slaving Society of Guadeloupe in the 1750s.

90. On Sir John Lambert, see G. E. Cokayne, ed., *Complete Baronetage*, v. 5 (Exeter, 1906), pp. 10–11; and Herbert Luthy, *La Banque Protestante en France...*, v. 2 (Paris, 1961), pp. 319–20. Lambert's grandfather Sir John Lambert I (1666–1723), an eminent Huguenot merchant who had fled to England in 1685 and subsequently loaned Queen Anne £400,000, was later exiled for the part he played in the South Sea Bubble. *The Case of Samuel Shepherd, John Lambert, and John James David, Merchants of London* (London, 1713); *The Appellant's Case: Sir John Lambert, Bart., Appellant v. Sir Daniel O'Carrol* (London, 1731); and Agnew, *Protestant Exiles*, p. 497.

plantations in Guadeloupe and Saint Domingue, which suffered severely from the interruption of trade during the Seven Years' War. To this end, Premord contracted with Oswald for 7,500 slaves. Over a five-year period, the proprietors agreed to deliver 1,500 "prime slaves" each year to the Society, to be divided among four different ships that would arrive on the African coast four times annually.[91] Premord was to pay £22 per slave, and payment was to be made by Lambert to Oswald in bills of exchange drawn on Paris according to a prearranged timetable.[92] The sex, age, and height of the slaves were all specified in great detail.[93] Two-thirds of the slaves were to be men. In any delivery of 350 slaves, 120 were to be men younger than 27; 80 boys above 4'4"; 34 boys between 3'10" and 4'3"; 25 "women-girls"; and 21 girls between 4' and 4'3". Heavy penalties were stipulated for noncompliance by either party.[94]

By the time the last contract ship left Bance Island in March 1768, bound for Saint Domingue, Grant, Oswald & Co. had placed 4,847 slaves on board 14 ships sent by the Honfleur Society. The contract had averaged 969 slaves per year for five years and 346 slaves per vessel, dramatically more than the 1763–1768 averages maintained by London slavers (219 slaves per vessel) and Liverpool slavers (235 slaves).[95]

On the African coast, execution of the contract posed few problems: while the arrangement seriously strained the factory's capacity, necessitating more factories and workers, only occasionally did the agents incur demurrage charges or fail to deliver the agreed-upon number of

---

91. There is some disagreement on the numbers involved. The data suggest 1,200 per year (3 shiploads of 400 per ship), but contemporary observations are higher. Premord's agent mentioned 1,500 slaves and four ships (Mettas, "Honfleur," p. 14) and Tweed concurred (*Considerations*, pp. 65–67), but Francis Rogue alluded to 2,000 slaves per year, and Nicolas Lion said the contract agreed on six ships, four loads of slaves to the New World and two loads of indigo to France (Mettas, "Honfleur," p. 14).

92. T 70/29/308r. £22 in 1762 amounts to £1,492 or $2,219 in 1994. Factory prices were high. Presumably, they were deemed acceptable by the fast turnaround of ships that resulted from doing business with the factory. The French armateur Foache, who struck a contract two years earlier, summed up the reason for higher prices: "La longueur des voyages est un objet très désavantageux." Villiers, "Les Bases," p. 171.

93. Tweed, *Considerations*, pp. 65–67.

94. If the Society should not accept the number of slaves which it had agreed to accept, it would have to pay the proprietors £9 for every unaccepted slave. Moreover, the Society's ships were to spend two months on the coast, waiting for the factory to fill the order and, if the agents could not supply the contracted number of slaves in the two-month period, the factory would have to pay the Society £30 in demurrage fees for every day that the ship lingered on the coast. To further discourage noncompliance, the parties agreed to an additional £5,000 penalty. Tweed, *Considerations*, pp. 65–67.

95. David Richardson, "The Eighteenth-Century British Slave Trade," *Research in Economic History*, v. 12 (1989), Appendix.

slaves. It was in Europe where the operation broke down. Difficulties arose over the manner of remittance. Time was of the essence, since payment for one cargo of slaves had to precede delivery of the next.[96] Under the arrangement, Premord asked Lambert to sell the Society a bill of exchange, which the Society would remit to Grant, Oswald & Co. The London firm handed the bill to the "drawee" stipulated on the bill and received cash. Lambert drew bills on his correspondent in London that were payable in a specified number of days. If the correspondent had in his control funds belonging to Lambert, he debited Lambert's account for the sum of the bills; if he did not, he would obtain funds by drawing and selling other bills on Lambert. On several occasions, however, the drawee declined to accept the bill of exchange and returned it to Grant, Oswald & Co., because he had no Lambert funds and he knew Lambert could not pay other bills drawn on him; Lambert had neither sufficient cash reserves in Paris nor sufficient credit balances in London. Lambert, in turn, had insufficient reserves, because the Honfleur Society had not paid him, and the Honfleur Society had not paid Lambert because it had insufficient income.[97]

The situation became intolerable late in 1766. Believing Premord's assurances of quick remittance and reimbursement, Lambert had advanced the Society considerable sums of money from his own reserves, but repayment was not forthcoming. Premord was unable to pay because "the high price of goods in America" made the collection of "considerable returns" from planters an extremely slow process. Moreover, the conduct of the trade made the operation extremely uncertain: ship captains and Caribbean agents supposedly failed to submit receipts acknowledging the acceptance of slaves by the captain or auctioneer in America.[98] Premord contemplated bypassing Lambert altogether in order to eliminate the commission fee, but Grant and Oswald balked at such a risky arrangement and the entire scheme ground to a halt. The

96. Sudlows, Oswald Papers, Sir Alexander Grant to Richard Oswald, September 22, 1767. For contemporary discussion of the art of managing bills of exchange, see Beawes, *Lex Mercatoria Rediviva*; Timothy Cunningham, *Laws of Bills of Exchange* (London, 1760), and *The Merchant's Lawyer* (London, 1761); and the excellent summary in Joseph Chitty, *A Treatise on the Laws of Bills of Exchange* (London, 1799). A succinct modern account appears in McCusker, *Money and Exchange*, pp. 18–22.
97. Richard Oswald & Co. to Hornetener, Walker & Co., November 29, 1768, and Sir John Lambert to Oswald & Co., August 18, December 15, 1766, Oswald Papers, Sudlows.
98. Sir John Lambert to Oswald & Co., December 15, 1766, and John Aird to Richard Oswald, September 4, 1766, Oswald Papers, Sudlows. See Mettas, "Honfleur," p. 16, on the problem of slow returns plaguing Premord. Mettas believes that Premord's turnaround time was unusually fast, a condition that irreparably strained his capital resources. Of equal importance was the fact that there was a substantial postwar depression in progress.

only legal remedy available to Grant, Oswald & Co. was to "protest" Premord's bills for nonpayment or nonacceptance and then sue on the protested bill in a commercial court. "Embarrassment & unpunctuality" in payment vexed the owners into terminating the contract early in 1768.[99]

Despite its early demise, the contract had a profound impact on Grant, Oswald & Co.'s slaving. It brought the partners significant profit: gross margins totaled £28,000, averaging £2,000 per delivery or £5,600 per year.[100] While company ventures and private trades may have been even more profitable on a per slave or per ship basis, these proceeds were the most concentrated and sustained of those produced by any of the various marketing arrangements.[101] The French contract also significantly changed the partners' way of doing business. On one level, the additional demand for slaves directly spurred expansion. The proprietors' response, as we have already noticed, was to add more personnel and erect more buildings on the island, and move procurement inland beyond the factory to the outfactories.[102] On another level, the contract also introduced joint ventures with foreigners into the service portfolio of the associates. Willingness to respond to increased demand regardless of nationality meant that the flow of slaves turned into a flood. Even though Premord's missteps made any future dealings with the Honfleur Society impossible, the London partners willingly entertained the possibility of doing business with other foreigners. Although it is not clear

99. Sir John Lambert to Oswald & Co., August 18, 1766, and Sir Alexander Grant to Richard Oswald, August 29, 1767, Oswald & Co. to Hornetener, Walker & Co., November 29, 1768, Oswald Papers, Sudlows. The debts remained unpaid as late as December 1768.

100. £28,000 in 1763–68 amounts to £1,898,560 or $2,823,880 in 1994. The factory purchased prime slaves from the Africans for an average 65 bars in 1762–63 (Tweed, *Considerations*, pp. 65–67). If a bar equaled 5 shillings (Low to Grant, January 30, 1762), and if 20 shillings equaled 1 pound (McCusker, *Money and Exchange*, pp. 9, 35), then the factory bought slaves for £16,25 and sold them for £22. The gross margin is before the deduction of factory and counting-house expenses. Total factory expenses amortized over a 25-year period amounted to £240 per year. Counting-house expenses are not known. See Appendix IV.

101. Profits were also made on company indigo sent to France on the Society's ships. Itemizations of indigo profits can be found in Série d5b6, 0298, Archives de Paris. These profits are not included in the present discussion.

102. Expansion in volume did not occur in all sectors of distribution. There exists correspondence suggesting that the restrictive nature of the French contract (a claim on the first 1,500 slaves of each year) retarded the development of other outlets, like the satisfaction of personal needs. In planning to ship captive Africans to East Florida and Jamaica, Oswald and Grant were guarded about the prospects of success, since they could only purchase slaves with bills of exchange; Grant, at least, found that it was easier to buy needed laborers in Jamaica. Richard Oswald to James Grant, May 25, 1767, BCM 295; and Sir Alexander Grant to Richard Oswald, August 29, 1767, Oswald Papers, Sudlows.

whether they signed formal contracts with other foreign merchants, it is certain that they continued to fill the holds of foreign armateurs throughout the 1770s.[103] As far as the associates were concerned, the future lay with big contracts. Only the American Revolutionary War frustrated the realization of this goal.[104]

The number of slaves that the factory exported was high. In his groundbreaking study of trans-Atlantic slaving, Philip Curtin states that the 1760s saw the exportation of 5,300 slaves from Sierra Leone. The data collected and analyzed here, however, indicate that his projection was too low, since Bance Island, only one part of Sierra Leone and the Windward Coast, sent nearly twice that number in the 1760s.[105] And the tentative and conservative total estimate of 12,929 Africans for the period 1748–1784 represents only a minimum outflow. The eighteenth century saw the peak in the volume of the trade, and the rise of Sierra Leone as a source and, in both developments, Bance Island played a critical role. If the most recent estimates of slave exports from all Africa are accurate, Bance Island's exports during the period 1750–69 (9,655 slaves) constitute 6 percent of the British exports from Sierra Leone

103. Sir Alexander Grant to Richard Oswald, September 22, 1767, Oswald Papers, Sudlows; and Robert Alexander to Richard Oswald, December 15, 1768 (referring a request from "a considerable house in France" to Oswald & Co.), Oswald Papers, EUL. See also Mettas, *Répertoire*, v. 2, pp. 173–76.

104. After the War for America had ended, Oswald's nephews forged an agreement with a Danish firm to provide it with approximately 3,500 slaves during 1785 and 1786. Some uncertainty exists about the actual number of slaves exported under the Danish contract. Both Golberry, *Travels*, p. 249, and Pierre Labarthe, *Voyage au Senegal pendant les années 1784 et 1785* (Paris, 1802) state that over 3,000 slaves were sold to Danish traders and another 4,000 sent by British traders to British colonies. John Matthews told Parliament that, in 1785, 3,000 to 3,500 slaves were taken from the coast, of which 3,000 were taken by the English. Robert Norris testified that the Windward Coast produced 5,000 annually and that the British exported 38,000 from the entire continent each year and sold 1,500–2,000 to the Danish. *Report of the Lords of the Committee of Council on the Present State of the Trade to Africa* (London, 1789), in *British Sessional Papers, 1731–1800: House of Commons: Accounts and Papers*, v. 26: 1789, no. 646a, pt. 1, pp. 34–38. Elsewhere, in *A Short Account of the African Slave Trade* (London, 1789), p. 5, Robert Norris stated that the Danish took 6,000.

105. Curtin, *Atlantic Slave Trade*, pp. 221, 226. For revisions of Curtin's projections, see Paul E. Lovejoy, "The Volume of the Atlantic Slave Trade: A Synthesis," *Journal of African History*, v. 23 (1982), pp. 483–85. In his recalculation, Lovejoy claims that the British held 41 percent of the eighteenth-century trade, the Portuguese 29 percent, and the French 19 percent. In absolute numbers, the British took away 45,200 slaves in 1751–60 and 108,000 in 1761–70. The estimation of exports from the Windward Coast has been particularly troublesome. Jones and Johnson have suggested that Curtin's geographic attributions were misconstrued in the case of Sierra Leone, but, until they provide new projections for that part of Africa, Curtin's figures must stand. Adam Jones and Marion Johnson, "Slaves from the Windward Coast," *Journal of African History*, v. 21 (1980), pp. 17–34.

(172,840) and 2 percent of all countries' exports from the entire west coast of Africa (641,570).[106]

Embarrassment and Neglect

The outbreak of the American Revolutionary War stopped this flow of human cargo and so closed an important chapter in the history of Bance Island. For twenty-eight years, under the direction of Grant, Oswald & Co., the factory had served as an important commercial center where slaves and goods were acquired by barter and then shipped across the Atlantic. War shut down this warehouse. According to contemporaries, "the extreme embarrassment under which the English labored during the war ... forced them to neglect their possessions in Africa." Bance Island was slowly "deprived of every resource." The fort received no assistance after 1775. By 1778, there were only 17 whites at work there, down from a high of 44 ten years before. Not surprisingly, the French took advantage of their distress. On March 12, 1779, the French commander de Pontdevez seized all British ships in the island's vicinity: he sent the slave-laden *Providence* and *Hereford* to Saint Domingue; appropriated the *Tom* and *Fortitude* to French use; sent the ivory-filled *Juno* back to France; and burned what was left. He next turned on the fort and, within six days, turned it into "a heap of Ruins."[107]

The agents and some of the workers stayed on to rebuild the fort, but progress was slow. By 1785, a want of facilities still impeded the resumption of trade.[108] Construction lagged in part because the ownership had changed. In 1770, Sargent lost interest and sold his share to Oswald; in 1771, Mill died having bequeathed his share to Oswald; finally,

106. Curtin's and Lovejoy's recalculations have been revised by David Richardson. "Slave Exports from West and West-Central Africa, 1700–1810: New Estimates of Volume and Distribution," *Journal of African History*, v. 30 (1989), pp. 10, 13, and Table 7, and "Eighteenth-Century British Slave Trade," pp. 157–72. According to Richardson, during the period 1700–1809, the British exported 47%, the Portuguese 28%, and the French 16%. Together, from all parts of West Africa, the British, Portuguese, French, and Dutch exported 561,000 in 1750–59 and 751,000 in 1760–69. From the Windward Coast and Sierra Leone, the British exported approximately 47,250 (18.8% of the total) in 1750–59, and approximately 125,590 (32.1%) in 1760–69. Richardson does not account for French slavers taking slaves from British factories like Bance, however. Furthermore, systematic study of the commerce of individual private traders – Afro-European merchants or English outport traders – could only increase the figures.

107. Golberry, *Travels*, v. 2, p. 247; SP 89/84/327, 342, 344, 346–47; and J. Machat, *Documents sur les Établissements Français de L'Afrique Occidentale au XVIIIe Siècle* (Paris, 1906), p. 124 and n. 1.

108. William Crosbie to Richard Oswald, September 23, 1780, Oswald Papers, Sudlows; and Golberry, *Travels*, p. 246.

Grant died the following year and left his shares to his brother, a Speyside farmer who had no interest in trade. By the time of de Pontdevez's attack, Oswald owned five-ninths of the concern, Grant's executors three-ninths, and Sir John Boyd the remaining ninth. But Boyd was preoccupied with the fluctuating fortunes of his Caribbean plantations, and Grant's executors were harassed by the payment of creditors. Even Oswald, with his mind on the war in America, had little time to devote to the venture.[109]

In 1784, the reduced and crumbling partnership put the factory up for sale. The Grants' attorney placed three notices in the *Public Advertiser* in late September announcing the private sale of the

> whole of the several Islands, situated in the River Sierra Leon, and of that valuable Property, consisting of a Fort, with all Manner of spacious and convenient Buildings for carrying on the Slave Trade; and a Number of . . . trusty valuable Slaves, belonging to the Company, Natives of the Island, and all of them Tradesmen, Sailors, useful Servants, and Handicraftsmen; besides several Brigs, Sloops, and other small Craft; the Supplies of Merchandize sent from England for Trade, and what remains on Hand for the Use of the Settlement, with many other Articles too numerous to be inserted in an Advertisement.[110]

Despite the "peculiar Advantages among the Natives" and the desirable "Situation" enjoyed by the island, no buyer came forward. When Oswald died several weeks later, control passed to his nephews, John and Alexander Anderson.

Rather than sell the island, the Andersons worked to revive its trade. They purchased the outstanding shares from Grant's executors and Boyd. They invested in new buildings on the island and at the outfactories. When the buildings were sufficiently repaired, they resumed the traffic

---

109. In the early 1770s, Oswald had contemplated pulling out of the concern. Henry Laurens to John Lewis Gervais, January 20, 1773, *The Papers of Henry Laurens*, v. 8, p. 530. In the end, Oswald decided to persist but, later in the decade, he distanced himself from the operation by retiring to Ayrshire. His wartime activities are chronicled in Thomas Townshend to Lord Grantham, September 14, 1782, Grafton Papers 423/81, Suffolk Record Office, Ipswich; and "Notes on English Possessions on West Coast of Africa," c. September 1782, Shelburne Papers, v. 87, f. 350, Clements Library, Ann Arbor. When given the chance to protect his African possessions during the 1782 peace negotiations in Paris, he paid them scant attention. In 1782, he referred to a "Scheme of the African Trade" that he had written, but no copy of this memorandum has come to light. Only after he had returned to London in 1783 did Oswald ask Lord Grantham to "except" Bance Island "in case of any new Priviledges being given to the French." Richard Oswald to Lord Grantham, February 10, 1783, L30/14/290, Bedfordshire Record Office, Bedford.

110. *The Public Advertiser*, September 11, 24, 25, 1784.

in slaves, sending many of their own ships to the Caribbean and providing slaves to many slavers from the outports and colonies. Nevertheless, Bance Island never again reached its former level of preparedness,
and abolition rendered the factory all but "useless." The Andersons
continued to ship large numbers of slaves through the end of 1800. But,
in the ensuing years, sensing the end was near, they began to pull out.
When their attempt to sell the property to the Government failed, they
ceased operations in 1811. The seventy-five-year experiment in "free
trade" and "absolute dominion" ended amid entrepreneurial fatigue,
bureaucratic shuffling, and imperial reorganization, much as it had
begun.[111]

A "General Rendezvous"

The associates' buildup of Bance Island's factory roughly coincided with
a worldwide rise in the demand for sugar and slaves, and the imperial
struggle of the Seven Years' War, at the heart of which was a fight for
Europe's supply of sugar. This war, in particular, greatly facilitated the
proprietors' backward integration into trans-Atlantic slaving; it magni-
fied its profitability several times over. During the war, at least after
1759, Britain's naval supremacy more or less ensured safe transit with
little competition for the Atlantic sea lanes. Moreover, war contracting
and colonial subsidies fueled a boom in consumption that lasted at least
through the end of the war. But it was after the war that the conflict's
greatest legacy became apparent. The war had nearly destroyed the
French slave trade in West Africa, and thereby crippled French plantations in the French West Indies, depriving them of needed laborers. It
left a substantial foreign demand in Guadeloupe, Martinique, and Sainte
Domingue for factory slaves. At the same time, with the addition of
sugar islands to the British domain and their increase in sugar production, it created a hungry British demand for factory slaves, too. Britain's
conquests opened new markets for British goods and provided access
to staple goods at cheap prices. The war did not lead to a "complete
suspension of trade" in West Africa, as some historians have averred;
on the contrary, it encouraged unparalleled economic activity and expansion, for the fort as for the empire.[112] Trade on the island did not

111. For a detailed history of the island under the direction of the Andersons, see Hancock,
    "Citizen of the World," pp. 718–24.
112. Martin, ed., *Journal*, pp. 8, 10. Martin notwithstanding, there is little reason to
    believe the war retarded growth anywhere in the empire, except perhaps the Philip-
    pines, where the Filipinos were more interested in insurrection than trade.

fall off and facilities did not break down until the onset of the American Revolution.

This future was not obvious when Grant, Oswald & Co. purchased the factory in 1748. Indeed, the extent to which the expansion of the empire would carry their project forward was unimagined; their thoughts were fixed on far more specific, immediate concerns. The RAC had had more than its share of difficulties, and the private trading interests were highly divided. During the mid- to late-1740s, London's African trade reached a nadir, and the prospects for improvement were hardly auspicious. They were especially bleak for the associates, inasmuch as they were Londoners in a trade that in the previous two decades had come to be dominated by outport merchants. By preempting other traders through a large, well-timed investment in a sector of the market no longer controlled by established interests, they overcame the handicaps of their late and "foreign" entry into the trade. They obtained political recognition and legal warranty of their operation; attracted financing; provided for the myriad needs of defense, labor, and commerce; and developed and organized a general system of trade between Europe, Africa, America, and Asia, without the aid of the Government or Government-sanctioned monopolies.

To overcome the obstacles, the associates consciously forged extensive personal, geographical, and operational connections that made their sprawling network profitable. No other branch of British-American commerce was so global in extent, so much in need of coordination as was the trade in slaves. The associates drew together the divergent, increasingly international aspects of that trade. They called upon individual skills and services that, until then, had had little to do with one another. They marshaled a wider array of assets – capital, information, contacts, and materials – than had their predecessors, or indeed than did most of their competitors. Propelled by the ordinary, diachronic desire to increase capital, achieve economies in costs, manage risks, and enter new markets across the seas, the proprietors came to share skills and assets to a remarkable degree. In this they were distinctive.[113]

We can view the associates' commercial integration from several perspectives. On a personal level, each partner contributed the resources of his own individual business to further the work of the joint slaving venture. The Boyds are a good example of how the partners combined

113. As Davis notes, many shipping and enterprise shares were held by passive investors, and the degree of involvement varied among them. *The Rise*, pp. 101, 135. What is noteworthy about Bance Island is that none of the partners was passive: they knew one another well, contributed regularly to the supply of the operation, and frequently discussed matters relating to the allocation and use of firm resources.

far-flung contacts and abilities. George Fryer, who managed the Boyds' victualing contracts in Jamaica, sold Bance Island to the partners. Paul Boyd, Augustus's brother and a merchant in Waterford, supplied the factory with Irish beef and butter. Henry Laurens, who had previously acted as the Boyds' correspondent in South Carolina and provided them with supplies for their Caribbean estates, managed American slave sales for the company. As absentee sugar planters of St. Christopher, the Boyds themselves took some of the factory slaves; and their correspondent on the island, Messrs. James & Baillies, handled many more. Finally, as a Director of the East India Company for much of the 1750s and 1760s, John Boyd wielded influence in the London trading world and worked on Bance Island's behalf.

The East India connection was critical, since so many of the goods required for an African trade came from the subcontinent. At the East India Company, Boyd saw to it that his fellow proprietors received favorable concessions in the sale of goods. Sargent and Grant became two of the biggest purchasers of India cloth from the Company's warehouses in Leadenhall Street, and Grant's partner Johnston became one of the largest buyers of medicinal supplies. In turn, they supplied the Bance Island factory and the newly formed Company of Merchants Trading to Africa.[114]

Sargent's inclusion in the partnership brought a ready supply of goods and assured access to the world of London finance. From their house in Mincing Lane, Sargent, Stratton, Aufrere, Chambers, Cooke, Gardiner, and Rolleston combined an India trade in cottons, a Hamburg trade in German linens, and a Levant trade in Persian and Turkish silks. The Bance Island proprietors drew from all three regional sources to obtain cloth for barter in Sierra Leone. The northern European contacts of the Sargent group gave the proprietors access to the primary source of munitions in Europe; its largely West Country origins brought the partners ties to the dominant slave-trading ports of Bristol and Liverpool, and Britain's center of ammunition and arms in Birmingham and Manchester. Both sets of domestic connections provided the slaving firm with correspondents in the English outports and brought ships to its African anchorage. As directors of the Bank of England, Sargent, Stratton,

114. Boyd was present as a Director or Deputy Chairman at meetings of the Court of Directors when associates' (in particular, Grant's) nominees received coveted appointments as factors and writers and favorable treatment in obtaining trading concessions. B 75/247, 443–44, 469–70, 483, 487–88, 499, 532; B 77/36, 210; B 79/126, 140, 192, 205, 215, 285; B 80/445, IOL; and D 22/78r, IOL. For instances of associates (Sargent II, Johnston, Aufrere, and Grant) making sizable purchases from or deliveries to the Company, see B 75 (1758–60)/33, 44, 63, 134, 150, 398, 404, 439; B 76 (1760–61)/48, 116, 139, 151, 212, IOL.

and Cooke also brought financial expertise and access to commercial credit.

Richard Oswald contributed management skills to the conduct of Bance Island's trade. He and Mill supervised the accounts, conducted the correspondence, and handled the financial transactions, much as they did the affairs of their American correspondents. They were ambitious men, who pushed for bigger size, greater volume, and smoother operations. Maintaining good relations with other African traders was eased by the presence of their partner Robert Scott on the nine-man committee that controlled the new Company of Merchants, much as it was assisted in a later period by the tenure of Sargent's partners Aufrere and Chambers. Like the other associates, Oswald, Mill, and Scott came to regard Sierra Leone as a desirable destination for the various commodities they peddled through their own commercial channels. Tobacco and sugar that Oswald and Mill took from the Chesapeake and Caribbean ended up in the island's warehouse; rum from Mill's Carriacou and Tobago plantations drew African chiefs to the palaver; Scottish tartans that Oswald bought from former friends in Glasgow were shipped to Sierra Leone; and wine that Scott, Pringle & Co. loaded in Madeira lubricated the often tortuous barter.

On a less personal, more systemic level, the factory also represented the work of intensive coordination. In the waters of Bance Island's anchorage lay the ships of friends, neighbors, strangers, and enemies. In its storehouses were piled the fruits of both East and West. A free port in the southeast Atlantic, the entrepôt linked the African hinterland with English cities (London, Bristol, Lancaster, and Liverpool), British American colonies (Massachusetts, Rhode Island, Maryland, Virginia, South Carolina, Georgia, East Florida, and the West Indian sugar islands), Asian manufactories (India, Turkey, Persia, and Iran), and even countries Britain was at odds with economically or militarily (German principalities, France, Denmark and, to a lesser extent, Holland, and Portugal). Bance Island's operations were a good example of trade overcoming differences among members of a globalizing economy.

The factory on Bance Island served a critical, coordinating function in the associates' trans-Atlantic, and increasingly global, commerce. From the start, it was an opportunistic adventure that required quick and flexible responses to make it profitable. With its defenses able to fend off unwanted advance, and its commercial facilities and staff second to none by the end of the Seven Years' War, the factory enabled the proprietors to ply an extensive trade far into the interior and out across the ocean. Much of this work of commercial integration was both necessitated and aided by the expansion of Britain's empire. It was performed by relatives, friends, and strangers who were employed at the factory, given valuable firsthand exposure to Atlantic commerce, and later promoted to man the associates' ships as captains (William Cogill, Tublay James, Richard Savage, John Stephens, David Stirling, and Alexander Taylor); run their plantations as attorneys or overseers (John Bowman); oil the wheels of credit and commission as their correspondents in the West Indies (John Davidson, Peter Davidson, and Thomas Grant), North America (John Anderson and James Robertson), or India (Alexander Davidson); manage their affairs in London (John Donaldson); or even become competitors (John Aird) or critics (James Tweed). Running down the roster of factory personnel introduces the reader to the men who became the middle managers of the partners' global business empire.[115] The nearly complete control of the commercial circuit that these employees helped bring about smoothed the relationship between supply and demand. This business, conducted on an international scale, made the prospects of a full outward-bound voyage extremely likely, since both settlement and traders were entirely dependent upon the mother country for their provisions and supplies, and it ensured a ship full of slaves to the West Indies or North America. On the other side of the ocean, the associates' plantations, possessions, and commercial contacts ensured a ship full of commodities on an inward-bound voyage to London. Their competitive position in one market, such as the Caribbean sugar trade, was strengthened by their competitive position in other trades, like the African slave trade.

Such domination was rare. In the case of Grant, Oswald, and the other slaving associates, it goes far toward explaining why they, and not others, so successfully managed to make profits in this branch of commerce. At a time when the empire was growing and the number of consumers desiring British sugar and slaves was increasing at a dramatic rate, the island functioned as a critical node in an increasingly international commercial system – a system in which economic opportunity and individual initiative drove the push to integrate backward in a search for new commercial regions, new trade goods, and new business strategies.

115. Alexander McTaggart to Richard Oswald, September 3, 1766, Oswald Papers, Sudlows. The impact of former employees was not restricted to the associates' own business. For an example of Oswald recommending his workers to others, see Richard Oswald to Governor Grant, 1769, BCM 295.

7

Government Contracting: "A Work of Hercules"

IN 1754, AS THE SIX SLAVE FACTORY PROPRIETORS debated plans for their depot's rebuilding, Europeans again went to war. The military conflict started in North America, in the Pennsylvania backcountry and along the Nova Scotia frontier, where the fear of French encroachments and intrigues led Governor William Shirley of Massachusetts to launch an expedition to rout the French in the Kennebec River area. By spring 1755, two Irish regiments under Major General Edward Braddock were dispatched to Virginia. But it was not until the conflict between the British and the French became intertwined with another long-standing European conflict, the struggle between Prussia and Austria over supremacy in Germany, that the provincial theater of war emerged as secondary to the continental theater. France, Austria's ally, attacked the British-occupied island of Minorca in May 1756; Prussia invaded Saxony three months later; and Austria officially declared war on Prussia in January 1757. At first the affair was wholly continental – Austria and France lining up against Prussia, Hesse-Cassel, Hanover, Saxe-Coburg Gotha, Buckeburg, and Wolfenbuttel – but it quickly spread far beyond. For Britain's House of Hanover, the Franco-Austrian alliance represented a threat to its territories in Europe and a test of its alliance with Prussia. Never one to pass up a good fight, it entered the fray, paying the expenses of Hanoverians and Hessians, later extending its support to remaining allies, and finally sending nearly 15,000 of its own soldiers to Germany in 1758.[1] For London's overseas merchants, the war presented the chance of a lifetime.

By the end of the war, the "Combined Army," as the forces of Britain, Prussia, and their allies encamped west of the Elbe were called, numbered more than 101,000 soldiers, and Britain provisioned 96 percent of them. To this task was added that of provisioning at least

---

1. Sir Reginald Savory, *His Britannic Majesty's Army in Germany during the Seven Years War* (London, 1966), pp. 1–115, 442–47; and J. W. Fortescue, *A History of the British Army*, v. 2 (London, 1899), pp. 339–57.

70,000 British sailors and soldiers on the high seas and in the Americas. The operation was, the most recent historian of the war notes, "a large force by contemporary standards," for no previous eighteenth-century army had exceeded 80,000 troops. Its provisioning "represented not only a far greater commitment than Britain had previously undertaken, but also a task of considerable complexity."[2] It was a task well-suited to the associates' skills.

When war broke out in 1755, the associates were no strangers to military provisioning. They had witnessed the work of friends like Laurence Dundas during the War of Austrian Succession. In the aftermath of that war, they took up contracting themselves as an extension of their shipping and trading business. They found they could use the same resources they employed in other areas of enterprise – ships and men – with the government as a client. For those victualers who shipped contract goods, for instance, the same vessels could carry the Government's and their other clients' supplies. Moreover, the counting-house routines they devised were similar. Seizing opportunities in the late 1740s and early 1750s, the Boyds provided foods to the naval station at Kingston; Grant supplied the Navy Board in London with sea provisions; and Oswald furnished the Navy Board with stores like turpentine and tar from North Carolina.[3] But it was not until the Seven Years' War that the associates turned to contracting as more than an adjunct to shipping and trading. Although they still exploited the complementarity of contracting and shipping and trading, in wartime they made government contracting a separate enterprise in their business portfolio. Their military supply operations spanned the globe from India to Jamaica. In building them, they had to invest – employing men and purchasing goods and ships – on a larger scale than ever had before, including what they had wrought on Bance Island.

The navy employed the greatest number of the associates.[4] Expanding

2. Hamish M. Little, "The Treasury, the Commissariat and the Supply of the Combined Army in Germany during the Seven Years' War (1756–1763)" (Ph.D. dissert., University of London, 1981), pp. 32–33. I am indebted to Fred Anderson for the numbers of British forces in the Americas; they do not include militia-men, provincials, or civilian artificers.

3. The Boyds' contracts: Adm 110/16/242–46 (October 24, 1750); and Adm 111/35 (June 29–30, 1748). Grant's supply: GD 345/1163/2/44x: Alexander Grant to Sir Archibald Grant, January 27, 1754. Oswald's sales: James Murray to Richard Oswald, James Murray Letter Books, passim, Massachusetts Historical Society, Boston; and GD 248/168/1–4.

4. Two branches of the navy awarded contracts – the Navy Board concerning itself with ships, the Victualing Board with food – while the army's Ordnance Board concerned itself with almost everything else (guns, ammunition, stores, fortifications, and artillery and wagon trains). The Victualling Office preferred to obtain supplies in England or Ireland, rather than overseas, since it was "easier to control preparations and dispatch."

their prewar efforts, Augustus and John Boyd shipped beef (1747–60) and sea provisions (1748–60) to feed the 14,000 sailors and soldiers at the naval station in Kingston; in addition, they supplied beef and butter (1756–57) to the station in Plymouth, and sea provisions (1757–58) and beef (1763–64) to the station in Waterford.⁵ The Kingston contract was a major undertaking, requiring them to overcome the obstacles raised by distance; Jamaica being 4,000 miles from London, there arose problems of capture, spoilage, and disease. Having their provisions "arrive on time, and fit for consumption" required considerable coordination of transoceanic resources. Since Waterford was a major distribution center for beef and butter, and the home of Augustus Boyd's brother and cousins, many of whom were themselves export merchants, the Boyds called upon family contacts to buy, assemble, package, and deliver contract foods to the navy, there and at Plymouth. With similar family contacts in New England and "intimate acquaintance" with the navy's Treasurer Sir Gilbert Eliot, Sir Alexander Grant won the contract to supply the Nova Scotia naval station with bread, beer, rum, beef, pork, pease, oatmeal, rice, butter, and cheese (1759–62). When the war was over, he handed the contract over to John Mill, who serviced the garrison for another year.⁶

One of the more distinctive wartime contracts was the packet boat franchise granted by the Treasury and Post Office to John Sargent II and Richard Stratton in 1755. Looking back over the century's wars with France, the Government could not help but recognize the lack of safe and regular channels of aid and communication, especially along the important Britain/Caribbean axis. Postal services had been instituted during the War of Spanish Succession and again during the War of

N. A. M. Rodger, *The Wooden World: An Anatomy of the Georgian Navy* (London, 1986), pp. 35–36. For a more recent analysis of victualing, see Duncan Crewe, *Yellow Jack and the Worm* (Liverpool, 1994), chs. 1, 4, esp. pp. 5–7.

5. Jamaica contracts: Adm 110/16/242–46 (October 24, 1750); and Adm 111/35 (June 29–30, 1748). Belfast and Plymouth contracts: Adm 111/43 (January 28–31, 1756); Adm 110/18/212 (February 24, 1756); Adm 110/18/454–55 (February 7, 1757). Waterford contracts: Adm 111/46 (June 3, 1757), and Adm 111/56 (December 21–28, 1763). For the role that Americans played in the performance of the Boyds' victualing contracts, see *The Papers of Henry Laurens*, v. 1, pp. 329, 340–41, 366, v. 2, pp. 3–4, 20–21, 94–95, 182–84, 195–96, 237–38, 272–73, 325–26, 351–52, 422–23, v. 3, pp. 20, 39, 193–94, and v. 4, pp. 166–68.

6. Crewe, *Yellow Jack*, p. 156. Grant's and Mill's contracts are recorded in: Adm 111/49 (July 6, 11, 1759); National Maritime Museum, Adm/B/32 (June 15, 1759, April 28, 1760); Adm 111/53 (June 2, 7, 1762); and National Maritime Museum, Adm/D/33 (August 27, 1762). During the war, Grant also continued to strike agreements with individual captains for supplying ships in the West Indian and East Indian squadrons. GD 345/1180/37: Sir Alexander Grant to Captain Archibald Grant, March 6, 1760; and GD 248/178/2/1: Sir Alexander Grant to Sir Ludovick Grant, January 16, 1762.

Austrian Succession, but these had lapsed with peace. It was not until the Seven Years' War that the Government committed itself to a permanent postal service. Six months after the Newcastle Ministry sent Major General Braddock to Virginia, the Postmaster General, a brother of Stratton's godfather, granted Stratton and Sargent the exclusive privilege of carrying mail between Falmouth in southwestern England and the West Indies; four other franchisees carried mail to the Helvoetsluys, Leghorn, Lisbon, and New York. The two associates furnished four ships for the duration of the war. Each vessel weighed 150 tons, carried 26 seamen, and possessed 8 carriage guns and 6 swivel guns, each vessel undertaking two round-trip voyages per year to Barbados, Montserrat, Antigua, Nevis, St. Christopher, and Jamaica. For their services, Sargent and Stratton received quarterly payments of £2,230 per ship and numerous perquisites; their boats, for instance, were not subjected to customs searches and so avoided restrictions in the goods they could import. They earned £13,200 per year or £4,400 per voyage from the contract over the course of the war; the return on their initial outlay for these voyages was a fat 70 percent.[7]

Army contracting brought the greatest absolute profits to the contractors among the associates, although this was neither obvious nor assured before the fact. The army's traditional system of military supply was informal, irregular, and inefficient. Before 1688, soldiers' everyday needs for food, drink, clothing, and shelter were supplied largely by civilians. At home, citizens fed and clothed the army through individual contracts, and innkeepers quartered the troops; abroad, where the rights of the individual were not so zealously guarded, householders were forced to provide shelter, and shopkeepers, merchants, and sutlers often supplied the troops camped in their neighborhood. A distinctively British fear of standing armies kept supply operations disorganized, erratic, and localized. The Commissariat, the department in the army directly charged with responsibility for military supply, was never able to impose order. It shared responsibilities among a multitude of agencies: the civilian Treasury was responsible for food; the Ordnance Board for transport and shelter; the War Office for medicine and equipment; and the navy for overseas travel. Jurisdictions and functions overlapped, and there was much duplication and waste of materiel and manpower. From

---

7. £13,200 in 1755–63 amounts to £1,012,328 or $1,505,716 in 1994. Everard Fawkener to Treasury Lords, October 21, 1755, Post 1/8/250–54; Estimate, Post 1/8/259; Articles, November 6, 1755, Post 51/3; T 29/32/344, 346; *London Gazette*, October 25, 1755; and Hancock, "Citizen of the World," pp. 436–37. For further information, see L. E. Britnor, *The History of the Sailing Packets to the West Indies* (London, 1973); Kenneth Ellis, *The Post Office in the Eighteenth Century* (London, 1958), pp. 7–8, 44; and Steele, *English Atlantic*, ch. 9.

time to time, the Commissariat tried to introduce efficient acquisition and distribution methods, but with little success.[8]

After 1688, down to the Seven Years' War, this system of supply persisted largely intact. Some minor changes were introduced to cope with the increase in the scale of the wars waged by William III and his successors: as each new international conflict arose, the number of soldiers, the extent of their needs, and the size of the army's supply organization increased. It became increasingly difficult to supply the growing number of soldiers informally by living off the land, or by the welter of competing agencies, all with other responsibilities.[9] As a result, the army increasingly turned from the Commissariat and relied on contracting with one or two civilian merchants, whose activities were supervised by the Treasury, in order to provide a complete military supply service.[10]

British merchants who supplied the troops served as either senior "commissaries" (junior commissaries were mainly Germans) or "contractors." The choice between the two was usually determined by the bureaucrats' and generals' acceptance or rejection of the practice of private contractors performing high-level tasks in the army. A commissary was an appointed officer who drew up lists of necessaries and managed the procurement process; a contractor was a civilian merchant who, for a fee fixed by contract, furnished the supplies. A commissary reported to his superiors in the army, and shouldered a variety of military responsibilities; in principle, a contractor reported only to the Treasury in London and executed only the tasks outlined in his agreement. A commissary was restricted to dealing with officially sanctioned providers of materiel or finance; a contractor could draw on sources untapped by or unknown to the army. A commissary was forced to accept "a very low standard of material comfort"; the contractor, by contrast, could and often did live in substantial ease. Lastly, the commissary's rewards were generally limited to his salary and its perquisites, although the financial

8. Material in this and the following paragraphs is drawn from Little, "The Commissariat," ch. 1; John Childs, *The British Army of William III, 1689–1702* (Manchester, 1982), pp. 247–53; John Childs, *Armies and Warfare in Europe, 1648–1789* (Manchester, 1987), pp. 111–14; and D. W. Jones, *War and Economy in the Age of William III and Marlborough* (Oxford, 1988), pp. 28–39. On victualing, see Crowe, *Yellow Jack and the Worm*, ch. 4.

9. The differences in scale are revealed by comparing data for contracting in the War of Spanish Succession and the Seven Years' War. Cf. Add. Mss. 1,771/7, and Portland Loan 29/45f/44–259, BL; the published volumes of Treasury Board minutes for the period 1702–13; Ivor F. Burton, "The Secretary at War and the Administration of the Army during the War of Spanish Succession" (Ph.D. dissert., University of London, 1960), pp. 312–52; and Little, "The Commissariat."

10. John Perjes, "Army Provisioning, Logistics and Strategy in the Second Half of the 17th Century," *Acta Historica Academiae Scientiarum Hungaricae*, v. 16 (1970), pp. 1–52.

rewards of the senior commissaries were generous enough; a contractor's profits were limited only by his guile, his ability to trade, and his
competition for the contracts.[11]

Oswald, who had previously supplied the navy with tar and turpentine, became the biggest of the contractors among the associates when,
during the Seven Years' War, the army realized that its resources to
satisfy its needs were alarmingly inadequate. His involvement may have
been a special case, given the size of his undertaking, the fact that he
produced the goods he supplied, the amount of his profits, and the
disruption that personal management in Germany brought to his daily
London routine; yet the opportunity and the way he managed it were
not atypical.[12] From 1756 onward, he and his partner Mill supplied
bread and bread wagons to the British and Allied forces, first during the
summer encampments in southern England and later in Germany. Under similar agreements, they supplied hospital and infirmary wagons to
the British forces, baggage wagons to Prince Ferdinand's Prussian train
and, for the Board of Ordnance, artillery wagons to the British troops
in 1760 and 1761.[13] Despite the inefficiencies of the military supply
system, Oswald and Mill combined their experiences and contacts in

11. Little, "The Commissariat," pp. 84–85. Little correctly highlights the high level of
    salaries for Commissariat directors and the benefits that could accrue to them (such
    as lump sums upon appointment and allowances for forage, transport, clerical assist-
    ance, quarters, etc.), but these were enjoyed only by directors. The division between
    contractor and commissary was never completely clear. Significantly, when the word
    "entrepreneur" first appeared in English in the fifteenth century, for instance, it was
    used to describe men of battle, managers, or controllers of defensive operations; in the
    post-1688 period, the meaning is extended to comprehend military suppliers, denoting
    both contractor and commissary.
12. Midway through the war, Oswald also joined the Commissariat, as the army's own
    Commissary for the Supply in the Hesse Campaign; near the end of the war, he
    became the Ordnance Board's Commissary for the Supervision of the Artillery Trains.
    Oswald was the Hesse Commissary from February 1759 to June 1760. T 1/396/145,
    134: Thomas Orby Hunter to Richard Oswald, March 14, 18, 1759; and T 64/96/
    25–29: Thomas Orby Hunter to Samuel Martin, February 11, 1759. Oswald was the
    Artillery Train Commissary from June to December 1762. C 12/268/33: Davie v.
    Oswald, 1769. John Levett also served as a commissary in Germany, and after the
    war he supplied arrack to the military settlements of the East India Company. East
    India Company Consultations, January 3, 1774: John Levett to President and Council
    of Calcutta, February 13, 1774, National Archives of India, New Delhi.
13. On the summer bread contract, see T 1/365/33 (March 27, 1756); T 1/368/35 (April
    29, 1756); T 1/375/137–40 (c. April 1757); T 29/33/44–5 (May 4, 1758); and T 1/
    376/84 (May 30, 1758). The continental bread supply is detailed in Ann Arbor,
    Clements Library, Shelburne Papers, v. 154C: Richard Oswald, "Answers," ff. 64–66.
    Hospital, infirmary, and baggage services are discussed in Little, "The Commissariat,"
    p. 270 n. 3, citing a letter of Richard Oswald, October 1761, and a memorandum
    entitled "Wagons and Horses Furnished by Richard Oswald," both in the Dundas of
    Beechwood Muniments. See also "Instructions for Hatton," 1759, Add. Mss. 32,905/
    149. Record of the Ordnance contract appears in C 12/268/33: Davie v. Oswald,
    1769. The work of the Ordnance Office awaits study.

shipping and trading, planting, and slaving to fulfill their contracts with distinction.

Oswald's continental supply was another instance of the associates' backward integration, since he produced and distributed the bread himself. It got underway in mid-1758, when he won a contract to provision the troops in Germany, as he had been doing in southern England. In preparing for the army's initial entry into Germany, the army and the Treasury jointly drew up a preliminary list of necessaries for the stationing of the troops: bread, straw for tents, wood "for boyling the soldiers' kettles," hospitals, forage for horses, and wagons "to do all manner of Service." This first list was imprecise, refined only after weeks of subsequent deliberation among all concerned parties; in the end, it was decided they would need to feed an estimated 22,680 men and 55,440 horses; for seven weeks, this would require 277,829 loaves of bread, 271,656 rations of forage, 39,708 trusses of straw, and 3,333,960 pounds of wood. With this list in hand, the Treasury approached possible suppliers. Regarding "the character of the person" (something they never specified more precisely) as "no less essential . . . than the cheapness of the contract," the Treasury Lords invited proposals from certain "persons of credit and character" to provide them the goods. Oswald was not considered because he had never served as a contractor abroad, and the Treasury Lords deemed foreign military experience absolutely necessary. The merchants they did approach were either occupied or reluctant to extend themselves on such an extensive scale, and so submitted no bids.[14]

The Treasury Lords considered public bidding a last resort, even though it was widely agreed that public bidding produced results. Thus, with reluctance, the Treasury ran "publick advertisements" in the London newspapers for one week in July 1758, requesting "Proposals for Furnishing Bread wagons and Bread for the use of His Majesty's Troops now going abroad." To its relief, two merchants whom they had already passed over but still considered "honourable" submitted competing proposals: Richard Oswald and Abraham Prado. Assisted by David Graeme, an army officer he had known since childhood, Oswald won the contract with the lower of the two bids. What Graeme and Oswald sensed, and what the Treasury officials expected, too, was that the army's requirements would be large, fluctuating, and constantly revised.[15]

---

14. T 1/384; T 29/31; T 29/33/64–65; T 1/385/76, 82; and T 1/386/73.
15. T 29/33/68–69: July 13, 1758; *The London Gazette*, July 13, 1758; and T 1/386/73: October 23, 1758. The quantity to be delivered was not specified. Would-be contractors were to enumerate the price of a loaf made entirely of wheat; of a loaf made of two-thirds wheat and one-third rye; and of a cart, driver, and four horses. They were to send their bids "sealed up" to the Treasury Secretary before July 25. Similar procedures had been adopted before. T 29/32/461: May 10, 1757; *The London Gazette*, May 14, 1757; and T 29/32/464: May 14, 1757.

Before Oswald and Graeme could get started, however, a typical wartime snafu had to be set aright. The Commander-in-Chief, Prince Ferdinand of Brunswick, refused to have any truck with private merchants as military suppliers. To such men, he would have to divulge the locations of magazines; over such men, he would have little control. So, Whitehall hastily devised a new plan to accommodate the Prince: the Hanoverian Chancellery would supply all troops in Germany; only if the delivery should falter would Ferdinand employ merchants. But, then, Ferdinand changed his mind and engaged Prado, who had gone to Germany to lobby Ferdinand directly and, at the same time, the Hanoverian Chancellery declared itself unable to perform the work. In late August, after it learned of Hanover's refusal, but before it learned of Prado's appointment, the Treasury ordered acceptance of Oswald. For over a month, confusion reigned, and the army's stores dwindled. Alarmed at the possibility of starving troops, the Commander-in-Chief of the British Forces in Germany, the Duke of Marlborough, looked into the matter, dickered with Prado over price, and drafted a tentative agreement with him. Just at that moment, Oswald, who had spent his time lobbying in London, appeared in Germany and handed the Duke the Treasury order of late August. Marlborough recanted and ordered new bids from both parties.[16]

Oswald's personal links to the Ministry allowed him to defeat Prado. The Earl of Bute recommended the associate to Lord George Sackville, who in turn persuaded Prince Ferdinand to rethink acceptance of Oswald. The merchant secured the support of Henry Legge, the Chancellor of the Exchequer. He obtained the backing of his kinsman James Oswald of Dunnikier, a member of the Board of Trade, who, in turn, opened the doors for the meeting with Marlborough in Germany. And he got one of his oldest friends, Samuel Martin, an erstwhile Caribbean planter who was now one of the two Treasury Secretaries, to "say something or other" about him in Chambers. Facing such support, Marlborough and Ferdinand backed down and accepted the Treasury's choice.[17]

16. T 1/386/73; T 1/385/86: Treasury Lords to Commissary General Robert Boyd, August 30, 1758; T 1/385/88: Tentative Agreement with Abraham Prado, August 31, 1758; T 1/386/73; and T 1/384/56: Duke of Marlborough to Duke of Newcastle, September 11, 1758. Prince Ferdinand's opinion appears in F. von Westphalen, *Geschichte der Feldzuge des Herzogs Ferdinand von Braunschweig-Luneburg*, v. 3 (Berlin, 1871), p. 338.

17. John Mill to Earl of Bute, September 19, 1758, Bute Papers, Undated #95, Mountstuart, Isle of Bute; Henry Bilson Legge to James Oswald, September 29, 1758, James Oswald Papers, Autograph Letter #17, Hockworthy House, Wellington, Somerset; Richard Oswald to James Oswald, c. October 1758, in *Memorials of the Public Life and Character of the Right Honorable James Oswald of Dunnikier* (Edinburgh, 1825), pp. 295–300; and Richard Oswald to James Oswald, October 16, 1758, James Oswald

"[A]ccustomed in a mercantile way to enter into transactions of consequence upon honour without written evidence," Oswald did not press for a formal rendering of the agreement, and a final written accord was not signed until May 1759. Orally, Oswald agreed to provide bread from the middle of September 1758 onward. He was to supply the British troops in Germany with wheat bread, "as may be ordered, in Loaves of 6 pounds English weight, or any other weight that may be ordered." He was to establish a sufficient number of magazines and "lay therein sufficient Quantities of Wheat from time to time," "keep up and constantly supply the stores thereof," and provide ovens for baking. The bread was to be delivered to the Quarter-Master of the Troops at magazines. With respect to transportation, Oswald was to provide "all such waggons, as may be ordered, with good Horses, Harness and necessary Utensils, with proper Servants for the Management of them." The contract would continue as long as the Commissariat thought necessary; it could be terminated upon two weeks' notice.[18]

For its part, the Treasury granted Oswald significant privileges. He was exempted from all customs and tolls, in a land where border tariffs were devastating impediments to travel and trade.[19] At seaports, he was to be furnished with carriages "for transporting to the Magazines all such Wheat as he may bring from Foreign Parts." If he paid for transportation, he was to be "allowed" its expense, as well as the cost "for removing or transporting any Wheat or Flour in Magazine, to different places" when his own bread wagons were insufficient. When in enemy country, he was to be furnished with granaries, ovens, mills, and firewood, as well as quarters and lodgings for his employees, "at the same Rates as his Majesty's Electoral Troops" received. Forage for the bread-wagon horses was to be provided by the King's magazines, when Oswald was not allowed "a freedom of Forage"; when the privilege was granted, he could obtain his own forage and charge the Crown. At all times, his

Papers, Hockworthy House, Wellington, Somerset. On acceptance of Oswald, see T 1/384/63: Abraham Hume to Treasury Lords, October 23, 1758; T 1/385/111: Duke of Newcastle to Robert Boyd, October 25, 1758; T 1/384/66: Michael Hatton to James Tierney, November 24, 1758; and T 1/384/68: Memorial of Mill, November 29, 1758.

18. Richard Oswald to James Oswald, October 16, 1758, James Oswald Papers, Hockworthy House, Wellington, Somerset. In February 1759, the Treasury composed a tentative draft, which appears in T 1/395/387–94. See also T 29/33/141–44; and Richard Oswald, Answers, ff. 64–66 [hereinafter "Answers"], Shelburne Papers, v. 154C, Clements Library, Ann Arbor, Mich.

19. There were at least 32 toll gates on the Weser between Elsfleth and Munden. Little, "The Commissariat," p. 44. Before 1800, there were 314 sovereign states and 1,475 separate estates, each able to impose its own customs duties. Koppel S. Pinson, *Modern Germany: Its History and Civilization*, 2nd ed. (New York, 1966), p. 5.

magazines were to be given "sufficient convoys & guards." Moreover, Oswald was to be compensated "for any Losses or Damages" inflicted on his wagons, magazines, or stores by enemy action or "unavoidable accidents of Fire or Plunder" and for the value of any stores remaining at the termination of the contract.[20]

By the time Oswald's contract was reduced to writing in 1759, supply was in full swing. Deliveries had begun two weeks after the Commander-in-Chief approved the agreement the previous September, and they continued until March 1763.[21] Over this four-and-one-half-year period, Oswald imported wheat and flour from England or bought it in Holland and Germany, baked more than 5 million loaves of bread in large field bakeries, stored them in magazines under his control, and distributed them to the battalions and regiments when needed. At war's end, Oswald was regularly servicing forty-three battalions of British cavalry and infantry, who consumed a hearty share of the ninety tons of bread that was daily doled out. Throughout the war, Oswald's operation was nothing less than "a work of Hercules." Its gargantuan proportions and the "extreme hurry" in which it was carried out required him to coordinate ingredients, buildings, and employees, and accommodate the uncontrollable elements of harvest, weather, transport, and personnel.[22] Oswald's experience in long-distance shipping and trading and in commission merchandising gave him skills in procurement, distribution, and accounting that were tailor-made for the task at hand. When Malachy Postlethwayt voiced his famous dictum – "the art of war is now become a science, and, indeed, a trading one" – he was pointing as much to the importance of businessmen in supplying the troops as to anything else.[23]

Making his own bread was Oswald's first and chief concern. He

20. For similar allowances granted to Oswald by the Board of Ordnance, see T 1/409/ 218: Laurence Dundas to Colonel Pierson, September 10, 1761. On the whole, the contract favored the contractor. Other than the right of termination, no penalty clauses were inserted. No delivery schedules were fixed. No mention was made of the mode of transport, the protection of perishables, the kind of containers, and the volume and weight. Richard Oswald, Observations, ff. 50–51 [hereinafter "Observations"], Shelburne Papers, v. 154C, Clements Library, Ann Arbor. Oswald agreed to provide bread in either English or Munster weight; the choice was to be made by the army.

21. T 1/385/103: Michael Hatton to Duke of Newcastle, September 24, 1758; and Observations, f. 1.

22. Little, "The Commissariat," p. 216. Delivery usually occurred "in a regimental way" but occasionally "when wanted." For example, in times of distress, Oswald's magazine keepers and bakers felt obliged to keep "Open House," providing bread to all who demanded it. Observations, ff. 16–7, 1, 10–11, 14.

23. Postlethwayt, *Universal Dictionary*, v. 1, p. 335.

preferred to import wheat and flour in sacks from Britain: German wheat was inferior in quality to British wheat, he believed, and scarce in quantity, since rye was favored by Germans. Yet, as the war progressed, he relied increasingly on local Jewish-German suppliers to whom he had been introduced by his bankers in Amsterdam and correspondents in Rotterdam. From these brokers, he also received water for turning the wheels of portable grinding mills, wood for fueling bakehouse ovens, containers for holding baked six-pound loaves, and horses and carts for transporting the loaves, flour, and wheat.[24]

All ingredients converged on the magazine, the center of Oswald's world in Germany and, in many respects, an analogue to his London counting-house. The magazine was "indispensable" not only to promote "the success of operations, but also in order to spare the troops and the population, and to maintain discipline." Near the end of the war, fifty-five magazines served the combined army, and Oswald managed a third of them. From Bremen in the north to Fritzlar in the south, from Deventer in the west to Brunswick in the east – Oswald's magazines, mapped in Illustration 7.1, fed troops encamped over an area of 66,000 square miles. He sited these magazines in such a way that, when one depot or subcontractor failed, another was there to step in and perform the service without inordinate delay. The magazines were storehouses for wheat, flour, and bread, offices for the contractor, and hotels for the staff. Generally, they stood next to wheat-grinding and bread-baking facilities. If Oswald had his choice, he employed a local grinding mill, but occasionally he built his own. Such was not the case with the bakehouse, which he always built anew and on an immense scale. He staffed one bakery with 300 employees: a director, several master bakers, 6 assistant master-bakers, 40 bakers, and 250 underbakers and assistants.[25] In addition to this army of bakers, each magazine employed at least one secretary; a keeper to supervise operations in the contractor's absence; and several accounting clerks to accept grain and flour, pay suppliers, record the quantities received and disbursed, and draw

---

24. Observations, ff. 22, 32–33. The British officers did not allow their troops to consume the less wholesome rye or "ammunition" (one-third wheat, two-thirds rye) loaves. Little, "The Commissariat," pp. 216–17. The prejudice against rye bread may have been justified, for unseen micro-fungi like the ergot – a tiny, black shell that thrives on molding ears of rye in cold, wet climates – can produce psychotic episodes, gangrene, and cardiac arrest. On brokers, see T 1/417/189–97.
25. Perjes, "Army Provisioning," p. 25; T 1/417/32–33: July 15, 1762; Observations, f. 14; and Little, "The Commissariat," pp. 217–21. Oswald's bakehouses were of two kinds: fixed, and portable. Portable bakeries followed the main body of the army, usually twelve miles behind.

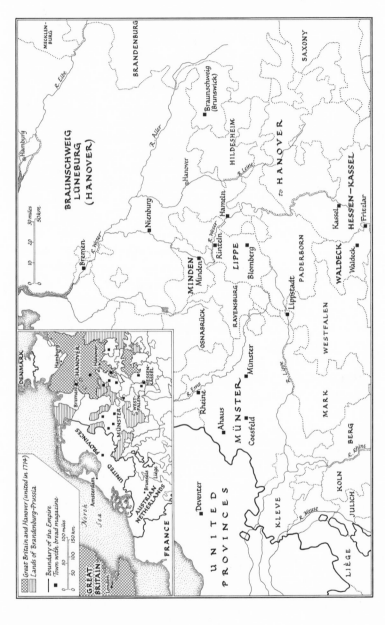

Illustration 7.1 A Map of Germany (1758–63), with the Locations of Richard Oswald's Bread Magazines. Drawn by Reginald Piggott.

up weekly and daily reports of provision levels for the commissary who was charged with inspecting the books and stores.[26] A multitude of Boors (German peasants) were also hired on an occasional basis as stallmasters, conductors, drivers, porters, and laborers; the whole of the transport operation, in fact, was conducted by these Boors. Lastly, there were guards, maintained at the contractor's expense, who safeguarded the magazine facilities and transport wagons. Workers were always in short supply and always a source of worry for a contractor obsessed with meeting obligations on time.[27]

Initially, Oswald and Graeme shared financial and administrative responsibilities equally but, two years into the operation, the associate bought out Graeme and assumed sole direction. Control, for Oswald, meant continual personal oversight. He rented comfortable rooms in the town nearest a magazine and visited his facilities daily; for the last three years of the war, his wife joined him, staying with Oswald or following twelve miles behind with the portable bakery when he visited the troops. On site, he ordered and cajoled the men he had placed in charge and with whom he generally had prior acquaintance: experts familiar with army procedure, like David Graeme or John Levett; locals knowledgeable in European languages and dialects and familiar with the supply capabilities of the region; and relatives, like his illegitimate son Richard and John Mill's cousin James. He ordered all who worked for him to cooperate with anyone else in the organization, and to communicate with anyone who might be affected.[28]

"Uninterrupted attention" to employees, facilities, and ingredients resulted in a competent and satisfactory execution of the contract. None of Oswald's loaves, for example, remained unbaked in the middle, which might have caused sickness among the soldiers. Almost all his disbursals

---

26. The reports of the magazines are housed in the Niedersachsisches Hauptstaatsarchiv, in Hannover, Germany. See, for example, Hann. 9e/1066/II/33–34. Commissariat-run magazines were subject to especially stringent reporting requirements. T 1/413/364–69 (c. 1761). On the difficulty of coordinating the extensive sets of accounts, see Oswald's own description, in Observations, f. 11. It was not until the war was over that Oswald "could bring all those persons together to a settled comptoir, by which I could have it in my power to get the articles [amounts], which I had a right to charge on the Crown, properly explained, sworn to, and attested by a Magistrate."

27. Transport was left to Germans, who were "at liberty to hire their waggons as they thought proper." The contractors "could get their assistance, or, if they refused, could force them . . . to pay them for the same in ready money." Observations, ff. 26–28; and David Graeme to Lt.-Col. Hotham, January 10, 1760, DDHO 4/1, Archives, University of Hull.

28. Articles, September 28, 1760, and Mary Oswald Letter Book, Oswald Papers, Sudlows. On the use of experts and locals, see T 1/385/76: Treasury Lords to Commissary General Robert Boyd, July 1758; T 1/385/73: July 28, 1758; and T 1/417/441: December 5, 1759.

of bread were regular and plentiful, in strong contrast to the nearly annual breakdown in the Commissariat's supply of the German troops.[29] Yet, coordinating ingredients, buildings, and people was not without its troubles. The climate, weather, and conditions of Germany often worked against the execution of the contracts. Weather materially affected the supply, since rye, while plentiful, quickly molded in Germany's cold and wet climate, and rye bread rotted in five days. Weather also bedeviled delivery. In March 1760, for example, ice and snow stopped shipments in the vicinity of the Cassel magazine for four weeks. For those charged with overseeing supply, "the anxieties" were "beyond expression." Later in the same year, after the troops reached their cantonments in Marienmunster, "violent snows & rains fell" and, for eight succeeding days, the River Nethe northwest of Cassel was "impassable." Neither the portable ovens nor the flour could move forward. Oswald made several attempts to cross it but, on each occasion, some of his bakers and horses drowned. He finally gave up. Bread rotted or went stale in the sack on one side of the river, while the troops went hungry on the other.[30] Compounding the problems of climate and weather was the dilapidated state of Germany's transportation infrastructure. Many roads were simply constructed, and most were nothing more than dirt paths. Water travel was often impeded by rain, which left the rivers and canals without apparent banks at a time when the roads were impassable. "The scarcity, delay and difficulty" caused by the transport facilities inflicted "real evil" and "universal distress" on the whole army.[31]

Perhaps even more than natural conditions and weather or climatic constraints, war itself frustrated the speedy execution of the contracts. War made the harvest unpredictable, and the crop even more scarce. The preferred comestible, wheat, was not commonly grown in Germany or Holland. The voracious Combined Army devoured what little wheat the countries it visited grew. And forced attempts to grow more grain either exhausted the soil or ran up against impossibility. In the final years of the war, many villages were so depopulated that nearly a third of all cropland went untilled. One army officer found himself so strapped that he was obliged to order hay, straw, and other provisions from as far north as East Friesland at the northern tip of Holland and as far east as the Elbe.[32] In times of emergency, when the march was rapid and the distance long, the exhausted army camped in one corner of the country

---

29. Observations, f. 11; and Samuel Martin to —, September 10, 1762, D/HV/B/4/23, Buckingham Record Office, Aylesbury.
30. T 1/405/193: Michael Hatton to Samuel Martin, May 10, 1760; T 29/34/56: Michael Hatton to Treasury Lords, April 30, 1761; and Observations, ff. 36–38.
31. Little, "The Commissariat," p. 216.
32. T 29/34/65–66: Michael Hatton to Samuel Martin, May 2, 1761.

and consumed its stores, and Oswald was obliged to bring them bread from afar. Their long-distance need created another problem for the contractor: obtaining workers in a depopulated region. Stores were low because there were few farmers to till the ground. Transport was slow because there were few Boors to drive the wagons. For instance, when the ice-choked Weser River became navigable again in April 1760, "the Boats were stopped for want of Men to draw them, and frequently lay empty for want of hands to load them." And when the supplies eventually reached Cassel, Oswald could get neither men nor wagons to transport flour and forage from the river to the magazine. Since the Commissariat typically provided little assistance, Oswald had no alternative but "to try the Boors," tempting them with ready money to lend him a hand, and generally this method succeeded. Yet Boor transport created its own nightmares: often the associate was required to advance cash as security; frequently his flour and bread were damaged by the Boor custom of transporting in open carriages; and the Boors fed themselves and their horses out of his stores.[33]

One final problem Oswald faced was timely payment. With the Seven Years' War, as with all wars, the Government and the army were extremely slow in discharging their debts. During the conflict, ministers and officers were slow in giving advances, and contractors were constantly in advance for large sums to local suppliers; at war's end, securing payment was even more arduous. When he returned to Britain, Oswald set about drawing up an account; but verification took eighteen months, and he could not tender his claim to the Audit Office until spring 1765. Because of irregularities in documentation, the Auditor decided that the Office would allow only a "mutual equitable composition" and, for the next six years, Oswald fought for the acceptance of vouchers and the deductibility of expenses. A final report was not issued until 1771, but even that did not quiet matters: Oswald's estate was not fully reimbursed until 1804![34]

33. Observations, ff. 3–6.
34. T 1/421/327; and Laurence Dundas to Messrs. Muilman & Sons, October 31, 1761, to James Craufurd, October 31, 1761, to Col. Pierson, October 31, 1761, and to Peter Taylor, January 6, 1762, Laurence Dundas Letter Book, Ms. 8,425, NLS. There were four steps to payment: (1) the contractor bought grain or flour from a supplier and obtained a receipt; (2) he gave the receipt to a Commissary of Account, who issued a certificate of acknowledgment; (3) the contractor submitted the certificate to the Deputy Paymaster in the field or to the Treasury and received a warrant that was payable on demand; and (4) he could exchange half of the amount of the warrant in cash, the other half in Exchequer Bills. T 29/36/304, 341, 352: May 17, 20, 1765. After the war, the warrants could also be exchanged for 4 percent Navy Stock. More than any other subject during the war, complaints about payment filled the ears of the Treasury Lords; after the war, the noise was deafening. See the Treasury minutes for April 29, May 2, 10, 1762. On later problems of procuring payment, see Observations, ff. 12–13, 49.

For his services in coordinating the supply of the army, Oswald was well rewarded.[35] This, however, was not so apparent in his earlier contract to supply the troops in southern England in 1756. In this agreement, Oswald "low-balled" the price of bread. He agreed to provide bread for 25,000 men – wheat bread at 6.1 pence per six-pound loaf and rye bread at 5.9 pence per six-pound loaf.[36] Since the price of wheat loaves in London averaged 8.2 pence per six-pound loaf in 1756, Oswald was selling bread to the army for about 75% of the market price.[37] On this basis, and considering only bread, the 1756 contract may have been only marginally profitable.

Once contractual relations were established and Oswald was asked to submit a second bid in 1757, his price rose 4.4 pence to 11.0 pence per loaf. To some extent, Oswald's price reflected the shortage of wheat brought on by severe drought and the drain of supplies from southern England on account of the war: the average price of bread in London rose from 8.2 pence in 1756 to 10.2 pence the following year.[38] All the same, Oswald's contract price rose from a 25% discount from the

---

35. Any determination of Net Income that applies the basic profit equation to governmental records must proceed with caution. Since nowhere did Oswald detail the costs of the goods he provided the army or the expense he incurred, the Expense of Goods Sold must be approximated according to the price of bread published in contemporary newspapers. The Expense represents a maximum amount; lower cost levels almost surely prevailed. Oswald's English supply depots probably had their own field ovens, and his German bread magazines certainly had their own baking facilities; by using them, Oswald did not have to pay the market price of bread. Oswald asked the Victualling Board in 1756 to lend him use of the oven at its Chatham office in order to bake army bread, but the Navy could not spare the oven. Adm 111/44 (May 21, 1756). In Germany, army rations "were sometimes cooked in the ordinary bakehouse of a town . . . but such facilities were rarely adequate"; it became common for contractors to construct new stone or brick ovens. Little, "The Commissariat," p. 217. On the "new" use of iron ovens, see T 64/96/53–54: March 11, 1759. Likewise, since at no time did the contractor specify the sums he paid for transport to Germany, wages of employees, office supplies, or other basic operating costs, the Expense of Contracting must be dispensed with. For the cost of producing bread, see Little, "The Commissariat," pp. 217–21, 373–75. Oswald was to pay all transport costs to the water landing nearest the army. T 1/385/67, 73. For the cost of shipping grain from England to Germany (original purchase + Channel transport + sacks + demurrage), see Little, "The Commissariat," pp. 367–71; for the cost of water travel and wagon hire, see Observations, ff. 31–32.
36. T 1/365/33: Richard Oswald to Treasury Lords, March 27, 1756; and T 64/133.
37. *The Gentleman's Magazine* lists monthly average market prices for one-peck wheat loaves (17 1bs., 6 oz.); the 1756 average was 23.8 pence per peck loaf. A six-pound loaf should have cost Oswald 8.2 pence in the London market. The figures given by Sir William Beveridge, *Prices and Wages in England*, v. 1, p. 424, and B. R. Mitchell, *British Historical Statistics* (Cambridge, 1981), p. 770, are considerably higher than the figures based on monthly magazine listings; the latter are used here.
38. W. G. Hoskins, "Harvest Fluctuations and English Economic History, 1620–1759," *Agricultural History Review*, v. 16 (1968), pp. 31–32. In 1756, wheat bread fetched the second highest price of the century.

market price to an 8% premium. Oswald received £27,374 on the 1757 supply contract, of which bread figured as 56% of the total value.[39] If his profit rate on bread was 31%, then his profit on the bread under the second army contract was £4,684.[40]

The third contract to supply the British and Hessian troops with bread and bread wagons was Oswald's largest and by far the most rewarding. Under this agreement, Oswald provided the troops with wheat bread at an average of 8.5 pence per six-pound loaf. In wartime Germany, he probably produced a six-pound wheat loaf for 3.5 pence on average; contract bread, therefore, had a markup of 5 pence per loaf, or 143%.[41] Oswald reported that he supplied 5,395,426 loaves of bread, for which he charged the army £191,088. At 3.5 pence per loaf, this bread cost Oswald £79,000 to make. He, therefore, earned £112,000 on four and one-half years' supply of bread.[42] To this sum, Oswald added income from the supply of goods other than bread, as well as from previous encampment contracts and two commissary contracts.[43]

At the time, one question was raised above others: did military contractors like the associates make inordinate profits by taking advantage of

39. T 1/375/138: Estimate, 1757; T 1/375/137, 139, 140: 1757; and T 29/32/464: May 19, 1757. The account appears in AO 1/174/510: November 11, 1758. For conflicting assessments, see AO 1/174/511 (£12,608), and T 1/376/84 (£27,276).

40. £4,684 in 1757 is approximately £319,309 or $474,934 in 1994. The first camp price schedule was 25% below market price. If one hypothesizes Oswald broke even on this contract, his behavior was designed to make himself known as an honorable, reliable contractor. On the second 1757 contract, he charged 108% of market price. If he could still produce the bread at 75% of the market price, he realized a gain of 33% of the market price, or 31% of his contract price. Profit calculations include allowance for transport and capital costs in building temporary ovens and the like.

41. Oswald's contract (November 1758 – April 1763) is detailed in five distinct sources: T 1/385/67, 73; T 1/385/111; T 29/33/98–100; AO 1/191/599; and "Answers," ff. 64–66. The initial contract price seems to have been 8.00 pence per six-pound wheat loaf, but was twice revised upward and "the average of the three prices of the contract" was 8.50 pence. "Observations," ff. 48, 37. On costs in Germany, see Little, "The Commissariat," p. 375 (the market price of bread in Germany was 5.94 grot per six-pound loaf on average); and McCusker, *Money and Exchange*, pp. 63, 79 (1 grot = .58 pence; 5.94 grot = 3.43 pence).

42. £112,000 in 1758–62 is approximately £8,589,452 or $12,775,778 in 1994. T 1/428/40–41: Memo on Mr. Oswald's Contracts for Bread & Wagons, 1763 (total = £763,415); and AO 1/191/599: Account, declared January 16, 1794 (total = £763,415). Elsewhere, he claimed he received Treasury warrants for £688,886 by May 1765 on his German contract; to this figure, he added £3,904 as Charges on the Crown and £115,346 as Charges on the Government. Observations, ff. 8–9.

43. Little suggests that Oswald made £9,341 as the Commissariat's Superintendent of English and Hessian Wagon Trains in 1763, keeping 14% of what he charged the army as profit. "The Commissariat," pp. 381–86. Laurence Dundas made £29,455, keeping 17%. Little's calculations are somewhat suspect, however, since he misconstrued the accounting and interpreted the "Discharges" as market price valuations of what Oswald paid out, rather than as contract prices.

the Government? Many men of letters and affairs thought so. Robert Burns savagely satirized Oswald as a "Plunderer of Armies." In Tobias Smollett's picaresque novel *The Expedition of Humphrey Clinker* (1771), the itinerant Matthew Bramble vilifies "agents, commissaries, and contractors" inasmuch as they had "fattened, in two successive wars, on the blood of the nation." He links them with other "upstarts of fortune" – Caribbean planters, African slavers, East Indian nabobs, stock market speculators, and (he sniffs) "men of low birth." (Clinker's description is certainly on target for the associates, for they filled all but the nabob category.) Smollett's contemporaries excoriated these characters as enemies "assailing insular and agricultural England," while many men of affairs attacked the militarized expansion of the empire as little more than a cabalistic ploy of merchants and contractors of Scots, Jewish, and European extraction.[44]

The answer to the question of inappropriate profiteering is twofold. Certainly contracting profits were enormous, by any early-modern standard. In no shorter period could a merchant make a greater amount of money than by executing government contracts in a time of war. These profits were another consequence of the growth of militarism and the empire. In the history of the British empire leading to the Seven Years' War, it is almost a truism that wars trimmed the sails of transoceanic merchants and decreased their opportunities for profits in shipping and trade. During the Seven Years' War, in contrast, commerce generally flourished. After the Battles of Lagos (August 1759) and Quiberon Bay (November 1759), the French navy had barely a ship in the Atlantic. British naval supremacy at last meant something, cutting the disruption of trade to a minimum. Disasters at the beginning of the war, such as the Battles of the Wilderness (1755), Minorca (1756), and Hastenbeck (1757), were commercially unimportant. British and American merchants

44. James Kinsley, ed., *The Poems and Songs of Burns*, v. 1 (Oxford, 1968), p. 447; James M. Holzman, *The Nabobs in England: A Study of the Returned Anglo-Indian, 1760–1785* (New York, 1926), p. 15; and *The Public Advertiser*, January 31, 1778. Recent historical investigation suggests that Smollett and the critics overdrew the case for peculation and turpitude. Little, "The Commissariat." Oswald, for instance, was certainly known for his proper commercial and financial behavior. Prince Ferdinand praised Oswald's performance, remarking that "the British have sent me Commissaries fit to be Generals, and Generals not fit to be Commissaries." Anon., "The Oswalds of Caithness," *Northern Ensign* (April 16, 1910), n.p. Lesser men repeated the praise. According to the head of the Commissariat, Oswald acted "for the public service only, in the most handsome and disinterested manner possible"; he spared "no expense to fulfill every contract he is concerned for in the noblest manner." T 1/405/84: Major Richard Pierson to Samuel Martin, October 18, 1760; and T 1/405/191–92: Michael Hatton to Samuel Martin, May 2, 1760. At the end of the war, Oswald was the only contractor that Treasury Secretary Samuel Martin could call "useful and good." Samuel Martin to —, September 10, 1762, D/HV/B/4/23, Buckingham Record Office, Aylesbury.

found themselves relatively free from attack, except from the odd pri-
vateer, and ready to absorb the custom of French planters. As we have
already seen in the expansion of the associates' slaving operations on
Bance Island, these enterprisers were working in both the Atlantic and
Western Europe. Not all of the associates who served as contractors
and victualers earned Oswald's stupendous profits, yet, with safe travel
and the increased opportunities for supply, they all multiplied their
fortunes several times over by seizing the opportunity to feed Britain's
soldiers and sailors. Their profit-making and that of merchants like
them deserves close investigation.

Moreover, government contractors took advantage of the scarcity of
their skills in commercial integration. The problem the Government
faced was that it needed merchant-contractors because they were the
only ones with sufficiently developed logistical skills and resources. Early-
modern warfare, always a nightmare to manage, created extraordinary
supply problems when, as in the Seven Years' War, its scale dramatically increased. The associates saw in this war a chance to sell the state
their skills in coordinating, distributing, and producing services and
goods. Oswald, for instance, was familiar with the rights and obligations of contracting parties, understood the intricacies of accounting,
and knew how to wend his way through the maze of foreign currencies,
customs duties, and government offices. Replicating systems that had
worked in his shipping and trading, planting, and slaving businesses,
Oswald integrated his bread supply operations as he did his baggage-,
artillery-, and hospital-wagon operations: he marshaled resources
(financing, grain, and equipment) and skills (financiers, grain distribu-
tors, bread bakers, transport suppliers, and depot employees) from around
the Atlantic commercial world; and, to meet war's complex logistical
challenges, he deployed these resources by relying on relatives and friends,
running his service like a family operation, and insisting on personal,
attentive, on-site management.

8

Financing: "Turning the Great Wheel of Unfathomable Commerce Round"

THE ASSOCIATES' CAREERS DEMONSTRATE the ability of outsiders to acquire substantial fortunes in the commercially expansive years between 1748 and 1776. These merchants departed for America or, less commonly, remained and trained in Britain in their late teens; set up London commission merchandising houses that specialized in shipping and trading during the 1730s and 1740s; entered the American planting business and the African slave trade during the 1740s and 1750s; and executed government contracts between 1748 and 1763. Finally, as we will explore in the rest of this book, during the 1760s, 1770s, and 1780s, they withdrew money from trade and invested in placements that marked them as "men of property."

Financing has always been a necessary instrument of commerce. This chapter considers four questions about that side of the associates' businesses: How did they finance their initial entry into London commission merchandising and their subsequent push into principal enterprising? What borrowing and lending did they do? How did they use banks? And, on becoming successful, where did they invest the cash that their businesses threw off? Answers to these questions are not as fully evidenced, unfortunately, as are answers to questions about the operational side of the associates' businesses. With respect to creating an initial stake, business and personal letters occasionally provide us with a glimpse of family gifts and legacies, but such letters are rare for the associates, especially in the early years of their training. The business records of the associates' firms have been lost. While personal and business letters have been preserved by their descendants, the account books generally stayed in London. Oswald's records are a case in point. On his death in 1784, after the balances were transcribed to the Andersons' account in a new set of books, the records were transferred to a strongbox in the office of Charlton Palmer, Oswald's attorney, who lived across the street at 18 Philpot Lane. They remained there until Palmer moved to

Fishmongers' Hall in 1795; on his death two years later, they passed to his partners Rowland and William Maltby, who took them with them when they moved to Lincoln's Inn Fields. The Maltby firm kept the records through at least the middle of the nineteenth century, when the firm and its partners disappear from legal directories and its books were lost.[1]

The wills of parents, relatives, partners, and colleagues help fill some of the informational gaps left by the lack of business records. Apprenticeship documents may supplement testamentary accounts, but they shed little light on men who, as a practice, did not sign formal articles. Marriage agreements and personal correspondence do shed some light on the acquisition of dowries. The evidence on borrowing and lending is just as exiguous. Since neither balance sheets nor account books have survived, the extent of activity must be built up from correspondence, court records, and wills. Borrowing from banks is the one exception, for bank records are comparatively complete and intact, and the records of London and regional banks can be combed for instances of associate borrowing and usage. Outside investments made late in life are also easy to track. Government debt has left detailed records now kept in England's public archives, although not all publicly held companies' ledgers and very few privately held companies' accounts have survived. The acquisition of land, the ultimate outside investment, is much less easy to trace. Private correspondence and local histories provide some clues. Local records are less helpful. Scotland's General and Particular Registers of Sasines, for instance, are an invaluable source, but they are silent on price and acreage; and no central English analogue to them exists. Only in the colonies is it possible, if the records have survived, to reconstruct the associates' real estate portfolios from land patents, land conveyances, and legal records. Thus, an examination of all available records concerning the sources of the associates' capital is an examination of relatively few, widely divergent records.

Creating an Initial Stake

In the middle decades of the eighteenth century, starting up in overseas trade generally required large amounts of capital. According to a 1747 trade manual, the work of a general overseas merchant required "unlimited" funds; the author of a subsequent guide thought it necessary to have £3,000 to £4,000 "to engage in foreign trade to any great

1. See John Browne's *General Law List* published annually in London between 1775 and 1854.

advantage," whereas an apothecary, retail cheesemonger, or upholsterer might need only £100, and a retail linen-draper, pawnbroker, or pewterer only £1,000.[2] Thus, the associates needed relatively large sums of money to go it alone or enter into partnership: a house would have to be leased and furnished, supplies ordered, clerks hired, warehouses rented, and, among other things, bonds warranting the return of trans-Atlantic cargo submitted to government officers. To meet these demands, the associates financed their own houses principally from small family legacies, their previous business earnings, and marriage dowries. They fit the caricature of the young man who keeps his eyes and ears open and his nose to the grindstone, and then marries for money.

Not counting the second-generation associates John Boyd and John Sargent III, only four of the other twenty-one associates received money from their parents – hardly surprising, given their backgrounds. Although it may have been the practice of "the first and richest familys" to furnish their sons with "large capitals . . . on their introduction" into business, it does not seem to have been the practice of the associates' families. There is no documentable distribution of a "portion" (the part of an estate that goes to an heir before the giver has died) to an associate during the life of his father. Michael Herries may have received a portion – two farms – in 1739, but the evidence is unclear. Furthermore, there is only one instance of a deceased father's estate going to an associate before the latter established himself as a merchant: John Levett, when he was orphaned in Turkey at age seven. The only other associates known to have received significant inheritances from parents – John Sargent II and George Aufrere – did so late in life, well after they had succeeded in business. This lack of family funds is probably typical of people from the margins; indeed, it probably helps explain their

2. £4,000 in 1747 is approximately £348,183 or $517,881 in 1994. Scant evidence survives to document the capitalization of individual mercantile firms. Levels varied with trade and region. Campbell, *London Tradesman* (London, 1747); J. Collyer, *Parents and Guardians Directory* (London, 1761); and Earle, *English Middle Class*, p. 107. As for the associates, the firm in which Aufrere first worked had a high capital stock of £9,000 sterling. Peregrine Cust to Sir John Cust, September-December 1744, in Elizabeth Cust, ed., *Records of the Cust Family, Series II: 1550–1779* (London, 1909), pp. 257–58. Many region-specific trades required much less. Mackaill, Melville, and Young, West African slave-traders, had £2,100. C 12/808/2: Johnson v. Oswald. Grant suggested that the Gordon firm in Jamaica maintain £2,000. Lewis Gordon to Sir Robert Gordon, January 3, 1760, Gordon Papers, La.II. 498, EUL. And Oswald advised John Lewis Gervais in South Carolina to reserve £1,373. Henry Laurens to John Lewis Gervais, January 1, 1773, *The Papers of Henry Laurens*, v. 5, p. 517. These may be low, however. The St. Christopher planter John Pinney speaks of £4,000–5,000 for a Caribbean partnership. Pares, *West India Fortune*, p. 171. And, before 1776, typical Chesapeake tobacco firms required between £5,000 and £20,000. Price, *Capital and Credit*, p. 38.

movement from home and into colonial trade. From what is known about legacies, it appears that the creation of entails and legal customs respecting the property of intestate fathers favored eldest sons and excluded most children from enjoying whatever real-property wealth their fathers possessed at death. It is possible that a similar bias also operated against sons generally when it came to the distribution of portions; fathers, whether landowners, businessmen, or professionals, were reluctant to entrust a sizable amount of money to a son who had not yet proven himself.[3]

In contrast, extended families, including grandparents, granduncles and grandaunts, godparents, and cousins, figured as an important source of start-up capital. Almost all of the associates inherited something early in their careers, at a point when they were settling themselves "in an independent way" in London. Upon the 1751 death of his cousin George Arnold, John Sargent II received £6,000 in cash, a house in London, a house in Surrey, two estates in Devon, and what remained after the payment of debts and legacies, just as he was setting up his own shop in Mincing Lane. Through his wife, he received another £400 in 1751 upon the death of her mother's sister's husband. Similarly, before 1750, Thomas Birch inherited half of two freehold estates in Hertfordshire and Bedfordshire from a rich uncle and two leasehold lots in St. Paul's Churchyard from a maternal grandmother. And two large sugar plantations on St. Christopher came from his maternal grand-mother when John Boyd turned twenty-six and entered the counting-house. Bequests of this kind were generally used "in the course" of establishing one's "trade and merchandize."[4]

3. Grant notes the behavior of the richest families in GD 345/1180/1765. On Levett, Sargent, and Aufrere, see Commons Sergeant's Book, v. 6, ff. 141–42, Orphans' Court Papers, COLRO; PROB 11/889/333–34: Will of John Sargent I, proved October 11, 1762; Agnew, *Protestant Exiles*, v. 2, p. 337; and RD, December 29, 1739, SRO. According to T. M. Devine, Glasgow merchants often set aside money so that their children would have the wherewithal to purchase a "stock in trade." "An Eighteenth-Century Business Elite: Glasgow–West India Merchants, c. 1750–1815," *Scottish History Review*, v. 57 (1978), p. 47. Recently, Earle has suggested that the most common source of funds before 1730 were parents. *English Middle Class*, p. 108.
4. On Sargent, see PROB 11, 197 Busby, Will of George Arnold (proved July 1, 1751); and PROB 11/789/q. 244: Will of Lancelot Rolleston, proved August 12, 1751. On Birch, see PROB 11/1000, Will of Thomas Birch (proved August 27, 1774). Birch inherited the other half on the death of his sister Penelope in 1763. PROB 11/895/q. 107: Will of Penelope Birch, proved February 19, 1763. On Boyd, see C 54/5,818/13–19 (citing Indenture of October 26–27, 1743). Another associate, Christopher Cham-bers, inherited a £1,000 trust set up by his uncle Lancelot Rolleston, Mrs. Sargent's aunt's husband. PROB 11/789/q. 244. See also legacies involving Grant in PROB 11/891/ff. 295–96: Will of Elizabeth Dicker. Among other Londoners trading to America, initial capitalization came from the immediate family, but subsequent money came from distant relatives and friends. Roberts, "Samuel Storke," p. 149.

Membership in a commercial group opened as many financial doors as familial assistance, and the importance of commercial acquaintances over blood relations gradually increased over the course of the associates' careers. Because they were outsiders, only five of the associates underwent the "genteel servitude" of formal apprenticeship: Aufrere, Sargent II, John Gardiner, Cooke, and Levett.[5] The rest of the associates' apprenticeships were informal. For a fee, established merchants took them as teenagers into their counting-houses and assigned them the tasks of copying letters and keeping accounts. Oswald's cousins followed this practice in training Oswald, for instance, and he did much the same thing with the Andersons. These early counting-house experiences often led to their accumulating the financial resources of former masters and partners. Aufrere, we know, assumed the bulk of the business of his erstwhile master, the Cornhill linen-draper Sir William Smith and, later, that of his business colleague Peregrine Cust, with whom he had worked in the 1740s. So, too, did Sargent II, who took over the firm once headed by his former master George Arnold; years later, Sargent took over the sizable Levant correspondence of his contracting partner Stratton. Similarly, Oswald acquired all of Mill's business assets on Mill's death of a "Paralytick Stroke" in 1771. Nearly all of the associates were given a financial stake in the operations they joined when young: they represented their merchants as overseas factors; shared the benefits of firm prizes; and joined the firm as junior partners, owning shares in vessels and receiving a percentage of profits.[6]

One substantial source of business profit earned early in their careers took the form of prize money garnered from privateering, the capture of enemy ships in time of war. Most large-scale trans-Atlantic merchants obtained letters of marque and reprisal from the Admiralty that permitted their vessels to capture French ships during the War of Jenkins' Ear, and such auxiliary military activities brought them substantial if unpredictable riches. On one occasion in 1744, an Oswald vessel captured a French ship off the coast of Ireland and, in the sale of the vessel and its cargo brought the three Oswalds thousands of pounds in windfall

---

5. On apprenticeship and its decline, see Glass, "Socio-economic status and occupation in the City of London at the end of the seventeenth century," in A. Hollaender and W. Kellaway, eds., *Studies in London History* (London, 1969), p. 385; J. R. Kellett, "The breakdown of Guild and Corporation control over the handicraft and retail trades of London," *Economic History Review*, 2nd ser., v. 10 (1957–58), pp. 388–89; and William F. Kahl, "Apprenticeship and the Freedom of the London Livery Companies, 1690–1750," *Guildhall Miscellany*, v. 7 (1956), pp. 17–20.

6. PROB 11/r. 793 (1752 London March 77 Bettesworth): Will of Sir William Smith; PROB 11 (71 Ducarel; proved February 21, 1785): Will of Peregrine Cust; PROB 11 (1751 Busby; proved July 1751): Will of George Arnold; PROB 11 (proved January 3, 1759): Will of Richard Stratton; PROB 11/975/118v–122r (proved November 18, 1771): Will of John Mill; and SRO, CS 234/R/2/23: Scott v. Mill, May 23, 1776.

profits. Young Oswald's share of several such sales – £15,000 – enabled him to go to London in 1745 and establish his independent shipping and trading practice there. From just one similar operation later in the decade, John Boyd reaped £1,400.[7]

After working their way into partnerships and earning start-up stakes for their own firms, the associates married well. Of the seventeen associates who married, each gained money, property, or connections from their wives. Marriage was "a highly commercial business" whose usefulness was never lost on an enterprising group of suitors struggling to fix themselves in London's society. To the associates, marriage was a process of economic alliance or exchange, similar to other kinds of commercial transaction. Marriage "without the acquisition of an estate at the same time" would lessen "the security of creditors very considerably," and marriage to a woman of fortune eased the often frequent capital and credit needs of young firms. Most associates married relatively late, during their thirties or forties; their average age at first marriage was thirty-six, nearly ten years older than the national average, and toward the end of the first stage of their capital accumulation.[8]

To her marriage, each of the seventeen associates' wives brought a dowry, which commonly included several estates, trust money, and personal goods.[9] In a typical arrangement, John Boyd acquired a dowry of £3,000 in 1749 on marrying the daughter of William Bumsted of

7. £15,000 in 1745 is approximately £1,419,366 or $2,111,136 in 1994; £1,400 in 1748 is approximately £116,786, or $173,706 in 1994. For privateering permits, see HCA 26/23/6r (Grant, *Pompey*, January 1745), 7r (Grant & Johnston, *Westmoreland*, January 1745), 23r (Oswald, *Gordon*, January 1745); HCA 26/24/26r (Augustus Boyd, *Jenny*, November 1745), 149r (Grant & Johnston, *Westmoreland*, September 1746); HCA 26/26/53r (Grant & Johnston, *Westmoreland*, November 1747), 114r (the Boyds, *Rowland*, February 1748). On Boyd, see Simmons and Thomas, eds., *Proceedings and Debates*, v. 1, p. 135. On Oswald, see E 504/28/1 (July 11–12, 1744), SRO; and Carlyle, *Anecdotes*, p. 45. For later windfall profits reaped by Grant, see, GD 248/99/6/22: Sir Alexander Grant to Sir Ludovick Grant, May 3, 1766.

8. The Andersons, Aufrere, Birch, the Boyds, Chambers, Samuel Gardiner, Grant, Herries, Johnston, Oswald, Rolleston, the Sargents, Scott, and Trevanion all married. On marriage, see Henry Laurens to John Lewis Gervais, January 21, 1774, *The Papers of Henry Laurens*, v. 9, p. 247; Borsay, *English Urban Renaissance*, pp. 243–48; and Langford, *Public Life*, p. 6. National averages at first marriage appear in E. A. Wrigley and R. S. Schofield, *The Population History of England*, Table 7.26, p. 255.

9. Clay, "Marriage, Inheritance," pp. 503–18, provides a summary of the historiography of marital property and argues that, in 1600–1815, brides with large inheritances were quite scarce; it was far more likely to find brides with large portions. This may be true for the early eighteenth century, when only rich men married wealthy heiresses and daughters. Earle, *English Middle Class*, p. 141. But the sample studied here suggests that it is not true from 1740 onward, when men without property but with significant commercial prospects experienced no difficulty marrying heiresses, unless of course their late marriage age reflects a difficulty; no contemporary information corroborates the supposition. Marriage contracts frequently placed a bride's dowry along with balancing property from the groom's family in the hands of trustees to protect the interest of the wife and her children, but no such contracts were signed by the associates.

Upton, a wealthy Warwickshire squire. Similarly, through marrying Mary Ramsay, the only child of Jamaica merchant Alexander Ramsay, Oswald inherited a Jamaican estate worth £8,000 – one of the grandest houses in Kingston, a counting-house, its shipping and trading operation, 103 slaves, and a share in one of the island's largest sugar plantations. One year after the marriage, Oswald used part of Ramsay's estate to secure the repayment of a loan he had taken for the improvement of the Bance Island slave factory.[10] In addition to her dowry, the associate gained complete power over his wife's freehold and chattel interests.[11] The choice of a marriage partner was a strategic step. "A fair Wife with empty pockets" was "like a noble house without Furniture, Showy but Useless."[12]

The associates who married also acquired contacts in the commercial or political sector from the match. By marrying the daughter of a prominent West Indian judge, Augustus Boyd rose in St. Christopher society and, later, gained the custom of London's absentee planters who had been friends of his father-in-law. For the same reason, Dr. Alexander Grant found it easier to acquire plantations in Jamaica, to leave the island for London and, in the metropolis, to attract American correspondents, for his father-in-law's reputation preceded him in each instance and eased the task. The Huguenot George Aufrere's marriage to a first cousin of the Earl of Exeter linked him to a large family of great wealth, extensive property, and political clout, all of which the merchant availed himself when setting his own affairs in order in the early 1750s. By marrying Anne Blackburn before moving to London, Michael Herries gained entree to London's Turkey trading world, which would have otherwise been closed to an outsider. And, in almost proverbial fashion, a number of associates married their masters' or partners' daughters, "clinching the connexion" to the firm and "elevating" the merchant in the community of traders. Robert Scott married his partner's eldest daughter, for instance, and John Trevanion wed John Boyd's

10. £3,000 in 1749 is approximately £245,942 or $365,809 in 1994; £8,000 in 1738 is approximately £711,009 or $1,057,541 in 1994. C 54/5818/13–19 (Indenture, September 20, 1749); and Inventory of Alexander Ramsay, Probate Inventories, Island Record Office, Spanishtown April 26, 1738. Oswald mortgaged a Jamaica court decree worth £5,524 which had been entrusted to Ramsay's trustees. Ramsay also got an annual rent of £200 from her Kingston properties. Crop Accounts, 1/B/11/4/1, f. 181, Jamaica Archives. Lest one think marital alliances were completely one-sided, see the details of Birch's marriage settlement in PROB 11/1000.

11. William Holdsworth, *A History of English Law*, 4th ed., v. 3 (London, 1935), pp. 525–27.

12. Barnard, *A Present for an Apprentice*, p. 68. For Grant's observations on marriage, see GD 345/1180/1765: Sir Alexander Grant to Captain Archibald Grant, December 27, 1764.

eldest daughter. Through both wives they acquired the contacts to go it alone commercially. And Alexander Anderson, by marrying the daughter of Richard Oswald's nephew and heir George at a time when Anderson was establishing himself in London, acquired access to one of Glasgow's larger sugar and tobacco trading networks.[13]

Borrowing and Lending

No merchant borrowed if he could draw on his own funds or those of his wife and, for much of their careers, the associates were cash-rich, especially after executing government contracts. Still, even when their resources were slim, they did not let the lack of cash stand in the way of new enterprise. When external events, such as the extraordinary purchase of land, the unexpected bankruptcy of a client, or the capture of overseas plantations by the enemy, momentarily stripped them of capital, as they did in the late 1760s and 1770s, the associates resorted to "extraordinary borrowing" (which the associates simply referred to as "borrowing"). Borrowing, in this sense, was distinguished from ordinary extensions of commercial credit which formed the foundation of all business in this period. Transferring funds by dealing in bills of exchange, granting and receiving book credit, making use of shop credit – such transactions were largely taken for granted by large-scale traders at midcentury.

But extraordinary borrowing was a different matter. Such borrowing was viewed by the associates as a possible first step toward financial and moral bankruptcy; borrowing beyond the capacity to repay or for conspicuous consumption in "a Life of Riot and Debauchery" was to be avoided. One should borrow, they believed, only to preserve capital stock in time of crisis or create or augment capital stock in order to take advantage of an extraordinary commercial opportunity and, then, only when the prospects for rapid repayment seemed optimistic.[14] But, being

13. PROB 11/911/q. 321; Playfair, *British Family Antiquity*, pp. 200–01; G. R. Dennis, *The Cecil Family* (Boston, 1914), p. 138; C 12/2288/36: Bate v. Bate; Pringle, *Records of the Pringles*, pp. 175–76; *Gentleman's Magazine*, v. 43 (1773), p. 303; and *An Act to Exonerate the Trustees of Richard Oswald of Auchincruive* (London, 1831).
14. GD 345/1162/3/30: Sir Alexander Grant to Sir Archibald Grant, December 23, 1752. See also Daniel Defoe, *The Complete English Tradesman*, 4th ed., v. 2 (London, 1738), pp. 1, 7, 13, 24; Barnard, *A Present for an Apprentice*, pp. 6, 16, 29; Postlethwayt, *Universal Dictionary*, v. 2, p. 626; and *Dumfries Weekly Magazine*, March 1, 1774, pp. 359–60. An analysis of prescriptive literature on the subject appears in Margaret R. Hunt, "English Urban Families in Trade, 1660–1800: The Culture of Early Modern Capitalism" (Ph.D. dissert., New York University, 1986), pp. 58–64.

cash-rich, they found few occasions to call upon others; instead, they were lenders during the middle and later years of their careers.[15]

In principle, private loans were simple affairs: a lender granted a borrower the use of a sum of money with the conditions that interest be paid for the period of use and that the principal be returned to the lender by a stipulated date.[16] Between 1713 and 1800, the legal maximum rate of interest a lender could charge in Britain was 5%; in the colonies, 6% to 8%.[17] Loans of cash or credit were debited from the borrower's account in the lender's books; in exchange, the lender received a promise to repay (an oral agreement or a promissory note), a bond, a transferable court judgment, or a mortgage securing repayment with property. The borrower's indebtedness was certified by a deed, and the deed was registered with local officials.[18]

In practice, private loans could be quite complex, however. If the loan was used to extinguish prior debts, the lender had to authenticate and consolidate the claims upon the borrower and then rank them in the order of repayment. A loan often became the subject of litigation between the lender and the borrower or his relatives.[19] And then there was the task of regaining the principal, the performance of which was

15. Earlier in the century, Londoners also participated in the market as lenders. Earle, *English Middle Class*, pp. 121–22, 362 n. 19. Some 15% of the gross assets of the 375 London citizens (some 9% of the gross assets of the merchants in the sample) whose estates were administered by the Orphans' Court were invested in personal loans, which Earle distinguishes from trade credit, which occupied 38% (36%).

16. "Loan" here denotes a sum directly lent at interest; it excludes a bank overdraft which was a short-term loan with interest. Grant regularly maintained overdrafts with Coutts & Co. and the British Linen Co.

17. The maximum of 5% and treble damages for violation was laid down in 1713 by 12 Anne 2, c. 16. The rate of interest actually affixed was determined by the convenience of the lender, the nature of the security given by the borrower, and the relation between lender and borrower. L. S. Pressnell, "The Rate of Interest in the Eighteenth Century," in L. S. Pressnell, ed., *Studies in the Industrial Revolution* (London, 1960), p. 186. Money being more abundant in London than elsewhere, interest rates were generally lower in the metropolis. Joseph B. Matthews, *The Law of Money-Lending, Past and Present* (London, 1906), p. 23; and T. S. Ashton, *An Economic History of England* (London, 1955), p. 26.

18. On the mortgage market, see Pressnell, "The Rate,", pp. 178–214; Robert Bell, *Lectures on Conveyancing* (Edinburgh, 1800); Robert Bell, *Outline of Lectures on the Law of Scotland* (Edinburgh, 1827); Charles Shepherd, *The Colonial Practice of St. Vincent* (London, 1822), pp. 48–60, 112–25; George Smith, *The Laws of Grenada* (London, 1808); and Hancock, "Borrowing and Lending in the Colonial Caribbean" (paper presented at the 1991 annual meeting of the American Historical Association).

19. Some 26% of all associates' lawsuits concerned notes, bonds, and mortgages for the nonpayment of loans; nearly a quarter of Grant's suits and more than a third of Oswald's suits concerned unrepaid loans. Legal Database. One particularly troublesome suit is recorded in Alexander Grant to Earl of Home, July 28, 1744, Box 25, Bundle 4; Lady Home to ——, September 10, 1744, Box 34, Bundle 1; and Alexander Grant to Earl of Home, September 18, 1744, Box 25, Bundle 4, Douglas-Home Muniments.

frustrated by numerous difficulties.[20] One impediment was psychological: the associates were loathe to push debt reclamation beyond personal appeals and threats to more rigorous measures, such as securing the debt, obtaining collateral, or suing, because they felt that rigidly severe collection threatened the harmony of mercantile community relations.[21] Additional obstacles were structural. Physical distance created some problems. The lack of proximity meant that a merchant had fewer chances to give and supervise "effectual orders about" the repayment or the reclamation "being soon finished in some shape or other."[22] But perhaps the greatest structural impediments were legal. The difference between the laws that prevailed in different jurisdictions often impeded legal pursuit. Even if the borrower lived nearby, the law was often inadequate. One could not proceed against all of the debtor's property; money and stock were exempted. One could, of course, proceed against the debtor's person; but one could not proceed simultaneously against both his person and his attachable property. And even if the law was adequate, the courts were slow, expensive, and, inasmuch as they raised the specter of countersuits, vexatious.

There were two good business reasons to lend money. First of all, lending was profitable. The associates usually lent at the maximum 5% rate in Britain and 6% or 8% in the colonies.[23] Such rates compared favorably to the 4% interest that navy and victualing bills paid, the 2% to 7% average rates of return they achieved through speculation in the Funds, and the 6% they earned in trans-Atlantic slaving.[24] One £10,000

20. Many loans were never repaid. In Oswald's case, 22% of the loans he had granted were unpaid at his death. See also Julian Hoppit, "The Use and Abuse of Credit in Eighteenth-Century England," in McKendrick and Outhwaite, eds., *Business Life*, pp. 64–77; and Sheridan, *Sugar and Slavery*, pp. 274–75.
21. The thousands of debt cases in London courts may suggest that, in the end, harmonious relations counted for little. The associates, therefore, may have been exceptional in their relative avoidance of litigation; but, until further work on litigation and litigiousness is done, any conclusion is conjectural.
22. GD 110/529: Richard Oswald to Sir Hew Dalrymple, January 5, 1750.
23. Pares, *Merchants and Planters*, pp. 49–50. They sometimes imposed lower rates. John Mill's loan of £12,000 at 4 1/2% to the Bank of Scotland was one instance. Directors' Minutes, November 22, 1766, Bank of Scotland Archives, 6/6/2/18–19, Edinburgh. But nowhere was money easily borrowed at 4 or 4 1/2%. GD 345/1165/2, 23: Sir Alexander Grant to Sir Archibald Grant, August 14; 1759. Higher rates generally prevailed overseas. GD 345/1162/5/43: Alexander Grant to Sir Archibald Grant, January 16, 1753; and Thomas Cooper and David McCord, eds., *The Statutes at Large of South Carolina*, v. 3 (Columbia, S.C., 1836), pp. 105–08, 709–12, and v. 4 (1841), pp. 363–65.
24. Rodger, *Wooden World*, p. 96; Table 4 and Appendix III, below. In addition, government consols earned 5%; land, 4%; and Caribbean sugar estates, between 3% and 14%. Ashton, *Economic Fluctuations*, Table 9; Robert C. Allen, "The Price of Freehold Land and the Interest Rate in the Seventeenth and Eighteenth Centuries," *Economic History Review*, 2nd ser., v. 41 (1988), pp. 33–50; and Ward, *British West Indian Slavery*, p. 48.

loan to the Earl of Home, for instance, brought Grant £500 each year in interest payments; by 1759, these payments had totaled £8,500.[25] Lending could also be profitable if the borrower defaulted. Default added much acreage to the associates' real estate portfolios. Robert Scott and his partner John Pringle, for example, extended a loan of £4,000 to a Grenada planter in the early 1760s and, when the planter defaulted in 1766, they claimed title to three coffee and cotton plantations that had been put up as security; two years later, the new owners sold the estates at a considerable profit. This cycle – secured loan, default, vesting, and resale – recurred frequently among the associates, especially for Grant and Oswald. Lenders who took advantage of the considerable rise of estate values in the period 1750–75 made substantial profits on their original outlay.[26] Furthermore, loan profitability was enhanced by lending's flexibility. This was especially true in the case of loans with unspecified terms which the associates could call in at their desire. Such a legal technicality made it an ideal mechanism for accumulating land.

Lending also created or cemented "power and influence." One way to exert control over others, Samuel Johnson once instructed Oswald's neighbor James Boswell, was to lend "sums of money to your neighbours, perhaps at small interest, perhaps at no interest," privately, "and always having their bonds in your possession." A lender gained a firm hold over the livelihood of the borrower by such measures. Sometimes an associate might take possession of the borrower's strongbox. More often he might assume management of personal income. Most frequently he might gain the right to claim the proceeds of provincial or foreign estates and, therein, new outlets for his merchandising business: in order to pay off his debt, the borrower consigned his crops to the associate's London house. At least £3,300 worth of unrefined muscovado sugar went to Grant in partial repayment of Home's debts between 1750 and 1756, and a similar amount went to him with instructions to sell on Home's account for a fee.[27]

The associates were especially active lenders in the years between the Peace of Paris (1763) and outbreak of the Revolution (1775); their

---

25. Approximately £862,562 or $1,282,958 in 1994. The history of the loan is recorded in Douglas-Home Muniments, 6/7–9, 25/1–4, 26/1, and 34/1–2.
26. Approximately £256,155 or $381,000 in 1994. Indentures, December 23–24, 1768, May 9, 1769, Deed Book, v. N1, ff. 412–33, Supreme Court Registry, St. Georges, Grenada. Magazines and newspapers were filled with reports of the rising value and growing foreclosure of Caribbean estates. *Scot's Magazine*, v. 33 (1771), p. 440.
27. Frederick A. Pottle and William K. Wimsatt, Jr., eds., *Boswell for the Defense, 1769–1774* (New York, 1959), p. 85. On the Home loan, see Hancock, "Citizen of the World," pp. 308–17.

lending peaked in the aftermath of the Banking Crisis of 1772–73. Oswald's papers give an extremely detailed account of his lending. No record of Oswald extending loans before 1763 has survived, although he would have been unusual if he lent nothing before the war; the silence is probably due to the disappearance of his counting-house papers in the nineteenth century. Between his return from Germany in 1763 and his death in 1784, he made at least 83 loans for sums ranging from £55 to £40,000. Private lending at interest above £1,000 was not unusual for him. Nearly two-thirds of his loans exceeded £1,000; the average loan equalled £4,175.[28]

Isolated references in less detailed manuscript collections indicate that Grant, Sargent II, Birch, Scott, Mill, and Johnston all lent similar amounts of money, over and above the hundreds of small £5 to £10 loans given to relatives.[29] While some scholars have argued that eighteenth-century merchants primarily made small loans, this position is not substantiated by the associates' lending portfolios.[30] They lent large sums, based on close familiarity with the recipient. The associates did not lend equally to all comers. Oswald gave four-fifths of his loans to Scots, and most of these, like Charles Dalrymple of Orangefield, Rev. Steel of Gadgirth, and James Wilson of Kilmarnock, were neighbors in Ayrshire or sufferers in the collapse of Oswald's Ayr Bank. Peers, baronets, officeholders,

28. Oswald's lending is detailed in "Citizen of the World," Appendix 2.
29. Grant: Grant loaned £10,000 to the Earl of Home in the early 1740s, and in the following decade he loaned Judge Charles Dawes of Jamaica at least £11,000 at 8%. GD 345/1162/5/43: Alexander Grant to Sir Archibald Grant, January 16, 1753. Other loans include – £1,349 to Gov. Edward Trelawney; £1,000 to Hugh Rose in 1752 [GD 248/175/3: Alexander Grant to Sir Ludovick Grant, July 17, 1752; Sir Ludovick Grant to Alexander Grant, July 17, 1752; and Sir Ludovick Grant to Alexander Grant, July 22, 1752]; £10,000 to Earl of Home in 1744 [Douglas-Home Muniments, Box 27, Bundle 2: Memorial, 1764]; £1,000 to Nathaniel Child in 1752 [Edinburgh, Bank of Scotland Customer Ledgers, v. 1752/53, 6/39/3/f. 95]; £500 to John Spottiswoode in 1768 [C 24/1788: Harman v. Spottiswoode, Sir Alexander Grant Deposition, January 11, 1771]; and £3,500 to Hugh McKay in 1769–1770 [Jamaica Archives, Court of Error, v. 4, ff. 197–98]. Sargent II and Birch: £331 to Mackaill, Melville & Young [C 12/808/2: Answer of Mill and Oswald, sched. 1, sub July 20, 1754]. Scott: £5,000 to Richard Oswald [Jamaica Archives, Deeds, v. 146, ff. 64–67]; and £10,000 to Sir Laurence Dundas, July 9, 1765 [Zetland Papers, North Yorkshire Record Office, Northallerton]. Mill: £1,000 to Charles Mill, August 29, 1767; £1,500 to Archibald Scott [Register of Deeds sub December 5, 1765, SRO]; £7,000 to Archibald Scott [Particular Register of Sasines, v. 28, f. 369, September 15, 1768, SRO]; and £3,000 to Lord Adam Gordon [Register of Deeds, November 23, 1770, SRO]. See also Frances N. Mason, ed., *John Norton & Sons* (Richmond, 1937), p. 235, for a loan from Mill to Virginia planter Robert Nicholas. Johnston: £2,000 to two merchants in Montserrat [Deeds, v. 8, #1711, Montserrat Courthouse].
30. Pressnell, "The Rate," p. 185; and Price, *Capital and Credit*, pp. 54–55. Price's conclusion, while true for Scottish merchants in Scotland, does not adequately describe London practice.

lawyers, merchants, and farmers – the London merchant preferred no one group above another, as long as they came from his homeland, or experienced a grievance to which Oswald had in some way contributed. Oswald never made loans to unknown individuals with unproven abilities. Approached by one Darney and asked to supply a nobleman with £30,000, Oswald turned the emissary away empty-handed when Darney refused to divulge the grandee's name. When loans were used as short-term investments, knowing one's debtors and having some nonfinancial hold over them were the guiding principles when determining whether to lend.[31]

In contrast to their willingness to lend, the associates were reluctant to borrow. Although outport merchants seeking to supplement their own resources "borrowed extensively on bond for the medium or long term," this group of Londoners usually avoided extraordinary borrowing. Pure loans not tied to credit transactions played only a minor role in the associates' financing efforts, except at times of extreme commercial need or distress. Only one instance of collective borrowing from individual or corporate lenders has been uncovered: a loan of £4,500 from an unknown source that enabled the Bance Island proprietors to finance the operating costs of the factory during the first years of their ownership.[32] The only instance of Oswald's individual borrowing occurred when he took £5,000 from Scott in order to pay his share of the Bance Island refurbishment.[33] Toward the ends of their careers, Mill and Grant jointly borrowed £2,000 to fund northern improvements; Grant accepted £13,777 from Oswald to set his Jamaican plantations aright; and Alexander Johnston borrowed £8,300 to add to his Scottish estates.[34] In each of these instances of individual borrowing, the associate borrowed to take advantage of agricultural opportunities at a time

31. Michael Herries to Richard Oswald, August 6, 1764, Oswald Letter Book, v. 2, p. 338, SRO.
32. *Journals of the House of Commons*, v. 26, p. 258.
33. Approximately £435,228 or $647,349 in 1994. Oswald assigned part of his wife's dowry to Robert Scott in exchange for £5,000 in cash; the claim was reassigned in 1765. Deeds, v. 146, ff. 64–67 (September 13, 30, 1751), v. 217, f. 82 (April 18, 1765), Island Record Office, Spanishtown.
34. On the loan to Mill and Grant of May 1, 1769, see Powers of Attorney Book, v. 63, f. 27, Jamaica Archives. On the loan to Grant of May 15, 1771, see Probate Inventories, Richard Oswald (dated August 21, 1786), Island Record Office, Spanishtown; and Sederunt Book, Grant Papers, Tomintoul House. On the loans to Johnston, see Sudlows, Oswald Papers, Michael Herries to Richard Oswald, August 6, 1772; *Gentleman's Magazine*, v. 40 (1772), p. 392; Montserrat Deeds, v. 10, # 2146 (October 29, 1772); and CS 238/O/1/24 (Conveyance, November 16, 1773) and CS 228/O/2/4 (Transfer, November 16, 1773, Bond, March 4, 1775), SRO. Other associates' lesser borrowing are recorded in Kent Record Office, U 969/T 1/17, 19, Maidstone; Michael Herries to Andrew Cochrane, February 22, 1770, Oswald Letter Book, SRO.

when his own end-of-career resources were heavily directed toward straightening out overseas plantation finances or extricating himself from the mess created by the bankruptcies of friends or correspondents.

The record of the associates' borrowing from banks is complete, and it reinforces the conclusion that their borrowing was light. On only five recorded occasions did Oswald borrow from a bank. Barclay, Bevan & Co. lent him money four times on a short-term demand basis; and each amount was repaid within the year: £6,000 in 1769, £1,000 in 1774, £1,000 in 1775, and £1,000 in 1778. The Bank of Scotland also advanced Oswald £2,300 in 1773.[35] These five transactions, negotiated to allow him to continue his agricultural improvements in southwestern Scotland, were unique to Oswald; no other record of institutional borrowing has survived. Professional bankers may have been lending money, but not to the associates.[36]

About the only associate to borrow extensively was John Boyd, in a period when he was financially embarrassed. In the late 1760s and 1770s, his Caribbean plantations experienced trouble unlike any that he had known before. The extraordinary mid-1760s boom in colonial trade glutted the London sugar market by 1769, and Boyd found his Caribbean sugar fetching lower prices. At the same time, the disturbances in America, especially the nonimportation agreements that sprang up in response to the Townshend Acts, disturbed patterns of trade and frustrated further enterprise. The greatest shock, however, came from the City. Boyd loaned £9,000 in stock to supporters of his friend Laurence Sulivan in October 1768 in order to assure the election of Sulivan and his men to the India Company's Court of Directors. But when the election was over, Sulivan's supporters refused to return the stock to Boyd or pay him fair market value. Boyd was devastated.[37] He struggled

35. Barclay's Bank Archives, London; and Court of Directors' Minutes, 6/6/3, ff. 8–9 (June 7, 1773), Bank of Scotland Archives, Edinburgh.

36. It is probably incorrect to suggest, as does D. M. Joslin, that large-scale London merchants were usually the recipients of such loans. D. M. Joslin, "London Private Bankers, 1720–1785," *Economic History Review*, 2nd ser., v. 7 (1954), p. 173.

37. Stock Ledger, L/AG/14/5/16/105 (October 5, 1768), IOL. At the center of Sulivan's machinations was the Great Scheme of 1768–69, a fund of £100,000 put together by a coalition of twenty-three investors for the splitting of stock; buyers of the split stock agreed to return the stock after the election at a fixed price of 280. The investors met financial disaster, however, when the stock fell below the return price and the buyers refused to keep their word. Sutherland, *India Company*, pp. 188–93; and Shelburne Papers, Bowood, Calne, Wiltshire. According to J. G. Parker, Boyd participated in "the Great Scheme." "The Directors of the East India Company, 1754–1790" (Ph.D. dissert., University of Edinburgh, 1977), p. 184. Parker, however, confuses the "Great Scheme" with other stock splitting plans supervised by Sulivan. Boyd's split was connected with Manship, Sulivan, and Van Sittart, and not with the Great Scheme investors. HMC, *Report on Palk Papers* (London, 1922), no. 97.

to recover from the speculative nightmare, but in vain. To facilitate the acquisition and buildup of seven new plantations in Grenada and Dominica, Boyd borrowed nearly £5,000 from Oswald in March 1771, but the loan further stretched his resources.[38] Boyd was particularly unlucky in where he lodged his money. Not only did William Neale, a mercer in Ludgate Street to whom Boyd had lent £1,500, find himself unable to repay, but Colebrooke, Lesingham & Binns, a bank which held at least £18,000 for Boyd, also stopped payment of claims upon it and finally went bankrupt in 1777.[39] Boyd's load was lightened in 1780 when his protégé the nabob Paul Benfield returned from Madras and loaned him £14,000, but this relief was temporary. In a fit of pique, Benfield demanded repayment, and Boyd was thrown back into uncertainty and vulnerability. Not until Nathaniel Smith, once a clerk in Boyd's counting-house and now an India Director, loaned him £56,000 did the associate regain his fiscal composure and begin the long, slow process of repayment.[40]

Use of Banks

Boyd's use of Colebrooke's bank is revealing, insofar as it suggests alternative means of financial management used by the associates. During the second half of the eighteenth century, Britain was undergoing a revolution in banking. The number of private banks in the metropolis nearly tripled between 1754 and 1774, from eighteen to fifty-two and,

38. Michael Herries to Richard Oswald, August 12, 1774, Oswald Papers, Sudlows.
39. There seems to be no connection between Henry Neale the banker and William Neale. The latter is somewhat mysterious: he appears in Mortimer's *Universal Director* (1763), Baldwin's *Complete Guide* (1772) and Kent's *London Directory* (1774), but he has no entry in Baldwin's 1777 trade directory or thereafter; moreover, there is no mention of him in the bankruptcy records at the PRO. It is most likely that, rather than going bankrupt (as John Baker avers), Neale called in his creditors for a less than full settlement. Philip C. Yorke, ed., *The Diary of John Baker* (London, 1931), p. 314. This makes even more sense when we remember that, as a West African and West Indian merchant, Boyd's firm would have been buying domestic textiles from inland traders like William Neale. I am indebted to Jacob Price for many of these points. Colebrooke's life is chronicled in Namier and Brooke, eds., *House of Commons*, v. 2, pp. 235–37; Lucy Sutherland, "Sir George Colebrooke's World Corner in Alum," *Economic History*, v. 3 (1936), pp. 237–58; and Parker, "Directors," Appendix. On Boyd's involvement with Colebrooke, see Laurence Sulivan to Robert Palk, September 15, 1774, in HMC, *Palk*, p. 243; and Parker, "Directors," Appendix. Colebrooke was indebted to other associates. London, Christie, Manson & Woods, Catalogue of Colebrooke sale, April 1774; E 112/1653/2521; and E 112/1654/2549.
40. John Boyd Jr. to Sir Robert Murray Keith, February 18, 1780, Add.Mss. 35518/107; John Boyd Jr. to Sir Robert Murray Keith, December 9, 1780, Add.Mss. 35520/138; John Boyd Jr. to Sir Robert Murray Keith, December 22, 1780, Add.Mss. 35521/204; and John Boyd Jr. to Sir Robert Murray Keith, March 27, 1781, Add.Mss. 35522/4, BL.

in the counties, especially of Scotland, a demand for credit, bills drawn on London, or specie led to a similar rise.⁴¹ For the growing business community, these banks functioned as lending institutions, discount houses for processing commercial bills and contracting warrants, and safe havens for investment or retirement capital. Private banks "afforded such aids" to liquidity and credit "as might seem incredible to those who have not had access" to them. Although it is commonly thought by historians that merchants drew extensively on all these services, the associates primarily viewed the banks, in ordinary times, as safe depositories.⁴² As we have already seen, the associates' borrowing from banks was light and selective. Their own firms' reserves were too large to warrant drawing on banks. For similar reasons, they seldom assigned contracting or commercial bills to the banks before the bills had matured, receiving less than face value and letting the banks realize the gain upon maturity. They rarely used their cash accounts to write drafts; nor did they use their bank balances as collateral for loans.⁴³

John Sargent II was the first associate to leave a record of direct dealings with a bank, when he deposited £2,414 with the Bank of England in November 1741.⁴⁴ Before the decade was over, Grant had

41. For a good discussion of English banking, see Joslin, "London Private Bankers," p. 173; Frank T. Melton, "Deposit Banking in London, 1700–1790," *Business History*, v. 28 (1986), p. 49; and Wilson, *Gentlemen-Merchants*, pp. 153–58. The number of banks is given in Price, *Capital and Credit*, p. 70. Joslin, "London Private Banks," pp. 173, 180–81, gives slightly different statistics: twenty-seven in 1745 and fifty-one in 1776. On the "financial revolution" in Scotland, see Alastair Durie, "Lairds, Improvement, Banking, and Industry in Eighteenth-Century Scotland," in T. M. Devine, ed., *Lairds and Improvement in the Scotland of the Enlightenment* (Edinburgh, 1978), pp. 21–30; C. W. Munn, "The Scottish Provincial Banking Companies, 1747–1864" (Ph.D. dissert., University of Glasgow, 1975), p. 55; Slaven, *The Development*, p. 50; and Ms. 4,796 (October 1–8, 1769), NLS.

42. Sir Archibald Grant, *Thoughts Concerning Banks and the Paper-Currency of Scotland* (Edinburgh, 1763); *The Edinburgh Advertiser*, January 6, 1764, p. 10, February 21, 1764, p. 113, November 23, 1764, pp. 329–30, December 4, 1764, p. 353, and January 25, 1765, p. 57; and, for Sir Alexander Grant's views on banking, Sir Alexander Grant to Sir Robert Gordon, March 27, 1764, Gordon Papers, La.II.498, NLS. Cf. Joslin, "London Private Bankers," p. 173; Price, *Capital and Credit*, p. 94; and McCusker, *Money and Exchange*, pp. 19–27.

43. The three functions are detailed in Grant, *Thoughts*. On discounting, see B. L. Anderson, "Money and the Structure of Credit in the Eighteenth Century," *Business History*, v. 12 (1970), pp. 85–101; and McCusker, *Money and Exchange*, pp. 19–22. For the associates' discounting, see Discount Books, 2/23, 6/2, 7/16, 11/1, Barclay's Bank (54 Lombard St.), London; Current Account Ledgers, 6/39/3/95, 6/39/4/170, Bank of Scotland Archives. The discounting of warrants was especially complex. "Observations," ff. 2, 75; and Beveridge, *Prices*, pp. 519–22.

44. The following conclusions are based on an extensive search of all available ledgers and records kept by banks with which the associates could have done business. The following banks were included – Bank of England, Barclays, Childs, Coutts, Drummonds, Goslings, and Hoares and, in Scotland, the Bank of Scotland, Royal

a cash account with Coutts & Co., and Oswald and Scott had cash accounts with the British Linen Company. During the 1750s and early 1760s, the number of associate accounts increased; following the conclusion of hostilities in 1763, it shot up again, as the younger generation of associates joined the ranks of depositors.[45] London bankers treated cash accounts on a demand basis and gave no interest, but most associates placed small amounts of capital in London banks, in large measure because they eased matters in times of crisis and facilitated discretionary expenditures.[46] As Graph 8.1 shows us, the total of the associates' bank accounts – personal, firm, and trustee – at all banks grew from £2,000 in 1745–54, to £7,000 in 1755–63, to £12,000 in 1764–73.[47]

Grant's and Oswald's individual bank balances (the total of each associate's individual holdings) are representative of most associates who left their cash with banks. Grant maintained small bank accounts continuously from 1741 to his death in 1772. Except during 1763, when he held £3,013, his end-of-year balances averaged £136 per year and were distributed between no more than two banks at any one time. Oswald maintained somewhat higher balances. From 1749 to 1784, he averaged £835 at the end of each year at one London bank and two Scottish banks. When Oswald needed to withdraw cash in order to pay for the purchase of Government securities, he drew on his London bank; when he needed ready money to pay farmworkers, seed suppliers, or local booksellers in southwestern Scotland, he opened accounts with the Glasgow Arms Bank and the Ayr Bank. The amounts involved were small: Oswald, for instance, never kept more than £200 at any one time at the main Ayr office, and never more than £300 at its Dumfries branch.[48]

Bank of Scotland, and Glasgow Arms Bank. Accounts of fourteen associates were examined; accounts for Alexander Anderson, John Anderson and John Sargent III were not examined; accounts for Thomas Birch, Augustus Boyd, John Gardiner, John Levett, Alexander Johnston, and Robert Scott were not found. Amounts lodged with some banks, such as the Ayr Bank, while discernible from private correspondence or personal wills, could not be verified with ledgers and were therefore not included in the numerical analysis, although considered in the narrative.

45. 1750–63: Aufrere, Chambers, Cooke, Grant, and Stratton; 1763–85: John Boyd, Samuel Gardiner, Rolleston, Sargent III, Trevanion, and Wood.

46. Smith, *Wealth of Nations*, v. 1, p. 92; Auchincruive Ledger "1775," p. 36, Oswald Papers, Sudlows; Hopeton House Muniments, HH1/18/3/B; McMillan, "The Ayr Bank," p. 8; and Price, *Capital and Credit*, pp. 82–83.

47. £2,000 in 1745–54 is approximately £171,347 or $254,858 in 1994; £12,000 in 1764–73 is approximately £780,287 or $1,160,584 in 1994.

48. £835 in 1749–84 is approximately £57,855 or $86,053 in 1994. On Oswald's use of local banks to fund improvements, see Auchincruive Ledger "1775," Oswald Papers, Sudlows; to set aside money for purchases of stocks and shares, see John Anderson to Richard Oswald, September 25, 1780, Oswald Papers, Sudlows.

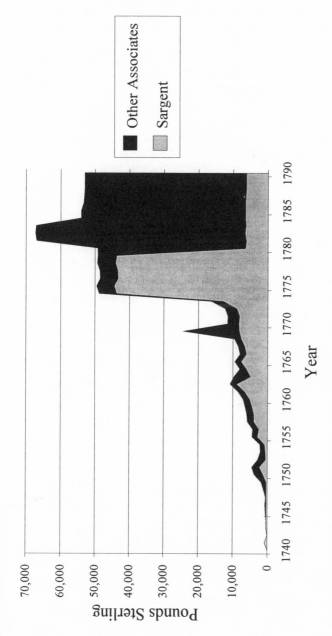

Graph 8.1 Bank Balances: Sargent and Other Associates, 1740–90

Source: Private Drawing Office Ledgers 216–333, Bank of England Archives, Roehampton; Customer Accounts Ledgers 49, 57, 65, Hoares Bank, London; Discount Books 1–18, Barclays Bank (main office), and Customer Accounts Ledgers, Goslings Bank (Barclays Bank Fleet Street branch office), London; Customer Accounts Ledgers, Childs Bank, London; Ledgers 18–96, Coutts Bank, London; Current Account Ledger, 6/39/1–11, British Linen Bank, Bank of Scotland Archives, Edinburgh; Ship Bank Customer Ledgers 1769–72, in TD 161/3, Strathclyde Regional Archives, Glasgow; and Auchincruive Ledger "1775," Oswald Papers, Sudlows.

The one exception among the associates to the generally slight use of banks as safe depositories was John Sargent II who, during the 1770s and 1780s, kept large amounts in his personal and firm cash accounts at the Bank of England. Sargent increased his cash reserves in 1750, raising his personal balances to £1,300; upon inheriting the substantial estate of his cousin George Arnold the following year, he nearly doubled them again. Such moves paved the way for his election to the Bank Directorate in 1753. After 1757, his personal end-of-year balance never fell below £4,500; and, between 1763 and 1790, it seldom varied from £6,500. Throughout the course of his partnership with Aufrere, Cooke, and Chambers, his firm balance averaged £2,500 at the end of each year; after he dissolved and reorganized the firm, it averaged £37,000 for seven years; only in 1780 did it return to its pre-1774 level. The ties of the two Sargents and Cooke to the Bank's Directorate, their need to demonstrate an economic stake in the institution during their time on the Board, and their desire to maintain influence once tenure had ceased go part of the way toward explaining such large deposits. The vitriolic disagreements and career shifts among partners in the Sargent firms and the resulting changes in membership go the rest of the way: large reserves were sensible, perhaps necessary, since quick liquidation of the previous firm's debts required substantial amounts of ready cash. The period of Sargent's atypically large reserves – 1774–80 – was punctuated with two such firm reorganizations.

Outside Investments

Merchants typically invested in a wide array of business and financial assets, in addition to their holdings of cash, silver, and art: (1) their own businesses and partnerships; (2) other people's ventures; (3) privately owned companies with illiquid shares; (4) publicly owned monied companies' annuities and stock; (5) government debt; and (6) land.[49] As their careers advanced, their own businesses and partnerships shifted from being absorbers of funds to being generators of funds that they could then invest in other people's businesses, shares, annuities, stocks, government debt, and land. The largest part of an associate's portfolio was his own business, either solely owned or in concert with partners, and these we have examined in the preceding four chapters. But the associates did not stop with their own concerns; they consistently invested in other people's businesses, relatively small private companies and

---

49. On the diversity of investments, see Hancock, "'Domestic Bubbling,'" *Economic History Review*, v. 47 (November 1994), pp. 683–85.

corporations whose stock was not publicly floated or quoted. Sir Alexander Grant, for instance, became a shareholder in the English Mines of Manor venture and the English York Buildings Company.[50] In the North, in the 1740s, he bought shares in a company that harvested Speyside timber; a decade later, he invested in the Aberdeen Whaling Company; and, in the 1760s, he backed the Forth-Clyde Canal Company.[51] Oswald also cultivated a number of northern interests – a Pittenweem carpet venture, the Forth-Clyde Canal, and a Kilmarnock woolen factory – whose records have not survived.[52] The shares of some private companies, such as small banks or improvement societies, were in principle tradable but were floated in markets characterized by little organization and activity. Investment in insurance companies, for example, was common among the associates.[53] Oswald and Scott each owned shares in the Sun Fire Insurance, while Sargent's partners Aufrere and Birch each held shares in the London Assurance and the Royal Exchange Assurance, respectively. Unfortunately, the records of purchases and sales are almost nonexistent for these companies, and their prices were infrequently published in newspapers and magazines. Similarly, the records of the British Linen Company bank survive, but the demand for its stock was so low and its transfer so rare that the price was never listed. As a rule, these adventures are poorly documented. The exceptions to this paucity of evidence are their activities in the market for monied company stocks and shares and government debt, and in the market for land. The remainder of this chapter takes up these investments.

---

50. GD 345/1154/13: Francis Grant to John Coutts, May 12, 1748. Alexander Grant held one of twelve shares in the mining venture.
51. GD 345/1161/3/107x, 106x, 114, 104, 11: Alexander Grant to Sir Archibald Grant, July 16, 30, September 1, 16, November 18, 1752; Anon., *Extracts from the records of the Convention of royal burghs*, pp. 269–70; and *Edinburgh Advertiser*, November 11, 1768.
52. George Chalmers to Richard Oswald, November 15, 1768, Oswald Papers, EUL; *Edinburgh Advertiser*, November 11, 1768; Register of Sasines, April 19, 1769, SRO; and William Coats to Richard Oswald, November 19, 1768, and Wilson & Co. to Richard Oswald, November 13, 1770, Oswald Papers, Sudlows.
53. Oswald's insurance holdings were purely financial. For these, see C 12/1081/6: Answer of John and Alexander Anderson, sched. 2, sub February 14, 1785. Oswald held only six shares of Sun Fire Office stock that earned £39 per year; fifty shares were needed for nomination to the Directorate. P. G. M. Dickson, *The Sun Fire Insurance Office, 1710–1960* (London, 1960), p. 265. The holdings of other associates were more politically motivated. Aufrere bought forty shares (£1,000) of London Assurance stock, just enough to facilitate his nomination to the Directorate. London Assurance Stock Ledger, Ms. 8,743B, f. 588 (October 10, 1764), COLRO. Birch, a Director of the Royal Exchange Assurance, owned a similar amount in that company. For Scott's service as a Director of the Sun Fire Insurance, see *The Court and City Register* (London, 1765), p. 259, (London, 1771), p. 218.

Funds

The century spanning 1688–1788 provided investors like the associates with unprecedented opportunities in the Funds.[54] In this period, permanent, public Funds were not "a matter entirely unknown" in Britain, as they had been before 1688.[55] An organized market, marked by the presence of a group of professional brokers, the public quotation of prices, and a permanent, central location for trading, was firmly fixed by early in the eighteenth century. As government spending on war exceeded parliamentary provisions, successive ministries financed expenditures by taking up loans and mortgaging future revenues. The mountain of state debt grew throughout the century, especially when Pitt struggled to redress the imbalance between debt and income via expanded taxes during the Seven Years' War (1755–63). Much of the new debt was "funded" – issued in the form of tradable notes called annuities – and Britain's merchants played a prominent role in organizing

54. In the century spanning the Glorious Revolution and the American Revolution, the term "Funds" usually referred to "the public security that is given to the people" by the state for "money borrowed of them," either by "appointing a bank to repay the sums borrowed, or appropriating certain taxes for the discharge thereof"; it also connoted the offerings of public ("monied") companies like the East India Company or, less frequently, of smaller private companies. R. Rolt, *A New Dictionary of Trade and Commerce*, 2nd ed. (London, 1761), sub "funds."

55. Scholarship has been largely silent on this question with respect to eighteenth-century Britain. The subject of early-modern investment in the Funds has received only meager attention in the last several decades. Most historians have concentrated on how the market organized itself, what securities it offered and, how, through the funding of debt, it subsidized the expansion of the state. K. G. Davies, "Joint stock investment in the later seventeenth century," *Economic History Review*, 2nd ser., v. 4 (1952), p. 283; Dickson, *Financial Revolution*, pp. 457–520; S. R. Cope, "The Stock Exchange Revisited: A New Look at the Market in Securities in London in the Eighteenth Century," *Economica*, v. 45 (1978), pp. 1–21; and P. Mirowski, "The Rise (and Retreat) of a Market: English Joint Stock Shares in the Eighteenth Century," *Journal of Economic History*, v. 41 (1981), p. 576. Details about the role of the various market instruments funding the national debt are sketched in Dickson, *Financial Revolution*, pp. 486–520; and Mirowski, "Rise," pp. 560–66. The focus has been on the aggregate market and economy, rather than on the investment behavior of market participants. Few historians or economists have assessed the ways middle-class investors operated within the system, or the ways financiers interacted with the state in the years after 1740 when consumer demand and overseas production soared. Exceptions to this macrocosmic approach are Alice Carter, "Analysis of Public Indebtedness in Eighteenth-Century England," *Bulletin of the Institute of Historical Research*, v. 24 (1953), pp. 173–81; H. V. Bowen, "Investment and Empire in the Later Eighteenth Century," *Economic History Review*, 2nd ser., v. 42 (1989), pp. 186–206; and Earle, *English Middle Class*, pp. 143–50. Looking at the portfolios of London businessmen who died and left orphans between 1690 and 1720, Earle found that "investment in company stocks and bonds" was "fairly exclusive, being reserved mainly for the wealthy, particularly wealthy merchants," that 48 percent of their investments were made in the Funds, and that businessmen tended to invest more as they got older. The present analysis examines the important work of such investors. The work of underwriting and brokerage is recounted in detail in Hancock, "Citizen of the World," ch. 7.

and operating the market for these notes. In the later decades of their lives, the "Funds" provided the associates with an important means of making and managing money.[56]

We can synthesize a collective Funds portfolio for Grant, Oswald, Sargent, and seven other associates who speculated in the Funds. In essence, this collective portfolio is a recumulation of individual and joint accounts of the associates who invested and acted as trustees. Graph 8.2 tracks the changes in this collective portfolio over the entire period. Starting in the mid-1740s at £1,000, the associates' investments rose dramatically at the end of the Seven Years' War to a peak of over £250,000 in the mid-1760s and then fell off in the early 1770s. Short of the progress of the war and the pace of the government's payments for their wartime services, few major imperial and economic events seem to have exerted much influence on their portfolios; the rise and fall of investments seems to have been untouched, for instance, by the breakdown in Anglo-American relations between wars or the Credit Crisis of 1772–73. Reconciling and valuing their portfolios at the end of each year, we find that these ten associates each held, on average, £2,630 of traded securities at the end of each of the 50 years between 1740 and 1790. At the same time, Grant, Oswald, Sargent, and their seven associates managed a sizable amount of stocks and securities in trust for others between 1750 and 1785 – on average, £19,000 at the end of each year. Sometimes, the value of the trusts could be very large. In 1765, for instance, they collectively held £121,000 in trust for others, in addition to £74,000 in their own accounts.[57]

The rest of this inquiry focuses on Grant, Oswald, and Sargent, who in the peak year of the ten associates' investing owned just over one-third of the recumulated collective portfolio. For these three merchants, we can reconstruct individual portfolios, since they invested directly as individual investors or trustees, not as partners. The scale of Grant's holdings was average for the three: his portfolio averaged £2,580 at the end of each year over a period of 26 years (1747–72). Oswald's investments were larger, averaging £8,500 over 38 years (1747–84), and Sargent's were smaller, averaging £1,160 over 43 years (1748–90).[58]

56. Dickson, *Financial*; and Brewer, *Sinews*, pp. 114–26. For a list of war-induced offerings, see *Accounts and Papers* (Parliamentary Papers 1890–91, XLVIII), "Report by the Secretary and Comptroller General of the Proceedings of the Commissioners for the Reduction of the National Debt," pp. 95–136; and *Accounts and Papers* (Parliamentary Papers 1898, LII), "History of the National Debt, from 1694 to 1786," pp. 24–75.

57. £121,000 in 1765 is approximately £8,189,891 and $12,181,480 in 1994; £74,000 in 1765 is approximately £5,008,694 and $7,449,831 in 1994.

58. £2,580 in 1747–52 is approximately £218,090 or $324,383 in 1994; £8,500 in 1747–84 is approximately £594,469 or $884,201 in 1994; and £1,160 in 1748–90 is approximatley £78,655 or $116,989 in 1994.

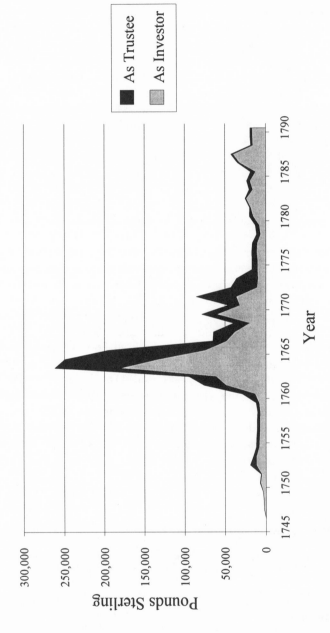

Graph 8.2 Recumulated Funds Investments, 1747–90

We can organize their investments into "positions" – a position being an investment in a security from the time the associate added it to his portfolio until the time he reduced his holding to zero. Often, there were both purchases and sales within the period of a position. Table 8.1 summarizes the three associates' positions. Amount Earned shows the sum of dividends and trading gains or losses over the period a position was held. Rate of Return is the internal rate of return (annual rate) that the associate earned on the position for its entire length, taking into account both dividends and trading gains or losses. Real Rate of Return adjusts the rate of return to account for changes in the price level according to Elizabeth Schumpeter's price series for the eighteenth century. (The inflation adjustments are rather crude, because price changes within years had to be interpolated into the series.)

Two different kinds of behavior can be discerned in these individual portfolios: what might be called "speculation," seeking short-term trading gains, holding more positions, and trading more heavily and frequently, yet ironically often for less profit; and "long-term investing," holding fewer positions and trading less often but, ultimately, making more money.[59]

Sir Alexander Grant's portfolio suggests that he was the closest thing to a speculator among the associates. Fascinated by the market for shares, he scrutinized it closely each day. He was convinced that he could win profit and power by manipulating it. Acting on this conviction and ruled by the enthusiasm of the moment, he worked in bursts. In his investments, he was neither systematic nor methodical; he was no planner, even though he was attentive to the minutiae of the Exchange. He often wavered and vacillated, making up his mind only after hearing what others had to say. However, once he was convinced that he had the correct solution, Grant pursued matters with a vengeance. Even if

---

59. "Speculative" is a slippery term. The idea of the "speculator" as someone who bought or sold to gain from a rise or fall in market value seems to have been first expressed in print during the Seven Years' War, although it surely predates that conflict, for it was extensively discussed by the Scholastics. The concept was almost impossible to define since any asset could become speculative. Still, contemporaries attempted to distinguish speculation from regular trading, placing all things on a continuum: investing in lands or depositing in banks, for instance, were usually regarded as less speculative than buying Funds. Explicit in the meaning of such terms was (1) the speed that the value of the commodity could rise or fall and (2) the fact that investors acted on their beliefs that a rise or fall would occur. Implicit, here, were observers' beliefs that (1) speculators behaved irregularly, buying in large quantities or in frequent bursts, and (2) they had access to information about the probability of market fluctuations that others did not. S. T. Janssen, *Smuggling Laid Open in all its . . . Destructive Branches* (London, 1763), p. 28; and Smith, *Wealth of Nations*, v. 1, pp. 130–31 (I.x.b.38).

Table 8.1   Returns from Publicly Traded Funds

Fund	Opening date	Closing date	Amount earned	Rate of return	Real rate of return	Days held	Years held
Alexander Grant				(£)	(%)	(%)	
3½% East India annuities	15/10/1750	16/05/1753	361	6.3	9.0	944	2.6
3½% South Sea annuities	12/20/1752	05/03/1753	19	8.9	11.5	75	0.2
3% Consolidated annuities	22/09/1752	14/11/1752	1	3.3	5.8	53	0.1
	22/10/1761	17/09/1762	251	9.2	9.7	330	0.9
	24/09/1762	30/03/1769	(86)	-0.8	-1.7	2,379	6.5
	21/05/1770	06/06/1771	12	1.2	-2.6	381	1.0
	20/11/1771	06/07/1771	38	9.5	2.3	229	0.6
3% East India annuities	15/10/1750	17/12/1751	51	5.6	10.1	428	1.2
	20/12/1752	02/11/1754	30	5.7	10.1	682	1.9
3% Reduced annuities	24/05/1765	13/01/1767	7	5.0	6.5	599	1.6
4% Consolidated annuities	22/06/1767	18/04/1769	80	5.0	5.9	666	1.8
Bank of England stock	25/06/1760	05/02/1761	(31)	-4.6	1.4	225	0.6
East India stock	24/01/1749	03/11/1753	262	6.2	8.4	1,744	4.8
	22/02/1755	10/03/1763	133	2.1	1.6	2,938	8.0
	13/05/1763	11/04/1765	(61)	-2.4	-4.9	699	1.9
	05/12/1765	04/08/1766	500	49.7	51.7	242	0.7
	05/03/1767	02/08/1770	(41)	-0.4	-0.3	1,246	3.4
	25/09/1770	17/09/1771	188	20.7	15.0	357	1.0
	03/10/1771	30/06/1772	39	5.0	-2.0	271	0.7
Navy stock	03/05/1763	14/09/1763	(342)	-10.7	-12.6	134	0.4
	12/01/1764	14/01/1764	5	50.0	50.0	2	0.0
	03/07/1765	30/10/1765	18	5.5	6.5	119	0.3
Total/Average of priced Funds			1,434	2.7	2.6	670	1.8
British Linen Bank stock*	01/05/1747	31/05/1753				2,222	6.1
	31/05/1753	08/02/1769				5,732	15.1
Average of all Funds						946	2.6
Richard Oswald							
3% Consolidated annuities	20/03/1764	24/04/1766	828	5.5	3.4	765	2.1
3% Reduced annuities	08/04/1766	18/06/1766	11	6.8	7.9	71	0.2
4% Consolidated annuities I	07/06/1764	22/04/1766	1,175	6.5	5.1	684	1.9
	24/11/1780	06/11/1784	2,086	9.7	7.3	1,443	4.0
Consolidated Long annuities	28/06/1764	05/08/1772	47	5.5	5.5	2,960	8.1
	24/11/1780	06/11/1784	11	8.5	7.2	1,443	4.0
East India stock	28/02/1764	06/11/1784	1,008	4.6	3.9	7,557	20.7
Navy stock	27/10/1763	03/21/1764	5,882	11.9	9.6	146	0.4
	21/03/1764	25/12/1767	13,335	7.7	6.7	1,374	3.8
Total/Average of Priced Funds			24,382	8.3	6.9	1,827	5.0
British Linen Bank stock*	03/03/1747	27/08/1748				451	1.2
	16/02/1775	21/06/1785				3,778	10.4
Average of all Funds						1,879	5.1

Table 8.1   *Cont'd*

Fund	Opening date	Closing date	Amount earned	Rate of return	Real rate of return	Days held	Years held
John Sargent							
3% Reduced annuities	05/09/1771	20/09/1791	31	3.6	2.9	7,320	20.1
Bank of England stock	10/01/1748	30/05/1783	1,063	2.0	1.5	12,924	35.4
Consolidated Long annuities	28/06/1764	19/08/1772	24	5.1	4.4	2,974	8.1
	19/05/1773	03/02/1775	2	6.8	8.4	625	1.7
	25/11/1782	10/11/1784	2	8.2	6.8	716	2.0
East India stock	09/08/1766	23/09/1766	20	8.0	11.4	45	0.1
Total/Average of Priced Funds			1,142	2.1	1.6	4,101	11.2

Notes: The rate of return used here is the internal rate of return on cash flows associated with the position.   A position is defined as the entire history of an investment between the first purchase and the time when the balance was netted to zero. Grant, for example, had seven positions in India stock, because he brought his balance to zero on seven different occasions. Here it is assumed (1) that the investment was paid for or payment was received on the date of the transaction, (2) that dividend and interest payments were issued and received on the official dividend date, and (3) that no registration or broker fees were incurred.   For examples of Oswald drawing from the bank to pay for stock purchases by installment, see John Anderson to Richard Oswald, September 25, 1780, and Account, September 28, 1780, Oswald Letter Book, v. 2, ff. 92, 107, SRO.

To calculate real rates of return, all cash figures were converted to their equivalent in 1721 pounds sterling (1721 being a year in which the price index was 100), using Elizabeth Schumpeter's index of eighteenth-century prices.   "English prices and public finance, 1660-1822," *Review of Economic Statistics*, v. 20 (1938), 21-37.   With these figures, average rates across positions were calculated.   An average rate is the joint internal rate of return on all of the positions, discounting each position back to its own first purchase date.

An asterisk (*) notes that there is no purchase or sale price information for British Linen Company stock.   Therefore, it appears as a separate entry in the table.

Sources

Quantity: Bank of England Archives: Bank Stock, Ledgers 37-57;   South Sea Old Annuities (1st Subscription), Ledgers 47, 53 and 55;   South Sea 3½% Annuities (1751 Subscription), Ledgers;   Consolidated Long Annuities, Ledgers 1761-1807;   4% Navy Stock, Ledgers, 1749, 1760-67, 1784-95;   Reduced 3% Annuities, Ledgers C-NN;   Consolidated 3% Annuities, Ledgers 1-10;   Consolidated 4% Annuities (First), Ledgers 1760-73;   and Consolidated 4% Annuities (Second), Ledgers 1777-1811.

India Office Library: India Stock Ledgers, L/AG/14/5/10-26, and Sheila Lambert, ed., *Sessional Papers of the Eighteenth Century* (Wilmington, Del., 1975), v. 26, #3, 157;   and India Annuities, 3½% Ledgers, 1750-56; 3% Ledgers, L/AG/14/5/252-68.

Public Record Office, Kew Gardens: South Sea Stock papers.

Bank of Scotland Archives: British Linen Company Stock Ledgers, 6/32/1, 6/35/1-3, and 6/37/25.

Scottish Record Office: Royal Bank of Scotland Stockholders List, in GD 18/5882 ('A list of the names of the proprietors of the Royal Bank of Scotland,' 14 Feb. 1752).

Price: The data are weekly prices taken from *Gentlemen's Magazine* (first choice), *London Magazine* (second choice), and thereafter *Lloyd's List*, *London Chronicle*, or *Public Advertiser*.   Wednesday's price is the price usually selected, but if the midweek price was not listed then Thursday's price is used, and if there is no Thursday price, then Tuesday's price and so on until a price is found for the week.   Not all weeks have prices and as a result there are some gaps, on account of failures to record prices or the transfer books being closed.

Dividend: Information on stock dividends is found in Sir John Clapham, *The Bank of England: A History* (Cambridge, 1945); K.N. Chaudhuri, *The Trading World of Asia and the English East India Company, 1660-1760* (Cambridge, 1978);   and Bowen, "Investment," p. 191.

he got "burned," he seldom abandoned an idea; rather, he pulled back momentarily and regrouped for another attempt.

We detect evidence of Grant's combative characteristics in Table 8.1. Grant maintained 24 positions over 24 years, more than double the number of positions that his friend and partner Oswald held, even though the average value of Oswald's portfolio was more than triple Grant's. Grant held his average position for 2.6 years, and he held 17 of the 24 positions for less than two years. Grant's first burst in the Funds came in the 1750s. The value of his portfolio peaked in 1752, when he held £7,500 on his own account, and another £8,000 as trustee for others. Between 1750 and 1754, he opened 6 new positions and closed out 7. Except for maintaining positions in the British Linen Company and the East India Company, he did not involve himself again in the market until 1760. He speculated persistently after the war. Finally, in early 1769, he closed out all of his positions except for India stock and retired from the market for one year, after which he returned to dabble slightly until his death in 1772.

On his own account, Grant negotiated 143 trades over 24 years, nearly 6 trades per year. Some 41% of these trades occurred between January 1762 and December 1765, in the immediate aftermath of the Seven Years' War, when he was receiving payments for previously rendered victualing services. During those four years, he traded 59 times. In 1763, his busiest year, he made 34 trades, fewer than 3 trades per month. By modern standards, his behavior was hardly demonic! Overall, Grant made nearly twice as many trades per year as his fellow associates.

Frequency of trading, however, did not translate into high levels of profit. In spite (or because) of being the most frequent trader among the associates, Sir Alexander Grant reaped fleeting rewards. From his first purchase in the late 1740s to his death in 1772, he earned only £1,434 in the market, as both investor and trustee. Before accounting for dividends, he suffered trading losses of £487. Before 1760, he closed out 7 positions; on each of the 6 positions we can price, he realized a small increase or at least no loss. After 1760, his success was more mixed: Grant lost on 5 of the 11 positions he opened in the 1760s. Still, loathe to give up what he thought was a good idea, he continued to push. The 4 positions he opened in the early 1770s all made him a profit, and he spent the last month of his life issuing sale orders from his deathbed in Westminster.

It is interesting that Grant made more money in the offerings of the East India Company, in which he was a Proprietor, than he did in total. From India Funds, he made £1,462; from all offerings, he made only

£1,434. Thus, he experienced a net loss on all other Funds. Although there is no direct evidence on this point, this pattern is certainly suspicious of what today we would call "insider trading." As a Proprietor and a close partner of the Director John Boyd, Grant was in a good position to benefit from early warning and accurate "advice." Outside of East India Funds, Grant experienced a net loss of £28 on 12 positions in 6 securities between 1752 and 1772. Over all his trading in 22 positions between 1749 and 1772, Grant's average rate of return was 2.7% per year. Changes in the price level reduce this average rate of return slightly.

Whereas Grant worked in bursts and seldom questioned the wisdom of his initial decisions, Oswald paced himself and continually fretted about the past. A close manager, Oswald loved the operational side of business, whether the tobacco trade or the Funds market. He was tremendously well-organized and efficient, the closest thing to a machine the associates knew. But Oswald was also both ambitious and insecure: he was seldom satisfied with results and constantly pushed for larger and larger profits. At the same time, he was extremely averse to risky ventures. Many of these general business traits were reflected in Oswald's personal portfolio. He held only British Linen stock before 1760, but made a dramatic appearance on the Funds stage in the years that followed the Peace of Paris of 1763. Some 92% of Oswald's Funds purchases occurred in the 25 months after the signing of the preliminary articles of peace, by which time he had received roughly £800,000 on his German contracts. Between 1763 and his death in 1784, Oswald held 11 positions in 8 Funds, and held them for 5.1 years on average. Six of these 11 positions he held for 4 or more years. At its peak in 1764, his portfolio was worth more than £100,000. But, by 1767, it had dropped to £1,389. He was less interested than Grant in constantly adjusting his portfolio. Over the course of the 38 years that he was in the market, Oswald negotiated 129 trades, 72% of them between 1763 and 1766, after returning from Germany. Outside of that 4-year period, there is record of only 36 Oswald trades – about one per year. However, these may have been augmented by trades that were never registered or whose registrations have not survived.

Oswald, the largest volume trader, was the most successful in turning a profit. (And he was, perhaps, the least typical investor for such gains.) Not once did he experience a loss on a position. By the end of his trading career, he had made £24,382, and had earned an average annual return of 8.3% on his investments. The range of his returns was narrower than Grant's; Oswald never achieved a profit rate of more than 11.9% or less than 4.6% on any position.

Sargent behaved more like Oswald than like Grant, although the similarity is not exact. Linen trader, Bank director, postal contractor, and M. P., John Sargent was one of the most serious-minded of the associates, a group not noted for its levity. Everything he did, he did for a reason or purpose and, once he had fixed on it, he stuck to it with dogged loyalty. At the same time, he was extremely frugal and spent only when he thought it absolutely necessary. Perhaps for these reasons, he maintained fewer positions (only 6) but held them longer than any other associate – 11.2 years on average. Even if his extraordinary 35-year holding of Bank stock is excepted, his positions still averaged 6.4 years.

Sargent traded less actively than Grant, and even less than Oswald. Unlike Grant, and something of a prude, Sargent abhorred speculation merely for the sake of quick gains. He was the archetypal "long-term" investor: holding securities for relatively long periods. His episodic bursts of buying and selling were generally tied to the acquisition or dissolution of a trust. Of the three merchants, Sargent was the most willing to accept such investment responsibilities for others and, from the mid-1750s onward, his trust investments dwarfed his personal investments. Between 1748 and 1790, the end-of-year value of Sargent's personal portfolio ranged between £2,878 in 1752 and £28 in 1784; it averaged £1,164 per year.

The Fund that Sargent held the longest was Bank stock, an investment that entitled him to nomination to the Directorate, and later ensured that his voice would be heard at the table: initially, he bought £400 (nominal value) of stock in 1748; three years later, he increased his account to £2,000 and maintained this level throughout his tenure as Director; after he stepped down, he reduced his holdings to £1,400 in 1767, to £1,000 in 1769, and to £100 in 1773; he finally closed the position in 1783. Only in the 1760s did Sargent add relatively insignificant amounts of 3 Per Cent Reduced and Consolidated Long annuities. Of Reduced, he purchased £50 (nominal value) in 1771 and then shelved the certificate; he may have forgotten it, for it remained in his portfolio to his death in 1791. In contrast, he constantly dabbled in Long annuities for nearly ten years until he sold out in the aftermath of the banking crisis of 1772.

Sargent's profits are an interesting reflection of "long-term" investment behavior. Between 1748 and 1784, he made £1,142 on six positions and earned an average rate of return of 2.1%. It is true that, in one two-month speculation in India stock, at the height of a speculating frenzy in that stock in 1766, he earned at an annual rate of 8.0%, but such gains were unusual for him, and did not amount to much in pounds, anyway. The norm of 2.1% was set by the much larger quantity of Bank stock that he held for 35 years; if it is removed from his portfolio, his investments returned an average 5.1%.[60]

Why did generally prudent men like Grant, Oswald, and Sargent invest in the Funds? While some political insiders like William Burke, Lord Clive, or Lord Holland may have made a killing in the market for shares, Grant, Oswald, and Sargent, like most investors, realized only modest gains.[61] They seem to have considered investment in the Funds a safe way to put money to work for short periods of time. All of them were government contractors, and they returned from the Seven Years' War with tens of thousands of pounds sterling in Treasury warrants, Ordnance certificates, and Victualing Board bills. Half of these were payable on demand and could be cashed at the Bank of England drawing office; the rest had to be exchanged for government annuities or sold to third parties to raise cash.[62] Until Oswald and other contractors decided on an ultimate use for such pay, whether acquiring land, building houses, or plowing it into new business ventures, they needed a secure, liquid, and not unprofitable store of value. As we see in Graph 8.3, the associates' investments in the Funds fell just as they moved their capital into longer-term investments like land.[63]

In addition to using the Funds as a store of value, the associates used some investments – Grant's in the East India Company, Sargent's in the Bank of England – to increase the merchant's power in company affairs.

60. For profit rate in alternative pursuits, see Grassby, "Rate of Profit," pp. 721–74; Ward, *British West-Indian Slavery*, p. 48; and P. Mirowski, "Adam Smith, Empiricism, and the Rate of Profits in Eighteenth-Century England," *History of Political Economy*, v. 14 (1982), pp. 178–98.
61. H. V. Bowen "Lord Clive and Speculation in East India Company Stock, 1766," *Historical Journal*, v. 30 (1987), pp. 914, 918. On Company speculations in the 1760s, Lord Clive made at least £51,993, Lord Holland £41,958, and William Burke, £12,000.
62. Hancock, "Citizen of the World," p. 293. For example, under "An act for granting annuities to satisfy certain navy, victualing and transport bills" (3 Geo. III, c. 9), contractors who held Navy, Victualing, Ordnance, or Treasury certificates were entitled to exchange the state's debt for 4 Per Cent Navy Stock annuities.
63. On Oswald's contracting pay, see T 1/428/40–41, and AO 1/191/599; "Observations," ff. 8–9; and "Answers," ff. 64–66. On the movement of money into land, see Sudlows, Oswald Papers, Michael Herries to Richard Oswald, 16 September 1774. Earlier, Oswald had used £5,000 of 4 Per Cent Navy stock to clear a bill at the Bank of England. Idem., Michael Herries to Richard Oswald, 9 July 1765. It should be clear from Graph 8.3 that the Funds are measured in pounds and the lands in acres and, so, not directly comparable. Still, since it is the timing that is important here, the comparison holds with respect to what the associates did with their money – whether plowing it into business or land.

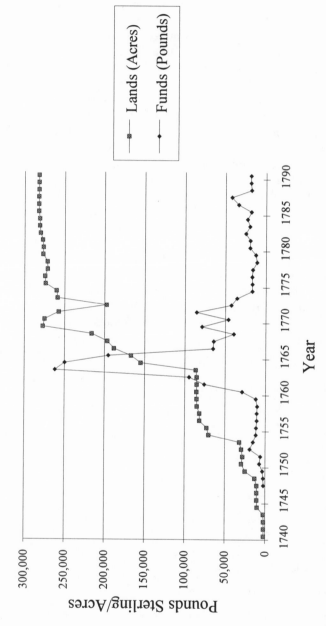

Graph 8.3 Recumulated Funds Investments v. Lands Investments 1740–90

Grant, Sargent, and Oswald maintained 15 positions in India and other monied company stocks for an average 5.5 years, more than twice as long as they held their 21 positions in government securities.[64] Sargent held his Bank stock for 35 years, and John Boyd nurtured his India stock for 28 years. In both cases, their holding coincided with their service as Directors. Grant and Oswald, being sizable purchasers of India goods used in their African trade, held their India stock 23 years and 20 years, respectively.[65]

Owning stock was "the key to success" in the East India Company's politics. Owning £500 (nominal value) of stock qualified the proprietor to vote in the Company's legislature, known as the General Court. Since "in the final instance the appointment and dismissal of Company servants was vested in the General Court," those individuals who sought lucrative appointments on the subcontinent for themselves, relatives, and friends or who hoped for favorable commercial treatment did well to acquire the minimum £500.[66] As a Director and holder of a sizable amount of Company stock, John Boyd secured overseas positions for his partners and their dependents. In autumn 1759, for instance, when Boyd served as Deputy Chairman, he secured factorships and writerships for his future son-in-law John Trevanion, as well as for Grant's nephew Alexander Davidson, and Walton Steevens, the nephew of one of Grant's Jamaica cronies. At the same time, he moved the powerful Committee of Correspondence on which he sat to appoint his cousin John Caillaud a major in the Company's forces at Madras, and to ensure the succession of Grant's nephew Captain Alexander Grant as a major in the Bengal troops. Years later, he named to a Madras engineering post a

64. But Sargent did have one twenty-year position in 3 Per Cent Reduced annuities.
65. Boyd's portfolio was heavily weighted in the direction of the India Company. During the 1760s, when he was most engaged, he purchased £100 of Consolidated Long annuities, £200 of East India annuities, and £37,000 of India stock. For his splitting, see IOL, Stock Ledgers, sub March 9, 1763, and October 5, 1768. Boyd may have also created eight votes on January 24, 1770. Other associates who created fictitious votes were Oswald's partners Scott and Mill. Idem., March 10, 1761, May 20, 1761, March 8, 1763, and May 7, 1763. In the other companies, Sargent and his two partners Stratton and Cooke purchased enough shares to entitle them to a seat on the Bank's Directorate. Scott also held enough shares in the South Seas Company to become a Director. W. M. Acres, *The Bank of England from Within*, v. 2 (London, 1931), p. 621; and [South Seas Company,] *A List of the Names of the Corporation of the Governor and Company of Merchants Trading to the South Seas* (London, 1748), p. 8.
66. Bowen, "Investment," p. 189; and Sutherland, *East India Company*, p. 7. John Boyd, Grant, Herries, Levett, Mill, Oswald, and Scott held a minimum number of shares. Stock Ledgers, 1748–1807, IOL. The 1773 Regulating Act (13 Geo. III, c. 64) raised the voting minimum to £1,000, increased the time one had to own stock before voting, and introduced a proportional system in which one could have more than one vote.

lodger in his own home and a childhood friend of Trevanion, Paul Benfield, the fabulous, notorious nabob later pilloried by Burke.[67]

The associates who invested also found the possibility of making a killing in the Funds, although this turned out to be more promise than reality. Here, the associates were attentive to current affairs. Eighteenth-century Funds prices generally fell in the first years of war and rose as peace was being concluded. As a result, yields on government securities and company annuities rose in time of war and fell in time of peace.[68] As one of Oswald's friends noticed, during the last two years of the Seven Years' War, the low prices of the Funds encouraged several gentlemen "to take up all the money either owing to them or that they could borrow in Scotland, in order to purchase into the publick Funds," so that they could take advantage of high yields and the potential increase in their value when peace broke out. Using this logic, in 1761, Mill bought £33,550 and Grant £7,850 of 3 Per Cent Consols.[69]

Investing was part of the associates' lives. They warily used the Funds when they received more cash than they could profitably reinvest in their businesses and in order to exercise political power within joint-stock companies. The great age of associate investment in the Funds immediately preceded or coincided with a period marked by their appearance on the stage of commercial politics and their especially intense involvement in building estates and plantations. Financial investments like the Funds enabled merchants like Grant, Oswald, and Sargent to buy land and erect new structures in the agricultural, transportation, manufacturing, philanthropic, and colonial sectors of the economy, to safeguard their personal wealth, and to enhance their reputations as gentlemen.

Lands

The connection between Funds and lands was by no means coincidental. Both were outlets for capital that was not being plowed back into

---

67. On Boyd's securing appointments for family and friends, see B 75/443–44, 532 (Trevanion), 487–88, 532 (Davidson), 469–70, 483, 487 (Steevens), 499 (Cuming), 247 (Grant) and D 22/78r (Caillaud), IOL. On Benfield, see B 79/126, 140, 285 (August 1763, January 1764), IOL. Boyd's dealings with Benfield are recounted in greater detail in Hancock, "Citizen of the World," ch. 1.

68. "Yield" is a comparison of the annual dividend to the capital invested. I am using it not in the eighteenth-century sense which expressed the annual payments as a fixed percentage of face value, but in the modern sense of the dividend rate on the purchase price. If prices were below par, then yields were higher than the stated interest rate; if above par, yields were lower.

69. William Mure, ed., *Selections from the Family Papers at Caldwell*, v. 1, pt. II (Glasgow, 1854), p. 211; and Henry Hamilton, "Scotland's Balance of Payments Problem in 1762," *Economic History Review*, 2nd ser., v. 1 (1953), p. 344.

the associates' businesses; with this capital, they built estates in England, Scotland, and America and increased their holdings as age and wealth advanced. Graph 8.3 recumulates their landholdings. While the significance of these holdings to the associates is fully explored in the next chapter, it is worth noting here that the extent of landownership was great. Nine associates owned 13,000 acres around the world at the end of the War of Austrian Succession in 1748. Six years later, at the outset of the Seven Years' War, ten held 74,000 acres. Their total acreage nearly doubled in 1764 and, by the time of the Battles of Lexington and Concord, the associates owned 275,000 acres worldwide. In all, between 1745 and 1785, their landholding had grown nearly twenty-seven-fold.[70]

Economic historians studying landowning have argued that, as the eighteenth century wore on, land in England came to be held in fewer and fewer hands; very large estates increased in number and proportion of the land; and, as they took a greater share of each county, the consolidators squeezed out the lesser gentry and common freeholders. There resulted a "chronic and serious shortage" of land. These trends, it is held, continued through the second half of the century, although the rate of consolidation diminished somewhat.[71] This argument, however,

70. In contrast, only 25% of London citizens who left orphans in 1690–1730 appear to have owned or leased land. Earle, *English Middle Class*, p. 153. Earle, however, does not attempt to trace the holdings of freehold land, and no one has studied in detail the proportion of land to other assets.

71. Appendix VI. On landholding, see Habakkuk, "English Landownership," pp. 2–17; Habakkuk, "The English Land Market in the Eighteenth Century," in J. S. Bromley and E. H. Kossman, eds., *Britain and the Netherlands* (London, 1960), pp. 154–73; and Mingay, *English Landed Society*, pp. 50–79. Younger historians have argued that the Habakkuk/Mingay view should not be adopted wholesale: they assert there was no shortage of land in the middle of the century to discourage land transfers; there was no want of money with which to buy it; and land was not the most profitable investment open to purchasers. Clay, "Marriage," pp. 513–14; Clay, "The Price of Freehold Land and the Interest Rate in the Seventeenth and Eighteenth Centuries," *Economic History Review*, 2nd ser., v. 27 (1974), pp. 173–89; and Allen, "The Price of Freehold Land," pp. 33–51. The argument that land was not the most profitable investment is particularly muddied. In the early eighteenth century, Defoe stated that the gross return on investment in land was 5%. *The Complete English Tradesman*, v. 2 (London, 1726–27), pp. i, 159–82. At roughly the same time, the net return was 3%. Early, *English Middle Class*, p. 152. Returns appear to have stayed fairly stable throughout the late 1770s and early 1780s. One of Grant's friends noted that land in the vicinity of Montrose would earn "little better than 3 pr ct for your money" in 1760. Walter Tullideph to Duncan Grant, March 28, 1760, Tullideph Letter Book, v. 3, SRO. A recent study by Allen provides similar results. "The Price of Freehold Land," p. 34. Later in the century, the rate rose. In 1778, Oswald stated that he could get 4% from land; by 1783, he was getting 5%. Andrew Grant and John Fordyce to Richard Oswald, March 31, 1778, Samuel Mitchelson to Richard Oswald, April 20, 1778, and Richard Oswald to Samuel Mitchelson Jr., June 4, 1783, Oswald Papers, Sudlows. None of the arguments accounts for the nonquantifiable, nonfinancial benefits of land.

is based on a limited number of examples – a handful of individuals in England alone. On the evidence of the associates' activities, large-scale London merchants who had the desire and money to invest were not prevented from establishing estates by a lack of land or a consolidation in ownership among a traditional landed elite.[72] When their individual holdings are recumulated, it appears the associates owned over 150,000 acres in Britain and another 125,000 acres overseas during most of the period from 1770 through 1785. London's overseas traders did not avoid purchasing land in the counties, as some historians have suggested, or in the colonies, as most historians have ignored.[73]

Estate-building occurred relatively late in the associates' lives.[74] For most of them, it arose in the decades that followed the Seven Years' War, when they had reached a certain age and degree of prosperity. They tended to buy and hold land, not speculate and sell. At home, their most common strategy was to buy a large county estate and, through a series of small purchases of adjoining lands, add to the core. Grant did this at Dalvey, John Boyd at Danson Hill, Oswald at Auchincruive, and Sargent II at Halstead Place. They preferred freehold over other types of land ownership: they held 99% of their land in freehold, plus a little land leased in urban or suburban communities. Landowning was more than just "an extension of the leasehold market."[75]

When Alexander Grant purchased a large agricultural estate in northeastern Scotland in January 1749 and made his first purchase of India Company stock five months later, he could not have foreseen the events of the 1750s and 1760s and the extent to which an international war would increase Britain's territory overseas and assure her naval supremacy. Nor would this diffident yet determined merchant have predicted the extent to which imperial growth would augment his own trade and capital, protect his financial investments, and give him the wherewithal to make many more. Yet, at the same time, he would not

72. For a long time, historians thought that merchants were heavy investors in the land market. Accordingly, some historians have argued that early seventeenth-century merchants bought large tracts of land. Lang, "Social Origins," p. 40. Others have argued that Georgian merchants preferred to place their investible money elsewhere. Earle, *English Middle Class*, pp. 152–57; Wilson, *Gentleman Merchants*, p. 227; and Pocock, "Augustan Perception," pp. 69–72.

73. At the end of the period under study here, each associate or his estate owned or leased on average 13,455 acres in the counties and colonies. When the substantial and possibly atypical holdings of Grant (71,139 acres), Mill (18,762 acres), and Oswald (174,410 acres) are removed from the sample, the average drops to 1,014 acres.

74. Cf. Clay, "The Price of Freehold Land," p. 185.

75. Habakkuk, "English Land Market," p. 158; and Earle, *English Middle Class*, pp. 148, 155.

have been surprised by the outcome. Grant and his associates had always considered trans-Atlantic commerce and finance to be one great interlocking enterprise: earning fees from commission merchandising, marriage to a Jamaican planter heiress, the management of Caribbean plantations, trade in sugar, wartime privateering, naval victualing, speculation in the Funds (especially in those Funds borne of or strengthened by the Seven Years' War), the acquisition of land, and the like, were all parts of the trans-Atlantic whole. Financing, in the words of Henry Laurens, his South Carolina correspondent, was both the instrument which turned "the Great Wheel of Unfathomable Commerce Round" and the stuff of commerce itself.[76] Fittingly, land, the ultimate investment, was both an outlet for capital and a necessary commercial transaction. As we will see in the pages that remain, it was also a means of acquiring a powerful, secure, and devisable stake in society.

76. Henry Laurens to James Knight, June 12, 1764, *Papers of Henry Laurens*, v. 4, p. 311.

PART III

Becoming a Gentleman

9

The Urge to Improve

IN 1763, AT THE CLOSE OF BRITAIN'S most extensive and expensive war to date, the associates could be found back at work in their small and orderly counting-houses, moving employees, ships, and commodities around the Atlantic-centered world. They were Americans, Scots, Irish, Huguenots, Midlanders, or West Country-men, who could look back upon modest, even humble origins, years of living abroad and serving people across the seas. In London, they had set themselves up in trades marked by growth and relative openness to outsiders, in large measure because they were outsiders themselves, with few connections to the ruling cliques in commerce. Over the years, they remedied that situation and, by the time of the signing of the Peace of Paris in 1763, they were undeniable successes. War and slavery had enabled them to build fortunes. Their position in commercial society was confirmed. They were called on to fill government contracts, underwrite government bonds, lend much-needed capital, serve as advisors to the Government, and lead the development of new lands in America.

But this does not account for the whole of their lives; in particular, it does not account for their own movement through society. For all their successes, the associates were still frustrated in the fulfillment of their social desires. They had gained great wealth, as well as significant political influence, but they were still regarded as marginal figures in society. Standing outside the peerage, baronetage, and established landed gentry, they lacked social status. To gain respect and station, they had to insinuate themselves into the world inhabited by men of noble birth and high office by working to be seen as "gentlemen." The entry into the world of Britain's gentlemen, of course, required first that the associates attain wealth and age. But wealth and age alone were not sufficient. In addition, their acceptance depended on actively taking up the multifaceted work of "improvement," building upon the empire of ideas and programs we can call the practical Enlightenment. This chapter and the one that follows recount the associates' movement from the periphery to the center of society, their ascent into the realm of the gentleman.

Gentlemen and Improvers

The definition of the gentility the associates sought was inexact at the time, and historians have not done much to clarify the matter. Some have argued that the eighteenth-century conception of gentility was more rigid than that of earlier periods, although to date the preponderance of evidence suggests that "the precise attributes of a gentleman" became increasingly vague, and contemporary attitudes toward gentility increasingly liberal during the period. Before the Glorious Revolution of 1688, a few objective tests determined who was a gentleman. Noble birth was one obvious mark, as were high rank in the royal service and high standing in the professions – the army, clergy, or law. Possession of land served to confirm the nobleman's or civil servant's respectability.[1] Few passed these objective tests, however. In the decades following 1688, the men who served the state's burgeoning bureaucracy or made fortunes from trans-Atlantic commerce grew in number, in importance, and in the resources at their command. In response, a deportmental rather than a hereditary or professional definition of gentility gained currency: one was a gentleman if one looked and acted the part.[2] Certain characteristics of behavior became marks of gentlemanly status: a good education, "a genteel dress and carriage," refined external behavior, and the financial wherewithal to support this polished style of living. By the time the associates were setting up shop in London, businessmen previously shunned by those of noble birth or high rank could acquire the benefit of being addressed as gentlemen. "The term *Gentleman*" was commonly used by the 1760s to designate "Him, who merits this denomination: the Man elevated above the vulgar" and distinguished either by his "superior accomplishments" or "by his high birth and dignity of station."[3]

Daniel Defoe sensed the liberalization of the definition of "gentility,"

1. In this regard, the nature of the possession, the size of the holding, and the relation of the holder to the land (whether, for instance, he had to work the land himself) were also significant. As a result, the relation of land to respectability could become blurred, for in some instances mere yeomen could be considered gentlemen.
2. The debate about whether gentility was a function of birth or virtue was in some respects old by 1600. It had roots in ancient ethical theory and found expression in various forms after 1400. What was new in the eighteenth century was an emphasis on sensibility and manners. I am indebted to David Sacks for impressing this point (and many more) in this and the following chapter.
3. Peter Borsay, *The English Urban Renaissance: Culture and Society in the Provincial Town, 1660–1760* (Oxford, 1989), pp. 225–56; Peter Laslett, *The World We Have Lost: England before the Industrial Age*, 2nd ed. (New York, 1971), pp. 23–54; George Lillo, *The London Merchant* (London, 1731), Act 1, Scene 1; and *Monthly Review*, v. 24 (1761), p. 119. Borsay's material is compelling, although it overemphasizes fashionable pastimes and products. Further research on the subject is needed.

this new emphasis on manners and sensibility, well before the 1760s when he remarked that trade was so far "from being inconsistent with a gentleman, that, in short, trade in England makes gentlemen, and has peopled this nation with gentlemen." As he was fond of doing, Defoe made acquiring status seem easy; it was not. The taint of trade lingered long after deportmental characteristics had been acquired; hostility and suspicion still dogged aspiring businessmen in the second half of the century. Horace Walpole expressed surprise that merchants could behave like gentlemen, and many less colorful men made the same point. In *An Estimate of the Manners and Principles of the Times* (1757), the minister John Brown noticed that generous merchants were the exception, not the rule, and that "Sons and Relations of Men of Quality," but not of merchants, had "a prior Claim to all high Employments in the State" – a sentiment Adam Smith shared twenty years later. The economist Josiah Tucker in his *Instructions for Travellers* (1758) similarly acknowledged that a merchant frequently failed to "meet with Respect equal to his large and acquired Fortune." Yet Tucker was more sanguine about the son of a merchant: "if he gives his Son a liberal and accomplished Education – the Birth and Calling of the Father are sunk in the Son; and the Son is reputed, if his Carriage is suitable, a Gentleman in all Companies, though without serving in the Army, without Patent, Pedigree, or Creation." The very flexibility of deportmental characteristics like education or dress, of course, made the attainment of gentility far from certain, and economically successful men of the middling ranks devised a variety of strategies to minimize the uncertainty. By "the continuous purchase and display of cultural products," some men and women "signaled" their entry into genteel society; a more straightforward program of rural improvements enabled others, like the associates, to become civilized and sociable citizens of their world.[4]

The associates wrapped their quest for gentility in the cloak of improvement. As a word, "improvement" first appeared in the early

4. Daniel Defoe, *The Complete English Tradesman* (Gloucester, 1981), p. 216; Daniel Defoe, *Robinson Crusoe* (Oxford, 1840), p. 265; John Brown, *An Estimate of the Manners and Morals of the Times* (London, 1757), pp. 130, 160, 207; Smith, *Wealth of Nations*, v. 2, pp. 713–14 (V.i.b.8–11); Josiah Tucker, *Instructions for Travellers* (Dublin, 1758), sub "Are the English Nobility & Gentry more disposed to Town Residences?"; and Borsay, *Urban Renaissance*, p. 231. Economists have treated the idea of "signalling" at length. Thorstein Veblen's *The Theory of the Leisure Class* (New York, 1899) is the classical reference: conspicuous consumption in a competitive society, according to Veblen, was used by individuals to signal wealth; from wealth, observers inferred status and power. More recently, A. Michael Spence has developed the concept more in *Market Signaling: Informational Transfer in Hiring and Related Screening Processes* (Cambridge, 1974). I would like to thank Peter Coclanis for bringing Spence's work to my attention.

fourteenth century. From the start, it denoted turning something to good account or profit, and was usually reserved for discussions of farming. Its earliest appearance, in the Year Book of Edward I for 1302, refers to the reclamation of waste or unoccupied land through enclosure and planting. In the seventeenth century, Bacon spoke of "the culture and manurance of minds in youth" in 1605 and, later, Clarendon extended the meaning of "Improver" to describe an individual who cultivated his own character. The meaning of "improvement" and its variants quickly stretched to connote nonagricultural activities. By Cromwell's time, it was common to speak – although seldom in the same breath or by the same author – of improvement as a moral or spiritual edification, an act of textual interpretation, or a lucrative investment of money. Often the word was used synonymously with "change." By the early 1700s, in a sense that hearkened back to Clarendon's use of "Improver," it had come to embrace the cultivation of body or mind. Richard Steele's "Man of the Town" had "very little improvement" but what he had "got from plays," much as the minister Robert South looked to London as "the best place of improvement." Under the Georges, one could improve one's station and "renown."[5]

By the time the associates settled in London, men of letters were writing expansively on the subject. Clerics offered _An Improvement of the Doctrine of Earthquakes_ (1755) and lectures on _The Proper Improvement of Divine Judgements_ (1758). Merchants issued _Some Observations for Improvement of Trade_ (1732) and _An Essay on the Improvement of the Woolen Manufactures_ (1741). The mental and educational advancement of would-be gentlemen came in for special treatment: _The Complete Letter-Writer: Or Polite English Secretary_ (1761) contained examples of "elegant letters" for "the improvement of style," and critics like Addison and Steele were extracted in _Short Histories for the Improvement of the Mind_ (1762). "The earth itself,"

5. Year Books of 30–31 Edward I (Rolls), 19; [Langtoft], Ms. Oxf. Fairf.24 lf 12; and Francis Bacon, _The Advancement of Learning_ (1605), ed. G. W. Kitchin (London, 1973), p. 151 (XIX.2). For "improver," see Edward Hyde, Earl of Clarendon, _The History of the Rebellion and Civil Wars in England_, v.1 (written 1647; London, 1702), ss. 15, 132; and Walter Blith, _The English Improver; or A New Survey of Husbandry_ (London, 1649). Contemporaneous nonagricultural uses of "improvement" appear in Thomas Stanley, _The History of Philosophy_, v. 3 (London, 1656–60), 75/2; and J. Clerk, _Faithfull Steward_ (London, 1655), p. 30. Late-seventeenth- and eighteenth-century cultural references include: Waller, _To a Person of Honour_ (London, 1698); Steele, _Spectator_, v. 1. p. 276 (# 41, par. 2: April 17, 1711); Robert South, _Twelve Sermons Preached upon Several Occasions_, v. 5 (London, 1727), pp. 1–48; and John Milton, _Works_, ed. Thomas Birch, v. 1 (London, 1753), p. 3. See also Joan Thirsk, _Economic Policy and Projects: The Development of a Consumer Society in Early Modern England_ (Oxford, 1978); and Joyce Appleby, _Economic Thought and Ideology in Seventeenth-Century England_ (Princeton, 1978).

Priestley summed up in 1782, was "in a state of improvement." Broccoli, conversation, education, "free and candid inquiry," quadrilles, emetic powders, painting, shorthand, midwifery: almost anything could be improved.[6]

The Seven Years' War ushered in Britain's great "Age of Improvement" by providing financial resources in an unprecedented volume to effect the improving schemes of nouveaux riches like the associates. Coming when it did, at a time when rural depopulation and economic depression were clouding the minds of men of affairs, this "Age" pricked the consciences of such men to move beyond mere self-promotion to reverse the perceived economic decline or stasis of the community.[7] Improvement societies sprang up during the Seven Years' War, and their memberships soared; their projects included social experiments as often as projects of pure personal aggrandizement. In London, the Society for the Encouragement of Arts, Manufactures, and Commerce brought together an impressive array of interested citizens and, in the counties, specifically agricultural societies performed similar services. All but the Boyds and Herries were members of the London Society, and most were members of its county analogues. Improvement was not all talk, however. Improvers also acted, developing estates, growing crops, promoting transportation and industrial projects, patronizing charities, and pushing an agenda of commercial and agricultural legislation in Parliament.

6. Joseph Priestley, *Institutes of Natural and Revealed Religion*, 2nd ed., v. 1 (London, 1982), pp. 18–19. Agricultural references include: George Stanhope, *A Paraphrase and Comment upon the Epistles and Gospels*, v. 3 (London, 1705), p. 29; Defoe, *Robinson Grusoe*, p. 365; Stephen Switzer, *The Country Gentleman's Companion: or, Ancient Husbandry Restored; and Modern Husbandry Improved* (London, 1732); Richard Bradley, *The Country Gentleman and Farmer's Monthly Director; Containing Necessary Instructions for the Management and Improvement of a Farm* (London, 1727); E.B., *Frugal Husbandry Expressed in Short Rules and Directions for the Growth and Improvement of Hops* (London, 1740); *A Dissertation on the Chief Obstacles to the Improvement of Land* (Aberdeen, 1760); John Baker, *Some Hints for the Better Improvement of Husbandry* (London, 1762); *Foreign Essays on Agriculture and Arts . . . for the Improvement of British Husbandry* (London, 1765); Arthur Young, *Farmer's Letters to the People of England* (London, 1767), p. 250; Oliver Goldsmith, *She Stoops to Conquer* (1773), in *Collected Works*, ed. A. Friedman, v. 5 (Oxford, 1966), p. 115; Richard Twiss. *A Tour of Ireland in 1775* (London, 1776), pp. 65–66; and Smith, *Wealth of Nations*, p. 13 (I.i.1).

7. H. J. Habakkuk, "English Landownership, 1680–1740," *Economic History Review*, v. 10 (1940), p. 13. For contemporary impressions of stagnation and decline, see Robert Selby to Richard Oswald, October 2, 1768, Oswald Papers, Sudlows; John Maxwell to William Pulteney, December 16, 1773, Pulteney Papers, PU 1560, Huntington Library; and James Anderson to Earl of Shelburne, May 28, 1782, Shelburne Papers, v. 67, ff. 247–63, Clements Library. The most recent author to discuss the concern for decline and the fear of depopulation in the 1770s is Bailyn, in *Voyagers*, pp. 30–57. See also Dalphy Fagerstrom, "The American Revolutionary Movement in Scottish Opinion, 1763 to 1783" (Ph.D. dissert., University of Edinburgh, 1951), pp. 89, 90, 210.

All the associates worked in this way, some more and some less; since those who appear to be lesser improvers are also those about whom we know the least, their contributions may have been more substantial than we know. All the associates ascribed to a neo-Baconian belief in the possibility of bettering man's condition by promoting character, agriculture, industry, and commerce; and they acted on this belief.[8]

The associates invoked the concept of improvement to describe the whole gamut of activities they regarded as necessary for becoming gentlemen.[9] The steps they took to prove themselves gentlemen were laid out in the books that lined their libraries and in the essays that filled their newspapers or magazines. One typical self-help author argued that one could identify a gentleman, first, "when improving his lands" and, thereafter, when "enriching his tenants," when "his beneficence may be read in the looks of the poor," and when "his house is open, not with the stiffness of a public day, that tells the neighbourhood he would not be perplexed at another time, but with all the hospitality of an ancient Baron." The accuracy of this assessment is borne out by the associates' experience. To later generations, their steps may seem formulaic: estates, farms, amenities for the community, and political offices. Yet each step reflected the importance the associates had achieved in the mercantile and political worlds, and enhanced and reinforced that status further.

8. Membership Index, Royal Society of Arts, London; Henry T. Wood, *A History of the Royal Society of Arts* (London, 1913); and Derek Hudson and Kenneth Luckhurst, *The Royal Society of Arts, 1754–1954* (London, 1954), pp. 149–67. The older Royal Society and the younger Royal Society for the Improvement of Natural Knowledge also took part in improvement discussions. For details on local societies in Scotland, see GD 345/1166/4/19; GD 248/351/11–3: Alexander Chalmers to James Grant, April 21, 1787; *The Edinburgh Advertiser*, July 13, 1764; *The Dumfries Weekly Journal*, May 4, 1779, pp. 3c–4a; and *Select Transactions of the Honourable the Society of Improvers in the Knowledge of Agriculture in Scotland* (Edinburgh, 1743). After 1748, Ayrshire had its own "Society for Improving of Agriculture and Manufactures in the Shire of Ayr." R. H. Campbell, "The Scottish Improvers and the Course of Agrarian Change in the Eighteenth Century," in L. M. Cullen and T. C. Smout, eds., *Comparative Aspects of Scottish and Irish Economic and Social History, 1600–1900* (Edinburgh, 1977), pp. 204–15; and James E. Handley, *The Agricultural Revolution in Scotland* (Glasgow, 1963), pp. 73–76. Although the work of Scottish improvement societies has been closely scrutinized, that of their counterparts in English counties, such as the Bath & West of England Society or the Smithfield Club, has been woefully neglected. Neither G. E. Mingay, *English Landed Society in the Eighteenth Century* (London, 1963) nor G. E. Mingay and J. D. Chambers, *The Agricultural Revolution, 1750–1880* (New York, 1966) mentions society activity.

9. GD 345/1161/1/48: Alexander Grant to Sir Archibald Grant, March 7, 1751; GD 345/1164/3/95: Alexander Grant to Sir Archibald Grant, September 3, 1756; GD 345/1166/4/33–34: Alexander Grant to Sir Archibald Grant, October 25, 1760; John Stevenson to Richard Oswald, November 28, 1764, Oswald Papers, EUL; John Maxwell to Richard Oswald, May 1, 1767, May 22, 1776, Oswald Letter Book, v. 3, ff. 39, 207; and Samuel Mitchelson Jr. to Richard Oswald, October 20, 1778, Oswald Papers, Sudlows.

Through a polite, industrious, and moral improvement program, they created (or thought they created) a better life for others, and thereby solidified the status of gentlemen for themselves and their families. Contrary to what Adam Smith wrote in 1776, the pursuit of wealth was not plagued by a tendency to indolence, and the presence of wealth did not render its holders incapable of altering their surroundings for what most men of the affairs deemed the better.[10]

Lands

A world "without property was almost inconceivable" to seventeenth- and eighteenth-century Britons. Time and again, social commentators espoused its primacy. The Dean of Peterborough considered it "the true basis and measure of power" in 1730. Subscribers to the 1742 *London Magazine* were reminded that "Property" was their "Deity." John Brown, in his *Thoughts on Civil Liberty, on Licentiousness, and Faction* (1765), affirmed the popular belief that "Power follows Property." Property exerted such force because it was both economic and social. "A larger Proportion of Property," the Dean of Lincoln noted in 1752, "gives a Superior Weight, and Dignity, and Authority." Such was conventional wisdom. When the manufacturer George Phillips set out in 1792 to describe the "sufficient influence" of property, he voiced a consensus: "Its splendour dazzles the weak, awes the timid, abashes the modest...."[11]

The associates shared their countrymen's view of property. If their holdings are recumulated, it appears they increased their acreage twenty-seven-fold between 1745 and 1785, as we see in Graph 9.1. Upon moving to London, the associates acquired leaseholds in the City. Initially, these consisted of counting-houses that they also used as dwelling-houses, such as Sargent's at 38 Mincing Lane and Oswald's at 17 Philpot Lane. As they prospered, they separated home from office and moved their lodgings to townhouses in more fashionable suburbs like Westminster – Augustus Boyd, Grant, and Oswald on Great George Street, Sargent on Downing Street, and John Boyd on Grafton Street – and Chelsea – where Aufrere took up Robert Walpole's old mansion.[12]

10. John Trussler, *The Way to Be Rich and Respectable* (London, 1775), p. 6; Smith, *Wealth of Nations*, v. 1, pp. 265 (I.xi.p.8) and 385–86 (III.ii.7); and Notebook of Improvements by Patrick, Earl of Dumfries, 1768–1803, Dumfries Papers A-1098, Dumfries House, Cumnock.

11. These quotations appear in Paul Langford's excellent *Public Life and the Propertied Englishman, 1698–1798* (Oxford, 1991), pp. 4, 51–53.

12. With respect to nineteen associates about whom some property-holding information is known, thirteen were still leasing counting-houses at the time of their death.

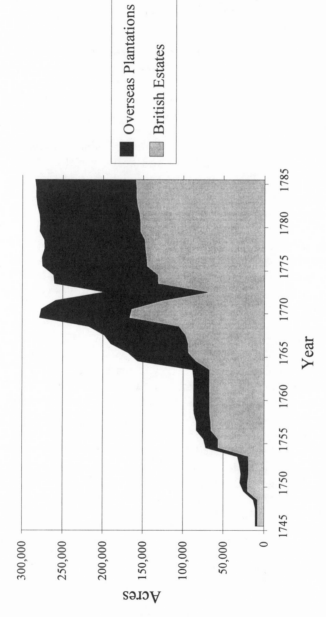

Graph 9.1 Recumulated Lands Investments, 1745–85

At the same time that they made their first purchases in the City, the associates also bought overseas plantations, and continued to do so for the rest of their careers.[13] At the same time that they moved their lodgings to townhouses, they also bought villas in the country. The villa, with 5 to 100 acres of land, was leased for a term of years and located no farther than a day's journey from London. Its "convenient neighborhood" – northwestern Kent, northern Surrey, or southwestern Essex – enjoyed easy access to the City, as Illustration 9.1 demonstrates, and a community inhabited by similarly situated individuals. John Boyd's Kent, for instance, was home to the villas of at least a dozen prominent Caribbean expatriates, such as the Mays, the Longs, the Boyds, the Kenyons, the Mannings, the Butlers, the Duports, the Malcolms, the Adyes, and the Willetts. The compactness and convenience of these villas stood in contrast "to the magnificence and extensive range of the country seats,"[14] another kind of country estate acquired by the associates. Country seats were generally purchased even later than villas

Townhouses, although grander, bore a strong resemblance to counting-houses. Sargent's Downing Street residence is detailed in Butler, Ewart Mss., ZBU/BB/6/13, Northumberland Record Office. A much more detailed picture of Oswald's house at 14 Great George Street is contained in C 12/1070/12: Oswald v. Christie (1783). On Grant's townhouse, see *Survey of London*, v. 10, pp. 28–29. On Aufrere's townhouse, see Thomas Faulkner, *An Historical and Topographical Description of Chelsea and Its Environs* (London, 1819), and Reginald Blunt, *Paradise Row, or a Broken Piece of Old Chelsea* (London, 1906), pp. 139–42. Information on the neighborhoods into which the associates were moving appears in London County Council, *Survey of London*, v. 10 (London, 1926), pp. 21–55. On townhouses generally, see Cruickshank and Wyld, *London: The Art of Georgian Building*, pp. 18–38, 82–221; and Summerson, *Georgian London*, pp. 38–39, 44–56.

13. Nine (39%) associates owned foreign plantations, as we saw in Chapter 5: the Boyds, Grant, Herries, Mill, Oswald, Scott, Trevanion, and Wood. These nine were all West Indian or North American merchants; all but Herries owned Caribbean land. Only members of the Sargent circle resisted buying overseas plantations.

14. The following associates leased villas: Alexander Anderson (Staines, Surrey), Augustus Boyd (Lewisham, Kent), John Boyd (Bexleyheath, Kent), Chambers (Dedham, Essex), Cooke (Walthamstow, Essex); Samuel Gardiner (Walthamstow and West Ham, Essex); Grant (Eltham, Kent, and Leatherhead, Surrey); Herries (Kingsland Place, Middlesex); Mill (Hampstead, Middlesex); Oswald (Eltham, Kent, and Brighthelmstone, Sussex); Rolleston (Camberwell, Surrey); Sargent II (Crayford, Kent); Scott (Camberwell, Surrey, and Blackheath, Kent); Stratton (Charlton, Kent); and Trevanion (Windsor, Berkshire). The average distance from these villas to the Royal Exchange at the center of London was fourteen miles. Grant's "Bookham Grove" is described in John Harvey, "A Short History of Bookham," *Proceedings of the Leatherhead & District Local History Society*, v. 1, n. 4 (1950), pp. 18–19, and v. 1, n. 8 (1954), pp. 13–25; Nicolaus Pevsner and Ian Nairn, rev. Bridget Cherry, *Surrey* (Harmondsworth, 1971), pp. 264–65; and S. E. D. Fortescue, *People and Places: Great and Little Bookham* (Great Bookham, 1975), pp. 14, 50–53. On villas generally, see Charles Middleton, *Picturesque and Architectural Views for Cottages, Farmhouses and Country Villas* (London, 1793), p. 9. I am grateful to Clare Taylor for information on Kent's Caribbean families.

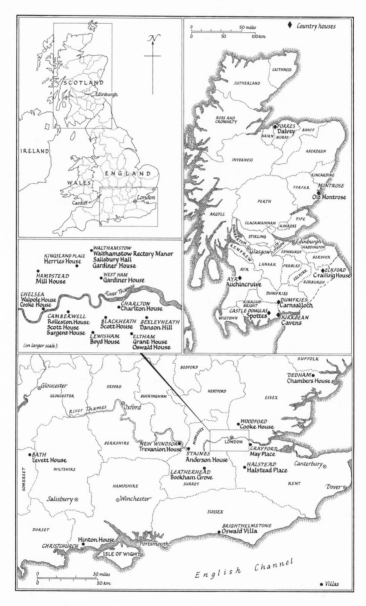

Illustration 9.1 A Map of England and Scotland, with the Locations of the Associates' Country Houses and Villas. Drawn by Reginald Piggott.

and, in the case of most of them, they replaced villas.[15] Except for John Boyd and Grant, the associates started buying country seats in the aftermath of the Seven Years' War. Having achieved commercial success in their businesses by middle age, they found in the counties opportunities to invest and chances to solidify their claims to respectability. They made good on these opportunities by forging links to the specific geographical communities where they bought. They had no desire to live in a world set apart from the rhythms of everyday life; rather, they worked to become community members who actively integrated the various parts of the economy.

Because Oswald's improving was typical and better documented than the other associates', his purchases deserve detailed scrutiny.[16] The timing of his push into the market for land is significant. As Graph 9.2 shows, before the Seven Years' War ended, Oswald owned or leased one house in the City, two commercial tracts along the James River in Virginia, a financial interest in a sugar plantation in Jamaica, and a share of an island in West Africa. Peace and the prosperity that followed from his wartime contracting required him to search for a secure way to invest the money he had made on his German contracts. In one year, he bought, 5,614 acres outright and 9,056 on mortgage in Scotland, where he had owned nothing before; over the next two years, he further augmented his Scottish holdings. Additional purchases occurred in 1773, when Oswald increased his Scottish acreage nearly fivefold to 77,519 acres. His Scottish estates peaked in 1782 at 102,679 acres.[17]

Oswald focused most of his efforts on the barony of Auchincruive, a vast tract situated on the northern bank of the River Ayr, five miles east of Ayr and sixty miles south of Glasgow.[18] The estate was an ancient

15. The following owned freehold county estates: Birch (Hertfordshire, and Bedfordshire); John Boyd (Kent); Chambers (Essex); Cooke (Essex); Samuel Gardiner (Essex); Grant (Inverness, Nairn, Elgin and Forres, and Moray); Herries (Kirkcudbright, and Dumfries); Johnston (Dumfries); Levett (Hampshire); Mill (Forfar); Oswald (Ayr, and Kirkcudbright); Sargent II (Kent); and Sargent III (Surrey).

16. The holdings of John Boyd, Grant, and Sargent II are detailed in Hancock, "Citizen," pp. 753–68.

17. This tally might buttress George Eyre-Todd's claim that Oswald took advantage of the Ayr Bank Crisis in 1772 and made large purchases of land from afflicted customers of the Bank. *History of Glasgow*, v. 3 (Glasgow, 1934), p. 261. But there is absolutely no evidence that those who sold to Oswald had suffered from the financial improprieties of the Ayr Bank. Mirroring this British rise, his North American holdings grew in the 1760s, from 5,000 acres in Virginia and Jamaica to 50,000 acres scattered between Nova Scotia and East Florida. Abroad, during the years 1770–84, his already substantial real estate portfolio increased 31 percent as he expanded into East Florida and the eastern Caribbean.

18. The meaning of "Auchincruive" is unclear. Neither John Sinclair nor George Chalmers provides a definitive suggestion. Sinclair, *The Statistical Account of Scotland*, v. 7 (Edinburgh, 1793), pp. 353–60; and Chalmers, *Caledonia*, v. 6 (Paisley, 1890), pp.

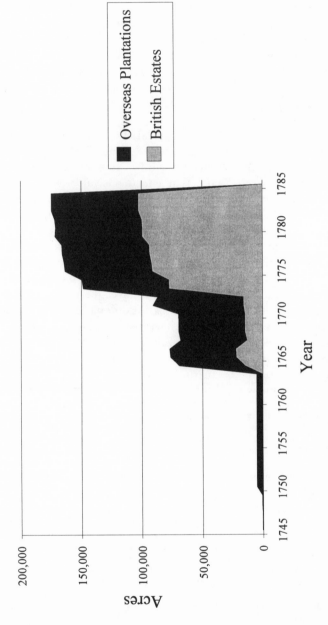

Graph 9.2 Richard Oswald's Lands Investments, 1745–84

property that had recently come into the possession of James Murray of Broughton, an owner of lands in Wigtown and Kirkcudbright, a friend of Rockingham, and a cousin of Oswald's North Carolina client James Murray.[19] Although information about the property under Murray is sketchy, it appears that some sort of house existed before he arrived there and that Murray engaged the Adam brothers to design and build another house near the original. It was this property and mansion, "the main agents through which a person established social position,"[20] that Oswald purchased in July 1764.[21]

The associates bought land in the counties with increasing frequency and in growing volume in the quarter-century after the Seven Years' War, mostly during the last two or three decades of their lives. Beyond

514–15. It may denote "the field of the sheepfold." Anon., "Country Homes of Scotland, No. 85: Auchincruive, Ayr," *The Scots Pictorial*, February 24, 1923, p. 183. Or it may denote "field of trees." Kathleen Knox, "A History of the Gardens at Auchincruive" (B.S. Honors thesis, University of Strathclyde/West of Scotland College of Agriculture, 1981), p. 1.

19. The estate was owned by the Wallace family until 1374 and thereafter by the Cathcart family until 1758, when Murray purchased it from the 9th Baron Cathcart. *Burke's Peerage and Baronetage*, v. 1, p. 498; and Namier and Brooke, eds., *House of Commons*, v. 3, pp. 184–85. For Murray's purchase, see GD 117/1: Sasine, August 6, 1483; GD 10/941/2; GD 10/937; and GD 10/1421/6/282,825: Lord Cathcart to James Murray, April 7, 1755, and John Syme to Charles Brown, January 5, 1758.

20. Borsay, *English Urban Renaissance*, p. 232. One 1723 observer mentioned "Lord Cathcart's house of Auchencroof half a mile to the southeast of the Kirk" of St. Quivox, with large orchards and "a pleasant dry situation, hansome avenues and vistoes on all sydes of the house." Arthur Mitchell, ed., *Geographical Collections Relating to Scotland Made by Walter Macfarlane*, v. 1 (Edinburgh, 1906), p. 411. The 1758 sale also refers to a "Tower Fortalice Manor Place." Knox, "Gardens," p. 1; "Plan of the Gardens of Auchencroff the Seat of the Honorable Charles Cathcart, Master of Cathcart," copied in 1813 from an original drawing, and "Plan of Auchencroff . . . copied in 1813 from an Original drawn by William Boutcher in 1713 [1723]," West of Scotland College of Agriculture Library, Auchincruive, Ayr. Though these two surveys focus mainly on the gardens and grounds, both plans indicate the presence of a house on roughly the same site as the house completed by Oswald. While no mention of a house appears in Murray's newspaper advertisements in January 1764, Oswald's subsequent correspondence with his Ayr factors makes sense only if some structure existed. This was in all probability the beginning of the new edifice designed by the Adam brothers. Plans, now in the Soane Museum, were drawn up by the Adam brothers and inscribed "Auchincruive" for "John Murray Esqe at Broughton."

21. In January 1764, after Murray decided he no longer needed a third Scottish estate and could do without Auchincruive, he placed four advertisements in the *Edinburgh Evening Courant*. Interested parties were to write to his agent, the attorney George Muir, for the particulars of the property and sale; an auction was to be held at John's Coffeehouse in Edinburgh at 5 P.M. on January 12. When no purchasers appeared, the auction was rescheduled for January 24. When no purchasers came forward again, the sale was thrown into private negotiation and, in the ensuing months, Oswald's attorney struck a deal with Muir. Auchincruive was transferred on July 15. *Edinburgh Evening Courant*, January 9, 14, 20, 23; and *Caledonian Mercury*, January 23, 1764; General Register of Sasines, v. 251, ff. 371–79, 379–83, 383–88, SRO; and Disposition from James Murray to Richard Oswald, September 6, 1764, SRA-Glasgow.

these observations, it is difficult to generalize. John Sargent II made one moderate-sized purchase and stopped. John Boyd leased a villa at Danson Hill in 1753, bought it several years later, and augmented it with similar moderate-sized tracts of contiguous farmland over the remainder of his life. Alexander Grant and Richard Oswald first made large purchases, and later increased their estates with investments in surrounding farms and in neighboring counties. What tied these four different approaches together was the purpose underlying them – the attainment of "Superior Weight, and Dignity, and Authority." But before we turn to what land brought them, we should understand what it did not bring.

In principle, landowning made money; but, in fact, it seldom did, at least for the associates. In the fourth quarter of the century, economists began to argue that farming was "a precarious employment for a man to place his dependence on" and that the profits from agriculture "seem to have no superiority over those of other employments." These experts were reporting the lessons learned before them by men like Oswald and Grant. With all "judicious men in trade," the associates knew they could "far better improve their money than by investing it in land." Historians have recently calculated the "scanty returns" that could be expected from land, no more than 3 1/4 percent per year. Far greater rewards, perhaps 20 percent, could be made in commerce.[22]

And if, in principle, landowning also provided a residence, in practice, it seldom did. Although many of the associates regularly visited their lands and estates, only Herries bought a country seat with the intention of permanently residing there; the associates' identities were too closely tied to London, and often months went by without a visit to nearby villas. After buying the Dalvey estate in Moray, Grant disavowed any plans to retire to the North or even to make it a retreat; true to his word, he visited this demesne only eight times in twenty-seven years. Mill visited Old Montrose on three occasions in the last decade of his life. And Scott went to Crailing Hall even less frequently.[23]

The associates bought freehold estates to establish their heirs' economic security and their family's social standing, rather than to provide them with returns and residences. This function of owning land – "leaving a legacy" – went to the heart of the enhancement of their status, and was the primary motivating factor at work in building their estates.

22. Smith, *Wealth of Nations*, v. 1, p. 374 (II.v.37); William Marshall, *The Rural Economy of the Midland Counties*, v. 2 (London, 1790), p. 139; GD 345/1164/3/95: Sir Alexander Grant to Sir Archibald Grant, September 3, 1756; GD 345/1166/4/33–34x, 23: Sir Alexander Grant to Sir Archibald Grant, October 25, 1760, August 14, 1759; and Allen, "Price of Freehold Land," p. 34.

23. GD 345/1160/3/1: Alexander Grant to Sir Archibald Grant, January 1, 1750; and GD 345/1179/282: Alexander Grant to Captain Archibald Grant, October 9, 1755.

Years before he bought Dalvey, for example, Grant broadcast his desire to find "a small purchase" on which to settle his younger brother; and, when the London merchant finally bought the estate, he placed his brother's family in the main house. While Grant's brother, in the merchant's opinion was childish and needy, he was still the father of the childless merchant's heirs. Even though he had no plans or desire to live in the North himself, Grant was very willing "to furnish money to render the place agreeable to whomsoever it may fall" after him. Land would provide "for the future generation's benefit" and "prevent disputes" among successors.[24]

The act of leaving a legacy, of course, was not solely directed to the heir or family. Land, with a sufficiently high valued rent, was also "the key to participation in local and national politics." It enabled an owner to sit as a member of the lieutenancy, a commissioner of supply, or a heretor of the parish. Possession of English freehold land valued at or above 40 shillings per annum, or ownership of a Scottish superiority valued at £400 Scots (£35 sterling) qualified an owner to select parliamentary representatives. "Property was a foundation on which a parliamentary interest could be built," as Sir Lewis Namier pointed out years ago, for the more votes a family had, the more political influence it possessed.[25]

When Grant pointed out to the chief of the clan that his "having an estate" in Inverness and Nairn "will add a little to your interest," he was being disingenuous.[26] By buying Dalvey, his family stood to gain by a rise in social profile; a country estate, if "ornamented and improved," did "Honour to the Owner, and raises the Emulation of others." In the social sphere, Grant realized, "a Gentleman" could not promote his

---

24. GD 248/172/3/12: Alexander Grant to Sir Ludovick Grant, March 2, 1747; GD 345/1160/3/1: Alexander Grant to Sir Archibald Grant, January 1, 1750; GD 345/1179/282: Alexander Grant to Captain Archibald Grant, October 9, 1755; and GD 345/1165/1/114: Sir Alexander Grant to Sir Archibald Grant, October 24, 1758.
25. Namier and Brooke, *House of Commons*, v. 1, pp. 2, 13, 38, 43; and Ann E. Whetstone, *Scottish County Government in the Eighteenth and Nineteenth Centuries* (Edinburgh, 1981), pp. 74–75, 139. A citizen could also qualify as an elector by possessing 40 shillings "of the auld extent" but, by 1750, recourse to this method was infrequent. William Ferguson, "The Electoral System in the Scottish Counties before 1832," *Miscellany Two* (Edinburgh, 1984), pp. 267, 276.
26. GD 248/173/3: Alexander Grant to Sir Ludovick Grant, July 15, September 12, 1749; and GD 248/221/2: Sir Alexander Grant to Sir James Grant, February 12, 1767. Under the Property Qualification Act of 1711, an owner of land valued at £600 or more could stand as a county representative. Pickering, *Statutes at Large*, v. 12 (1764), pp. 89–92; and B. W. Hill, *The Growth of Parliamentary Parties, 1689–1742* (London, 1976), p. 131. Yet, see John Plumb's *The Growth of Political Stability in England, 1675–1725* (London, 1967), p. 143, which argues that the Act "failed totally."

interest "in any way with greater advantage" than by acquiring and improving land. To look like "a county gentleman," it was "absolutely necessary" to buy land.[27] Land demonstrated good character. Buying and improving land balanced the purportedly lavish and indolent life style of corrupt Londoners with the virtuous *via activa* of simple and productive farmers. It created "some timeless Elysium," a spa to which London merchants like the associates could resort for clean air and clear thinking. Good character, in their minds, had scientific and religious dimensions. Owning land obligated them to concern themselves with the productivity of the region, and to experiment with ways to improve it. But improving land was as much an act of repentance and reformation as it was of scientific experimentation; it was a commitment to agricultural society. Accordingly, they believed that "God gave Man the earth *ut operatur*," and they felt that it was incumbent on Man "to repent of his sins & improve the ground."[28]

It is within this context that we should view the oft-stated desire to help, to be useful, to assist the public – a wish that was central to the associates' acquisition of land. "We are all born, or ought to be [born], to serve one another." Since "the original destination of man" was "to cultivate the ground," service (as Grant defined it) started with the purchase of land and the build-up of estates. But it did not end there. Increasing the capacity of one's estates meant promoting the welfare of one's community. Not coincidentally, just as he was purchasing his estate, Grant decided on a motto for his family crest: *te favente virebo*, that is, "I will grow green serving you."[29]

Farms

Closely linked to the landed estate was the component that has been most commonly considered in discussions of improvement – the farm. Eighteenth-century thinkers as different as Adam Smith and Edward Gibbon agreed that agriculture was the crucial sector of the national and imperial economy, and that the farm was the most important institution. Smith, in fact, believed that agriculture was the most productive economic activity, with manufacturing following it, and commerce last.

27. John Maxwell to William Pulteney, December 16, 1773, Pulteney Papers, PU 1560; John Sargent to Benjamin Franklin, January 3, 1783, American Philosophical Society, Philadelphia; and Tucker, *Instructions*.
28. GD 345/1160/31: Alexander Grant to Sir Archibald Grant, January 1, 1750; Walter Johnstone to William Pulteney, April 18, 1761, Pulteney Papers, PU 719, Huntington Library, San Marino; and Smith, *Wealth of Nations*, v. 1, p. 378 (III.i.3).
29. Richard Oswald to Caleb Whitefoord, April 15, 1784, Add.Mss. 36,596, BL; GD 345/1162/3/31x: Alexander Grant to Sir James Johnstone, December 23, 1752; and John Stevenson to Richard Oswald, November 28, 1764, Oswald Papers, EUL.

The natural order of things, as he described it, was agricultural. Gibbon, writing one year after the publication of *The Wealth of Nations*, echoed Smith's sentiment, contending for different reasons that agriculture was "the foundation of manufactures," since "the productions of nature are the materials of art." Both agreed that land was central to preserving virtue in a republic.[30] The equation of virtue with the work of the farm rang true with Georgian readers who believed that one of the principal tasks of society, in an economic sense, was "the forceful imposition of culture upon what was wild." All activity was in this sense "farming": breeding, cultivating, building harbors and roads, and shipping were viewed as "Imperial Works, and worthy Kings." Not a few contemporaries agreed with Jonathan Swift that farmers (broadly defined) "do more essential service" to their country "than the whole race of politicians put together."[31]

Within this web of ideological meanings was situated a relation among self-improvement, farming, and social improvement. Farming established the independence of the landowner and humanized the wild countryside. Lord Kames, the contemporary of Smith and Gibbon and the friend of Grant and Oswald, was one who saw the connections clearly. He opened *The Gentleman Farmer* (1776), which he hoped would be used by "gentlemen of land-estates," with the admission that agriculture was "of all occupations the best adapted to gentlemen in a private station." It required "a degree of exercise, which is the best preservative of health." It kept "the mind always awake, and in an enlivening degree of agitation." Most importantly, it merged private and public interests. "How pleasing to think," he concluded, "that every step a man makes for his own good, promotes that of his country!" While we may regard Kames's analysis of gentlemen-farmers "serving their country and themselves at home, which is genuine patriotism," as overwrought, this was the construction placed upon farming by the associates themselves.[32]

By the eighteenth century, an "agricultural revolution" was sweeping the land.[33] Kames's "science" and "rational principles" were being applied

---

30. Smith, *Wealth of Nations*, v. 1, p. 360 (II.v.1–2); and Gibbon, *Decline and Fall*, v. 1. p. 54.
31. Pope, *Epistle IV: To Richard Boyle, Earl of Burlington* (London, 1731); Jonathan Swift, *Gulliver's Travels* (London, 1965), p. 126; and James Thomson, *Liberty, The Castle of Indolence and Other Poems* (Oxford, 1986), p. 204 (ii.19). See also Shields, *Oracles of Empire*, p. 71; and Maren-Sofie Rostvig, *The Happy Man: Studies in the Metamorphoses of a Classical Ideal*, v. 2 (Oslo, 1958).
32. Henry Home, Lord Kames, *The Gentleman Farmer*, 4th ed. (first published, 1776; Edinburgh, 1798), pp. xiv, xvi, xviii, 37.
33. The term "agricultural revolution" was first applied to the eighteenth century by Naomi Riches, *The Agricultural Revolution in Norfolk* (Chapel Hill, 1937), a revision of her 1934 University of Chicago Ph.D. dissertation.

to agriculture by men like Oswald and Grant. Gentlemen farmers formed agricultural reading and discussion groups in the first half of the century, in London, where the associates were active members, and in almost every major market town. The force of these groups was especially strong in Scotland, where the first society in Europe was founded in Edinburgh (1723). Numerous offshoots sprang up in the succeeding decades: Buchan (1730); East Lothian (1736); Ayr (1748); Aberdeen (by 1752); Elgin (by 1763); and Dumfries and Galloway (1776). For the associates, these groups were a means of bringing new ideas to their attention, as well as of promoting intercourse between themselves and the hereditary agricultural elite. The work of the societies was assisted by an outpouring of practical and theoretical writing on the "new" farming that presented agriculture and husbandry as "a rational and intelligible system."[34] Around 1750, writers began to render a more scientific account of farming practice, praising certain methods and denigrating others. No longer were agricultural treatises primarily a regurgitation of facts, a compendium of ancients, or a moral and spiritual rumination on the activities of farmers. Many writers now expressed concern for the social relations that characterized the estate. Others writers outlined general theories and tried to create systematic, scientific, profit-driven programs for enhanced production. Experts focused on actual experiences, recorded by contemporaries and subjected to revision by readers.[35]

At the same time, gentlemen farmers implemented more vigorous programs of agricultural reform on the lands they had purchased with the windfalls of war and trade. Old farming methods were stopped and new ones adopted. The number of acres under cultivation grew, and output rose by 40 or 50 percent over the course of the century.[36] Land

34. Handley, *Agricultural Revolution*, p. 74. An excellent discussion of the opportunities and problems faced by the Dumfries, Wigtown, and Kirkcudbright Society appears in Edward J. Cowan, "Agricultural Improvement," *Transactions of the Dumfries and Galloway Natural History and Antiquarian Society*, v. 53 (1977–78), pp. 157–67. For society-sponsored writing, see Maxwell, ed., *Select Transactions*.

35. Mingay and Chambers, *Agricultural Revolution*, p. 73; and William Doyle, *The Old European Order, 1660–1800* (Oxford, 1978), p. 22. Among the earlier writers were William Ellis, John Lawrence, Jethro Tull, and Grant's grandfather William Mackintosh. Cf. William Mackintosh, *Essay on the Husbandry of Scotland* (Edinburgh, 1730); and Sir Archibald Grant of Monymusk, *The Farmer's New-Year's Gift to His Countrymen* (Edinburgh, 1757), *Dissertation on the Chief Obstacles to the Improvement of Land* . . . (Edinburgh, 1760), and *Practical Farmer's Pocket-Companion* (Edinburgh, 1766). Keith Tribe discusses the shift from early eighteenth-century analysis to "a new mode of writing." *Land, Labour and Economic Discourse* (London, 1978), ch. 4.

36. Mingay and Chambers, *Agricultural Revolution*, p. 34; and A. H. John, "The Course of Agricultural Change, 1660–1760," in L. S. Pressnell, ed., *Studies in the Industrial Revolution* (London, 1960), p. 152. For the view that growth slowed in 1750–1800, see R. V. Jackson, "Growth and Deceleration in English Agriculture, 1660–1790," *Economic History Review*, 2nd ser., v. 38 (1985), pp. 333, 349–50.

enclosure reached its peak in the middle decades of the century, perhaps later in Scotland than in England. The open field and runrig (land in separate ridges tilled by different tenants) systems were slowly replaced by enclosure and parcel consolidation. Improvers were aggressively investing in farming infrastructure at the same time. In the early 1700s, for instance, Oswald's Kirkcudbrightshire had no mills, no cattle, and only two carts for hire; neither wheat nor potatoes were grown. After 1750, agricultural change quickened and new tools, techniques, and crops were introduced and became widespread, so that, by 1770, farming in that county was almost unrecognizable to those who had known it before – new crops like turnips, new tools like Small's plough, new crop rotation schemes, rectangular fields and trimmed hedges, and better market facilities. In Scotland, "farmers of some more than common substance or ingenuity" were encouraged "by chances of uncommon profite from pretty large tracts of land" to think of agriculture and husbandry "as a science and trade." In the process, they made themselves appear respectable, drawing attention to what were considered "Roman" virtues like independence and productivity, and exercising a kind of lordship that they imagined had prevailed in Tudor and Stuart Britain.[37]

Oswald, Grant, Mill, Scott, Herries, and the Andersons participated in Scotland's agricultural renaissance, laying their lands "under regulations to inclose and plant" and settling tenants "upon the farm" for "a limited time." The associates pushed their agricultural improvement program in three phases.[38] Fixing "marches" (that is, settling boundaries) had to be done first. Land was not a good investment if it lacked sound title or was saddled with encumbrances. The associates, therefore, extinguished prior claims to the land or, at least, worked to insulate their heirs against them, sometimes by resorting to third-party arbitrators who renegotiated and straightened bounds for them. Enclosing the lands surveyed followed hard on settling boundaries. Everywhere the level of the legal and physical protection of agricultural investments was impressive: the number of enclosure Acts passed by Parliament rose from approximately 25 in the 1720s, to 137 in the 1750s, to 660 in the 1770s. Many more areas were enclosed by neighborly agreement, for which no Act was required. In Moray, Grant always raised borders from quicks and trees along his boundaries as

37. GD 1/268/1: John Maxwell to William M. Herries, February 8, 1811; T. Smout and A. Fenton, "Scottish Agriculture before the Improvers – An Explanation," *The Agricultural History Review*, v. 13 (1965), pp. 73, 82; Slaven, *Development*, pp. 62–64, 67–77; and R. H. Campbell, "The Population of the South–West of Scotland from the Mid-Eighteenth Century to 1911," *Transactions of the Dumfries and Galloway Natural History and Antiquarian Society*, v. 60 (1985), pp. 83, 88, 91.
38. Cf. Grant, "Friendly Hints," c. 1764, in Fraser, *Chiefs of Grant*, v. 2, pp. 442–44; and Notebook, Dumfries Papers A1098, Dumfries House, Cumnock.

soon as the ink was dry on his agreements, and Oswald did the same
in Ayr, to separate their lands from the intrusion of outsiders. This
practice, they argued, raised legal safeguards and promoted greater
efficiencies in farming, by separating animals from crops and preventing
the former from despoiling the latter.[39]

Having settled the boundaries and enclosed the properties, the associates had to decide whether to lease the lands to tenants or develop the
farms themselves. Treatise writers and celebrated improvers of the day
urged them to lease, and they seem to have done so in most instances,
especially since London merchants had little time to oversee their farms
personally. Oswald granted all but the home farms at Auchincruive and
Cavens to tenants, and Grant, Johnson, Mill, and Scott did the same on
their estates. The associates' leases provided for relatively high levels of
landlord cooperation with the tenants – a show of beneficence was a
mark of gentility – in exchange for carrying out detailed programs of
improvement. In one typical twenty-one-year lease struck in 1766,
Oswald agreed to build a house, a barn, and a stable for the tenant and
a dike to defend the property against flooding from high tides, and to
pay all public assessments on the property, except multures (tolls of
grain or flour paid to the local miller). In return, the tenant agreed to
pay £150 per year for the first seven years, and £200 per year thereafter; above the rent, he agreed to pay 6 percent interest on expenditures
incurred by enclosing, dividing, and draining the farm; and to implement
a comprehensive "plan of management" for manuring "croft" land and
rotating crops over three years. Penalties in the form of additional rent
were charged for overcropping. Outfield arable land and "bogue pasture ground" were subjected to similarly restrictive regulations.[40]

On both their home farms and their tenanted estates, the associates

39. Information for this and the following paragraph appears in GD 345/1160/4/75–76x:
   Sir Archibald Grant, Report, October 1750; GD 125/30/loose: Sir Alexander Grant
   to Hugh Rose, October 29, 1763; and John Maxwell to Richard Oswald, September
   28, 1766, Oswald Letter Book, SRO. On boundaries, see Richard Oswald to Robert
   Wallace, November 24, 1769, Robert Wallace to Richard Oswald, November 28,
   1769, Oswald Papers, Sudlows; and John Maxwell to Richard Oswald, March 1, 1770,
   Oswald Letter Book, v. 3, f. 73. On enclosure, see GD 248/99/6/26: Sir Alexander
   Grant to Sir Ludovick Grant, October 2, 1766; GD 248/681/4: Lord Findlater to Sir
   Alexander Grant, July 1, 1769; GD 345/1171/1769: Sir Alexander Grant to Sir Archibald
   Grant, September 22, 1769; John Maxwell to William Johnston, March 19, 1764, and
   George Malcolm to William Johnston, April 7, 1767, Pulteney Papers, PU 1560, and
   PU 860, Huntington Library, San Marino; and Pawson, *Transport*, pp. 128–29.
40. Typical leases are discussed in Oswald Letter Book, v. 3, ff. 23–26, 39, September 8,
   1766, May 1, 1767, SRO; Memo, October 19–21, August 1, 1774, Oswald Papers,
   Sudlows; Richard Oswald to John Maxwell, December 9, 1780, Oswald Letter Book,
   v. 3, ff. 259–60. Sir Archibald had already advised Alexander Grant to set out his
   entire estate on long leases. GD 345/1160/4/75–76x. A discussion of risk and the
   rental contract appears in Avner Offer, "Farm Tenure and Land Values in England,
   c. 1750–1950," *Economic History Review*, v. 44 (1991), pp. 6, 11–13.

reworked lands that had been neglected for generations. Soils had to be leveled, wetlands drained, and crops introduced. Often, the associates employed old methods, like burning and blasting, but they also experimented with new methods and machines, like the contraption Oswald brought from Jamaica to uproot trees.[41] Once freed of stones and stumps, the lands had to be plowed, fertilized, and sown with grasses, crops, or trees, if they were not turned into pasture. It was this aspect of farming that the associates most enjoyed. At Auchincruive and Cavens, Oswald tried new plows that had been exhibited at the meetings of the London Society for the Encouragement of Arts, Manufactures, and Commerce. He tested new forms of fertilizer and, after numerous trials, boasted of a particularly promising concoction of lime and manure. Through trial and error, he eventually earned great acclaim for his "improvement of the soil" and succeeded in drawing the attention of Scotland to the potential of the wet clay and sandy soil of Ayrshire when improved with his mixture. Better fertilizer, he was convinced, raised the likelihood of an increase in pasture yield, which in turn enhanced the quality of the livestock.[42] In fertilizing and other improving matters, Oswald adhered when he could to the principles enumerated by Jethro Tull and Oswald's neighbor William Craik.[43] On Craik's advice, Oswald ordered his farmers to place potato and turnip seeds in holes and furrows "in the drill way," rather than broadcasting them with the wind. He had

41. Sir Alexander Grant to Sir Robert Gordon, March 27, 1764, La.II.498, EUL; John Maxwell to Richard Oswald, March 5, 1766, Oswald Letter Book, v. 3, f. 17, SRO; John Maxwell to William Johnston, November 26, 1764, George Malcolm to William Pulteney, March 12, 1771, Pulteney Papers, PU 1538 and PU 1516, Huntington Library, San Marino.
42. Agriculture Committee Minute Books, 1766–67, ff. 1–2, 23–24, 54–58, 60–61, Royal Society of Arts, London; and Description, 1775, Pulteney Papers, PU 1675, Huntington Library, San Marino. On manure, see John Maxwell to Richard Oswald, December 23, 1774, Oswald Letter Book, v. 3, f. 157; and Memo, August 18, 1770, Oswald Papers, Sudlows. Liming releases inert organic fertilizers in the soil. In the 1770s, the value of shell lime was well-known; with "its peculiar Unctuousness as well as Strength," it was "a most valuable and lasting Manure." *The London Chronicle*, April 25–27, 1758; and James Alexander, *A Dissertation on Quick Lime* (Glasgow, 1779). After 1750, the use of lime in Ayrshire was widespread. C. A. Whatley, "The Industrialization of Ayrshire" (University of Strathclyde, Ph.D. dissert, 1975), pp. 311–16. Oswald's work in Ayrshire was reported in Andrew Wight, *A Present State of Husbandry*, v. 3 (Edinburgh, 1777), pp. 200–01. At Auchincruive and Cavens, Oswald dug lime quarries; to supplement their supply, he arranged for a boat to make regular trips between Ireland and Ayr. In Moray, Grant used a mixture of dung and lime. GD 345/1160/4/75–76x.
43. GD 1/168/1: John Maxwell to William Herries, February 8, 1811. On Craik, see G. W. Shirley, "Two Pioneer Galloway Agriculturalists – Robert Maxwell of Arkland and William Craik of Arbigland," *Transactions of the Dumfries and Galloway Natural History and Antiquarian Society*, 3rd ser., v. 13 (1927), pp. 129–61; "Account of William Craik, Esq., of Arbigland," *The Farmer's Magazine*, No. 46 (1811), pp. 145–65; and A. Truckell, W. Duncan, and T. Scott, *Kirkbean: Parish and Kirk* (Kirkbean, 1976).

them till the ground throughout the year with an English plow. And he required them to integrate new fodder crops into a three- or six-year rotation, imposing what agricultural historians have so frequently considered to be the fundamental improvement of the age.[44]

If Oswald succeeded in his improvements, it was because he proceeded cautiously, experimenting with new techniques and treating his workers leniently by the standards of the time. Although it is not the image of the improver passed down by contemporary or subsequent commentators, a picture of Oswald as a landlord fiercely intent on establishing close, long-term relations with his workers and tenants emerges from his estate correspondence. He delegated responsibility to capable and reliable farm managers; in the unusual situation that they failed him, he moved quickly to replace them. He let to tenants that he regarded as virtuous and trustworthy, after subjecting them to a grueling round of interviews and getting them to agree to his program for the land. He assisted them with housing, training, and a lenient consideration of arrears. The respect and love of one's laborers, he knew from his treatises and actual experiences, was a mark of polite status. In managing his tenants and estates in this manner, he was projecting an image of a latter-day paterfamilias, an hospitable "Ancient Baron."[45] In

44. John Maxwell to Richard Oswald, June 17, 1769, October 16, 1776, Oswald Letter Book, v. 3, ff. 63, 213, SRO. Oswald used both the Rotherham plow and James Small's swing plow rather than the more cumbersome Scotch plow. Plowing was a difficult task, especially in southwestern Scotland where farmers had to cope with "excessive moisture, a fugitive sun, and soils" that were often waterlogged. Slaven, *Development*, pp. 58–78. On crop rotations, see John Maxwell to Richard Oswald, September 8, 1766, October 16, 1776, Oswald Letter Book, v. 3, ff. 23–26, 213, SRO; Memo, October 20, 1770, Oswald Papers, Sudlows; Scheme, September 13, 1776, Pulteney Papers, PU 1615; and Mingay and Chambers, *Agricultural Revolution*, p. 54. Suggestions about plants were obtained from a variety of sources: personal acquaintances, seed societies, professional gardeners, and publications. On Oswald obtaining plants and seeds from Edinburgh, see John Maxwell to Richard Oswald, December 7, 1772, December 23, 1774, Oswald Letter Book, v. 3, ff. 17, 116–18, 157, SRO; and Memo, March 5, 1766, April 1, 15, 1770, Maxwell Letter Book, Oswald Papers, Sudlows. Newspapers were filled with advertisements of gardening books and plant specimens. *The Edinburgh Advertiser*, June 18, 1765; January 28, February 16, 1768; and January 20, 1769. Georgian books on farming are cataloged in G. E. Fussell, *Chronological List of Early Agricultural Works in the Library of the Ministry of Agriculture and Fisheries* (London, 1930), pp. 5–21.

45. Factors, like John Maxwell of Terraughty, were often active in the affairs of several landowners at the same time. Maxwell served not only Oswald but also the Duke of Queensberry and the Earl of Nithsdale. On the work of a factor, see Ian D. Grant, "Landlord and Land Management in Northeastern Scotland, 1750–1850" (University of Edinburgh, Ph.D. dissert, 1978), pp. 206–22. Maxwell's son William was made supervisor at Auchincruive in 1770, but was fired for mismanaging funds. John Maxwell to Richard Oswald, February 9, 1775, October 16, 1776, July 11, 1778, and February 15, 1779, Oswald Letter Book, v. 3, ff. 161–63, 213–27, SRO. On lenient treatment of tenants, see John Maxwell to Richard Oswald, March 6, 1784, Oswald Letter Book, v. 3, ff. 316–19, SRO.

assuming the mantle of agricultural virtue, investing in the county, and exercising virtuous lordship over its people – enriching what his library books, chimney reliefs, and oil paintings reminded him was the basis of a civilized society – Oswald argued his case for inclusion in the society of gentlemen. By politely beating the hereditary rulers of the neighborhood at their own game with a regimen of industry, competence, and control in farming, Oswald could join the ranks of gentlemen.

"Works of Lasting Benefit to the Country"

In playing the part of the county laird, the associates also worked on revivifying local economies. In particular, they focused their energies on three areas of life in the countryside: transportation, manufacture, and philanthropy. They worked alone and in cooperation with their neighbors, especially the traditional county elites; and often they combined commercial with charitable goals, doing well by doing good. In all of these activities, they sought to build a good bourgeois elysium: fiscally sound, morally virtuous, and commercial successful.

The third quarter of the eighteenth century was a boom time for transportation. The changes wrought during these years laid the foundation for nearly all subsequent economic advances in Britain, by connecting and widening her markets. "Good roads, canals, and navigable rivers," Adam Smith claimed, were "the greatest of all improvements," and recent scholarship upholds the boast: whether by sea, river, or road, "local and regional markets were linked together through steadily improving transport services, which distributed goods."[46] In southeastern England, southwestern Scotland, and northeastern Scotland, the associates played their part in building roads and bridges[47] and, to a lesser extent, canals and lighthouses.[48] They used their business and

---

46. Smith, *Wealth of Nations*, p. 163 (I.xi.b.5); and Brewer, *Sinews*, p. 183.
47. On roads, see Pawson, *Transport*, pp. 13, 91, 113–15; and Alexander K. Goodwin, "Road Development in Ayrshire, 1750–1835" (M.Litt. thesis, University of Strathclyde, 1970), p. 26.
48. On canals, see *The London Chronicle*, June 20, 23, 1767; Barker, "The Beginnings of the Canal Age," pp. 1–22; Jean Lindsay, *The Canals of Scotland* (Newton Abbot, 1968), ch. 1; and "The Great Canal," *Issues in Accountability*, v. 3, pp. 30–31. The first large-scale canal in England, the Sankey canal, was opened in 1757. Most of the Scottish associates were involved in a later project linking the Firth of Forth to the Firth of Clyde. They gave generously: Grant (£200), Mill (£1,000), Scott (£1,000), and Oswald (£1,000). A List, 1767, H 654/76–79; Memorial, 1777, H 655/88A-9; and Reconsideration 1778, H 655/90, Hopeton House. They attended its stockholder meetings and lobbied for it in Parliament. GD 248/221/2: Sir Alexander Grant to Sir James Grant, April 28, May 5, 1767, Sir Alexander Grant to Sir Ludovick Grant, April 30, 1767; GD 248/99/6/41: Sir Alexander Grant to Sir Ludovick Grant, December

social networks to obtain expert assistance for their projects; they drew upon their management experience to bring together laborers and supplies in construction projects; and they provided financial support for new construction and offered moral support to other projectors.

Consider Oswald's Ayrshire. At midcentury, the county was known for the ruinous condition of its roads; the soil was deep in some places, rugged and narrow in others; many roads were "impassable in Winter, for wheel carriages and horses, and very dangerous for travellers."[49] Most roads were made of clay and gravel, and only a few had stone strips in the center to ease the horses' movement. Road construction and repair were the responsibility of individual landowners and justice-of-the-peace trusts, but both groups, seriously strapped for cash and unable to muster sufficient labor, neglected their charges. It was not until 1766 that concerned residents – many, like Oswald, new to the district – banded together to search for a remedy, having given up on official channels.[50] The corrective they chose was the "public" turnpike trust. Compared to justice-of-the-peace trusts, the public turnpike trusts vested decision-making power in local landowners as trustees, who possessed a greater stake in the outcome than did appointed officeholders. Compared to individual landowners, the turnpike trustees had more money at their disposal – gifts, subscriptions, loans, and toll earnings collected by the trustees – and were therefore better equipped to support administrators and pay laborers. Prodded by Oswald and several

22, 1767; and Hope Mss., H 655/117, Hopeton House. On lighthouses, see *Journals of the House of Commons*, v. 27, p. 361 (January 15, 1756; March 3, 1756); Renwick, ed., *Extracts*, v. 6 (1911), pp. 472, 522; R. W. Munro, *Scottish Lighthouses* (Stornoway, Lewis, 1979), pp. 43–47; John Maxwell to Richard Oswald, October 17, 1781, Oswald Letter Book, v. 3, f. 275; A. Graham and A. Truckell, "Old Harbours in the Solway Firth," *Transactions of the Dumfries and Galloway Natural History and Antiquarian Society*, 3rd ser., v. 52 (1976–77), pp. 139–40; Munro, *Scottish Lighthouses*, pp. 42–43; and Geoffrey Stell, "Southerness Lighthouse," *Transactions of the Dumfries and Galloway Natural History and Antiquarian Society*, 3rd ser., v. 59 (1984), pp. 64–69.

49. On Ayr's roads, see Earl of Cassilis, Patrick Boyle, and Alexander Boswell to [Earl of Loudoun], February 13, 1759, and Earl of Dumfries to Earl of Loudoun, July 31, 1760, Loudoun Papers, LO (Scotch) 7,318, and 11,002. Dumfries roads were no better. George Malcolm to William Pulteney, April 26, 1770, Pulteney Papers, PU 905, Huntington Library, San Marino. For road building in Kirkcudbright, see C. A. S. Maitland, *Commissioners of Supply for the Stewartry of Kirkcudbright, 1728–1828* (Dalbeattie, 1933), pp. 82–93; and Alexander Anderson, "The Development of the Road System in the Stewartry of Kirkcudbright, 1590–1890," *Transactions of the Dumfries and Galloway Natural History and Antiquarian Society*, 3rd ser., v. 44 (1967), pp. 204–22.

50. Goodwin, "Road Development," pp. 20–22. In discussing late eighteenth-century road building, Whetstone, in *County Government*, places too much emphasis on government work.

other landowners, Parliament conferred its approval on the arrangement in a Private Act of 1767, the first of its kind in Scotland.[51]

Trustees were appointed and met for the next twenty years. They assumed responsibility for all the roads in Ayr, and delegated supervision of individual roads to subsidiary committees. At the first general meeting of the trust, Oswald was named a member and, over the years, he sat on four subcommittees. He attended whenever he was in residence at Auchincruive; at other times, he sent his factor as proxy.[52] He supported construction projects, even when the roads did not abut his properties; on one occasion, he gave £200 toward the building of a distant road and, on another occasion, absorbed the entire cost of building a toll house. He involved himself in all aspects of road repair. Given his love of minutiae and problem-solving, he relished the chance to advise others on construction, whether the subject was materials, drainage, or dimensions. Selecting routes to be repaired was a less congenial assignment, since it interfered with the improvements of one's neighbors, but he did not shy away from this job; indeed, he seemed to relish mapping the roads. The result was the complete transformation of Ayr's transportation infrastructure: old roads on which coal could not have been carried more than two miles in 1763 were fully traversable in 1784, and four new roads, 100 miles in all, which did not exist when he bought Auchincruive were by his death major arteries connecting various parts of the county to its center. Some fifty-six new roads were laid down in Ayr between 1766 and 1775 and, for most projects, Oswald provided some assistance.[53] By the last decade of his life, bridges and

51. Whetstone, *County Government*, pp. 81–88. On the 1767 Act (7 Geo. III, c. 106), see Pickering, *Statutes at Large*, v. 27, p. 616; and *Journal of the House of Commons*, v. 31, pp. 73, 400, 412, 415. After 1766, many counties followed Ayr's example and applied to Parliament for the right to commandeer statute labor. Pawson, *Transport*, p. 91; and Whetstone, *County Government*, pp. 86–87.

52. CO 3/4/1/5,7,10,11,204, SRA-Ayr; and Goodwin, "Road Development," pp. 33, 141. On Oswald in Ayr, see CO 3/4/1/5,7,10,11,204, SRA-Ayr. From July 1767, he sat on the Ayr-Mauchline-Douglas committee, the Ayr-Ochiltree-Sanquhar committee, the Ayr-Shawsbridge-Galston-Strathaven committee and, after June 1774, the Ayr-Coylston-St. Quivox-Monckton committee. He was also named to a committee for ascertaining the valuation of parishes by which the conversion of statute labor might take place. He attended four countywide meetings in the first two years: October 28, 29, 1767; September 7, October 5, 1768. Thereafter, his attendance was more sporadic: August 9, 1772; August 29, 1776; and June 7, 1780. CO 3/4/1/20,28,156,257,289 and CO 3/5/3/62–65, SRA-Ayr.

53. Robert Wallace to Richard Oswald, November 28, 1769, Memo, May 20, August 18, 1770, and William Cunningham to Richard Oswald, July 22, 1780, Oswald Papers, Sudlows; John Maxwell to Richard Oswald, May 22, 1776, Oswald Letter Book, v. 3, f. 207; Earl of Loudoun to Richard Oswald, September 8, 1767, Alexander Montgomerie to Richard Oswald, October 1, 1767, Earl of Loudoun to Richard Oswald, October 7, 1767, Alexander Forsyth to Richard Oswald, August 8, 1768,

roads he had built and financed linked his estate to the town of Ayr and its harbor, the limeworks and coalworks he had opened in the neighborhood, his new salt pans north of the town, a local wool factory in which he was a partner, other properties he owned in Kirkcudbright, and the cities of Glasgow, Edinburgh, and London.[54]

Building roads hardly fits our idea of Georgian gentility, yet it produced some of the most public examples of good works performed by aspiring gentlemen. In justifying these activities to themselves, the associates drew the analogy to charity. As Oswald tells it, he once heard "a very good sermon" on charity and it "left some impression." But he thought it

> a great pity that the dignity of the pulpit will not admit of a particular application to the mending of bad roads – which I think have as just a claim to the exercise of those virtues as most other cases of distress. Of this I was strongly convinced on a visit we lately made at Stair. It's a great loss that Mr. Steel [the minister] travels generally on horseback. If he went in a carriage as we did, I'm sure he would pick out a Text that would be of Lasting Benefit to the Country.

Oswald viewed road building as the moral equivalent of poor relief: county employment rose with the turnpike trusts' addition of contract and trust laborers, often paupers and the elderly, and good roads reduced the isolation of the country "as the active interchange of commodities and ideas superseded the encapsulation of early eighteenth-century life." His altruism was, of course, partially self-serving. Good roads made his life and his improvements easier. They enhanced the look of his neighborhood, which in turn polished his image. Oswald and men like him believed that good roads separated them from "a people only emerging from a state of barbarism." Moreover, they gave him another opportunity to mix with his social superiors. Ayr's committee rosters show Oswald working with the most genteel members of Ayr society. At these meetings, he gained a social quid pro quo because, in laying out the roads and funding their construction, he came to the aid of his

---

Earl of Dumfries to Richard Oswald, March 8, 1770, and David Limond to Richard Oswald, November 14, 1770, April 6, 7, 29, October 19, 26, 1776, January 16, 1777, Oswald Papers, Sudlows.

54. Oswald was not the only associate interested in roads. For Grant, see GD 345/1165/2/23: Sir Alexander Grant to Sir Archibald Grant, August 14, 1759; James Stewart Mackenzie to Sir Robert Gordon, October 24, 1763, Sir Alexander Grant to Sir Robert Gordon, October 27, 1763, Sir Alexander Grant to Sir Robert Gordon, February 16, March 27, 1764, Gordon Papers, La.II.498, EUL; GD 248/178/2/24: Sir Robert Gordon to Sir Ludovick Grant, February 5, 1764. For John Boyd, see St. Mary's Vestry Minutes, May 3, 1768, Hall Place, Bexley, Kent. For Herries, see Petition of David Lamont, July 10, 1798, SP 2079, Signet Library Edinburgh.

neighbors and created a form of debt that on more than one occasion was remembered long after his death.[55]

The associates also participated in local industrial ventures. We know from other sources that, in establishing themselves as urban gentlemen, Leeds and Glasgow merchants acquired shares in a large number of manufacturing ventures and, in time, came to dominate their regions' industries.[56] London merchants who moved into the counties in the second half of the century did the same. Even an incomplete reconstruction of the associates' industrial portfolios suggests a wider range of commitment than is generally recognized. They invested in maritime undertakings, especially whaling[57]; the making of cloth, mainly wool[58]; mining, particularly salt, coal, and lime[59]; and the production of building

55. GD 3/5: Richard Oswald to Alexander Montgomerie, October 20, 1771; Gibbon, *Decline*, v. 1, pp. 43, 50–51; Slaven, *Development*, p. 65; Macpherson, *Annals*, v. 3, p. 360; Goodwin, "Development," p. 108.

56. T. M. Devine, "The Colonial Trades and Industrial Investment in Scotland, c. 1700–1815," *Economic History Review*, 2nd ser., v. 29 (1976), pp. 3–4; and Wilson *Gentlemen Merchants*, pp. 137–58.

57. Grant was a director of the Inverness Fishing Chamber and the Aberdeen Whale Fishery. Magistrates to Alexander Grant, February 23, 1751, Highland Regional Archives, Inverness; GD 248/175/2: Alexander Grant to Sir Ludovick Grant, November 25, 1752; *Aberdeen Journal*, June 30, 1752, June 26, 1753; GD 345/1161/3/107x, 106x, 114, 104, 11: Alexander Grant to Sir Archibald Grant, July 16, 30, September 1, 19, October 26, November 18, 1752; GD 345/1162/2/17x: Alexander Grant to Sir Archibald Grant, March 1, 1753; W. Duncan, "Aberdeen and the Whaling Industry," *Northern Scotland*, v. 3 (1977), pp. 49–52; and R. Michie, "Northern Whale Fishing," *Northern Scotland*, v. 3 (1977–78), pp. 62–63. Grant also expressed interest in establishing a salmon "factory" near his Moray estate. GD 345/1160/4/149: Alexander Grant to Sir Archibald Grant, July 15, 1749, December 22, 1750, March 7, 1751.

58. Oswald was a partner in the Kilmarnock Woolen Factory (Cuninghame & Co.). Archibald McKay, *The History of Kilmarnock*, 4th ed. (Kilmarnock, 1880), pp. 108–11. He also owned shares in James Wilson & Co. of Kilmarnock. James Wilson & Co. to Richard Oswald, November 3, 1770; William Boyd to Richard Oswald, December 17, 1773, Oswald Papers, Sudlows; and Particular Register of Sasines-Ayr, v. 22, ff. 4–9 (June 19, 1773), SRO. In 1766, he worked to establish a Turkey carpet factory near Ayr. Daniel Bloom to Richard Oswald, October 23, 1766, Oswald Papers, EUL. On cloth manufacturing in Ayr, see R. H. Campbell, ed., *States of the Annual Progress of the Linen Manufacture, 1727–1754* (Edinburgh, 1964), pp. v–x; Alastair Durie, "The Scottish Linen Industry in the Eighteenth Century: Some Aspects of Expansion," in L. M. Cullen and T. C. Smout, eds., *Comparative Aspects of Scottish and Irish Economic History, 1600–1900* (Edinburgh, 1977), pp. 88–99; and Annette M. Smith, "State Aid to Industry – An Eighteenth Century Example," in T. M. Devine, ed., *Lairds and Improvements in the Scotland of the Enlightenment* (Edinburgh, 1978), pp. 47–58.

59. Oswald dug lime pits and coal mines near his estates. Maxwell Letter Book, August 31, 1772, Oswald Papers, Sudlows. On coal and lime, see Ian Donnachie, "The Lime Industry in South-West Scotland," *Transactions of the Dumfries and Galloway Natural History and Antiquarian Society*, 3rd ser., v. 48 (1971), pp. 146–52; Robert Douglas, "Coal-Mining in Fife in the Second Half of the Eighteenth Century," in G. Barrow, ed., *The Scottish Tradition: Essays in Honour of Ronald Gordon Cant* (Edinburgh, 1974), pp. 211–22; J. Nef, *The Rise of the British Coal Industry*, v. 1 (London, 1966); and Slaven, *Development*, pp. 111–14.

materials, such as lumber, rope, iron, and glass.[60] In most of these endeavors, they were not sleeping partners but active principals, taking charge of the support or management of operations. The profusion of their schemes for underdeveloped hinterlands is striking, particularly when we remember that the associates lived elsewhere for most of the year and that the lines of their businesses stretched not inland but outward across the seas.

In Oswald's Ayrshire, beginning in the 1740s and lasting through 1800, industrial activity was on the rise. In large part, this growth was driven by Irish demand for Ayrshire linen and coal. Local consumption also grew, for, as Ayr's population expanded and its economy developed, the need for coal, lime, and salt increased. Entrepreneurs built new salt pans, lime quarries, and coal mines to supply such materials. The salt pans Oswald ran at Maryburgh, several miles north of the town of Ayr, were one instance of this. Oswald bought his salt pans with ten acres of land at the same time that he bought Auchincruive, but at first he let the pans sit idle. Eventually, in 1766, he ordered two pan plates from a Boness distributor and installed them the following April. At the same time, he ordered the building of two pan houses to cover the plates and a dwelling house for the keeper of the pans. Production commenced in June 1767.[61] By 1772, his salt output had risen to 6,500 pounds. At first, Oswald managed the operation directly but,

---

60. No satisfactory study of the eighteenth-century timber industry in Scotland exists. Previous treatments have largely ignored the Spey Valley and the large contract held by Grant. Anderson, *Scottish Forestry*, v. 1, pp. 440–43, 450, 473–74; George A. Dixon, "William Lorimer on Forestry in the Central Highlands in the Early 1760s," *Scottish Forestry*, v. 29 (1975), pp. 191–210; W. Forsyth, *In the Shadow of Cairngorm: Chronicles of the United Parishes of Abernethy and Kincardine* (Inverness, 1900), pp. 198–203; David Nairne, "Notes on Highland Woods, Ancient and Modern," *Transactions of the Gaelic Society of Inverness*, v. 17 (1890–91), pp. 170–221; and H. Steven and A. Carlisle, *The Native Pinewoods of Scotland* (Edinburgh, 1959), pp. 111–21. Yet extensive documentation does exist for such a study. GD 248 (1741–56). In the 1760s, Grant became involved in an attempt to manufacture wooden drain pipes in the Spey Valley and market them in London. Fraser, *Chiefs of Grant*, v. 2 (1883), p. 448; and GD 248/99/6/34–35, 40: Sir Alexander Grant to Sir Ludovick Grant, March 10, 12, August 20, 1767.

61. Salt-processing is detailed in Ephraim Chambers, *Cyclopedia*, v. 2 (London, 1728), pp. 13–14; Whatley, "Industrialization," pp. 193–209, "Scottish Salt Making in the Eighteenth Century," *Scottish History*, v. 52 (1982), pp. 2–26; "'That Important and Necessary Article': The Salt Industry and Its Trade in Fife and Tayside, c. 1570–1850," *Abertay Historical Society Publications*, v. 22 (1984), pp. 10–65; and "Sales of Scottish Marine Salt, 1714–1832," *Scottish Economic and Social History*, v. 6 (1986), pp. 4–17. Oddly, Whatley ignores salt-making in Ayrshire, one of the three great salt-producing regions of Scotland. On Maryburgh, see Charles Addison & Sons to Richard Oswald, August 26, 1766, Oswald Papers, EUL; and William Lockhart to Richard Oswald, April 15, May 16, 1767, Oswald Papers, Sudlows.

as it became profitable, he leased the pans to a local enterpriser. During his ownership, the pans were the pride of Ayrshire and the talk of Britain.[62]

Industrial improvement fostered a reputation for service to the community that was part of the profile of a gentleman. These local ventures were not wholly eleemosynary, of course. They were also instances of investment opportunism. As a large landowner in the county, Oswald had the chance to spot opportunities for industrial investment and, because his factor lived there year-round, he could supervise them closely, if indirectly. They were also expressions of paternalism. As would-be lairds, the associates were predisposed "to promote a spirit of industry" and to help those in need of financial and managerial assistance. Traditionally, local lairds of noble birth, like Lords Dumfries, Loudoun, or Cassilis, assumed responsibility for invigorating moribund businesses, but by the middle decades of the century they were turning for help to new men of action with their management experience and full purses. In the 1770s, for instance, Dumfries came to Oswald for assistance with an ailing pencil and porcelain factory. Helping manufacture salt, wool, lumber, or oil moved a merchant "from behind his counter into the vacant place of the gentleman," as Henry Fielding phrased it. A gentleman not only "enriched his own capacity" but also gave life to his community's industries.[63]

One final instance of gentlemanly benevolence can be found in the associates' charitable giving. Philanthropy gripped these merchants' imaginations, as it did many others' in the period. Since each county landowner was a heretor of his parish and so responsible for church property, the associates' charitable contributions often took the form of church construction. In 1765, for instance, Mill erected a new east loft for himself in the Maryton Kirk, not far from his Old Montrose estate. Two years later, Oswald added a new aisle to the church of St. Quivox Parish less than a mile from Auchincruive and, in the mid-1770s, he paid for a new Kirkbean Kirk in southeastern Kirkcudbrightshire, on

---

62. Salt production and usage can be estimated from "salt charge vouchers" recorded by the salt officers whose responsibility it was to collect salt duties and track the sale of salt. The vouchers are kept in the SRO. They are not free of interpretative problems, however, since they are incomplete. Cf. the voucher-based figures given here to the Abstracts found in Acc. 5,381/39/1, NLS. In 1771, Oswald had been approached by James Montgomerie of Ayr, who asked for a lease to the salt works, but Oswald refused. He accepted the following year. GD 213/56/1: James Montgomerie to Richard Oswald, August 3, 1771.

63. Dumfries Papers, A 1098, Dumfries House, Cumnock; Henry Fielding, "An Enquiry into the Causes of the Late Increase in Robbers," in J. Browne, ed., *The Works of Henry Fielding*, v. 10 (London, 1871), p. 360; and *The Weekly Register*, February 6, 1731.

the edge of his Cavens estate.[64] A loft, an aisle, or a pew allowed each merchant a perch from which he could strike the pose of the laird. Not to have such ecclesiastical paraphernalia "was unthinkable for proper-tied people," for, as one late-century Gloucestershire minister rather brazenly admitted, improvements to "the Church shew the wealth and religious zeal of the Inhabitants." Church improvements advertised the heretor's claim to gentility, boldly summed up in the large banners emblazoned with new coats of arms tacked to the front of the loft; they also reflected the respectability of his neighborhood.[65] The heretors did not ignore the poor of the parish either; most substantial poor relief came in the form of alms or trusts given by the lairds. Oswald, for instance, gave to the poor of St. Quivox on an annual basis, Mill on his deathbed set up a £1,000 trust for the poor of Maryton, and Herries on his demise established a similar fund for Haugh of Urr.[66]

In London, the associates likewise proffered alms, although they were more narrowly focused in their metropolitan giving. Fellow merchants who had fallen on hard times were especially favored by this group of merchants who had once considered themselves outsiders. After the *Public Advertiser* announced the opening of a fund for "the Relief of a Person who was formerly a Merchant in a considerable Way, but, by very great Losses and Sickness in his Family, [was] reduced to the greatest Distress," the associates and other "charitable and well-disposed persons" sent their contributions to the New York and Por-tugal Coffeehouses in the Summer of 1765. On other occasions, they were moved to contribute to funds aiding residents of disaster-stricken communities. When a good part of the City of London burned in 1748, most associates gave at least £5 toward relief; and when the Boyds' Basseterre, on St. Christopher, was ravaged by earthquake and fire in the mid-1770s, John Trevanion headed up the organizing committee and talked the associates into contributing similar amounts. War, in particular, could always prize open their pocketbooks, and these "gen-tlemen" aided many an indigent soldier with contributions collected

64. CH 2/259/2/130, SRO; Chalmers, *Caledonia*, v. 6, p. 515; Rev. William McQuhae to Richard Oswald, June 1, 1967, Sudlows, Oswald Papes; and John Maxwell to Richard Oswald, February 5, March 22, May 22, 1776, Oswald Letter Book, v. 3, ff. 201, 205, 207.
65. Langford, *Public Life*, pp. 21–22, quoting the diary of Rev. Samuel Viner.
66. CH 2/319/2/84–85, 95–97, 2/319/3/2, 7–8 (St. Quivox), SRA-Ayr; and CH 2/259/2/149–50 (Maryton), SRO. For bequests in wills, see Wills of John Mill (1771), Richard Oswald (1784), and Michael Herries (1800), SRO; David Frew, *The Parish of Urr: Civil and Ecclesiastical: A History* (Dalbeattie, 1909), p. 284; and Montrose, Town Hall, John Mill's Mortification Book, 1/9/6. For other instances of the associ-ates' assisting the poor, see GD 248/176/1/43: Duncan McIntosh to Lachlan Grant Jr., May 15, 1753; and GD 248/346/3/32: Advertisement, March 11, 1761.

during the 1745 Rebellion, the Seven Years' War, and the American Revolution.[67]

The associates' contemporaries regarded the middle decades of the eighteenth century as the "great age of benevolence." And, while the volume of support is debatable, there was undeniably a more dramatic outpouring of philanthropic giving by men farther down the social ladder than had previously occurred. Of the 138 donors who gave to at least three of London's major foundations between 1740 and 1770, more than half were men of commerce – financiers, stockbrokers, company directors, merchants, and manufacturers. Merchants "controlled charitable finance and spending" at Britain's center, modeling their foundations on joint-stock companies and channeling their energies to entrepreneurial programs. More often than not, these programs strove to help men and women beneath them on the social ladder, and to prevent them from needing to claim additional alms or assistance in the future.[68] Throughout the 1750s, 1760s, and 1770s, the associates supported and, in many cases, governed at least nine of these programmatic foundations: the Magdalen House for Penitent Prostitutes, the London Hospital, the Lying-in-Charity for Delivering Poor Married Women at their Own Habitation, the Foundling Hospital, St. George's Hospital, the Scots Corporation, the Smallpox Hospital, the Marine Society, and the Trinity House.[69]

67. *Public Advertiser*, July 12, 1765, p. 3. For disaster relief, see *London Magazine*, (March 1748), pp. 139–40; *General Advertiser*, September 13–14, 1748; and *Public Advertiser*, January 1, 1777. For wartime assistance, see *The Report from the Committee of the Guild-Hall Subscription Towards the Relief, Support and Encouragement of the Soldiers Employed in Suppressing the Rebellion in 1745* (London, 1747); *London Evening Post*, January 5, 1760, p. 1; and *Public Advertiser*, October 16, 31, 1775.

68. Donna Andrew, *Philanthropy and Police* (Princeton, 1990), pp. 3, 11–12, 88–90. For early eighteenth-century comment on the charity of merchants, see Alexander Chalmers, ed., *The Spectator*, v. 2 (New York, 1853), pp. 402–05. The material in this paragraph and the following is drawn from Donna T. Andrew's dissertation, "London Charity in the Eighteenth Century" (Ph.D. dissert., University of Toronto, 1977), pp. 141–47, later published as *Philanthropy and Police*. Ms. Andrew has graciously supplied me with information about their membership. Less illuminating studies of London charity include Sampson Low, Jr., *The Charities of London* (London, 1863); and Betsy Rodgers, *Cloak of Charity: Studies in Eighteenth-Century Philanthropy* (London, 1949). For histories of the associates' charities, see Ruth K. McClure, *Coram's Children: The London Foundling Hospital in the Eighteenth Century* (New Haven, 1981); J. Blomfield, *St. George's, 1733–1933* (London, 1933); James S. Taylor, *Jonas Hanway: Founder of the Marine Society: Charity and Policy in Eighteenth-Century Britain* (London, 1985); and G. G. Harris, *The Trinity House of Deptford, 1514–1660* (London, 1969).

69. Magdalen House: Augustus Boyd, Grant. London Hospital: Augustus Boyd, Grant. Lying-in-Charity: John Boyd. Foundling Hospital: John Boyd, Sargent II, Stratton. St. George's Hospital: Grant. Scots Corporation: Grant, Johnston, Mill, Oswald, Scott.

The Magdalen House for Penitent Prostitutes is a good example of associate-sponsored aid through reform.[70] The House was the brain-child of Jonas Hanway, a friend of Aufrere, Grant, and Sargent, each of whom he had recommended for membership in London's Society for the Encouragement of Arts, Manufactures, and Commerce. The idea for such a house first surfaced in 1750, but nothing came of it until Hanway took it up again in 1757. The problem that Hanway publicized was a large and intractable one for City residents and aspiring gentlemen alike. Could those "who think of their duty," Hanway asked, "look on, and see such crowds of females become the prey of penury, infamy and disease?" The likes of the associates thought not and, with their help, the Magdalen House opened its doors in August 1758.

Sir Alexander Grant served as one of the Magdalen's charter vice-presidents. "Eminent in rank and fortune, as well as distinguished for piety," he supported, lobbied, and pushed its program for thirteen years.[71] A variety of reasons drew him in: religious feeling (he respected the injunction "Thou shalt not commit adultery"); public health (he believed the program would "stop the progress of diseases"); and social stability (he hoped the hospital would check libertinism, increase the incidence of marriage, and advance virtue and industry). Grant believed that a prostitute was "anathema to the community, a fountainhead of crime and vice and an outstanding threat to the peace of society"; worst

Smallpox Hospital: Grant. Marine Society: Sargent II, Wood. Trinity House: Stratton. The records of the Magdalen House are available only as they were recorded in contemporary pamphlets. The Marine Society's Donations and Legacies Book is at the National Maritime Museum, Greenwich, Kent. The Foundling Hospital archives are at the Greater London Record Office.

70. Membership Index, Royal Society of Arts, London. Robert Dingley first proposed the idea of such a charity to Hanway in 1750 and struggled to win support of the plan for the next seven years. Samuel Johnson's *The Rambler*, n. 107 (March 19, 1751); *Gentleman's Magazine*, v. 21 (1751), pp. 163–65; John M. Hutchins, *Jonas Hanway, 1712–1786* (London, 1940), pp. 111–12; and S. B. P. Pearce, *An Ideal in the Working: The Story of Magdalen Hospital, 1758 to 1958* (London, 1958), p. 9. For discussion of an appropriate name for the charity, see *The Public Advertiser*, April 19, 1758, p. 2. The story of the Magdalen Charity can be pieced together from various eighteenth-century reports. Gough/London/112, #2: Jonas Hanway to Robert Dingley, February 18, 1758, and #3: *The Plan of the Magdalen House for the Reception of Penitent Prostitutes* (London: 1758), pp. 22–24, Bodleian Library, Oxford. See also Anon., *The Origin of the London Magdalen Hospital* (Wellington, Somerset, after 1872); Hutchins, *Hanway*, ch. 5; Pearce, *An Ideal*, passim; and Taylor, *Hanway*, pp. 75–79.

71. Grant was an important conduit of information and membership. Because of his solicitations, Sir Archibald Grant and Lord Bute joined. GD 345/1166/3/40x: Sir Alexander Grant to Sir Archibald Grant, July 17, 1760; and Sir Alexander Grant to Charles Jenkinson, February 24, 1762, Add.Mss. 38,198/84. He hounded many relatives into joining, contributing, attending its Sunday services, and dining in Billiter Lane with "the Great Traveller" Jonas Hanway. GD 345/1180/1763: Sir Archibald Grant to Captain Archibald Grant, — 19, January 25, February 1, 1763, Sir Alexander Grant to Captain Archibald Grant, January 22, 1763. There were more Grants in the lists than members of any other family.

of all, she was an ungrateful and unproductive citizen of an increasingly consumer-oriented society, a drain on the productivity of her self and her clients. But retribution was no way to release her economic skills. Reformation was a better means of promoting economic growth and moral correction.[72]

The "asylum" that these "eminent gentlemen" built was a relentless experiment in social redevelopment. Saving the prostitute occurred in three stages: repentance, reform, and resettlement. To assure themselves of full repentance, the charity's Governors conducted a series of grueling interviews which were difficult to pass. Believing that old, hardened prostitutes could not easily reform themselves, they preferred young, relatively inexperienced women. Once a candidate was interviewed, approved, and admitted into the House, the rigorous process of reform began. She was given whatever medical treatment she required and a set of gray woolen clothes. Henceforth, she was called by her first name only. As the Governors felt that purgation of the past was the best means of reform, she was even directed to refrain from speaking to other penitents, especially about former activities, and from seeing anyone connected to her past life. She was given her own bed, which was surrounded by heavy drapes, materially sealed off from temptation. Once separated from any reminder of her waywardness, she was administered a heavy dose of religion – numerous readings and mandatory attendance at two daily chapel services, where the Governors peered at her from behind a screen. Only after repentance and reform could she think of re-entering the world she had left. At this third stage, the Governors took great pains to see that she did not slip back into old habits. They contacted her family and her more reputable acquaintances, and they provided her with what they considered to be a marketable skill, usually knitting, that would keep her "from idleness" and, as an added benefit, contribute to the upkeep of the House. Eventually, they placed her in service.

As its founders knew, a project "of this sort opens . . . a vast field for improvement." Domestic industry, such as knitting, spinning, and weaving carpets, was one outlet for the Magdalens' new-found skills, but the Governors and subscribers were more intrigued by the prospects raised by overseas expansion and settlement, and the House became one of Britain's first "imperial charities."[73] Sir Alexander Grant, in particular,

---

72. Andrew, "London Charity," pp. 141–42, discusses the grounds for widespread support. See also *A Plan for Establishing a Charity-House, or Charity Houses, for the Reception of Repenting Prostitutes* (London, 1758), pp. vii–x. On the results of the program, see letters by former inmates in *The London Chronicle*, May 23–26, 1761, pp. 501–02. Cf. Jonas Hanway, *Virtue in Humble Life* (London, 1774), p. v.

73. Taylor, *Hanway*, p. xiii. Taylor refers to the mind-set of the charities as "Christian mercantilism."

saw the Magdalens' need for employment as an opportunity to promote the settlement of Britain's new American colonies. In characteristic haste, he secured the election of his cousin, the new Governor of East Florida, to the House's ruling Board and, in the same letter that he informed the Governor of his election, proposed transporting reformed prostitutes to America where they could serve as wives and workers. At his own expense, Sir Alexander proposed to select four penitents "of the middling rank" and send them to St. Augustine where they would await the Governor's orders. Apparently, the Governor was less than thrilled at this act of charity, and he declined to reply. But before the Governor had even received the letter, the London merchant dispatched the four women. Even after word flew back of the Governor's displeasure, Sir Alexander was still undeterred and sent several more in the next two years. Only when he learned that the first four had fallen "back into their former manner" did the stubborn merchant reluctantly "give up that" speculation.[74]

The associates' charitable programs were designed to build a fiscally sound, numerically populous, morally virtuous, and commercially skilled community through rehabilitation (the Magdalen), repopulation (the Foundling Hospital, the Lying-In-Charity, and numerous medical hospitals), education (the Marine Society, the Magdalen, and the Scots Corporation), and relief (the Scots Corporation). Like most informed men of the day, the associates feared a cataclysm from depopulation and vice. The many neighborhood hospitals that sprang up during their careers ensured the birth and health of children in a country noted for its declining population but expanding empire. Their institutions emphasized the moral and economic value of work at every turn: Magdalens were trained to weave Turkey carpets, Marine boys to steer ships, and Scots pensioners' children to perform clerical duties. They were, Jonas Hanway tells us, "afraid of the infection," whether from prostitution, sickness, or unemployment.[75] The associates helped devise and run social

74. Jonas Hanway to Robert Dingley, February 18, 1758, Gough/London/112/#2/Letter 5, Bodleian Library, Oxford; and Taylor, *Hanway*, p. xii. The idea of settling colonies with reformed prostitutes was first expressed by Rev. William Dodd, *A Sermon*, 2nd ed. (London, 1759), pp. x–xi. The House admitted many women each year but placed relatively few. This imbalance was beginning to trouble its Governors by the mid-1760s. Andrew, "London Charity," p. 154. On the Florida connection, see Sir Alexander Grant to Governor James Grant, June 17, 1767, February 1, 1769, February 8, 1770, BCM 402; Sir Alexander Grant to Governor Grant, June 19, 1767, BCM 344; and Governor Grant to Sir Alexander Grant, June 28, 1769, BCM Bound Letter Book.
75. On population and philanthropy, see Hanway, *Reflections*, p. 289. Disease was perceived as the manifestation of a vitiated constitution. Illness was commonly viewed as "a deeply significant life-event, integral to the sufferer's whole being, spiritual, moral and physical." Roy Porter, *Disease, Medicine and Society in England, 1550–1866* (London, 1987), p. 25.

programs to cure the infection by molding the behavior and thinking of "sick" individuals, and shaping the economic and social relationships that linked the citizenry together.

Parliamentary Service: "An Opportunity of Proving Myself"

One of the best ways to promote an improvement program that would advance both industry and morality and, at the same time, burnish the reputation of the improver by making him appear patriotic and polite was to engage in politics at the national level. Nearly a third of the associates – Grant, Sargent II, Aufrere, Stratton, Sargent III, and Trevanion – pushed for a seat in the House of Commons. Throughout their tenures, they used their power primarily to safeguard their commercial, agricultural, and social interests.

Sir Alexander Grant's activity in the House was typical for these associates. Tirelessly tending to the work of its committees, he (among other things) led the drive for parliamentary approval of and funding for the canal linking the Firth of Forth to the Firth of Clyde. He sat on numerous private road repair or construction committees, regardless of whether the roads were in Moray or Norfolk. And he used his rank as one of the more senior City businessmen to promote subsidies for various entrepreneurial ventures, such as salmon and herring fisheries and pipe manufactories in northern Scotland, and employment schemes designed to teach poor girls in the Highlands how to spin and market their cloth. Not surprisingly, commerce – local, national, and international – was his primary political concern. Indeed, it was as an expert on commercial matters that Grant made his greatest mark. Throughout his tenure, he was regarded by both the House and the Ministry as an especially well-informed spokesman for West Indian and North American affairs. When he first rose to speak in March 1763, he provided expert testimony in behalf of those who would impose a tax on cider, detailing the beneficial effects of the tax on the sugar and rum trade.[76] On other occasions, he lectured the Government on the intricacies of

---

76. Malmesbury Papers, Box 16, March 1763, Hampshire Record Office, Winchester. In December 1763, he described to the House the rough treatment he had received during the Royal Exchange riot over the burning of the *North Briton*. Box 17, December 8, 1763; and *London Chronicle*, December 6, 1763. The following February, he "repeated a coffee-house conversation of pragmatic Londoners" who said that Grenville's Sugar Act should be repealed. Box 18, February 10, 1764. On March 8, 1764, he sided with those who wanted to make merchant M.P.s liable to bankruptcy and "talked strongly about some Merts purchasing a seat here on purpose for a protection." Box 18, 1764.

Jamaica currency, pushed for a reduction on the import duty for brandy, and took a strong stand against petitions calling for the relaxation of customs duties levied on sugar imported from foreign countries. In 1764, he worked to obtain payment to his namesake Alexander Grant for his service as a Contractor for the Indian Trade in Canada and, the following year, he called for the repayment of Nova Scotia merchants who had supplied the navy and army with provisions.[77]

John Sargent II was likewise sought after as an expert in commercial affairs, especially those that related to America. In the reorganization of the empire that followed the Peace of 1763, he was in a strong position to advise ministers and House members on the intricacies of imperial financing, having been a Director of the Bank of England from 1753 and remaining so through 1767.[78] He was doubly valuable to them, given his knowledge of specific colonies, since he also served as the agent of Pennsylvania and New York during his tenure. Personal connections to Benjamin Franklin, for instance, had won him the agency for Pennsylvania.[79] In 1760, three years after he had first met Franklin, Pennsylvania needed someone in London to receive, invest, and disburse to its creditors the money it had been allotted by Parliament; and "the electric Philosopher" recommended Sargent to the Assembly. For over six years, Sargent's firm collected the colony's money from the Exchequer, placed it in an interest-free account that they opened at the Bank of England, paid debts incurred by the colony, and generally represented its citizens' concerns.[80] During the controversy about the Government's

77. *Journal of the Commissioners for Trade and Plantations*, v. 1759–63, pp. 90–91 (February 29, 1760); T 1/424/115: February 18, 1763; T 29/35/291–92: February 2, 1764; T 1/43/71: February 8, 1764; T 29/35/300: February 9, 1764; and Sir Alexander Grant to Charles Jenkinson, June 14, 1765, Add.Mss. 38,204/270, BL.
78. Acres, *The Bank of England*, v. 2, p. 619.
79. Sargent's friendship with Franklin was close. As tokens of that friendship, Sargent and Aufrere received three Franklin portraits – one by David Martin, one by Benjamin West, and another by an unknown artist. Oswald received two. Sellers, *Benjamin Franklin in Portraiture*. Moreover, young William Temple Franklin lodged with the Sargents in London in 1784. John Sargent to Benjamin Franklin, November 14, 1784, American Philosophical Society, Philadelphia.
80. Sargent was Pennsylvania's financial agent through September 1766. Its legislature first appointed Sargent's firm on October 18, 1760 to handle the 1758 grant, and reappointed it the following year to manage the 1759 grant. *Pennsylvania Archives*, 8th ser., v. 6, pp. 5,166, 5,262, 5,341, 5,358, 5,441; v. 7, pp. 5,900–08. Sargent, Aufrere & Co. rendered its last account in September 1766. During the 1760s and 1770s, he was also Franklin's private banker. *Papers of Benjamin Franklin*, v. 14 (1970), p. 170, v. 19 (1975), p. 41. On Sargent's endowment of annual essays, see *Papers*, v. 10, pp. 143–44; William B. Reed, *Life and Correspondence of Joseph Reed*, v. 1 (Philadelphia, 1847), p. 40; and *Papers*, v. 13, pp. 279–80. The essays were published as *Four Dissertations on the Reciprocal Advantages of a Perpetual Union between Great Britain and Her American Colonies* (Philadelphia, 1766).

most noted act of imperial economic integration – the Stamp Act – Sargent represented the colony of New York before Parliament; and, although he personally adopted a neutral position in the debate itself, he pressed New York's position, defended Franklin's support for repeal, and after the vote for repeal warmly defended repeal itself.[81]

In Sargent's case, the associate worked as an "active instrument" for "the improvement of America" even after he departed Parliament.[82] Although, in his stubbornly modest way, he described his activity simply as providing "a little relief not worth mentioning," the services he rendered were substantial. He assisted friends and clients in the colonies, like Connecticut's William Samuel Johnson and Pennsylvania's Benjamin Franklin. In London, he lobbied for redress of "the alarming state" of the American trade. And he aided William Pitt, Lord Chatham, one of America's most evidently ardent advocates. Although he neither espoused radical positions nor directly worked to aid the cause of independence, he was, significantly, one of the first Englishmen to congratulate Franklin on the peace.[83]

81. Sargent was appointed New York's political agent in December 1765 and charged with presenting the colony's Stamp Act petitions to the Committee of the Whole House. *Proceedings of the General Assembly of the Colony of New York*, v. 2, pp. 802–07; Anon., "Letters of Dennys DeBerdt, 1757–1770," *Publications of the Colonial Society of Massachusetts*, v. 13 (1912), pp. 317–18; Edmund B. O'Callaghan, ed., *Documents Relating to the Colonial History of the State of New York*, v. 7 (Albany, 1856), p. 908; *Journal of the Legislative Council of New York*, v. 2 (Albany, 1861), p. 1653; and *The Colonial Laws of New York*, v. 4 (Albany, 1899), pp. 1002–03. For his services, New York awarded him with "a piece of plate" as "a memorial of the gratitude of this colony in acting as special agent, for which he generously declined any gratuity."

82. Not all associates sided with Sargent, Though he did not approve of "many steps that have been taken" by the King's Government in the area of American affairs, Grant, for instance, thought it "madness" to countenance rebellious proceedings in the colonies, since, if tolerated, they "will root out all order amongst us." Sir Alexander Grant to John Powell, December 25, 1769, Grant Papers, Tomintoul House.

83. John Sargent to Benjamin Franklin, January 3, 1783, American Philosophical Society, Philadelphia; William Samuel Johnson to John Sargent, November 10, 1771, October 31, 1772, and November 13, 1773, William Samuel Johnson Papers, Connecticut Historical Society, Hartford. In 1775, he arranged for a meeting of merchants involved in American commerce and, as the agent for New York, petitioned Parliament for the protection of the American trade; he pushed for withholding the petition from publication, but his initiative was overruled and the petition was presented on February 7. *Maryland Gazette*, March 16, 1775; *London Chronicle*, January 5–7, 9, 1775; *Georgia Gazette*, March 29, April 26, 1775; Main Papers (February 7, 1775), House of Lords Record Office, London; and *Correspondence of Edmund Burke*, v. 3, p. 113 (February 9, 1775). On Pitt, see PRO-KG, PRO 30/8/55/I/81: John Sargent to Earl of Chatham, March 31, 1777. Sargent was Pitt's host at Downing Street during Pitt's last illness. William R. Anson, ed., *Autobiography and Political Correspondence of Augustus Hervey, 3rd Duke of Grafton* (London, 1898), p. 302. On Sargent and the peace, see John Sargent to Benjamin Franklin, January 28, 1783, American Philosophical Society, Philadelphia.

Well before the end of the American Revolutionary War, indeed by the time the Stamp Act was repealed, Sargent II doubted his ability to effect change through Parliament, finding his efforts to promote commercial exchange and maintain commercial harmony frustrated by the state of national politics. Most of the other associates in office agreed with him; significantly, all but Sargent III held office only briefly. By the 1760s, groups of the elite in the countries, the boroughs, and increasingly Whitehall itself chose the candidates who would sit in the House. The status of a candidate's family and the pressure of a candidate's patron commonly caused elections to be decided beforehand and in private. Such had not been the state of affairs a century before when, around the time of the English Civil War and the Restoration, religious and political ideologies, organized parties, multiple candidates, and contested elections all began to contribute to "the rage of party." But by the early eighteenth century, the furor had subsided. A smaller proportion of elections were contested, and the growth of the share of the population that could vote was checked. This is not to say that the associates' age did not see fundamental political change, for the popular protest movements they often decried, such as the one led by John Wilkes, unleashed new forces in the political arena which, over the succeeding 100 years, significantly altered the system.[84] Nevertheless, parliamentary politics was a highly personalized and selective process. Seemingly public matters like the administration of trade and building of economic infrastructure were handled as the local, particular, "private" concerns of the Members. Only occasionally did Parliament take up great matters of state, imperial reorganization, or political reform.

When he took his seat, Sargent II, like Grant, viewed the Commons as a place to promote his improvements. He first gained office by virtue of his wealth. In 1753, Lord Montagu, the patron of Midhurst, in West Sussex, needed money. Sargent had it, and what was euphemistically labeled a £1,500 "loan" bought Sargent a recommendation to Montagu's constituency. Sargent won decisively at the election the following year. But his hold on the seat was not secure and, when the Montagus decided to handle their own affairs in 1760, he found himself without a patron.[85]

---

84. J. H. Plumb, "The Growth of the Electorate in England from 1600 to 1715," *Past & Present*, v. 45 (1969), pp. 90–116; J. A. Cannon, *Parliamentary Reform, 1640–1832* (Cambridge, 1973), pp. 49–50; and Mark Kishlansky, *Parliamentary Selection: Social and Political Change in Early Modern England* (Cambridge, 1986). On the fundamental changes introduced in the 1760s, see John Brewer, *Party Ideology and Popular Politics at the Accession of George III* (Cambridge, 1976).

85. Sargent's parliamentary activities are summarized in Namier and Brooke, eds., *House of Commons*, v. 3, pp. 404–05. The call for the election went out on January 16, 1754, and the election was held on January 25. Despite Sargent's boast that he was "fixed with my Lord for life," Montagu's support during the contest was lukewarm, and it was only Sargent's pertinacity, expended "at a dear rate," that overcame the

He struggled for the next five years to find another place.[86] Finally, with the help of George Grenville, Sargent returned to Parliament in 1765 as the representative of West Looe, Cornwall. Membership in the House provided him the "opportunity of proving myself."[87] Throughout his second term, however, Sargent experienced one disappointment after another, as individual allegiance came to be more important than substantive measures.[88] He remained loyal to Grenville long after the

opposition. Cowdray Mss. 4,797, West Sussex Record Office, Chichester. On political alignment, see Party List, 1754, Add.Mss. 33,034/183–88, BL. In the middle decades of the eighteenth century, the quickest route to political promotion was financial support of those in high places and it is for this reason that Sargent eagerly subscribed £6,000 to Newcastle's 1757 Loan. *Subscribers to a Loan* (London, 1757). In Parliament, Sargent used his influence to promote the Montagus's affairs. Over the course of 1760, however, Lord Montagu took the management of his family's affairs out of Sargent's hands and entrusted them to his son. John Sargent to Duke of Newcastle, July 2, 1760, Add.Mss. 32,908/21, BL.

86. He applied to the Duke of Newcastle but, despite Sargent's previous financial support of the Duke, Newcastle would not back him. The associate then offered his "sincere devotion" to the Earl of Bute; but devotion, it seems, was not what Bute wanted, and Sargent received only a polite reply. Unable to secure backing, he stepped down. The loss rankled him. In his years of political exile, he strove to curry favor with "the Great Commoner" William Pitt and slowly bought the support of New Shoreham's political corporation. At the same time, he began to speak out more vocally on trade matters, on one occasion calling for free trade in Senegal, on another joining other trans-Atlantic merchants in support of the peace of 1763 and, on still another, urging the cultivation of hemp in North America. His politics in these years became more closely tied to business than they had before. John Sargent to Joseph Shippen, October 27, 1761, Shippen Papers, v. 5, p. 169, Historical Society of Pennsylvania, Philadelphia. He was successful in his drive to win New Shoreham's constituency; by 1765, Grenville and Rockingham were asking him for advice on the choice of its representative. George Grenville to John Sargent, October 9, 20, 28, 1765, and George Grenville to Topham Beauclerk, October 28, 1765, Stowe Mss. 7/2, Huntington Library, San Marino. For his political positions, see CO 388/50/72: December 16, 1762; *London Gazette*, May 21, 1763; and CO 323/17/I: November 30, 1763.

87. Sargent had applied to Bute in April 1764 for help with the Midhurst by-election. Sargent had hoped to stand against Bamber Gascoyne, George Grenville's nominee, and to do so he needed Bute's assistance, but Bute ignored his plea. Bute Papers, "1764, #323," April 12, 1764, Mountstuart, Isle of Bute. Sargent next turned to Gascoyne's patron Grenville and received more favorable treatment. Grenville recommended Sargent to James Buller as a suitable candidate to fill a vacancy at Buller's borough of West Looe in Cornwall. George Grenville to James Buller, November 1, 17, December 29, 1764, Stowe Mss. 7/2, Huntington Library, San Marino. Negotiations with Grenville, Buller, and Sargent lasted through December, and ended on a positive note; Sargent was elected in January 1765 and, after a contest, was seated. George Grenville to James Buller, December 11, 1764, and Account, February 9, 1765, Buller Mss. BO 23/7/2–3, West Looe, Cornwall.

88. After Grenville fell from power and went into Opposition in July 1765, Sargent was listed as a member of the Grenville/Bedford group. Later, he officially joined the Opposition in early 1767 to maintain the land tax at its present levels. Labaree, ed., *Papers*, v. 13 (1969), p. 292 (citing a letter written by Sargent & Co., August 2, 1766, and published by the *Pennsylvania Gazette*, October 2, 1766); List, December 1766, Wentworth-Woodhouse Muniments, R86, Sheffield City Libraries; and Add.Mss. 33,001/357–63: March 2, 1767 ("Bedford & Grenville"), and 33,002/470–73: February-March 1767 ("Grenville"), BL.

minister's fall from power in June 1765, but by 1768 he had had enough. He quit Parliament "without regret."[89]

At roughly the same time, but for different reasons, Grant too found the internecine battles among personalities and parties more frustrating and less rewarding then he had expected. He had first run for election as the M.P. for the Inverness Burghs in 1754, but failed in his bid, in large measure because he failed to win the support of the chief of the clan. After his defeat, he built a base of support among the politically connected Scots in London, ran again in 1761, and was unanimously elected as the Burghs' representative.[90] Politically, he referred to himself as "The Miller of Mansfield," after the protagonist in a short contemporary drama that recounted the virtues of a country gentleman whose only loyalty was to the King, but in self-description Grant was somewhat disingenuous.[91] Throughout his tenure, he was loyal to whomever held the reigns of power. Initially he sided with Bute, and supported Bute's peace, for instance, in 1763. After Bute's fall from power, he sided with Grenville, while continuing to maintain close ties to Bute's party. He opposed John Wilkes and the repeal of the cider tax. Later, after Grenville's fall in 1765, he supported Rockingham. But political maneuvering in the House did him little good with his constituency; when an Indian nabob named Hector Munro returned to Scotland and stripped him of his local support by buying the votes of the Inverness Burghs councilors, Grant lost his seat. Grant and Sargent alike found themselves unable to push their schemes of commercial and agricultural improvement through Parliament and unwilling to succumb to "the venality of the times." Accordingly, they stepped down. The "opportunity for proving" themselves and improving their surroundings through direct involvement in national politics proved more trouble than it was worth.[92]

---

89. John Sargent to George Grenville, March 9, 1768, in J. R. G. Tomlinson, ed., *Additional Grenville Papers, 1763–1765* (London, 1962), p. 262.
90. Moray District Record Office, ZBFo/A2/4/321–26, Forres; Inverness Burgh Council Minutes, April 14, 1761, Highland Regional Archives, Inverness; and Fortrose Burgh Council Minutes, April 13, 1761, B 28/8/3, SRO.
91. GD 248/672/5/55: Sir Alexander Grant to James Grant, July 27, 1765; Robert Dodsley, *The Miller of Mansfiled: A Dramatic Tale* (London, 1737).
92. Add.Mss. 32,974/25 (June 1765), BL; List, December 1766, Wentworth-Woodhouse Manuscripts R 86, Sheffield City Libraries, Sheffield; Add.Mss. 33,037/37 (February–March 1767: Grant is "Bute's Friend" and votes for a 2 shilling land tax), 33,002/470–73 (February–March 1767: Grant is of Bute party), 33,001/357–603 (March 2, 1767: Grant is "For the Administration"), BL; and GD 345/1171/1768: Sir Alexander Grant to Sir Archibald Grant, August 25, 1768. But, in an unusual display of independence, he opposed Rockingham on the repeal of the Stamp Act in February 1766, supporting the Act and expressing indignation at letting "our colonies spit in our faces." On Grant and the Stamp Act, see Namier and Brooke, eds., *House of Commons*, v. 2, p. 528; and *The Debates and Proceedings of the British House of Commons*, v. 7 (London, 1972), pp. 143, 292.

In the minds of the associates, giving to charities, revivifying industry, rebuilding roads, and reclaiming land, whether at home or abroad, whether in one's private capacity or as a representative in Parliament, were acts of "justice and benevolence" which themselves formed "a great part of the character of a gentleman and a man of honor." Such behavior expressed social leadership, appropriated the authority long exercised by the hereditary and landed elites, and manifested religious conviction. In the gifts and trusts they set up to remedy the effects of economic and social decline, the associates and others donned the mantle of that authority, caring for the victims of the commercial society that they had helped create. In extending alms to the needy and facilitating their employment, the associates demonstrated their power and influence over others in society. Bernard Mandeville, whose influence on Georgian thought is still immeasurable, overstressed the self-interest of charitable givers and society improvers when he pronounced that "Pride and Vanity have built more Hospitals than all other Virtues together"; and he overlooked the force of Christian duty and emotional gratification that accompanied many of the gifts. But his point is important: most philanthropists needed to be seen as gentlemen. The desire for praise, for the reputation that clung to the praiseworthy, and for "the Satisfaction there is in Ordering" and directing those beneath them in rank moved the associates to give and to work as they had never done before.[93]

93. Borsay, *English Urban Renaissance*, p. 252; and Bernard Mandeville, *The Fable of the Bees*, ed. Philip Heath (Harmondsworth, 1970), pp. 264, 269, 287.

10

The Way to Be Rich and Respectable

W HEN MEN ENGAGED IN THE CIVIL SERVICE, the legal profession, and City finance and commerce were accepted, at least in principle, into the ranks of gentlemen, they began to sink large amounts of capital into lands, farms, transportation and manufacturing ventures, and philanthropic programs in order to solidify their status. But improvement was not just something done to the land and its inhabitants. Given the mixture of motivations underlying the social improvements noted in the previous chapter, improvement was also something done to an individual's identity, indeed to his very self. The most material expressions of the associates' desire to become gentlemen are the houses they built, the art collections and libraries they filled them with, and the gardens they planted surrounding them. In the ensuing centuries, their properties have been broken up and sold, their farms dissolved, their roads replaced or rerouted, and their canals, lighthouses, and factories allowed to fall to ruin; in most cases, though, the houses still stand and they speak volumes "about the way owners and occupants saw themselves and wished to be seen by others."[1]

Houses

House building lay at the heart of the construction of social identity. The era in which the associates built was a feverish one for construction in general. There were, for instance, 389 new country houses and villas built in England between 1660 and 1760; this construction took place at four times the rate in the middle of the eighteenth century that it had in the late seventeenth century.[2] As part of the "subtle" shift that occurred

1. Borsay, *English Urban Renaissance*, p. 232.
2. Charles S. Smith, "Supply and Demand in English Country House Building, 1660–1740," *Oxford Art Journal*, v. 11 (1988), pp. 3–9. Smith's conclusions question the findings of Lawrence and Jeanne Stone in *An Open Elite? England, 1540–1880* (Oxford, 1984) and call for a more thoroughgoing investigation of social mobility.

in "the composition of the landed elite in the decades after the Hanoverian accession," some twenty associates acquired county or suburban properties between 1745 and 1785, near the end of this house-building boom.[3] The villa owners of this group changed their houses but little: like John Sargent II or Sir Alexander Grant, they moved into preexisting structures situated on small plots of land, modified them only slightly, and paid scant attention to the enveloping greensward. (See Illustrations 10.1–10.4.) But an equal number had enough land on which to build a large "gentleman's seat" and, in fact, erected or at least planned to erect such a mansion house (Illustrations 10.5–10.7). As their greatest expenditures on polite display, these houses are rich in significance. Country seats can illustrate good or bad contemporary architectural taste, and domestic or foreign stylistic influence, but they can also substantiate individual personalities, social roles, and polite strategies. Although there were many differences among the associates' mansions, some similarities emerge. Oswald's house, for instance, is typical in its formal features and its symbolic meanings, and will therefore be singled out for analysis here.[4]

A mansion stood on the north side of the River Ayr at the center of the Auchincruive estate when James Murray acquired the property in the late 1750s, but he found the house old-fashioned, insubstantial, and altogether unsuitable. He commissioned the Scottish architects John, Robert, and James Adam to draw up plans for a new residence on the high knoll overlooking the water. At least two side views and three

---

3. Smith, "Supply," p. 8. No material has surfaced about houses owned by John Anderson, John Gardiner, or William Wood.
4. Some country houses are relatively well-documented. Oswald's Auchincruive is discussed in Anon., "Auchincruive, Ayr," *The Scots Pictorial*, February 24, 1923; Arthur Oswald, "Auchincruive, Ayrshire," *Country Life*, December 7, 1923; and J. Kirkwood, "Auchincruive House" (pamphlet for Ayrshire Archaeological and Natural History Society, n.d.). Boyd's Danson is detailed in Danson Deeds, Local Studies History Library, Hall Place, Bexley; and Hancock, "Citizen of the World," pp. 835–56. Grant's Dalvey is described in GD 248/672/5/53: Sir Alexander Grant to James Grant, October 11, 1764; Percy L. Parker, ed., *The Journal of John Wesley* (Chicago, 1977), p. 275. This is probably the same building that Sir John Clerk of Penicuik sketched in his "Notebook" and that Sir Archibald detailed in his 1750 "Sketch and Explication." GD 18; and GD 345/1160/4/77x. What is depicted is not the square Palladian house that now stands on the hill overlooking the Findhorn Valley, a post-1772 mansion datable from beams and nails. For Johnston's Carnsalloch, see Isaac Ware, *A Complete Body of Architecture* (London, 1756), pls. 54–55; and *The Scottish Field* (April 1957), pp. 25–27. Mill's building program at Old Montrose is recorded in a "Decreet Arbitral" between Mill and the architect Robert Robinson. Register of Deeds, RD 3/229/2/598–99 (December 19–22, 1770), SRO; and Howard Colvin, *A Biographical Dictionary of British Architects, 1600–1840* (London, 1978), p. 702. Herries' Spottes, Levett's Hinton, Sargent III's Lavington, and Scott's Crailing Hall are poorly documented, but the structures remain and have been personally inspected by the author.

Illustration 10.1 John Sargent II's May Place, Crayford, Kent. J. Greig engraving, 1820. *From*: Thomas K. Cromwell, *Excursions through Kent* (London, 1820), p. 190. *Courtesy*: Hall Place, Bexley Library, Bexley, Kent.

floor plans for a central-block house with two pavilion wings were drawn, and construction began in the early 1760s (Illustrations 10.8–10.12). By the time Oswald acquired Auchincruive in 1764, a foundation had been laid, exterior walls erected, and the timbering and tiling of roofs begun. Oswald decided to continue the project according to the Adam plan, but he reduced the grand design in both appearance and scale.[5]

The grand Adam design for a villa with wings was an expression of prevailing genteel taste, vying with the most ambitious designs of courtiers and peers in its Palladian purity. Rather than a "vast and emphatic" "double pile" with a suite of parade rooms, Auchincruive was to possess a villa design – "roughly square in plan, with its main elevations consisting of a three-bay pedimented centre, often expressed as an applied

5. The Adam design and the resulting house were not oriented exactly east/west or north/south. Rather, the two principal facades looked south-southwest and north-northeast, respectively. In the present discussion, the convention that "south" means south-southwest will be adopted. The Adam plans are housed in London, Sir John Soane Museum, Adam Drawings, v. 44, nn. 60–64.

Illustration 10.2 William Cooke's Salisbury Hall, Walthamstow, Essex. *Courtesy*: Vestry House Museum, London Borough of Waltham Forest.

Illustration 10.3 Sir Alexander Grant's Bookham Grove, Great Bookham, Surrey. Painting by John Hassell. *Courtesy:* Lambeth Archives, London.

Illustration 10.4 William Cooke's Walthamstow Rectory Manor, Walthamstow, Essex: North Facade. *Courtesy:* Vestry House Museum, London Borough of Waltham Forest.

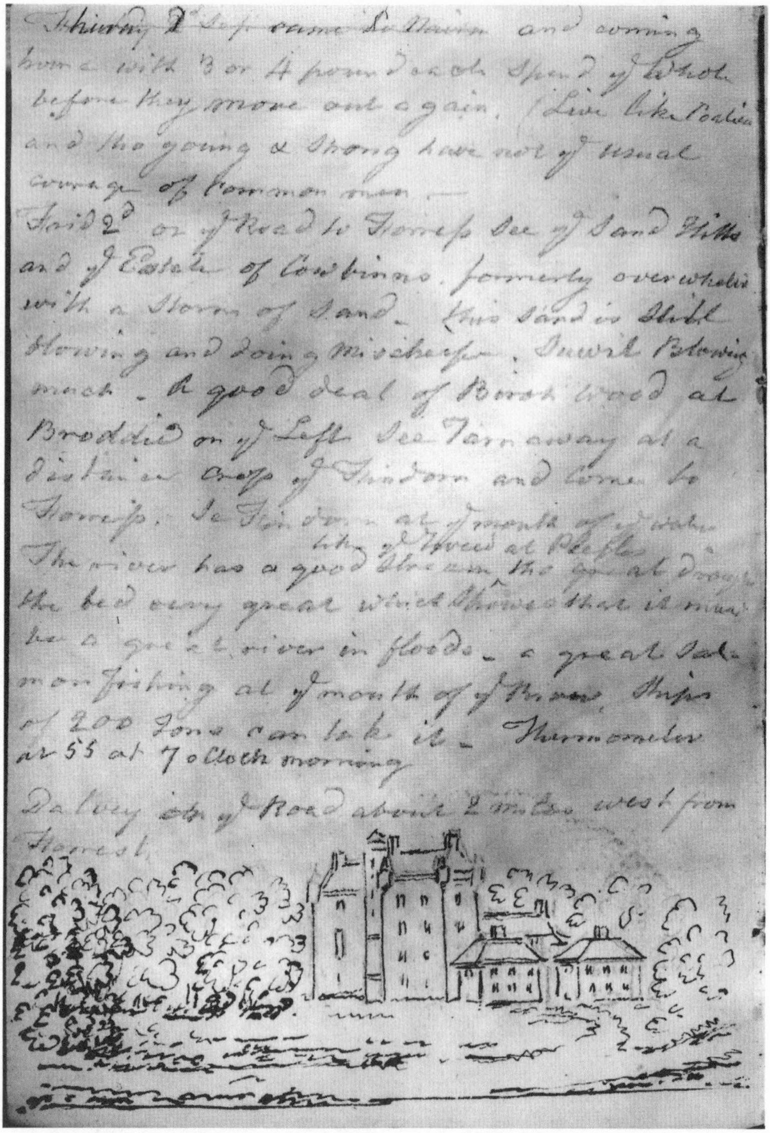

Illustration 10.5 Sir Alexander Grant's Dalvey, Forres, Moray. Page from Notebook of Sir John Clerk of Penicuik, GD 18/2118/24, SRO. *Courtesy*: Scottish Record Office, Edinburgh.

Illustration 10.6 Michael Herries's Spottes, Haugh of Urr, Kirkcudbright. *Courtesy:* Sir Michael Herries, Kt.

Illustration 10.7 Alexander Johnston's Carnsalloch, Kirkton, Dumfries. *Courtesy:* Christopher Campbell-Johnston, Esq., Salwarpe, Worcestershire.

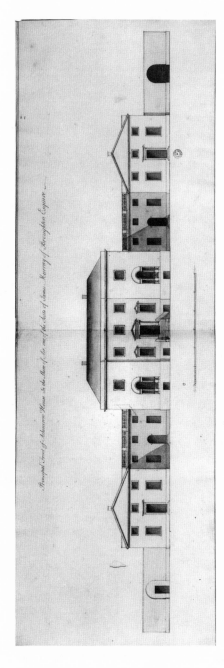

Illustration 10.8 Richard Oswald's Auchincruive, St. Quivox, Ayr: Plan of the Park-Side Facade, Adam Drawings, *v.* 44, no. 60. *Courtesy:* Sir John Soane's Museum, London.

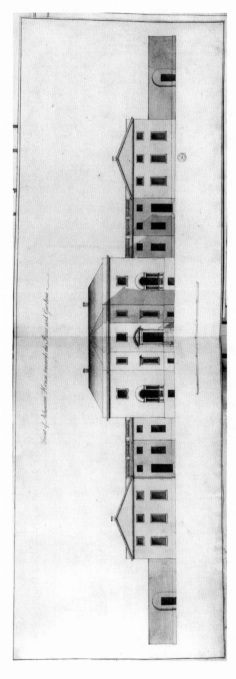

Front of Schwevon House toward the House and Gardens

Illustration 10.9 Auchincruive Plan of the River-Side Facade, Adam Drawings, v. 44, no. 61. *Courtesy:* Sir John Soane's Museum, London.

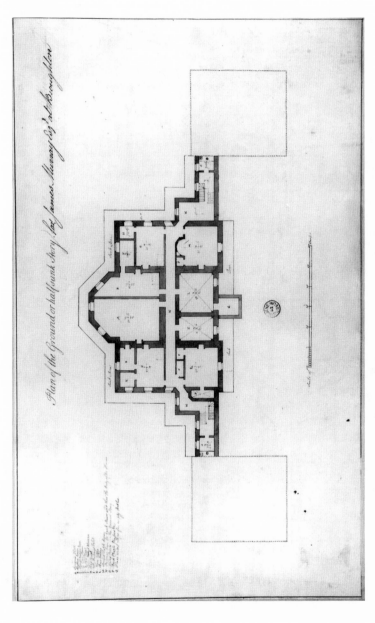

Illustration 10.10 Auchincruive: Plan of the Ground or Half-Sunk Story, Adam Drawings, *v.* 44, no. 62. *Courtesy:* Sir John Soane's Museum, London.

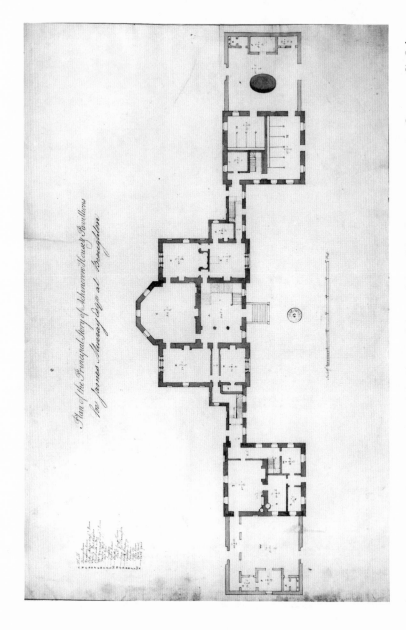

Illustration 10.11 Auchincruive: Plan of the Principal Story, Adam Drawings, v. 44, no. 63. *Courtesy:* Sir John Soane's Museum, London.

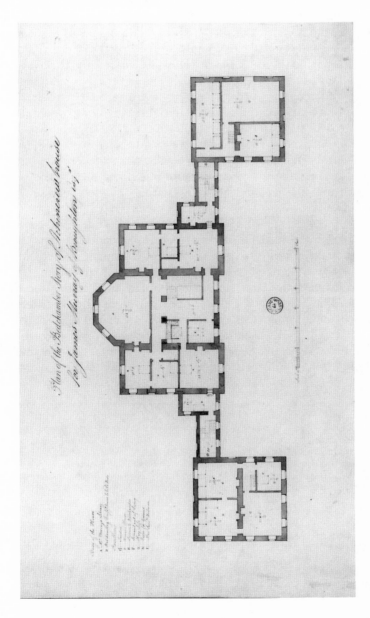

Illustration 10.12 Auchincruive: Plan of the Bedchamber Story, Adam Drawings, v. 44, no. 64. *Courtesy:* Sir John Soane's Museum, London.

or fully developed portico, and single bays to each side."[6] The main part was to be 75 feet long and 45 feet wide, and to have four stories – half-sunk ground; principal; bedchamber; and attic. Two nearly square two-story pavilions were to project forward on either side of the south-facing facade of the main block and connect to it by short arcades; beyond each pavilion were to run screen walls enclosing a kitchen garden and a wash house. The result would be an effective interplay of advancing and receding surfaces along two fronts, each 230 feet in length: the south-facing facade, broken into three divisions, would look out over the river and gardens, and the north-facing facade over wooded parkland. The Adam brothers hoped to give Auchincruive a grand appearance, with a symmetrical face and a regular succession of pedimented windows. Yet unlike many grander, more traditional piles, there were no columns and pilasters, no niches with statues, and no windows with splayed surrounds.

Oswald occupied a subsidiary house on the estate while he personally supervised construction. He ordered materials from London, chimney tiles and wainscotting from Rotterdam, timber from Germany and Norway, and bells from Glasgow. He stocked his park with pheasants from China and fortified his farms with lime from Dublin. Drawing on networks he had built up over the course of his career, he brought together a cadre of nationally renowned architects, decorators, and foremen from London, and skilled and unskilled laborers from the surrounding countryside. Before 1764 was up, he initiated a search for a factor who would supervise the running of the home farm and handle tenant matters.[7]

6. John Summerson described the two principal classes of country houses designed during the 1700s: "the greater house," and the more compact villa. "The Classical Country House in 18th-Century England," *Journal of the Royal Society of Arts*, v. 107 (1959), pp. 541–53. Examples of "the greater house" can be found in Wanstead, Essex (Lord Castelmain) and Houghton, Norfolk (Robert Walpole). It consisted of an oblong divided along the long axis by a spine wall; along the short axis were two principal rooms – the hall and saloon. Wings were attached to the central block. Interest in an imposing style of architecture waned after 1740, and was replaced by the villa plan. On villas, see Peter Leach, *James Paine* (London, 1988), p. 50. The first important British house of "the villa revival" was James Paine's Heath House, Yorkshire, built in 1744–45, but the style did not take firm root for two decades.

7. Michael Herries to Richard Oswald, August 14, 1764, Oswald Letter Book, v. 2, ff. 340–41; Receipt, August 14, 1764, William Laird to Richard Oswald, August 16, 17, 21, 1764, Oswald Papers, Sudlows; James Lockhart to Richard Oswald, December 22, 26, 1764, Oswald Papers, EUL; George Baird to Richard Oswald, August 24, 1764, Oswald Letter Book, v. 2, f. 1, SRO; and Archibald Bogle to Richard Oswald, September 28, 1764, Oswald Papers, Sudlows. Timber used in the construction of the house was generally foreign. William Laird to Richard Oswald, May 12, 1768, Oswald Papers, Sudlows. For final touches, see Robert Fall to Richard Oswald, November 23, 1764, James Gordon to Richard Oswald, November 4, 1764, William Cunningham to Richard Oswald, October 30, 1764, Contract, October 15, 1764; and George Baird to Richard Oswald, September 20, 1764, Oswald Papers, Sudlows.

Rough construction took four years, from 1764 to 1768. Oswald studied the progress with enthusiasm, his ardor evidenced by an unending flow of letters between his office in London and his factor in Ayr, as well as frequent trips to the site. The year 1765, for example, was marked by selection of materials, supervision of construction, and opening of stone, lime, and coal quarries in outlying fields so that his workmen had a ready supply of building materials. As time went on, his concerns shifted from construction to finish. He selected manuscript boxes which the Adam brothers assured him were worthy of the nobility and, later, he tinkered with the designs for the doors, windows, and shutters.[8]

Oswald made the important decisions himself, although in making up his mind he relied heavily on the Adam family. At Auchincruive, the brothers exceeded their usual attentiveness. In early 1766, John Adam visited the site and sketched designs for sash windows with brass pulleys; the following March, James Adam prepared ceiling and chimney drawings and sent window materials (Illustrations 10.13 and 10.14). Since "the different parts" were "at full size & particularly mark'd for what purposes" they were intended, the workmen should have made no mistake in executing them, but "if they should require any farther explanation," James offered on-site inspection, and another brother offered "to obey" Oswald's call "at any time." This they provided free of charge.[9]

Despite Oswald's enthusiastic attention and the help he received from his architects, work dragged on through 1767. The May report from his factor, while typical, was hardly encouraging:

> The whole work in your New House goes on very slowly and in short I have no pleasure in looking at what is done & a doing. I do wish & intreat that you could find some more able person to direct and conduct the execution of the work in the principal story

8. John Adam to Richard Oswald, March 11, 1765, Oswald Papers, Sudlows.
9. John Miller to Richard Oswald, February 20, April 10, 1766, Oswald Papers, EUL; James Adam to Richard Oswald, July 21, 1766, Oswald Papers, Sudlows; Adam Papers, v. 11, nn. 221–23, and v. 22, nn. 219–21, Sir John Soane's Museum; and, on the individual help offered by the brothers, John Adam to Richard Oswald, November 7, 1767, Oswald Papers, EUL. The Adam firm was well-equipped to provide a wide range of building materials to its clients, since it owned a timber and wood business, a brick works, a stone operation, and a building supply company. Alastair Rowan, "After the Adelphi," *Journal of the Royal Society of Architecture*, v. 122 (1974), pp. 667–68. For examples of the Adam brothers assisting Oswald's building, see James Adam to Richard Oswald, August 16, 1766, Oswald Papers, Sudlows. Oswald wanted Ratcliffe Crown glass for the principal story windows and London Crown glass on the ground and attic stories, but the contractor sent inferior grades. Only after James Adam threatened the supplier was the undesirable glass replaced. For Adam's unwillingness to take payment, see James Adam to Richard Oswald, September 4, 1767, Oswald Papers, Sudlows; and John Adam to Richard Oswald, November 6, 1767, Oswald Papers, EUL.

Illustration 10.13 Auchincruive: Design of the Ceiling for the Hall, Adam Drawings, v. 11, no. 221. *Courtesy:* ~~Sir John Soane's Museum, London.~~

(Hall Chimney Piece for Richard Oswald Esqr.)

Illustration 10.14 Auchincruive: Design of the Hall Chimney Piece, Adam Drawings, v. —, no. 220. *Courtesy:* Sir John Sonane's Museum, London.

so that you may have some comfort in the possessing of it. The ornaments that are made look in general very heavie & are not clean done.

Spurred on by such reports, Oswald quickly hired a master carpenter from London. At the same time, he began to fill the house with his belongings – china, sofas covered with green damask silk, cases of wine and port. More capable craftsmen coupled with his personal attention seem to have finally succeeded in rousing the laborers and, by year's end, work on the exterior was substantially complete. Enough had been done to warrant fixing the date "1767" to a rainwater gutter-head immediately below the entrance-facade parapet.[10] By 1768, the roof of the southwestern kitchen and laundry wing having been finished and the decoration of secondary rooms having begun in earnest, the house was complete enough to move into.[11]

Auchincruive was not finished until 1771 and, by that time, it was a decidedly different building from the Adam plan. We have an early nineteenth-century print and two early twentieth-century photographs of the 1771 structure (Illustrations 10.15–10.17). From these views, we see how Oswald's execution changed the original Adam design.[12] Auchincruive was more modest in scale and plain in detailing than the Adams planned. Rather than triangular or segmentally curved pediments above the main block's principal-story windows, Oswald overrode the

10. John Maxwell to Richard Oswald, May 1, 1767, Oswald Letter Book, v. 3, f. 39, SRO; Richard Oswald to William Crouch, Carpenter, May 19, 1767, containing Crouch's contract, and William Lockhart to Richard Oswald, June 10, 1767, Oswald Papers, Sudlows. Other than that Oswald chose Crouch as the carpenter, almost nothing is known about him. He seems to have procured ideas from treatises and contemporaneous projects. We know that he was a London joiner who subscribed to Paine's *Plans*. Geoffrey Beard, *Craftsmen and Interior Decoration in England, 1660–1820* (London, 1981), p. 254. Culzean Castle, the seat of the Earl of Cassilis and the best example of Adam architecture in southwestern Scotland, was on his mind. Earl of Cassilis to Richard Oswald, February 19, 1770, Oswald Papers, Sudlows. On the completion of the exterior, see William Lockhart to Richard Oswald, June 24, 1767, David Robertson to Richard Oswald, September 19, 1767, Oswald Papers, Sudlows.
11. Robert Selby to Richard Oswald, June 4 1768, Oswald Papers, Sudlows; George Baird to Richard Oswald, July 5, 1768, Oswald Letter Book, v. 2, f. 32, John Maxwell to Richard Oswald, July 23, 1768, and George Baird to Richard Oswald, October 12, 1768, v. 2, f. 36 SRO. For the official date of occupation, see E 326/1/12–15, SRO. Window taxes were annually assessed on all inhabited buildings. In 1766, Oswald was charged for twenty-four windows; two years later, he paid for seventy-seven.
12. The engraving in Illustration 10.15 bears an 1807 watermark. Its caption reads "The Home of Richard A. Oswald," who died in 1819. Its interpretation is fraught with difficulty: the central portion of the main block is recessed, rather than protruding, which would have been the case had the Adam design been followed exactly. It is probably most accurately viewed as the northern park-side facade and a southwestern wing, with liberties having been taken in drawing the details.

Illustration 10.15 Auchincruive: Park-Side Facade. Drawing by J. Denholm. Engraving by Robert Scott (1807).
Courtesy: Royal Commission of the Ancient and Historical Monuments of Scotland.

Illustration 10.16 Auchincruive: Park-Side Facade. *Courtesy:* Royal Commission of the Ancient and Historical Monuments of Scotland, Edinburgh.

Illustration 10.17 Auchincruive: River-Side Facade. *Courtesy:* Royal Commission of the Ancient and Historical Monuments of Scotland, Edinburgh.

brothers' order and repeated the simple, flat-surfaced lintels that appear everywhere else on the building. Rather than the single Palladian window, considered by contemporaries to be "calculated for show, and very pompous in their nature," that Adam wanted for the side divisions of the principal story, Oswald set a pair of plain, rectangular windows identical to the plain rectangular windows used in the rest of the house.[13] The facade is flat and severely unadorned. The Adam scheme called for a solid parapet with urns atop the roof, but Oswald allowed only the balustrade. In the pavilion, he omitted the Adam parapet altogether, maintaining clean lines and saving some money. All walls were rendered with rough material: cement and sand peppered with crushed stone and gravel. Plain stonework dominated: it edged the main block's three sections in the two plain courses below the principal story and in the parapet of the main block. The windows on the half-sunk story were likewise framed by plain moldings. Few references to classical architecture complicated this rough and stony exterior: no temple fronts, no pediments above windows, no windows with arches, and no giant pilasters or columns.

Compared to the other principal country houses of Ayrshire, Auchincruive is simpler and less ostentatious. In reflecting on the eighteenth century, art historians have understandably focused on the grand style of building, but there was also a simpler style, and it is in this plainer tradition that Auchincruive and most other associate houses fall.[14] For

13. Ware, *Complete Body*, p. 467.
14. The "grand style" of housing has understandably caught the attention of architectural historians. It can be glimpsed in the buildings erected by several of the associates' acquaintances: Cally House, the principal seat of James Murray of Broughton, from whom Oswald bought Auchincruive [William Adam, *Vitruvius Scoticus*, pls. 111–13]; Kenwood House, the London villa of Oswald's friend Lord Mansfield [*The Works of Robert and James Adam*, ed. Henry H. Reed (New York, 1980), v. 1, n. 2, pls. 1–8]; the Whitehall townhouse of Sargent II's fellow speculator Sir Matthew Featherstonehaugh [James Paine, *Plans, Elevations and Sections of Noblemen's and Gentlemen's Houses*, v. 1 (London, 1767), pp. 26–32]; and the homes of Oswald's army acquaintances: Abraham Hume's Wormley Bury [Arthur T. Bolton, "Wormley Bury, Hertfordshire," *Country Life*, v. 37 (January 30, 1915), pp. 144–49]; Peter Taylor's Purbrook Park [Anon., "Topographical Descriptions of Farlington, Hants," *Gentleman's Magazine* (1800), pp. 729–31, and Nicolaus Pevsner and David Lloyd, *Hampshire and the Isle of Wight* (Harmondsworth, 1967), p. 472]; and Laurence Dundas's Aske Hall in Yorkshire [Northallerton, North Yorkshire Record Office, Zetland Papers, Aske House surveys; F. O. Morris, *A Series of Picturesque Views of Noblemen and Gentlemen of Great Britain and Ireland*, v. 5 (London, 1882), pp. 24–27; G. Bernard Wood, "Tower Houses of Yorkshire," *Country Life*, December 15, 1960, pp. 1,480–82; and Christopher S. Sykes, "The Raising of Aske," *Interiors*, July-August 1985, pp. 137–49], as well as the more imposing Moor Park in suburban Hertfordshire [L. W., "Moor Park," *Country Life*, January 6, 13, 1912, pp. 18–26, 56–62; John Harris, "The Dundas Empire," *Apollo*, v. 86 (September 1967), pp. 170–79; and T. P. Hudson, "Moor Park, Leoni and Sir James Thornhill," *The Burlington Magazine*, v. 113 (1971), pp. 657–61].

every Henry Hoare or Laurence Dundas, merchants building fabulous piles, there were at least three merchants who fit Isaac Ware's generic description of the gentleman-builder from London who built "for convenience more than magnificence" and wanted "the house handsome though not pompous."[15] Auchincruive was to project the image of a gentleman of stoic stability, free from greedy or passionate display, unmoved by the confusion of urban life, and submissive to an emerging order of respectability that reckoned restraint as its hallmark.

Within the house are similar echoes of this gentility and restraint.[16] Although the interior has been greatly modified since Oswald's death, the original arrangement and decoration are not difficult to reconstitute. Like most associates' houses, Auchincruive had a typical, late-eighteenth-century villa floor plan: nearly square, with a long axis comprised of three rooms on the river side and three rooms on the park side, and a short axis dominated by a centrally placed entrance hall and drawing room (Illustration 10.18). One entered the house via a flight of stairs rising to the principal story from a carriage run at the center of the south front. The entrance Hall was a large rectangle, 60 feet by 35 feet. The Hall's 15-foot walls were paneled with wood, painted white, and adorned with fluted pilasters and a narrow Doric frieze with alternating triglyphs and metopes emblazoned with the sun. On the ceiling, Robert Adam intermixed one large rectangle with several smaller squares; around the rectangle, he wove classical festoons and various circles, from the largest of which sprouted olive stems, branches, and leaves (Illustration 10.13). In the Hall's white Italian marble fireplace, he insisted on a carved frieze of coiling vine tendrils and young birds plucking at grapes. In olives and grapes, motifs requested by Oswald, Adam found a fitting emblem of the improvements Oswald later introduced on the estate. Flowering branches of olive, ancient symbols of victory and fame, suggest Oswald's mixed reasons for coming to the countryside: returning from the battlefields of Germany with the fruits of war in his purse, he desired to breathe life into the poor and depopulated countryside and, at the same time, win for himself personal fame and the esteem of gentlemen. In writing to his factor or his neighbors in Ayrshire, Oswald often likened himself to the laurel that sprouted during Minerva's contest with Neptune or as the dove that brought a sprig of olive back to

15. The idea of a class-based architectural style would not have struck Georgian owners as peculiar. In one of the most popular Palladian texts of the century, Isaac Ware highlighted elements appropriate "for a house of a merchant in trade." *Complete Body*, pp. 293–94, 406.
16. This was in keeping with Palladian dictates. Palladian architects generally adhered to a principle of relating the interior and exterior through "the contrast between the well-proportioned austere facade, and the rich, almost rococo interior." Cruickshank and Wyld, *London*, p. 35.

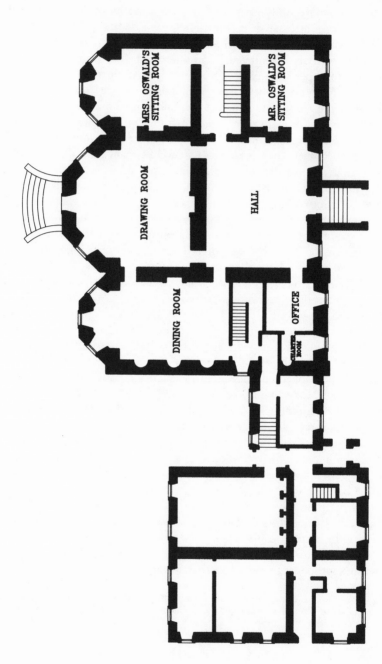

Illustration 10.18 Auchincruive: Principal Floor Plan as of 1784. Drawing by Hugh Adams Russell.

the ark.[17] He insisted on repeating the olive, laurel, and grape motifs wherever they could be conveniently introduced. In a similar vein, in the two public rooms adjoining the Hall, Oswald's Sitting Room and the Office/Charter Room, he expressed his dual interest in agricultural productivity and personal gain by decorating their cornices with a classical frieze of the thyrsus, a wand tipped with a pine cone, a symbol of fertility characterizing Bacchus and the Satyrs, and entwined with ivy, a symbol of regeneration.

While imposing, the public Hall and the rooms that adjoined it were not the most significant spaces in Oswald's house. What struck the visitor to Auchincruive was the preponderance of private spaces placed at the front and the top of the house. Auchincruive did not have the circuit of reception rooms around a central hall and staircase that characterized the larger, grander country houses of Britain; rather it had a string of smaller, more intimate conversation rooms. A Dining Room was situated in the northwestern corner of the main block, where an Adam carving of vines articulated themes of food, harvest, and hope on the ceiling, and two white Italian marble sideboards similarly decorated with vines bespoke agricultural abundance. Here, Oswald hung his favorite eating and drinking scenes – Hans Rottenhammer's *Feast of the Gods* and Palamedes's *The Flemish Supper* – and biblical scenes from the early life of Christ. The festivity of the room stood in strong contrast to the more severe style of Mrs. Oswald's Sitting Room, where heavy doors with bold pediments, enriched architraves, and pronounced keystones, as well as graphic scenes from the lives of St. Catharine, St. John, and humorless burghers, recalled an earlier, less consumer-driven era.

The centrally situated Drawing Room dominated the park-side suite. This hexagonal space was topped with an Adam ceiling and paneled in rare Central American woods. Its marble chimney-piece had been shipped directly from Italy by Oswald's correspondent in Leghorn. In front of its fire, the Oswalds held receptions that drew most of Ayrshire's worthies – the Dumfries, the Kennedys, the Cassilis, the Millars. As the carvings of winged putti plucking or piping musical instruments above the doors suggest, the room frequently doubled as a concert hall and game room, complete with "checking" board, shuttle cock, and billiard table. Unlike neighboring rooms, its focus was not upward to the lessons of the paintings – there were few of these here, and mainly of the

17. In the eighteenth century, the vine commonly symbolized paradisiacal fertility. John Gay, "Wine: A Poem" (1709), in *John Gay: Poetry and Prose*, ed. V. A. Dearing, v. 1 (Oxford, 1974), p. 23, ll. 76–84.

light Canaletto variety – but outward through a door and two floor-to-ceiling windows to the vistas of the parkland.[18]

At the two ends of the house, between the public and private suites, staircases connected the floors. Oswald discarded Adam's unusual idea for a single staircase rising out of the Hall in favor of a more restrained Palladian solution: two small and inconspicuous stairs tucked away at the ends of the house. Above the principal story lay a bedchamber floor divided by a long passage running east-to-west. Here were the most private areas of the house: bedrooms, dressing-rooms, and private sitting-rooms. Directly above the Drawing Room, lay Oswald's favorite – a redwood Library whose cases had been fitted by the London master carpenter with sliding glass panes. By midcentury, books were no longer "the accoutrements of the expert"; they "had become a part of everyday life" and "the common property of the family and its guests." For someone as dedicated to the useful application of self-won knowledge as Oswald, the library was a repository of books on new accounting methods, new agricultural techniques, new colonial lands, and polite behavior.[19]

Auchincruive's interior possesses some features of grandeur – including marble chimney-pieces, rare wood paneling, ornately molded door frames, sculpted ceilings, and references to classical architecture with festoons, friezes, and entablatures – but these features do not dominate. The internal arrangement and decoration, like the external features, were meant to signify "a man of parts." In interpreting that phrase for himself, Oswald took special liberties with the decorative room plans drawn up by the Adams. In the Hall and Dining Room, he replaced commissioned designs for the marble chimney-pieces with his own simpler designs incorporating the olive and grape motifs he had introduced elsewhere. He introduced Italian marbles and rare woods into the private quarters, and there was no want of silk. But, as in his counting-house, there was little gold and silver ornamentation. Only the Hall was reserved for the display of wealth and power. Though there were many paintings, there were no separate galleries for art. The only collection Oswald showcased lay at the center of the house, where the Library's extensive set of books on improvement and empire set a practical, informational tone. Auchincruive was the home of a man whose origins

18. George Baird to Richard Oswald, September 27, 1771, Oswald Letter Book, v. 2, SRO. John Levett's brother Francis Levett purchased marble chimney-piece sculptures for Oswald in Leghorn, Italy. John Levett to Richard Oswald, September 12, 1764, Oswald Papers, Sudlows. Most carvings and freestanding sculptures were the work of local Ayr craftsmen. "1775" Auchincruive Ledger, f. 19 Oswald Papers, Sudlows.

19. Mark Girouard, *Life in the English Country House: A Social and Architectural History* (Harmondsworth, 1980), pp. 180, 206. Additional bedrooms were on the attic story.

were humble, whose traditions were malleable, whose fortunes were self-made, and whose refinements were self-taught. Perhaps because of this self-reliant bent, his house was an amalgam of elements that accurately revealed the builder: the plainness of its exterior, the comfortable yet restrained luxury of its interior, the centrality of the library, and the self-improving nature of its contents.

Art Collections

Collecting art, like building houses, reflected, enhanced, and reinforced the associates' emerging gentility. Not just "outward Appearance, Clothing and Equipage" but "rational Abilities, . . . [and] real knowledge" of the arts also distinguished "the well-bred Gentleman." There was, the associates' contemporaries felt, "an Air of Mien" which "comes no other Way" than by exposure to and possession of art works. "[A] taste" for painting or sculpture became "a man of fashion very well," since "the title of Connoisseur" of painting or sculpture was "the safest passport in every fashionable society."[20]

Much like mere ownership of land, mere introduction to art was not sufficient to project their gentility. "Persons of all ranks and degrees" could "set up for connoisseurs, and even the lowest people talk familiarly of Hannibal Scratchi, Paul Varnish, and Raphael Angelo." The mark of a true gentleman was not only that he bought and possessed art, but that he did so with knowledge, appreciation, and discernment – that is, with "taste." Throughout the century, a knowledge of painting demonstrated a gentleman's differences from a member of a lower social group. When conversation turned "upon Painting, a Gentleman that is a *Connoisseur* is distinguished, as one that has Wit and Learning. . . . Not to be a *Connoisseur* on such an Occasion either silences a Gentleman and Hurts his Character; Or he makes a Worse Figure in pretending to be what he is not to those who see his ignorance."[21]

The associates were singled out by contemporaries as "connoisseurs" known for the "taste" of their collections, which they pieced together by various means. One of the more common ways was foreign travel; indeed, some critics denied "merit" to anyone who had "not travelled two or three thousand miles to acquire" works of art. Britain had no long-standing, productive painting profession at home to patronize, so

20. Stephen Philpot, *Essays on the Advantage of A Polite Education Joined with a Learned One* (London, 1747), intro., p. xii; Bonamy Dobree, ed., *The Letters of Philip Dormer Stanhope, 4th Earl of Chesterfield*, v. 4 (New York, 1932), p. 106; and Goldsmith, *Citizen of the World*, pp. 113–14 (Letter XXXIV).

21. *The Fugitive Miscellany*, v. 2 (London, 1775), p. 24; and Jonathan Richardson, *Argument in Behalf of the Science of a Connoisseur, in Two Discourses* (London, 1719), pp. 217–22.

acquisitive Georgian collectors looked to Europe in the middle decades of the century. There, they found the opportunity to collect works of art and educate themselves in the artistic styles with which a gentleman was to be conversant. In *New Letters from an English Traveller* (1781), Martin Sherlock reported that

> Nothing is so useful as travelling to those who know how to profit by it. Nature is seen in all her shades, and in all her extremes. If the mind of the traveller be virtuous, it will be confirmed in the love of virtue, and in the abhorrence of vice. . . . If the traveller has the seeds of one or of several talents, he will find men of the first merit in every line, who will think it a pleasure to encourage and unfold those seeds, and to communicate himself.

The traveler saw "those countries which are famous as scenes of so many actors in History," and "the seeing" was "highly conducive to the enlarging and opening of the understanding." Visiting Europe was "the best, indeed, the only way of learning how to weigh the perfections and imperfections of our own country." "Continental peregrinations" were a form of education and a mark of the educated.[22]

John Boyd was one associate who took the Tour. He first went abroad in the early 1770s and, later, following the grant of a baronetcy in 1775, took his family on a more extensive, year-long tour of France, Switzerland, Italy, the Low Countries, and Russia. Other associates made similar trips. In Aufrere's case, the merchant's family took up a lengthy residence in Rome, where he studied painting and music and found for his daughter a husband, an Englishman also on tour. Before leaving for Italy, he had bought and studied all ten volumes of Bernard de Montfaucon's *The Antiquities of Italy*, a book to which he continually referred when making purchases in subsequent years.[23] The places an associate visited influenced his collection, for he returned with works

22. *Literary Magazine*, v. 1 (1756), p. 465; Martin Sherlock, *New Letters from an English Traveller* (London, 1781), pp. 147–49; John Boyd, Jr., to Sir Robert Murray Keith, June 2, 1776, July 17, 1787, Add.Mss. 33,126 and Add.Mss. 35,538/284. The purposes of travel are outlined by Tucker in *Instructions*, p. 1. The route of the typical Tour is described in Andrew W. Moore, *Norfolk & the Grand Tour* (Norfolk, 1985), p. 14.

23. On Boyd, see *The London Gazette*, May 20, 1775, p. 1; John Boyd to Sir Robert Murray Keith, August 8, 1775, Add.Mss. 35,509/161, BL; and Patrick Home to Chase, November 22, 1775, Home-Robertson Papers, Paxton House, Berwickshire. The Boyds were in Caserta, north of Naples, the following January visiting Sir William Hamilton; in Rome by March; and in Venice by April. Patrick Home to Ninian Home, March 12, 1776, Home Robertson Papers, Paxton House; Note dei Forstieri 760: April 31, 1776, Venetian State Archives. On Aufrere, see Yarborough, *Brocklesbyana*, pp. 102–04; Account, AND 5/9/37, Lincolnshire Archives Office; PROB 11: Will of Aufrere, proved 1801. On Chambers, see L. Dutens to H. Mann, October 12, 1763, SP Foreign 105/315/276, PRO; and James Martin, Manuscript Diary of His Tour (1763–65), v. 2: December 31, 1763, v. 3: May 7, June 5, 1764, BL.

from those countries and he continued to collect the works of their artists back in London. The wide range of Boyd's collection can be explained, in part, by the extensive nature of his pan-European travels, while Aufrere, resident in Italy, favored Italian artists above all others.

Not all merchants took the Tour; indeed, Tourists formed a minority of the merchants who collected. As far as can be determined, Oswald never went on a Tour, although during his five years in Germany he based his bread contracting operations at Cassel, where the Landgraf was feverishly amassing one of Europe's finest collections of antique sculptures. It would have been unlikely for Oswald to have returned empty-handed from Germany; we know he returned from his diplomatic service in Paris in 1782 with twenty-eight trunks of paintings and prints. He could also draw on his principal Continental correspondents, the Amsterdam Hopes, renowned for their collection of Dutch and Flemish masters, and their connections to northern European art dealers.[24]

Most associates opted to stay put in London and have the art come to them. If artists had London studios (an unusual situation, except for portraitists) or if their works appeared in annual exhibitions or estate auctions, merchants could negotiate the purchases themselves. John Boyd acquired George Barret's *Morning Scene in Wales* from one of the Society for the Encouragement of Arts, Manufactures, and Commerce's annual shows, and he bought two *Views of Italy* by Richard Wilson at the 1774 sale of Boyd's bankrupt banker Colebrooke's personal property. In subsequent decades, he acquired Lodovico Caracci's *St. Francis*, Luca Giordano's *Venus at the Forge of Vulcan*, Rembrandt's *Portrait of His Mother*, and Daniel Seghers's *Festoon of Flora* at auctions held by Sir William Hamilton and the heirs of Lord Londonderry.[25]

Direct purchases from an exhibition, at auction, or on Tour brought some items into the associates' collections, but they bought most of

24. *Aufklarung und Klassizismus in Hessen-Kassel unter Landgraf Friedrich II, 1760–1785* (Kassel, 1979), pp. 242–92; and Marten G. Buist, *At Spes Non Fracta: Hope & Co., 1770–1815: Merchant Bankers and Diplomats at Work* (The Hague, 1974), pp. 486–94.

25. General auctions started in England about 1676; in Scotland, perhaps as early as 1668. The first picture auction was held in London in 1682. Iain Pears, *The Discovery of Painting: The Growth of Interest in the Arts, 1680–1768* (New Haven, 1988), p. 57; and "Auctions and Auction Rooms," *Notes and Queries*, 7th ser., v. 8, pp. 384, 477 (November 16, December 14, 1889). For the Colebrooke sale, see Christie, *A Catalogue of the Superb Collection of Pictures* (London, April 22–33, 1775) (Christie's annotated copy). The proceeds of the sale were divided between two of Colebrooke's creditors – the associate George Aufrere and the attorney Thomas Ansell. For Boyd's art, see *A Catalogue of a Genuine Collection of Valuable Pictures by the Most Admired Masters of the Italian, French, Flemish, and Dutch Schools. . . . The Property of Sir John Boyd, Bart., Deceased, By whom they were collected during a long Residence in Italy, And now removed from his Seat in Kent* (London, H. Phillips, March 18–19, 1800); and *A Catalogue . . .* (London, Coxe, Burrell & Foster, May 7–8, 1805).

their art through agents. Relatives, friends, and acquaintances sometimes purchased paintings and statues for them. John Ainslie, the companion of Oswald's illegitimate son Richard, bought prints for the
merchant when Ainslie and the younger Oswald traveled to France and
Belgium. In June 1766, Ainslie waited on Robert Strange the engraver
"to ask his advice considering the prints" Oswald desired, and then
accompanied Strange "to the place where they might be seen" and
purchased. In the same year, John Boyd relied on an even more elaborate chain of acquaintance to procure landscapes from Parisian painter
Joseph Vernet: the French painter Charles Pavillon was working on a
series of wall murals for Boyd's Dining Room at Danson, when Boyd
requested that he ask the Parisian painter Louis Michel Van Loo, one
of Pavillon's friends, to ask Vernet, one of Van Loo's friends, for a large
landscape with a waterfall.[26] On other occasions, professional agents
acquired art for the associates. Aufrere regularly called upon the services of Sir Joshua Reynolds, as agent as well as advisor.[27] Others
tapped the services of dealers like Matthew Brettingham, Thomas Jenkins,
and Gavin Hamilton, who scoured the Italian countryside in search of
artifacts for buyers back home. John Boyd, one of Hamilton's clients,
acquired with the dealer's help a second-century Roman vase from an
excavation of the villa of Emperor Antoninus Pius just south of Rome
(Illustration 10.19).[28] Even the fiercely independent Grant called on his

26. John Ainslie to Richard, June 25, 1766, Oswald Papers, Sudlows; Michael Herries to
   John Ainslie, September 2, 1766, Oswald Letter Book, v. 2, f. 346, SRO; and Leon
   Lagrange, *Les Vernet* (Paris, 1864), pp. 347, 365.
27. For instance, Pocketbooks of Sir Joshua Reynolds, 1770–90, sub October 14, 1765,
   October 24, 1766, and February 4, 1767, Royal Academy of Art; and Sir Joshua
   Reynolds to Sir William Hamilton, June 17, 1770, *The Letters of Sir Joshua Reynolds*,
   ed. F. W. Hilles (London, 1929), p. 27. See also Francis Broun, "Sir Joshua Reynolds'
   Collection of Paintings," vol. 1 (Ph.D. dissert., Princeton University, 1987), ch. 2.
28. The marble "Danson Vase" was excavated in 1772–73 by Gavin Hamilton from
   Monte Cagnolo/Cagnola, one kilometer northeast of Civita Livinia. The "Vase with
   Bacchanalians" was restored "with great attention," probably by Charles Townley.
   Hamilton considered it "inferior to none extant." "Hamilton's Letters," pp. 313, 321;
   GD 248/226/4/2. Contemporaries described it as "one of the most beautiful vases,
   perhaps in the world." Francis H. Taylor, *The Taste of Angels: A History of Art
   Collecting from Rameses to Napoleon* (Boston, 1948), p. 492. Three angles of the
   vase appear in G. B. Piranesi, *Vasi, Candelabra, Cippi, Sarcofagi, . . .* , v. 1 (Rome,
   1775), pls. 57–59. The sculpture represents fauns "of diverse ages" gathering grapes,
   placing them in baskets, and passing through the mountains. Boyd bought the nine-
   foot vase from Hamilton when Boyd was travelling on the Continent in 1775–76 and
   placed it in the Entrance Hall of Danson Hill. The vase was sold with the estate in
   1806; the purchaser sold it to the British Museum, where it is now displayed as
   Sculpture No. 2,502. Guy Colburn, "Civita Lavinia, The Site of Ancient Lanuvium,"
   American Journal of Archaeology, v. 18 (1914), pp. 24–25; Carlo Pietrangeli, *Scavi
   Scoperte di Antichita Sotto Il Pontificato di Pio VI* (Rome, 1958), pp. 111, 153; and
   Mark Jones, ed., *Fake? The Art of Deception* (London, 1990), pp. 132–35. Some
   uncertainty about the site of the vase has been caused by Piranesi stating that it was
   found at Hadrian's Villa in 1769. There is no evidence to substantiate Piranesi's claim.

Illustration 10.19 The Danson Vase. British Museum, Sculpture #2, 502, London. *Courtesy*: British Museum, London.

cousin Abbé Peter Grant, an exile in Rome who supported the Pretender, introduced British collectors to impoverished papal families, and acted as agent. Many "valuable Collections of Pictures" in Britain were built upon "the frequent ruins and dispersion of the finest Galleries in Rome and other Cities" with the help of such men.[29]

29. Horace Walpole, *Aedes Walpolianiae* (London, 1747), p. viii. The collecting of Italian art by the British during the 1700s is briefly discussed by Francis Haskell and Nicholas Penny, *Taste and the Antique: The Lure of Classical Sculpture, 1500–1900* (New Haven, 1981), p. 66, but they restrict their comments to antique sculpture. See also Denys Sutton, "The Lure of the Antique," *Apollo*, v. 119 (1984), pp. 312, 315. The role played by the wily Abbé Peter Grant in the acquisition of Italian art deserves a full-scale study. Mention of him appears in L. Lewis, *Connoisseurs and Secret Agents*

Sometimes the owner, his family, or a visitor made a list of the collections that were put together in these ways by merchants "ambitious to be thought" of as discriminating "judges of painting."[30] The Earl of Exeter, Aufrere's cousin by marriage and the owner of one of late Georgian England's finest private art collections, used the early morning hours when staying at the homes of friends to record their collections. His diary and Aufrere's own published list allows us to reconstitute Aufrere's collection. Similarly, the factor's list of paintings drawn up at Oswald's death, and the auctioneer's catalogue of paintings sold soon after Sir John Boyd's death assist the search.[31] These three collections, whose lists are complete, were relatively extensive: Aufrere's collection had nearly 150 paintings; Boyd's, more than 250; and Oswald's, 81. In fact, Aufrere owned one of the fifty "most distinguished collections" pieced together in the final quarter of the century, a collection that Sir Joshua Reynolds valued at £200,000.[32]

in *Eighteenth-Century Rome* (London, 1961), pp. 123–24, 130, 144–45, 160, 167–68, 217, 222, 232–33; and Fraser, *Chiefs of Grant*, v. 1, pp. 444–45, v. 2, pp. 446, 533–39, 551–58.

30. Emily J. Climenson, ed., *Passages from the Diary of Mrs. Philip Powys* (London, 1899), p. 63. As a group, merchants have never figured prominently in a discussion of collecting. For the collecting of Joseph Smith, the British Consul in Venice, see Francis Haskell, *Patrons and Painters* (New York, 1971), pp. 299–310; and Frances Vivian, *Il Console Smith* (Vicenza, 1971). The collections of Samson Gideon, Sir Laurence Dundas, Sir George Colebrooke, and Robert Udney are discussed in Denys Sutton, "New Trends," *Apollo*, v. 116 (December 1982), pp. 364–69, and "Cross Currents in Taste," ibid., pp. 373–76. Gideon's art collection of thirty-nine paintings is listed in [Thomas Martyn,] *The English Connoisseur*, v. 1 (London, 1766), pp. 12–14. Dundas's purchase of furniture, tapestries, and pictures is discussed in *Apollo*, v. 86 (September 1967), pp. 170–225. Catalogues of Henry Hope's collection are reproduced in Buist, *At Spes Non Fracta*, pp. 486–94. Other merchants' catalogues are listed in Frits Lugt, *Répertoire des Catalogues de Ventes*, v. 1 (The Hague, 1938). For an extremely rare example of merchants commenting on art, see Robert Harvey's Journal, 1773–74, and John Patteson's Letters, 1768–71 and 1778+, both in the Norfolk Record Office. Oswald, Boyd, and Aufrere are discussed below. Sargent II was a patron of Parisian artist Joseph Vernet: in 1764, he ordered three paintings "to the fantasy of" Vernet and, in 1765, he ordered a large marine- or landscape. Lagrange, *Vernet*, pp. 344–45. In the 1770s, he procured a landscape by Giovanni Both. Lincolnshire, Stamford, Burghley House, Library M. R. P. A. Orlandi, *Abecedario Pittorico*, p. 244, Lord Exeter's marginalia.

31. On Exeter, see Burghley House, *Abecedario*, marginalia; and Taylor, *Taste of Angels*, pp. 451–53. The handwritten Oswald list appears in a separate volume of the Oswald Papers at Sudlows. Supplementary information is provided by published sales catalogues. Christie, *A Catalogue of the Pictures of a Gentleman* (London, December 31, 1808); and Sotheby, Wilkinson & Hodge, *Catalogue of Important Pictures by Old Masters of the English & Continental Schools, Including the Properties of . . . R. A. Oswald, Esq.* (London, June 14, 1922), pp. 16–25.

32. Approximately £11,492,144 or $17,093,185 in 1994. Gustav F. Waagen, *Treasures of Art in Great Britain*, v. 1 (London, 1854), pp. 26–27; and *Scots Magazine*, v. 66 (1804), p. 728.

Inaccuracies abound in contemporary lists such as these; misunderstandings and misattributions were legion. Many works were not what they purported to be, given the difficulties of verification. The compiler often did not really know whether the picture was in fact painted by the named artist, and he relied on customary attribution, usually the word of a seller or broker. Few paintings attributed to Rembrandt in the eighteenth century, for instance, were painted by Rembrandt. If we cannot find the picture to verify the attribution, we are left with contemporary claims. Moreover, Aufrere's is the only complete extant collection for the associates. Not having the other collections in toto, we are forced to piece them together. This is difficult because few artists mentioned in Georgian collections have been the subject of historical investigation, fewer still have had their oeuvre catalogued, and their works have often been destroyed or sequestered in undisclosed private collections. Among the eighty-one paintings once owned by Oswald, only Canaletto's *Piazza San Marco Looking South*, two versions of Joseph Wright's copy of Duplessis's portrait of Benjamin Franklin, William Denune's portrait of Richard Oswald, and Johann Zoffany's portrait of Mrs. Oswald (Illustrations 2.5 and 2.6) can be traced with any certainty. Several other paintings seem likely candidates – but the paucity of works and the inability to verify paintings on his list make a full, detailed analysis of Oswald's art nearly impossible.[33]

From the lists, however, we can make a few generalizations about the nationalities, periods, and subject matters in the associates' art collections. Consider the paintings Oswald brought to Auchincruive between 1763 and 1784. Nearly half were seventeenth-century works, one-quarter dated from his own century, one-eighth came from the fifteenth and sixteenth centuries, and the remainder cannot be dated. Along with a taste for seventeenth-century painting went an appreciation of Dutch and Flemish artistry: nearly half of his paintings were by artists who had lived and worked in the Netherlands. In this regard, Oswald was

33. Pears, *Discovery of Painting*, p. 66. For Oswald's Canaletto, see W. G. Constable, *Canaletto*, v. 2 (Oxford, 1962), pp. 206–07, n. 48(a). One of the Wright copies of the Franklin portrait, now at Yale University, was made for Oswald during the 1782 peace negotiations; another copy, now at the Boston Public Library, was commissioned by Oswald and given to his brother or nephew. Sellers, *Benjamin Franklin*, pp. 415–18, pls. 8, 25. It is probable that the Birmingham City Art Gallery's *Falstaff Reviewing His Recruits* by Francis Hayman, acquired from an anonymous seller in a year when the scion of the Oswalds was selling off family treasures, belonged to Oswald. Brian Allen, *Francis Hayman* (New Haven, 1987), p. 179. Likewise, it is probable that Frans Francken II's *Solomon's Idolatry*, now at the Getty Museum in Malibu, California, belonged to Oswald. Of Franklin's portrait, it is interesting to note that Sargent II also owned a portrait painted by David Martin, and Aufrere owned two copies of it.

in step with a growing British interest in the naturalistic landscapes of Netherlandish artists like Hobbema and Ruisdael. The only other artists who stood out in his collection were the Italians, whose contribution comprised more than a third of the set. French, British, and German artists together formed only one-tenth of the collection.[34]

Oswald's paintings often told biblical or religious stories (27% of the paintings). Works such as Antonio Balestra's *St. John Preaching* and *The Beheading of St. John*, Pompeo Batoni's *The Holy Family*, Andrea Locatelli's *The Flight into Egypt*, and Frans Francken II's *Solomon's Idolatry* dominated rooms at Auchincruive. Landscape scenes, a quarter (25%) of the collection, were almost as common. Two types of subjects rounded out the group: classical and mythological subjects, such as Rubens's *Bacchanalian Feast* and Anticone's *Diana and Endymion*, and an equal number of "conversation" pieces, such as Pieter de Hooch's *Musical Conversation*, Anthonie Palamedes's *Flemish Supper*, Gerard Ter Borch's *Girls Making Lace*, and Francis Hayman's *Sir John Falstaff Raising Recruits*.

This thoroughly orthodox interest in seventeenth-century Dutch and Italian artists and in biblical and landscape themes also runs through the collections amassed by the other associates. More than half of the paintings in Aufrere's villa in Chelsea expressed biblical or religious themes (54%), dated from the 1600s (62%), and were the works of Italian artists (68%). Individual tastes changed the balance somewhat: although one-half of John Boyd's paintings dated from the seventeenth century and over one-third depicted landscapes or marinescapes, more than one-third of his paintings were from his own century and only one-fifth represented biblical or religious themes. With this interest in contemporary works went an interest in English artists: nearly one-quarter of John Boyd's paintings were the work of English artists, one-quarter Dutch artists, and almost as many Italian artists. Boyd seems to have been unique among the associates in his interest in English and contemporary art.

34. Appendix VII. During this period, Italy was "the single most important source of high quality works," and Italian paintings of the first half of the seventeenth century the most highly valued. Dutch and Flemish paintings were almost as highly esteemed. French painters and artists of the High Renaissance and earlier periods were "in a decided minority." Between 1762 and 1774, 47 percent of the paintings imported into Britain came from Italy, 18 percent from France, and 15 percent from Holland. Pears, *Discovery of Painting*, pp. 166–68, 210, Table 2. In the 1700s, regional distribution was a function of both taste and availability. Italy and Holland had a large artistic output, and their exports to Britain were large. Nearly constant war with France made French works less available. Tariff barriers erected and enforced by Spain made it more expensive for Englishmen to acquire Spanish paintings than works from any other country. Ibid., pp. 54–55.

The subjects favored in the collections for which complete lists have survived were polite, industrious, and moral; their inclusion in these collections further solidified the merchants' emerging status as discriminating gentlemen. The art frequently reflected the good life as the owners knew it. Views of their houses and gardens, pictures of their horses and cows, and still-lifes of dead game and fresh food confirmed their comfort and gentility. Many paintings were blatantly preoccupied with wealth. Three views of Danson by George Barret, Elias Martin, and Richard Wilson (Illustration 10.20), hung on the walls of Boyd's Westminster townhouse, and two more were ordered from Thomas Malton and Richard Corbould for Danson itself (Illustrations 10.21). All of these views accentuated the prominence of the house and the importance of its owner; in these pictures, as in the more stylized views of the Italian campagna sketched by Moucheron, one finds scenes of fields, ponds, hunts, and country pleasures – representations of the harmonious elysium that they thought they were constructing for themselves.[35] Elsewhere, groaning boards of ripe fruit (Stanover), dead game (Weenix), and plump sheep (Dujardin) reified the plenty that the associates were encouraging on their estates through technical improvements. Hunting scenes, represented by Morland's *Spaniels Hunting* or *Pointers in a Landscape*, evoked appropriate pastimes for a gentleman of means, although there is no indication that any of the associates actually did hunt, shoot, or fish.

In these idealized scenes, tenants often toil in the shadow of or stand apart from the laird, who stands for the associate. Domenico Fetti's *The Lord of the Vineyard Hiring Laborers*, in Aufrere's collection, is no mere courtly figure (Illustration 10.22). Fetti's lord, actually Christ, is seated in the lower right of the canvas, and he points downward to the spade on which a laborer is leaning. His demeanor is impurely polite, and he is conversing with the tenant rather than ordering him about. Yet he is unmistakably the lord, with a bright white frock, a jaunty red hat topped by silver and green feathers, and a dramatic gesture that leaves few to wonder who is in charge. The painting represents the improved personal stations the associates attained, as well as the improved agricultural relations they tried to introduce on their estates.

The assumption of power could be hidden and the association with the pastoral strengthened, as it was in Sir Joshua Reynolds's Mrs. *Pelham Feeding Poultry* (Illustration 10.23), a portrait commissioned by Aufrere in the year of his daughter's marriage to Charles Anderson Pelham.

35. Leon Battista Alberti, *The Ten Books of Architecture*, trans. James Leoni, v. 2 (London, 1966), p. 804, cited in Margaretha Lagerlof, *Ideal Landscape* (New Haven, 1990), p. 5.

Illustration 10.20 Sir John Boyd's Danson Hill, Bexleyheath, Kent. Painting by Richard Wilson. *Courtesy*: Bexley Libraries and Museums Department, Hall Place, Bexley, Kent.

Illustration 10.21 Sir John Boyd's Danson Hill, Bexleyheath, Kent. Painting by Thomas Malton, c. 1790. *Courtesy*: Ashmoleon Museum, University of Oxford.

Sophia Aufrere Pelham, standing before a toy dairy, wears a flowered dress and holds a sieve from which she feeds chickens and pigeons, a British version of Marie Antoinette playing with her barnyard animals at Versailles. But whatever the disguise, the message was the same: in the art they put on their walls, the associates found images in which polite, industrious, moral lords – in other words, their own idealized selves – replaced the traditional rulers of society.

These overseas traders also reminded themselves and others of their engagement with commerce by hanging the marinescapes of Dutch, French, and English painters on their walls, in much the same way that they placed representations of Africans on their coats of arms or their dinner service. As a shipper and trader, Aufrere could recognize his calling in Willem Van de Velde the Younger's *A Calm*. Equally, John Boyd could perceive his trade in idealized representations of shipping, like Charles Brooking's *Sea View* and Ludolf Bakhuyzen's *Vessels Passing a Buoy*; realistic accounts of mariners hauling a small vessel to higher ground in the midst of a tremendous rolling tide, like Joseph Turner's *Sea Shore with a Tremendous Rolling Tide*, which Boyd found at the Royal Academy exhibition in 1797; or graphic depictions of shipping and trading, like Turner's *Fishermen Coming Ashore at Sunset*,

Illustration 10.22 *The Lord of the Vineyard Hiring Laborers*, by Domenico Fetti. *Courtesy*: Dresden Gemaldegalerie Altemeister, Dresden, Germany (copy); Private Collection, United Kingdom (original).

Illustration 10.23 *Mrs. Pelham Feeding Poultry*, by Sir Joshua Reynolds. *Courtesy*: Private Collection, United Kingdom.

Previous to a Gale (Illustration 10.24). These paintings were generally realistic and factual. "Through the angle of each spar, the set of each sail, the tension or slackness of each rope," or the actions of each sailor, the owner and viewer witnessed the makings of sea-borne trade and heroicized Britain's emergence as a prosperous mercantile empire.[36] In a more allegorical fashion, Aufrere found an apposite symbol of the Englishman taming the world and reducing it to order in Bernini's impressive statue of *Neptune & Triton*, which he placed in an octagonal summerhouse overlooking the Thames. As seen in Illustration 10.25, Neptune stands on a shell, as on a chariot, gliding atop the ocean, from which his son the merman Triton emerges, blowing on a conch shell. Amid a raging storm, Neptune throws his copper trident into the sea to quell the tumult. Thus presented, Neptune "the master of navigation" provided Aufrere with an emblem of "absolute dominion over the tumultuous waters of the world."[37]

Placing ancient and classical subjects on one's walls could clearly trumpet the merit of one's accomplishments. The depictions of antiquity in the associates' art collections tended to classicize the owners and highlight traits of the eighteenth-century gentleman. Such presentation served as social camouflage by which the merchant instructed others and reminded himself of the legitimacy of new wealth in polite society. The analogy with Rome subtly undergirt their claim to social recognition by associating them with older, "nobler," "higher" principles. Thus, they cast their surroundings not in terms of modern Britain but ancient Rome. Their houses bore Roman architectural and decorative effects: muted brick colors, an assertive principal story, and restrained door cases on the outside and, on the inside, "useful" rooms, handsome but not extravagant finishes, and collections of valuables. Their gardens were styled after the re-creations of the Roman Campagna painted by Claude and Dughet, artists whom they displayed prominently on their

36. *Charles Brooking, 1723–1759* (Bristol, 1966), p. 4.
37. Reynolds bought the statue from Thomas Jenkins in Rome in 1786. Two different reports of the statue's later purchase survive. Some scholars suggest Aufrere's son-in-law Charles Anderson Pelham, Baron Yarborough, bought it in 1794. William T. Whitley, *Artists and Their Friends in England, 1700–1799* (London, 1928), pp. 181–82; John Pope-Hennessy, *Catalogue of Italian Sculpture in the Victoria and Albert Museum* (London, 1964), pp. 596–600; and Broun, "Reynolds' Collection," pp. 60–61. It is more likely that Aufrere bought the sculpture at Ralph's Exhibition in 1792 for £500, with the sculptor Nollekens acting as his agent. Receipt from Edmond Malone to Joseph Nollekens, July 27, 1792, Yale University Beinecke Library, New Haven; R. Wittkower, "Bernini Studies – I: The Group of Neptune and Triton," *Burlington Magazine*, v. 94 (March 1952), pp. 68–76; Tessa Murdoch, "Louis Francois Roubiliac and His Huguenot Connections," *Proceedings of the Huguenot Society of London*, v. 24 (1983), p. 3; Joseph Spence, *Polymetis* (London, 1755), pp. 65, 218–19; and Charles Scribner III, *Gianlorenzo Bernini* (New York 1991), pl. 7.

Illustration 10.24 *Fishermen Coming Ashore at Sunset, Previous to a Gale* (The Mildmay Seapiece), by Joseph M. W. Turner. Present Whereabouts Unknown. *From:* Joseph M. W. Turner, *Liber Studiorum*, v. 2 (London, 1812). *Courtesy:* Houghton Library, Harvard University.

Illustration 10.25 *Neptune & Triton*, by Gianolorenzo Bernini. *Courtesy*: Victoria & Albert Museum, London.

walls. Their halls were filled with the sarcophagi of Roman senators and generals (Illustrations 10.26 and 10.27) or, better, busts of themselves in Roman garb (Illustrations 10.28 and 10.29). The busts of George Aufrere by Joseph Nollekens and Arabella Aufrere by Louis Francois Roubiliac sensitively ascribe a Roman nobility to the sitters.[38]

38. The Nollekens bust of George Aufrere is signed and dated 1777. It may have been commissioned by Aufrere's son-in-law Charles Anderson-Pelham. John Lord, "Joseph Nollekens and Lord Yarborough: Documents and Drawings," *Burlington Magazine*

Cippo antico di marmo che si vede presso il Signor Giorgio Aufrere Cavaliere Inglese nella sua Villa a Chelsea

Illustration 10.26 Cinerarium of Saenia Longina. *From*: G. B. Piranesi, *Vasi*, . . . , v. 2, pl. 46. *Courtesy*: Houghton Library, Harvard University.

Such "Romanness" brought distinct advantages. It established them as learned men, steeped in the traditions and truths of antiquity, and also implied senatorial status, to be shared with established families. "No compliment" could impart "a more flattering idea to an Englishman,

(December 1988), pp. 915–20. The Roubiliac bust of Arabella Bate Aufrere was signed and dated 1748, at the time of her marriage to Aufrere. Tessa Murdoch, "Louis Francois Roubiliac and His Huguenot Connections," *Proceedings of the Huguenot Society of London*, v. 24 (1983), pp. 29–30.

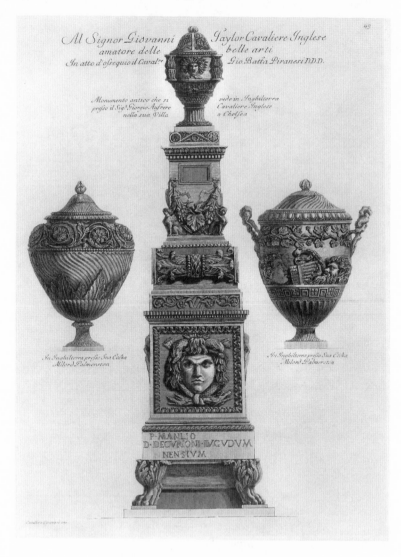

Illustration 10.27 Cinerarium of P. Manlio. *From*: G. B. Piranesi, *Vasi*, . . . , v. 1, pl. 49. *Courtesy*: Houghton Library, Harvard University, Cambridge, Mass.

Illustration 10.28 Bust of George Aufrere, by Joseph Nollekens. *Courtesy*: Private Collection, United Kingdom.

Illustration 10.29 Bust of Arabella Aufrere, by Louis François Roubiliac. *Courtesy*: Private Collection, United Kingdom.

than that which compares him to an old Roman," the political controversialist and social commentator John Shebbeare noticed; the "valour, prudence, love of liberty and his country, with those other eminent qualities of our illustrious predecessors, are the attributes which he receives with most delight."[39] In the very different world of Rome's republic, men like the associates would have gained a high and respected social position by rising through the *cursus honorum*, a series of public employments. Viewed through the lens of classical architecture and art, the associates' admission into the corridors of political power and the salons of polite society seems quite natural.

Themes of *politesse* were reinforced by themes of pastoral industry. These found their best expression in the full and detailed dramatization of the life and work of the peasantry. An interest in this low life is hardly surprising among men eager to appear landed and genteel. In the hundred years after the Glorious Revolution, the growth in shipping and trading, the rise of commercial agriculture, and the shift in the interests of the aristocracy and civil service from royal court to private estate encouraged "a new appreciation of the value of industriousness" and awakened a visual interest in its artistic representation. "This realization made the old pastoral ideal less than entirely adequate" and encouraged the evocation of an alternate image of the countryside that viewed "work together with leisure," an image that was "truer to actual experience."[40]

A painting by Christian Dietrich that Aufrere collected shows this interest in industry. In *The Farrier's Shop*, two men ready the tools needed to shoe a horse, while the unsuspecting animal munches on hay. In the background, under the shelter of a dovecote, a mother tends to the needs of her two children. No excuse is made for the dirt, grime, or squalor. The mood is one of sympathy, even interest. Depicted on the canvas are people who run the full gamut of emotion and know the full range of experience, but whose primary concern is work. These were the economic agents of a prior day, highly romanticized. As described in the pamphlets the associate collected in his library, these people in the shop were the reservoir of Britain's wealth who, at the same time, were capable of an almost arcadian enjoyment of work. In this painting, as in most of the associates' other genre paintings and landscapes, the clarity of composition, the skillful handling of light, and the richness of detail leave an impression that tranquillity pervades the world of the working Boor. One finds no forced evictions, no deserted villages. Rather,

39. John Shebbeare, *Letters from England*, v. 1 (London, 1756), p. 1.
40. David H. Solkin, *Richard Wilson: The Landscape of Reaction* (London, 1982), pp. 22–23.

Illustration 10.30 *Peasants Playing Cards*, by Andries Both. *Courtesy*: Private Collection, United Kingdom.

the tenants and workers on the estates go about their daily lives in a way they relish. Three young peasant men depicted by Andries Both in Illustration 10.30 are seated, two hover behind, and yet another lies down beside them on the ground. One of the players holds his cards in his hands, seeming to hesitate; they are already open, but not yet laid on the ground. His friends watch intently as another opponent examines his cards. Beyond them, caught in the sultry light of full summer, a young man is un-self-consciously bathing close to a bridge, over which passes a man with a donkey, basket, and cart. Everything here is thoroughly composed. But for the crumbling castle and ruined pile which loom above the players, there is little here that marks the use or abuse of arbitrary power and the presence or futility of excess and vanity.

The virtue of a simple, industrious country life is enunciated time and again in the associates' collections. Farming received special emphasis, whether in Morland's *A Winter Scene*, Wilson's *A Sunny Evening*, or the many landscapes by Philips Wouwermans. In every associate's collection, agriculture outstripped trade three to one as a theme. Whereas commerce was often maligned as a base and self-serving pursuit, farming was universally deemed a high calling and a manifestation of Kames's "genuine patriotism," and it was frequently depicted as a pursuit of the gods. In Danson's Dining Room, for instance, Boyd ordered the French painter Charles Pavillon to depict the gods responsible for the promotion of agriculture and art: a goddess by a blasted oak tree (probably Pomona), a goddess with a pitcher of wine, a goddess with a sheaf of wheat (Ceres), a goddess playing a zither in honor of the sun, a goddess playing a flute (a Muse), and a goddess with a mask (Momus, the patron of criticism). Above the doors, putti clutch grapes or flutes and sport with goats or parrots; above the fireplace, in a painted *Sacrifice to Bacchus*, the fertility god is surrounded by women carrying tambourines and offering bushels of grapes. Few who looked up from the table would fail to connect farming, fertility, and deity. Throughout Boyd's house, too, the emblems of the crop that Oswald and Grant hoped to grow in Florida – grapes – appeared as they did in all the associates' newly built houses, intertwining themes of nobility, abundance, regeneration, and liberty. Agriculture was regarded as one of the few truly virtuous sectors of the Georgian economy, and so it was anything but whimsical for the associates to choose it as a subject for viewing. Agricultural paintings were visual words in a language of social legitimation. Like Adam's marble carvings at Auchincruive, Pavillon's dining room cycle at Danson softened, perhaps cloaked, the commercial origins of the associates' wealth, and implied a precommercial interest in the soil.

The emphasis on agriculture is only one step removed from an emphasis on morality and, in the numerous biblical and religious paintings of the associates, the moral message was explicit. None of the associates left an extensive record of active religiosity, yet religious themes dominated in more than half of Aufrere's collection, and made up a fifth of Boyd's collection. One suspects the associates expressed their faith indirectly by surrounding themselves with religious painting. The acquisition or frequent viewing of an *Il Reposo*, Crucifixion, or *Mater Dolorosa* was, in this way, an indirect act of devotion.[41]

The associates' religious art was dominated by forceful figures who

41. Joseph Alsop, *The Rare Art Traditions* (New York, 1982), pp. 122, 126. Over one-half of the collections amassed by the broker Robert Strange was devoted to religious themes.

Illustration 10.31 *The Ascent of Christ/Christ Falling beneath the Cross*, by Peter Paul Rubens. *Courtesy*: Private Collection, United Kingdom.

vigorously opposed contemporary hierarchies and insisted on Christian virtues, or heroic characters who performed acts of charity. Rubens's *Ascent of Christ*, which Aufrere displayed in his Drawing Room, narrates the story of Jesus carrying his own Cross (Illustration 10.31). The Cross is large and heavy; the mood is one of sympathetic pity. Christ, falling beneath the weight of the Cross, is assisted by a youth who lifts his burden and a woman who wipes his face. In this painting, Aufrere chose a widely recognized symbol of the burden of true charity that the Christian must carry throughout his life. The associates regarded charity as the cardinal human virtue, demanding both a love for one's God and a love for one's neighbors. Whether it was Elijah and the Widow of Zaraphath, who gave him food, or Elisha and the Rich Woman of Shunem, who bestowed friendship on him, the paintings selected by the associates laid emphasis on the active expression of charity. One could not have mistaken the moral of Domenico Fetti's *Lord of the Vineyard* or the message of Sebastian Bourdon's massive seven-part *Works of Mercy* or its importance to the Huguenot merchant Aufrere: feeding the hungry, receiving the stranger, freeing the captive, giving drink to the thirsty, clothing the naked, burying the dead and, the subject of Illustration 10.32, healing the sick. No matter how hard a gentleman might labor, these pictures suggested, he would not necessarily partake of salvation if he should be wanting in charity, although admittedly the love of fellow men was extended only to other whites. Ironically, it does not appear to have occurred to these slave traders, holding up "freeing the captive" and the like as a moral imperative, that true charity might include black Africans. In artistic litanies of good works, the associates mirrored the programs they were implementing among white men and women through their own philanthropic programs.

One other related theme, righteous resistance, appears frequently among the paintings of saints: the ascetic John the Baptist repudiating Herod for marrying his brother's wife; the husband Joseph taking Mary and Christ away into Egypt in defiance of Herod; the secret believer Sebastian supporting his fellow Christians in defiance of Roman law and, after surviving an execution of arrows, returning to confront the emperor; the Roman Christian Cecilia who converted and wed a Roman nobleman; and the preacher Dominic challenging the Albigensian heresy in southern France.

Among these stories, that of Susannah and the Elders especially caught the associates' fancy. In Susannah, the associates' contemporaries found an example of naive virtue triumphing over villainy. On Romanelli's canvas (Illustration 10.33), two lecherous elders of the exiled Babylonian community pounce upon the young wife of a prosperous Jew, Susannah, who is taking her toilet in the garden. As it appeared in Aufrere's Drawing Room, they threaten to expose her, falsely, as an adulteress, unless she submits to their sexual demands. Spurning them, she is condemned to death, and only the eleventh hour intercession of Daniel saved her from destruction. Wherever the scene was viewed – Aufrere owned three versions, Oswald one – there was, apart from undeniable titillation, an example of the triumph of the young and new in capturing

Illustration 10.32 *Seven Works of Mercy: Healing the Sick,* by Sebastian Bourdon. *Courtesy:* John & Mable Ringling Museum of Art, Sarasota.

Illustration 10.33 *Susannah & the Elders*, by Giovanni Francesco Romanelli. *Courtesy:* Private Collection, United Kingdom.

the attention of the old and established, as well as the ultimate delivery from evil of those restraining lust out of principle.[42]

The associates' collections form a commentary on the dangers of moral failure to Western civilization. In nonreligious ways, the ruined temples and vases of Wilson, Panini, Codazzi, and Piranesi, the broken columns and bent cypresses of Weenix, and the imposing piles of Stonehenge sketched by Serres implied that even the richest and strongest civilization could crumble. "The pleasing reflections from those venerable Relicts of antient Roman Grandeur," one Tourist noted, showed the collector "how Time erases everything; for those noble and immense Edifices were certainly (by their manner of building) intended to stand for ever."[43] The ancient sarcophagi collected by Aufrere ghoulishly dramatized the same point. And the boxes of volcanic sulfur that Boyd brought back with him from Naples after the eruption of Mount Vesuvius in 1767, over which hung J. B. A. Tierce's *The Eruption of Mount Vesuvius* and *The Fall of Tivoli*, made the connection in even more graphic terms, linking the past to the present. Ruins, whether in Italy, books, or one's garden, provided a lesson in history, "illustrating the changeable fortunes to which human endeavors were subject over time."[44] The threat of decay, whether natural or man-made, continued into the modern age. Even commercial success was implicated. If he had any

---

42. Aufrere owned a Romanelli, Parmigianino, and Paolo Veronese; Oswald, a Barbieri. On Veronese's "Susannah," see Luisa Vertova, "Some Late Works by Veronese," *Burlington Magazine*, v. 102 (February 1960), pp. 68–71; and Beverly L. Brown, "Replication and the Art of Veronese," in *Retaining the Original: Multiple Originals, Copies, and Reproductions* (Washington, D.C., 1989), pp. 111–24. One should not overlook the possible voyeuristic pull of such drawings. Voyeurism received vivid expression in Thomas Rowlandson's pornographic drawing of Susannah, where the maiden provocatively exposes herself to two wizened art collectors. Gert Schiff, ed., *The Amorous Illustrations of Thomas Rowlandson* (London, 1989), p. xxxiv. On spying, generally, see Ronald Paulson, *Rowlandson: A New Interpretation* (Oxford, 1972), pp. 80–83. Artists were fond of depicting connoisseurs examining pictures of naked women on an easel. Cf. John Oliver's print "Colonel Charteris Contemplating the Venus of Titian" (1766), Rowlandson's etching "Satyr and Nymph (after Poussin)," and James Gillray's "A Cognoscenti contemplating ye Beauties of ye Antique," to Nicolas Poussin's painting of *Sleeping Venus Surprised by Satyrs* which was purchased by Aufrere.

43. Jonathan Skelton to William Herring, June 7, 1758, in "The Letters of Jonathan Skelton," *The Walpole Society*, v. 36 (1960), p. 45.

44. Aufrere's sarcophagi appear in Piranesi, *Vasi*, v. 1, pls. 96, 47. For the sepulchral chest of Saenia Longina, now at Brocklesby Park, see Adolf Michaelis, *Ancient Marbles in Great Britain*, trans. G. A. M. Fennell (Cambridge, 1882); and A. H. Smith, *A Catalogue of Antiquities in the Collection of the Earl of Yarborough at Brocklesby Park* (London, 1897). Of the cinerarium of P. Manlio, no trace remains. On ruins, see Laurence Goldstein, *Ruins and Empire: The Evolution of a Theme in Augustan and Romantic Literature* (Pittsburgh, 1977), pp. 5–8, 13, 59–72. 95–113; and Solkin, *Wilson*, p. 28.

doubt about the ruinous influence exerted by commercial wealth, Boyd needed only to look up at Rembrandt's *The Vanity of Riches, or The Miser Reflecting on their Uncertainty* to remind himself that desire and appetite might triumph over valuable activity.

Collecting art was one way that socially lesser men could compete with peers of the realm. Much of what the associates bought was conventionally polite, industrious, and moral, and closely followed current fashion. These were expensive, if conventional, marks of gentility. Two marinescapes by Vernet cost Sargent £216 in 1764, at a time when a small "gentleman" farmer could support himself, a wife, four children, and five servants in the country for £400.[45] Expensive collecting was a mark of a man of means; knowledgeable and tasteful collecting, which might also embrace a well-disguised passion to collect the beautiful and rare, allowed the outsider to create a respectable place for himself in society.

Gardens

The need for an appropriate display of and use for new wealth shaped the associates' improvement programs outside the house, as it did within. In 1739, the author of *Common Sense* noted that everyone

> is to be *doing something at his Place*, as the fashionable Phrase is; and you hardly meet with any Body, who, after the first Compliments, does not inform you, that he is *in Mortar* and *moving of Earth*: the modest terms for Building and Gardening. *One large Room*, a *Serpentine River*, and a *Wood*, are become the most absolute Necessaries of Life, without which a Gentleman of the smallest Fortune thinks he makes no Figure in his Country.[46]

In providing themselves with these "Necessaries of Life," the associates could have drawn on three distinct gardening styles: formal, poetic, and informal.[47] The "formal garden" of the seventeenth century, favored by French and German princes, was usually a series of repetitive geometric enclosures situated along an axial vista. The "poetic garden" rose in the early eighteenth century as a British alternative to the European formal geometrical garden, and was usually "constructed as a free-form allegorical critique of Walpolean politics." Broad themes dear to the heart

45. Approximately £15,132 or $22,506 in 1994. Lagrange, *Vernet*, p. 344–45; and Trussler, *The Way*.

46. Quoted in Elizabeth Manwaring, *Italian Landscape in Eighteenth-Century England* (New York, 1925), p. 133.

47. Christopher Hussey, *English Gardens and Landscapes, 1700–1750* (London, 1967), chs. 1–3.

of Opposition Whigs – such as the triumph of virtue over vice, of the past over the present, or of Britain in an international order – found expression in a linked series of garden monuments, such as those erected at the home of the banker Henry Hoare at Stourhead and Viscount Cobham at Stowe. But, in planting their gardens, the associates copied neither the formal nor the poetic model. They had no desire to amuse in the French manner, nor to make partisan statements. Rather, they were intent on keeping abreast of changing fashion, which came to embrace the creation, indeed the glorification, of open frontiers. As the nation became more confident in the international realm, so its gardens came to connect the park to the countryside, the horizon, and far beyond. Accordingly, around their new houses, the associates laid "informal" gardens, and they executed these with polish, if not genius. Their gardens gave them the opportunity to collect their thoughts, indulge their fantasies and, according to Paul Langford, appear more landed than they really were.[48] The associates developed their gardens in a style associated with the work of Lancelot "Capability" Brown and his circular, rather than axial, planning. Brown himself was involved in laying out Boyd's policies at Danson and Aufrere's son-in-law's park at Brocklesby. But a gentleman-gardener did not need to employ Brown or one of his students to produce similar effects.

Auchincruive is a good example of Brownian gardening creating an effect "as if the Golden Age was revived."[49] Here Oswald interpreted the task of gardening broadly, and work proceeded on several levels. His first efforts were directed toward the untenanted farms and hilly mounts that surrounded the house. Oswald and his full-time gardener adopted the "late and now universal taste" of "throwing a large extent . . . into lawns of grass" and planting trees. Since "trees still constituted the most obvious and, in the long run, the most profitable part of improvement," Oswald reintroduced trees and hedges into the landscape on a massive scale, mixing domestic and foreign species, with trees and shrubs from Florida and Jamaica crowding out bushes and flowers from Bengal and China. This global forest was enlivened by two simple bridges over the Ayr, a graveled "Walk" along the river, a terraced wall that rose dramatically from the Walk to the mansion above, a dam and a cascade, an open-air theater, and a tea-house.[50]

48. Langford, *Public Life*, pp. 12–13.
49. Henry Hoare to Lord Bruce, October 12, 1771, in Kenneth Woodbridge, *Landscape and Antiquity: Aspects of English Culture at Stourhead, 1718 to 1838* (Oxford, 1970), p. 63–64.
50. William Boutcher, Jr., *A Treatise on Forest Trees* (Edinburgh, 1775), quoted in Alan Tait, *The Landscape Garden in Scotland, 1735–1835* (Edinburgh, 1980), p. 10; and

The tea-house is an intriguing commentary on Oswald's attempt at defining his own gentility (Illustrations 10.34 and 10.35).[51] As drawn by Robert Adam and executed by local craftsmen, it bears a simple yet striking design. Two concentric drums, one placed above the other, are topped by a conical roof. Four round turrets support the outer wall of the lower drum; twelve tall relieving arches unify the exterior facade of the upper drum. At the center of each arch is a small circle classically ornamented with acanthus leaves. The top of the drum is banded with a projecting machicolated cornice and battlements. Alastair Rowan has correctly labeled this "a hybrid style of varied origins," synthesizing ancient and medieval, foreign and domestic emblemata: a design based on Theodoric's sixth-century mausoleum at Ravenna, the capital of the West; a slated, conical roof topped by a ball-finial, the hallmark of Scotland's feudal vernacular tradition; and a cornice modeled after Renaissance precedents.[52] Oswald could enter through one of four arches in the lower drum, and follow a circular passage surrounding the servants' hall (with a plain Doric cornice and chimney-piece) and kitchen (with the most up-to-date heating and serving apparatus), to a curved staircase that rose to the upper drum. Climbing the short distance, the gentleman of Auchincruive could take tea or drink seltzer with the lairds of the county in a replica of the tomb of the man who had once ruled all Italy and had aimed to steep his own Ostrogothic people in civilizing Roman traditions. From its heights, Oswald, a man of many worlds, could look out over "the pretty Landskip of his own Possessions": Claude-like fields, newly dug lime pits, industrious and

Tait, *Landscape Garden*, p. 100. Hand-in-hand with his attempt to reforest, Oswald cleared salable trees from many areas of the estate. Account of Work, March 1770, Memorandum, December 8, 1772, Oswald Papers, Sudlows; and Mark L. Anderson, *A History of Scottish Forestry*, v. 1 (London, 1967), p. 438. The sale of the timber and its patriotic connection to gardening is discussed in Alexander Pope, *Epistle IV: To Richard Boyle* (1731), ll. 187–88; and Robert Williams, "Rural Economy and the Antique in the English Landscape Garden," *Journal of Garden History*, v. 7 (1987), pp. 78–90.

51. Alastair Rowan, "Robert Adam's Last Castles," *Country Life* (August 22, 1974), p. 494–97, and "After the Adelphi: Forgotten Years in the Adam Brothers' Practice," *Journal of the Royal Society of Arts*, v. 122 (1974), pp. 690–91. The teahouse was drawn in 1778. It is not clear when construction began, but the structure was complete by December 1783; in March 1784, the factor was plastering the upper floor, and installing its doors and windows. Richard Oswald to William McCall, December 12, 1782, and William McCall to Richard Oswald, March 4, 1783, Oswald Papers, Sudlows.

52. Rowan, "After the Adelphi," p. 691; and Geoffrey Beard, *The Work of Robert Adam* (Edinburgh, 1978), pp. 17, 52. As he had done in the mansion, Oswald simplified Adam's grand plan by replacing an exterior double stair rising from the ground to the tearoom floor with a simpler interior stair.

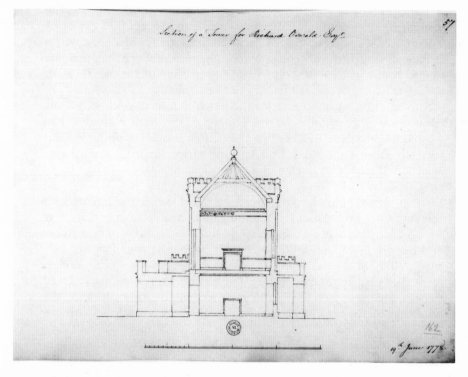

Illustration 10.34 Auchincruive Tea-House. Robert Adam Plan of Tower Interior, Adam Drawings, v. 19, no. 162. *Courtesy*: Sir John Soane's Museum, London.

contented tenants, the growing town of Ayr, and the Salvatorian sea beyond.[53]

More intensive and controlled gardening was conducted behind an enclosure 1,000 feet north of the mansion, at the end of a grassy, sheep-

53. D. F. Bond, ed., *The Spectator*, v. 3 (Oxford, 1965), p. 552 (No. 414: June 25, 1712). The congruence between gardening and painting is discussed by Manwaring, *Italian Landscape*, ch. 6; and H. F. Clark, "Eighteenth-Century Elysiums: The Role of 'Association' in the Landscape Movement," *Journal of the Warburg & Courtauld Institute*, v. 6 (1943), pp. 163–89. For authors viewing landscapes in pictorial terms, see Robert Potter, *Holkham* (London, 1759); *The Rise and Progress of the Present Taste in Planting Parks, Pleasure Grounds, Gardens, etc.* (London, 1767); Horace Walpole, "Essay on Gardening," *Anecdotes of Painting*, 4th ed. (London, 1771); William Mason, *The English Garden* (London, 1772), bk. 1, ll. 216–39; Richard Graves, "Love of Order," in *Euphrosyne* (London, 1773), v. 1, pp. 7–8, 19–21, v. 2, p. 79; and *An Essay on the Different Natural Situations of Gardens* (London, 1774). It was not uncommon for landowners to design garden views with pictures in mind. Schulz, *Paradise*, pp. 22–23; and Manwaring, *Italian Landscape*, p. 172.

Illustration 10.35 Auchincruive Tea-House. *Courtesy*: Royal Commission of the Ancient and Historical Monuments of Scotland, Edinburgh.

filled park. Here, in contrast to the intentional lack of cultivation elsewhere, control, order, and practicality were the ruling principles. The outer walls formed a rough rectangle, divided into two spaces by two parallel crescent-shaped internal walls. The upper, northern space was used as a kitchen garden, complete with orchards of nectarines, apples, apricots, pears, and peaches and beds of potatoes, barley, rye, and clover.[54] In the northwest corner, Oswald built a greenhouse that he decorated with classical cornices, friezes with olive and grape motifs, and molded architraves. In this "glittering Fane, where rare and alien Plants might safely flower" with the aid of a central brick heating pit, Oswald raised the pineapples that he sent to friends as tokens of his

54. The walls (3.5 meters high) of the enclosed garden formed a service walkway, six meters wide. On orchards, see Maxwell Letter Book, A State of Affairs, May 18, 1773, Oswald Papers, Sudlows.

affection and the seeds he sent to his overseers in Florida. Against the south side of the southern curved wall, flued and heated by a series of grates, he set a range of lean-to glass hothouses. The first in Scotland, these hothouses were filled with fig trees, grape vines, sugar cane, and nut bushes planted in pots. Below them, the lower, southern plot served as the estate's ornamental garden; it was split in half by two yew hedges leading down to statues of Adam and Eve (reminding Oswald of life before the Fall), an American tulip tree (reminding him of overseas plantations) and, in the distance, the river Ayr.[55]

By 1774, when work on the gardens was complete and the task of cultivating new and unusual plants in full swing, Oswald was reputed to have "the finest Garden & most elegant Glass House and Hot House" in Scotland.[56] Here were all the outward trappings of current fashionable taste – lawns, gardens, ponds, and temples – that allowed the merchant to cut a "Figure in his County." Oswald cast before his neighbors an image of boundless territory – not far off in the case of one who owned a sizable fraction of Ayrshire and a third of Kirkcudbrightshire – and even the specter of romanticism. Yet the overwhelming message from his gardens was one of control. Oswald's penchant for order, regularity, and symmetry and his legendary frugality exhibited themselves in the installation of tightly compartmentalized seedbeds and narrow, straight, and well-groomed gravel paths. His desire to manage production found vent in the building of espaliers for training and grafting fruit, and the installation of stoves to alter the natural growing patterns of plants he forced from seed.

Built with the windfalls of war and the profits of trans-Atlantic slaving, the house, the art collection, and the garden were the private expressions of the station to which the associates aspired and largely acceded.

55. Memo, November 17, December 8, 1772, March 1773, Oswald Papers, Sudlows. Access to the hothouse grates was gained by a sixty-five-meter tunnel beneath the service walkway dividing the two walls. William Lockhart to Richard Oswald, April 4, 1767, Maxwell Letter Book, Memo, July 22, 1770, Account, May 12, June 2, July 7, 1772, March, June 8, 1773, Oswald Papers, Sudlows. For commemoration of glass hothouses, see Mason, *English Garden*, bk. IV, ll. 217–18, 230. On the divisions of the garden, see Thomas Lauder to Richard Oswald, August 22, September 1, 1778, Oswald Papers, Sudlows. The growth of greenhouses and hothouses in Britain deserves scholarly attention. For brief mention of the origins of enclosed greenhouse gardening there, see Stefan Koppelkamm, *Glasshouses and Wintergardens of the Nineteenth Century*, trans. Katharine Talbot (New York, 1981), pp. 10–16; and Priscilla Boniface, *The Garden Room* (London, 1982), pp. i–ii.
56. John Henry to Richard Oswald, September 6, 1774, Oswald Paper, Sudlows. Oswald hired the son of the gardener at Kilkerran House to oversee the gardens in his absence. For later opinion, see William Aiton, *General View of the Agriculture of the County of Ayr* (Edinburgh, 1811).

As befitted their natural, "Roman" lordship, these expressions were classical, grand, expensive, rooted in the land and its produce, and concerned with proper relations among the classes and occupations of society. As was appropriate for arrivistes, these expressions were archaic, modest, virtuous, and concerned with improvement and learning. They reflect the tightrope that successful men of affairs had to walk in the eighteenth century if they were to integrate themselves into society. By and large they succeeded: the Earls of Dumfries and Cassilis took tea with Oswald while gaining his advice on manure, seeds, the manufacture of pencils, and their financial affairs; the Grants visited the Argylls and the Butes; Augustus Boyd's son John became a baronet; while Aufrere bequeathed one of the most "distinguished collections" of painting and sculpture in the country to his descendants, the future Earls of Yarborough. In the social world, the associates were undeniable successes.

Mercantile Legacies: *"Industrious Friends"*

THE ASSOCIATES WERE AMONG the most dynamic agents in eigh-teenth-century British and American economic, social, and political life. By the time they died, they had long since shed the mantles of outsiders and won commercial success, social acceptance, and political power. Their strategies of commercial integration had made them rich. Their strategies of polite improvement had won them reception in any society. Their contributions to the emerging "fiscal-military" state had earned them a place among those who ruled the empire.

The legacies left by these integrating and improving associates be-speak their rise to wealth, esteem and, in many cases, high office. When Augustus Boyd died in August 1765 at the advanced age of eighty-eight, he had lived his last years in extreme comfort, just one block from the epicenter of Britain's constantly expanding, increasingly commercial empire. The erstwhile Scots-Irish immigrant who had settled in St. Christopher and later established himself in London left an estate worth over £50,000. To his wife, he bequeathed £800 in cash and an annuity of £800 drawn from the proceeds of one of his St. Christopher estates; leasehold properties in Westminster and Lewisham; jewels, rings, and watches; 1,200 ounces of silver plate; china and linen; and carriages, chariots, coaches, horses, and equipage. To his five grandchildren, he bequeathed annuities totaling £2,400. To his brothers and sisters, nieces, nephews, employees, and servants, he granted annuities totaling another £2,250. Finally, he left the Magdalen House and the London Hospital each a £50 annuity. His only child, John, who was later to receive a baronetcy and become one of the country's great art collectors, inher-ited the remainder, most notably the 180-acre "Castle" plantation and the 214-acre "Stones Fort" estate in St. Christopher, a house in Basseterre, and two 1,400-acre sugar plantations in St. Croix; together his overseas properties earned him £9,000 a year.[1]

1. PROB 11/r. 911/q. 321/f. 278 (proved September 11, 1765); Henry H. Drake, ed., *Hasted's History of Kent, Part I* (London, 1886), p. 261. £50,000 in 1765 is approx-imately £3,384,250 or $5,042,533 in 1994.

Sir Alexander Grant was a man of even greater resources. At his death in 1772, he left an estate stretching from Scotland and England to Africa, Jamaica, Florida, and Nova Scotia and valued at £93,000. He gave his houses in Westminster and Surrey, an annuity of £1,200, and various personal possessions to his wife; he left his Scottish estates to his only brother; and he assigned his Jamaican plantations to trustees, who were to divide the profits among his nieces and nephews.[2] But Grant's reputation was built on more than wealth or office alone, for he had forged sturdy links to the Court and Whitehall. Twenty years before, after reclaiming a baronetcy for his family, he had befriended the Earl of Bute and, through Bute, the Prince of Wales; the Prince, on becoming George III, "somewhat distinguished" the merchant as "a favorite." He became a frequent visitor to the Court and a guest at royal functions, such as the Prince of Wales' birthday party in 1762 and the Queen's birthday party the following year. The invitations, like the supporters he received for his coat of arms, were tokens of the favor which the temperamental Londoner had so lovingly cultivated.[3]

After leaving Parliament in 1768, Grant severed all ties to Scotland and permanently fixed his home in the City.[4] With an insider's cache of information and a fervent love of gossip and theater, this supremely digressive man of affairs who was hopelessly addicted to cashews and sweetmeats could be good company, and toward his wife and a handful of intimates, he expressed affection and enthusiasm. Yet most who met him thought him blunt, convinced of his own importance, moralistic, and, above all, painfully tenacious at wielding power. He was a difficult man to work with, or for – exacting, meddling, angry, sometimes physically violent. Driven by this need to dominate, Grant found retirement impossible. While he first talked of reducing his commitments in 1763, it was not until 1770, at the age of sixty-five, that he actually turned his business over to three relatives. Even then, leisure was painful. Exercising vigorously all his life and unwilling to give up now, he ordered a new mahogany exercising horse in the last year of his life; but he found exercise no substitute for work, and he returned to the

2. Sederunt Book, ff. 13–20, Grant Papers, Tomintoul House; PROB 11/1772/Middx Nov 403 (proved November 26, 1772); GD 176/828; and Answer, February 1786, Signet Library, 686/18, Edinburgh. £93,000 in 1772 is approximately £5,417,499 or $8,057,880 in 1994.

3. GD 345/1180/86, 141: Sir Alexander Grant to Captain Archibald Grant, January 6, July 14, 1761; Sir Alexander Grant to Charles Jenkinson, July 7, 1761, Add.Mss. 38,197, BL; and GD 248/99/6/3: Sir Alexander Grant to Sir Ludovick Grant, July 21, 1761.

4. GD 345/1171/2/90: Sir Alexander Grant to Sir Archibald Grant, November 3, 1767; GD 345/1171/1/125: Sir Alexander Grant to Sir Archibald Grant, December 5, 1767; and *Edinburgh Advertiser*, April 22, 29, May 3, 13, June 3, 1768.

counting-house within the year.⁵ His return was brief, though. In June 1772, Sir Alexander was "in a dangerous way" and, one month later, "rather worse" – he could no longer hold a pen and could barely utter a syllable. By the time he breathed his last on August 1, he had come to be known as "a Man of Parts, a Lover of his Country, Benevolent, Generous, Hospitable, [and] Honest" – a man of means and station who had moved far beyond the world of a plantation doctor who learned his craft in a correspondence course and leased an acre on the western edge of the British empire.⁶

As representative as Grant's accomplishments were for his cohort, none was more emblematic of the economic and social distance the associates had traveled than the legacy left by Richard Oswald. When he died in November 1784, this child of Caithness who got his first break collecting debts in Virginia and Jamaica for his cousins left behind a sterling reputation and a sizable estate. This "truly Good Man," as Benjamin Franklin described him, left an estate worth £500,000 in land, money due him on bonds and mortgages, claims upon the Government, stocks and annuities, and bank accounts. The bulk of his assets, including the picture collection that was "a specimen" of his "good taste," went to his wife, in trust for his nephew and heirs, yet substantial legacies and annuities were left to friends in Scotland, Germany, India, Jamaica, and Georgia.⁷ To focus on Oswald's personal gains and social mobility alone, however, is misleading, for his influence in the wider world was extensive.

Indeed this book has suggested that the associates' most durable legacy was something less tangible than wealth, titles, roads, or political "access," something that reached beyond their heirs or their countrymen it was the integration and improvement of the British Atlantic community.

5. Sir Alexander Grant to John Gordon, October 14, 1769, Sir Alexander Grant to Alexander Grant, December 25, 1769, Sir Alexander Grant to John Grant, March 1772, Sir Alexander Grant Letter Book, and Sederunt Book, October 19, 1773, Gr⸌ Papers, Tomintoul House.
6. GD 248/179/1/116, 130: Ludovick Grant to James Grant, June 24, J. 11, 1772; Sir Alexander Grant to Col. Grant, July 6, 1772, Grant Papers, Tomintoul House; Robert Grant to Governor Grant, July 30, 1772, BCM 661; William Grant to Governor Grant, August 1772, BCM 674; GD 248/50/3/60: Charles Grant to James Grant, August 8, 1772; and GD 345/1172/1772: Captain Archibald Grant to Sir Archibald Grant. The body of the restless Scot was carried on a fishing smack to Moray and buried at Dalvey alongside the remains of his father; the corpses of an unnamed daughter and his wife's cousin Elizabeth Dicker accompanied him. For Gordon's high opinion, see Sir Robert Gordon to Robert Gordon, Jr., November 10, 1756, La.II.498, EUL.
7. *The Glasgow Mercury*, November 6, 18, 1784; *The Morning Chronicle*, November 12, 1784, p. 3; *The Times*, January 11, 1785, p. 3; and CC 5,508/687–747. £500,000 in 1784 is approximately £28,600,751 or $42,540,185 in 1994.

By considering Britain's overseas colonies and investments not as a set of discrete and severable commercial projects but as a single entity, all parts of which were linked to the center where they lived and worked, the associates, in the course of managing their own business operations, granted a bequest of immense significance. Given this lifetime contribution, it is only fitting that the associate Richard Oswald was chosen to negotiate the peace that formally ended the American Revolutionary War and molded the Atlantic community into a new and different whole.[8]

To what extent was the British Atlantic community more integrated in 1785 upon Richard Oswald's death than fifty years earlier, when Augustus Boyd arrived in London? The question deserves a fuller answer than this volume has delivered. By design, this study has focused on only one side of the question: the actions of individuals working in the metropolis and promoting trans-Atlantic exchange. Nevertheless, we can identify five areas in which the associates and merchants like them made a real difference: increasing the scope of the empire, deepening its infrastructure, expanding its trade, peopling its shores and hinterlands, and spreading the new optimistic, experimental ideas of the Enlightenment.

The British empire was larger and more complex by the end of the eighteenth century. Those years witnessed a strengthening of England's dominion over Scotland and Ireland and, through the reclamation of wasteland, a revivification of local economies along the "inner periphery." Overseas, British territory increased fivefold between the capture of Jamaica in 1655 and the Peace of Paris in 1763. The peace found British settlements scattered as far west as western Pennsylvania and as far east as eastern Bengal. Moreover, the end of the Seven Years' War unleashed a fury of speculation and expansion. By the outbreak of the American Revolution, a host of land schemes were afoot which, had war not intervened, would have officially moved the pale of colonial rule as far west as the Mississippi River.

The associates helped to open up Britain's hinterlands and connect them to the center. They led the charge in the development of new lands: Grant and Oswald in Nova Scotia, Sargent in the Ohio Country, Oswald in Carolina, Oswald and Herries in Georgia, Grant, Oswald,

---

8. Oswald's work as peace negotiator is the best-documented episode in his life. It is summarized in Richard B. Morris, *The Peacemakers* (New York, 1965), and analyzed in Charles R. Ritcheson, "'To An Astonishing Degree Unfit for the Task': Britain's Peacemakers, 1782–1783," in Ronald Hoffman and Peter Albert, eds., *Peace and the Peacemakers: The Treaty of 1783* (Charlottesville, 1986), pp. 70–100.

Herries, and Mill in Florida, and eight of the associates in the West Indies. In all, between 1740 and 1790, they acquired approximately 120,000 acres of undeveloped land in America and actively planted half of them, managing at least thirty-five of their own plantations from afar. Nor did they restrict their activities to America, for they actively engaged in the establishment of "colonies in the countryside" back home in the much-neglected fields of the counties.

The far-flung empire in which the associates worked also had a deeper infrastructure by 1785. An increase in the frequency of trans-Atlantic voyages, the expansion of regular postal services to the West Indies, New York, and Nova Scotia, and the presence of new or improved port facilities, coupled with the decrease in the dangers of trans-Atlantic voyaging from the decline of piracy, eased the flow of goods, people, and information between Europe and America. The proliferation of newspapers, the introduction of more postal coaches and routes, and the construction of roads, bridges, and ferries incorporated relatively inaccessible parts of America and Britain into the global trading world. The Atlantic community shrank as the eighteenth century progressed, even as constituent members of the empire declared their independence from one another.

The associates helped create this infrastructure to support the work of their American plantations and county estates. They extended development capital and credit to American planters and merchants in the Caribbean and lower South, and landowners and farmers in the counties. They provided postal services to the West Indies. They also undertook a host of smaller, location-specific improvements: commissioning better maps and charts of the Sierra Leone estuary and the St. Mary River; building better harbors in St. Augustine and Ayr, and lighthouses off the coasts of Glasgow and Kirkcudbright; and laying more roads between Ayrshire estates and the metropolis and between Florida's plantations and the South Carolina Low Country.

Over the course of the eighteenth century, Britons and Americans also gained access to more and more varied goods. The annual value of exports and re-exports from England and Wales to the thirteen colonies that became the United States more than tripled between 1735 and 1785. During the same half-century, trade made more diverse goods available in all parts of the empire; by its end, it was not unusual to find East Indian or German wares in back-country Carolina stores. Urban communities grew, standards of living rose, and the new, recognizably modern strain of consumerism appeared, together with the belief that city-dwellers and country folk alike were increasingly acquisitive and materialistic. The bilateral exchange between Britain and America in nearly all things but slaves persisted and continued to flourish, at least through the end of the century.[9]

From the first day they set foot in London, the associates formed part of the conveyor belt of trade goods. They sent into the Atlantic, Baltic, Mediterranean, and Indian seas more than 450 trading voyages over the course of forty years, ships laden with plantation supplies, trade goods, and assorted manufactures from Britain and northern Europe, wine and salt from Southern Europe and the Wine Islands, slaves, gold, and ivory from Africa, and returning with sugar, molasses, rum, tobacco, and fish. They provided their correspondents and clients from Massachusetts to Tobago with the wherewithal to conduct trade and cultivate staples, from sugar casks and grinding mills to stationery supplies, and everyday necessities, from stockings and magazines to tea and wine. As middlemen chiefly responsible for receiving and selling colonial sugar, tobacco, wheat, and timber, the associates on their outbound vessels provided American colonists with finished goods that were not manufactured in the colonies or at least were not available as cheaply there. Wigs, watches, mahogany bedsteads, and counting-house safes that could be bolted to the floor – almost anything that an American desired flowed through their warehouses along the Thames. At the entrepôt they established at Bance Island, the associates combined goods and peoples from India, Turkey, Italy, Germany, France, Britain, and America to obtain the slaves whose labor would build what the associates called the "New World" on the other side of the Atlantic.

In the size, growth, and diversity of the peoples in the New World, we find another indicator of Atlantic integration, as increasingly the Atlantic community was one large labor market. Between 1730 and 1790, America's total white and black population grew from 629,000 to 3,932,000. This rise depended heavily on a large and increasing flow of European and British migrants and African slaves into America. Because white migrants flocked to America from all parts of Europe and Britain, America had a much greater ethnic diversity in 1785 than it did in 1735. "After 1760, the increase in immigration became so great that

---

9. Elizabeth B. Schumpeter, *English Overseas Trade Statistics, 1697–1808* (Oxford, 1960), pp. 17–18, tables V–VI; Curtis P. Nettels, *The Emergence of a National Economy, 1775–1815* (New York, 1962), pp. 44–48; Gordon C. Bjork, "The Weaning of the American Economy: Independence, Market Changes, and Economic Development," *Journal of Economic History,* v. 24 (1964), p. 557; James F. Shepherd Jr. and Samuel H. Williamson, "The Coastal Trade of the British North American Colonies, 1768–1772," *Journal of Economic History,* v. 32 (1972), pp. 783–810; and United States Bureau of the Census, *Historical Statistics of the United States, Colonial Times to 1970,* v. 2 (Washington, D.C., 1975), pp. 1176–94.

it constituted a social force in itself." In addition, between 1731 and 1790, approximately 1.5 million slaves were shipped to British America.[10]

The associates helped to people America by moving people around the world, some to settle and others to serve, constructing a community of interests in the Atlantic. Throughout their London careers, the associates were deeply involved in the intercontinental transfer of labor. They drew relatives, friends, and unnamed workers from their homeland to work and live overseas as their agents and employees. Grant's nephews, the Davidsons, and Oswald's magazine clerk, John Lewis Gervais, went out to America with their recommendation, worked for them on their plantations or represented their interests in the cities, and eventually settled there. Moreover, the associates provided passage for men, women, and children from Ireland, Scotland, Wales, England, and many parts of Europe. Grant brought Scots settlers to Jamaica in the 1740s, and Oswald brought religious refugees and indentured servants to Nova Scotia, Florida, and other parts of America in the 1750s, 1760s, and 1770s. While it is impossible to determine precisely how large this flow of labor was, the constant reference to it in their correspondence suggests it was considerable. At the same time, the associates shipped nearly 13,000 West Africans from Bance Island to Grenada, St. Christopher, Jamaica, Florida, Georgia, the Carolinas, and Virginia to work American fields and staff American houses.

The exchange of science, technology, and practical ideas also helped to connect men and women on both sides of the Atlantic. Botanical and agricultural information and samples were exchanged through letters and publicized in writings, and actual attempts to grow crops were encouraged through monetary rewards backed by British organizations like the Society for the Improvement of Arts, Manufactures, and Commerce. Both British county farmers and American creole planters and industrialists traveling abroad investigated strategies for enhancing the productivity of their lands and workers. Americans often introduced crops and methods first tested and espoused in Britain, while in the last few decades of the eighteenth century American inventions and labor systems also influenced industrial production and agriculture in the Old World.[11]

10. United States Bureau of the Census, *Historical Statistics*, v. 2, p. 1168 (Series Z2–8); Curtin, *Atlantic Slave Trade*, p. 150; Henry A. Gemery, "European Emigration to North America, 1700–1820: Numbers and Quasi-Numbers," *Perspectives in American History*, New Ser., v. 1 (1984), p. 322; and Bailyn, *Voyagers*, ch. 1, esp. pp. 7, 24.
11. Indigo and rice cultivation and production, in which new methods and techniques for controlling water and cleaning grain were gradually employed, are two examples of this. Joyce E. Chaplin, *An Anxious Pursuit: Agricultural Innovation and Modernity in the Lower South, 1730–1815* (Chapel Hill, 1993), pp. 108–17, 134–58.

The associates were a part of integrating the oceanic community in this way, too, by spreading new technologies and ideas, especially in agriculture and engineering. Wherever they established plantations, the associates introduced new crops, tools, and techniques that they had first heard about and tried in Britain. Indigo, grapes, figs, cottons, sugar, spices – almost any crop was worth attempting. In effect, America was the associates' laboratory. Grant continually tinkered with new and different methods to harness water power, and thereby control floods and promote irrigation, to eradicate crop blight, or to increase the production of rum. On his own plantations, Oswald followed current recipes in building more efficient grinding mills and improving the quality of his indigo. Some of the ideas the associates spread were political and commercial, especially the idea of a larger British world, united and enhanced by trade in an international environment. Most of them had long been convinced of the primary importance of commercial amity and exchange. Concerned, for instance, that the commercial bonds which held the empire together were fraying in the 1760s, Sargent endowed a medal for the best essay on "the Reciprocal Advantages of a Perpetual Union." When Oswald sanctioned severing political ties in 1782, he defended it as strengthening more general ties across the Atlantic.

Oswald's best-known "improvement" was managed, not in "the great desart" of Scotland or in the bug-infested swamps of Florida, but in the hotel rooms of Paris and Passy. In 1795, the English radical and political economist Benjamin Vaughan wrote to James Monroe, then Minister to France for the newly formed United States, who had inquired about this improvement. The reply was revealing.

Thirteen years before, in planning for the peace that was to terminate the War for America, it had been necessary "to have a negotiator acquainted with mercantile & military affairs; yet few of the English merchants had seen at once America & an army, & most of them have their business & consequently their knowledge confined to one particular object." It had been "requisite to have a person . . . devoid of the pride of aristocracy, without being suspected of democracy, . . . a man old in experience yet, with a versatility of mind and temper, capable of entering into new affairs." The negotiator eventually selected, Oswald, had had these and other "points to recommend him." "His great wealth, procured by his own judicious arrangements, enabled him to be independent." In trans-Atlantic commerce, he had become "accustomed to transactions upon a large scale & of a novel nature," which demanded not only "original ideas" but also the "experience . . . to correct them." "His age was very senior. [He] thought for himself. His manners were such that, though perfectly simple, he was admitted into all company;

his sincerity was relied upon at first and, though not given to deceive others, he was yet too experienced & observant to be long deceived himself." The negotiator's "views were philanthropic & expanded, & his sense was sound; and, though he had little or no scholarship, yet being retired in his habits he knew many valuable books on government & on political affairs." Moreover, Vaughan noted, he "had resided in various parts of America; & he knew not a little of Europe." It did not hurt that Britain's representative was "the most intimate & respected friend" of one of the American negotiators, Henry Laurens, and acquainted with and connected to another, Benjamin Franklin. Britain's envoy was chosen, in short, because he was "much acquainted with the world & its concerns."[12]

These plump encomia to Richard Oswald provide vivid testimony of how completely one associate had shed the outsider's marginal status that had marked him at the outset of his London business career. No longer was he a man lacking in resources and standing, devoid of a place in London's largely English community. George III thought Oswald the "fittest Instrument for the renewal of . . . friendly intercourse" with the colonies. In introducing the associate to Franklin, the Earl of Shelburne, Secretary of State for Home, Irish, and Colonial Affairs under Rockingham, described Oswald as "an Honest man, and . . . the fittest for the purpose. He is a pacifical man, and conversant in those negotiations, which are most Interesting to Mankind." These traits made Shelburne "prefer him to any of our Speculative Friends, or to any person of higher Rank." Franklin, whose extensive connections to the associates were never once mentioned during the course of the negotiations,[13] found him "a wise and honest Man," whose "Moderation,

---

12. Benjamin Vaughan to James Monroe, September 18, 1795, James Monroe Papers, Series 1, Reel 1, Library of Congress, Washington, D.C.; and Notes of Benjamin Vaughan, 1782–83, f. 1, Vaughan Papers, American Philosophical Society, Philadelphia.

13. Sir Alexander Grant had discounted bills of exchange for Benjamin Franklin, and Lady Grant was a regular visitor at the home of Franklin's landlady Margaret Stevenson in Craven Street. Labaree, ed., *Papers of Benjamin Franklin*, v. 7 (1963), pp. 367–68, v. 10 (1966), pp. 381–82. Oswald and Franklin were both involved in Nova Scotia and East Florida land speculation in the 1760s, and Oswald met Franklin in London at a meeting of the East Florida Society on February 24, 1765. Rogers, "East Florida Society," p. 488, n. 46. For over twenty-five years, Franklin also lived next door to Oswald's friend and Ayrshire neighbor Caleb Whitefoord, who in 1782 served as Oswald's secretary in Paris. Finally, Sargent II had gained the Pennsylvania finance agency through his friend Franklin and, later, in the 1760s and 1770s, succeeded in winning the involvement of Franklin in the Walpole Company's Vandalia project for the Ohio Country. Sargent first met Franklin in 1757 at the London home of a mutual friend, Colonel William Deane, and the two became close friends. Whenever Franklin was in Britain, Sargent's home in Kent was open and his bottle uncorked. Labaree, ed., *Papers of Benjamin Franklin*, v. 7, p. 321. The friendship with Franklin is documented in v. 9, p. 124, v. 20, pp. 312–13, and v. 21, p. 547. The associates' ties to Henry Laurens were almost as strong. The Boyds had dealt with him in executing

prudent Counsels, and sound Judgement may contribute much, not only
to the speedy Conclusion of a Peace, but to the framing of such a Peace
as may be firm and long-lasting." John Adams was struck by his sincerity, and John Jay, his "candid and proper manner." "No man," it
was agreed, would "ever be found with better qualifications or dispositions"; "no Man would deny Mr. Oswald's fitness for his Station."[14]
At the outset of the war, the man who would become Britain's negotiator had been adamantly opposed to the colonies' cause. During the
late 1770s, he felt Britain should quell the insurrection overseas and
crush her opponents and, as late as mid-July 1782, he felt "the Americans are, or ought to be, under the British Government."[15] A "permanent & happy constitution" for the colonies, ruled by a Viceroy or Lord

their Jamaica naval station victualing contracts and supplying their St. Christopher
plantations from the late-1740s onward, and they introduced him to Oswald. Oswald's
acquaintance with the Charlestonian was indeed, as Vaughan averred, "intimate and
respected." Oswald had corresponded with Laurens since 1756 and acted as his
metropolitan agent; he had hosted Laurens when the American stayed in London;
and, most famously, when Laurens was imprisoned in the Tower from October 1780
through December 1781, he worked for his release. Together, Richard Oswald and
Edmund Burke worked for Laurens's freedom; and, on December 31, 1781, Oswald and
his nephew John Anderson posted bail. Henry Laurens, "A Narrative of the Capture
. . . ," *Collections of the South Carolina Historical Society*, v. 1 (1857), pp. 18–83;
John Anderson to Richard Oswald, September 28, October 4, 7, 1780, Oswald Letter
Book, v. 3, ff. 94–96, 100; and Stevens, ed., *Facsimiles*, nn. 959–60, 965, 973, 988.
14. Earl of Shelburne to Benjamin Franklin, April 6, 28, 1782, in Smyth, ed., *Writings of
Benjamin Franklin*, v. 8, pp. 462, 483; John Fortescue, ed., *The Correspondence of
King George the Third from 1760 to 1783*, v. 6 (London, 1928), p. 22; Benjamin
Franklin to Earl of Shelburne, April 18, May 13, 1782, Benjamin Franklin to Richard
Oswald, June 27, 1782, in Smyth, ed., *Writings*, v. 8, pp. 466, 497, 554–55; John
Adams to Robert Livingston, November 6, 1782, and John Adams to Richard Oswald,
February 14, 1783, in Charles F. Adams, ed., *The Works of John Adams*, v. 7
(Boston, 1852), pp. 660–61 and v. 8 (Boston, 1853), p. 41; John Jay to Robert
Livingston, November 17, 1782, in Henry P. Johnston, ed., *The Correspondence and
Public Papers of John Jay*, v. 2 (New York, 1983), p. 376; and William Cobbet, *The
Parliamentary History of England*, v. 23 (London, 1814), p. 413. Cf. John Pownall
to Earl of Dartmouth, February 9, 1775, in Benjamin F. Stevens, ed., *Facsimiles of
Manuscripts in European Archives Relating to America, 1773–1783* . . . , v. 24 (London, 1895), no. 2031.
15. See Oswald's memoranda in various repositories. At Ann Arbor, University of Michi-
gan, Clements Library, see (1) Supplement to the Papers of August, September 1779;
(2) General Observations Relative to the Present State of the War, September 1779;
(3) Plan for an Alliance with Russia in order to Carry on the American War, April
12, 1781. At Charlottesville, University of Virginia, McGregor Library, see (4) Memorial Relative to Elizabeth River & Hampton Road in Virginia, June 26, 1779; (5)
Memorandum Relative to the Plan for an Alliance with Russia, August 2, 1781; (6)
Heads of a Conversation with Mr. Laurens, August 14, 1781, P.S. August 17, 1781;
(7) Memorandum, August 15, 1781; (8) Memorandum On the Folly of Invading
Virginia, the Strategic Importance of Portsmouth, and the Need for Civilian Control
of the Military, August 15–17, 1781. A modern edition of these memoranda appears
in Hancock, ed., "Pen and Ink" (forthcoming). Oswald's tone was more conciliatory
in letters to Americans. Richard Oswald to Henry Laurens, April 12, 1778, in *Papers
of Henry Laurens*, v. 13, pp. 107–13.

Lieutenant and a Privy Council, he thought, would be the best solution.[16] But over the course of the 1782 negotiations he moved toward reconciliation. The realities of the situation – especially the distance between the two countries, which prevented any effective control by Britain, and the growing strength of America – caused him to agree to many of the American requests. So to did the logic of an internationalism forged over a long, successful career. He readily acquiesced, for he had always valued a community of economic interests – one in which Britain's interests ranked higher than America's, of course – more than he had esteemed imperial symbolism and political connections.[17] Having lived in America during the 1730s and 1740s, and traded with Americans for over forty years, he knew the depth of American animosity and the extent to which Britain could and could not force her former colonists to do her bidding. Britain's "enemies" had "the ball at their foot," in Oswald's estimation, and any British approach would have to be realistic.[18]

In Paris, Oswald set out to "satisfy the Americans in such a manner as to have a chance of soothing them into neutrality," and so sanctioned, and even encouraged, what some considered pro-American positions. Most importantly, Oswald advised granting America unconditional independence, and counseled Shelburne to alter his commission so that he could negotiate with the "Thirteen United States of America" rather than Britain's "Colonies and Plantations." The associate recognized the liberating psychological impact that this recognition would have in making America independent "of all other nations" before a treaty was signed, rather than as the first article of the treaty.[19]

In addition to rendering America neutral, Oswald sought to maintain and extend harmonious commercial relations between the two countries. He insisted that the British allow the Americans the right to fish in Newfoundland's waters and to dry their catch on its banks. When pressed by the "Great Men" in London, he persuaded the Americans to dry their fish on the banks of the unsettled bays, harbors, and creeks of Labrador, the Magdalen Islands, and Nova Scotia, rather than in Newfoundland itself, a provision that emerged as Article 3 of the Treaty.[20]

16. CO 5/8/II/288–307; and FO 97/15/35. Cf. FO 95/511/7/May 6.
17. Ritcheson, "To an Astonishing Degree," p. 100.
18. FO 97/157/17: Oswald to Shelburne, July 8, 1782; and Richard Oswald, May 31, 1782, cited in Morris, *The Peacemakers*, p. 276.
19. Richard Oswald to Earl of Shelburne, July 11, 1782, Shelburne Papers 70/27/2, Clements Library, Ann Arbor; FO 95/511: Richard Oswald to Thomas Townshend, August 15, 17, 1782; FO 27/2: Richard Oswald to Thomas Townshend, September 10, 1782; Richard Oswald to Earl of Shelburne, September 11, 1782; and Minute of September 19, 1782, Shelburne Papers, 71/85–92, Clements Library, Ann Arbor.
20. Richard Oswald to Thomas Townshend, September 19, 1782, and Richard Oswald to Thomas Townshend, November 30, 1782, Shelburne Papers, 71/221–39 and 70/416–21, Clements Library, Ann Arbor.

Oswald also championed the cause of the Loyalists in the colonies; he arranged the compromise whereby Congress was to recommend relief to the States and grant amnesty to those who had remained loyal to the Crown, a compromise that became Articles 5 and 6.[21] Believing in "a mutuality of commerce," he enthusiastically backed Jay's unsuccessful proposal for Britain to retake West Florida from Spain. A return to prewar control of West Florida would provide "the Command of the Mouth of the Mississippi, and the navigation thereof" and a watch upon the Caribbean, as well as "an Entrepot" for "the Trade of the great back Country of all the Provinces of the 13 States that would naturally go to the Southward" and "a beneficial Connection with those States." Considering that "the Atlantic Side of said States lies open to the same correspondence with us as formerly," there would be reason to hope that, "in a mercantile view," the mother country would "not lose much by the Change that has happened." In Oswald's understanding of the linkage between America and Britain, commercial integration was the most important achievement to preserve. The West Florida deal, eventually shelved, would have provided Loyalists seeking asylum both a safe haven and a market. It would have given British merchants free navigation on the Mississippi River and partial control of its trade. British commissaries, in particular, would have benefited from the cheap supply of cattle in the Carolinas and Georgia. In Oswald's opinion, the long-term commercial advantages Britain would sustain by a tie to America were too great to forgo by total separation. The new United States would "grow out of the reach of comparison as to consequence with almost any nation in Europe" and, yet, because of its preoccupation with its backcountry, would not soon become a country of manufacturers. It was therefore in Britain's best economic interests to effect a "renewal of former correspondence and friendship," a "wise association" of mutually beneficial commercial exchange.[22]

After signing the Preliminary Articles in November and returning to London the following January, Oswald sought respite with his family and friends, dividing his days between his new townhouse in Westminster and his improved estates in southwestern Scotland. At his table, he

21. CO 5/8/317: Oswald to American Commissioners; Henry Strachey to American Commissioners, November 25, 1782, Richard Oswald to Thomas Townshend, November 30, 1782, Shelburne Papers, v. 70, Clements Library, Ann Arbor; and John Adams, *Diary*, v. 3, pp. 69–70.
22. FO 27/2: Richard Oswald to Thomas Townshend, October 5, 7, 1782; Benjamin Vaughan to Earl of Shelburne, October 3, 1782, Vaughan Papers, Massachusetts Historical Society, Boston; Richard Oswald to Thomas Townshend, October 8, 1782, Shelburne Papers 70, and Richard Oswald to Earl of Shelburne, October 3, 1782, Shelburne Papers 71/127–28, Clements Library, Ann Arbor.

mixed members of the British political and social establishment like the Dukes of Dorset and Queensberry, John Pownall, and the Earls of Shelburne, Cassilis, and Eglintoun with counting-house cronies like Robert Pringle and Thomas Brown.[23] Despite the social whirl, America was never far from Oswald's thoughts. He found consolation in the fact that the terms he had hammered out with Franklin, Adams, Jay, and Laurens were accepted without revision as the Final Articles of Peace when the treaty was signed in September 1783.[24] In London, he entertained the American negotiators before their return to the United States and, later, served as their correspondent: it was Oswald, for instance, who procured a copy of Captain Cook's *Voyages* for Franklin. From time to time, he attempted to secure repayment of loans he had made to Virginia and Carolina planters years before, but he only fitfully dabbled in business, having handed the daily management of his firm over to his nephews, the Andersons. He participated in local Scottish politics and pushed his rural improvements, pruning the shrubs and dusting the plants he had had brought from Florida and Grenada.[25] He and his wife left Westminster for his great horticultural "laboratory in the North" in early September 1784. Punctilious as always, he gave detailed instructions on the cleaning and painting of his Great George Street townhouse. But Richard Oswald did not live to see the results. The "Peacemaker" died in his bedroom in Ayrshire at 6 A.M. on November 6, 1784, after "a transit of one short hour." The friend, the relatives, and the factor who looked on as he breathed his last witnessed the passing of a true citizen of the world.[26]

Oswald, the other associates, and international merchants like them established and solidified a canon for businessmen-of-affairs that is still

23. This reflected the makeup of Oswald's neighborhood in Westminster, where he daily encountered both national politicians and commercial enterprisers, aristocrats, nabobs, widows, merchants, and lawyers. From his windows, he could watch the comings and goings of Charles Morgan, Mrs. Augustus Boyd, Thomas Parker, Sir Alexander and Lady Grant, William Sumner, Joshua Smith, Sir George Nares, and Naphtali Franks. London County Council, *The Survey of London*, v. 10 (London, 1926), pp. 21–55.

24. Benjamin Franklin to Richard Oswald, January 14, 1783, in Smyth, ed., *Writings*, v. 9, pp. 3–4; and Richard Oswald to Caleb Whitefoord, April 5, 1783, in W. A. S. Hewins, ed., *The Whitefoord Papers* (Oxford, 1898), pp. 185–87.

25. Laurens Papers, 7/12 (April 2, 1783), South Carolina Historical Society, Charleston; Richard Oswald to Caleb Whitefoord, June 1, 1784, in Hewins, ed., *Whitefoord Papers*, p. 192; Richard Oswald to Benjamin Franklin, June 8, 1784, Bache Collection, American Philosophical Society, Philadelphia; and John Maxwell to Richard Oswald, April 23, 1784, Oswald Letter Book, v. 3, ff. 320–22, SRO.

26. John Anderson to Richard Oswald, Oswald Letter Book, v. 2, ff. 104, 108, SRO; Minute of Oswald's Death, November 6, 1784, Oswald Papers, Sudlows.

in place centuries later, perhaps even more so in America than in Britain and Europe. They were practical, sometimes pedestrian men concerned with precise matters of detail who, after becoming successful in business, moved beyond commercial ventures into the realms of art, agriculture, science, and public affairs, carrying their ameliorative ideas about economically and socially viable communities with them. These metropolitan enterprisers operated in ways that, if you believe the business press, are being rediscovered at the end of the twentieth century: managing global operations with loosely bound sets of ventures, associations, and organizations, and a strong emphasis on flexible and ad hoc action. The origins and centuries-long development of these approaches merit further analysis.

The associates and other merchants like them – marginal, opportunistic, global, improving, and integrative – were in accord with what we can call their century's "practical Enlightenment." They were the necessary men of that moment. They were not philosophers; they did not rule in the grand realm of ideas. All the same, they were as caught up in innovative, investigative efforts, and as confident of the possibilities of human reason and endeavor in controlling the environment as those in the intellectual sphere. They were opportunistic seekers of advantage, careful implementers and coordinators, and quick adherents of ideas and plans devised by others. These were the men who made things work – their own businesses, their City's commerce, Britain's expanding empire in the Atlantic and far beyond. Using their practical, detailed knowledge, they carved out a new place for enterprise and entrepreneurs in the world.

Appendixes

Associates' Genealogies

Appendix I.1 *Boyd Family*

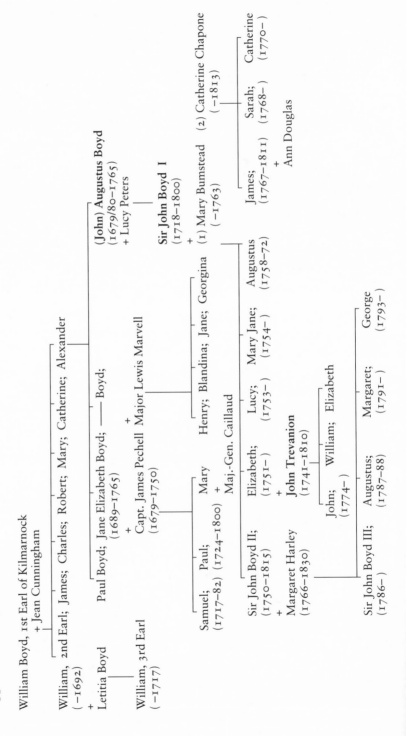

Appendix I.2 *Grant Family*

Duncan MaCondacht Grant

| John Grant of McConnochie | Donald Grant of Kinveachy | Sueton Grant of Inverlaidnan | John Grant ("More") |

Sueton Grant

Sir James Grant (–1695)   (Sir) Ludovick Grant (–1701)

Duncan Grant   Sir Sueton Grant (–1701)

James Grant (–1665)   Donald Grant (–1735)

Alexander   James   John   Robert   Elizabeth   Margaret

Mary Cooke (–1744)   Robert Cooke, Sr.
+
Robert Elbridge (–1727)

Sir Patrick Grant (1654–1755)
+
Lydia Mackintosh

Sir Ludovick (–1790)   Janet
+
Margaret Innes (–1782)   — Davidson

Sir Alexander Grant (1705–72)
+
Elizabeth (1717–92)

Elizabeth Elbridge   Robert Jr.
+
Samuel Dicker

Alexander   Lydia
+
William Falconar Lewis Grant

Margaret   Peter   Patrick

Gilbert   Hugh   James

Alexander; (1760–1825)   James; (1751–1816)   Peter; (1820–)   Charles;   John;   Robert;   Louis; (–1779)   Marjory;   Elizabeth;   Margaret

Appendix I.3 *Oswald Family*

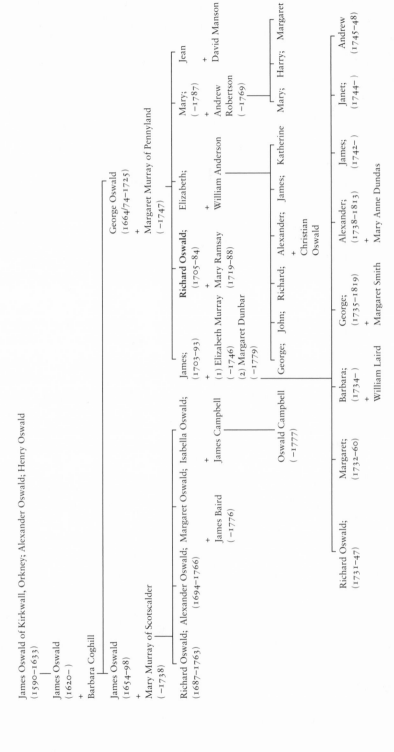

Appendix I.4 *Sargent/Arnold Family*

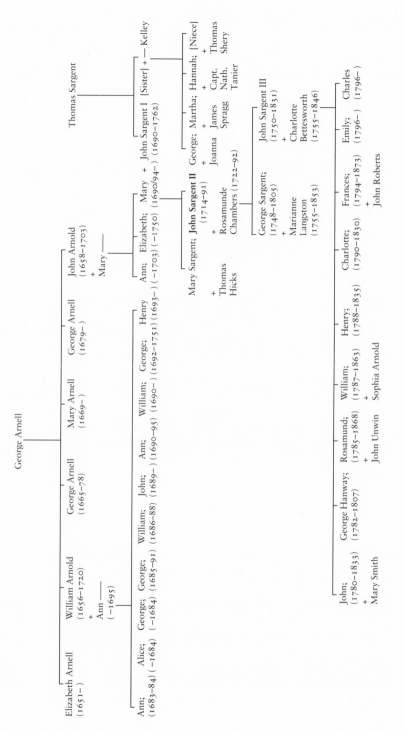

Appendix I.4 *Aufrere/Chambers/Rolleston Family*

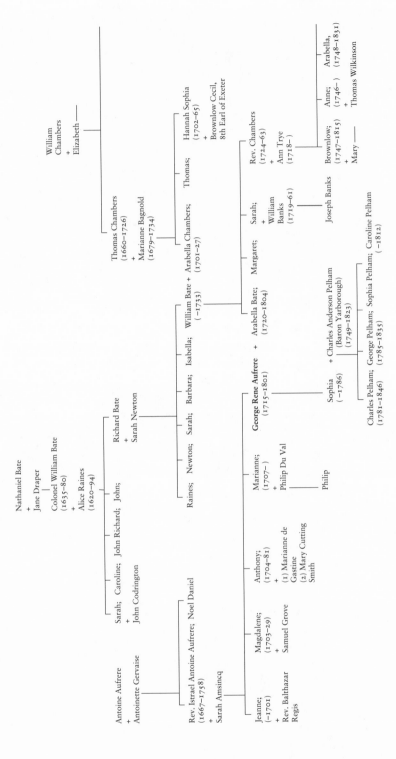

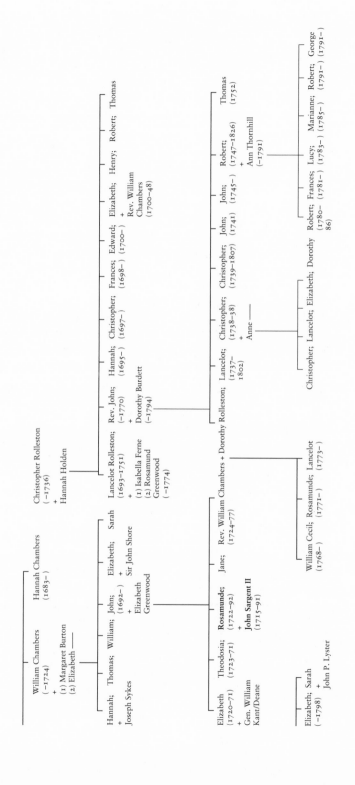

Sources for the Shipping Database

In the present analysis, information from the port books and Naval Office Shipping Lists is combined with references culled from other British and foreign sources, especially central government records and newspapers. Newspapers are frequently ignored as a source of shipping data. To date, the best study of the general dimensions of London's trade (French, "Trade and Shipping") ignores them entirely, although the most thorough and illuminating investigation of voyaging patterns involving an outport (Kenneth Morgan, *Bristol and the Atlantic Trade*) makes use of them in reconstructing round-trip voyages. Newspapers and all other sources provide the historian with the clearest possible focus on the globalization of the associates' ship trade from 1745 to 1785.

The basic sources of information are the books once kept by customs officers, both domestic and colonial. Unfortunately, in 1896–99, the Public Record Office destroyed nearly all the London port-books for the period after 1696. *First Report of the Royal Commission on the Public Records . . . [of] England and Wales, in House of Commons Sessional Papers, 1912–1913*, xliv, Part I (cd. 6361), pp. 9, 18, Part II, Appendix (cd. 6395), pp. 45–51, Part III, Minutes (cd. 6396), pp. 166–67.

The records for outports (referred to here as "port-books") and for colonial ports ("Naval Office Shipping Lists" or NOSL) serve as the principal source of information but provide a serious underestimate of shipping activities. In the case of Augustus and John Boyd's victualing shipments to Jamaica, for instance, no Irish records exist to document the export of provisions from Ireland to Jamaica, because all Irish port records were destroyed by fire; no Philadelphia records exist to document the export of grains from Philadelphia to Jamaica because such exports were duty-free.

Nevertheless, the NOSL present the most detailed account of the shipping of the twenty-three associates, a group of traders for whom no account books and firm records have survived. For additional discussion of these and similar problems in using port records, see Higgins, "Charleston," p. 126; and Peter V. Bergstrom, *Markets and Merchants:*

Economic Diversification in Colonian Virginia, 1700–1775 (New York, 1985), pp. 4–7. The records that contain information about the comings and goings of ships must be used with care. Ralph Davis, "Shipping Records," *Archives*, v. 7, pp. 135–42; Doerflinger, *A Vigorous Spirit*, pp. 366–87; French, "Trade and Shipping"; Rupert Jarvis, "Sources for the History of Ports," *Journal of Transport History*, v. 3 (1955), pp. 76–93; Levett, *For Want of Trade*; John J. McCusker and Russell R. Menard, *Economy of British America*, pp. 76–78; Walter Minchinton, *The Naval Office Shipping Lists*; and D. M. Woodward, "Short Guides to Records: "Port Books," *History*, v. 55 (June 1970), pp. 207–10.

Shipping records
  British ports
    PRO-KG, ADM 7/78–98, Mediterranean Passes; ADM 68/194–202, Seamen's Sixpence
    PRO-CL, E 504/5, 15/2, 28/1, English Outport Books
    SRO, E 190/248/9, 190/249/10, Scottish Outport Books
  Colonial ports
    Rhode Island: Rhode Island Lists, National Archives Depository, Waltham, Mass.
    Pennsylvania: Computer Print-out of Shipping List, Historical Society of Pennsylvania, Philadelphia
    Virginia: CO5/1446–1447
    South Carolina: CO5/510–11
    Georgia: CO 5/710
    East Florida: CO 5/573
    Jamaica: CO 142/15–19
    St. Christopher: CO 243/1/15; T 1/512
    Antigua: T 1/512
    Grenada: CO 106/1
    West Africa: T 70/144, 633, 1263; CO 388/45/11 and 388/46/1
  Foreign ports
    Hamburg, Staatsarchiv: Angaben; Ankünften
    Rotterdam, Gemeente-archief: Zeetijdingen; Rotterdamse courant; Notarial Archives
    Paris, Archives de Paris, Serie d5B6/0298
  Contemporary newspapers
    British: *Lloyd's List*; *Lloyd's Register*; *London Chronicle*
    American: *The Virginia Gazette*; *The South-Carolina Gazette*; *The Georgia Gazette*
    Caribbean: *Gazette Sainte-Domingue*; *Petites affiches americaines*; *Affiches americaines*

Manuscript collections

Macpherson-Grant Muniments, Bundles 250, 295, 359, 552, and
Bound Letter Books of Governor James Grant, Ballindalloch
Castle, Aviemore, Scotland

Grant of Castle Grant Papers (GD 248/168–75), Grant of
Monymusk Papers (GD 345/1761), and Oswald Letter Books,
SRO, Edinburgh, Scotland

Mss. 5025, 9811, NLS, Edinburgh, Scotland

Home Papers, The Hirsel, Coldstream, Berwickshire, Scotland

Herries Papers, Spottes, Castle Douglas, Kirkcudbrightshire,
Scotland

Radcliffe Papers, Levant Accounts, Hertfordshire Record Office,
Hertford

Add.Mss. 237,071/362–64, BL, London

ADM 3/54, ADM 111/50, T 1 (allowances to ship arms, 1745–
65), and T 64/49, PRO-KG, London

Court of Chancery records, C 11/632, C 12/1036/12, C 31/187/
84, and C 107/68/tied bundle, PRO-CL, London

Main Papers, sub March 13, 1764, and February 19,1766, Manuscript Division, House of Lords, London

Ms. 8,741/1, Guildhall Library, London

Oswald Papers, Sudlows, Shedfield

James Murray Letter Books and Papers, Massachusetts Historical
Society, Boston

Printed, unpublished, and private sources

Coughtry, Jay, *The Notorious Triangle*, pp. 241–73

Craig, R., and R., Jarvis, eds., *Liverpool Registry of Merchant
Ships*, pp. 19, 61–67, 77, 81, 91, 104, 119

Cunningham, Timothy, *The Law of Bills of Exchange*, pp. 340–
51

Hardy, Charles, *A Register of Shipping*, pp. 42–44, 54–57, 70–
73, 82–85, 98–99

Mettas, Jean, *Répertoire des expeditions Negrieres françaises au
XVIII siècle*, v. 2 (Paris, 1978)

Minchinton, Walter, et al., eds., *Virginia Slave Trade Statistics,
1698–1775* (Richmond, 1984), pp. 143–51

Richardson, David, University of Hull, England

Schofield, Maurice, Widnes, Chester, England

Grant's Jamaican Plantations, 1752–1772

Table AIII.1   Grant's Jamaican Plantations, 1752-72

Estate[a]	Year Acquired	Beginning[b]			Ending[c]		
		Acres	Slaves	Price[d]	Acres	Slaves	Price
Charlemont	1752-63	903	137	5,000	903	133	6,705
Albion and Eden[e]	1752-68	2,640	-[f]	4,800			
Albion					1,519	-	17,770
Eden					1,120	-	15,723
Dalvey	1765-68	2,023+	284+	21,055	2,023	161	9,876
Epsom Pen	1765	77	-	216	77	22	2,027
Crawle	1765	662	191	7,714	-	-	-
Berwick	1768	2,161	-	14,286	2,161	141	9,244
Rio Magno Pen	1768	-	-	-			
Total		10,066	675	59,071	7,803	457	61,345

(a) Albion and Eden were situated in the northern parish of St. Mary; Charlemont, Crawle, Berwick and Rio Magno Pen were located in the central parish of St. Thomas in the Vale; and Epsom Pen was located in the central parish of St. Catherine.   Combining four earlier estates (Saul's River, Plaintain Garden River, Bowden, and Wheelerfield), the Dalvey plantation was situated in the easternmost parish of St. Thomas in the East.   Epsom and Rio Magno were technically not sugar plantations but livestock and subsistence estates that supplied the other sugar works.

(b) Beginning amounts for year, acreage, slaves, and prices are culled from Deed Books, Old Series, vols. 146-256 passim, at the Island Record Office, Spanishtown, Jamaica.   Ending figures are based on Sir Alexander Grant's estate inventory in Probate Inventory, v. 1773, February 15, 1773, Inventory of Sir Alexander Grant; and the values of his estates given in Sederunt Book, Grant Papers, Tomintoul House. Production amounts are recorded in Crop Accounts, 1/B/11/4/1/1-6, sub estate name, Jamaica Archives, Spanishtown.

(c) Ending figures are based on Grant's 1772 probate inventory. The Crawle estate is not listed in this inventory. Furthermore, acreages are not mentioned. It is assumed that the number of acres remained the same, if neither pruchases of adjacent land, sales, or mortgages were recorded in the Deed Books. Finally, the 1772 valuations probably do not include land values.

(d) Price figures have been commuted to English pounds sterling from Jamaica island currency.

(e) Albion and Eden plantations were owned jointly by Sir Alexander Grant and Alexander Grant of Achoynanie until 1768, when the lands were divided by casting lots. Sir Alexander acquired Albion, the value of which (with its 215 slaves) was then reassessed from £17,770 to £12,803. The new value takes into consideration both land and slaves.

(f) '-' signifies no available data.

Sources: Jamaica Archives, Spanishtown: Crop Accounts, 1/B/11/4, v. 2, ff. 127-28; v. 3, ff. 58, 221; v.4, ff. 1-3, 27, 33; v.5, ff. 22, 75, 93, 139, 199; and v. 6, ff. 22-23, 52, 144-46, 148-50, 156.

The Associates' Profits from Planting and Slaving

Planting

Determining how much sugar and rum an associate's estates produced and exported and how much the commodities made upon sale in London is no easy matter.[1] One needs figures for plantation production, trans-Atlantic shipping, and metropolitan sale, but the figures for any one function in any one year are sketchy, and are never available for all three functions in the same year.

Profit calculations may be "golden dreams and visionary computations," overkill, for there is every indication that planters simply computed expected income and regulated expenditure accordingly, with little heed to invisible debts and charges.[2] Yet an effort is worth making. Two sources ease the difficulty of determining quantity and value: port records detailing quantities of exports and imports; and crop accounts filed with the Jamaica Island Secretary by factors and overseers.[3] When combined with contemporary prices of sugar and rum, these sources allow us to make fairly rough but relatively reliable estimates of production.

---

1. For a discussion of the problems in determining profits in the 1600s, see Richard Grassby, "The Rate of Profit in Seventeenth-Century England," *English Historical Review*, v. 84 (1969), pp. 721–24. The problems are not much different for the eighteenth century. Ward, in *British West-Indian Slavery*, p. 48, has calculated that sugar planting between 1749 and 1832 ranged between 3.4% and 13.5% and averaged 8–10%. In contrast, English land earned profits at a gross rate of 3.1–4.0% per year (Allen, "Price of Freehold Land," p. 34; the mortgage interest rates fluctuated between 3.5% and 4.5% in 1721–94), government securities at a rate of 5% or less (Ashton, *Economic Fluctuations*, Table 9), and seventeen British firms between 1728 and 1826 averaged profit rates of 13% (ranging from 9% to 18%) (Philip Mirowski, "Adam Smith, Empiricism, and the Rate of Profit in Eighteenth-Century England," *History of Political Economy*, v. 14 (1982), pp. 178–98). Mirowski's high figures stand in strong contrast to those of other historians and as indications of the overall profitability of British investment are subject to criticism on the grounds of the unrepresentative nature of his sample firms; still, as possible alternative investments available to London merchants, their rating can stand.

2. *American Husbandry*, p. xxix.

3. Richard B Sheridan, "The Wealth of Jamaica in the Eighteenth Century," *Economic History Review*, 2nd ser., v. 18 (1965), p. 294.

It is possible to calculate with caution what Grant's crops might have realized upon sale in London. On the revenue side, crop accounts are spotty and the reporting gaps are significant. On the expense side, critical facts – such as production expenses, capital appreciation or depreciation costs, or voyaging and handling fees – are hard to find. Still the task is not impossible.[4] Revenue data extrapolated from shipping data in port records cover a wider expanse of time (22 years, 1747–68) and a broader spectrum of activity (both correspondent service and personal enterprise) than do data culled from existing plantation records. From the records completed by the customs officers recording the contents of each vessel arriving at or departing from Jamaica, one can compile a list of all goods on all Grant ships. Further, one can postulate that common rates prevailed on all Grant ships for wastage,[5] prior and island expense,[6]

4. Only J. R. Ward has examined problems of calculation in any detail. "The Profitability of Sugar Planting in the British West Indies," *Economic History Review*, 2nd ser., v. 31 (1978), p. 199. His method of estimating profit is largely adopted here.
5. Ward believes that 14% of the total inbound weight was lost on the trans-Atlantic voyage. "Profitability," p. 199. McCusker suggests a higher degree of loss: 25%. "The Rum Trade," p. 139.
6. Prior Expense: Capital charges of ship and its outfit and running costs of wages, victuals, repairs, port charges, and miscellaneous items. Detailed accounts of outset costs are rare. A lawsuit between partners Grant, Johnston, and Gardiner and their captain produced a complete itemization of costs incurred on a bilateral voyage of the *Neptune* (1747–48): £508 for ship, wages and in-transit expenses, and £478 for port expenses. C 11/631/32: Ogilvie v. Grant. A King's Bench case about the insurance of another Grant ship, *The Prince of Orange* (1757–58), valued ship, outset and provisions at £1,182. Cunningham, *Bills of Exchange*, p. 345.
   Wartime expense of £1,000 for ship and men are detailed for the 1747–1748 sugar-and-rum voyage of Alexander Grant's *Neptune* in a Chancery lawsuit waged by its captain. C 11/631/32: Ogilvie v. Grant, Bill of Complaint, 1749. £1,000 amounted to 9% of Net Revenue. Ten years later, Grant's *Prince of Orange* incurred outset costs of £1,182 for ship and men. Cunningham, *Bills of Exchange*, p. 345. In contrast, Davis estimates a 150-ton Virginia trading vessel cost £1,650 and a 200-ton Virginia trading ship cost £2,200 in outset expenses. "Earnings of Capital in the English Shipping Industry, 1670–1730," *Journal of Economic History*, v. 17 (1957), pp. 410–11. Wartime expenses were, of course, greater than peacetime costs. Compare the per-voyage replacement value of one of Sargent and Stratton's packet boats to the West Indies (£1,900 during the Seven Years' War) to the value claimed by their successor (£1,210). According to Davis, *The Rise*, pp. 365–78, capital and running costs did not change noticeably between 1725 and 1775.
   Island Expense: Wages, stock, supplies, repairs, and taxes. Information on island expenses is sketchy. In 1752, Grant's factor deducted 38% from Before-Wastage Revenue in the London Market. Jamaica Archives, Crop Accounts, v. 2, ff. 127–28. Planter and historian Edward Long estimated that "contingent" charges varied from 29% on a 300-acre estate to 33% on 900 acres. Long, *History*, pp. 460, 462. Any percentage poses problems, since the proportion of expenses to receipts varied with the size and age of the plantation, weather conditions, or pestilence.
   The only academic itemization of Island Expenses per se appears in Long, *History*, pp. 460–62; and the review of *American Husbandry*, pp. xxiv–xxv. According to Long,

insurance,[7] freight,[8] customs duties,[9] sales,[10] and total subsequent expense.[11]

An adaptation of the profit equation provides a useful starting point[12]:

between 29% and 33% of Revenue was spent on island stores, wages, repairs, stock and supplies. The anonymous reviewer gives a higher number: 30–41%. On Albion and Eden estates, island expenses = 38% of plantation receipts. But see also John Campbell's list in *Candid and Impartial Considerations on the Nature of the Sugar Trade* (London, 1763), pp. 22–23.

But most planters conflated prior and island expense. Mesopotamia, for example, was a sugar estate in western Jamaica. From 1751 to 1775, its owner spent £7,488 for slaves, and £10,536 on supplies. "Net Proceeds in England" = £69,679; Total Expenses = £18,024; Gross Proceeds = £85,484. Previous Expense and non-slave Island Expense, therefore, was 26% of Net Profit, 21% of Gross Profit. "Mesopotamia Returns, 1751–77," Clarendon Papers, Ms. b37, Bodleian Library, Manuscripts Department, Oxford. See also the accounts of Spring plantation, a moderate-sized sugar estate in western Jamaica with an average of 106 to 124 slaves. Smyth of Ashton Court Papers, AC/WO/16, Bristol Record Office.

7. Ward, "Profitability," p. 200. According to Richardson, "Profits," p. 71, outbound rates (as a percentage of outlay) were 7.5% in peace and 15% in war; inbound rates 2% in peace and 4% in war. Cunningham, *Bills of Exchange*, pp. 338–41, provides different figures: in war with convoy, outbound = 11%, and inbound = 13%. Cunningham cites the case of a Grant ship leaving Jamaica without convoy and paid 30% in wartime but could have cut its costs in half by going with convoy.

8. Ward, "Profitability," p. 199.

9. Lowell J. Ragatz, comp., *Statistics for the Study of British Caribbean Economic History, 1763–1833* (London, 1928), p. 11. Two fascinating contemporary handbooks give substance to the claim that "the Laws of the Customs formed a very difficult Science." Henry Crouch, *A Complete View of the British Customs*, 5th ed. (London, 1764); and Samuel Baldwin, *A Survey of the British Customs* (London, 1770).

10. An "Account of Sugar Sales, 1762–78" at Bristol, in the Bristol Record Office (WO/16/50).

11. Taken together: According to the Bristol account, Subsequent Expenses were divided among insurance, freight, import duty, storage, and brokerage costs and were calculated as the difference between Gross Proceeds (£11,450) and Net Proceeds (£8,069). This amounted to 30% of Gross Proceeds. Sheridan, in "A Rejoinder," *Economic History Review*, 2nd ser., v. 21 (April 1968), Table 2, calls them "invisible items" and assigns them 38.1%.

For each crop and cargo, it is assumed that the entire crop of sugar and rum was sent to England, that the entire cargo was sold in the open market at the current price, and that brokerage fees (usually 1/8%) were not incurred. A 30% assessment, therefore, should be valid, since Grant shipped all his sugar and rum to the mother country. See Crop Accounts, v. 6, ff. 22–23, 36, 44, 52, 121, 130, 144–50, 156, 159, 164, 218, Jamaica Archives. Molasses could have been used on his plantations or sold to locals. Cocoa, corn, pimento, plantain, and livestock were always used by the planter or sold to his neighbors.

Even so, this final value does not take into consideration the depreciation of the hull or the risk of loss. On these matters, see Davis, "Earnings," pp. 411–12, who sets the value at 4% and 4%, respectively.

12. The difficulties in estimating profits (especially in estimating net income from operations and capital appreciation and depreciation) are discussed in Hancock, "Citizen of the World," pp. 400–01.

Revenue in London Market
- Wastage
= Total Revenue (Gross Profit)

Prior London Expense (Outset and Invoice)
+ Island Expense
+ Subsequent London Expense
= Total Expense

Net Income from Operations (Revenue less Expense)
+ Capital Appreciation/Depreciation of Plantation
= Profit

Using this equation, one can construct an interesting comparison from port records. Some 44 of the shipments that Grant sent as either agent or principal contained on average 201 hogsheads, 28 tierces, and 4 casks of sugar (373,908 pounds) and 31 puncheons and 2 casks of rum (3,585 gallons).[13] (Table AIV.1). In terms of value, each of these ships carried on average £6,686 in sugar and £2,683 in rum. Only 30 of these voyages, however, were made on Grant's own account.[14] Total Before-Duty Revenue (Gross Profit) from the 30 voyages in these years was £341,335, Total Expenses were £267,919, and Net Income amounted to £73,416. On average, preduty profits were £2,447 per voyage and £6,118 per year during the 12 years of the 30 voyages.[15]

Estimation from port records sets only an upper limit on possible profits from planting, since many ships also contained the cargoes of clients and strangers. Additional, confirming information comes from plantation records, which can be combined with what one knows about shipping activities and costs. Employing the plantation records data from the period for which the information is most complete (1766–71) (Table AIV.2) and assuming (as most contemporaries and historians have done) that wastage was 15%, prior London and island expenses were 33% of before-wastage possible revenue in the London market, and subsequent expenses were 30% of total revenue, one derives the following profit for the seven plantations in the six-year period:

Revenue in London Market	£152,828
- Wastage	22,924
= Total Revenue (Gross Profit)	129,904

13. These statistics do not incorporate information from those sugar ships that were lost at sea or taken by the enemy.
14. Those voyages which were not undertaken primarily for Grant's own account are marked in Table AIV.1 with an asterisk.
15. £2,447 in 1747–68 is approximately £186,911 or $278,007 in 1994; £6,118 in 1747–68 is approximately £467,314 or $695,074 in 1994.

Prior London Expense	19,800
(assuming 18 voyages)	
+ Island Expense	50,433
+ <u>Subsequent London Expense</u>	38,971
= Total Expense	109,204
Net Income from Operations	£20,700

Thus, before adjusting for appreciation or depreciation of plantations between 1766 and 1771, I estimate that Grant made approximately £20,000 in total or £3,450 on average per year.[16]

Not surprisingly, the port-record average is almost double the crop-account average for the period 1766–71.[17] If the rate of profit represents "the net annual rate of return on capital" solely invested in the planting and commodity trade,[18] then Grant achieved a return of 44% on his outlay for voyages but only a return of 29% on his outlay for plantations. Whatever the measure, however, these were phenomenal profit rates compared to the 5% to 15% profit levels that were reached on other plantations in the West Indies and in other West Indian trading houses in Britain.[19] When it came to Caribbean planting, an associate's efforts brought large returns.

16. £20,000 in 1766–71 is approximately £1,326,094 or $ 1,972,405 in 1994. £3,450 in 1766–71 is approximately £228,751 or $340,240 in 1994. The estates did appreciate in value, of course, but no reliable information survives to document the rise. The only instance of both beginning and near-end value is that of Albion and Eden, but the shockingly low price Grant paid for the properties and the shady circumstances surrounding the deal caution against using it as an example. C 12/1014/13: Barclay v. Grant, 1765.

17. Another method of determining profit also exists – multiplying the total weight of the commodity by its average freight rate. Based on 15,790,032 pounds of sugar at 36 shillings per cwt, and on 157,410 gallons of rum at 9 shillings per gallon: In the case of sugar, Grant should have earned £284,615 total and on average £9,487 per expedition; and in the case of rum £72,232 total and £2,408 per venture. Combining the two averages, the result – £11,895 per voyage – exceeds the preceding estimate by 367%.

18. Grassby, "Rate of Profit," p. 724. In the present study, the "rate of profit" is calculated by dividing the Total Profit (also known as the Net Income) by the sum of both Prior Expense and Island Expense.

19. Ward, *British West-Indian Slavery*, p. 48; Richard Pares, *West India Fortune*, p. 320; Pares, *Yankees and Creoles* (Cambridge, Mass., 1956), p. 143; Pares, *Merchants and Planter* (Cambridge, 1960), p. 38; and Ralph Davis, *Aleppo and Devonshire Square*, c. 13. See also Vilar, *Catalogue*, III, pp. 300, 324 (10–28%). Cf. Stein, *French Sugar Business*, p. 85 (5–6%); Davis, *Rise*, Chs. 16–17 (2–3%); and Brulez, p. 83. On profit rates in Jamaica, see the review of *American Husbandry* (from 3% to 16%, 5% and 9%), Long, *History* (10%), and the author of *American Husbandry* (15–30%).

Table AIV.1 Grant's Jamaican Ships' Receipts (calculated from port records), 1747-68

Departure Date	Sugar Weight	Value	Rum Volume	Value	Total Value	Wastage	Total Revenue	Total Expense	Net Income
27/11/1747	334,686	7,161	8,360	2,926	10,087	1,513	8,574	7,001	1,573
05/06/1750*	33,180	461			461	69	392	1,370	(978)
10/06/1750*	16,590	231			231	35	196	1,235	(1,039)
18/06/1750*	66,360	922			922	138	784	1,639	(856)
15/07/1750*	24,885	346			346	52	294	1,302	(1,008)
01/08/1750*	58,065	807			807	121	686	15,772	(886)
08/07/1751*	16,590	253			253	38		1,248	(1,033)
29/09/1751*	49,770	759			759	114	215	1,544	(899)
28/04/1752	547,480	10,580	4,400	8,503	19,083	2,862	645	12,264	3,957
06/07/1752	535,030	10,339	3,740	7,228	17,567	2,635	16,221	11,377	3,555
21/04/1753	559,900	9,238	3,300	1,383	10,621	1,593	14,932	7,313	1,715
03/05/1753	597,230	9,854	3,300	1,383	11,237	1,686	9,028	7,674	1,878
10/04/1754	313,143	5,594	1,870	784	6,378	957	9,551	4,831	590
19/04/1754	497,700	8,891	5,500	2,305	11,196	16,799	5,421	7,650	1,867
10/07/1754	522,580	9,336			9,336	1,400	9,517	6,561	1,374
22/07/1754*	49,770	889			889	133	7,936	1,620	(864)
27/08/1754	394,000	7,039	660	277	7,315	1,097	6,218	5,379	839
10/02/1755	547,460	9,780	4,400	1,474	11,254	1,688	9,566	7,684	1,882
25/06/1755*	33,180	593			593	89	504	1,447	(943)
30/06/1755*	49,770	889			889	133	756	1,620	(864)
01/07/1755	200,739	3,586			3,586	538	3,048	3,198	(150)
01/07/1755*	16,590	296			296	44	252	1,273	(1,021)
03/07/1755**	49,770	889			889	133	756	1,620	(864)
03/07/1755	107,830	1,926	1,100	369	2,295	344	1,951	2,443	(492)

Date								
18/05/1757	165,900	3,076	5,500	1,843	4,918	738	4,181	3,977	203
20/06/1757	605,530	11,227	7,700	2,580	13,806	2,071	11,735	9,177	2,559
20/07/1759*	18,249	417			417	63	355	1,344	(989)
14/06/1762	720,805	14,658	13,080	8,332	22,989	3,448	19,541	14,549	4,992
14/06/1762	505,164	10,273	2,200	1,302	11,574	1,736	9,838	7,871	1,967
14/06/1762	526,720	10,711	10,450	6,184	16,895	2,534	14,360	10,983	3,377
17/06/1762	668,149	13,587	3,300	1,953	15,540	2,331	13,209	10,191	3,018
10/05/1763	850,200	13,816	11,000	17,875	31,691	4,754	26,937	19,639	7,298
24/07/1763	671,870	10,918	9,900	16,088	27,005	4,051	22,955	16,898	6,056
10/08/1763	1,094,830	17,791	1,650	2,681	20,472	3,071	17,401	13,076	4,325
20/08/1764	580,650	9,436	3,300	5,363	14,798	2,220	12,578	9,757	2,821
10/05/1764	331,800	5,101	5,500	2,750	7,851	1,178	6,674	5,693	981
18/05/1764	497,700	7,652	2,200	1,100	8,752	1,313	7,439	6,220	1,219
15/06/1764*	179,172	2,755	327	163	2,918	438	2,480	2,807	(327)
11/07/1764	559,380	8,600	1,980	990	9,590	1,439	8,152	6,710	1,441
10/05/1765	609,915	11,613	7,590	3,795	15,408	2,311	13,097	10,114	2,983
04/07/1765	558,374	10,631	7,590	4,175	14,806	2,221	12,585	9,761	2,824
15/07/1765	616,607	11,740	14,740	8,107	19,847	2,977	16,870	12,711	4,160
03/05/1766	554,101	10,603	7,040	3,872	14,475	2,171	12,304	9,568	2,736
06/07/1768	514,559	8,920	5,060	2,277	11,197	1,680	9,517	7,650	1,867
Total	16,451,973	294,184	157,737	118,056	412,241	61,836	350,405	289,561	60,844

Sources

Quantity: See source note to Table 4.1.
Price of sugar and rum: See source note to Table AIV.2.
Wastage: See fn. 5 in this appendix for assumed percentages.
Total Expense: See fn. 6 in this appendix for known and estimated costs.

Appendix IV

Table AIV.2 Grant's Jamaican Plantations' Receipts (calculated from crop accounts), 1752-71

Date[a]	Sugar Weight[b]	Value[c]	Rum Volume	Value	Total Value
1752	190,785	3,687	2,090	810	4,497
1757	284,930	5,283	9,900	3,317	8,599
1766	486,075	9,301	16,940	9,317	18,618
1767	852,308	15,307	14,630	7,315	22,622
1768	893,780	15,494	26,070	11,732	27,225
1769	595,166	11,073	19,360	8,954	20,027
1770	811,251	14,603	31,460	14,550	29,153
1771	963,879	17,784	36,630	17,399	35,183

(a) Crop years have been translated to calendar years.

(b) When reducing the contents of eighteenth-century cargo containers to common units, John McCusker and Russell Menard advise caution: "Imported and exported goods travelled in a myriad of packages, most of which varied in size by time, by point of origin, and by commodity, and had many different names and different capacities." *The Economy of British America*, pp. 76-77. An examination of Alexander Grant's cargo containers produces the following equivalencies:

    sugar -   1 hogshead = 1,659 pounds, 1 tierce = 1,244 pounds, 1 cask = 415 pounds;

    molasses - 1 hogshead = 106 gallons, 1 cask = 64 gallons, 1 barrel = 32 gallons;

    rum -   1 puncheon = 110 gallons, 1 cask = 110 gallons.

These equivalencies agree with Beckford, *Account*, pp. 80-82, and McCusker, "The Rum Trade," Appendix, pp. 789-94, 818-19, 826-30. In the present discussion, I have adopted the amounts for weights and measures assigned by McCusker. Weights are in pounds, and volumes in gallons.

(c) Values pose a separate problem. In the present discussion, "market value" or "London value" denotes an amount calculated by multiplying quantities of plantation produce or ship cargoes reported by island or port officials by the prices of sugar or rum in London, based on the prices listed in Sheridan, *Sugar and Slavery*, Appendix 5, pp. 496-97, Appendix 6, p. 498, and McCusker, "The Rum Trade," Table E16, pp. 1067-1068, Table E44, p. 1143. There are no extant price series for sugars sold in Jamaica. "Jamaica value" denotes an amount assessed or accepted by a colony official and stated in the island Crop Accounts; amounts given as island currency have been changed to British sterling, following the exchange ratios listed in McCusker, *Money and Exchange*, pp. 252-53.

Sources

    Quantity: See source notes to Table AIV.1.

    Price: Sheridan, *Sugar and Slavery*, Appendices 5 and 6; and McCusker, "The Rum Trade," Tables E16, E44.

Slaving

Determining the amount of profit the associates made is no easier for slaving than it is for planting.[20] The basic profit equation is the same: the difference between revenue (the Total Contribution from Selling Slaves and Other Goods) and expense (the Total Expense incurred by purchasing ships and slaves, outfitting and insuring ships and cargo, transporting slaves and cargo, marketing them, and in general running the operation). Yet there the similarity ends. Factory expenses should be included, plantation expenses excluded, and shipping expenses augmented by the addition of a new side to the trade polygon. And unfortunately one can never ascertain the expense of managing and running the enterprise as a whole, which included the costs of the London office and the island factory, the returns to the capital employed in the business, and the opportunity costs of the principals' time.

Of course, in spite of such obstacles, one can make reasonable estimates of "typical" contributions for the various forms of associate slaving. One can calculate the Contribution from Selling Slaves (I in Table AIV.3), from information that lies buried in government files, contemporary newspapers, and associate correspondence and accounts.[21] Estimating the Contribution from Selling Other Goods (II) and the Expense

20. The debate over profits made from slaving has been keen. Decades, ago, Eric Williams, in *Capitalism and Slavery* (London, 1944), argued that profits were enormous; and several recent historians, Joseph Inikori and William Darity, have made the same claim. But most historians now disagree.

    A lively exchange has occurred over the exact amount of the profits and the structure of the market that produced them. Robert P. Thomas and Richard N. Bean argue that the slave trade was a nearly perfect competitive industry dominated by a small number of big merchants. "The Fishers of Men," pp. 885–914. Commercial practice, rather than economic theory, has been examined at great length by those historians (like Roger Anstey) who make use of aggregate data or those historians (like Francis Hyde and David Richardson) who analyze individual behavior. Roger Anstey, *The African Slave Trade and British Abolition* (London, 1975); Francis B. Hyde, Bradbury Parkinson, and Sheila Marriner, "The Nature and Profitability of the Liverpool Slave Trade," *Economic History Review*, 2nd ser., v. 5 (1953), pp. 368–77; and David Richardson, "Profitability in the British-Liverpool Slave Trade," *Revue francaise d'histoire d'Outre Mer*, v. 52 (1975) pp. 301–08.

    The full debate begins with Anstey's *Slave Trade*; it can be pieced together from the footnotes of several recent contributions by David Richardson and William Darity. See, for example, Richardson, "Accounting for Profits in the British Trade in Slaves: Reply to William Darity," *Explorations in Economic History*, v. 26 (1989), pp. 492–99; and most recently Richardson, "The Eighteenth Century British Slave Trade: Estimates of its Volume and Distribution," *Research in Economic History*, v. 12 (1989), pp. 151–95. In recent years, the principal disagreement has been over the price-per-slave that Darity and Joseph Inikori use in their calculations involving the 1780s.

21. For sale and purchase prices, see [Tweed], *Considerations*, pp. 65–67; and C 12/1036/12: Oswald v. Wallace, Complaint, January 3, 1773.

Appendix IV

Table AIV.3   Associates' Slave Trading, 1748-84

Company Expeditions

Number of expeditions	34
Span of years	35
Contribution - slaves	£121,021
Contribution - other goods	£30,255
Gross contribution	£151,276
Initial voyaging expense	£138,075
Subsequent voyaging expense	?
Net contribution	£13,201
per expedition	£388
per year	£367
Rate of contribution	6%

Personal and Private Deliveries

Number of deliveries	10
Span of years	21
Contribution - slaves	£21,927
Net contribution	£21,927
per delivery	£2,193
per year	£1,044

Contract Deliveries

Number of deliveries	15
Span of years	5
Contribution - slaves	£26,005
Net contribution	£26,005
per delivery	£1,734
per year	£5,201

Total Activity

Number of expeditions and deliveries	59
Span of years	36
Total net contribution	£61,133
Total facilities expense	£30,292
Profit	£30,841
per expedition or delivery	£523
per year	£857

Sources

Quantity of slaves and goods: See source notes to Table 4.1.

Price of slaves and goods: See Oswald Papers, Sudlows; Ragatz, *Statistics*; and source note to Table 4.1.

Wastage and expense: See fnn. 5 and 6, Appendix IV.

of Managing and Running the Operation is a different kettle of fish. Many components are missing, some incomplete, and others unreliable; they are susceptible only to the crudest of measurements. In the case of Revenue Made From the Sale of Other Goods, for example, there is a disturbing lack of continuous and specific reporting.[22] Thus, one is thrown back upon models erected from voyages for which such revenues are known. Two voyages serve as guides: Liverpool merchant William Davenport's ship *Hawke* earned a contribution from the sale of other goods that was 25% of the contribution from the sale of slaves on its first voyage in 1779, and 103% on its second voyage the following year. When known values exceeded these estimates, one can plug them into the profit equation; but, when they do not exist, the more conservative of the two contribution rates (25%) can be used.[23] Itemization of General Expenses Relating to Production and Voyaging (III) is as rare as information about Revenue from Selling Other Goods. In short supply are – costs of the factory's upkeep, construction, depreciation, provisioning, and insurance[24]; costs of wages paid to employees[25]; costs of the purchase, depreciation, furnishing, and outfitting of slaving

22. When slaves were the principal cargo, other African goods were overlooked or omitted in the customs accounts and, when such goods did receive mention, they were often described simply as "dry goods." Or despite the fact that Sierra Leone ivory tusks ("elephants' teeth") were considered "the very best of all Guinea, being very white and large," their quantity and price were seldom noted by captains or officers. Barbot, "A Description of the Coasts of North- and South-Guinea . . . ," in Churchill, comp., *A Collection*, v. 5, p. 102. The Bance Island factory's ships often carried gold, silver, tortoise shell, and grain from the associates' clients, but their shipments are infrequently recorded. An exception is C 12/808/2: Johnson v. Oswald, Answer of Oswald, scheds. 1–4.

23. Hyde et al., "Nature," pp. 375–76. On the 1779 voyage, other goods (ivory and freight) contribution = £3,499, and slaves contribution = £13,874. On the 1780 voyage, other goods (sugar, cotton, coffee, and oil) contribution = £10,130, and slave contribution = £9,831. Richardson, "Profits," pp. 76–77, warns about the exceptional nature of the *Hawke*'s profits. But the appearance of the ship (its build and outfit) and the pattern of its first voyage mirror those of many of the trading vessels sent out by Grant, Oswald & Co. The "other goods" revenue made on its first voyage is adopted here.

24. Information about the purchase price of the factory and the cost of its upkeep is detailed in the *Journals of the House of Commons*, v. 26, p. 258. A guess about annual factory expenses can be made with the assistance of an account of expense during the first fifty-eight months of Grant, Oswald & Co.'s ownership that the partners submitted to Parliament in 1752: the partners had acquired the island free of charge, but the previous owner required them to buy its inventory for £3,947, the repayment of which, if the principal and interest were amortized over a twenty-five-year period in equal installments at 10%, averaged £441 per year; factory expenses in the first fifty-eight months totaled £1,159 and averaged £240 per year. Similarly, no information is available on the costs incurred in the London counting-house; London time and services are therefore omitted from the estimation.

25. David Richardson has postulated that mid-century wages amounted to £169 per voyage. "Costs of Survival," p. 192.

vessels[26]; and costs of transporting and marketing slaves.[27] Of all the expenses, voyaging costs (transport and supply) are the most elusive. What one does know is that voyaging expenses were considerable: one African voyage of a Bristol slaver had an initial outlay of £5,693 in 1774[28]; and William Davenport's initial outlay on African trips averaged £4,375 between 1757 and 1784.[29] Since Davenport's voyages closely resembled Bance Island's slaving ventures, their middle-of-the-road figure of £4,375 is used here. This estimate, of course, certainly exaggerates the amount spent; but, given the tenuousness of the evidence it is prudent to postulate it here. The use of this "consensus" figure is a convenience only, and is not meant to deny the possibility of variance.[30]

26. In 1749, the purchase and outfit of a Bristol slaver cost £16 per ton. Nearly forty years later, the expense for a Liverpool slaver was roughly the same, although a British ship trading to the West Indies cost only £9 per ton. Richardson, "Costs of Survival," p. 184. Davis, "Earnings," pp. 411–12, set the cost of depreciation at 4% and of the risk of loss at 4%.
27. On the 1771–72 voyage of the associates' *Africa*, the expense of selling slaves amounted to 4.67% of the revenue from selling slaves. C 12/1036/1/2: Oswald v. Wallace, Bill of Complaint, January 2, 1773. These expenses included the captain's coast commission, slave-trading privileges extended to certain employees, and doctor's money. For higher estimates, see Hyde et al., "Nature," pp. 365–67 (*Hawke* in 1779 = 19.43%; *Hawke* in 1780 = 16.02%). According to Richardson, the cost of managing slaves in the middle passage during the late 1780s was £2 per head. This cost included the expense of additional fittings (armaments, netting, and shackles), of extra food and medicine (5% of total exports), and of additional crewmen to supervise the slaves. Overall transport costs were higher – £7 per head. "Costs of Survival," pp. 185, 192, 183.
28. Minchinton, "The Voyage," p. 198. Initial working capital = £3,200; purchase and refitting = £1,247; and cargo and duties = £4,446.
29. Richardson, "Profits," pp. 82–87.
30. The only specific itemization of outlay for one of the associates' African ventures lies buried in the files of the Court of Chancery. C 12/808/2, C 12/808/5, C 12/814/31: Johnson v. Oswald, 1760–61, especially Answer of Richard Oswald and John Mill (February 11, 1761) and its four schedules. The case involved Mill and Oswald's administration of the estate of the African trader Thomas Melville, Jr., who died in January 1756. In the Answer submitted to the Court, the two associates provided an account of four African ventures that averaged £1,577 in outlay and related costs. The Answer lists outset costs (ship, outfit, wages, insurance, miscellaneous, and cargo) for four African ships: *Prince Edward*, May 1751 (£1,681); *Prince Edward*, August 1752 (£1,810); *Mercury*, December 1752 (£1,391); and *Richard*, March 1753 (£1,311). Since these figures reflect only initial outlay, rather than initial *and* subsequent outlay, and many goods were not accounted for until well after the return of the vessel, they are not used here.
   Virginia trading expeditions between 1725 and 1775 generally averaged outset costs of £2,850. Davis, *The Rise*, p. 378. But when a trader moved from bilateral to trilateral or multilateral trading, as did Grant and Oswald, costs like insurance rose. Cunningham, *Bills of Exchange*, p. 378.
   Another way to estimate outset costs is suggested by Anstey, *British Slave Trade*, p. 30: multiplying the average tonnage of the fleet in question by an outset cost per ton per annum adjusted for price change (1761–70: £45.8/ton; 1771–75: £50/ton).
   No evidence of intermediate and inbound expenses has been uncovered and as a result they are omitted in the present analysis. Their omission should not be construed as a statement of their unimportance.

Table AIV.3 summarizes the results of the estimation of earnings. Like all estimates, these numbers have their limitations, yet at the same time they provoke some interesting speculation on one aspect of the business of London enterprisers that is rare, suggestive, and trustworthy. Here, in aggregate, the net contribution from the sale of slaves and other goods in Africa, the West Indies, and North America totaled £61,133, facilities expenses £30,292, and overall profit £30,841 on an initial fixed investment worth £4,000.[31]

If one breaks down the aggregate according to average profits per expedition, average markup, and contribution rate, by expedition or year, different aspects are revealed. First of all, average profits per expedition or delivery varied markedly between and within kinds of operations. Trans-Atlantic voyages sponsored by the partnership averaged £388 per expedition, whereas deliveries on contract to French merchants in Africa averaged £1,734 per delivery and deliveries to private traders working the coast averaged £2,193 per delivery.[32] Secondly, looking at the average markup added upon sale to the buying price of the slave in each category (company expeditions, deliveries on contract, and deliveries to individual partners and private traders), one finds that no one markup prevailed – 33% on average for the French contract (swinging between 12% and 46%), 92% (between 47% and 181%) for the private sales, and 137% (between 59% and 430%) for the company expeditions between Africa and the West Indies or North America.[33] Finally, if one takes a similar measure of the contribution rate, representing the increase of net contribution on the initial voyage expense (the money made over and above the amount of the initial investment in company ventures), one finds that a surprisingly low average contribution rate of 6% prevailed on trans-Atlantic slave voyages supervised by the associates.[34]

This average of 6%, however, hides the fact that there were more losses than gains and that there were wide fluctuations in contribution rates between 222% and −94%. True, high profits may have been realized from time to time; in 1766–67, for example, a single round-trip voyage of the associates' ship *Africa* may have made nearly £10,000 in

31. Alternative slaving profits (incorporating both low and high voyaging expenses as well as both low and high other goods revenue) are arranged by date and kind of negotiation, in Hancock, "Citizen," Appendix 10 a–d. The data for the present discussion are taken from Appendix 10d. £4,000 in 1749 is approximately £327,922 or $487,745 in 1994.
32. £388 in 1749–84 is approximately £26,884 or $39,986 in 1994; £1,734 is approximately £120,145 or $178,071; and £2,193 is approximately £151,948 or $226,004.
33. The markup on slaves is calculated by dividing the contribution from sale of slaves by the expense of purchasing the slaves. Hancock, "Citizen," Appendix 10d, col. 11.
34. The contribution rate is calculated by dividing the contribution from the expedition by the expedition expense that was paid in advance. Hancock, "Citizen," Appendix 10d, col. 19.

contribution from its expedition. But such an amazing success could just as easily be followed by a devastating loss; the slave trade, whether managed from Bristol, Liverpool, or London, was always beset by "[g]reat risk and uncertainty."[35]

Just as average profits on different slaving operations varied, so the contribution rates of slaving expeditions increased and stabilized with the passage of time and the acquisition of experience in oceanic shipping. The peacetime period from 1749 to 1755, when the firm was first learning the trade, was marked by continuous loss. During the Seven Years' War, there was marked improvement: the company experienced only two losses on eight ships in seven years. Thereafter, in the period leading up to the American War, success was less predictable, with twelve losses in twenty voyages; yet the average contribution rate fell only slightly and high wins were as frequent as near misses. Clearly, as the associates became more familiar with slaving, their success (as measured by positive and increasing profit amounts) grew in frequency and size. Only the death of three partners and the outbreak of the American Revolution frustrated continued growth.

The foregoing, extremely conservative analysis of associate profit-making is a rough analysis at best but a valuable one insofar as it allows one to note broad comparisons. In particular, it reveals but a slight difference in reward levels between London and outport slave traders. The average contribution rates of company expeditions managed by the London associates differed only marginally from the less "modest" profit rates that were achieved by their competitors in Liverpool and Bristol; whereas the associates most likely gained at a contribution rate on company expeditions of 6%, their outport counterparts (by the most liberal calculation to date) never generally averaged profits per voyage of 8% or 10%.[36]

35. Hyde et al., "The Nature," p. 369.
36. Anstey, *African Slave Trade*, p. 47 (1761–70: 8.2%; 1771–80: 12.1%; 1781–90: 10.7%); Stein, *French Sugar Business*, p. 37, and Richardson, "Profitability," p. 304 (67 Davenport ventures, 1757–84: 17% per venture). Adjusted for duration and remittance, Davenport earned on average about 10.5% on adjusted outlay annually, 8.1% on initial outlay. Ibid., p. 305. The calculations of Anstey and Richardson have been severely criticized by Inikori, in "Market Structure," p. 761 (1757–76: 14%; 1779–84: 51.6%). In revising Anstey, Darity suggests between 16.0% and 17.3% as likely rates. "Profitability," p. 382. This low rate of return for associate voyages is matched by that of a French slave-trading firm in 1776–84 (6%). Jean Meyer, *L'Armement nantais dans la deuxieme moitie du XVIIIe siecle* (Paris, 1969). The Dutch and the Danes earned even less. Anstey, "Volume," pp. 3–31.

A further relative comparison may also be significant: slave profits were not as large as plantation profits or contracting profits. Even with the possibility of sizable errors in the estimates, slaving was on the low end. But if one introduces a high figure for Other Goods Revenue, the rate of contribution is 71%.

Bance Island Efficiency Levels, 1748–1776

Table AV.1:   Bance Island Efficiency Levels, 1748-76

	1748/12/19	1750/11/18	1751/8/19	1751/1/2	1752/3/1	1756/8/14	1757/7/28
State of Repair	"very bad" guns	"indifferent"	"very much out" of repair walls	"insecure" walls	"very much decayed & out of repair"	"good"	"good"
People							
Whites							
Agents	1 Melwin	-	2 Staple, S. McLeod, J.	1 Staple, S.	-	-	2 McLeish, G. Stephens, J.
Factors							3
Others	4	-	8	9	-	-	23
Masters	-	-	2	3		-	5
Total	5	8	12	13		32	45
% Scots			25%	15%			
Blacks							
Men	-	21	23	19	-	60	60
Women		4	16	14		16	16
Boys		3	18	7		36	13
Girls		-	16	4		37	4
Total		28	73	44		149	93
Vessels		9	8	5		6	6
Artillery							
Cannon							
Total	13	25	25	25	-	28	28
Mounted		10	10	10		-	-
Unmounted		15	15	15		-	-
or 12 pound							
9 pound		10	10	10		-	10
6 pound		-	-	-		-	-
3&4 pound		3	3	3		-	6
1&2 pound		12	12	12		-	12
Shot (rounds)							
12 pound	-	-	-	-	-	-	-
9 pound		-	135	135		-	-
6 pound		-	47	47		-	-
3&4 pound		-	205	205		-	-
1 pound		-	-	-		-	-
Total		-	387	387		900	900
Grape & Chain	-	-	129	129	-	-	-
Powder (barrels)	-	10	6	6	-	30	-
Small Arms							
Muskets	-	-	40	40	-	60	60
Swords		-	40	40		60	60
Bayonets		-	-	-		60	60
Pistols		-	-	-		20	20
Drums		-	-	-		-	-
Lanthorns		-	-	-		-	-
Miscellaneous		-	21	21		30	20

Table AV.1   *Cont'd*

1758/6/28	1762/1/26	1763/5/26	1765/5/9	1769/3/29	1770/2/16	1773/11/30	1776/1/15
					"almost decayed"	"good"	
2	2	1	2	2	-		2
Aird, J.	Aird, J.	Aird, J.	Stirling, D.	Knight, T.			Knight, T.
James, T.	Tweed, J.		Teise, G.	Davidson, A.			McIntosh, A.
3	3	5	3	5		-	-
30	11	23	19	29		-	4+
7	3	5	6	8		-	-
42	19	34	30	44		33	6+
21%	-	32%	33%	23%		-	-
75	105	197	137	24	-	137	51
15	30	26	-	-		-	29
-	-	5	-	-		-	50
-	-	5	-	-		-	28
90	135	233	137	24		137	158
7	3	17	10	-	-	10	6
-	42	25	28	57	-	28	30
-	-	8	22	25		28	-
-	-	17	6	32		-	-
-	-	-	-	-		-	-
-	6	6	6	6		-	-
-	10	10	10	10		-	16
-	-	-	-	-		-	-
-	26	9	12	41		-	14
-	300	300	300	-	-	-	-
300	400	350					
	-	-	-				
	350	150	350				
	-	-	"great quantity"				
	950	850	1,000		"sufficient		
					quantity"		
	650	-	"great deal"	-	-	-	-
"great	"large	25	-	-	-	-	-
stock"	quantity"						
40	40	40	-	-	-	-	-
40	40	40					
40	-	40					
40	-	-					
-	-	-					
24	-	-					
80	-	40					

The Associates' Landownership, 1745–85

Table AVI.1   Distribution of Lands Owned by Type

Year	London Counting- or Town House	Villa	Country Seat	Overseas Plantation	Total
1745	6	0	8,377	2,116	10,499
	7	0	8,377	2,116	10,500
	7	0	8,377	2,116	10,500
	6	0	8,377	4,618	13,001
	12	50	20,514	4,618	25,194
1750	11	100	20,514	8,956	29,581
	11	150	19,138	8,956	28,255
	11	200	19,141	10,359	29,711
	11	200	19,446	12,681	32,338
	12	200	56,562	14,958	71,732
1755	13	200	56,562	17,589	74,364
	12	300	65,425	17,589	83,326
	12	350	65,425	17,681	83,468
	11	350	67,015	19,191	86,567
	25	350	67,116	19,500	86,991
1760	25	350	67,125	19,535	87,035
	25	350	67,198	19,435	87,008
	26	350	67,198	19,435	87,009
	27	400	67,199	20,638	88,264
	28	400	83,928	72,342	156,698
1765	25	300	93,725	74,662	168,712
	30	300	93,949	95,728	190,007
	31	350	96,928	101,108	198,417
	31	250	105,208	112,455	217,944
	27	335	166,648	111,942	278,952
1770	27	385	164,503	112,203	277,118
	27	285	125,938	132,593	258,843
	28	200	69,895	129,102	199,225
	29	200	13,102	128,951	142,282
	29	200	131,510	129,723	261,462
1775	29	200	145,078	129,970	275,277
	29	200	145,874	129,970	276,073
	29	200	147,349	125,260	272,838
	30	480	147,736	124,837	273,083
	29	480	153,300	124,333	278,646
1780	32	580	153,300	124,333	278,245
	33	580	154,199	124,333	279,145
	33	580	156,840	124,333	281,786
	30	1,752	156,940	124,333	283,055
	30	1,802	156,933	124,333	283,098
1785	30	1,802	157,873	124,685	284,390

Sources

London: Tax Assessment Record Books, and Trade Directories, Guildhall Library, London.

England: Wills, PRO-CL, London; Title Deeds, Kent Record Office, Maidstone; Danson Deeds, Hall Place Local Studies Library, Bexley; Title Deeds, Essex Record Office, Colchester; Title Deeds, Devon Record Office, Exeter.

Scotland: Register of Deeds, Register of Sasines, Grant of Castle Grant Papers, Grant of Monymusk Papers, Oswald Letter Books, SRO, Edinburgh; Oswald Papers, NLS, Edinburgh; Herries Papers, Spottes, Haugh of Urr; Oswald Papers, Sudlows; Sir John Sinclair, *The Statistical Account of Scotland*.

Abroad:

Africa	*Journal of the House of Commons*, v. 1752; Oswald Papers, Sudlows.
Jamaica	Land Patents, v. 19, 21, 24, 26, 30, 31, Jamaica Archives, Spanishtown, Jamaica; Deed Record Books, vols. 81, 83, 97, 102, 106, 146, 153, 157, 159-161, 163, 173-174, 176-182, 184, 191, 194, 199, 205, 214-215, 218, 220, 226-227, 229-230, 245-248.
St. Croix	Landlister, 1751-76, Danish National Archives, Copenhagen; Landlister, 1758, 1766, National Archives, Washington, D.C.
St. Kitts	Boyd Mortgages, Public Record Office of Northern Ireland, Belfast; Hugh Alexander Boyd Collection, Ballycastle, Northern Ireland; Close Rolls, PRO-CL, London.
Antigua	Deed Books, Will Books, Probate Inventories, Supreme Court Archives, St. John's.
St. Vincent	Island Secretary Register Books, Supreme Court Registry, Kingstown, St. Vincent.
Grenada	Island Secretary Register Books, Supreme Court Registry, St. George's; Close Rolls, PRO-CL.
Tobago	Island Secretary Register Books, Public Library, Scarborough, Tobago.
East Florida	*Acts of the Privy Council*, vols. 4-6.
Georgia	Property Deed Books, Georgia Department of Archives and History, Atlanta; *Proceedings of the Georgia Historical Society*.
S. Carolina	Property Deed Books, South Carolina Department of Archives and History, Columbia; *The Papers of Henry Laurens*.
Virginia	*The Virginia Gazette*.
Nova Scotia	Egmont Papers, BL, London; Public Archives of Nova Scotia, Halifax; *Acts of the Privy Council*, vols. 4-6

The Associates' Art Collections

Appendix VII

Table AVII.1   Distribution of Paintings, by Century, Nationality, and Genre

Century	15th	16th	17th	18th	Unknown
Aufrere					
Number of works purchased	3	43	93	8	2
	2%	29%	62%	5%	1%
Boyd					
Number	0	37	121	88	9
	0%	15%	47%	35%	4%
Oswald					
Number	2	8	40	20	11
	2%	10%	49%	25%	14%

Nationality	Italian	French	Dutch	Flemish	German	English	Austrian	Swiss	Spanish	Unknown
Aufrere										
Number	101	20	11	10	5	1	0	0	0	1
	68%	13%	7%	7%	3%	1%	0%	0%	0%	1%
Boyd										
Number	55	26	61	33	8	59	1	1	2	9
	22%	10%	24%	13%	3%	23%	0%	0%	1%	4%
Oswald										
Number	28	2	16	18	2	4	0	0	0	11
	35%	2%	20%	22%	2%	5%	0%	0%	0%	14%

Genre	Religious	Landscape & Marinescape	Genre	Myth	Portrait	History & Battle	Animal	Other	Total
Aufrere									
Number	101	20	11	10	5	1	0	0	149
	68%	13%	7%	7%	3%	1%	0%	0%	100%
Boyd									
Number	55	26	61	33	8	59	1	1	255
	22%	10%	24%	13%	3%	23%	0%	0%	100%
Oswald									
Number	28	2	16	18	2	4	0	0	81
	35%	2%	20%	22%	2%	5%	0%	0%	100%

George Aufrere's Art Collection

Dressing Room

Rembrandt H. Van Rijn	*An Old Man's Head*
Nicolas Poussin	*A Sacrifice to Pan*
Raphael [after]	*St. John*
Albrecht Durer	*The Ascension*
Francesco Albani [after]	*The Rest on the Flight into Egypt*
Francesco Vanni	*A Boy Lying on a Bed*
Peter Paul Rubens	*His Wife*
Giovanni Francesco Grimaldi (Bolognese)	*A Landscape with Figures*
Federico Zuccaro	*A Venetian General*
Jacopo Bassano	*The Encampment of Israelites*
Jacopo Tintoretto	*A Venetian Nobleman*
Pietro Paolo Veglia	*The Nativity*
Pietro Paolo Veglia	*The Adoration of the Magi*
Sebastien Bourdon	*Releasing the Prisoners*
Sebastien Bourdon	*Healing the Sick*
Carlo Dolci	*Ecce Agnus Dei*
Benardino Luini [after]	*Christ Disputing with the Elders*
Gaspar Dughet	*A Landscape with a Hermit Reading*
Gaspar Dughet	*A Landscape with a Hermit Seated*
Philips Wouwermans	*A Landscape with Figures*
Philips Wouwermans	*A Landscape with Figures*

Back Dressing Room

Giovanni Antonio De Sacchis (Pordenone)	*The Binding of St. Sebastian*
Carlo Maratti	*A Magdalen*
Michelangelo Cerquozzi (di Battaglia)	*A Rehearsal of an Italian Comedy*
Giuseppe Grisoni	*A Landscape with the Sibyl's Temple*
Salvator Rosa	*Harlequin*
Salvator Rosa	*Scaramouche*
Giovanni Paolo Panini	*The Ruins of Rome*
Michelangelo Cerquozzi (di Battaglia)	*A Battle*
Michelangelo Cerquozzi (di Battaglia)	*A Battle*
Giovanni Lanfranco	*A Sketch of a Picture at Burghley House*
Giovanni Guercino [after]	*Madam de la Valiere as the Magdalen*
Antonio Tempesta	*Moonlight*
Filippo Lauri	*A Landscape with Figures*
Domenico Zampieri (Domenichino)	*A Magdalen*
Francesco Solimena	*Virgin & Child*
Filippo Lauri	*The Magdalen Reclining*

Ante-Room

Pieter Van Laer, or Sebastien Bourdon	*A Battle*
Andrea Sacchi	*The Death of Abel*
Paul Bril	*A Landscape with Figures*
Paul Bril	*A Landscape with Figures*
Willem Van De Velde the Younger	*A Calm*
Leonardo Da Vinci	*Christ Holding a Type of the Trinity*
Giovanni Battista Salvi (Sassoferrato)	*The Virgin's Head*
Carlo Maratti	*The Virgin's Head*
Federico Barocci	*The Rest on the Flight into Egypt*
Michele Rocca (Parmigianino)	*Susannah & the Elders*
Michele Rocca (Parmigianino)	*David & Bathsheba*
Domenico Zampieri (Domenichino)	*Perseus & Andromeda*
Francesco De Rossi	*Tobit & the Angel*
Pieter Van Laer	*A Conversation*
Andries Dirksz. Both	*Peasants Playing Cards*
Charles Le Brun	*Hercules & Hersione*
Domenico Zampieri (Domenichino)	*The Baptism of Christ by John*
Claude Lorrain (Claude Gellee)	*A Landscape with Figures*
Salvator Rosa	*A Battle*
Paolo Veronese	*Emperor Augustus & the Sibyl*

Dining Room

Pietro Da Cortona	*Emperor Augustus & the Sibyl*
Guido Reni	*Cupid with a Laurel Crown in His Hand*
Giovanni Guercino	*A Cosmographer*
Raphael	*The Virgin, Joseph & Young Christ*
Antonio Allegri Correggio	*The Head of St. Catherine*
Domenico Fetti	*The Lord of the Vineyard Hiring Laborers*
Raphael	*The Virgin, Child, St. John, & St. Anne*
Gaspar Dughet	*A Landscape with an Aqueduct*
Andries Both and Philips Wouwermans	*A Landscape*
Ippolito Scarcellino Da Ferrara	*The Flight into Egypt*
Salvator Rosa	*A Rocky View near Salerno*
Pier Francesco Mola	*A Landscape: The Prodigal Son*
Martin De Vos	*The Death of St. Dominic*
Carlo Maratti	*The Death of St. Joseph*
Bartolommeo Biscaino	*Christ & the Samaritan Woman*
Bartolommeo Biscaino	*Noli Me Tangere*
Claude Lorrain (Claude Gellée)	*A View in the Campagna of Rome*
Salvator Rosa	*A Lake Surrounded by Rocky Mountains*
Bartolommeo Schidone	*The Virgin & Child*
Titian	*The Holy Family & St. Catherine*

Guido Reni	*Mater Dolorosa*
Paolo Caliari Veronese	*Susannah & the Elders*
Paolo Caliari Veronese	*Rebecca Receiving Presents at the Well*
Nicolas Poussin	*Rinaldo & Armida*
Nicolas Poussin	*Sleeping Venus Surprised by Satyrs*
Girolamo Mazzola (Parmigiano)	*The Virgin, Child, St. John & St. Margaret*
Girolamo Mazzola (Parmigiano)	*The Virgin, St. Catherine & Others*
Pier Francesco Mola	*The Muse of Imitation*
Guido Reni	*A Sibyl*

Withdrawing Room

Paolo Caliari Veronese	*A Balladsinger in a Group of Figures*
Claude Lorrain (Claude Gellee)	*A Landscape*
Sebastien Bourdon	*Feeding the Hungry*
Sebastien Bourdon	*Receiving Strangers*
Sebastien Bourdon	*Giving Drink to the Thirsty*
Sebastien Bourdon	*Clothing the Naked*
Sebastien Bourdon	*Burying the Dead*
Pier Francesco Mola	*Elijah & the Widow of Zaraphath*
Pier Francesco Mola	*Elisha & the Rich Woman of Shunem*
Adriaen Van Ostade	*A Balladsinger in a Group of Figures*
Sebastiano Veneziano Del Piombo	*The Descent from the Cross*
Girolamo Mazzola (Parmigiano)	*The Entombment of Christ*
Peter Paul Rubens	*Christ Falling beneath the Cross*
Giorgio da Castelfranco (Giorgione)	*The Dalmatian Prisoner*
Luca Giordano	*St. John Preaching in the Wilderness*
Luca Giordano	*The Conversion of St. Paul*
Hans Rottenhammer I & Jan Brueghel	*The Virgin, Child & St. John*
Hans Rottenhammer I & Jan Brueghel	*The Martyrdom of St. Cecilia*
Giovanni Francesco Romanelli	*Susannah & the Elders*
Paolo Caliari Veronese	*Don Carlos, Prince of Spain*
Titian	*A Boy Playing a Lute*
Bernardino Gatti	*The Mystic Marriage of St. Catherine*
Girolamo Mazzola (Parmigiano)	*The Virgin & Child*
Agostino Carracci	*An Angel*
Agostino Carracci	*The Virgin*
David Teniers the Younger	*A Landscape with Ruins & Gypsies*
David Teniers the Younger	*A Landscape with Mountains & Capuchins*

Cabinet between the Drawing Room and the Back Drawing Room

Giovanni Battista Salvi (Sassoferrato)	*The Virgin & Child*
Jean Baptiste Blin	*Flowers in a Vase*
Jean Baptiste Blin	*Flowers in a Vase*
Federico Barocci	*The Rest on the Flight into Egypt*
Francesco De Rossi (Salviati)	*The Salutation*
Alessandro Varotari (Padovanino)	*Endymion Asleep*
Christian Dietrich	*The Farrier's Shop*
Cornelis Van Poelenburgh	*Nymphs Dancing*
Unknown	*A Landscape*
Jacopo Tintoretto	*The Creation of Eve*
Benedetto Luti	*A Woman's Head*
Benedetto Luti	*A Woman's Head*
Federico Barocci	*The Magdalen with a Skull*
David Teniers the Younger	*Fishermen*
Carlo Maratti	*The Wise Men's Offering*
Andrea Sacchi	*Cain & Abel*
Carletto Veronese	*The Salutation*
Carlo Dolci	*The Head of the Young Christ*
Alessandro Tiarini	*The Vision of St. Francis*
John Powell [after Joshua Reynolds]	*A Sketch: Mrs. Pelham Feeding Poultry*
Filippo Lauri	*Christ Calling St. Peter*
Hans Rottenhammer I	*The Virgin & Child*
Girolamo Mazzola (Parmigiano)	*A Group of Boys*
Lodovico Carracci	*Padre Eterno*
Innocenzo Da Imola	*The Virgin, Child, Sts Francis & Catherine*
Henri Van Steenwyk & Frans Francken II	*The Interior of a Church in Antwerp*
Giovanni Francesco Grimaldi (Bolognese)	*A Landscape with Figures*

Passage to the China Closet

Luca Giordano	*Mars & Venus with Cupid*
Jacopo Bassano	*An Angel Appearing to the Shepherds*
Sebastien Bourdon	*A Corps De Guarde*
Salvator Rosa	*A Landscape with Figures*
Antonio Tempesta	*Moonlight*
Pompeo Batoni	*The Sacrifice of Iphigenia*
Sir Anthony Van Dyck	*The Adoration of the Shepherds*

Tapestry Room

Guido Reni	*Salome Receiving the Head of John*
Eoli	*Ruins in Perspective*

Source: A Catalogue of Mr. Aufrere's Pictures (London, 1791).

Sir John Boyd's Art Collection

Francesco Albani	*A Landscape with Figures*
David Allan [after Guido]	*Aurora*
David Allan	*Cupid & Psyche*
David Allan	*The Origin of Painting*
David Allan [after Albani]	*Charity*
David Allan [after Guercino]	*The Prodigal Son*
David Allan [after Guercino]	*Card Players*
David Allan [after Guercino]	*The Fortune Teller*
David Allan [after Guido]	*The Annunciation*
David Allan [after Guido]	*The Salutation*
Anon.	*View of Richmond Bridge & Hill*
Anon.	*The Parting of the Red Sea*
Anon.	*Dogs Disturbing Swans from Their Rest*
Anon.	*Henry VIII*
Anon.	*Edward VI*
Anon.	*A Boy's Head*
Anon. [after Canaletto]	*View of St. Mark's Place in Venice*
Anon. [after Titian]	*The Adoration of the Shepherds*
Jacques D'Arthois	*A Landscape with Cattle*
William Ashford	*A Landscape in the Vicinity of Dublin*
William Ashford	*A Landscape with Figures & Cattle*
Ludolf Bakhuyzen	*A Sea View: Vessels Passing a Buoy*
Thomas Barker	*Crazy Jane*
George Barret	*A Landscape with Figures & Buildings*
George Barret	*A Morning Landscape in Wales*
George Barret	*A Moonlight Landscape in Wales*
George Barret	*A Perspective View of Danson*
Jacopo Bassano	*The Angel Appearing to the Shepherds*
Jacopo Bassano	*The Birth of Christ*
Cornelis Pietersz. Bega	*A Conversation*
Nicholas P. Berchem	*A Landscape with Figures & Cattle*
Nicholas P. Berchem	*A Landscape with Figures & Cattle*
Nicholas P. Berchem and Adam Pynacker	*A Cabinet Picture*
Nicholas P. Berchem and Adam Pynacker	*A Cabinet Picture*
Jan Frans Van Bloemen	*Women Washing Linen in an Aqueduct*
Andries Both	*A Landscape with River, Ships & Cattle*
Andries Both	*Giving Refreshment to the Sick & Lame*
Richard Brakenburg	*Interior of a School*
Richard Brakenburg	*Interior of a School*

Bartholomaus Breenberg	*The Centurion*
Bartholomaus Breenberg	*Nymphs in Conversation*
Bartholomaus Breenberg and Cornelis Poelenburgh	*Nymphs Bathing*
Bartholomaus Breenberg and Cornelis Poelenburgh	*Nymphs Reposing after a Bath*
Charles Brooking	*A Sea View*
Charles Brooking	*A Sea View*
Jan Brueghel the Elder	*A Landscape with Figures*
Jan Brueghel the Elder	*A Landscape*
Jan Brueghel the Elder	*A Conversation*
Jan Van De Capelle	*Market Boats Coming Up a River*
Annibale Carracci	*Mater Dolorosa*
Annibale Carracci	*Pluto & Cerberus*
Lodovico Carracci	*St. Francis in a Trance with an Angel*
Jan Chalon	*Landscape*
Jan Chalon	*Landscape*
Viviano Codazzi	*Ruins with Figures*
Sebastiano Conca	*A Fountain with Figures & Cattle*
Antonio Allegri Correggio	*Ecce Homo*
Antonio Allegri Correggio	*A Magdalen*
Pietro Da Cortona	*Venus & Cupid*
Pietro Da Cortona	*Europa*
Pietro Da Cortona	*Europa*
Pietro Da Cortona	*The Infant Bacchus with Nymphs & Satyrs*
Pietro Da Cortona	*The Virgin & Child*
Aelbert Cuyp	*A Landscape with Figures & Horses*
Aelbert Cuyp	*A Landscape with Cows & Boats*
Aelbert Cuyp	*A View on the Rhine*
Etienne Delaulne	*A Landscape*
Etienne Delaulne	*A Landscape*
Etienne Delaulne	*A Moonlight Landscape*
Christian Dietrich	*A Landscape with Figures*
Christian Dietrich	*A Landscape with Figures*
Carlo Dolci	*The Virgin*
Gaspar Dughet	*A Landscape*
Gaspar Dughet	*A Landscape with Figures & Sheep*
Gaspar Dughet	*A Landscape with Figures & Buildings*
Gaspar Dughet [circle of]	*A Landscape with Figures*
Gaspar Dughet [circle of]	*A Grove*
Karel Dujardin	*A Landscape with Cows & Sheep*
Adam Elsheimer	*The Nativity*
Adam Elsheimer [after Raphael]	*The Nativity*
Adam Elsheimer [after Raphael]	*The Adoration of the Shepherds*
Domenico Fetti	*Turks Smoking*
Frans Francken II	*An Incantation*
Frans Francken II	*Moses Striking the Rock*

Benevenuto Da Garofolo	*The Virgin & Child*
Cristofano Gherardi	*The Union of the Arts: An Allegory*
Luca Giordano	*Alpheus & Arethusa*
Luca Giordano	*Venus at the Forge of Vulcan*
Jan Gossaert	*The Wise Men's Offering*
Jan Griffier I	*View on the Rhine*
Jan Griffier I	*View on the Rhine*
Giovanni Francesco Grimaldi [Bolognese]	*A Picture with Pictures in the Foreground*
Giovanni Francesco Guercino	*Rebecca Showing Her Bracelet*
Giovanni Francesco Guercino	*A Man in Ruff & Armor*
Johan Philipp Hackaert	*A View near Rome with Figures*
Johan Philipp Hackaert	*A View near Rome with Figures*
Johan Philipp Hackaert	*A Landscape with Figures & Cattle*
Johan Philipp Hackaert	*A Landscape with Figures & Cattle*
Joris Van Der Hagen	*A Landscape with Figures Hunting*
Gavin Hamilton	*Paris & Helen*
Gavin Hamilton	*Narcissus*
Gavin Hamilton	*Helen*
Anton Hickel	*The Princesse De Lamballe*
Meindert Hobbema	*A Landscape with a Cataract & Buildings*
Robert Home [after Raphael]	*The Virgin & Child*
Melchior D'Hondecoeter	*Birds & Fowl*
Jean Huber	*Voltaire & His Maid*
Julius Caesar Ibbetson	*A Farm Yard at Chale in the Isle of Wight*
Julius Caesar Ibbetson	*Steep Hill & Cove in the Isle of Wight*
Julius Caesar Ibbetson	*A Landscape with Figures*
Julius Caesar Ibbetson	*A Landscape with Figures*
Julius Caesar Ibbetson	*Border Stone at Borrowdale, Cumberland*
Julius Caesar Ibbetson	*A Sea Shore*
Cornelius Johnson I	*Lord Stafford in Armor*
Jacob Jordaens	*The Flight into Egypt*
Pieter Van Laer (II Bamboccio)	*The Interior of a Cave*
Pieter Van Laer (II Bamboccio)	*The Flight into Egypt: A Moonlight Scene*
Pieter Van Laer (II Bamboccio)	*The Prodigal Son with Figures & Cattle*
Filippo Lauri	*An Allegory*
Filippo Lauri	*An Allegory*
Charles Andre Van Loo	*Rinaldo & Armida*
Isaack Luttichuys	*Henry Duke of Gloucester in Armor*
Carlo Maratti	*The Virgin & Child*
Carlo Maratti	*The Virgin & Child*
Elias Martin	*A View of the Back of Danson*
Michelangelo	*The Crucifixion*
Michiel J. Van Miereveld	*William, Prince of Orange*

Willem Van Mieris	*Ceres & Bacchus*
Willem Van Mieris	*A Conversation*
Pierre Mignard	*The Baptism of Christ*
William Miller	*The Resurrection*
Pier Francesco Mola	*A Landscape with Figures*
Pier Francesco Mola	*A Landscape with St. Bruno*
Pier Francesco Mola	*A Landscape*
Jan Mienze Molenaer	*Boors Regaling*
Jan Mienze Molenaer	*Family Grace before a Repast*
Jean Baptiste Monnoyer I	*A Flower Piece*
Moore	*A View through a Cave*
Moore	*A View through a Cave*
George Morland	*Shipwrecked Sailors in a Storm*
George Morland	*The Saving of a Wreck after a Storm*
George Morland	*A Scene in a Wood with Rustic Figures*
George Morland	*A Chelsea Pensioner & Two Ladies*
George Morland	*Heskerton Grove near Woodbridge*
George Morland	*A Young Porker Feasting on Cabbage*
George Morland	*The Painter at His Easel*
George Morland	*A Cottager, Daughter & Dog Going Home*
George Morland	*The Antiquarian*
George Morland	*A Butcher's Slaughter House: Exterior*
George Morland	*A Woodscape with Figures*
George Morland	*A Sow & Pigs*
George Morland	*Pointers in a Landscape*
George Morland	*Two Donkeys*
George Morland	*Spaniels Hunting*
George Morland	*Pigs outside a Barn*
Isaac De Moucheron	*A Castle with River & Figures*
Francisco Mueda	*The Sacrifice of Iphigenia*
Bartolome Esteban Murillo	*The Virgin & Child*
Peeter Neefs the Elder	*An Interior of a Church*
Peeter Neefs the Elder	*An Interior of the Antwerp Great Church*
Peeter Neefs the Elder	*An Interior of a Cathedral: A Perspective*
Ocheali	*A View in Rome*
Ocheali	*A View in Rome*
John Opie	*King Richard*
Isaack Van Ostade	*Travellers Stopping at a Cabaret*
Jean Baptiste Oudry	*A Dog & Swans*
Anthonie Palamedes II and Adriaen Van Der Werff	*A Battle*
Anthonie Palamedes II and Adriaen Van Der Werff	*A Battle*

Giovanni Paolo Panini	*Ruins*
Pierre Patel I	*A Landscape with Bridge &*
	Columns
Egbert Van Der Poel	*A View of Scheveling*
Cornelis Van Poelenburgh	*Sleeping Diana Observed by a Satyr*
Paulus Potter [school]	*A Landscape with Cows & Horses*
Nicolas Poussin	*The Dead Christ*
Nicolas Poussin	*A Boy & a Girl*
Nicolas Poussin	*A Landscape with Buildings &*
	Figures
Nicolas Poussin	*A Landscape with Buildings &*
	Figures
Nicolas Poussin & Gaspar Dughet	*Solemn Grandees*
Raphael	*St. John & the Infant Christ*
Guido Reni	*A Capuchin's Head*
Guido Reni	*St. John & the Lamb*
Rembrandt H. Van Rijn	*Tycho Brahe in His Study*
Rembrandt H. Van Rijn	*The Vanity of Riches*
Rembrandt H. Van Rijn	*Portrait of His Mother*
George Romney	*A Recumbent Wood Nymph*
Salvator Rosa	*A Landscape with Figures & Horses*
Hans Rottenhammer I	*The Triumph of Cupid*
Hans Rottenhammer I	*The Holy Family*
Peter Paul Rubens	*A Lady in Black with a Ruff*
Peter Paul Rubens	*An Old Man's Head*
Peter Paul Rubens	*A Man's Head*
Peter Paul Rubens	*A Man's Head*
Peter Paul Rubens	*A Man's Head*
Peter Paul Rubens	*Love & War*
Peter Paul Rubens	*Venus & Mars*
Peter Paul Rubens [after Zuccarro]	*Sir Francis Walsingham*
Peter Paul Rubens and Jacques	*Tigers in a Landscape*
D'Arthois	
Jacob Van Ruisdael	*A Cataract in Mountainous Country*
Jacob Van Ruisdael [after]	*A Landscape with Figures*
Christian Georg Schuz	*A Landscape with a Cataract*
Samuel Scott	*A Sea Storm with Ships*
Daniel Seghers and Cornelis Van	*A Circular Festoon with Beautiful*
Poelenburgh	*Flora*
Dominic Serres	*Boats & Vessels*
Dominic Serres	*View of Stonehenge*
Giovanni Andrea Sirani	*The Madonna's Head*
Stanover	*Fruit*
Stanover	*Fruit*
Henri Van Steenwyk	*St. Peter in Prison*
Herman Van Swanevelt	*A Landscape*
Herman Van Swanevelt	*A Picture*
David Teniers the Younger	*An Interior*
David Teniers the Younger	*A Scene with Figures*
David Teniers the Younger	*Armour & Military Accoutrements*

David Teniers the Younger	*The Temptation of St. Anthony*
David Teniers the Younger	*Beggars*
David Teniers the Younger	*Card Players*
David Teniers the Younger	*An Incantation*
David Teniers the Younger	*A Landscape with Figures*
David Teniers the Younger	*A Small Head*
David Teniers the Younger	*A Man Writing at a Desk*
Jean Baptiste Antoine Tierce	*The Eruption of Mt. Vesuvius*
Jean Baptiste Antoine Tierce	*The Fall of Tivoli*
Jean Baptiste Antoine Tierce	*Nero's Baths*
Jean Baptiste Antoine Tierce	*The Fall of Terme*
Jacopo Tintoretto	*Young Man Playing a Guitar*
Titian	*Recumbent Venus*
Titian	*The Magdalen*
Titian	*The Holy Family & St. Elizabeth*
Joseph Mallard William Turner	*The Sea Shore with a Great Rolling Tide*
Joseph Mallard William Turner	*View of a Fish Market on the Dutch Coast*
Joseph Mallard William Turner	*Port Du Diable in Switzerland*
Joseph Mallard William Turner	*Perspective of a Bridge with a Hermit*
Francesco Vanni	*The Virgin, Child, Joseph & an Angel*
Diego R. Velasquez	*The Penitential Magdalen*
Adriaen Van De Velde	*A Landscape, with Cows, Horses & Sheep*
Willem Van De Velde the Younger	*A Sea Storm*
Willem Van De Velde the Younger	*Shipping*
Willem Van De Velde the Younger	*A Sea Engagement*
Willem Van De Velde the Younger and Brooking	*A Sea View with Figures and Ships*
Willem Van De Velde the Younger and Brooking	*A Sea View*
Claude Joseph Vernet	*An Evening View on the Sea Coast*
Claude Joseph Vernet	*A Sea View with Figures*
Claude Joseph Vernet	*A Sea View with Figures*
Claude Joseph Vernet	*A Sea View with Ships*
Claude Joseph Vernet	*A Storm with a Shipwreck near the Rocks*
Claude Joseph Vernet	*A Moonlight View with Figures & a Fire*
Paolo Caliari Veronese	*The Marriage of St. Catherine*
Paolo Caliari Veronese	*Christ among the Doctors*
Paolo Caliari Veronese	*St. Peter Weeping*
Paolo Caliari Veronese	*Cleopatra*
Paolo Caliari Veronese [after Guido]	*Abraham Preparing to Sacrifice Isaac*
Daniel Vertangen	*Salamacis*
Simon De Vlieger	*A Sea View*

Simon De Vos	*Christ's Passage to the Mount of Olives*
Jean Antoine Watteau	*Soldiers Seated beneath a Tent*
Jean Antoine Watteau	*The Halt of an Army before a Meal*
Jean Antoine Watteau [copy of Correggio]	*Venus & Cupid*
Jan Baptist Weenix	*A Sea Port with Broken Column & Figures*
Jan Baptist Weenix	*Dead Partridges*
Adriaen Van Der Werff	*The Virgin & Child*
Adriaen Van Der Werff	*A Nymph & a Shepherd*
Francis Wheatley	*Cottage Charity*
Gerard Wigmana	*The Virgin & Child*
Richard Wilson	*A Landscape with Figures, Ruins & Water*
Richard Wilson	*A Landscape with Figures*
Richard Wilson	*A Landscape: Strada Nomentana*
Richard Wilson	*A Sunny Evening*
Philips Wouwermans	*A Winter Scene with Figures & a Bridge*
Philips Wouwermans	*An Encampment*
Joseph Wright	*A Landscape with a Lake beneath a Mount*
Joseph Wright	*A Seaport beneath a Castle*
Renier Zeeman	*A Brisk Gale with Dutch Sloops*
Francesco Zuccarelli	*The Flight into Egypt*
Francesco Zuccarelli	*A Landscape*
Francesco Zuccarelli	*A Landscape with Figures*
Francesco Zuccarelli	*A Landscape with Figures & Water*

Source: A Catalogue of a Genuine Collection of Valuable Pictures by the Most Admired Masters of the Italian, French, Flemish and Dutch Schools, ... The Property of Sir John Boyd, Bart., Deceased, By whom they were collected during a Long Residence in Italy, And now removed from his Seat in Kent (London, H. Phillips, March 18–19, 1800), and *A Catalogue ...* (London, Coxe, Burrell & Foster, May 7–8, 1805).

Richard Oswald's Art Collection

Francesco Albani	*Venus & Adonis*
Giovanni Battista Anticone	*Diana & Endymion*
Anon.	*A Sacred Procession*
Anon.	*St. Catherine*
Anon.	*A Landscape*
Anon.	*A Landscape*
Anon.	*A Landscape*
Anon.	*A Landscape*
Anon.	*The Magdalen*
Anon.	*Finding Monk*
Antonio Balestra	*The Beheading of St. John*
Antonio Balestra	*St. John Preaching*
Gia Francesco Barbieri	*Susannah & the Elders*
Pompeo Girolamo Batoni	*The Holy Family*
Bartolommeo Biscaino	*Christ in the Temple*
Ambrogio di Stefano Borgognone	*St. Paul Preaching*
Benedetto Caliari	*The Woman of Cana*
Carlo Caliari (Caliafari)	*A View of Venice*
Antonio Canal (Canaletto)	*A View of Venice*
Antonio Canal (Canaletto)	*A View of Venice*
Paolo Emilio Capi	*Venus Blinding*
Annibale Carracci	*The Death of Abel*
Valerio Castello	*The Virgin & Child*
Giovanni Benedetto Castiglione	*A Landscape*
Aelbert Cuyp	*A Landscape with Cattle*
William Denune	*Richard Oswald*
Gerbrandt Van Den Eeckhourt	*Corps De Guarde*
Frans Francken I	*Passover*
Frans Francken I	*The Adoration of the Maji*
Frans Francken I	*The Marriage Feast*
Frans Francken II	*Solomon's Idolatry*
Luca Giordano	*Joseph Being Sold by His Brothers*
Jean Josefsz. Van Goyen	*Cattle*
Jean Josefsz. Van Goyen	*A Landscape*
Alberti Guido	*The Virgin & Child*
Van Hastie	*The Birth of Erichthonius*
Francis Hayman	*Sir John Falstaff Raising Recruits*
Willem Van Herp	*Clothing the Naked*
Pieter De Hooch	*A Musical Conversation*
Jan Josef Horemans II	*A Conversation*
Jan Josef Horemans II	*A Butcher's Shop*
Filippo Lauri	*Ceres Returning Thanks for the Harvest*
Sir Pieter Van Der Faes Lely	*Dead Game*
Sir Pieter Van Der Faes Lely	*Dead Game*
Andrea Locatelli	*The Flight into Egypt*
Adam Frans Van Der Meulen	*A Landscape*

Adam Frans Van Der Meulen	*A Landscape*
Domenico Mona	*A Battle*
Hieronymus Van Der My	*Venus & Aeneas*
Aert Van Der Neer	*Moonlight*
Anthonie Palamedes I	*A Flemish Supper: The Oyster Feast*
Giovanni Paolo Panini	*Ruins*
Giovanni Paolo Panini	*Ruins*
Cornelis Van Poelenburgh	*Diana & Aektion*
Rembrandt Hermansz. Van Rijn	*An Old Man & a Woman*
Olivier F. Rocque	*Venus*
Olivier F. Rocque	*Diana*
Willem Romeyn	*Cattle*
Philipp Peter Roos (Rosa Da Tivoli)	*Cattle*
Hans Rottenhammer I	*The Feast of the Gods*
Peter Paul Rubens	*A Bacchanalian Feast*
Eduaert Snayers	*A Battle*
Eduaert Snayers	*A Battle*
Frans Snyders	*Dead Game*
Francesco Solimena	*Tobit & the Angel*
David Teniers the Younger	*A Landscape*
David Teniers the Younger	*An Encampment*
David Teniers the Younger	*The Sack of a Village by Banditti*
Gerard Ter Borch	*Girls Making Lace*
Francesco Cavaliere Trevisani	*The Visitation of Elizabeth*
Francesco Cavaliere Trevisani	*Mary*
Claude Joseph Vernet	*A Landscape*
Abraham Willaerts	*A Landscape*
Abraham Willaerts	*A Landscape*
Thomas Willeboirts	*Perseus & Andromeda*
Philips Wouwermans	*A Landscape*
Philips Wouwermans	*The Stag Chase*
Joseph Wright	*Benjamin Franklin*
Johann Zoffany	*Mary Ramsay Oswald*

Source: "Pictures belonging to Mr. Oswald" (unpublished manuscript, Oswald Papers, Sudlows).

Unpublished Sources

Canada
  Nova Scotia, Halifax
    Nova Scotia Archives
      Nova Scotia Land Records
  Ontario, Toronto
    Archives of Canada
      Nova Scotia Land Records

France
  Paris
    Archives de France
      Papers relating to West Africa
    Archives de Paris
      Premord Accounts
    Ministère des Relations Extérieures, Archives des Affaires Étrangères
      Papers relating to 1782–83 Peace Negotiations

Germany
  Hannover
    Niedersachsisches Staatsarchiv
      Ferdinand of Brunswick-Wolfenbuttel Papers

India
  New Delhi
    National Archives of India
      Home Proceedings, 1770–76

Portugal
  Lisbon
    Arquivo Nacional da Torre do Tombo
      Provedoria e Junta da Real Fazienda do Funchal
        Madeira Port Records
      Alfàndega do Funchal
        Madeira Port Records

Spain
  Madrid
    Archivo Historico Nacional
      Seccion de Estado, Bundles 4203–3885
        Papers relating to 1782–83 Peace Negotiations
  Seville
    Archivo General de Indias
      Santa Fe 389–90, 447, 1167
        Cartegena Slave Contract Papers
  Valladolid
    Archivo General de Simancas
      Secretaria de Estado: Francia
        Papers relating to 1782–83 Peace Negotiations

Sweden
  Uppsala
    University Library
      Henry Smeathman Diary

United Kingdom
  Aberdeen
    Aberdeen University Library
      Montcoffer Lodge/Duff House Papers
  Aberystwyth
    National Library of Wales, Manuscripts Department
      Clive Manuscripts
  Aviemore
    Ballindalloch Castle
      Macpherson-Grant Papers (Governor James Grant Papers)
  Aylesbury
    Buckinghamshire Record Office
      Howard-Vyse Manuscripts
  Ayr
    Carnegie Library
      Ayr Burgh Records
    Strathclyde Regional Archives
      Commission of Supply Minute Books
      St. Quivox Parish Records
      Turnpike Trust Minute Books
      Valuation Rolls

Bedford
 Bedfordshire Record Office
  Grantham Papers
  Orlebar Manuscripts
Belfast
 Public Record Office
Bentham
 Mr. E. P. English
  Mills Letterbooks, 7 vols.
Bexley
 Hall Place, Local Studies Library
  Bexley Parish Records
  Danson Deeds
Bristol
 Bristol Record Office
  Woolnough Papers
  Alexander Grant of Achoynanie Papers
 Bristol University Library
  Pinney Papers
Bury St. Edmunds
 Suffolk Record Office
  Grafton Papers
Calne
 Bowood (The Earl of Shelburne)
  Shelburne Papers
Chichester
 West Sussex Record Office
  Cowdray Manuscripts
Coldstream
 The Hirsel (Baron Home of the Hirsel)
  9th Earl of Home Correspondence
Cumnock
 Dumfries House (The Marquis of Bute)
  Dumfries and Loudoun Papers
Dumfries
 Dumfries Archives Centre
  Dumfries Town Council Minutes
 Dumfries Museum
  Merchant's Account Book
  Planter's Account Book
Dundee
 Glamis Castle (The Earl of Strathmore)
  Strathmore Papers

Dunfermline
  Broomhall (The Earl of Elgin)
    Papers of 9th–11th Earls of Elgin
Edinburgh
  Bank of Scotland
    Bank of Scotland Accounts
    British Linen Bank Accounts and Letters
  Edinburgh University Library
    Laing Manuscripts, Gordonstoun Papers
    Oswald Papers
  Hopetoun House (The Marquis of Linlithgow)
    Hope Family Papers
  National Library of Scotland
    Sir Laurence Dundas Letterbook
    Caddell of Grange Papers
    Fettercairn (Sir William Forbes) Papers
    Alexander Houston & Co. Letter- and Account-Books
    Lauriston Castle Collection, Delvine Papers
    Mure of Caldwell Papers
  Royal Bank of Scotland
    Minutes of Directors
  Signet Library
    Printed Papers of the Court of Sessions

Scottish Record Office – General Register House

B 6	Ayr Burgh Records
B 28	Fortrose Burgh Records
CC 1–8	Commissary Court Records (Wills)
CH 2	Parish Records: St. Quivox, Thurso, Wick, & Urr
E 106	Exchequer Records: Valuation Rolls
E 326	Exchequer Records: Window Tax Records
E 504	Exchequer Records: Customs Collectors' Quarterly Accounts (Port Books)
E 536	Ayr Salt Collectors' Quarterly Accounts
GD 1/32	Grant of Monymusk Papers
GD 1/268	Herries of Halldykes Papers
GD 1/306	Alexander Oliphant & Co. Letterbook
GD 1/618	George Oswald of Scotstoun Papers
GD 3	Earl of Eglintoun Papers
GD 10	Murray of Broughton Papers
GD 18	Clerk of Penicuik Papers
GD 25	Marquis of Ailsa Papers

GD 44	Gordon of Castle Gordon Papers
GD 58	Carron Iron Company Records
GD 109	John Hamilton of Bargany Letters
GD 110	Hamilton-Dalrymple of North Berwick Papers
GD 117	Cathcart of Carleton Papers
GD 125	Rose of Kilravock Papers
GD 135	Stair Manuscripts
GD 142/8	Hamilton of Pinmore Papers
GD 171	Forbes of Callendar Papers
GD 213	Oswald of Auchincruive Letterbooks
GD 219	Murray of Murraythwaite Papers
GD 224	Duke of Buccleuch Muniments
GD 248	Grant of Seafield (Castle Grant) Papers, and Cullen House Papers
GD 345	Grant of Monymusk Papers
RD 2–4	Register of Deeds
RS	Register of Sasines

Scottish Record Office – West Register House

CE 1	Scottish Customs Board Minute Books
CE 60	Glasgow and Greenock Minute Books
CS 19–29	Court of Sessions Extracted Processes
CS 228–39	Court of Sessions Unextracted Processes
RHP	Register House Plans

Exeter
    Devon Record Office
        George Arnold and John Sargent II Land Leases
Flichity
    Tomintoul House (Sir Patrick Grant of Dalvey)
        Plantation and Sederunt Books of Sir Alexander Grant
            Estate
Forres
    Brodie Castle (The Brodie of Brodie)
        Brodie Papers
    Town Hall, Burgh Council Minutes
Galashiels
    Gala House
        William Makdougall Letters
Glasgow
    Glasgow University Archives
        Hamilton of Rozelle Papers

Houston House
  Alexander Speirs Letters and Accounts
  Mitchell Library, Rare Book and Manuscript Room
  Bogle Papers
  Strathclyde Regional Archives
    Campbell of Succoth Papers
    Mitchell Johnston, Solicitor Collection
    Register of Burgh Deeds
    Stirling of Keir Papers
Greenwich
  National Maritime Museum
    Letters of Admiralty Board, Navy Board, and Victualing Board
    Dockyard Records
    Marine Society Records
Haugh of Urr
  Spottes (Sir Michael Herries)
    Michael Herries Papers
Hertford
  Hertfordshire Record Office
    Radcliffe Family of Hitchin Priory Papers
Hull
  Hull University Library (Brynmor Jones Library)
    Sir Charles Hotham Thompson Papers
Inverary
  Inverary Castle (The Duke of Argyll)
    Argyll Muniments, Calendar of Craigforth Papers
Kelty
  Blair Adam (Mr. Adam)
    Adam Brothers Correspondence
Lincoln
  Lincolnshire Record Office
    Cust Papers, Letters of Peregrine Cust
    Monson Papers, Journal of Thomas Thistlewood
    Yarborough Papers, Letters and Accounts of Charles
      Anderson-Pelham
London
  Bank of England Archives
    Bank Private Drawing Office Ledgers
    Government Annuity Ledgers
  Barclays Bank (54 Lombard Street)
    Records of Fraeme, Barclay & Co.
    Records of Barclay, Bevan & Co.

British Library
  Bathurst Papers (Loan 57)
  Egerton Manuscripts
    Henry Cavendish Parliamentary Diary
    Earl of Hertford Papers
  Grenville Papers
  Hastings Papers
  Kings' Manuscripts
    Transcripts Relating to West Africa
    Governor Grant's Reports on East Florida
    W. G. J. DeBrahm's Report of the General Survey
    Adam Gordon's Journal of an Officer in East Florida
  Long Papers
  Marlborough Papers
  Newcastle Papers
Corporation of London Record Office
  Court of Orphans Records
  Court of Decrees (Court of Conscience) Records
  Freedom Records
  General Assessment Land Tax Records
Coutts & Co. (440 Strand)
  Customer Account Ledgers
General Post Office, Archives Department
  Treasury Letterbooks
  General Accounts
  Overseas Mail Sea Contracts
Guildhall Library and Archives
  Edward Grace Letterbook
  General Assessment Land Tax Records
  Insurance Company Records (Royal Exchange & Sun Office)
  Livery Company Records (Grocers & Haberdashers)
C. Hoare & Co. (37 Fleet Street)
  Customer Account Ledgers
House of Lords
  Main Papers
India Office Library
  Minutes of Court of Directors
  General Correspondence
  Accountant General's Papers: Bond and Stock Ledgers
  Proceedings (Consultations) of the Government in India:
    Bengal Consultations: Mayor's Court Records
    Bengal Public Proceedings
    Bengal Revenue Proceedings

National Westminster Bank
  Bristol Old Bank Records
  Prescotts, Grote Bank Records
  Smyth & Payne Bank Records

Public Record Office – Chancery Lane

C 11–12	Chancery Proceedings, Six Clerks Series
C 24	Chancery Town Depositions
C 31	Chancery Affidavits
C 33	Chancery Entry Books of Decrees
C 38	Masters' Reports and Certificates
CP 40	Court of Common Pleas Plea Rolls
E 112	Exchequer Bills and Answers
KB 122	King's Bench Judgment Rolls
KB 125	King's Bench Entry Book of Rules
PROB 11	Wills

Public Record Office – Kew Gardens

ADM 2	Admiralty Out-Letters
ADM 3	Minutes of the Admiralty Board
ADM 106	Navy Board Records
ADM 110	Victualing Board Out-Letters
ADM 111	Victualing Board In-Letters
AO 1	Declared Accounts
AO 12	American Loyalist Claims
BT 6	Board of Trade General Miscellanea
CO 5	America and West Indies Original Correspondence
CO 101	Grenada Original Correspondence
CO 106	Grenada Miscellanea
CO 137	Jamaica Original Correspondence
CO 142	Jamaica Miscellanea
CO 152	Leeward Islands Original Correspondence
CO 217	Nova Scotia Original Correspondence
CO 267	Sierra Leone Original Correspondence
CO 285	Tobago Original Correspondence
CO 318	West Indies Original Correspondence
CO 323–24	Colonies General Original Correspondence
CO 388	Board of Trade Original Correspondence
FO 27	General Correspondence: France
HO 42	George III Correspondence
IR 1	Apprenticeship Books
PRO 30/8	Chatham Papers

T 1	Treasury Board Papers
T 27	Treasury Out-Letters
T 28	Treasury Various
T 29	Minutes of Treasury Board
T 36	Accounts/Scotland: Miscellaneous Returns
T 47	Duty Registers (Carriage, Plate, and Servants)
T 52	King's Warrants of Letters Patent
T 64	Miscellanea Various
	Correspondence with Hunter and Munchausen
	Accounts, Letters and Warrants
T 70	African Companies' Papers
T 77	East Florida Claims Commission
T 79	American Loyalist Claims Commission
T 98	Treasury Board Supplementary Papers
WO 1	War Office In-Letters

Royal Academy of Art
  Sir William Chambers Letters
  Sir Joshua Reynolds Pocketbooks, 1770–90
Royal Bank of Scotland (49 Charing Cross)
  Drummonds Bank Customer Account Ledgers
Royal Bank of Scotland (20 Birchin Lane)
  Childs Bank Customer Account Ledgers
  William & Glyn Records
Royal Geographic Society
  African Association Papers
  Banks Papers (copies)
Royal Society of Arts
  Committee Minutes
  Correspondence
  Membership Rolls
Sir John Soane's Museum
  Robert Adam Drawings of Auchincruive
University of London, Goldsmiths Library
  Manuscripts
University of London, Institute of Commonwealth Studies
  Minutes of Committee of West India Planters and
    Merchants
Maidstone
  Kent Record Office
  Danson Hill Deeds

Halstead Place Deeds
Halstead Parish Records
Matlock
  Chatsworth (The Duke of Devonshire)
    Devonshire Papers, 1757 Subscribed Loan Papers
Maybole
  Blairquhan (Mr. James Hunter-Blair)
    James Hunter Blair Papers
Montrose
  Town Hall
    Montrose Town Council Minutes
    Bridge of Dun Papers
Nairn
  Nairn District Council Office
    Nairn Burgh Council Minutes
Newcastle-upon-Tyne
  Northumberland Record Office
    Sir John Hussey Delaval Papers
    Riddell Papers, Buchanan Accounts
Northallerton
  North Yorkshire Record Office
    John Hamilton of Sundrum Papers
    Zetland Archives, Sir Laurence Dundas Papers
Nottingham
  University of Nottingham Library
    Newcastle Papers
Oxford
  Bodleian Library
    Laurence Sulivan Papers
    George Macartney Papers
    Rhodes House Library
    "State of Carriacou"
Perth
  Scone Palace (The Earl of Mansfield)
    Judge Mansfield Notebooks
Rothesay
  Mountstuart (The Marquis of Bute)
    Bute Papers
Shedfield
  Sudlows (Admiral Sir Julian Oswald)
    Richard Oswald Papers

Sheffield
  Sheffield City Libraries
    Wentworth-Woodhouse Manuscripts, Rockingham Papers
Stafford
  Sandon Hall (Mrs. Jane Waley)
    Nathaniel Ryder Papers, Letters and Journals
  Staffordshire Record Office
    Dartmouth Manuscripts, Oswald Memoranda, and Letters
Thornhill
  Drumlanrig Castle (The Duke of Buccleuch)
    Drumlanrig Castle Factor's Accounts
Wellington
  Hockworthy House (Mrs. Daphne Burton)
    James Oswald of Dunnikier Papers
Wick
  Caithness District Council Office
    Thurso Baillie Court Records
    Wick Town Council Minutes
Winchester
  Hampshire Record Office
    Harris Manuscripts

United States
  Ann Arbor
    Clements Library
      Lansdowne (Shelburne) Papers
      Richard Oswald Memoranda
      Henry Strachey Papers
      Thomas Townshend Papers
  Boston
    Boston Public Library
      Winthrop Papers
    Massachusetts Historical Society
      Samuel Cary Manuscripts
      Everett Papers
      James Murray Letterbooks and Letters
  Charleston
    South Carolina Historical Society
      John Lewis Gervais Letters
      Henry Laurens Papers

Columbia
  South Carolina Department of Archives and History
    Colonial Land Plats
Hartford
  Connecticut Historical Society
    William Samuel Johnson Papers
New Haven
  Beinecke Library
    Pequot Papers
    Osborne Collection (Danson Drawing)
New York
  New York Historical Society
    John Lewis Gervais Letters
    Henry Laurens' Manuscript Journal of "Voyage and Captivity
      and Confinement"
    Daniel Wier Letterbook
  New York Public Library
    Bancroft Collection Miscellaneous Transcripts
      David Hartley Correspondence
    Emmet Collection
    Tomlinson Collection
Philadelphia
  American Philosophical Society
    Benjamin Franklin Papers
    Benjamin Vaughan Papers
  Historical Society of Pennsylvania
    Boudinot Papers
    Hand Papers
    Shippen Papers
    Vane Papers
    Weir Papers
Providence
  Rhode Island Historical Society
    John Sargent II Letters
San Marino
  Huntington Library
    Clarkson Papers
    Grenville Papers
    Macaulay Papers, Diary of Zachary Macaulay
    William Johnston Pulteney Papers
    Thomas Townshend Papers

West Indies
 Antigua
  St. John's, Supreme Court House
   Court Records
   Deeds
   Wills
 Grenada
  St. George's, Supreme Court House
   Common Pleas Records
   Deeds
 Jamaica
  Kingston
   National Library of Jamaica
    Plantation Plats
   University of West Indies/Mona Campus
    David Mill Deeds relating to Carriacou
  Spanishtown
   Island Record Office
    Deeds, Old Series
    Probate Inventories
    Last Wills
  Jamaica Archives
    Chancery Records
    Court of Error Records
    Crop Accounts
    Grand Court Records
    Land Patents
    Powers of Attorney
 Montserrat
  Plymouth, Public Library
   Court Records
   Deeds
 St. Vincent
  Kingstown, Supreme Court
   Common Pleas and Court of Error Records
   Deeds
 Tobago
  Scarborough, Supreme Court, Public Library
   Deeds

Index